SOCIOLOGY
A BRIEF INTRODUCTION

SOCIOLOGY
A BRIEF INTRODUCTION

RICHARD T. SCHAEFER
Western Illinois University

ROBERT P. LAMM

McGRAW-HILL, INC.
New York   St. Louis   San Francisco   Auckland   Bogotá
Caracas   Lisbon   London   Madrid   Mexico City   Milan
Montreal   New Delhi   San Juan
Singapore   Sydney   Tokyo   Toronto

SOCIOLOGY: A Brief Introduction

Copyright © 1994 by McGraw-Hill, Inc. All rights
reserved. Portions of this text were taken from *Sociology,*
Fourth Edition. Copyright © 1992, 1989, 1986, 1983 by
McGraw-Hill, Inc. All rights reserved. Printed in the
United States of America. Except as permitted under
the United States Copyright Act of 1976, no part of this
publication may be reproduced or distributed in any
form or by any means, or stored in a data base or
retrieval system, without the prior written permission of
the publisher.

Acknowledgments appear on pages 411–413, and on
this page by reference.

This book is printed on acid-free paper.

    3 4 5 6 7 8 9 0 VNH VNH 9 0 9 8 7 6 5

ISBN 0-07-055033-6

INTERNATIONAL EDITION

Copyright © 1994

Exclusive rights by McGraw-Hill, Inc. for manufacture
and export. This book cannot be re-exported from the
country to which it is consigned by McGraw-Hill. The
International Edition is not available in North America.

When ordering this title, use ISBN 0-07-113667-3

This book was set in New Baskerville
by York Graphic Services, Inc.
The editors were Rhona Robbin, Phillip A. Butcher,
and Susan Gamer;
the designer was Joan E. O'Connor;
the production supervisor was Kathryn Porzio.
The photo editor was Elyse Rieder.
The permissions editor was Elsa Peterson.
Drawings were done by Fine Line Illustrations, Inc.
Von Hoffmann Press, Inc., was printer and binder.

Cover Credit:
August Macke: WOMAN IN THE GREEN JACKET, 1913,
Rheinisches Bildarchiv, Museum Ludwig, Cologne.

Library of Congress Cataloging-in-Publication Data

Schaefer, Richard T.
    Sociology: a brief introduction / Richard T.
    Schaefer, Robert P. Lamm.
        p.   cm.
    Includes bibliographical references and indexes.
    ISBN 0-07-055033-6 (acid-free paper)
    1. Sociology.   2. United States—Social
        conditions—1980–
    I. Lamm, Robert P.   II. Title.
HM51.S345   1994
301—dc20   93-9830

ABOUT
THE AUTHORS

Richard T. Schaefer, born and raised in Chicago, is Professor of Sociology and Dean of the College of Arts and Sciences at Western Illinois University. He received his B.A. in sociology from Northwestern University and his M.A. and Ph.D. from the University of Chicago. He has taught introductory sociology for 24 years to students in colleges, adult education programs, nursing programs, and a maximum-security prison. He is the author of the well-received *Racial and Ethnic Groups* (Harper Collins, 1993), now in its fifth edition. His articles and book reviews have appeared in many journals, including *American Journal of Sociology, Phylon: Review of Race and Culture, Contemporary Sociology, Sociology and Social Research,* and *Teaching Sociology.* He was recently elected president of the Midwest Sociological Society.

Robert P. Lamm is a New York-based freelance writer with extensive experience on social science textbooks and supplements. His essays, profiles, reviews, and fiction have appeared in two anthologies and in more than 30 periodicals in the United States, Canada, and Great Britain. He received his B.A. in political science from Yale University, also studied at Sarah Lawrence College, and has taught at Yale, Queens College, and the New School for Social Research. He is a longtime activist in the National Writers Union.

Schaefer and Lamm have collaborated on all four editions of *Sociology* (McGraw-Hill, 1992) and its supplements. They served as editors of the reader *Introducing Sociology* (McGraw-Hill, 1987).

To my nephew, John Leeseberg
R.T.S.

In memory of the Jewish fighters
of the Warsaw Ghetto Revolt,
which began on April 19, 1943
R.P.L.

CONTENTS
IN BRIEF

CONTENTS

LIST
OF BOXES

PREFACE

After 24 years of teaching sociology to students in colleges, adult education programs, nursing programs, an overseas program based in London, and even a maximum-security prison, I am firmly convinced that the discipline can play a valuable role in teaching critical thinking skills. Sociology can help students to better understand the workings of their own society and other cultures. Through the distinctive emphasis on social policy found in this text, students will be shown how the sociological imagination can be useful in examining such public policy issues as multiculturalism, child care, the AIDS crisis, national health insurance, domestic violence, and disability rights.

The introductory course in sociology is taught in a variety of formats according to a bewildering array of academic calendars. Despite this, the first four editions of *Sociology* have been well received and used at more than 400 schools, including just about every type of institution of higher education. However, it has become clear that some instructors rarely draw on the full 20 chapters of *Sociology* and instead seek a more concise overview of the discipline that will permit them to assign additional material or projects. Consequently, the present volume was developed in response to these requests for a brief introduction to sociology.

Sociology: A Brief Introduction includes all the distinctive features that have been popular with instructors and students who use the more comprehensive volume, including three especially important focal points:

- *Strong and balanced coverage of theoretical perspectives throughout the text.* The functionalist, conflict, and interactionist perspectives are introduced, defined, and contrasted in Chapter 1. We explore their distinctive views of such topics as culture (Chapter 2), social institutions (Chapter 4), deviance (Chapter 5), stratification by gender (Chapter 8), education (Chapter 10), and health and illness (Chapter 12).
- *Consistent coverage of issues affecting women in all chapters, not solely the chapter on gender.* Examples of such coverage include social policy sections on child care (Chapter 4), affirmative action (Chapter 7), abortion (Chapter 8), domestic violence (Chapter 9), and sexual harassment (Chapter 11); boxes on sexism in language (Box 2-1), the effects of divorce on female and male children (Box 9-2), and sexism in medical research (Box 12-1); and special sections on the treatment of women in education (Chapter 10) and on women in politics (Chapter 11).

• *Use of cross-cultural material throughout the text.*
Examples of such coverage include sections on colonialism and neocolonialism, modernization, and multinational corporations (Chapter 6); boxes on international crime rates (Box 5-2), race relations in Brazil (Box 7-1), aging worldwide (Box 8-2), liberation theology (Box 10-1), and Japan's declining fertility rate (Box 12-2); and discussion of the health care systems of Canada, Sweden, and Great Britain in the social policy section on national health insurance (Chapter 12).

As in our longer text, we take great care to introduce the basic concepts and research methods of sociology and to reinforce this material in all chapters. The most recent data are included, making this book even more current than the fourth edition of *Sociology*. Finally, the 12 social policy sections appearing in the brief edition (beginning with Chapter 2) apply sociological principles and theories to important social and political issues that are being debated by contemporary policymakers and by the general public.

CONTENT

Sociology: A Brief Introduction is divided into 13 chapters which study human behavior concisely from the perspective of sociologists. The opening chapter ("The Sociological View") presents a brief history of the discipline and introduces the basic theories and research methods employed in sociology.

The next four chapters focus on key sociological concepts. Chapter 2 ("Culture") illustrates how sociologists study the behavior we have learned and share. Chapter 3 ("Socialization") reveals how humans are most distinctively social animals who learn the attitudes and behavior viewed as appropriate in their particular cultures. We examine interactions within small groups and large bureaucracies in Chapter 4 ("Social Structure, Groups, and Organizations"). Chapter 5 ("Deviance and Social Control") reviews how we conform to and deviate from established social norms.

In the next three chapters, we consider the social hierarchies present in societies. Chapter 6 ("Stratification in the United States and World-

wide") introduces us to the presence of social inequality; while Chapter 7 ("Racial and Ethnic Inequality") and Chapter 8 ("Gender and Age Stratification") analyze specific types of inequality.

The following chapters examine the major social institutions of human society. Marriage, kinship, and divorce are only three of the topics examined in Chapter 9 ("The Family"). The remaining social institutions are considered in Chapter 10 ("Religion and Education") and Chapter 11 ("Government and the Economy").

The final chapters of the text introduce major themes in our changing world. Chapter 12 ("Health and Population") helps us understand the impact of these issues on our society and across the world. Chapter 13 ("Collective Behavior, Social Change, and Urbanization") presents sociological analysis of the process of change.

SPECIAL FEATURES

"Looking Ahead" Questions

Each chapter of *Sociology: A Brief Introduction* begins with "Looking Ahead"—a set of questions designed to interest students in the most important subjects and issues that will be raised.

Chapter Introduction

Following "Looking Ahead," a lively chapter introduction conveys the excitement of sociological inquiry. For example, the opening chapter begins with an examination of how sociologists view the growth of state lotteries in recent decades. Chapter 7 ("Racial and Ethnic Inequality") opens with a brief overview of the 1992 riots in Los Angeles and other cities. Chapter 10 ("Religion and Education") begins with a portrait of Islamic day schools in the United States which offer instruction to African American and immigrant youngsters.

Chapter Overview

Reflecting the positive responses to the format of *Sociology*, the introduction is again followed by a chapter overview that describes the content of the chapter in narrative form.

Key Terms

Careful attention has been given to presenting understandable and accurate definitions of each key term. These terms are highlighted in **_bold italics_** when they are first introduced. A list of key terms and definitions in each chapter—with page references—is found at the end of the chapter. In addition, the _glossary_ at the end of the book includes the definitions of the textbook's 340 key terms and the page references for each term.

Boxes

The boxes supplement the text discussions and are closely tied to the basic themes of each chapter. Certain boxes illustrate the application of sociological theories, such as the analysis of functionalist and conflict views of popular music in Chapter 1. Others provide detailed analysis of sociological research, such as the study of impression management by students after exams (see Box 3-1). Still other boxes focus on contemporary issues, such as the pervasive stereotype of Asian Americans as a "model minority" (see Box 7-2).

Illustrations and Tables

Like the boxes, the _photographs, cartoons, figures,_ and _tables_ are closely linked to the themes of the text, and their captions make the links explicit.

Social Policy Sections

The social policy sections play a critical role in helping students to think like sociologists. These sections focus on current and often controversial issues of public policy such as gun control (Chapter 5), welfare (Chapter 6), affirmative action (Chapter 7), and sexual harassment (Chapter 11). In all cases, students are shown the utility of sociological theory and research in understanding and resolving major political issues confronting policymakers and the general public. To help students appreciate the relevance of sociology in studying policy issues, each section begins with a set of questions designed to underscore the connection.

Chapter Summaries

Each chapter includes a brief numbered summary to aid students in reviewing the important themes.

Critical Thinking Questions

After the summary, three critical thinking questions are presented to help students learn to critically analyze the social world in which they participate. Such critical thinking is an essential element in the sociological imagination.

Additional Readings

An annotated list of additional readings concludes each chapter. These works have been selected because of their sociological soundness and their accessibility for introductory students.

References

Some 1,270 books, articles, government documents, scholarly presentations, dissertations, and pamphlets are included in the list of references at the end of the book. These materials have been listed with complete bibliographic information so that they can be retrieved easily by instructors or students. About 240 of these references were published in 1991, 1992, or 1993.

SUPPLEMENTS

Accompanying this textbook are the _Students' Guide_, the _Instructor's Resource Manual,_ and the _Test Bank._ I feel that it is important for all materials to be developed together, rather than written independently of each other. Consequently, these three supplements have been written by the same people responsible for preparation of this textbook: myself and my coauthor, Robert P. Lamm.

The _Students' Guide_ includes standard features such as detailed _key points_, definitions of _key terms, multiple-choice questions, fill-in questions,_ and _true-false questions._ All are keyed to specific pages in the textbook. Perhaps the most distinctive feature is the *social policy exercise,* which is closely tied to the social policy sections in the text.

The *Instructor's Resource Manual* provides sociology instructors with *additional lecture ideas* (including alternative social policy issues), *class discussion topics, topics for student research* (along with suggested research materials for each topic), and suggested *additional readings* (unlike those in the text itself, these are meant for instructors rather than students). Finally, *media materials* are suggested for each chapter, including audiotapes, videotapes, and films.

The *Test Bank* can be used with computerized test-generating systems. *Multiple-choice questions* are included for each chapter; they will be useful in testing students on basic sociological concepts, application of theoretical perspectives, and recall of important factual information. (All questions in the *Test Bank* are labeled as "definition," "application," or "information" questions.) Correct answers and page references are provided for all questions.

In addition to the printed format, the *Test Bank* is available in computerized form for use on IBM PCs and compatibles, Apple II and IIc computers, and the Apple Macintosh. Tests can also be prepared by our customized test service. The telephone number for Customized Tests is 800-888-EXAM. McGraw-Hill's local representative can help instructors obtain these supplements.

Finally, McGraw-Hill also makes available to adopters videos, interactive software, and other materials and services. For more details, contact McGraw-Hill's main office or your local McGraw-Hill representative.

ACKNOWLEDGMENTS

Robert P. Lamm serves as coauthor of this book and has been an integral part of my writing with McGraw-Hill since the first edition of *Sociology.*

Both Bob and I are deeply appreciative of the contributions to this project made by our editors. Phillip Butcher, our sociology editor, has provided insight, constructive criticism, and consistent encouragement. Rhona Robbin, a senior editor at McGraw-Hill, has worked as our development editor for more than 12 years. Her thoughtful, sensitive, and respectful guidance has certainly made this a better book.

Additional guidance and support were provided by Susan Gamer, editing supervisor; Sally Constable, marketing manager; Elyse Rieder, photo editor; Elsa Peterson, permissions editor; William O'Neal, copy editor; Joan O'Connor, designer; and Kathy Porzio, production supervisor. Special thanks go to Cybele Eidenschenk, assistant editor; and Kimberly Rainis, editorial assistant. Each handled a variety of administrative tasks cheerfully and reliably.

I have had the good fortune to be able to introduce students to sociology for many years. These students have been enormously helpful in spurring on my own sociological imagination. In ways I can fully appreciate but cannot fully acknowledge, their questions in class and queries in the hallway have found their way into this textbook.

Sociology: A Brief Introduction reflects many insightful suggestions made by eight sociologists who offered constructive and thorough evaluations: Joseph V. Domino, Texas A & M University; Jackie Eller, Middle Tennessee State University; Michael Givant, Adelphi University; Cheryl Kimberling, Tarrant County Junior College; Joel I. Nelson, University of Minnesota; Ellen Rosengarten, Sinclair Community College; Mwizenge S. Tembo, Bridgewater College; and Peter Turner, Herkimer County Community College. In addition, my colleagues at Western Illinois University have been most supportive.

As is evident from these acknowledgments, the preparation of a textbook is truly a team effort. The most valuable members of this effort continue to be my wife, Sandy; and my son, Peter. They provide the support so necessary in my creative and scholarly activities.

Richard T. Schaefer

SOCIOLOGY

A BRIEF INTRODUCTION

1

THE SOCIOLOGICAL VIEW

"This week's lottery numbers are 3, 11, 19, 31, 44, and 48." Millions of people across the United States wait anxiously for such announcements, hoping that their lottery tickets match the winning combinations. Winning the lottery may seem the only way for some of us to realize our dreams or simply to escape poverty.

As recently as 1960, lotteries were banned outright in each of the nation's 50 states. However, by 1992 lotteries not only were permitted but were *exclusively government-run* in at least 33 states, the District of Columbia, Puerto Rico, and the Virgin Islands. Nationwide, state lottery ticket sales reached $20.6 billion in the fiscal year that ended in July 1991 (Smothers, 1992).

Observers view government-run lotteries in a number of ways. A state legislator would probably be delighted that the state can receive millions of dollars in revenues without increasing taxes. A marketing specialist would be interested in how state governments use television, print media, and other promotional techniques in publicizing lotteries and increasing the number of customers. A consumer-protection advocate might also be concerned about advertising for lotteries, but would emphasize that it rarely specifies the odds against winning, relying instead on such phrases as "Everyone is a winner" and "All you need is a dollar and a dream." In fact, a lottery participant is six times more likely to be struck by lightning than to win the jackpot.

What if a sociologist considered the phenomenon of state lotteries? He or she would certainly note an apparent contradiction: state governments criminalize private gambling while aggressively promoting lotteries. The sociologist would also emphasize that states target low-income residents in their lottery promotions. Lottery terminals are more heavily concentrated in poor neighborhoods than in wealthy neighborhoods. Lottery advertisements are most frequent at the beginning of each month, when Social Security and public assistance checks arrive.

Are the poor more likely than the affluent to spend a high portion of their earnings for the very unlikely chance of becoming an instant millionaire? Sociologists would attempt to test that notion. For the sociologist, the growth of state lotteries represents an opportunity—not an opportunity to make a quick fortune, but rather an opportunity to learn more about our changing society (Mangalmurti and Cooke, 1991).

WHAT IS SOCIOLOGY?

The sociologist has a distinctive way of examining human interactions. *Sociology* is the systematic study of social behavior and human groups. It focuses primarily on the influence of social relationships on people's attitudes and behavior and on how societies are established and change. As a field of study, sociology has an extremely broad scope. Therefore, this textbook deals with families, gangs, business firms, political parties, schools, religions, and labor unions. It is concerned with love, poverty, conformity, discrimination, illness, alienation, overpopulation, and community.

Residents of Philadelphia are shown waiting in line to purchase lottery tickets. Sociologists point out that state governments criminalize private gambling while aggressively promoting lotteries.

The Sociological Imagination

In attempting to understand social behavior, sociologists rely on an unusual type of creative thinking. C. Wright Mills (1959) described such thinking as the *sociological imagination*—an awareness of the relationship between an individual and the wider society. This awareness allows people (not simply sociologists) to comprehend the links between their immediate, personal social settings and the remote, impersonal social world that surrounds them and helps to shape them.

A key element in the sociological imagination is the ability to view one's own society as an outsider would, rather than from the limited perspective of personal experiences and cultural biases. Thus, instead of simply accepting the fact that movie stars and rock stars are the "royalty" of our society, we could ask, in a more critical sense, why this is the case. Conceivably, an outsider who was unfamiliar with the United States might wonder why we are not as interested in meeting outstanding scientists, elementary school teachers, or architects.

Sociological imagination can bring new understanding to daily life around us—or even to our view of the past. For example, Claude Fischer (1988:211–233) studied gender differences in telephone use during the half century before World War II and the social meanings of these differences. During the period 1890–1940, telephones became common in middle-class urban homes as well as on many farms.

Fischer (1988:224) observes that, in the period under study, North American women "seemed to have a special affinity for the household telephone and that affinity seemed to involve sociability." He offers a number of possible explanations for this gender difference, among them:

- Women, especially homemakers, were typically more isolated from daily adult contact than men were. Therefore, telephone calls allowed many women to experience some of the social contact that their husbands found in the workplace.
- Women's traditional role as "social managers" for their families led to extensive telephone responsibilities in service to the household, the extended family, the friendship circle, and the community.

Fischer (1988:229) concludes that, like the bicycle and the automobile, the telephone served as a "technology of sociability" that allowed women to increase their social interactions. He adds that "men's jokes about this affinity are, perhaps, at base, simply a defensive acknowledgment of this difference between men and women in personal relations."

Sociology and Common Sense

Sociology focuses on the study of certain aspects of human behavior. Yet human behavior is something with which we all have experience and about which we all have at least a bit of knowledge. All of us might well have theories about why movie stars and rock stars receive so much attention and adulation. Our theories and suggestions come from our experiences and from a cherished source of wisdom—common sense.

In our daily lives, we rely on common sense to get us through many unfamiliar situations. However, this commonsense knowledge, while sometimes accurate, is not always reliable, because it rests on commonly held beliefs rather than on systematic analysis of facts. It was once considered "common sense" to accept that the earth was flat—a view rightly questioned by Pythagoras and Aristotle. Incorrect commonsense notions are not just a part of the distant past; they remain with us today.

In the United States, "common sense" tells us that when a racial minority group moves into a previously all-White neighborhood, property values decline. "Common sense" tells us that people panic when faced with natural disasters, such as floods and earthquakes, with the result that all social organization disintegrates. However, these particular commonsense notions—like the notion that the earth is flat—are *untrue;* neither of them is supported by sociological research. Race has been found to have little relationship to property values; such factors as zoning changes, overcrowding, and age of housing are more significant. Disasters do not generally produce panic. In the aftermath of natural disasters, greater social organization and structure emerge to deal with a community's problems.

Like other social scientists, sociologists do not accept something as a fact because "everyone knows it." Instead, each piece of information must be tested and recorded, then analyzed in relationship to other data. Sociology relies on scientific studies in order to describe and understand a social environment. At times, the findings of sociologists may seem like common sense because they deal with facets of everyday life. Yet it is important to stress that such findings have been *tested* by researchers. Common sense now tells us that the earth is round. But this particular commonsense notion is based on centuries of scientific work upholding the breakthrough made by Pythagoras and Aristotle.

In this chapter, the nature of sociology as a field of inquiry will be explored. We will evaluate the contributions of three pioneering thinkers—Émile Durkheim, Max Weber, and Karl Marx—to the development of sociology. A number of im-

Singer Gloria Estefan is shown distributing food to victims of Hurricane Andrew, which caused substantial damage in 1992. In the aftermath of natural disasters such as hurricanes, greater social organization and structure emerge to deal with a community's problems.

portant theoretical perspectives used by sociologists will be discussed. We will also describe the basic principles and stages of the scientific method and will present a number of techniques commonly used in sociological research, such as surveys, observation, and experiments. Finally, particular attention will be given to the ethical challenges that sociologists face in studying human behavior.

THE DEVELOPMENT OF SOCIOLOGY

People have always been curious about how we get along, what we do, and whom we select as our leaders. Philosophers and religious authorities of ancient societies and medieval societies made countless observations about human behavior. These observations were not tested or verified scientifically; nevertheless, they often became the foundation for moral codes. Several of the early social philosophers predicted that a systematic study of human behavior would one day emerge. Beginning in the nineteenth century, European theorists made pioneering contributions to the development of a science of human behavior.

Early Thinkers:
Comte, Martineau, and Spencer

In France, the nineteenth century was an unsettling time for that nation's intellectuals. The French monarchy had been deposed earlier in the revolution of 1789, and Napoleon had subsequently been defeated in his effort to conquer Europe. Amidst this chaos, philosophers considered how society might be improved. Auguste Comte (1798–1857), credited with being the most influential of these philosophers of the early 1800s, believed that a theoretical science of society and systematic investigation of behavior were needed to improve society.

Comte coined the term *sociology* to apply to the science of human behavior and insisted that sociology could make a critical contribution to a new and improved human community. Writing in the 1800s, Comte feared that France's stability had been permanently impaired by the excesses of the French Revolution. Yet he hoped that the study

Harriet Martineau (1802–1876), an English scholar, was an early pioneer of sociology who studied social behavior both in her native country and in the United States.

of social behavior in a systematic way would eventually lead to more rational human interactions. In Comte's hierarchy of sciences, sociology was at the top. He called it the "queen" and its practitioners "scientist-priests." This French theorist did not simply give sociology its name; he also presented a rather ambitious challenge to the fledgling discipline.

Scholars were able to learn of Comte's works largely through translations by the English sociologist Harriet Martineau (1802–1876). But Martineau was a path breaker in her own right as a sociologist; she offered insightful observations of the customs and social practices of both her native Britain and the United States. Martineau's book *Society in America* (1962, original edition 1837) examines religion, politics, child rearing, and immigration in the young nation. Martineau gives special attention to status distinctions and to such factors as gender and race.

Another important contributor to the discipline of sociology was Herbert Spencer (1820–1903). Writing from the vantage point of relatively prosperous Victorian England, Spencer did not feel compelled to correct or improve society; instead, he hoped to describe it better. Spencer was familiar with Comte's work but seemed more influenced by Charles Darwin's study *On the Origin of Species*. Drawing on Darwin's insights, Spencer used the concept of evolution of animals to explain how societies change over time. Similarly, he adapted Darwin's evolutionary view of the "survival of the fittest" by arguing that it is "natural" that some people are rich while others are poor.

Spencer's approach to societal change was extremely popular in his own lifetime. Indeed, he dominated scholarly thinking more than Comte did. Unlike Comte, Spencer suggested that societies are bound to change; therefore, one need not be highly critical of present social arrangements or work actively for social change. This viewpoint appealed to many influential people in Great Britain and the United States who had a vested interest in the status quo and who were suspicious of social thinkers who endorsed change. We will consider Spencer's views on society and social change in more detail in Chapter 13.

Émile Durkheim

Émile Durkheim's important theoretical work on suicide was but one of his many pioneering contributions to sociology. The son of a rabbi, Durkheim (1858–1917) was educated in both France and Germany. He established an impressive academic reputation and was appointed as one of the first professors of sociology in France. Above all, Durkheim will be remembered for his insistence that behavior cannot be fully understood in individualistic terms, that it must be understood within a larger social context.

In his research on suicide, Durkheim was primarily concerned not with the personalities of individual suicide victims, but rather with suicide *rates* and how they varied from country to country. As a result, when he looked at the number of suicides reported in 1869 in France, England, and Denmark, Durkheim also examined the populations of these nations to determine their rates of suicide. In doing so, he found that whereas England had only 67 reported suicides per million inhabitants, France had 135 per million and Denmark had 277 per million. Thus, in terms of national comparisons, the question became: "Why did Denmark have a comparatively high rate of reported suicides?"

Durkheim went much deeper into his investigation of suicide rates, and the result was his landmark work *Suicide,* published in 1897. Durkheim refused to automatically accept unproven explanations regarding suicide, including the beliefs that such deaths were caused by cosmic forces or by inherited tendencies. Instead, he focused on such problems as the cohesiveness or lack of cohesiveness of religious and occupational groups.

Durkheim's research suggested that suicide, while a solitary act, is related to group life. Protestants had much higher suicide rates than Catholics did; the unmarried had much higher rates than married people did; soldiers were more likely to take their lives than civilians were. In addition, it appeared that there were higher rates of suicide in times of peace than in times of war and revolution, and in times of economic instability and recession rather than in times of prosperity. Durkheim concluded that the suicide rates of a society reflected the extent to which people were or were not integrated into the group life of the society.

Like many other sociologists, Durkheim's interests were not limited to one aspect of social behavior. Later in this book, we will consider his thinking on crime and punishment, religion, and the workplace. Few sociologists have had such a dramatic impact on so many different areas within the discipline.

Max Weber

Another important theorist who contributed to the scientific study of society was Max Weber (pronounced "VAY-ber"). Born in Germany in 1864, Weber took his early academic training in legal and economic history, but he gradually developed an interest in sociology. Eventually, he became a professor at various German universities. Weber told his students that they should employ *Verstehen,* the German word for "understanding" or "insight," in their intellectual work.

He pointed out that much of our social behavior cannot be analyzed by the kinds of objective criteria we use to measure weight or temperature. To fully comprehend behavior, we must learn the subjective meanings people attach to their actions—how they themselves view and explain their behavior.

For example, suppose that sociologists were studying the social ranking of individuals in an electricians' union. Weber would expect researchers to employ *Verstehen* to determine the significance of the union's social hierarchy for its members. Sociologists would seek to learn how these electricians relate to union members of higher or lower status; they might examine the effects of seniority on standing within the union. While investigating these questions, researchers would take into account people's emotions, thoughts, beliefs, and attitudes (L. Coser, 1977:130).

We also owe credit to Weber for a key conceptual tool: the ideal type. An *ideal type* is a construct, a model that serves as a measuring rod against which actual cases can be evaluated. In his own works, Weber identified various characteristics of bureaucracy as an ideal type (these will be discussed in detail in Chapter 4). In presenting this model of bureaucracy, Weber was not describing any particular business, nor was he using the term *ideal* in a way that suggested a positive evaluation. Instead, his purpose was to provide a useful standard for measuring how bureaucratic an actual organization is (Gerth and Mills, 1958:219). Later in this textbook, the concept of ideal type will be used to study the family, religion, authority, and economic systems and to analyze bureaucracy.

Although their professional careers came at the same time, Émile Durkheim and Max Weber never met and probably were unaware of each other's existence, let alone ideas. This was certainly not true of the work of Karl Marx. Durkheim's thinking about the impact of the division of labor in industrial societies was related to Marx's writings, while Weber's concern for a value-free, objective sociology was a direct response to Marx's deeply held convictions. Thus, it is not surprising that Karl Marx is viewed as a major figure in the development of several social sciences, among them sociology (see Figure 1-1 on page 8).

Karl Marx

Karl Marx (1818–1883) shared with Durkheim and Weber a dual interest in abstract philosophical issues and in the concrete reality of everyday life. Unlike the others, Marx was so critical of existing institutions that a conventional academic career was impossible, and although he was born and educated in Germany, most of his life was spent in exile.

Marx's personal life was a difficult struggle. When a paper he had written was suppressed, he fled his native land and went to France. In Paris, he met Friedrich Engels (1820–1895), with whom he formed a lifelong friendship. They lived at a time when European and North American economic life was increasingly being dominated by the factory rather than the farm.

In 1847, Marx and Engels attended secret meetings in London of an illegal coalition of labor unions, the Communist League. The following year, they finished preparing a platform called *The Communist Manifesto,* in which they argued that the masses of people who have no resources other than their labor (whom they referred to as the *proletariat*) should unite to fight for the overthrow of capitalist societies. In the words of Marx and Engels:

> The history of all hitherto existing society is the history of class struggles. . . . The proletarians have nothing to lose but their chains. They have a world to win. WORKING MEN OF ALL COUNTRIES UNITE! (Feuer, 1959:7, 41).

After completing *The Communist Manifesto,* Marx returned to Germany, only to be expelled. He then moved to England, where he continued to write books and essays. Marx's life there was one of extreme poverty. He pawned most of his possessions, and several of his children died of malnutrition and disease. Marx clearly was an outsider in British society, a fact which may well have affected his view of western cultures (R. Collins and Makowsky, 1978:40).

Under Marx's analysis, society was fundamentally divided between classes who clash in pursuit of their own class interests. When he examined the industrial societies of his time, such as Germany, England, and the United States, he saw the factory as the center of conflict between the ex-

FIGURE 1-1 The Early Social Thinkers

Émile Durkheim
1858–1917

Max Weber
1864–1920

Karl Marx
1818–1883

Academic training	Philosophy	Law, economics, history, philosophy	Philosophy, law
Key works	1893 — *The Division of Labor in Society* 1897 — *Suicide: A Study in Sociology* 1912 — *Elementary Forms of Religious Life*	1904–1905 — *The Protestant Ethic and the Spirit of Capitalism* 1922 — *Wirtschaft und Gesellschaft*	1848 — *The Communist Manifesto* 1867 — *Das Kapital*

SOURCES: Left, Bibliothèque Nationale, Paris; middle, Culver Pictures; right, Culver Pictures.

Many of today's sociological studies draw on the work of three nineteenth-century thinkers: Durkheim, Weber, and Marx.

ploiters (the owners of the means of production) and the exploited (the workers). Marx viewed these relationships in systematic terms; that is, he believed that an entire system of economic, social, and political relationships had been established to maintain the power and dominance of the owners over the workers. Consequently, Marx and Engels argued that the working class needed to overthrow the existing class system. Marx's writings inspired those who were later to lead communist revolutions in Russia, China, Cuba, Vietnam, and elsewhere.

Even apart from the political revolutions that his work helped to foster, Marx's influence on contemporary thinking has been dramatic. Marx emphasized the *group* identifications and associations that influence an individual's place in society. As we have seen, this area of study is the major focus of contemporary sociology. Throughout this textbook, we will consider how membership in a particular gender classification, age group, racial group, or economic class affects a person's attitudes and behavior. In an important sense, this way of understanding society can be traced back to the pioneering work of Karl Marx.

Modern Developments

Sociology, as we know it in the 1990s, builds on the firm foundation that was developed by Émile Durkheim, Max Weber, and Karl Marx. However, the discipline of sociology has certainly not remained stagnant over the last century. Sociologists have gained new insights which have helped them to better understand the workings of society.

Charles Horton Cooley (1864–1929) was typical of the sociologists who became prominent in the early 1900s. Cooley was born in Ann Arbor, Michigan, and received his graduate training in economics but later became a sociology professor at the University of Michigan. Like other early sociologists, he had become interested in this "new" discipline while pursuing a related area of study.

Cooley shared the desire of Durkheim, Weber, and Marx to learn more about society. But to do so effectively, Cooley preferred to use the sociological perspective to look first at smaller units—intimate, face-to-face groups such as families, gangs, and friendship networks. He saw these groups as the seedbeds of society in the sense that they shape people's ideals, beliefs, values, and social nature. Cooley's work brought new understanding to groups of relatively small size.

In the early 1900s, many of the leading sociologists of the United States saw themselves as social reformers dedicated to systematically studying and then improving a corrupt society. They were genuinely concerned about the lives of immigrants in the nation's growing cities, whether these immigrants came from Europe or from the American south. Early female sociologists, in particular, were often active in poor urban areas as leaders of community centers known as *settlement houses*. For example, Jane Addams (1860–1935), a member of and speaker before the American Sociological Society, cofounded the famous Chicago settlement Hull House. Addams and other pioneering female sociologists commonly combined intellectual inquiry, social service work, and political activism—all with the goal of assisting the underprivileged and creating a more egalitarian society (Deegan, 1988).

By the middle of the twentieth century, however, the focus of the discipline had shifted. Sociologists restricted themselves to theorizing and gathering information, while the aim of transforming society was left to social workers and others. This shift away from social reform was accompanied by a growing commitment to scientific methods of research and to value-free interpretation of data.

Sociologist Robert Merton (1968:39–72) made an important contribution to the discipline by successfully combining theory and research. Born in 1910 of Slavic immigrant parents in Philadelphia, Merton subsequently won a scholarship to Temple University. He continued his studies at Harvard, where he acquired his lifelong interest in sociology. Merton's teaching career has been based at Columbia University.

Merton has produced a theory that is one of the most frequently cited explanations of deviant behavior. He noted different ways in which people attempt to achieve success in life. In his view, some may not share the socially agreed-upon goal of accumulating material goods or the accepted means of achieving this goal. For example, in Merton's classification scheme, "innovators" are people who accept the goal of pursuing material wealth but use illegal means to do so, including robbery, burglary, and extortion. Merton's explanation of crime is based on individual behavior—influenced by society's approved goals and means—yet it has wider applications. It helps to account for the high crime rates among the nation's poor, who may see no hope of advancing themselves through traditional roads to success. Merton's theory will be discussed in greater detail in Chapter 5.

Contemporary sociology reflects the diverse contributions of earlier theorists. As sociologists

Early female sociologists were often active in poor urban areas as leaders of community centers known as settlement houses. For example, Jane Addams (1860–1935) was a cofounder of the famous Chicago settlement, Hull House.

approach such topics as divorce, drug addiction, and religious cults, they can draw on the theoretical insights of the discipline's pioneers. A careful reader can hear Comte, Durkheim, Weber, Marx, Cooley, Addams, and many others speaking through the pages of current research. In describing the work of today's sociologists, it is helpful to examine a number of influential theories (also known as *perspectives*).

MAJOR THEORETICAL PERSPECTIVES

Sociologists view society in different ways. Some see the world basically as a stable and ongoing entity. They are impressed with the endurance of the family, organized religion, and other social institutions. Some sociologists see society as composed of many groups in conflict, competing for scarce resources. To other sociologists, the most fascinating aspects of the social world are the everyday, routine interactions among individuals that we sometimes take for granted. The three perspectives that are most widely used by sociologists will provide an introductory look at the discipline. These are the functionalist, conflict, and interactionist perspectives.

Functionalist Perspective

In the view of functionalists, society is like a living organism in which each part of the organism contributes to its survival. Therefore, the *functionalist perspective* emphasizes the way that parts of a society are structured to maintain its stability.

Talcott Parsons (1902–1979), a Harvard University sociologist, was a key figure in the development of functionalist theory. Parsons had been greatly influenced by the work of Émile Durkheim, Max Weber, and other European sociologists. For over four decades, Parsons dominated American sociology with his advocacy of functionalism. He saw any society as a vast network of connected parts, each of which contributes to the maintenance of the system as a whole. Under the functionalist approach, if an aspect of social life does not contribute to a society's stability or survival—if it does not serve some identifiably useful function or promote value consensus among

members of a society—it will not be passed on from one generation to the next.

As an example of the functionalist perspective, let us examine prostitution. Why is it that a practice so widely condemned continues to display such persistence and vitality? Functionalists suggest that prostitution satisfies needs of patrons that may not be readily met through more socially acceptable forms such as courtship or marriage. The "buyer" receives sex without any responsibility for procreation or sentimental attachment; at the same time, the "seller" gains a livelihood through this exchange.

Through such an examination, we can conclude that prostitution does perform certain functions that society seems to need. However, this is not to suggest that prostitution is a desirable or legitimate form of social behavior. Functionalists do not make such judgments and do not wish to condone the abuses or crimes that prostitutes and their clients may commit. Rather, advocates of the functionalist perspective hope to explain how an aspect of society that is so frequently attacked can nevertheless manage to survive (K. Davis, 1937).

Manifest and Latent Functions A university catalog typically presents various stated functions of the institution. It may inform us, for example, that the university intends to "offer each student a broad education in classical and contemporary thought, in the humanities, in the sciences, and in the arts." However, it would be quite a surprise to find a catalog which declared: "This university was founded in 1895 to keep people between the ages of 18 and 22 out of the job market, thus reducing unemployment." No college catalog will declare that this is the purpose of the university. Yet societal institutions serve many functions, some of them quite subtle. The university, in fact, *does* delay people's entry into the job market.

In order to better examine the functions of institutions, Robert Merton (1968:115–120) made an important distinction between manifest and latent functions. ***Manifest functions*** of institutions are open, stated, conscious functions. They involve the intended, recognized consequences of an aspect of society, such as the university's role in certifying academic competence and excellence. By contrast, ***latent functions*** are unconscious or unintended functions and may reflect hidden purposes of an institution. One latent function of universities is to serve as a meeting ground for people seeking marital partners.

Dysfunctions Functionalists acknowledge that not all parts of a society contribute to its stability all the time. A ***dysfunction*** is an element or a process of society that may actually disrupt a social system or lead to a decrease in stability.

Many dysfunctional behavior patterns, such as homicide, are widely regarded as undesirable. Yet dysfunctions should not automatically be interpreted as negative. The evaluation of a dysfunction depends on one's own values, or, as the saying goes, on "where you sit." For example, South Africa's wide-ranging system of racial segregation, known as *apartheid*, has been functional for the nation's Whites by raising them to a superior social and economic position. But it has been dysfunctional for Blacks, Asians, and people with mixed-race backgrounds—all of whom have been denied basic rights and have been relegated to second-class status.

Conflict Perspective

In contrast to functionalists' emphasis on stability and consensus, conflict sociologists see the social world in continual struggle. The ***conflict perspective*** assumes that social behavior is best understood in terms of conflict or tension between competing groups. Such conflict need not be violent; it can take the form of labor negotiations, party politics, competition between religious groups for members, or disputes over the federal budget.

As we saw earlier, Karl Marx viewed struggle between social classes as inevitable, given the exploitation of workers under capitalism. Expanding on Marx's work, sociologists and other social scientists have come to see conflict not merely as a class phenomenon but as a part of everyday life in all societies. Thus, in studying any culture, organization, or social group, sociologists want to know who benefits, who suffers, and who dominates at the expense of others. They are concerned with the conflicts between women and men, parents and children, cities and suburbs, and Whites and Blacks, to name only a few. In studying such questions, conflict theorists are interested in how society's institutions—including

Sociologist W.E.B. Du Bois (1868–1963), the first Black person to receive a doctorate from Harvard University, later helped organize the National Association for the Advancement of Colored People (NAACP). Conflict theory has encouraged sociology to include the views of Black scholars.

the family, government, religion, education, and the media—may help to maintain the privileges of some groups and keep others in a subservient position.

Obviously, there is a striking difference between the functionalist and conflict perspectives (see Box 1-1 on page 12). Conflict theorists are primarily concerned with the kinds of changes that conflict can bring about, whereas functionalists look for stability and consensus. The conflict model is viewed as more "radical" and "activist" because of its emphasis on social change and redistribution of resources. On the other hand, the functionalist perspective, because of its focus on the stability of society, is generally seen as more "conservative" (Dahrendorf, 1958).

11

THE SOCIOLOGICAL VIEW

BOX 1-1

FUNCTIONALIST AND CONFLICT VIEWS OF POPULAR MUSIC

We generally think of the functionalist and conflict perspectives as being applied to "serious" subjects such as the family, health care, and criminal behavior. Yet even popular music can be analyzed using these sociological approaches.

FUNCTIONALIST VIEW

Although intended primarily to entertain people, popular music serves definite social functions. For example, such music can bring people together and promote unity and stability. While Iran held 53 Americans as hostages during 1979 and 1980, people across the nation remembered them with yellow ribbons, and Tony Orlando's song "Tie a Yellow Ribbon 'Round the Old Oak Tree" achieved a new surge of popularity. Yellow ribbons continued to serve as a patriotic symbol when the United States greeted returning Desert Storm soldiers in 1991. Moreover, Bette Midler's song "From a Distance" expressed solidarity with troops serving in the Persian Gulf (Cooper, 1992).

From a functionalist perspective, popular music also promotes basic social values. The long tradition of gospel music suggests that faith in Jesus Christ will lead to salvation. In the 1960s, the Beatles told us that "All You Need Is Love." Then, during the era of the Vietnam War, they asked that we "Give Peace a Chance."

CONFLICT VIEW

Popular music can reflect the values of a particular age group and therefore intensify the battle between the generations. In the 1960s, folksinger Bob Dylan's "The Times They Are A-changin'" warned older people to get out of the way of the younger generation if they couldn't understand it. More recently, much of punk rock and alternative music (and costumes) is designed to shock conventional society and reflect the sense of alienation and outrage that its enthusiasts feel.

Popular music can also represent a direct political assault on established institutions. The Sex Pistols' "Anarchy in the U.K." and the Smiths' "The Queen Is Dead" attack the British monarchy. Many of the reggae songs of Bob Marley and the Wailers, such as "Burnin' and Lootin'," endorsed a revolution in Jamaica. Similarly, certain rap songs, among them Public Enemy's "Fight the Power" and Ice-T's "Cop Killer," challenge the established social order of the United States (Leland, 1992).

Finally, whereas functionalists emphasize that popular music promotes social values that bring people together, conflict theorists counter that popular music often focuses on injustices and on how certain groups of people are victimized by others. In this regard, Midnight Oil's "The Dead Heart" laments the mistreatment of Australia's native Aborigines, while Suzanne Vega's "Luka" and Garth Brooks's "The Thunder Rolls" both focus on the ugly reality of domestic violence.

Clearly, there is more to popular music than simply entertainment. Most songs have lyrics which carry explicit messages of one sort or another. From the functionalist approach, popular music reinforces societal values, while conflict theorists see popular music as another reflection of the political and social struggles within a society (Denisoff and Wahrman, 1983:23–26).

✳ Throughout most of the twentieth century, sociology in the United States was influenced primarily by the functionalist perspective. However, the conflict approach has become increasingly persuasive since the late 1960s. The widespread social unrest resulting from battles over civil rights, bitter divisions over the war in Vietnam, the rise of the feminist and gay liberation movements, the Watergate scandal, urban riots, and confrontations at abortion clinics offered support for the conflict approach—the view that our social world is characterized by continual struggle between competing groups. Currently, conflict theory is accepted within the discipline of sociology as one valid way to gain insight into a society.

One important contribution of conflict theory is that it has encouraged sociologists to view society through the eyes of segments of the population that rarely influence decision making. Early Black sociologists such as W. E. B. Du Bois (1868–1963) provided research that they hoped would assist the struggle for a racially egalitarian society. Du Bois had little patience for theorists such as Herbert Spencer who seemed content with the status quo. He advocated basic research on the lives of Blacks that would separate opinion from fact. Sociology, Du Bois contended, had to draw on scientific principles to study social problems like those experienced by Black Americans.

Similarly, feminist scholarship in sociology has enhanced our understanding of social behavior. A family's social standing is no longer viewed as defined solely by the husband's position and income. Feminist scholars have challenged stereotyping of women and have argued for a gender-balanced study of society in which women's experiences and contributions are as visible as those of men (Brewer, 1989; Komărovsky, 1991).

Interactionist Perspective

The functionalist and conflict perspectives both analyze behavior in terms of societywide patterns. However, many contemporary sociologists are more interested in understanding society as a whole through an examination of social interactions such as small groups conducting meetings, two friends talking casually with each other, a family celebrating a birthday, and so forth. The *interactionist perspective* generalizes about fundamental or everyday forms of social interaction. Interactionism is a sociological framework for viewing human beings as living in a world of meaningful objects. These "objects" may include material things, actions, other people, relationships, and even symbols (Henslin, 1972:95). Focusing on everyday behavior permits interactionists to better understand the larger society.

George Herbert Mead (1863–1931) is widely regarded as the founder of the interactionist perspective. Mead taught at the University of Chicago from 1893 until his death in 1931. Mead's sociological analysis, like that of Charles Horton Cooley, often focused on human interactions within one-to-one situations and small groups. Mead was interested in observing the most minute forms of communication—smiles, frowns, nodding of one's head—and in understanding how such individual behavior was influenced by the larger context of a group or society. However, despite his innovative views, Mead only occasionally wrote articles, and never a book. Most of his insights have been passed along to us through edited volumes of his lectures which his students published after his death.

Interactionists see symbols as an especially important part of human communication. In fact, the interactionist perspective is sometimes referred to as the *symbolic interactionist perspective*. Such researchers note that both a clenched fist and a salute have social meanings which are shared and understood by members of a society. In the United States, a salute symbolizes respect, while a clenched fist signifies defiance. However, in another culture different gestures might be used to convey a feeling of respect or defiance.

Let us examine how various societies portray suicide without the use of words. People in the United States point a finger at the head (shooting); urban Japanese bring a fist against the stomach (stabbing); and the South Fore of Papua New Guinea, clench a hand at the throat (hanging). These types of symbolic interaction are classified as forms of **nonverbal communication,** which can include many other gestures, facial expressions, and postures.

Since Mead's teachings have become well known, sociologists have expressed greater interest in the interactionist perspective. Many have moved away from what may have been an excessive preoccupation with the large-scale (macro) level of social behavior and have redirected their attention toward behavior which occurs in small groups (micro level). Erving Goffman (1922–1982) made a distinctive contribution by popularizing a particular type of interactionist method known as the **dramaturgical approach.** The dramaturgist compares everyday life to the setting of the theater and stage. Just as actors present certain images, all of us seek to present particular features of our personalities while we hide other qualities. Thus, in a class, we may feel the need to project a serious image; at a party, it may seem important to look relaxed and entertaining.

TABLE 1-1 Comparing the Major Theoretical Approaches

	FUNCTIONALIST	CONFLICT	INTERACTIONIST
VIEW OF SOCIETY	Stable, well-integrated	Characterized by tension and struggle between competing groups	Active in influencing and affecting everyday social interaction
LEVEL OF ANALYSIS EMPHASIZED	Large-scale (macro level)	Large-scale (macro level)	Smaller-scale (micro level) analysis as a way of understanding larger phenomena
VIEW OF SOCIAL CHANGE	Predictable, reinforcing	Change takes place all the time and may have positive consequences	Reflected in people's social positions and their communications with others
VIEW OF THE SOCIAL ORDER	Maintained through cooperation and consensus	Maintained through force and coercion	Maintained by shared understanding of everyday behavior
PROPONENTS	Émile Durkheim Talcott Parsons Robert Merton	Karl Marx W. E. B. Du Bois C. Wright Mills	George Herbert Mead Charles Horton Cooley Erving Goffman

This table shows how the three theoretical approaches can be compared along several important dimensions.

The Sociological Approach

Which perspective should a sociologist use in studying human behavior? Functionalist? Conflict? Interactionist?

Sociology makes use of all three approaches (see Table 1-1), since each of them offers unique insights into the same problem. Thus, in studying the continued high levels of unemployment in the United States, the functionalist might wish to study how unemployment reduces the demand for goods but increases the need for public services, thereby leading to new jobs in the government sector. The interactionist might encourage us to focus on the impact of unemployment on family life, as manifested in divorce, domestic violence, and dependence on drugs and alcohol. Researchers with a conflict perspective might draw our attention to the uneven distribution of unemployment within the labor force and how it is particularly likely to affect women and racial and ethnic minorities—those groups least likely to influence decision making about economic and social policy.

No one of these approaches to the issues related to unemployment is "correct." Within this textbook, it is assumed that we can gain the broadest understanding of our society by drawing on all three perspectives in the study of human behavior and institutions. These perspectives overlap as their interests coincide but can diverge according to the dictates of each approach and of the issue being studied. A sociologist's approach to a research problem is influenced in important ways by his or her theoretical orientation. However, all sociologists who wish to conduct effective research must follow the scientific method, which will be discussed in the next section.

CONDUCTING SOCIOLOGICAL RESEARCH

Effective sociological research can be quite thought-provoking. It may interest us in many new questions about social interactions that require further study. On the other hand, effective research is not always dramatic. In some cases, rather than raising additional questions, a study will confirm previous beliefs and findings. We will now examine the research process used in conducting sociological studies.

The Scientific Method

Like the typical woman or man on the street, the sociologist is interested in the central questions of our time. Are we lagging behind in our ability to feed the world population? Is the family falling apart? Why is there so much crime in the United States? Such issues concern most people, whether or not they have academic training. However, unlike the typical citizen, the sociologist has a commitment to the use of the scientific method in studying society. The *scientific method* is a systematic, organized series of steps that ensures maximum objectivity and consistency in researching a problem.

Many of us will never actually conduct scientific research. Nonetheless, it is important that we understand the scientific method, for it plays a major role in the workings of our society. Residents of the United States are constantly being bombarded with "facts" or "data." A television news report informs us that "one in every two marriages in this country now ends in divorce," yet Chapter 9 will show that this assertion is based on misleading statistics. Almost daily, advertisers cite supposedly scientific studies to prove that their products are superior. Such claims may be accurate or exaggerated. We can make better evaluations of such information—and will not be fooled so easily—if we are familiar with the standards of scientific research. As this chapter will indicate, the scientific method is quite stringent and demands that researchers adhere as strictly as possible to its basic principles.

The scientific method requires precise prepara-

tion in developing useful research. If investigators are not careful, research data that they collect may prove to be unacceptable for purposes of sociological study. There are five basic steps in the scientific method that sociologists and other researchers follow. These are (1) defining the problem, (2) reviewing the literature, (3) formulating the hypothesis, (4) selecting the research design and then collecting and analyzing data, and (5) developing the conclusion. An actual example will illustrate the workings of the scientific method.

In recent decades, women in the United States have increasingly entered occupations and careers that traditionally were reserved for men. As this change in the workplace evolved, the media persisted in typically portraying women in such traditional roles as mother and homemaker. Sociologists Penny Belknap and Wilbert Leonard, II

Sociologists Penny Belknap and Wilbert Leonard, II, analyzed sexual stereotyping in print advertisements appearing in major magazines so that they could better understand the images that the media are conveying to men and women in the United States.

(1991), devised a study to examine whether the media continue to show women primarily in these conventional roles.

These researchers began by *defining the problem*. The first step in any sociological research project is to state as clearly as possible what you hope to investigate. Belknap and Leonard noted that the media contribute to and perpetuate male dominance. They decided to analyze sexual stereotyping in print advertisements appearing in major magazines so they could better understand the images that the media are conveying to women and men in the United States.

The next step in their research was to *review the literature*. By conducting a review of the relevant scholarly studies and information, researchers refine the problem under study, clarify possible techniques to be used in collecting data, and eliminate or reduce the number of avoidable mistakes they make. Belknap and Leonard examined various studies of the roles of men and women portrayed in print advertisements. They were especially influenced by the work of interactionist theorist Erving Goffman (1979), who had emphasized that advertisements subtly convey the message that women are inferior and subordinate to men. For example, men are often shown as possessing power, authority, competence, and confidence, whereas women are often portrayed as being childlike and deferential.

After reviewing earlier research and drawing on the contributions of sociological theorists, the researchers then *formulate the hypothesis*. A **hypothesis** is a speculative statement about the relationship between two or more factors known as *variables*. Income, religion, occupation, and gender can all serve as variables in a study. We can define a *variable* as a measurable trait or characteristic that is subject to change under different conditions.

In formulating a hypothesis, researchers generally must suggest how one aspect of human behavior influences or affects another. If one variable is hypothesized to cause or influence another, social scientists call the first variable the **independent variable**. The second is termed the **dependent variable** because it is believed to be influenced by the independent variable. In their study of magazines' portrayal of women, Belknap

and Leonard were interested in the effect that a particular variable (type of magazine) might have on the images of women used in advertisements. As the causal or influencing characteristic, type of magazine ("traditional" or "modern") is the independent variable. The variable that Belknap and Leonard were trying to explain, portrayal of women in advertisements, is the dependent variable.

The researchers hypothesized that traditional magazines (*Good Housekeeping, Sports Illustrated,* and *Time*) would be more likely to portray women in subordinate positions (for example, being childlike and deferential) than would modern magazines (*Gentlemen's Quarterly, Ms.,* and *Rolling Stone*). In order to test a hypothesis and determine if it is supported or refuted, researchers need to *select a research design* and then *collect and analyze data*. In choosing a research design, Belknap and Leonard relied on a technique known as **content analysis,** which is the systematic coding and objective recording of data, guided by some rationale. The researchers examined approximately 170 print advertisements in each of the "traditional" and "modern" magazines to see if they showed women in a subordinate position.

After collecting and analyzing data, the researchers come to the final step in the scientific method; they *develop the conclusion*. Belknap and Leonard's content analysis revealed that advertisements in all six magazines under study tended to show women in subordinate positions. (It should be noted that this research was conducted *before Ms.* magazine stopped accepting advertising in 1990, in part because women continue to be treated as subordinate by many advertisers.) There was no substantial difference between the portrayal of women in traditional and modern magazines. Consequently, the researchers' findings *did not* support their hypothesis.

Does this mean that their study was a failure? Not at all. These findings remind us that researchers who use the scientific method may reach different conclusions from what they had expected, in turn generating ideas for further study (see Figure 1-2). Indeed, Belknap and Leonard recognize that there is a need for continuing research regarding the portrayal of women and men in advertising.

FIGURE 1-2 The Scientific Method

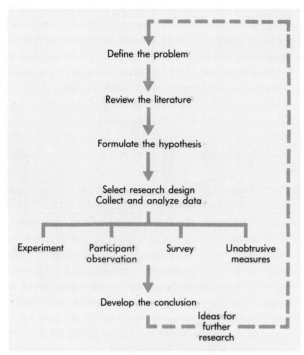

Define the problem

Review the literature

Formulate the hypothesis

Select research design
Collect and analyze data

Experiment — Participant observation — Survey — Unobtrusive measures

Develop the conclusion

Ideas for further research

The scientific method allows sociologists to objectively and logically evaluate the facts collected. This can lead to further ideas for sociological research.

Research Designs

An important aspect of sociological research is deciding how data should be collected. A *research design* is a detailed plan or method for obtaining data scientifically. Selection of a research design is a critical step for sociologists and requires creativity and ingenuity. This choice will directly influence both the cost of the project and the amount of time needed to collect the results of the research. Sociologists regularly use surveys, observation, experiments, and unobtrusive measures to generate data for their research.

Surveys   Almost all of us have responded to surveys of one kind or another. We may have been asked what kind of detergent we use, which presidential candidate we intend to vote for, or what

our favorite television program is. A *survey* is a study, generally in the form of an interview or questionnaire, which provides sociologists with information concerning how people think and act. Among our nation's best-known surveys of opinion are the Gallup poll and the Harris poll. As anyone who watches the news during presidential campaigns knows, these polls have become an important part of political life.

When you think of surveys, you may remember many "person on the street" interviews on local television news shows. While such interviews can be highly entertaining, they are not necessarily an accurate indication of public opinion. First, they reflect the opinions of only those people who appear at a certain location. Thus, such samples can be biased in favor of commuters, middle-class shoppers, or factory workers, depending on which street or area the newspeople select. Second, television interviews tend to attract outgoing people who are willing to appear on the air, while they frighten away others who may feel intimidated by a camera. A survey must be based on precise, representative sampling if it is to genuinely reflect a broad range of the population.

A *representative sample* is a selection from a larger population that is statistically found to be typical of that population. There are many kinds of samples, of which the random sample is frequently used by social scientists. For a *random sample,* every member of an entire population being studied has the same chance of being selected.

By using specialized sampling techniques, sociologists do not need to question everyone in a population. Thus, if researchers wanted to examine the opinions of people listed in a city directory (a book that, unlike the telephone directory, lists all households), they might call every tenth or fiftieth or hundredth name listed. This would constitute a random sample.

In preparing to conduct a survey, sociologists must not only develop representative samples; they must exercise great care in the wording of questions. An effective survey question must be simple and clear enough for people to understand it. It must also be specific enough so that there are no problems in interpreting the results. Even questions that are less structured ("What do

Doonesbury

BY GARRY TRUDEAU

Sociologists try to phrase questions carefully so that there will be no misunderstanding on the part of respondents. If a question is improperly worded (or biased, as in this cartoon), the results are useless for the researchers. Here, a less biased question would be: "Do you favor additional measures to reduce smoking in public places?"

you think of programming on educational television?") must be carefully phrased in order to solicit the type of information desired. Surveys can be indispensable sources of information, but only if the sampling is done properly and the questions are worded accurately.

There are two main forms of surveys: the ***interview*** and the ***questionnaire.*** Each of these forms of survey research has its own advantages. An interviewer can obtain a high response rate because people find it more difficult to turn down a personal request for an interview than to throw away a written questionnaire. In addition, a skillful interviewer can go beyond written questions and "probe" for a subject's underlying feelings and reasons. On the other hand, questionnaires have the advantage of being cheaper, especially when large samples are used.

Studies have shown that the gender (or race) of the researcher can have an impact on survey data. In 1990, the Eagleton Institute of Politics at Rutgers University confirmed that women were more likely to take strong "pro-choice" positions when questioned by a woman about the issue of abortion. For example, 84 percent of women interviewed by another woman agreed that the decision to have an abortion is a private matter that should be left to the woman to decide without government intervention. By contrast, only 64 percent of women interviewed by a man took the same position. Men's responses seemed unaffected by the gender of the researcher. Similarly,

people's responses to questions about housing discrimination may be influenced by the racial and ethnic background of the interviewer. The findings of the Eagleton Institute study underscore the careful attention that sociologists must give to all elements of the research design (Morin, 1990).

Observation When an investigator collects information through direct participation in and observation of a group, tribe, or community under study, he or she is engaged in ***observation.*** This research technique allows sociologists to examine certain behaviors and communities that could not be investigated through other methods. In some cases, the sociologist actually "joins" a group for a period of time to get an accurate sense of how it operates.

During the late 1930s, in a classic example of observation research, William F. Whyte moved into a low-income Italian neighborhood in Boston. For nearly four years, he was a member of the social circle of "corner boys" that he describes in *Street Corner Society*. Whyte revealed his identity to these men and joined in their conversations, bowling, and other leisure-time activities. His goal was to gain greater insight into the community that these men had established. As Whyte (1981:303) listened to Doc, the leader of the group, he "learned the answers to questions I would not even have had the sense to ask if I had been getting my information solely on an interviewing basis." Whyte's work was especially valuable, since, at the time, the academic world had little direct knowledge of the poor and tended to rely for information on the records of social service agencies, hospitals, and courts.

The initial challenge that Whyte faced—and that each participant observer must encounter—was to gain acceptance into an unfamiliar group. It is no simple matter for a college-trained sociologist to win the trust of a religious cult, a youth gang, a poor Appalachian community, or a circle of skid row residents. It requires a great deal of patience and an accepting, nonthreatening type of person.

A sociologist conducting observation research must retain a certain level of detachment from the group under study, even as he or she tries to understand how members feel. If the research is to be successful, the observer cannot allow the close associations or even friendships that inevitably develop to influence the conclusions of the study. Anson Shupe and David Bromley (1980), two sociologists who have used participant observation, have likened this challenge to that of "walking a tightrope." Despite working so hard to gain acceptance from the group being studied, the participant observer *must* maintain some degree of detachment.

In using observation studies, sociologists are well-aware that the presence of an observer may affect the behavior of the people being studied. The recognition of this phenomenon grew out of research conducted during the 1920s and 1930s at the Hawthorne plant of the Western Electric Company. A group of researchers headed by Elton Mayo set out to determine how the productivity of workers at this plant could be improved. Investigators examined the impact of variations in the intensity of light and variations in working hours on productivity. To their surprise, they found that *all* steps they took seemed to increase productivity. Even measures that seemed likely to have the opposite effect, such as reducing the amount of lighting in the plant, led to higher productivity.

Why did the plant's employees work harder even under less favorable conditions? Their behavior apparently was influenced by the greater attention being paid to workers in the course of the research. Since that time, sociologists have used the term **Hawthorne effect** when subjects of research perform in a manner different from their typical behavior because they realize that they are under observation.

Experiments When sociologists want to study a possible cause-and-effect relationship, they may conduct experiments. An ***experiment*** is an artificially created situation which allows the researcher to manipulate variables.

In the classic method of conducting an experiment, two groups of people are selected and matched for similar characteristics such as age or education. The subjects are then assigned by researchers to one of two groups—the experimental or control group. The ***experimental group*** is exposed to an independent variable; the ***control group*** is not. Thus, if scientists were testing a new type of antibiotic drug, they would administer injections of that drug to an experimental group but not to a control group.

Social psychologist Donna Desforges (Desforges et al., 1991) and her colleagues at Texas Christian University conducted an experiment (without use of a control group) to examine the impact of a positive work experience on people's negative stereotypes concerning former mental patients. As one part of this experiment, which involved a sample of 95 college students, each student was asked to participate in a cooperative learning exercise with another person (actually, a confederate working with the researchers). The students were given autobiographical essays supposedly written by their partners and learned that they were former mental patients (though, in fact, this was not the case).

Before starting the learning exercise, the students were asked to complete questionnaires about their anticipated attitudes toward working with their partners (whom they believed were former mental patients). During the performance of the exercises, the researchers' confederates displayed no unusual or aberrant behaviors. Then, once the exercises were completed, the students filled out questionnaires about how it actually felt to work with their partners.

Researchers found a significant difference in college students' attitudes after working with people whom they (falsely) believed to be former mental patients. After completing the learning exercises, these students registered more positive attitudes toward both their particular partners and former mental patients in general. Students who had initially expressed negative attitudes concerning former mental patients revealed more positive feelings after the exercises; those who had begun with positive attitudes toward former mental patients had even more positive attitudes afterward. In this experiment, the positive work experience *had* led to a more favorable view of former mental patients.

Conducting sociological research is more difficult, and therefore more costly, in the field than in a laboratory setting (often on a college campus). Consequently, as in the experiment described above, researchers must sometimes rely on samples composed entirely of college students. Such participants may or may not be representative of the larger public of the United States. There is an additional problem in using a laboratory setting: the responses of subjects in such settings may be different from their responses in less structured, real-life situations.

Unobtrusive Measures Social scientists from the University of Arizona studied people's spending and eating habits by examining household garbage left out on the street (Rathje, 1974). Sociologists Joan Luxenburg and Lloyd Klein (1984) monitored citizens' band radio broadcasts near a truck stop in Oklahoma to learn about a relatively new form of soliciting for prostitution. These are two unconventional examples of the use of unobtrusive measures in social scientific research.

Unobtrusive measures include a variety of research techniques that have no impact on who or what is being studied. These are designed as *nonreactive,* since people's behavior is not influenced. As an example, Émile Durkheim's statistical analysis of suicide neither increased nor decreased human self-destruction. Whereas subjects of an experiment are often aware that they are being watched—an awareness that can influence their behavior—this is not the case when unobtrusive measures are used. Consequently, sociologists can avoid the Hawthorne effect by employing unobtrusive methods (Webb et al., 1981).

One basic technique of unobtrusive measurement is the use of statistics, as in Durkheim's work. Crime statistics, census data, budgets of public agencies, and other archival data are all readily available to sociologists and other social scientists. Much of this information can be obtained at relatively low cost. For example, political scientist Gary Orfield (1987) was able to obtain computer tapes of enrollments by race for 36,000 schools from the U.S. Department of Education; these tapes helped him to conduct a major study of segregation of public schools in the 1980s.

There is one inherent problem, however, in relying on data collected by someone else: the researcher may not find exactly what is needed. Social scientists studying family violence can use statistics from police and social service agencies on *reported* cases of spouse abuse and child abuse. Yet such government bodies have no precise data on *all* cases of abuse.

Many social scientists find it useful to study cultural, economic, and political documents, including newspapers, periodicals, radio and television tapes, scripts, diaries, songs, folklore, and legal papers, to name a few examples. In examining these sources, researchers employ a type of unobtrusive measurement known as *content analysis.* As described earlier, Penny Belknap and Wilbert Leonard, II, used content analysis to study the portrayal of women in print advertisements.

Unobtrusive measures have proved to be valuable as a supplement to other research methods. For example, business firms use data from retail outlets on the advance order of gift wrap as an early indicator of holiday spending. Peter Appert, a Wall Street analyst, has even developed a gift wrap index. While the index is not foolproof, this unobtrusive measure has served as an accurate predictor of sales since it was first introduced in 1981 (Neuborne, 1991).

Ethics of Research

A biochemist cannot inject a serum into a human being unless it has been thoroughly tested. To do otherwise would be both unethical and illegal. Sociologists must also abide by certain specific standards in conducting research—by a **code of ethics.** The professional society of the discipline, the American Sociological Association (ASA), first published the *Code of Ethics* in 1971 (most recently revised in 1989), which put forth the following basic principles:

1 Maintain objectivity and integrity in research.
2 Respect the subject's right to privacy and to dignity.
3 Protect subjects from personal harm.
4 Preserve confidentiality.
5 Acknowledge research collaboration and assistance.
6 Disclose all sources of financial support (American Sociological Association, 1989).

On the surface, the basic principles of the ASA's *Code of Ethics* probably seem quite clear-cut. It may be difficult to imagine how they could lead to any disagreement or controversy. However, many delicate ethical questions cannot be resolved simply by reading the six points above. For example, should a sociologist engaged in observation research *always* protect the confidentiality of subjects? What if the subjects are members of a religious cult allegedly engaged in unethical and possibly illegal activities? In Box 1-2 (page 22), we consider this sensitive issue by examining the views of a sociologist who studied a highly controversial religious group (see also Heller, 1987; Shupe and Bromley, 1980).

Most sociological research uses *people* as sources of information—as respondents to survey questions, subjects of observation, or participants in experiments. In all cases, sociologists need to be certain that they are not invading the privacy of their subjects. Generally, this is handled by assuring those involved of anonymity and by guaranteeing that personal information disclosed will remain confidential. However, studies by Laud Humphreys and William Zellner raised important questions about the extent to which sociologists could threaten people's right to privacy.

Tearoom Trade Sociologist Laud Humphreys (1970a, 1970b, 1975) published a pioneering and controversial study of homosexual behavior in which he described the casual homosexual encounters between males meeting in public restrooms in parks. Such restrooms are sometimes called *tearooms* by homosexual men. As one consequence of this provocative research, the chancellor of the university where Humphreys was employed terminated his research grant and teaching contract.

In order to study the lifestyle of homosexual males in tearooms, Humphreys acted as a participant observer by serving as a "lookout," warning patrons when police or other strangers approached. While he was primarily interested in the behavior of these men, Humphreys also wanted to learn more about who they were and why they took such risks. Yet how could he obtain such information? Secrecy and silence were the norms of this sexual environment. Most of the men under study were unaware of Humphreys's identity and would not have consented to standard sociological interviews.

As a result, Humphreys decided on a research technique that some social scientists later saw as a violation of professional ethics. He recorded the license plate numbers of tearoom patrons, waited a year, changed his appearance, and then interviewed them in their homes. The interviews were conducted as part of a larger survey, but they did provide information that Humphreys felt was necessary for his work. While Humphreys's subjects consented to be interviewed, their agreement fell short of *informed* consent, since they were unaware of the true purpose of the study.

Although the researcher recognized each of the men interviewed from his observations in the restrooms, there was no indication that they recognized him. Humphreys learned that most of his subjects were in their middle thirties and married. They had an average of two children and tended to have at least some years of college education. Family members appeared to be unaware of the men's visits to park restrooms for casual homosexual encounters.

Even before the public outcry over his research began, Humphreys (1970b:167–173; 1975:175–232) was aware of the ethical questions that his study would raise. He exerted great care in maintaining the confidentiality of his subjects. Their real identities were recorded only on a master list kept in a safe-deposit box. The list was destroyed by Humphreys after the research was conducted.

For social scientists, the ethical problem in this research was not Humphreys's choice of subject

BOX 1-2

PRESERVING CONFIDENTIALITY

*I*n his book Doomsday Cult, *sociologist John Lofland (1977:xi) analyzes the "first five years in America (1959–1964) of an obscure end-of-the-world religion that went on to become nationally and internationally famous in the 1970s." He explains that this cult, which he refers to as the "Divine Precepts," or "DPs," is led by a Korean man who arrived in the United States in 1971. Lofland adds that, by the 1970s, the DPs had become widely viewed as a "powerful and nefarious social force that had to be countered."*

Many readers of Doomsday Cult *suspected that the DPs were, in fact, Reverend Sun Myung Moon's Unification church. However, after years of observation research, Lofland refused to break his initial promise of anonymity and reveal the real names of the DPs and their leader. At the end of the book, Lofland (1977:345–346) explains why he maintained this position:*

. . . First, I continue to have a personal and private obligation to the members with whom I spent many months. I am determined that they will not suffer infamy on my account, despite the fact that some have achieved infamy by their own actions. Second, I am a sociologist rather than an investigative journalist . . . , muckraker or other moralist. . . .

Sociologists must agree to protect the people they study in ex-

John Lofland.

Courtesy Lyn H. Lofland

change for permission to be privy to the secrets of social organization and social life. I made such an agreement with the group reported in this book, and although the fame of the group now makes it difficult to continue this protection, I must try. Anything less endangers the future of sociology itself, threatening to bring it into even more disrepute by giving credence to the charge that sociologists are merely one more breed of muckraker, whistle-blower, undercover agent, police spy, or worse. . . .

The position I offer above is not, of course, absolute. . . . There are a few circumstances in which I would not grant or continue the protections of anonymity. A prime one is if I believed that the DPs seriously threatened the pluralism of American society,

that they had any serious chance of taking over the United States government, I would try to stop them, and use personally identified information on members to do so. That is, a pluralistic and more or less free society is one indispensable condition of practicing sociology itself. I would not stand by and allow them to destroy my discipline (which they would do if they could) and the society that makes that discipline possible. In my judgment, they do not now nor are they ever likely to pose such a threat.

There is an interesting postscript to this story. Despite Lofland's firm efforts to protect the anonymity of the DPs and their leader, it was commonly assumed—and even flatly asserted in print by other scholars—that the DPs were indeed Moon's Unification church. By the early 1980s, Lofland (1985:120–121) finally concluded that the "'secret' had become absurdly obvious, so obvious that continuing the 'cover' seemed pointless." Consequently, in 1983, he asked the president of the United States' branch of the Unification church to release him from his 1962 agreement with church officials. This request was granted, but it was agreed that only the organization and its founder would be named by Lofland. He continues to protect the identities of the cult members whom he met during his years of observation research.

matter, but rather the deception involved. Patrons of the tearoom were not aware of Humphreys's purposes and were further misled about the real reasons for the household interviews. However, in the researcher's judgment, the value of his study justified the questionable means involved. Humphreys believed that, without the follow-up interviews, we would know little about the kinds of men who engage in tearoom sex and would be left with false stereotypes.

In addition, Humphreys believed that by describing such sexual interactions accurately, he would be able to dispel the myth that child molestation is a frequent practice in restrooms. One unintended consequence of the research was that it has been increasingly cited by attorneys seeking acquittal for clients arrested in public bathrooms. These lawyers have used the study to establish that such behavior is not unusual and typically involves consenting adults. A recent study of Canadian police records by sociologist Frederick Desroches (1990) supports Humphreys's earlier findings regarding tearoom sex. The majority of Canadian participants were married and many had children. Of 190 males studied who were involved in such sexual activities, only three were teenagers (two of whom were participating in tearoom sex together) and none were children (see also J. Gray, 1991).

Do these gains in our knowledge and understanding offset Humphreys's actions of encroaching on people's private lives and deceiving them during interviews? Essentially, in reflecting on the study, we are left with conflict between the right to know and the right to privacy. There is no easy resolution to this clash of principles. Yet we can certainly ask that sociologists be fully aware of the ethical implications of any such research techniques (I. Horowitz and Rainwater, 1970; Von Hoffman, 1970).

Accident or Suicide? A similar ethical issue—with the right to know posed against the right to privacy—became apparent in research on automobile accidents in which fatalities occur. Sociologist William Zellner (1978) wanted to learn if fatal car crashes are sometimes suicides that have been disguised as accidents in order to protect family and friends (and perhaps to collect otherwise unredeemable insurance benefits). These acts of "autocide" are by nature covert, even more so than the sexual behavior of Humphreys's subjects.

In his efforts to assess the frequency of such suicides, Zellner sought to interview the friends, coworkers, and family members of the deceased. He hoped to obtain information that would allow him to ascertain whether the deaths were accidental or purposeful. People approached for interviews were told that Zellner's goal was to contribute to a reduction of future accidents. For this reason (as they were falsely informed), Zellner wished to learn about the emotional characteristics of accident victims. No mention was made of the interviewer's suspicions of autocide, out of fear that potential respondents would refuse to meet with him.

Zellner eventually concluded that at least 12 percent of all fatal single-occupant crashes are suicides. This information could be valuable for society, particularly since some of the probable suicides actually killed or critically injured innocent bystanders in the process of taking their own lives. Yet the ethical questions still must be faced. Was Zellner's research unethical because he misrepresented the motives of his study and failed to obtain subjects' informed consent? Or was his deception justified by the social value of his findings?

As in the study of tearoom trade, the answers are not immediately apparent. Like Humphreys, Zellner appeared to have admirable motives and took great care in protecting confidentiality. Names of suspected suicides were not revealed to insurance companies, though Zellner did recommend that the insurance industry drop double indemnity (payment of twice the person's life insurance benefits in the event of accidental death) in the future.

Zellner's study raised an additional ethical issue: the possibility of harm to those who were interviewed. Subjects were asked if the deceased had "talked about suicide" and if they had spoken of how "bad or useless" they were. Could these questions have led people to guess the true intentions of the researcher? Perhaps, but according to Zellner, none of the informants voiced such suspicions. More seriously, might the study have caused the bereaved to *suspect* suicide—when before the survey they had accepted the deaths as accidental? Again, we have no evidence to suggest this, but we cannot be sure.

Given our uncertainty about this last question, was the research justified? Was Zellner taking too large a risk in asking the friends and families of the deceased victims if they had spoken of suicide before their death? Does the right to know outweigh the right to privacy in this type of situation? And who has the right to make such a judgment? In practice, as in Zellner's study, it is the *researcher*, not the subjects of inquiry, who makes the critical ethical decisions. Therefore, sociologists and other investigators bear the responsibility for establishing clear and sensitive boundaries for ethical scientific investigation.

Neutrality and Politics in Research The ethical considerations of sociologists lie not only in the methods used, but in the way that results are interpreted. Max Weber (1949:1–49, original edition 1904) recognized that sociologists would be influenced by their own personal values in selecting questions for research. In his view, that was perfectly acceptable, but under no conditions could a researcher allow his or her personal feelings to influence the interpretation of data. In Weber's phrase, sociologists must practice **value neutrality** in their research.

As part of this neutrality, investigators have an ethical obligation to accept research findings even when the data run counter to their own personal views, to theoretically based explanations, or to widely accepted beliefs. Durkheim countered popular conceptions when he reported that social (rather than supernatural) forces were an important factor in suicide. Similarly, Humphreys challenged traditional suspicions when he found that users of tearooms were not preying on adolescents or younger boys.

Some sociologists believe that it is impossible for scholars to prevent their personal values from influencing their work. As a result, Weber's call for value-free sociology has been criticized on the grounds that it leads the public to accept sociological conclusions without exploring the biases of the researchers. Furthermore, drawing on the conflict perspective, Alvin Gouldner (1970:439–440), among others, has suggested that sociologists may use objectivity as a sacred justification for remaining uncritical of existing institutions and centers of power. These arguments are attacks not so much on Weber himself as on how his goals have been incorrectly interpreted. As we have seen, Weber was quite clear that sociologists may bring values to their subject matter. In his view, however, they must not confuse their own values with the social reality under study (Bendix, 1968:495).

Peter Rossi (1987:73) admits that "in my professional work as a sociologist, my liberal inclinations have led me to undertake applied social research in the hope that . . . my research might contribute to the general liberal aim of social reform. . . ." Yet, in line with Weber's view of value neutrality, Rossi's commitment to rigorous research methods and objective interpretation of data has sometimes led him to controversial findings not necessarily supportive of his own liberal values. For example, when Rossi and a team of researchers carefully attempted to measure the extent of homelessness in Chicago in the mid-1980s, they arrived at estimates of the city's homeless population far below those offered (with little firm documentation) by the Chicago Coalition for the Homeless. As a result, Rossi was bitterly attacked by coalition members for hampering social reform efforts by minimizing the extent of homelessness. Having been through similar controversies before, Rossi (1987:79) concludes that "in the short term, good social research will often be greeted as a betrayal of one or another side to a particular controversy." But he insists that such applied research is exciting to do and can make important long-term contributions to our understanding of social problems.

Even the decision to conduct a study can spark partisan debate. In 1991, a challenge to a major research effort was partially fought off after the secretary of Health and Human Services announced that he was canceling funding for a five-year, $18 million national survey of teenage life in the United States. The survey had strong backing from the National Institutes of Health, but conservatives were troubled by the inclusion of questions on sexual behavior and pressured the Bush administration to kill the study. Intense debate followed, in which supporters of the research spoke of the need to better understand sexual behavior in light of the prevalence of teen pregnancy and sexually transmitted diseases (including AIDS). Subsequently, the House of Representatives, by a 2–1 vote, authorized the federal government to engage in surveys of sexual behavior. But the fate of the teen survey was left in doubt, underscoring the fact that studying social behavior can generate serious controversy (COSSA, 1991).

As this example illustrates, the issue of value neutrality becomes especially delicate when one considers the relationship of sociology to government. Indeed, in the United States, the federal government has become the major source of funding for sociological research. Yet Max Weber urged that sociology remain an autonomous discipline and not become unduly influenced by any one segment of society. According to his ideal of value neutrality, sociologists must remain free to reveal information that is embarrassing to government or, for that matter, is supportive of government institutions (L. Coser, 1977:219–222; Gouldner, 1962). Thus, researchers investigating a prison riot must be ready to examine objectively not only the behavior of inmates but also the conduct of prison officials before and during the outbreak. This may be more difficult if sociologists fear that findings critical of governmental institutions will jeopardize their chances of obtaining federal support for new research projects.

Although the American Sociological Association's *Code of Ethics* expects sociologists to disclose all funding sources, the code does not address the issue of whether sociologists who accept funding from a particular agency may also accept their perspective on what needs to be studied. Lewis Coser (1956:27) has argued that as sociologists in the United States have increasingly turned from basic sociological research to applied research for government agencies and the private sector, "they have relinquished to a large extent the freedom to choose their own problems, substituting the problems of their clients for those which might have

Shown is a camp for homeless people in Los Angeles. Sociologist Peter Rossi was attacked by the Chicago Coalition for the Homeless for hampering its efforts at social reform because his carefully researched estimate of the city's homeless population was far below that offered (with little firm documentation) by the coalition.

interested them on purely theoretical grounds." Viewed in this light, the importance of government funding for sociological studies raises troubling questions for those who cherish Weber's ideal of value neutrality in research.

CAREERS IN SOCIOLOGY

Figure 1-3 below summarizes sources of employment for those with B.A. or B.S. degrees in sociology. Like other liberal arts graduates, sociology majors can generally offer their employers essential job-related skills. Alumni find that their refinement in such areas as oral and written communication, interpersonal skills, problem solving, and critical thinking gives them an advantage over graduates who have pursued more technical degrees (Benner and Hitchcock, 1986).

Reflecting practical value of studying sociology, the figure shows that the areas of human services, business, and government offer important career opportunities for sociology graduates. Undergraduates are commonly advised to enroll in sociology courses and specialties best-suited to their career interests. For example, students hoping to become health planners would take a class in medical sociology; students seeking employment as social science research assistants would refine their skills in statistics and methods. Internships, such as placements at city planning agencies and survey research organizations, offer sociology undergraduates an important opportunity to prepare for careers. Studies show that students who choose an internship placement have less trouble finding jobs, obtain better jobs, and enjoy greater job satisfaction than students without such placements (Salem and Grabarek, 1986).

The primary source of employment for sociologists is higher education. About 75 percent of recent Ph.D. recipients in sociology sought employment in two-year community colleges, liberal arts colleges, and universities. These sociologists will teach not only majors committed to the discipline but also students hoping to become doctors, nurses, lawyers, police officers, and so forth (B. Huber, 1985).

For sociology students interested in academic careers, the road to a Ph.D. degree (or doctorate) can be long and difficult. This degree symbolizes competence in original research; each candidate must prepare a book-length study known as a *dissertation*. Typically, a graduate student in sociology will engage in four to six years of intensive work, including the time required to complete the dissertation. Yet this effort is no guarantee of a job as a sociology professor.

In the near future, the demand for teachers is expected to be uncertain, since there will be fewer students of college age. Consequently, anyone who launches an academic career must be prepared for competition in the job market for college teachers (American Sociological Association, 1991; B. Huber, 1985).

Of course, not all people working as sociologists teach or hold doctoral degrees. Government is the second-largest source of employment for people in

FIGURE 1-3 Where Sociology Graduates Find Employment

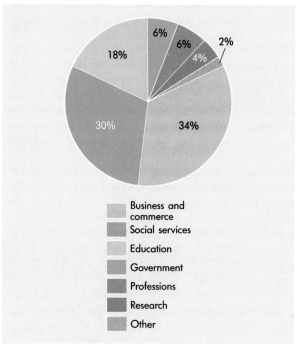

SOURCE: Watts and Ellis, 1989:301.

Graduates with baccalaureate degrees in sociology find employment in a number of areas, but particularly in business and commerce, social services, and education.

this discipline. The Census Bureau relies on people with sociological training to interpret data in a way that is useful for other government agencies and the general public. Virtually every agency depends on survey research—a field in which sociology students can specialize—in order to assess everything from community needs to the morale of the agency's own workers. In addition, people with sociological training can put their academic knowledge to effective use in probation and parole, health sciences, community development, and recreational services. Some people working in government or private industry have a master's degree (an M.A. or M.S.) in sociology; others have a bachelor's degree (a B.A. or B.S.).

It is clear that an increasing number of sociologists with graduate degrees are being hired by business firms, industry, hospitals, and nonprofit organizations. Indeed, studies show that many sociology graduates are making career changes from social services areas to business and commerce. As an undergraduate or graduate major, sociology is excellent preparation for employment in many parts of the business world (B. Huber, 1985, 1987; Watts and Ellis, 1989; Wilkinson, 1980).

SUMMARY

Sociology is the systematic study of social behavior and human groups. In this chapter, we examine the founders of the discipline, theoretical perspectives of contemporary sociology, the basic principles of the scientific method, and the various techniques used by sociologists in conducting research.

1 An important element in the **sociological imagination**—which is an awareness of the relationship between an individual and the wider society—is the ability to view our own society as an outsider might, rather than from the perspective of our limited experiences and cultural biases.

2 In his pioneering work *Suicide*, published in 1897, Émile Durkheim focused on social factors that contributed to the rates of suicide found among various groups and nations.

3 In contrast to the emphasis on stability which characterizes the **functionalist perspective** of sociology, the **conflict perspective** assumes that social behavior is best understood in terms of conflict between competing groups.

4 The **interactionist perspective** is primarily concerned with fundamental or everyday forms of interaction, including symbols and other types of **nonverbal communication**.

5 There are five basic steps in the **scientific method:** defining the problem, reviewing the literature, formulating the hypothesis, selecting the research design and then collecting and analyzing data, and developing the conclusion.

6 The two principal forms of **survey** research are the **interview** and the **questionnaire**.

7 Observation allows sociologists to study certain behaviors and communities that cannot be investigated through other research methods.

8 When sociologists want to study a cause-and-effect relationship, they may conduct an **experiment**.

9 Max Weber urged sociologists to practice **value neutrality** in their research by ensuring that their personal feelings do not influence the interpretation of data.

CRITICAL THINKING QUESTIONS

1 If a sociologist was present in a college cafeteria, what aspects of the social and work environment would be of particular interest because of his or her "sociological imagination"?

2 Suppose that your sociology instructor has asked you to do a study of homelessness in the area where your college is located. Which research technique (survey, observation, experiment, unobtrusive measurement) would you find most useful in studying homelessness? How would you use that technique to complete your assignment?

3 Can a sociologist genuinely maintain value neutrality while studying a group that he or she finds repugnant (for example, a White supremacist organization, a satanic cult, or a group of prison inmates convicted of rape)?

KEY TERMS

Code of ethics The standards of acceptable behavior developed by and for members of a profession. (page 21)

Conflict perspective A sociological approach which assumes that social behavior is best understood in terms of conflict or tension between competing groups. (11)

Content analysis The systematic coding and objective recording of data, guided by some rationale. (16)

Control group Subjects in an experiment who are not introduced to an independent variable by the researcher. (19)

Dependent variable The variable in a causal relationship which is subject to the influence of another variable. (16)

Dramaturgical approach A view of social interaction, popularized by Erving Goffman, under which people are examined as if they were theatrical performers. (13)

Dysfunction An element or a process of society that may disrupt a social system or lead to a decrease in stability. (11)

Experiment An artificially created situation which allows the researcher to manipulate variables. (19)

Experimental group Subjects in an experiment who are exposed to an independent variable introduced by a researcher. (19)

Functionalist perspective A sociological approach which emphasizes the way that parts of a society are structured to maintain its stability. (10)

Hawthorne effect The unintended influence that observers or experiments can have on their subjects. (19)

Hypothesis A speculative statement about the relationship between two or more variables. (16)

Ideal type A construct or model that serves as a measuring rod against which actual cases can be evaluated. (7)

Independent variable The variable in a causal relationship which, when altered, causes or influences a change in a second variable. (16)

Interactionist perspective A sociological approach which generalizes about fundamental or everyday forms of social interaction. (13)

Interview A face-to-face or telephone questioning of a respondent in order to obtain desired information. (18)

Latent functions Unconscious or unintended functions; hidden purposes. (10)

Manifest functions Open, stated, and conscious functions. (10)

Nonverbal communication The sending of messages through the use of posture, facial expressions, and gestures. (13)

Observation A research technique in which an investigator collects information through direct involvement with and observation of a group, tribe, or community. (18)

Questionnaire A printed research instrument employed to obtain desired information from a respondent. (18)

Random sample A sample for which every member of the entire population has the same chance of being selected. (17)

Representative sample A selection from a larger population that is statistically found to be typical of that population. (17)

Research design A detailed plan or method for obtaining data scientifically. (17)

Scientific method A systematic, organized series of steps that ensures maximum objectivity and consistency in researching a problem. (15)

Sociological imagination An awareness of the relationship between an individual and the wider society. (3)

Sociology The systematic study of social behavior and human groups. (2)

Survey A study, generally in the form of interviews or questionnaires, which provides sociologists and other researchers with information concerning how people think and act. (17)

Unobtrusive measures Research techniques in which the method of study has no influence on the subjects under investigation. (20)

Value neutrality Max Weber's term for objectivity of sociologists in the interpretation of data. (24)

Variable A measurable trait or characteristic that is subject to change under different conditions. (16)

Verstehen The German word for "understanding" or "insight"; used by Max Weber to stress the need for sociologists to take into account people's emotions, thoughts, beliefs, and attitudes. (6)

ADDITIONAL READINGS

Borgatta, Edgar F., and Marie L. Borgatta (eds.). *Encyclopedia of Sociology*. New York: Macmillan, 1992. A four-volume work that includes more than 350 signed essays on subjects ranging from "adulthood" to "work orientation." This encyclopedia is a good place to begin further reading or research.

Chafetz, Janet Saltzman. *Feminist Sociology: An Overview of Contemporary Theories*. Itasca, Ill.: Peacock, 1988. An overview of the major feminist theories in sociology that have emerged in the last two decades.

Miller, Delbert C. *Handbook of Research Design and Social Measurement* (5th ed.). Newbury Park, Calif.: Sage, 1991. A veritable encyclopedia of measures used in sociological studies; also includes guides to library research and writing of reports.

Schaefer, Richard T., and Robert P. Lamm (eds.). *Introducing Sociology*. New York: McGraw-Hill, 1987. A collection of 52 thought-provoking articles illustrating the sociological imagination.

Webb, Eugene J., Donald T. Campbell, Richard D. Schwartz, Lee Sechrest, and Janet Belew Grove. *Nonreactive Measures in the Social Sciences* (2d ed.). Boston: Houghton Mifflin, 1981. The authors identify unobtrusive methods of obtaining social science data other than questionnaires or interviews.

2

CULTURE

LOOKING AHEAD

- How do elements of a culture develop? How do they spread from one society to another?
- Why is language viewed by sociologists as the foundation of every culture?
- How are sanctions used to reinforce society's norms regarding proper behavior?
- Why are circus performers, computer hackers, and Appalachians all considered examples of subcultures?
- Should schools and colleges in the United States continue to focus on the traditions of western cultures? Or should they revise their curricula to give greater emphasis to African Americans, other racial and ethnic minorities, women, and nonwestern cultures?

During his 1992 visit to the Japanese city of Kashihara, President George Bush made a ceremonial stop at a Toys "Я" Us store that had recently opened. The president paid tribute to the ability of this New Jersey–based corporation to open large stores in Japan and many other countries. Indeed, the international growth of Toys "Я" Us in the 1990s is a vivid example of how a company can expand around the world by successfully adapting to the particular customs and needs of other cultures.

One central factor in this effort is a careful evaluation of the merchandise that will be offered. While marketing distinctive products from the United States in all of its international outlets, Toys "Я" Us must still cater to local tastes. Consequently, it sells porcelain dolls in Japan, wooden toys in Germany, and models of a high-speed train in France.

To be truly successful, however, an international marketer must often make changes in its management policies. According to Toys "Я" Us policy in the United States, cashiers should stand. Yet the London managers of a Toys "Я" Us outlet decided to revise that standard because the European custom is for cashiers to sit while working. "In every country we enter," notes Toys "Я" Us vice chairman Robert Nakasone, "we try to think globally and act locally" (A. Miller, 1992:47). Clearly, in extending its operations from North America to other continents, Toys "Я" Us managers are well-aware of substantial cultural differences. These differences in customs and behavior occur because people live in many different, unique cultures.

CULTURE AND SOCIETY

Culture is the totality of learned, socially transmitted behavior. It includes the ideas, values, and customs (as well as the sailboats, comic books, and birth control devices) of groups of people. Therefore, patriotic attachment to the American flag is an aspect of culture, as is the European custom that cashiers in retail stores sit rather than stand.

Sometimes people refer to a particular person as "very cultured" or to a city as having "lots of culture." That use of the term *culture* is different from our use in this textbook. In sociological terms, culture does not refer solely to the fine arts and refined intellectual taste. It consists of *all* objects and ideas within a society, including ice cream cones, rock music, and slang words. Sociologists consider both a portrait by Rembrandt and a portrait by a billboard painter to be aspects of a culture. A tribe that cultivates soil by hand has just as much of a culture as a people that relies on diesel-operated machinery. Thus, each people has a distinctive culture with its own characteristic ways of gathering and preparing food, constructing homes, structuring the family, and promoting standards of right and wrong.

Sharing a similar culture helps to define the

Shown is a Toys "Я" Us store that opened in Ami, Japan, in 1992. That same year, while visiting Japan, President George Bush paid tribute to the New Jersey–based corporation's ability to open its large stores in Japan and many other countries.

group to which we belong. A fairly large number of people are said to constitute a *society* when they live in the same territory, are relatively independent of people outside their area, and participate in a common culture. The city of Los Angeles is more populous than many nations of the world, yet sociologists do not consider it a society in its own right. Rather, it is seen as part of—and dependent on—the larger society of the United States.

A society is the largest form of human group. It consists of people who share a common heritage and culture. Members of the society learn this culture and transmit it from one generation to the next. They even preserve their distinctive culture through literature, art, video recordings, and other means of expression. If it were not for the social transmission of culture, each generation would have to reinvent television, not to mention the wheel.

Having a common culture also simplifies many day-to-day interactions. For example, if you plan to go to a movie theater in the United States, you know that you will not need to bring along a chair. When you are part of a society, there are many small (as well as more important) cultural patterns that you take for granted. Just as you assume that theaters will provide seats for the audience, you also assume that physicians will not disclose confi-

dential information, that banks will protect the money you deposit, and that parents will be careful when crossing the street with young children. All these assumptions reflect the basic values, beliefs, and customs of the culture of the United States.

Members of a society generally share a common language, and this fact also facilitates day-to-day exchanges with others. Language is a critical element of culture that sets humans apart from other species. When you ask a hardware store clerk for a flashlight, you do not need to draw a picture of the instrument. You share the same cultural term for a small, battery-operated, portable light. However, if you were in England and needed this item, you would have to ask for an "electric torch." Of course, even within the same society, a term can have a number of different meanings. In the United States, *grass* signifies both a plant eaten by grazing animals and an intoxicating drug.

The study of culture is an important part of contemporary sociological work. This chapter will examine the development of culture from its roots in the prehistoric human experience. The major aspects of culture—including language, norms, sanctions, and values—will be defined and explored. The discussion focuses both on general cultural practices found in all societies and on the wide variations that can distinguish one society from another. We will contrast the ways in which functionalist and conflict theorists view culture. The social policy section will look at the conflicts in cultural values which underlie current debates over the use of multicultural curricula in schools and colleges in the United States.

DEVELOPMENT OF CULTURE

Through advances in culture, human beings have come a long way from our prehistoric heritage. In the 1990s, we can send astronauts to the moon, split the atom, and prolong lives through heart transplants. The human species has produced such achievements as the ragtime compositions of Scott Joplin, the paintings of Van Gogh, the poetry of Emily Dickinson, and the novels of Dostoevsky. We can even analyze our innermost feelings through the insights of Sigmund Freud and other pioneers of psychology. In all these ways, we are remarkably different from other species of the animal kingdom.

The process of expanding culture has already been under way for thousands of years and will continue in the future. The first archeological evidence of humanlike primates places our ancestors back many millions of years. Some 2.5 million years ago people used tools and had containers for storage. From 35,000 years ago we have evidence of paintings, jewelry, and statues. By that time, elaborate ceremonies had already been developed for marriages, births, and deaths (Haviland, 1985).

Tracing the development of culture is not easy. Archeologists cannot "dig up" weddings, laws, or government, but they are able to locate items that point to the emergence of cultural traditions. Our early ancestors, the **hominids,** were primates that had characteristics of human beings. These curious and communicative creatures made important advances in the use of tools. Recent studies of chimpanzees in the wild have revealed that they frequently use sticks and other natural objects in ways learned from other members of the group. However, unlike chimpanzees, the hominids gradually made tools from increasingly durable materials. As a result, the items could be reused and refined into more effective implements.

Cultural Universals

Like the hominids, human beings have made dramatic cultural advances. Despite their differences, all societies have attempted to meet basic human needs by developing cultural universals. ***Cultural universals,*** such as language, are general practices found in every culture.

Anthropologist George Murdock (1945:124) compiled a list of cultural universals. The examples identified by Murdock include the following practices:

Athletic sports	Housing
Bodily adornment	Language
Calendar	Laws
Cooking	Marriage
Courtship	Medicine
Dancing	Music
Decorative art	Myths
Family	Numerals
Folklore	Personal names
Food habits	Property rights
Food taboos	Religion
Funeral ceremonies	Sexual restrictions
Games	Surgery
Gestures	Toolmaking
Gift giving	Trade
Hairstyles	Visiting

Many cultural universals are, in fact, adaptations to meet essential human needs, such as people's need for food, shelter, and clothing. Yet, although the cultural practices listed by Murdock may be universal, the manner in which they are expressed will vary from culture to culture. For example, one society may attempt to influence its weather by seeding clouds with dry ice particles to bring about rain. Another culture may offer sacrifices to the gods in order to end a long period of drought.

Like games, toys can be viewed as a cultural universal. In seeking to expand Toys "Я" Us to new international markets, the company's chairman, Charles Lazarus, stated that children around the world "all know what Nintendo is;

Cultural universals, such as bodily adornment and styles of dress, are general practices found in every culture. Shown in the traditional dress of their distinctive cultures are a woman from India, a man from New Guinea, and a family from Germany's Bavarian Alps.

they all know what Ninja Turtles are." However, as noted above, the manner in which cultural universals are expressed will vary. It is for this reason that Toys "Я" Us sells porcelain dolls in Japan, wooden toys in Germany, and models of a high-speed train in France. Children in these countries may all want Nintendo games and Ninja Turtle stuffed animals, but their other toy preferences may differ significantly (A. Miller, 1992:46).

While all cultures share certain general practices—such as cooking, gift giving, and dancing—the expression of any cultural universal in a society may change dramatically over time. Thus, the most popular styles of dancing in the United States during the 1990s are sure to be different from the styles dominant in the 1950s or the 1970s. Each generation, and each year, most human cultures change and expand through the processes of innovation and diffusion.

Innovation

The process of introducing an idea or object that is new to culture is known as **innovation.** There are two forms of innovation: discovery and invention. A **discovery** involves making known or sharing the existence of an aspect of reality. The finding of the DNA molecule and the identification of a new moon of Saturn are both acts of discovery. A significant factor in the process of discovery is the sharing of newfound knowledge with others. By contrast, an **invention** results when existing cultural items are combined into a form that did not exist before. The bow and arrow, the automobile, and the television are all examples of inventions, as are Protestantism and democracy.

Diffusion

One does not have to sample gourmet food to eat "foreign" foods. Breakfast cereal comes originally from Germany, candy from the Netherlands, chewing gum from Mexico, and the potato chip from the America of the Indians. The United States has also "exported" foods to other lands. Residents of many nations enjoy pizza, which was popularized in the United States. However, in Japan they add squid, in Australia it is eaten with pineapple, and in England people like kernels of corn with the cheese.

Just as a culture does not always discover or invent its foods, it may also adopt ideas, technology, and customs from other cultures. Sociologists use the term **diffusion** to refer to the process by which a cultural item is spread from group to group or society to society. Diffusion can occur through a variety of means, among them exploration, military conquest, missionary work, the influence of the mass media, and tourism.

Early in human history, culture changed rather slowly through discovery. As the number of discoveries in a culture increased, inventions became possible. The more inventions there were, the more rapidly further inventions could be created. In addition, as diverse cultures came into contact with one another, they could each take advantage of the other's innovations. Thus, when people in the United States read a newspaper, we look at characters invented by the ancient Semites, printed by a process invented in Germany, on a material invented in China (Linton, 1936:326–327).

Diffusion may take place over extremely long distances. The use of smoking tobacco began when Indian tribes in the Caribbean invented the habit of smoking the tobacco plant, where it grew wild. Over a period of hundreds of years, tobacco was acquired and cultivated by one neighboring tribe after another. Through diffusion, this practice traveled through Central America and across the North American continent (Kroeber, 1923: 211–214).

Even within a society, diffusion occurs as innovations—discoveries and inventions—gain wider acceptance. For example, "rap" was well established among certain inner-city Blacks long before most people in the United States were aware of this form of singing. A 1985 music video by the Chicago Bears football team helped to popularize rap; partly as a result, rap singing groups like Run-D.M.C. became known outside central cities.

While these examples show that diffusion is common within the United States and from culture to culture, it must be emphasized that diffusion of cultural traits does not occur automatically. Groups and societies resist ideas which seem too foreign as well as those which are perceived as threatening to their own beliefs and values. Each culture tends to be somewhat selective in what it absorbs from competing cultures. Europe accepted silk, the magnetic compass, chess, and gunpowder from the Chinese but rejected the teachings of Confucius as an ideology. Many people in the United States have accepted the idea of acupuncture, the Chinese practice of puncturing the body with needles to cure disease or relieve pain, but few have committed themselves to the philosophy behind acupuncture, which involves the idea that the human body contains equal but opposite forces called *yin* and *yang.*

Sociologist William F. Ogburn (1922:202–203) made a useful distinction between elements of material and nonmaterial culture. **Material culture** refers to the physical or technological aspects of our daily lives, including food items, houses, factories, and raw materials. **Nonmaterial culture** refers to ways of using material objects and to customs, beliefs, philosophies, governments, and patterns of communication. Generally, the nonmaterial culture is more resistant to change than the material culture is. Therefore, as we have seen, foreign ideas are viewed as more threatening to a culture than foreign products are. This is true both for residents of the United States and for other people of the world. We are more willing to use technological innovations that make our lives easier than we are ideologies that change our way of seeing the world.

Just as our society has selectively absorbed certain practices and beliefs from China and other nonwestern cultures, so too have these cultures been on the receiving end of cultural diffusion. While Japan has only 800,000 practicing Christians in its population of 120 million people, *Kurisumasu* (the Japanese term for "Christmas") is nevertheless a major holiday. Although *Kurisumasu* is not a religious observance, it is a highly commercial occasion, reflecting obvious American influences. The Japanese are encouraged to buy gifts as they pass through stores filled with tinseled Christmas trees and the sweet sound of Bing Crosby singing "White Christmas" (R. Yates, 1985).

ELEMENTS OF CULTURE

The uniqueness of each culture becomes evident when people from many societies come together. From 1975 to 1988, the number of foreign students attending colleges in the United States more than doubled. These visitors noticed how different their cultural practices were from ours. Asian students had to learn that a request from an instructor to arrange a conference is not necessarily a sign of disgrace. Instructors from the United States had to learn that if a foreign student avoids direct eye contact, it probably reflects shyness, not disrespect.

Each culture considers its own distinctive ways of handling basic societal tasks as "natural." But, in fact, methods of education, marital ceremonies, religious doctrines, and other aspects of culture are learned and transmitted through human interactions within specific societies. Lifelong residents of Naples will consider it natural to speak Italian, whereas lifelong residents of Buenos Aires will feel the same way about Spanish. Clearly, the citizens of each country have been shaped by the culture in which they live.

The Samal people of the southern Philippines—for whom fish are a main source of both food and income—have terms in their language for more than 70 different types of fishing and more than 250 different kinds of fish.

Language

Language tells us a great deal about a culture. In the old west, words such as *gelding, stallion, mare, piebald,* and *sorrel* were all used to describe one animal—the horse. Even if we knew little of this period of history, we could conclude from the list of terms that horses were quite important in this culture. As a result, they received an unusual degree of linguistic attention.

In the contemporary culture of the United States, the terms *convertible, dune buggy, van, four-wheel drive, sedan,* and *station wagon* are all employed to describe the same mechanical form of transportation. Perhaps the car is as important to us as the horse was to the residents of the old west. Similarly, the Samal people of the southern Philippines—for whom fish are a main source of both food and income—have terms for more than 70 types of fishing and for more than 250 different kinds of fish. The Slave Indians of northern Canada, who live in a rather frigid climate, have 14 terms to describe ice, including 8 for different kinds of "solid ice" and others for "seamed ice," "cracked ice," and "floating ice." Clearly, the priorities of a culture are reflected in its language (Basso, 1972:35; Carroll, 1956).

Language as the Foundation of Culture Language is the foundation of every culture, though particular languages differ in striking ways. ***Language*** is an abstract system of word meanings and symbols for all aspects of culture. Language includes speech, written characters, numerals, symbols, and gestures of nonverbal communication.

Language, of course, is not an exclusively human attribute. Even though they are incapable of human speech, primates such as chimpanzees have been able to use symbols to communicate. However, even at their most advanced level, animals operate with essentially a fixed set of signs with fixed meanings. By contrast, humans can manipulate symbols in order to express abstract concepts and rules and to expand human cultures.

In contrast to some other elements of culture, language permeates all parts of society. Certain cultural skills, such as cooking or carpentry, can be learned without the use of language through the process of imitation. However, it is impossible to transmit complex legal and religious systems to the next generation by watching to see how they are performed. You, for instance, could bang a gavel as a judge does, but you would never be able to understand legal reasoning without language. Therefore, people invariably depend on language for the use and transmission of the rest of a culture.

While language is a cultural universal, differences in the use of language are evident around the world. This is the case even when two countries use the same spoken language. For example, an English-speaking person from the United States who is visiting London may be puzzled the first time an English friend says "I'll ring you up." The friend means "I'll call you on the telephone."

Similarly, the meanings of nonverbal gestures vary from one culture to another. Whereas residents of the United States commonly use and attach positive meanings to the "thumbs up" gesture, this gesture has only vulgar connotations in Greece (Ekman et al., 1984).

Sapir-Whorf Hypothesis Language does more than simply describe reality; it also serves to *shape the reality of a culture.* For example, most people in the United States cannot easily make the verbal distinctions about ice that are possible in the Slave Indian culture. As a result, we may be somewhat less likely to notice such differences.

The role of language in interpreting the world for us has been advanced in the ***Sapir-Whorf hypothesis,*** which is named for two linguists. According to Sapir and Whorf, since people can conceptualize the world only through language, language precedes thought. Thus, the word symbols and grammar of a language organize the world for us. The Sapir-Whorf hypothesis also holds that language is not a "given." Rather, it is culturally determined and leads to different interpretations of reality by focusing our attention on certain phenomena.

This hypothesis is considered so important that it has been reprinted by the State Department in its training programs to sensitize foreign service officers to the subtle uses of language. However, many social scientists challenge the Sapir-Whorf hypothesis and argue that language does not determine human thought and behavior patterns. As a result, the hypothesis has been moderated somewhat to suggest that language may *influence* (rather than determine) behavior and interpretations of social reality (Carroll, 1953:46; Kay and Kempton, 1984; Martyna, 1983:34; Sapir, 1929).

Berlin and Kay (1991) have noted that humans possess the physical ability to make millions of color distinctions, yet languages differ in the number of colors that are recognized. The English language distinguishes between yellow and orange, but some other languages do not. In the Dugum Dani language of New Guinea's West Highlands, there are only two basic color terms—*modla* for "white" and *mili* for "black." By contrast, there are 11 basic terms in English. Russian and Hungarian, though, have 12 color terms. Russians have terms for light blue and dark blue, while Hungarians have terms for two different shades of red. Thus, in a literal sense, language may color how we see the world.

Gender-related language can reflect—although in itself it will not determine—the traditional acceptance of men and women in certain occupations. Each time we use a term like *mailman*, *policeman*, or *fireman*, we are implying (especially to young children) that these occupations can be filled only by males. Yet many women work as *letter carriers*, *police officers*, and *firefighters*—a fact that is being increasingly recognized and legitimized through the use of such nonsexist language (Martyna, 1983). Sexist biases of the English and Japanese languages are examined in Box 2-1 on page 40.

Just as language may encourage gender-related stereotypes, it can also transmit stereotypes related to race. Dictionaries published in the United States list, among the meanings of the adjective *black: dismal, gloomy* or *forbidding, destitute of moral light or goodness, atrocious, evil, threatening, clouded with anger*. Dictionaries also list *pure* and *innocent* among the meanings of the adjective *white*. Through such patterns of language, our culture reinforces positive associations with the term (and skin color) *white* and a negative association with *black*. Therefore, it is not surprising that a list which prevents people from working in a profession is called a *blacklist*, while a lie that we think of as somewhat acceptable is called a *white lie*.

Language is of interest to all three sociological perspectives. Functionalists emphasize the important role of language in unifying members of a society. By contrast, conflict theorists focus on the use of language to perpetuate divisions between groups and societies—as in the subtle and not-so-subtle sexism and racism expressed in communication. Interactionists study how people rely on shared definitions of phrases and expressions in both formal speech and everyday conversation.

Language can shape how we see, taste, smell, feel, and hear. It also influences the way we think about the people, ideas, and objects around us. A culture's most important norms, values, and sanctions are communicated to people through language. It is for these reasons that the introduction of new languages into a society is such a sensitive issue in many parts of the world.

Norms

All societies have ways of encouraging and enforcing what they view as appropriate behavior while discouraging and punishing what they consider to be improper behavior. "Put on some clean clothes for dinner" and "Thou shalt not kill" are examples of norms found in the culture of the United States; respect for older people is an example of norms of Japanese culture. *Norms* are established standards of behavior maintained by a society.

In order for a norm to become significant, it must be widely shared and understood. For example, in movie theaters in the United States, we typically expect that people will be quiet while the film is showing. Because of this norm, an usher can tell a member of the audience to stop talking so loudly. Of course, the application of this norm can vary, depending on the particular film and type of audience. People attending a serious artistic or political film will be more likely to insist on the norm of silence than those attending a slapstick comedy or horror movie.

Types of Norms Sociologists distinguish between norms in two ways. First, norms are classified as either formal or informal. *Formal norms* have generally been written down and involve strict rules for punishment of violators. In the United States, we often formalize norms into laws, which must be very precise in defining proper and improper behavior. In a political sense, *law* is the "body of rules, made by government for society, interpreted by the courts, and backed by the power of the state" (Cummings and Wise, 1989:550). Laws are an example of formal norms, although not the only type. The requirements for a college major and the rules of a card game are also considered formal norms.

By contrast, *informal norms* are generally understood but are not precisely recorded. Standards of proper dress are a common example of informal norms. Our society has no specific punishment or sanction for a person who comes to school or to college dressed quite differently from everyone else. Making fun of nonconforming students for their unusual choice of clothing is the most likely response (E. Gross and Stone, 1964; G. Stone, 1977).

BOX 2-1

SEXISM IN LANGUAGES: ENGLISH AND JAPANESE

Nancy Henley, Mykol Hamilton, and Barrie Thorne (1985:169) suggest that the sexist bias of the English language takes three principal forms: "It ignores, it defines, it deprecates."

IGNORING

English ignores females by favoring the masculine form for all generic uses, as in the sentence: "Each entrant in the competition should do his best." According to the rules of English grammar, it is incorrect to use "their best" as the singular form in the previous sentence. Moreover, usage of the "he or she" form ("Each entrant in the competition should do his or her best") is often attacked as being clumsy. Nevertheless, feminists insist that common use of male forms as generic makes women and girls invisible and implicitly suggests that maleness and masculine values are the standard for humanity and normality. For this reason, there has been resistance to use of terms like *mailman, policeman,* and *fireman* to represent the men and women who perform these occupations.

DEFINING

In the view of Henley and her colleagues (1985:170), "language both reflects and helps maintain women's secondary status in our society, by defining her and her place.'" The power to define

through naming is especially significant in this process. Married women traditionally lose their own names and take their husbands', while children generally take the names of their fathers and not their mothers. These traditions of naming reflect western legal traditions under which children were viewed as the property of their fathers and married women as the property of their husbands. The view of females as possessions is also evident in the practice of using female names and pronouns to refer to material possessions such as cars, machines, and ships.

DEPRECATING

There are clear differences in the words that are applied to male and female things which reflect men's dominant position in English-speaking societies. For example, women's work may be patronized as "pretty" or "nice," whereas men's work is more often honored as "masterful" or "brilliant." In many instances, a woman's occupation or profession is trivialized with the feminine ending *-ess* or *-ette;* thus, even a distinguished woman writer may be given second-class status as a *poetess* or an *authoress.* In a clear manifestation of sexism, terms of sexual insult in the English language are applied overwhelmingly to women. One researcher

found 220 terms for a sexually promiscuous woman but only 22 for a sexually promiscuous man (Stanley, 1977).

While the English language ignores, defines, and deprecates females, the same is true of languages around the world. The expressions commonly used by girls and boys in Japan underscore gender differences in that society. A boy can refer to himself by using the word *boku,* which means "I." But a girl cannot assert her existence and identity that boldly and easily; she must instead refer to herself with the pronoun *watashi.* This term is viewed as more polite and can be used by either sex. Similarly, a boy can end a sentence assertively by stating *"Samui yo"* ("It's cold, I say!"). But a girl is expected to say *"Samui wa"* ("It's cold, don't you think?"). For girls, proper usage dictates ending with a gentle question rather than a strong declaration.

Ellen Rudolph (1991:8), a photographer from the United States who lives in Tokyo, reports that Japanese parents and teachers serve as "vigilant linguistic police" who remind children to use only those forms of speech deemed appropriate for their sex. Girls who violate these gender codes are told *"Onnanoko na no ni,"* which means, "You're a girl, don't forget."

According to the informal norms of the culture of the United States, people may greet each other with a handshake or, in some cases, with a hug or a kiss. However, in the mountainous Asian kingdom of Bhutan, people greet each other by extending their tongues and hands.

Norms are also classified by their relative importance to society. When classified in this way, they are known as *mores* and *folkways*.

Mores (pronounced "MOR-ays") are norms deemed highly necessary to the welfare of a society, often because they embody the most cherished principles of a people. Each society demands obedience to its mores; violation can lead to severe penalties. Thus, the United States has strong mores against murder, treason, and child abuse that have been institutionalized into formal norms. *Folkways* are norms governing everyday behavior whose violation raises comparatively little concern. For example, walking up a "down" escalator in a department store challenges our standards of appropriate behavior, but it will not result in a fine or a jail sentence. Society is more likely to formalize mores than folkways. Nevertheless, folkways play an important role in shaping the daily behavior of members of a culture.

In many societies around the world, folkways exist to reinforce patterns of male dominance. Men's hierarchical position above women within the traditional Buddhist areas of southeast Asia is revealed in various folkways. In the sleeping cars of trains, women do not sleep in upper berths above men. In hospitals in which men are housed on the first floor, women patients will not be placed on the second floor. Even on clotheslines, folkways dictate male dominance: women's attire is hung lower than that of men (Bulle, 1987:4).

Acceptance of Norms Norms, whether mores or folkways, are not followed in all situations. In some cases, people evade a norm because they know it is weakly enforced. It is illegal in many states for teenagers to drink alcoholic beverages, yet drinking by minors is common throughout the nation. (In fact, teenage alcoholism is one of our country's most serious social problems.)

In some instances, behavior that appears to violate society's norms may actually represent adherence to the norms of one's particular group. Teenage drinkers often break the laws of a state government in order to conform to the standards of a peer group. Similarly, in India from the twelfth century until the 1840s, a secret religious-criminal group known as the *Thugs* murdered and robbed travelers as a way of life. Members closely followed the norms of their religion—which dictated even how victims were to be killed—and believed that their behavior was commanded and approved by their sacred goddess, Kali (Fannin, 1989).

Norms are also violated in some instances because one norm conflicts with another. For example, suppose that you live in an apartment building and one night hear the screams of the woman next door, who is being beaten by her husband. If you decide to intervene by ringing their doorbell or calling the police, you are *violating* the norm of "minding your own business" while, at the same time, *following* the norm of assisting a victim of violence.

Even when norms do not conflict, there are always exceptions to any norm. The same action, under different circumstances, can cause one to be viewed either as a hero or as a villain. Eavesdropping on telephone conversations is normally considered illegal and abhorrent. However, it can be done with a court order to obtain valid evidence for a criminal trial. A government agent who uses such methods to convict an organized crime baron may be praised. In our culture, even killing another human being is tolerated as a form of self-defense and is actually rewarded in warfare.

Acceptance of norms is subject to change, as the political, economic, and social conditions of a culture are transformed. For example, under traditional norms in the United States, a woman was expected to marry, rear children, and remain at home if her husband could support the family without her assistance. However, these norms have been changing in recent decades, in part as a result of the contemporary feminist movement (see Chapter 8). As support for traditional norms weakens, people will feel free to violate them more frequently and openly and will be less likely to receive serious negative sanctions for doing so.

Sanctions

What happens when people violate a widely shared and understood norm? Suppose that a football coach sends a twelfth player onto the field. Imagine a college graduate showing up in shorts for a job interview at a large bank. Or consider a driver who neglects to put any money into a parking meter. In each of these situations, the person will receive sanctions if his or her behavior is detected.

Sanctions are penalties and rewards for conduct concerning a social norm. Note that the concept of *reward* is included in this definition. Confor-

TABLE 2-1 Norms and Sanctions

| NORMS | SANCTIONS | |
	POSITIVE	NEGATIVE
Formal	Salary bonus	Demotion
	Testimonial dinner	Firing from a job
	Medal	Jail sentence
	Diploma	Expulsion
Informal	Smile	Frown
	Compliment	Humiliation
	Cheers	Ostracism

Sanctions serve to reinforce both formal and informal social norms.

mity to a norm can lead to positive sanctions such as a pay raise, a medal, a word of gratitude, or a pat on the back. Negative sanctions include fines, threats, imprisonment, and stares of contempt.

In Table 2-1, the relationship between norms and sanctions is summarized. As you can see in this table, the sanctions that are associated with formal norms (those written down and codified) tend to be formalized as well. If a coach sends too many players onto the field, the team will be penalized 15 yards. The college graduate who comes to the bank interview in shorts will probably be treated with contempt by bank officials and will almost certainly lose any chance of getting the job. The driver who fails to put money in the parking meter will be given a ticket and expected to pay a fine.

Implicit in the application of sanctions is *detecting* violations of norms or obedience to norms. A person cannot be penalized or rewarded unless someone with the power to provide sanctions is aware of the person's actions. Therefore, if none of the officials in the football game realizes that there is an extra player on the field, there will be no penalty. If the police do not see the car which is illegally parked, there will be no fine or ticket. Furthermore, there can be *improper* application of sanctions in certain situations. The referee may make an error in counting the number of football players and levy an undeserved penalty on one team for "too many players on the field."

The entire fabric of norms and sanctions in a culture reflects that culture's values and priorities.

The most cherished values will be most heavily sanctioned; matters regarded as less critical, on the other hand, will carry light and informal sanctions.

Values

Each individual develops his or her own personal goals and ambitions, yet culture provides a general set of objectives for members. _Values_ are these collective conceptions of what is considered good, desirable, and proper—or bad, undesirable, and improper—in a culture. They indicate what people in a culture prefer as well as what they find important and morally right (or wrong). Values may be specific, such as honoring one's parents and owning a home, or they may be more general, such as health, love, and democracy.

Values influence people's behavior and serve as criteria for evaluating the actions of others. There is often a direct relationship between the values, norms, and sanctions of a culture. For example, if a culture highly values the institution of marriage, it may have norms (and strict sanctions) which prohibit the act of adultery. If a culture views private property as a basic value, it will probably have laws against theft and vandalism.

The values of a culture may change, but most remain relatively stable during any one person's lifetime. Socially shared, intensely felt values are a fundamental part of our lives in the United States.

Obviously, not all 250 million people in this country agree on one set of goals. However, sociologist Robin Williams (1970:452–500) attempted to offer a list of basic values in the United States. His list included achievement, efficiency, material comfort, nationalism, equality, and the supremacy of science and reason over faith. Any such effort to describe our nation's values should be properly viewed as but a starting point in defining the national character. Nevertheless, a review of 27 different attempts to describe the "American value system," including the work of anthropologist Margaret Mead and sociologist Talcott Parsons, revealed an overall similarity to the values identified by Williams (Devine, 1972:185).

In his book _Continental Divide_, sociologist Seymour Martin Lipset (1990) contrasted the values of two superficially similar neighbors: the United States and Canada. According to survey data from many polls, people in the United States are more religious than Canadians and take more moralistic attitudes toward sex, pornography, and marriage. Whereas Canadians show greater concern for an orderly society and are more likely to favor a strong role for government, citizens of the United States show greater concern for liberty and are more supportive of limits on government power. In fact, people in the United States are more suspicious of "bigness" than Canadians—whether in terms of big government or private economic power.

One commonly cited barometer of the values of the United States is an annual questionnaire survey of attitudes of entering first-year college students; this survey focuses on an array of issues, beliefs, and life goals. For example, the 7 million respondents are asked if various values are personally important to them. Over the last 25 years, the value of "being very well off financially" has shown the strongest gain in popularity; the proportion of first-year college students who endorse this value as "essential" or "very important" rose from 40 percent in 1967 to 74 percent in 1991 (see Figure 2-1, page 44). By contrast, the value that has shown the most striking decline in endorsement by students is "developing a meaningful philosophy of life." While this value was the most popular in the 1967 survey, endorsed by more than 80 percent of respondents, it had fallen to seventh place on the list by 1991 and was endorsed by only 43 percent of respondents (Astin et al., 1987:23; 1991:26; Henkoff, 1989).

During the 1980s, there was growing support for values having to do with money, power, and status. At the same time, there was a decline in support for certain values having to do with social awareness and altruism, such as "helping others." However, by 1991 there was evidence that college students in the United States were once again turning toward social concerns. According to a nationwide survey, 40 percent of first-year students stated that "influencing social values" was a "very important goal." This was the highest score this value had registered over the 25-year history of the poll, exceeding even the 34 percent score in 1969 and 1970. Clearly, like other aspects of culture, such as language and norms, a nation's values are not necessarily fixed (Astin et al., 1991:26; Wiener, 1990).

FIGURE 2-1 Life Goals of First-Year College Students in the United States, 1967–1991

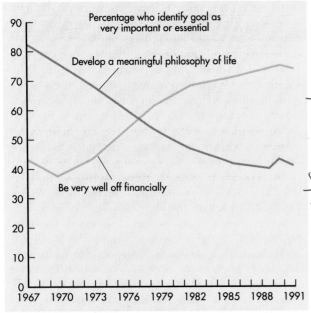

Percentage who identify goal as very important or essential

Develop a meaningful philosophy of life

Be very well off financially

SOURCE: UCLA Higher Education Research Institute, as reported in Astin et al., 1987:23, 97; 1991:26.

Over the last 25 years, entering first-year college students in the United States have become more concerned with being "very well off financially" and less concerned with developing "a meaningful philosophy of life."

CULTURAL VARIATION

Each culture has a unique character. Cultures adapt to meet specific sets of circumstances, such as climate, level of technology, population, and geography. This adaptation to different conditions is evident in differences in all elements of culture, including norms, sanctions, values, and language. Thus, despite the presence of cultural universals such as courtship and religion, there is still great diversity among the world's many cultures. Moreover, even within a single nation, certain segments of the populace will develop cultural patterns which differ from the patterns of the dominant society.

Aspects of Cultural Variation

Subcultures Older people living in housing for the elderly, workers in an offshore oil rig, rodeo cowboys, circus performers, and the Thugs of India—all are examples of what sociologists refer to as *subcultures.*

A **subculture** is a segment of society which shares a distinctive pattern of mores, folkways, and values which differ from the pattern of the larger society. In a sense, a subculture can be thought of as a culture existing within a larger, dominant culture. The existence of many subcultures is characteristic of complex societies such as the United States. Conflict theorists argue that subcultures often emerge because the dominant society has unsuccessfully attempted to suppress a practice which is regarded as improper, such as use of illegal drugs.

Members of a subculture participate in the dominant culture, while at the same time engaging in unique and distinctive forms of behavior. Frequently, a subculture will develop an **argot,** or specialized language, which distinguishes it from the wider society. Thus, the phrase "Smokey in a plain wrapper" has special meaning for truck drivers and others who listen to citizens' band radios (CBs). It indicates that a patrol officer is ahead on the road in an unmarked car. The phrase "bear in the woods giving out green stamps" means that the officer is giving out tickets, while "taking pictures" means that police are using a radar gun to monitor driving speeds.

Argot allows "insiders," the members of the subculture, to understand words with special meanings. It also establishes patterns of communication which cannot be understood by "outsiders." Sociologists associated with the interactionist perspective emphasize that language and symbols offer a powerful way for a subculture to maintain its identity. The particular argot of a given subculture, therefore, provides a feeling of cohesion for members and contributes to the development of a group identity (Halliday, 1978).

Subcultures develop in a number of ways. Often a subculture emerges because a segment of society faces problems or even privileges unique to its position. Subcultures may be based on common age (teenagers or old people), region (Appalachians), ethnic heritage (Cuban Americans), beliefs (a militant political group), or occupation (firefighters). Certain subcultures, such as that of computer "hackers," develop because of a shared interest or hobby. In still other subcultures, such as that of prison inmates, members have been excluded from normal society and are forced to develop alternative ways of living.

Countercultures Some subcultures conspicuously challenge the central norms and values of the prevailing culture. A ***counterculture*** is a subculture that rejects societal norms and values and seeks alternative lifestyles (J. Yinger, 1960). Countercultures are typically popular among the young, who have the least investment in the existing culture. In most cases, a person who is 20 years old can adjust to new cultural standards more easily than someone who has spent 60 years following the patterns of the dominant culture.

By the end of the 1960s, some writers claimed that an extensive counterculture had emerged in the United States, composed of young people who repudiated the technological orientation of our culture. This counterculture was viewed as including primarily political radicals and "hippies" who had "dropped out" of mainstream social institutions. These young men and women rejected the pressure to accumulate more and more cars, larger and larger homes, and an endless array of material goods. Instead, they expressed a desire to live in a culture based on more humanistic values, such as sharing, love, and coexistence with the environment. As a political force, the counterculture opposed the United States' involvement in the war in Vietnam and encouraged draft resistance (Flacks, 1971; Roszak, 1969).

By 1970, a new counterculture had surfaced in Great Britain. The Skinheads were young people with shaved heads who often sported suspenders and steel-toed shoes. Some Skinhead groups championed racist and anti-Semitic ideologies and engaged in vandalism, violence, and even murder. Immigrants from India and Pakistan became a common target of Skinhead attacks. (There were, however, other Skinhead groups that were explicitly *antiracist*.) Throughout the 1970s, the Skinhead counterculture gradually spread from Britain to Europe and North America. It is difficult to measure precisely the size of this counterculture, since Skinheads do not belong to a national or international organization. Nevertheless, according to one estimate, there were 5000 Skinheads in the United States in 1990 (*Economist,* 1990b; Hiro, 1973).

Henry Horenstein

A subculture is a segment of society which has a distinctive pattern of mores, folkways, and values which differ from the pattern of the larger society. Women athletes can be viewed as a subculture; shown are members of a "fast pitch" softball team from the American Women's Baseball Association.

Culture Shock Imagine that you are making your first trip to Poland, or Nigeria, or the People's Republic of China. You are staying in a small city in which the bus driver does not speak English, the currency is unfamiliar and puzzling, restaurants never serve food from the United States, and there is no movie theater. You find yourself feeling strangely disoriented, uncertain, out of place, even fearful. These are all indications that you may be experiencing ***culture shock.***

All of us, to some extent, take for granted the cultural practices of our society. As a result, it can be surprising and disturbing to realize that other cultures do not follow what we call the "American way of life." In fact, customs that seem strange to us are considered normal and proper in other cultures, which may see *our* mores and folkways as odd.

Culture shock over conflicting value systems is not limited to contacts between traditional and modern societies. We can experience culture shock within our own society. For instance, a conservative, churchgoing older person might feel bewildered or horrified at a punk rock concert. Similarly, given traditional notions about gender roles in our culture, many men might be shocked by a women's martial arts class with a female instructor.

People experience anxiety when they leave a familiar culture for an "alien" environment. When you are in a new and puzzling society, you can never be sure how others will react to your actions. Even the simplest gesture—offering to light a cigarette for someone else or leaving a tip in a restaurant—may be misunderstood and viewed as an insult. It is genuinely shocking to lose one's cultural bearings, though such an experience can educate us by clarifying our unquestioned cultural assumptions.

Attitudes toward Cultural Variation

Ethnocentrism Many everyday statements reflect our attitude that our culture is best. For example, we use terms such as *undeveloped, backward,* and *primitive* to refer to other societies. What "we" believe is a religion; what "they" believe is superstition and mythology (Spradley and McCurdy, 1980:28).

It is very tempting to evaluate the practices of other cultures on the basis of our own perspectives. Sociologist William Graham Sumner (1906:13–15) coined the term ***ethnocentrism*** to refer to the tendency to assume that one's culture and way of life are superior to all others. The ethnocentric person sees his or her own group as the center or defining point of culture and views all other cultures as deviations from what is "normal." As one manifestation of ethnocentrism, map exercises reveal that students in many nations draw maps in which their homelands are in the center of the world (see Figure 2-2).

The conflict approach to social behavior points out that ethnocentric value judgments serve to devalue groups and contribute to denial of equal opportunities. Psychologist Walter Stephan notes a typical example of ethnocentrism in New Mexico's schools. Both Hispanic and Native American cultures teach children to look down when they are being criticized by adults, yet many "Anglo" (non-Hispanic White) teachers believe that you should look someone in the eye when you are being criticized. "Anglo teachers can feel that these students are being disrespectful," notes Stephan. "That's the kind of misunderstanding that can evolve into stereotype and prejudice" (Goleman, 1991:C8).

Functionalists note that ethnocentrism serves to maintain a sense of solidarity by promoting group pride. Yet this type of social stability is established at the expense of other peoples. Denigrating other nations and cultures can enhance our own patriotic feelings and belief that our way of life is superior. Of course, ethnocentrism is hardly limited to citizens of the United States. Visitors from many African cultures are surprised at the disrespect that children in the United States show their parents. People from India may be repelled by our practice of living in the same household with dogs and cats. Many Islamic fundamentalists in the Arab world and Asia view the United States as corrupt, decadent, and doomed to destruction. All these people may feel comforted by membership in cultures that, in their view, are superior to ours.

Cultural Relativism It is not necessary to view all cultural variations with an assumption that one's own culture is more humane, more "civilized,"

FIGURE 2-2 Mental Maps of the World

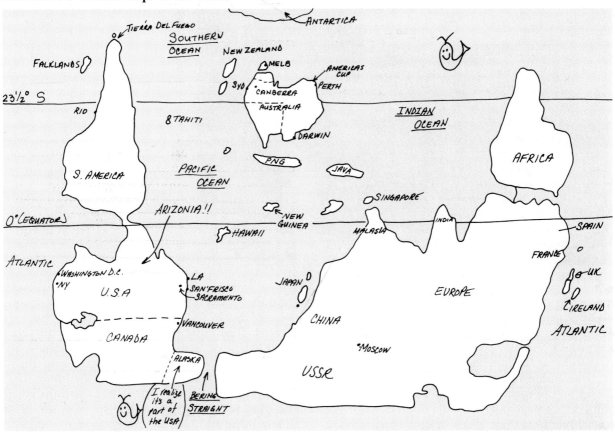

SOURCE: Saarinen, 1988:124.

How do we view the world? Do we see our own homeland in the center? In a map exercise, a student in the People's Republic of China saw China as central, while (as shown in this figure) an Australian student put Australia at the top.

and more advanced than others. While ethnocentrism evaluates foreign cultures using the familiar culture of the observer as a standard of correct behavior, **cultural relativism** views people's behavior from the perspective of their own culture. It places a priority on *understanding* other cultures, rather than dismissing them as "strange" or "exotic." Unlike ethnocentrism, cultural relativism employs the kind of value neutrality in scientific study that Max Weber saw as so important (see Chapter 1).

Cultural relativism stresses that different social contexts give rise to different norms and values. Thus practices such as polygamy, bullfighting, and monarchy are examined within the particular contexts of the cultures in which they are found.

While cultural relativism does not suggest that we must unquestionably accept every form of behavior characteristic of a culture, it does require a serious and unbiased effort to evaluate norms, values, and customs in light of the distinctive culture of which they are a part.

In practice, of course, the application of cultural relativism can raise delicate questions. In 1989, a Chinese immigrant man was convicted in a New York court of bludgeoning his wife to death with a hammer. However, the man was ac-

Xenocentrism *is the belief that the products, styles, or ideas of one's own society are inferior to those originating elsewhere. As one reflection of xenocentrism, people in the United States may prefer to buy foreign cars.*

quitted of the most serious charges against him, and was sentenced to only five years' probation, when the judge ruled that cultural considerations warranted leniency. The deceased woman had confessed to having had an extramarital affair, and the judge revealed that he had been influenced by the testimony of an expert on Chinese culture that husbands in China often exact severe punishment on their wives in such situations. In posttrial hearings, the judge declared that the defendant "took all his Chinese culture with him to the United States" and therefore was not fully responsible for his violent conduct. In response to this ruling, Brooklyn district attorney Elizabeth Holtzman angrily insisted: "There should be one standard of justice, not one that depends on the cultural background of the defendant. . . . Anyone who comes to this country must be prepared to live by and obey the laws of this country" (Rosario and Marcano, 1989:2).

There is an interesting extension of cultural relativism, referred to as *xenocentrism*. **Xenocentrism** is the belief that the products, styles, or ideas of one's society are inferior to those that originate elsewhere (W. Wilson et al., 1976). In a sense, it is a reverse ethnocentrism. For example, people in the United States often assume that French fashions or Japanese electronic devices are superior to our own. Are they, or are people

unduly charmed by the lure of goods from exotic places? Such fascination with British china or Danish glassware can be damaging to competitors in the United States. Some companies have responded by creating products that *sound* European like Häagen-Dazs ice cream (made in Teaneck, New Jersey) or Nike shoes (produced in Beaverton, Oregon). Conflict theorists are most likely to be troubled by the economic impact of xenocentrism in the developing world. Consumers in developing nations frequently turn their backs on locally produced goods and instead purchase items imported from Europe or North America.

CULTURE AND THE DOMINANT IDEOLOGY

As is readily apparent, sociologists regard culture as a highly significant concept, since it embraces all learned and shared behavior. Nevertheless, there are important differences in the ways in which functionalist and conflict theorists view culture. For example, we have seen that functionalists emphasize the role of language in unifying members of a society while conflict theorists focus on the use of language to perpetuate divisions between groups and societies.

Both sociological perspectives agree that culture and society are in harmony with each other, but for different reasons. Functionalists maintain that stability requires a consensus and the support of society's members; consequently, there are strong central values and common norms. This view of culture became popular in sociology beginning in the 1950s, having been borrowed from British anthropologists who saw cultural traits as all working toward stabilizing a culture. As we learned in Chapter 1, the functionalist view of culture can be used to explain why widely condemned social practices such as prostitution continue to survive. From a functionalist perspective, a cultural trait or practice will persist if it performs functions that society seems to need or contributes to overall social stability and consensus.

Conflict theorists concur with functionalists that a common culture may exist, but they argue that it serves to maintain the privileges of some groups while keeping others in a subservient position. A culture, therefore, may offer "reasons" (justifications) for unequal social arrangements. As noted in Chapter 1, Karl Marx identified values in the culture of capitalist societies that justified the exploitation of the working class. Today, a society's culture may seek to explain why Protestants enjoy greater privileges than Catholics (Northern Ireland), why the separate economic development of Blacks is behind that of Whites (South Africa), or why women can be expected to earn less than men (the United States and elsewhere).

The term *dominant ideology* is used to describe a set of cultural beliefs and practices that help to maintain powerful social, economic, and political interests. This concept was first used by Hungarian Marxist Georg Lukacs (1923) and Italian Marxist Antonio Gramsci (1929), but it did not gain an audience in the United States until the early 1970s. In Karl Marx's view, a capitalist society has a dominant ideology which serves the interests of the ruling class. Marx and Engels wrote in 1845:

The ideas of the ruling class are in every age the ruling ideas; i.e. the class which is the dominant *material* force of society is at the same time its dominant *intellectual* force (Bottomore, 1983:431).

From a conflict perspective, the social significance of the dominant ideology is that a society's most powerful groups and institutions not only control wealth and property; even more important, they control the means of producing beliefs about reality through religion, education, and the media. For example, if all of a society's most important institutions tell women that they should be subservient to men, this dominant ideology will help to control women and keep them in a subordinate position (Abercrombie et al., 1980, 1990; Robertson, 1988).

Functionalist and conflict theorists agree, again for different reasons, that variation exists within a culture. Functionalists view subcultures as variations of particular social environments and as evidence that differences can exist within a common culture. However, conflict theorists suggest that variation often reflects the inequality of social arrangements within a society. Consequently, from a conflict perspective, the challenge to dominant social norms by African American activists, the feminist movement, and the disability rights movement can be seen as a reflection of inequality based on race, gender, and disability status.

A growing number of social scientists believe that a "core culture" cannot be easily identified in the United States. The lack of consensus on national values, the diffusion of cultural traits, the diversity of our many subcultures, and the changing views of young people (refer back to Figure 2-1) all are cited in support of this viewpoint. Yet there is no way of denying that certain expressions of values have greater influence than others even in so complex a society as the United States (Abercrombie et al., 1980, 1990; Archer, 1988; Wuthnow and Witten, 1988:52–53).

We see, then, that neither the functionalist nor the conflict perspective can be used exclusively to explain all aspects of a culture. For example, the custom of tossing rice at a bride and groom can be traced back to the wish to have children and to the view of rice as a symbol of fertility, rather than to the powerlessness of the proletariat. Nevertheless, there are cultural practices in our society and others that benefit some to the detriment of many. They may indeed promote social stability and consensus—but at whose expense?

- How have changes in the population of the United States affected the debate over school and university curricula?

- What do scholars mean when they refer to the "canon"? What role should the canon play in the education of undergraduate students?

- How might functionalist and conflict theorists view the controversy over multiculturalism?

The culture of the United States can be compared to a kaleidoscope—the familiar optical device whose colors and patterns are formed by pieces of colored glass reflected from mirrors. As the viewer turns a set of mirrors in the kaleidoscope, he or she sees what appear to be an infinite variety of colorful images. Similarly, the culture of the United States is hardly static, especially with more than 1 million legal immigrants per year and a substantial number of illegal immigrants contributing to cultural diversity (Schaefer, 1992).

There is little doubt that the racial and ethnic makeup of the nation's schools and colleges is changing significantly. Sociologists have often been involved in documenting these changes and analyzing their social significance. In 1990, the entering first-year class at the University of California at Berkeley was 34 percent White, 30 percent of Asian descent, 22 percent of Mexican or Latin American descent, and 7 percent African American. At Stanford University, more than 40 percent of entering undergraduates are from African American, Native American, Asian or Asian American, or Mexican American backgrounds. While these racial and ethnic ratios are not evident at all schools and colleges across the country, they nevertheless reflect long-range population trends. According to projections, by the year 2080 the combined Black, Hispanic, and Asian populations of the United States may be approximately equal to the number of Whites (Bouvier and Davis, 1982; Stimpson, 1992:52).

As the racial and ethnic profile of student populations has changed, there has been increasing debate over the proper curriculum materials that should be used in school and college classrooms. Traditionalists believe that it is essential to focus on what is often called the *canon* of the best books of western civilization, including famous works by Shakespeare, Haw-

thorne, Melville, Hemingway, Faulkner, and others. By contrast, troubled by the fact that this canon overwhelmingly consists of White male authors from the United States or European backgrounds, advocates of *multiculturalism* insist that school and college curricula should be revised to give greater emphasis to the contributions and experiences of African Americans, other racial and ethnic minorities, women, and nonwestern peoples. Catharine Stimpson (1992:43–44), a former president of the Modern Language Association, suggests that multiculturalism "most often . . . means treating society as the home of several valuable but distinct racial and ethnic groups." While sociologists have not uniformly endorsed multiculturalism, they have long argued against any type of ethnocentric world view.

Viewed from a functionalist perspective, the traditional canon of western culture promotes stability, social solidarity, and consensus by helping to define the common values of the United States. These "great books" are said to speak across barriers of gender, race, religion, and geography and to provide a cultural heritage that all of us share. By contrast, however, conflict theorists might view the western canon as central to a dominant ideology that serves the interests of society's most powerful groups and institutions. From a conflict perspective, the movement in support of multiculturalism represents a challenge to long-standing inequities based on gender, race, and ethnicity.

Intense debate has erupted across the United States in school systems, colleges, and universities regarding efforts to introduce or protest multicultural curricula. At Stanford University, a required one-year course on western culture for incoming students focused on the traditional western canon. When critics argued that non-European works should be added to the reading list and that substantial attention should be given to issues of gender, race, and class, a long battle resulted. At the University of Texas in Austin, a proposal for a required writing course, Writing about Difference, was bitterly attacked. Defenders of the proposal argued that students would sharpen their writing skills while learning (through required readings) about cultural diversity, especially as it pertains to issues of race and gender. Those opposed to the proposal derided it as "Oppression English" and insisted that it brought a loaded political agenda into the class-

BOX 2-2

AFROCENTRICITY: PUTTING AFRICA AT THE CENTER

In the following selection, Molefi Kete Asante (1992:16–17, 21–22), a professor of African American studies at Temple University, explains the concept of Afrocentricity. Asante and other advocates of Afrocentricity hope to persuade schools and universities to adopt multicultural curricula that will place African and African American history and culture at the center of the intellectual experience.

. . . Afrocentricity is primarily an orientation to data. There are certainly data and facts which may be used by Afrocentrists in making analyses, but the principal component of the theoretical piece has to do with an orientation, a location, a position. Thus, I have explained in several books and articles that Afrocentricity is "a perspective which allows Africans to be subjects of historical experiences" rather than objects on the fringes of Europe. This means that the Afrocentrist is concerned with discovering in every case the centered place of the African. Of course, such a philosophical stance is not necessary for other disciplines; it is, however, the fundamental basis for African or African American studies. Otherwise, it seems to me that

Courtesy Molefi Kete Asante

Molefi Kete Asante.

what is being done in African American studies at some institutions might successfully be challenged as duplicating in content, theory, and method the essentially Eurocentric enterprises that are undertaken in the traditional departments.

African American studies, however, is not simply the study and teaching about African people, but it is the Afrocentric study of African phenomena; otherwise, we would have had African American studies for 100 years. But what existed before was not African American studies but rather a Eurocentric study of Africans. Some of these studies led to im-

portant findings and have been useful. So the Afrocentrists do not claim that historians, sociologists, literary critics, philosophers, and others do not make valuable contributions. Our claim is that by using a Eurocentric approach, they often ignore an important interpretive key to the African experience in America and elsewhere. . . .

Afrocentricity is not a matter of color but of perspective, that is, orientation to facts. The historian, sociologist, psychologist, and political scientist may examine the Battle of Gettysburg and see different elements or aspects because of the different emphases of the disciplines. In a similar manner, the Afrocentrist would look at the Civil War or any phenomenon involving African people and raise different questions than the Eurocentrist. These questions are not more or less correct but better in an interpretative sense if the person doing the asking wants to understand African phenomena in context. Since the Afrocentric perspective is not a racial perspective, but an orientation to data, anyone willing to submit to the rigid discipline of the field might become an Afrocentrist. . . .

room (Rothenberg, 1992; Searle, 1992:106–108; Will, 1992).

At the elementary and secondary school levels, New York State has been one of the centers of strife. In 1989, a task force appointed by the state commissioner of education released a controversial report entitled "A Curriculum of Inclusion." This examination of the state's history and social studies curriculum insisted that "African-Americans, Asian-Americans, Puerto Ricans/Latinos, and Native Americans have all

been the victims of an intellectual and educational oppression that has characterized the culture and institutions of the United States and the European world for centuries" (Ravitch, 1992:291; Smoler, 1992). In New York and elsewhere, some critics of traditional curricula have gone beyond a broad multicultural focus to advocate *Afrocentricity,* an approach that would place the African and African American experiences at the heart of cultural study (see Box 2-2, above).

An important voice opposing multiculturalism has been the National Association of Scholars (NAS). Founded in 1987, this organization has 2500 members, most of them professors and many of them political conservatives. Like other critics of multiculturalism, the NAS (1992) argues that radicals are threatening intellectual inquiry and academic freedom by demanding "politically correct" curricula. NAS members and other defenders of the traditional canon insist that the classic western intellectual tradition must be taught in schools and colleges in the United States because this tradition largely shaped the development of our culture. Moreover, works by Plato, Shakespeare, and others are seen as of such high intellectual and artistic quality that they will have meaning for *all* students, regardless of gender, race, or ethnicity (Kimball, 1992:64; Searle, 1992:88).

Defenders of multiculturalism counter that the traditional canon reflects the interests and perspectives of privileged White European males while largely ignoring the contributions of women, men of color, and working people. Henry Louis Gates, Jr. (1992:197), one of the nation's most distinguished African American scholars, suggests that the "return of 'the' canon, the canon of Western masterpieces, represents the return of an order in which my people were the subjugated, the voiceless, the invisible. . . ." Critics of the canon charge that placing the western cultural and intellectual heritage in a preeminent position represents an example of ethnocentrism and racism. In their view, a genuinely multicultural approach to education will help to empower female and non-White students while broadening our appreciation of humanity's multifaceted cultural and intellectual history (Rothenberg, 1992:265–266).

Sociologist Troy Duster (1991:B2) suggests that the controversy over multiculturalism is actually a "struggle over who gets to define the idea of America." Duster asks:

Are we essentially a nation with a common—or at least dominant—culture to which immigrants and "minorities" must adapt? Or is this a land in which ethnicity and difference are an accepted part of the whole; a land in which we affirm the richness of our differences and simultaneously try to forge agreement about basic values to guide public and social policy?

SUMMARY

Culture is the totality of learned, socially transmitted behavior. This chapter examines the basic elements which make up a culture, social practices which are common to all cultures, and variations which distinguish one culture from another.

1 The process of expanding human culture has already been under way for thousands of years and will continue in the future.

2 Anthropologist George Murdock has compiled a list of general practices found in every culture, including courtship, family, games, language, medicine, religion, and sexual restrictions.

3 Societies resist ideas which seem too foreign as well as those which are perceived as threatening to their own values and beliefs.

4 *Language* includes speech, written characters, numerals, symbols, and gestures and other forms of nonverbal communication.

5 Sociologists distinguish between *norms* in two ways. They are classified as either *formal* or *informal* norms and as *mores* or *folkways*.

6 The most cherished *values* of a culture will receive the heaviest sanctions; matters that are regarded as less critical, on the other hand, will carry light and informal sanctions.

7 Generally, members of a *subculture* are viewed as outsiders or deviants.

8 From a conflict perspective, the social significance of the concept of the *dominant ideology* is that the most powerful groups and institutions in a society control the means of producing beliefs about reality through religion, education, and the media.

9 Advocates of *multiculturalism* argue that the traditional curricula of schools and colleges in the United States should be revised to include more works by and about African Americans, other racial and ethnic minorities, and women.

CRITICAL THINKING QUESTIONS

1 Select three cultural universals from George Murdock's list and analyze them from a functionalist perspective. Why are these practices found in every culture? What functions do they serve?

2 Drawing on the theories and concepts presented in the chapter, apply sociological analysis to one subculture with which you are familiar. Describe the norms, values, argot, and sanctions evident in that subculture.

3 In what ways is the dominant ideology of the United States evident in the nation's literature, its music, its movies, its television programs, and its sporting events?

KEY TERMS

Argot Specialized language used by members of a group or subculture. (page 44)

Counterculture A subculture that rejects societal norms and values and seeks an alternative lifestyle. (45)

Cultural relativism The viewing of people's behavior from the perspective of their own culture. (47)

Cultural universals General practices found in every culture. (34)

Culture The totality of learned, socially transmitted behavior. (32)

Culture shock The feeling of surprise and disorientation that is experienced when people witness cultural practices different from their own. (46)

Diffusion The process by which a cultural item is spread from group to group or society to society. (36)

Discovery The process of making known or sharing the existence of an aspect of reality. (36)

Dominant ideology A set of cultural beliefs and practices that help to maintain powerful social, economic, and political interests. (49)

Ethnocentrism The tendency to assume that one's culture and way of life are superior to all others. (46)

Folkways Norms governing everyday social behavior whose violation raises comparatively little concern. (41)

Formal norms Norms which have generally been written down and which involve strict rules for punishment of violators. (39)

Hominids Primates that had characteristics of human beings. (34)

Informal norms Norms which are generally understood but which are not precisely recorded. (39)

Innovation The process of introducing new elements into a culture through either discovery or invention. (36)

Invention The combination of existing cultural items into a form that did not previously exist. (36)

Language An abstract system of word meanings and symbols for all aspects of culture. Language also includes gestures and other nonverbal communication. (38)

Law In a political sense, the body of rules made by government for society, interpreted by the courts, and backed by the power of the state. (39)

Material culture The physical or technological aspects of our daily lives. (36)

Mores Norms deemed highly necessary to the welfare of a society. (41)

Multiculturalism The effort to revise school and college curricula to give greater emphasis to the contributions and experiences of African Americans, other racial and ethnic minorities, women, and nonwestern peoples. (50)

Nonmaterial culture Cultural adjustments to material conditions, such as customs, beliefs, patterns of communication, and ways of using material objects. (36)

Norms Established standards of behavior maintained by a society. (39)

Sanctions Penalties and rewards for conduct concerning a social norm. (42)

Sapir-Whorf hypothesis A hypothesis concerning the role of language in shaping cultures. It holds that language is culturally determined and serves to influence our mode of thought. (38)

Society A fairly large number of people who live in the same territory, are relatively independent of people outside it, and participate in a common culture. (33)

Subculture A segment of society which shares a distinctive pattern of mores, folkways, and values which differ from the pattern of the larger society. (44)

Values Collective conceptions of what is considered good, desirable, and proper—or bad, undesirable, and improper—in a culture. (43)

Xenocentrism The belief that the products, styles, or ideas of one's society are inferior to those that originate elsewhere. (48)

ADDITIONAL READINGS

Abercrombie, Nicholas, Stephen Hill, and Bryan S. Turner (eds.). *Dominant Ideologies*. Cambridge, Mass.: Unwin Hyman, 1990. A critique of the view that common cultures emerge as ideological systems.

Bellah, Robert N., Richard Madsden, Anne Swidler, William M. Sullivan, and Steven M. Tipton. *Habits of the Heart: Individualism and Commitment in American Life*. Berkeley: University of California Press, 1985. Several social scientists team up to summarize the contemporary philosophy of the people of the United States as reflected in such values as individualism and commitment.

Berman, Paul (ed.). *Debating P.C.: The Controversy over Political Correctness on College Campuses*. New York: Dell, 1992. This timely anthology explores many aspects of the debate over multiculturalism and includes selections by Henry Louis Gates, Jr., Edward Said, Catharine Stimpson, George Will, Dinesh D'Souza, Molefi Kete Asante, Irving Howe, and Diane Ravitch.

Featherstone, Mike (ed.). *Global Culture: Nationalism, Globalization, and Modernity*. London: Sage, 1990. In this anthology, social scientists from many nations analyze the extent to which we are witnessing a globalization of culture.

Kraybill, Donald B. *The Riddle of Amish Culture*. Baltimore: Johns Hopkins University Press, 1989. Drawing on observation research in Lancaster County, Pennsylvania, Kraybill seeks to clarify how the Amish continue to prosper despite their resistance to technological change.

Wallerstein, Immanuel. *Geopolitics and Geoculture: Essays on the Changing World System*. Cambridge, Eng.: Cambridge University Press, 1991. Wallerstein argues that in light of the collapse of the iron curtain and the decline of the United States' dominance, a new world economy is emerging along with an accompanying "geoculture."

Weinstein, Deeva. *Heavy Metal: A Cultural Sociology*. New York: Lexington, 1992. A sociologist examines the subculture associated with "heavy metal" music and efforts to curtail this subculture.

3

SOCIALIZATION

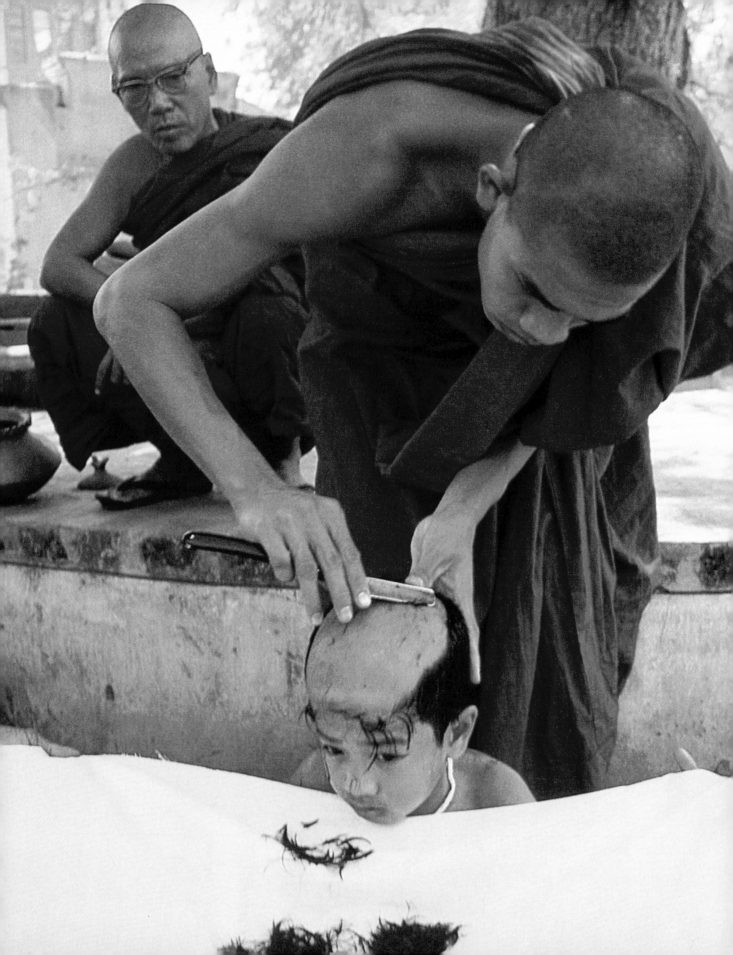

3

SOCIALIZATION

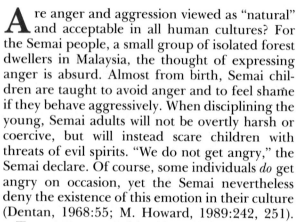

- What would happen if a child was reared in total isolation from other people?
- Will identical twins show similarities in personality traits, behavior, and intelligence if reared apart?
- How do we come to develop self-identity?

- How do the family, the school, the peer group, the mass media, the workplace, and the state contribute to the socialization process?
- What are the social implications of placing young children in child care centers?

Are anger and aggression viewed as "natural" and acceptable in all human cultures? For the Semai people, a small group of isolated forest dwellers in Malaysia, the thought of expressing anger is absurd. Almost from birth, Semai children are taught to avoid anger and to feel shame if they behave aggressively. When disciplining the young, Semai adults will not be overtly harsh or coercive, but will instead scare children with threats of evil spirits. "We do not get angry," the Semai declare. Of course, some individuals *do* get angry on occasion, yet the Semai nevertheless deny the existence of this emotion in their culture (Dentan, 1968:55; M. Howard, 1989:242, 251).

To someone reared in the United States or another western culture where there is much less compulsion to avoid anger, the Semai attitude toward aggression may seem surprising. If we assume that our culture is "normal" and superior to all others (thereby engaging in the kind of ethnocentrism discussed in Chapter 2), we may view the Semai as weak or peculiar. Yet, as we saw in Chapter 2, each culture has a unique character which shapes the values and behavior of its members.

Socialization is the process whereby people learn the attitudes, values, and actions appropriate to individuals as members of a particular culture. For example, Eskimos learn to enjoy eating the raw intestines of birds and fish, while Chinese people eat carp's head and the tripe (stomach tissue) of pigs. But most people in the United States have not been socialized to appreciate such foods.

Socialization occurs through human interactions. We will, of course, learn a great deal from the people most important in our lives—immediate family members, best friends, and teachers. But we also learn from people we see on the street, on television, and in films and magazines. On the micro level, socialization helps us to discover how to behave "properly" and what to expect from others if we follow (or challenge) society's norms and values. On the macro level, socialization provides for the passing on of a culture and thereby for the long-term continuance of a society.

Socialization affects the overall cultural practices of a society, and it also shapes our self-images. For example, in the United States, a person who is viewed as "too heavy" or "too short" does not conform to the ideal cultural standard. If the person is therefore judged unattractive, that evaluation can significantly influence his or her self-esteem. In this sense, socialization experiences can have an impact on the shaping of people's personalities. In everyday speech, the term ***personality*** refers to a person's typical patterns of attitudes, needs, characteristics, and behavior.

This chapter will examine the role of socialization in human development. It will begin by analyzing the debate concerning the interaction of heredity and environmental factors. Particular attention will be given to how people develop perceptions, feelings, and beliefs about themselves. The chapter will explore the lifelong nature of the socialization process, as well as important agents of socialization, among them the family, schools, and the media. Finally, the social policy section will focus on group child care for young children as a socialization experience.

THE ROLE OF SOCIALIZATION

Researchers have traditionally clashed over the relative importance of biological inheritance and environmental factors in human development. This debate has been called *nature versus nurture* (or *heredity versus environment*). Today, most social scientists have moved beyond this debate, acknowledging instead the *interaction* of these variables in shaping human development. However, we can better appreciate how hereditary and environmental factors interact and influence the socialization process if we first examine situations in which one factor operates almost entirely without the other (Homans, 1979).

Environment: The Impact of Isolation

For the first six years of her life, Isabelle lived in almost total seclusion in a darkened room. She had little contact with other people with the exception of her mother, who could neither speak nor hear. Isabelle's mother's parents had been so deeply ashamed of Isabelle's illegitimate birth that they kept her hidden away from the world. Ohio authorities finally discovered the child in 1938 when Isabelle's mother escaped from her parents' home, taking her daughter with her.

When she was discovered, despite being more than 6 years old, Isabelle could not speak. Her only communications with her mother had been by simple gestures. Verbally, Isabelle could merely make various croaking sounds. Marie Mason (1942:299), a speech specialist who worked closely with the child, observed that Isabelle

> . . . was apparently unaware of relationships of any kind. When presented with a ball, she held it in the palm of her hand, then reached out and stroked my face with it. Such behavior is comparable to that of a child of six months. She made no attempt to squeeze it, throw it, or bounce it.

Isabelle had been largely deprived of the typical interactions and socialization experiences of childhood. Since she had actually seen few people, she initially showed a strong fear of strangers and reacted almost like a wild animal when confronted with an unfamiliar person. As she became accustomed to seeing certain individuals, her reaction changed to one of extreme apathy. At first, it was believed that Isabelle was deaf, but she soon began to react to nearby sounds. On tests of maturity, she scored at the level of an infant rather than a 6-year-old.

Specialists developed a systematic training program to help Isabelle adapt to human relationships and socialization. After a few days of training, she made her first attempt to verbalize. Although she started slowly, Isabelle quickly passed through six years of development. In a little over two months, she was speaking in complete sentences. Nine months later, she could identify both words and sentences. Before Isabelle reached the age of 9, she was ready to attend school with other children. By her fourteenth year, she was in sixth grade, doing well in school, and was emotionally well-adjusted. Yet, without an opportunity to experience socialization in her first six years, Isabelle had been hardly human in the social sense when she was first discovered (K. Davis, 1940; 1947:435–437).

Isabelle's experience is important because there are relatively few cases of children deliberately reared in isolation. Her inability to communicate at the time of her discovery—despite her physical and cognitive potential to learn—and her remarkable progress over the next few years underscore the impact of socialization on human development.

The case study of Isabelle documents the adverse impact of extreme deprivation. Increasingly, researchers are emphasizing the importance of early socialization experiences for humans who grow up in more normal environments. It is now recognized that it is not enough to care for an infant's physical needs; parents must also concern themselves with children's social development. If children are discouraged from having friends, they will be deprived of social interactions with peers that are critical in their emotional growth.

Studies of animals raised in isolation also support the importance of socialization on development. Harry Harlow (1971), a researcher at the primate laboratory of the University of Wisconsin, conducted tests with rhesus monkeys that had

Rhesus monkeys display a need for social interaction when they cling to warm, terry cloth "substitute mothers." The monkey here is reaching for milk on a "mother" made of bare wire while remaining on the cloth "mother."

been raised away from their mothers and away from contact with other monkeys. As was the case with Isabelle, the rhesus monkeys raised in isolation were found to be fearful and easily frightened. They did not mate, and the females who were artificially inseminated became abusive mothers. Apparently, isolation had had a damaging effect on the monkeys.

A creative aspect of Harlow's experimentation was his use of "artificial mothers." In one such experiment, Harlow presented monkeys raised in isolation with two substitute mothers—one cloth-covered replica and one covered with wire which had the ability to offer milk. Monkey after monkey went to the wire mother for the life-giving milk, yet spent much more time clinging to the more motherlike cloth model. In this study, artificial mothers who provided a comforting physical sensation (conveyed by the terry cloth) were more highly valued that those that provided food. As a result, the infant monkeys developed greater social attachments from their need for warmth, comfort, and intimacy than from their need for milk.

Harlow found that the ill effects of being raised in isolation were often irreversible. However, we need to be cautious about drawing parallels between animal and human behavior. Human parents are not covered with cloth (or fur); they use more behavioral means of showing affection for their offspring. Nonetheless, Harlow's research suggests that the harmful consequences of isolation can apply to other primates besides humans (R. W. Brown, 1965:39).

The Influence of Heredity

Isolation studies may seem to suggest that inheritance can be dismissed as a factor in the social development of humans and animals. However, the interplay between hereditary and environmental factors is evident in two fascinating studies that began to produce results in 1987—one involving pairs of twins reared apart and the second examining the inheritability of a form of mental illness.

Inheritability and Traits of Twins Researchers at the Minnesota Center for Twin and Adoption Research are studying pairs of identical twins reared apart to determine what similarities, if any, they show in personality traits, behavior, and intelligence. Thus far, the preliminary results from the available twin studies indicate that both genetic factors and socialization experiences are influential in human development. Certain characteristics, such as twins' temperaments, voice patterns, and nervous habits, appear to be strikingly similar even in twins reared apart, thereby suggesting that these qualities may be linked to hereditary causes. However, there are far greater differences between identical twins reared apart in terms of attitudes, values, types of mates chosen, and even drinking habits. In examining clusters of personality traits among such twins, the Minnesota studies have found marked similarities in their tendency toward leadership or dominance, but significant differences in their need for intimacy, comfort, and assistance.

Researchers have also been impressed with the similar scores on intelligence tests of twin pairs reared apart. Most of the identical twins register scores even closer than those that would be expected if the same person took a test twice. At the same time, however, identical twins brought up in dramatically different social environments score quite differently on intelligence tests—a finding that supports the impact of socialization on human development (Bouchard, 1991).

Inheritability and Mental Illness Lancaster County, Pennsylvania, is hardly a likely site for scientific breakthroughs. Often the destination of tourists, this area is best known for its Amish communities. The Amish shun most modern conveniences, such as electricity, automobiles, radio, and television. They maintain their own schools and do not want their children socialized into many norms and values of the United States.

For 10 years, a team of psychiatrists and biologists (Egeland et al., 1987) studied the occurrence of manic-depressive behavior in three generations of Amish families. Victims of *manic depression* (or bipolar affective disorders) shift between the extreme emotional states of euphoria and depression. In studying this illness, scientists found that the Amish served as an excellent sample. Their communities keep accurate genealogical records; moreover, many environmental factors which contribute to manic depression, such as alcoholism, drug abuse, unemployment, and divorce, are extremely rare within the Amish subculture.

The findings of the Pennsylvania study suggest a hereditary basis for manic-depressive behavior, which is apparently linked to genes in the specific region of a chromosome. The researchers emphasize that this genetic characteristic neither guarantees nor precludes manic depression; they can report only that people with the characteristic

MacDonald/The Picture Cube

Members of Amish communities of Lancaster County, Pennsylvania, shun most modern conveniences, such as electricity, automobiles, radio, and television.

show a *predisposition* to manic-depressive behavior. Note that this degree of specificity was not present in the twin studies discussed earlier. There was no suggestion, for example, that a single gene could be linked to timidity.

In reviewing the studies of twin pairs and the Amish, one should proceed with some caution. Janice Egeland, head researcher for the Amish study, notes an encouraging aspect of findings which point to the importance of heredity in human development. "Too often," she argues, "personal embarrassment and social stigma are associated with an illness whose cause is beyond the control of the individual." By contrast, psychologist Leon Kamin fears that overgeneralizing from the Minnesota results—and granting too much importance to the impact of heredity—may be used to blame the poor and downtrodden for their condition. As the debate over nature versus nurture continues, we can anticipate numerous replications of these fascinating investigations to clarify the interplay between hereditary and environmental factors in human development (Leo, 1987; Plomin, 1989; Wallis, 1987:67).

Sociobiology

As part of the continuing debate on the relative influences of heredity and the environment, there has been renewed interest in sociobiology in recent years. *Sociobiology* is the systematic study of the biological bases of social behavior. Sociobiologists basically apply naturalist Charles Darwin's principles of natural selection to the study of social behavior. They assume that particular forms of behavior become genetically linked to a species if they contribute to its fitness to survive (van den Berghe, 1978:20). In its extreme form, sociobiology resembles biological determinism by suggesting that all behavior is the result of genetic or biological factors and that social interactions play no role in shaping people's conduct.

Sociobiology does not seek to describe individual behavior on the level of "Why is Fred more aggressive than Jim?" Rather, sociobiologists focus on how human nature is affected by the genetic composition of a group of people who share certain characteristics (such as men or women, or members of isolated tribal bands). In general, sociobiologists have stressed the basic genetic heritage that is shared by all humans and have shown little interest in speculating about alleged differences between racial groups or nationalities.

Many social scientists have strongly attacked the main tenets of sociobiology as expressed by Edward O. Wilson (1975, 1977, 1978), a zoologist at Harvard University. Some researchers insist that intellectual interest in sociobiology will only deflect serious study of the more significant factor influencing human behavior—socialization. Yet Lois Wladis Hoffman (1985), in her presidential address to the Society for the Psychological Study of Social Issues, argued that sociobiology poses a valuable challenge to social scientists to better document their own research. Interactionists, for example, could show how social behavior is not programmed by human biology, but instead adjusts continually to the attitudes and responses of others.

The conflict perspective shares with sociobiology a recognition that human beings do not like to be dominated, yet there the similarity ends. Conflict theorists (like functionalists and interactionists) believe that social reality is defined by people's behavior rather than by their genetic structure. Consequently, conflict theorists fear that the sociobiological approach could be used as an argument against efforts to assist disadvantaged people, such as schoolchildren who are not competing successfully (A. Caplan, 1978; M. Harris, 1980:514).

Wilson has argued that there should be parallel studies of human behavior with a focus on both genetic and social causes. Certainly most social scientists would agree with the sociobiologists' contention that there is a biological basis for social behavior. But there is less support for the more extreme positions taken by certain advocates of sociobiology (Gove, 1987; see also A. Fisher, 1992).

THE SELF AND SOCIALIZATION

We all have various perceptions, feelings, and beliefs about who we are and what we are like. We are not born with them. How, then, do we come to develop them? Do they change as we age?

Building on the work of George Herbert Mead (1964b), sociobiologists recognize that we create our own designation: the self. The *self* represents the sum total of people's conscious perception of their own identity as distinct from others. It is not a static phenomenon, but continues to develop and change throughout our lives.

Sociologists and psychologists alike have expressed interest in how the individual develops and modifies the sense of self as a result of social interaction. The work of sociologists Charles Horton Cooley and George Herbert Mead, pioneers of the interactionist approach, has been especially useful in furthering our understanding of these important issues (Gecas, 1982).

Sociological Approaches to the Self

Cooley: Looking-Glass Self In the early 1900s, Charles Horton Cooley advanced the belief that we learn who we are by interacting with others. Our view of ourselves, then, comes not only from direct contemplation of our personal qualities, but also from our impressions of how others perceive us. Cooley used the phrase ***looking-glass self*** to emphasize that the self is the product of our social interactions with other people.

The process of developing a self-identity or self-concept has three phases. First, we imagine how we present ourselves to others—to relatives, friends, even strangers on the street. Then we imagine how others evaluate us (attractive, intelligent, shy, or strange). Finally, we develop some sort of feeling about ourselves, such as respect or shame, as a result of these impressions. Earlier in the chapter, we saw that the concept of self in the Semai culture includes an image of non-aggressiveness (Cooley, 1902:152; M. Howard, 1989:249).

A critical but subtle aspect of Cooley's looking-glass self is that the self results from an individual's "imagination" of how others view him or her. As a result, we can develop self-identities based on incorrect perceptions of how others see us. A student may react strongly to an instructor's criticism and decide (wrongly) that the instructor views him or her as stupid. This can easily be converted into a negative self-identity through the following process: (1) the instructor criticized me, (2) the instructor must think that I'm stupid, (3) I *am* stupid. Yet self-identity is subject to change. If the student received an "A" at the end of the course, he or she might no longer feel stupid.

Mead: Stages of the Self George Herbert Mead (1930:706) acknowledged to Charles Horton Cooley that he was "profoundly indebted" to Cooley's "insight and constructive thought." We are in turn indebted to Mead for continuing Cooley's exploration of interactionist theory and for his contributions to sociological understanding of the self. Mead (1934, 1964a) developed a useful model of the process by which the self emerges, defined by three distinct stages.

During the *preparatory stage,* children merely imitate the people around them, especially family members with whom they continually interact. Thus, a small child will bang on a piece of wood while a parent is engaged in carpentry work or will try to throw a ball if an older sibling is doing so nearby.

As they grow older, children become more adept at using symbols to communicate with others. *Symbols* are the gestures, objects, and language which form the basis of human communication. By interacting with relatives and friends, as well as by watching cartoons on television and looking at picture books, children begin to understand the use of symbols. Like spoken languages, symbols vary from culture to culture and even between subcultures. "Thumbs up" is not always a positive gesture; nodding the head up and down does *not* always mean "yes." As part of the socialization process, children learn the symbols of their particular culture (Ekman et al., 1984).

Mead was among the first to analyze the relationship of symbols to socialization. As children develop skill in communicating through symbols, they gradually become more aware of social relationships. As a result, during the *play stage,* the child becomes able to imitate the actions of others, including adults. Just as an actor "becomes" a character, a child becomes a doctor, parent, superhero, or ship captain.

Mead noted that an important aspect of the play stage is role taking. ***Role taking*** is the process of mentally assuming the perspective of another, thereby enabling one to respond from that imagined viewpoint. For example, a young child will gradually learn when it is best to ask a parent for favors. If the parent usually comes home from work in a bad mood, the child will wait until after dinner when the parent is more relaxed and approachable. Although for children role taking may involve conforming to the behavior of others, for adolescents and adults role taking is more selective and creative (R. Turner, 1962).

In Mead's third stage, the *game stage,* the child of about 8 or 9 years old begins to consider several tasks and relationships simultaneously. At this point in development, children grasp not only their own social positions, but also those of others around them. Consider a girl or boy of this age who is part of a scout troop out on a weekend hike in the mountains. The child must understand what he or she is expected to do, but also must recognize the responsibilities of other scouts (as well as the leaders). This is the final stage of development under Mead's model; the child can now respond to numerous members of the social environment.

Mead uses the term **generalized others** to refer to the child's awareness of the attitudes, viewpoints, and expectations of society as a whole. Simply put, this concept suggests that when an individual acts, he or she takes into account an entire group of people. For example, a child who reaches this level of development will not act courteously merely to please a particular parent. Rather, the child comes to understand that courtesy is a widespread social value endorsed by parents, teachers, and religious leaders.

At this developmental stage, children can take a more sophisticated view of people and the social environment. They now understand what specific occupations and social positions are and no longer equate Mr. Williams only with the role of "librarian" or Ms. Franks only with "principal." It has become clear to the child that Mr. Williams can be a librarian, a parent, and a marathon runner at the same time and that Ms. Franks is one of many principals in our society. Thus, the child has reached a new level of sophistication in his or her observations of individuals and institutions.

Mead is best known for this theory of the self. According to Mead (1964b), the self begins as a privileged, central position in a person's world. Young children picture themselves as the focus of everything around them and find it difficult to consider the perspectives of others. For example, when shown a mountain scene and asked to describe what an observer on the opposite side of the mountain sees (such as a lake or hikers), young children nevertheless describe only objects visible from their own vantage point. This childhood tendency to place ourselves at the center of events never entirely disappears. When an instructor is ready to return term papers or examinations and mentions that certain students did exceptionally well, we often assume that we fall into that select group (Fenigstein, 1984).

As people mature, the self changes and begins to reflect greater concern about the reaction of others. Parents, friends, coworkers, coaches, and teachers are often among those who play a major role in shaping a person's self. Mead used the term **significant others** to refer to those individuals who are most important in the development of the self (Schlenker, 1985:12–13).

Goffman: Impression Management   As was seen in Chapter 1, the interactionist approach, which owes a great deal to both Cooley and Mead, emphasizes the micro (or small-scale) level of analysis. Thus, this sociological perspective is especially suited to an examination of how the self develops. Erving Goffman, a recent sociologist associated with the interactionist perspective, suggested that many of our daily activities involve attempts to convey impressions of who we are.

Early in life, the individual learns to slant his or her presentation of the self in order to create distinctive appearances and to satisfy particular audiences. Goffman (1959) refers to this altering of the presentation of the self as **impression management.** Box 3-1 provides an everyday example of this concept by describing how students engage in impression management after examination grades have been awarded.

In examining such everyday social interactions, Goffman makes so many explicit parallels to the theater that his view has been termed the **dramaturgical approach.** According to this perspective, people can be seen as resembling performers in action. For example, clerks may try to appear busier than they actually are if a supervisor happens to be watching them. Waiters and waitresses may "not see" a customer who wants more coffee if they are on a break.

BOX 3-1

IMPRESSION MANAGEMENT BY STUDENTS AFTER EXAMS

Sociologists Daniel Albas and Cheryl Albas (1988) drew upon Erving Goffman's concept of impression management to examine the strategies that college students employ to create desired appearances after grades have been awarded and examination papers returned. Albas and Albas divide these encounters into three categories: those between students who have all received high grades (Ace-Ace encounters), those between students who have received high grades and those who have received low or even failing grades (Ace-Bomber encounters), and those between students who have all received low grades (Bomber-Bomber encounters).

Ace-Ace encounters occur in a rather open atmosphere because there is comfort in sharing one's high mark with another high achiever. It is even acceptable to violate the norm of modesty and brag when among other Aces,

since, as one student admitted, "It's much easier to admit a high mark to someone who has done better than you, or at least as well."

Ace-Bomber encounters are often sensitive. Bombers generally attempt to avoid such exchanges because "you . . . emerge looking like the dumb one" or "feel like you are lazy or unreliable." When forced into interactions with Aces, Bombers work to appear gracious and congratulatory. For their part, Aces offer sympathy and support for the dissatisfied Bombers and even rationalize their own "lucky" high scores. To help Bombers save face, Aces may emphasize the difficulty and unfairness of the exam.

Bomber-Bomber encounters tend to be closed, reflecting the group effort to wall off the feared disdain of others. Yet, within the safety of these encounters, Bombers openly share their disappointment and engage in expressions

of mutual self-pity that they themselves call "pity parties." Face-saving excuses are developed for the Bombers' poor performances, such as "I wasn't feeling well all week" or "I had four exams and two papers due that week." If the grade distribution in a class included particularly low scores, Bombers may engage in scapegoating the professor, who will be attacked as a sadist, a slave driver, or simply an incompetent.

As is evident from these descriptions, students' impression-management strategies are constrained by society's informal norms regarding modesty and consideration for less successful peers. In classroom settings, as in the workplace and in other types of human interactions, efforts at impression management are most intense when status differentials are most pronounced—as in encounters between the high-scoring Aces and the low-scoring Bombers.

Face-work is another aspect of the self to which Goffman (1959) has drawn attention. Maintaining the proper image can be essential to continued social interaction; face-saving behavior must be initiated if the self suffers because of embarrassment or some form of rejection. Thus, for example, in response to a rejection at a singles' bar, a person may engage in face-work by saying, "I really wasn't feeling well anyway" or "There isn't an interesting person in this entire crowd."

Goffman's approach is generally regarded as an insightful perspective on everyday life, but it is not without its critics. Writing from a conflict perspective, sociologist Alvin Gouldner (1970) sees Goffman's work as implicitly reaffirming the sta-

tus quo, including social class inequalities. Using Gouldner's critique, one might ask if women and minorities are expected to deceive both themselves and others while paying homage to those in power. Moreover, sociologist Carol Brooks Gardner (1989) has suggested that Goffman's view of public places as innocuous settings in which strangers often interact politely gives insufficient attention to women's well-founded fear of the sexual harassment, assault, and rape that can occur there. In considering impression management and the other concepts developed by Goffman, sociologists must remember that by *describing* social reality one is not necessarily endorsing its harsh impact on many individuals and groups (S. Williams, 1986:357–358).

Erving Goffman (1922–1982) made a distinctive contribution to sociology by popularizing a particular type of interactionist method known as the dramaturgical approach.

Goffman's work represents a logical progression of the sociological efforts begun by Cooley and Mead on how personality is acquired through socialization and how we manage the presentation of our self to others. Cooley stressed the process by which we come to create a self; Mead focused on how the self develops as we learn to interact with others; Goffman emphasized the ways in which we consciously create images of ourselves for others.

Psychological Approaches to the Self

Psychologists have shared the interest of Cooley, Mead, and other sociologists in the development of the self. Early work in psychology, such as that of Sigmund Freud (1856–1939), stressed the role of inborn drives—among them the drive for sexual gratification—in channeling human behavior. Other psychologists, such as Jean Piaget and Lawrence Kohlberg, have emphasized the stages through which human beings progress as the self develops.

Like Cooley and Mead, Freud believed that the self is a social product. But unlike Cooley and Mead, he suggested that the self has components that are always fighting with each other. According to Freud, people are in constant conflict between their natural impulsive instincts and societal constraints. Part of us seeks limitless pleasure, while another part seeks out rational behavior. By interacting with others, we learn the expectations of society and then select behavior most appropriate to our own culture. (Of course, as Freud was well-aware, we sometimes distort reality and behave irrationally.)

Research on newborn babies by the Swiss child psychologist Jean Piaget (1896–1980) has underscored the importance of social interactions in developing a sense of self. Piaget found that newborns have no self in the sense of a looking-glass image. Ironically, though, they are quite self-centered; they demand that all attention be directed toward them. Newborns have not yet separated themselves from the universe of which they are a part. For these babies, the phrase "you and me" has no meaning; they understand only "me." However, as they mature, children are gradually socialized into social relationships even within their rather self-centered world.

In his well-known ***cognitive theory of development,*** Piaget (1954) identifies four stages in the development of children's thought processes. In the first, or *sensorimotor,* stage, young children use their senses to make discoveries. For example, through touching they discover that their hands are actually a part of themselves. During the second, or *preoperational,* stage, children begin to use words and symbols to distinguish objects and ideas. The milestone in the third, or *concrete operational,* stage is that children engage in more logical thinking. They learn that if a formless lump of clay is shaped into a snake, it is still the same clay. Finally, in the fourth, or *formal operational,* stage, adolescents are capable of sophisticated abstract thought and can deal with ideas and values in a logical manner.

Piaget has suggested that moral development becomes an important part of socialization as children become able to think more abstractly. When children learn the rules of a game such as checkers or jacks, they are learning to obey societal norms. Children under 8 years old display a rather basic level of morality: rules are rules, and there is no concept of "extenuating circumstances." However, as they mature, children become capable of greater autonomy and begin to experience moral dilemmas as to what constitutes proper behavior.

According to both Jean Piaget and Lawrence Kohlberg (1963, 1981), children give increasing attention to how people think and why they act in a particular way. As a result, children learn to evaluate the intentions behind norms and the consequences of norms in a much more sophisticated manner (see also Gilligan, 1982).

SOCIALIZATION AND THE LIFE CYCLE

Rites of Passage

The socialization process continues throughout all stages of the human life cycle. In cultures less complex than our own, stages of development are marked by specific ceremonies. Many societies have definite *rites of passage* that dramatize and validate changes in a person's status. For example, a young Aboriginal woman in Australia will be honored at a ceremony at the time of her first menstruation. During these festivities, her first, unborn daughter is betrothed to a grown man. Hence the expression is heard that "there is no such thing as an unmarried woman" (Goodale, 1971). For the Aborigines, there is a sharp dividing line between childhood and the responsibilities of adult life.

This is not the case in our culture, but several psychologists and sociologists have nonetheless assigned particular labels to various periods of socialization. In examining the socialization process in the United States, it is important to understand that we do not necessarily move from one stage to another in the clear-cut way that we are promoted from one grade in school to another. This may lead to some ambiguity and confusion as we develop our selves: At a certain age and

Many societies, including the United States, have definite rites of passage *that dramatize and validate changes in a person's status. A young Apache woman is shown taking part in a four-day ceremony to honor her first menstruation. Throughout the ceremony, elders and relatives will chant: "Walk with honor and dignity. Be strong! For you are the mother of a people." The Kota people of the Congo have a traditional rite of passage into adulthood whereby adolescent males paint themselves blue (viewed by the Kota as the color of death) to symbolize the death of childhood. Interestingly, as an accommodation to modern life in the Congo, this Kota rite of passage now takes place somewhat later in life so that young males can complete their public schooling.*

level of maturity, for instance, are we children or adolescents? At another, are we adolescents or adults?

The United States does bear some resemblance to simpler societies such as that of the Aborigines in that we have events marking the assumption of new roles and statuses—the wedding, for example, represents a rite of passage in our society. Yet there is no one ceremony that clearly marks the shift from childhood to adulthood. Instead, we go through a prolonged period of transition known as *adolescence*.

This transition varies depending on certain social factors, especially social class. A person from a poor background may not have any alternatives but to work full time at a rather early age. Because of the need to contribute to the family income or to become financially self-supporting, such a young person may not have the luxury of delaying entry into the labor force by continuing his or her education.

Some of the most difficult socialization challenges (and rites of passage) are encountered in the latter years of life. Assessing one's accomplishments, coping with declining physical abilities, experiencing retirement, and facing the inevitability of death may lead to painful adjustments. Old age is further complicated by the negative way in which the elderly are viewed and treated in many societies, including the United States. Older people's self-image may weaken if they are influenced by the common stereotype of the elderly as helpless and dependent. However, as we will explore more fully in Chapter 8, many older people continue to lead active, productive, fulfilled lives.

Anticipatory Socialization and Resocialization

The development of a social self is literally a lifelong transformation which begins in the crib and continues as one prepares for death. Two types of socialization occur at many points throughout the life cycle: anticipatory socialization and resocialization.

Preparation for many aspects of adult life begins with anticipatory socialization during childhood and adolescence and continues throughout our lives as we prepare for new responsibilities. *Anticipatory socialization* refers to the processes of socialization in which a person "rehearses" for future positions, occupations, and social relationships. A culture can function more efficiently and smoothly if members become acquainted with the norms, values, and behavior associated with a social position before actually assuming that status.

The process of anticipatory socialization is evident in the families of snakers (a term they prefer to *snake charmers*) in India. At the age of 5 or 6, the

son of a snaker will begin to touch the snakes he has observed all his life. The boy will soon learn how to catch snakes and will become familiar with the habits of each species. In snaker families, it is a matter of intense pride when a boy follows in the footsteps of his father, his grandfather, and earlier male ancestors (Skafte, 1979).

Occasionally, as we assume new social and occupational positions, we find it necessary to unlearn our previous orientation. *Resocialization* refers to the process of discarding former behavior patterns and accepting new ones as part of a transition in one's life. Such resocialization occurs throughout the human life cycle. It is required, for example, when a young father in the United States becomes absorbed in caring for his infant daughter or son. The father may have been socialized since his childhood to view tasks such as changing diapers, offering midnight feedings with a bottle, and taking the child to the pediatrician as "women's work." Suddenly, he finds himself a parent within a culture that is expecting fathers to become more involved in day-to-day child-rearing duties. This man not only needs to learn new skills but also must set aside his previous attitudes and behavior patterns regarding child rearing.

Resocialization in Total Institutions

In certain situations, people are voluntarily (or sometimes involuntarily) resocialized within a highly controlled social environment. Resocialization is particularly effective when it occurs within a total institution. Erving Goffman (1961) coined the term *total institutions* to refer to institutions, such as prisons, the military, mental hospitals, and convents, which regulate all aspects of a person's life under a single authority. The total institution is generally cut off from the rest of society and therefore provides for all the needs of its members. Quite literally, the crew of a merchant vessel at sea becomes part of a total institution. So elaborate are its requirements, so all-encompassing are its activities, that a total institution often represents a miniature society.

Goffman (1961) has identified four common traits of total institutions. First, all aspects of life are conducted in the same place and are under the control of a single authority. Second, any activities within the institution are conducted in the company of others in the same circumstances—for example, novices in a convent or army recruits. Third, the authorities devise rules and schedule activities without consulting participants. Finally, all aspects of life within a total institution are designed to fulfill the purpose of the organization. Thus, all activities in a monastery are centered on prayer and communion with God (Davies, 1989; P. Rose et al., 1979:321–322).

Individuality is often lost within total institutions. For example, upon entering prison to begin "doing time," a person may experience the humiliation of a ***degradation ceremony*** as he or she is stripped of clothing, jewelry, and other personal possessions (H. Garfinkel, 1956). Even the person's self is taken away to some extent; the prison inmate loses his or her name and becomes known to authorities as No. 72716. From this point on, daily routines are scheduled with little or no room for personal initiative. The institution is experienced as an overbearing social environment, and the individual becomes secondary and rather invisible.

Goffman's concept of a total institution alerts us to the negative aspects of depriving people of contact with the larger society. The power of such institutions in shaping people's behavior was disturbingly illustrated in a famous experiment by Philip Zimbardo (1972, 1974; C. Haney et al., 1973). He and a team of social psychologists carefully screened more than 70 college students for participation in a simulated prison. By a flip of a coin, half were arbitrarily designated as prisoners, the others as guards. The guards were allowed to make up their own rules for maintaining law, order, and respect.

After only six days of operation, Zimbardo and his colleagues were forced to end the experiment because the student guards had begun to take pleasure in cruel treatment of prisoners. About a third were tyrannical in their arbitrary use of power, while the remaining guards did not agree with this tough approach. At the same time, the prisoners meekly accepted their confinement and mistreatment. More recently, sociologist Ivan Fahs conducted several replications of Zimbardo's model prison experiment over a four-year period; he came to the same disturbing findings (E. Greene, 1987).

AGENTS OF SOCIALIZATION

As we have seen, the culture of the United States is defined by rather gradual movements from one stage of socialization to the next. The lifelong socialization process involves many different social forces which influence our lives and alter our self-images.

The family is the most important agent of socialization in the United States, especially for children. Five other agents of socialization will be given particular attention in this chapter: the school, the peer group, the mass media, the workplace, and the state. The role of religion in socializing young people into society's norms and values will be explored in Chapter 10.

Family

The family is the institution most closely associated with the process of socialization. Obviously, one of its primary functions is the care and rearing of children. We experience socialization first as babies and infants living in families; it is here that we develop an initial sense of self. Most parents seek to help their children become competent adolescents and self-sufficient adults, which means socializing them into the norms and values of both the family and the larger society. In this process, adults themselves experience socialization as they adjust to becoming spouses, parents, and in-laws (Gecas, 1981).

The lifelong process of learning begins shortly after birth. Since newborns can hear, see, smell, taste, and feel heat, cold, and pain, they orient themselves to the surrounding world. Human beings, especially family members, constitute an important part of the social environment of the newborn. People minister to the baby's needs by feeding, cleansing, and carrying the baby.

The family of a newborn and other caretakers are not concerned with teaching social skills per se. Nevertheless, babies are hardly asocial. An infant enters an organized society, becomes part of a generation, and typically enters into a family. Depending on how they are treated, infants can develop strong social attachments and dependency on others. Interestingly, the twentieth century has seen a prolonging of children's dependence on parents in the United States. As the

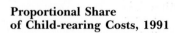

BOX 3-2

THE COST OF REARING A CHILD

Few societies assign a dollar value to child rearing, but a governmental research group in the United States offers annual estimates. For example, the estimated average cost of rearing a child from birth through age 17 for a two-parent, middle-income family with no more than five children living in the urban midwest will be $122,760. This cost will be $48,000 greater for high-income families and $35,000 less for lower-income families.

The accompanying figure shows the breakdown of this estimated average cost of $122,760 into such categories as housing, food, transportation, medical costs, and clothing. Since 1981, there has been a significant increase in the proportion of child-rearing costs attributable to education, while the proportional share for other items has declined (Family Economics Research Group, 1992:33–36).

Proportional Share of Child-rearing Costs, 1991

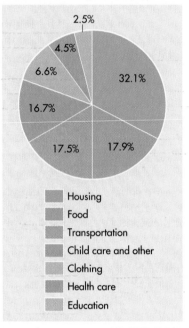

SOURCE: *Education Week*, 1991; Family Economics Research Group, 1992:34.

Of the estimated average cost of $122,760 for raising a child from birth through age 17 in a middle-income family in the urban midwest, the largest share (32.1 percent) will go to housing, while food will account for almost one-fifth (17.9 percent) of the total cost.

---

length of time devoted to parenthood has increased, the cost of rearing a child has escalated (see Box 3-2).

Most infants go through a relatively formal period of socialization generally called *habit training*. Schedules are imposed for eating and sleeping, the termination of breast or bottle feeding, and the acceptance of new foods. In these and other ways, infants can be viewed as objects of socialization, yet they also function as socializers. Even as the behavior of a baby is being modified by interactions with people and the environment, the baby is causing others to change their behavior patterns. The baby converts adults into mothers and fathers, who, in turn, assist him or her in progressing into childhood (Rheingold, 1969).

As both Charles Horton Cooley and George Herbert Mead noted, the development of the self is a critical aspect of the early years of one's life. In the United States, such social development includes exposure to cultural assumptions regarding sex differences. The term **gender roles** refers to expectations regarding the proper behavior, attitudes, and activities of males and females. For example, "toughness" has been traditionally seen as masculine—and desirable only in men—while "tenderness" has been viewed as feminine. As we will see in Chapter 8, other cultures do not necessarily assign these qualities to each gender in the way that our culture does.

As the primary agents of childhood socialization, parents play a critical role in guiding children into those gender roles deemed appropriate in a society. Other adults, older siblings, the mass media, and religious and educational institutions also have noticeable impact on a child's socialization into feminine and masculine norms. A culture may require that one sex or the other take primary responsibility for socialization of children, economic support of the family, or religious or intellectual leadership.

Like other elements of culture, socialization patterns are not fixed. In the last 20 years, there has, for example, been a sustained challenge to traditional gender-role socialization in the United States, owing in good part to the efforts of the feminist movement (see Chapter 8). Nevertheless, despite such changes, children growing up in the 1990s are hardly free of traditional gender roles. As Letty Cottin Pogrebin (1981:380), a founder and editor of *Ms.* magazine, wondered, how many parents would move a 6-year-old girl's toy chest into the room of their 6-year-old boy with confidence that he would enjoy its contents?

Interactionists remind us that socialization concerning not only masculinity and femininity, but also marriage and parenthood, begins in childhood as a part of family life. Children observe their parents as they express affection, deal with finances, quarrel, complain about in-laws, and so forth. This represents an informal process of anticipatory socialization. The child develops a ten-

tative model of what being married and being a parent are like. We will explore socialization for marriage and parenthood more fully in Chapter 9.

As we noted earlier, children function within the family as agents of socialization themselves. The term *reverse socialization* refers to the process whereby people who are normally being socialized are at the same time socializing their socializers. For example, young people may affect the way their parents (and other adults) dress, eat, and even think. Sociologist John Peters (1985) studied reverse socialization by surveying the parents of his college students in Canada. Peters found that these parents had been influenced by their children in such areas as sports, politics, clothing, physical appearance, and sexuality (see also Thorne, 1987:95). Anthropologist Margaret Mead (1970:65–91) has suggested that reverse socialization is greatest in societies undergoing rapid social change; in such societies, the young socialize the old to new customs and values.

School

Like the family, schools have an explicit mandate to socialize people in the United States—and especially children—into the norms and values of our culture. As conflict theorists Samuel Bowles and Herbert Gintis (1976) have observed, schools

David Young-Wolff/PhotoEdit

According to traditional gender roles in the United States, "toughness" has been seen as masculine—and desirable only in men and boys—while "tenderness" has been viewed as feminine.

In the United States and other cultures, schools serve socialization functions. During the 1980s, Japanese parents and educators were distressed to realize that children were gradually losing the knack of eating with chopsticks. Schools were chosen as the proper institution to remedy this situation.

in this country foster competition through systems of reward and punishment, such as grades and evaluations by teachers. Thus a child who is working intently to learn a new skill can nevertheless come to feel stupid and unsuccessful. However, as the self matures, children become capable of increasingly realistic assessments of their intellectual, physical, and social abilities.

Functionalists point out that, as agents of socialization, schools fulfill the function of teaching recruits the values and customs of the larger society. Conflict theorists concur with this observation, but add that schools can reinforce the divisive aspects of society, especially those of social class. For example, higher education in the United States is quite costly despite the existence of financial aid programs. Students from affluent backgrounds thus have an advantage in gaining access to universities and professional training. At the same time, less affluent young people may never receive the preparation that would qualify them for our society's best-paying and most prestigious jobs. The contrast between the functionalist and conflict views of education will be discussed in more detail in Chapter 10.

In teaching students the values and customs of the larger society, schools in the United States have traditionally socialized children into conventional gender roles. Professors of education Myra Sadker and David Sadker (1985:54) note that "although many believe that classroom sexism disap-

peared in the early '70s, it hasn't." Indeed, a report released in 1992 by the American Association of University Women (1992)—which summarized 1331 studies of girls in school—concludes that schools in the United States favor boys over girls.

According to this report, girls show a disturbing pattern of *downward* intellectual mobility compared with boys, resulting from differential treatment based on gender. Teachers praise boys more than girls and offer boys more academic assistance. Boys receive praise for the intellectual content of their work, whereas girls are more likely to be praised for being neat. Teachers reward boys for assertiveness (for example, calling out answers without raising their hands) while reprimanding girls for similar behavior. Finally, girls often are not expected or encouraged to pursue higher-level mathematics and science courses. The report concludes that girls are less likely than boys to reach their academic potential and insists that "the system must change" (American Association of University Women, 1992:84).

In other cultures as well, schools serve socialization functions. During the 1980s, for example, Japanese parents and educators were distressed to realize that children were gradually losing the knack of eating with chopsticks. Having been seduced by spoons and cheeseburgers, some children could not use *hashi* (chopsticks) at all. Consequently, schools were chosen as the proper institution to remedy this situation. Whereas only 10 percent of school lunch programs provided chopsticks in 1975, this figure had risen to 69 percent in 1983 and to 90 percent by the end of the decade (Hiatt, 1988).

Peer Group

As a child grows older, the family becomes somewhat less important in his or her social development. Instead, peer groups increasingly assume the role of George Herbert Mead's significant others. Within the peer group, young people associate with others who are approximately their own age and who often enjoy a similar social status. For example, in her observation research of sixth-, seventh-, and eighth-grade girls, sociologist Donna Eder (1985) observed that, at any time, most girls interact primarily with members of a single peer group. While each group's composition may change over the three-year period, it is generally a select few peers who are important to girls during this developmental period.

Gender differences are noteworthy in the social world of adolescents. Males are more likely to spend time in groups of males, while females are more likely to interact with a single other female. This pattern reflects differences in levels of emotional intimacy; teenage males are less likely to develop strong emotional ties than are females. Instead, males are more inclined to share in group activities. These patterns are evident among adolescents in many societies besides the United States (Dornbusch, 1989:248).

Peer groups, such as friendship cliques, youth gangs, and special-interest clubs, frequently assist adolescents in gaining some degree of independence from parents and other authority figures. As we will study in more detail in Chapter 5, conforming to peers' behavior is an example of the socialization process at work. If all of one's friends have successfully battled for the right to stay out until midnight on a Saturday night, it may seem essential to fight for the same privilege. Peer groups also provide for anticipatory socialization into new roles that the young person will later assume.

Teenagers imitate their friends in part because the peer group maintains a meaningful system of rewards and punishments. The group may encourage a young person to follow pursuits that society considers admirable, as in a school club

engaged in volunteer work in hospitals and nursing homes. On the other hand, the group may encourage someone to violate the culture's norms and values by driving recklessly, shoplifting, engaging in acts of vandalism, and the like.

Peer groups serve a valuable function by assisting the transition to adult responsibilities. At home, parents tend to dominate; at school, the teenager must contend with teachers and administrators. But, within the peer group, each member can assert himself or herself in a way that may not be possible elsewhere. Nevertheless, almost all adolescents in our culture remain economically dependent on their parents, and most are emotionally dependent as well.

Mass Media

In the last 75 years, such technological innovations as radio, motion pictures, recorded music, and television have become important agents of socialization. Television, in particular, is a critical force in the socialization of children in the United States. Many parents in essence allow the television set to become a child's favorite "playmate"; consequently, children in our society typically watch over three hours of television per day. Remarkably, between the ages of 6 and 18, the average young person spends more time watching the "tube" (15,000 to 16,000 hours) than working in school (13,000 hours). Apart from sleeping, watching television is the most time-consuming activity of young people.

Relative to other agents of socialization discussed earlier—such as family members, peers, and schools—television has certain distinctive characteristics. It permits imitation and role playing but does not encourage more complex forms of learning. Watching television is, above all, a passive experience; one sits back and waits to be entertained. Psychologist Urie Bronfenbrenner (1970), among others, has expressed concern about the "insidious influence" of television in encouraging children to forsake human interaction for passive viewing.

Critics of television are further alarmed by the programming that children view as they sit for hours in front of a television set. It is generally agreed that children (as well as adults) are exposed to a great deal of violence on television. On Saturday morning cartoon programs, a violent act is presented every two minutes. By the time of

Not only is television an important agent of socialization in the United States; it is even proving to have a significant influence in Samoa, where much of the programming comes from the United States.

high school graduation, a young person has witnessed some 18,000 fictional murders on television. Can watching so much violence have a numbing effect on one's sensibilities and moral values? Experiments document that children do tend to become more aggressive and hyperactive after viewing a violent sequence on television. Unfortunately, such studies measure only brief exposure; there are no conclusive data on the impact of television violence after weeks, months, and literally years of viewing.

Like other agents of socialization, television has traditionally portrayed and promoted conventional gender roles. A content analysis of child characters on prime-time television revealed that boys are shown as significantly more active, aggressive, and rational than girls. The two sexes are also shown as differing substantially in the types of activities in which they participate. Young girls on prime-time television talk on the telephone, read, and help with housework, whereas boys play sports, go on excursions, and get into mischief. In terms of socialization, television's portrayal of child characters is especially significant, since these characters may be the most meaningful for younger viewers (Peirce, 1989).

Even critics of the medium generally concede that television is not always a negative socializing influence. Creative programming such as *Sesame Street* can assist children in developing basic skills essential for schooling. In addition, television

programs and even commercials expose young people to lifestyles and cultures of which they are unaware. This entails not only children in the United States learning about life in "faraway lands," but also inner-city children learning about the lives of farm children and vice versa.

Not only does television educate viewers about members of other cultures and subcultures, it may even influence changes in self-identity. Researchers have long documented the strong differences between Puerto Ricans, Chicanos (Mexican Americans), Cuban Americans, and other Hispanic peoples. Yet the emergence of two nationwide Spanish-language television networks, Univision and Telemundo—watched in 1989 by three-fourths of all Hispanics—has blurred these distinctions somewhat and strengthened the common identity of these minorities as Hispanics. While minimizing certain subcultural differences, television appears to be having a unifying influence on the nation's growing Hispanic population (Mydans, 1989).

Television is unquestionably a powerful agent of socialization in the United States. Indeed, television seems to effectively socialize us to watch television: only 5 percent of adults watch less than

30 minutes per day! In view of the power of television, parents may need to monitor this aspect of a child's environment just as carefully as they evaluate teachers, playmates, and baby-sitters (Huesmann and Malamuth, 1986; Meyrowitz, 1985; R. Roberts, 1987).

While we have focused on criticisms of television as an agent of socialization, it is important to note that similar concerns have been raised regarding the content of popular music (especially rock music and "rap"), music videos, and motion pictures. These forms of entertainment, like television, serve as powerful agents of socialization for many young people in the United States and elsewhere. There has been continuing controversy about the content of music, music videos, and films—sometimes leading to celebrated court battles—as certain parents' organizations and religious groups challenge the intrusion of these media into the lives of children and adolescents.

Workplace

A fundamental aspect of human socialization involves learning to behave appropriately within an occupation. In the United States, working full time serves to confirm adult status; it is an indication to all that one has passed out of adolescence. In a sense, socialization into an occupation can represent both a harsh reality ("I have to work in order to buy food and pay the rent") and the realization of an ambition ("I've always wanted to be an airline pilot") (W. Moore, 1968:862).

Occupational socialization cannot be separated from the socialization experiences that occur during childhood and adolescence. We are most fully exposed to occupational roles through observing the work of our parents, of people whom we meet while they are performing their duties (doctors or firefighters, for example), and of people portrayed in the media (presidents, professional athletes, and so forth). These observations, along with the subtle messages we receive within a culture, help to shape—and often limit—the type of work we may consider.

Wilbert Moore (1968:871–880) has divided occupational socialization into four phases. The first phase is *career choice*, which involves selection of academic or vocational training appropriate for the desired job. If one hopes to become a physician, one must take certain courses, such as biology and chemistry, which are required of applicants to medical school. If one's goal is to become a violin maker, it will be useful to work as an apprentice for an expert practicing that craft.

The second phase identified by Moore is *anticipatory socialization*, which may last only a few months or extend for a period of years. Some children "inherit" their occupations because their parents run farms or "ma and pa" stores. In a sense, these young people are experiencing anticipatory socialization throughout childhood and adolescence as they observe their parents at work. In addition, some people *decide* on occupational goals at relatively early ages and never waver from their choices. A young woman or man may resolve to become a dancer at the age of 11 or 12; the entire adolescent period may focus on training for that future.

The third phase of occupational socialization—*conditioning and commitment*—occurs while one actually occupies the work-related role. *Conditioning* consists of reluctantly adjusting to the more unpleasant aspects of one's job. Most people find that the novelty of a new daily schedule quickly wears off and then realize that parts of the work experience are rather tedious. Moore uses the term *commitment* to refer to the enthusiastic acceptance of pleasurable duties that comes as the recruit identifies the positive tasks of an occupation.

In Moore's view, if a job proves to be satisfactory, the person will enter a fourth stage of socialization, which he calls *continuous commitment*. At this point, the job becomes an indistinguishable part of the person's self-identity. Violation of proper conduct becomes unthinkable. A person may choose to join professional associations, unions, or other groups which represent his or her occupation in the larger society.

Occupational socialization can be most intense immediately after one makes the transition from school to the job, but it continues through one's work history. Technological advances may alter the requirements of the position and necessitate some degree of resocialization. Thus, after years of working at typewriters, secretaries may find themselves adjusting to sophisticated word-processing equipment. In addition, many men and women change occupations, employers, or places of work during their adult years. Therefore, occupational socialization continues throughout a person's years in the labor market (Mortimer and Simmons, 1978:440–441; see also Becker et al., 1961; Ritzer, 1977).

The State

Social scientists have increasingly recognized the importance of the state as an agent of socialization because of its growing impact on the life cycle. Traditionally, family members have served as the primary caregivers in our culture, but in the twentieth century the family's protective function has steadily been transferred to outside agencies such as hospitals, mental health clinics, and insurance companies (Ogburn and Tibbits, 1934:661–778). Many of these agencies are run by the government; the rest are licensed and regulated by governmental bodies. In the social policy section, we will see that the state is under pressure to become a provider of child care, which would give it a new and direct role in the socialization of infants and young children.

In the past, the life cycle was influenced most significantly by heads of households and by local groups such as religious organizations. However, in the 1990s the individual as a citizen and an economic actor is influenced by national interests. For example, labor unions and political parties serve as intermediaries between the individual and the state.

The state has had a noteworthy impact on the life cycle by reinstituting the rites of passage that had disappeared in agricultural societies and in periods of early industrialization. For example, government regulations stipulate the ages at which a person may drive a car, drink alcohol, vote in elections, marry without parental permission, work overtime, and retire. These regulations do not constitute strict rites of passage: most 21-year-olds do not vote and most people choose their age of retirement without reference to government dictates. Still, by regulating the life cycle to some degree, the state shapes the socialization process by influencing our views of appropriate behavior at particular ages (Mayer and Schoepflin, 1989).

SOCIAL POLICY AND SOCIALIZATION

THE NEED FOR CHILD CARE

- Is it desirable to expose young children to the socializing influence of day care?
- In the view of conflict theorists, why does child care receive little government support?
- Should the costs of day care programs be paid by government, by the private sector, or entirely by parents?

The rise in single-parent families, increased job opportunities for women, and the need for additional family income have all propelled an increasing number of mothers of young children into the paid labor force of the United States (see Chapter 8). The majority of all mothers with children under the age of 6 are now in the paid labor force, and the number either working or looking for a job is expected to reach 70 percent by the year 2000. Who, then, will take care of the children of these women during work hours? For two-thirds of all 3- to 5-year-olds for whom national data are now available, the solution has become group child care programs. Day care centers have become the functional equivalent of the nuclear family, performing some of the nurturing and socialization functions previously handled only by family members (Holmes, 1990b).

Studies indicate that children placed in high-quality child care centers are not adversely affected by such experiences; in fact, good day care benefits children. The value of preschool programs was documented in a comparison of full-time Milwaukee preschoolers with a "non-nursery" group. Those children attending the preschool program from ages 3 months to 6 years showed significantly greater language development and greater gains on achievement tests than children in the non-nursery control group did. In addition, research conducted in the last few years indicates that children in day care or preschool programs are more self-sufficient. They react well to separation from their parents and tend to have more stimulating interactions when together. Finally, studies suggest that children may be better off in centers with well-trained care-

Feminists echo the concern of conflict theorists that high-quality child care receives little governmental support because it is regarded as "merely a way to let women work."

givers than cared for full time by mothers who are depressed and frustrated because they want to work outside the home (Galinsky, 1986; Garber and Herber, 1977; Shell, 1988).

Even if policymakers decide that publicly funded child care is desirable, they must determine the degree to which taxpayers should subsidize it. A number of European nations, including the Netherlands, Sweden, and Russia, provide preschool care at minimal or no cost. France has a comprehensive system of child care services which are largely financed by tax revenues, including free full-day preschool programs, subsidized day care centers, and licensed care in private homes for infants and toddlers. However, providing first-rate child care in the United States is anything but cheap, with a cost of $4000 a child per year not unusual in urban areas. Thus, a nationally financed system of child care could lead to staggering costs (Lawson, 1989).

Feminists echo the concern of conflict theorists that high-quality child care receives little governmental support because it is regarded as "merely a way to let women work." Nearly all child care workers (94 percent) are women; many find themselves in low-status, minimum wage jobs. The average salary of child care workers in the United States is only about $9000, and there are few fringe benefits. A child care teacher with a college degree earns only 45 percent as much as a similarly educated woman working in other occupations and only 27 percent as much as a similarly educated man. Although parents may complain of child care costs, the staff are, in effect, subsidizing children's care by working for low wages. Not surprisingly, there is a high turnover rate among child care teachers. In 1991, about 50 percent of the nation's day care programs reported turnover averaging half their

staff members each year (M. Elias, 1991; Hellmich, 1990; Reardon, 1989).

Thus far, few local communities have passed ordinances to encourage child care. What about the private sector? Companies are increasingly recognizing that child care can be good for business, since many employees view it as an important fringe benefit. Between 1984 and 1987, there was an increase of 50 percent in the number of companies that offered subsidized child care, financial assistance for child care, or child referral services. Still, even with this increase, as of 1990, only 13 percent of major corporations sponsored child care centers at or near their job sites. Even fewer companies offered discounts or vouchers for child care (F. Chapman, 1987; P. Taylor, 1991).

Many policymakers believe that parents—rather than government or the private sector—should be solely responsible for the costs of day care programs. Yet child care is often relied on because a parent is attempting to increase family income. Unless fees are kept to a minimum, the expenses of day care will wipe out the additional wages earned. Viewed from a conflict perspective, child care costs are an especially serious burden for lower-class families, who already find it hard to take advantage of limited job opportunities. Moreover, the difficulty of finding affordable child care has particularly serious implications for mothers who work (or wish to work) outside the home. Even if they enter the paid labor force, mothers may find their work performance and opportunities for advancement hindered by child care difficulties. Since child care is commonly viewed as a woman's responsibility, working mothers (rather than working fathers) are especially likely to bear the burden of these problems.

In a report issued in 1988, the Child Care Action

Campaign—a national coalition of leaders from government, the media, corporations, labor unions, religious groups, and women's groups—asserted that lack of adequate day care is weakening the economy of the United States. The report concludes that child care can expand the nation's labor pool, that early education can improve students' educational performance, that child care enables families to be financially self-sufficient, and that child care improves corporate productivity. In the view of the Child Care Action Campaign: "All sectors of our economy must make a significant investment in child care" (Reisman et al., 1988:10).

Public support for child care has risen markedly in the last two decades. In 1987, national surveys showed that 80 percent of adults favored the establishment of more day care services for children (compared with only 56 percent in 1970). In a 1989 survey, two-thirds of parents with children under 14 years of age agreed that government has an obligation to provide child care assistance, and 57 percent of these parents stated that employers have a similar responsibility. But, to date, most government officials and leaders of private enterprise continue to give low priority to the issue of child care. This is ironic given the importance of early childhood socialization to the intellectual and social development of future generations in the United States (Morin, 1989; S. Rebell, 1987).

In 1987, the Act for Better Child Care (known as the *ABC bill*) was introduced in Congress to make child care more affordable for low-income families and to increase the accessibility of high-quality child care for *all* families. The ABC bill continued to be a focal point of discussion for policymakers and was finally approved in greatly modified form in 1990 as the Child Care Act. Consisting of two parts, this act provided for both grants and tax credits to support child care. A total of $2.5 billion was authorized for grants to the states over the years 1991–1993, with most of this funding intended to assist low-income families in obtaining child care services. The new tax credits would allow parents to deduct out-of-pocket child care expenses from their income taxes. While this legislation provides much less financial support for child care than had been proposed years earlier, it nevertheless establishes a precedent for direct federal subsidies through the states for child care programs (Holmes, 1990a; Rovner, 1990).

SUMMARY

Socialization is the process whereby people learn the attitudes, values, and actions appropriate to individuals as members of a particular culture. This chapter examines the role of socialization in human development; the way in which people develop perceptions, feelings, and beliefs about themselves; and the lifelong nature of the socialization process.

1 Socialization affects the overall cultural practices of a society, and it also shapes the images that we hold of ourselves.

2 In the early 1900s, Charles Horton Cooley advanced the belief that we learn who we are by interacting with others.

3 George Herbert Mead is best known for his theory of the *self*. He proposed that as people mature, their selves begin to reflect their concern about reactions from others.

4 Erving Goffman has shown that many of our daily activities involve attempts to convey distinct impressions of who we are.

5 As the primary agents of socialization, parents play a critical role in guiding children into those *gender roles* deemed appropriate in a society.

6 Like the family, schools have an explicit mandate to socialize people in the United States—and especially children—into the norms and values of our culture.

7 We are most fully exposed to occupational roles through observing the work of our parents, of people whom we meet while they are performing their duties, and of people portrayed in the media.

8 By regulating the life cycle, the state shapes the socialization process by influencing our views of appropriate behavior at particular ages.

9 As more and more mothers of young children have entered the labor market of the United States, the demand for child care has increased dramatically.

CRITICAL THINKING QUESTIONS

1 Should social research in areas such as sociobiology be conducted even though many investigators believe that this analysis is potentially detrimental to large numbers of people?

what are the 6 agents of socialization?
Family, school, peer group, mass media, workplace + the state

2 Drawing on Erving Goffman's dramaturgical approach, discuss how the following groups engage in impression management: athletes, college instructors, parents, physicians, politicians.

3 How would functionalists and conflict theorists differ in their analyses of the mass media?

KEY TERMS

Anticipatory socialization Processes of socialization in which a person "rehearses" for future positions, occupations, and social relationships. (page 68)

Cognitive theory of development Jean Piaget's theory explaining how children's thought progresses through four stages. (66) *Sensorimotor, Preoperational, concrete, formal operational*

Degradation ceremony An aspect of the socialization process within total institutions, in which people are subjected to humiliating rituals. (69)

Dramaturgical approach A view of social interaction, popularized by Erving Goffman, under which people are examined as if they were theatrical performers. (64)

Face-work A term used by Erving Goffman to refer to people's efforts to maintain the proper image and avoid embarrassment in public. (65)

Gender roles Expectations regarding the proper behavior, attitudes, and activities of males and females. (70)

Generalized others A term used by George Herbert Mead to refer to the child's awareness of the attitudes, viewpoints, and expectations of society as a whole. (64)

Impression management A term used by Erving Goffman to refer to the altering of the presentation of the self in order to create distinctive appearances and satisfy particular audiences. (64)

Looking-glass self A phrase used by Charles Horton Cooley to emphasize that the self is the product of our social interactions with others. (63)

Personality In everyday speech, a person's typical patterns of attitudes, needs, characteristics, and behavior. (58)

Resocialization The process of discarding former behavior patterns and accepting new ones as part of a transition in one's life. (68)

Reverse socialization The process whereby people normally being socialized are at the same time socializing their socializers. (71)

Rites of passage Rituals marking the symbolic transition from one social position to another. (67)

Role taking The process of mentally assuming the perspective of another, thereby enabling one to respond from that imagined viewpoint. (63)

Self According to George Herbert Mead, the sum total of people's conscious perception of their identity as distinct from others. (63)

Significant others A term used by George Herbert Mead to refer to those individuals who are most important in the development of the self, such as parents, friends, and teachers. (64)

Socialization The process whereby people learn the attitudes, values, and actions appropriate to individuals as members of a particular culture. (58)

Sociobiology The systematic study of the biological bases of social behavior. (62)

Symbols The gestures, objects, and language which form the basis of human communication. (63)

Total institutions A term coined by Erving Goffman to refer to institutions which regulate all aspects of a person's life under a single authority, such as prisons, the military, mental hospitals, and convents. (68)

ADDITIONAL READINGS

Elkin, Frederick, and Gerald Handel. *The Child and Society: The Process of Socialization* (5th ed.). New York: Random House, 1989. This book reviews the social science literature on socialization, examines agents of socialization, and gives special emphasis to gender-role socialization.

Goffman, Erving. *The Presentation of Self in Everyday Life.* New York: Doubleday, 1959. Goffman demonstrates his interactionist theory that the self is managed in everyday situations in much the same way that a theatrical performer carries out a stage role.

Harlow, Harry F. *Learning to Love.* New York: Ballantine, 1971. This heavily illustrated book describes the landmark studies of behavior conducted at the Primate Research Center at the University of Wisconsin.

Klein, Abbie Gordon. *The Debate over Child Care, 1969–1990: A Sociohistorical Analysis.* Albany: State University of New York Press, 1992. A background view of child care services in the United States.

Lott, Bernice. *Women's Lives: Themes and Variations in Gender Learning.* Monterey, Calif.: Brooks/Cole, 1987. An overview of the socialization experiences of women in the United States.

Schlenker, Barry R. (ed.). *The Self and Social Life.* New York: McGraw-Hill, 1985. Social scientists, primarily psychologists, examine the concept of the self as an explanation of behavior.

4

SOCIAL STRUCTURE, GROUPS, AND ORGANIZATIONS

LOOKING AHEAD

- How do sociologists use the terms *status* and *role*?
- How is "networking" helpful in finding employment?
- How do the family, religion, and government contribute to a society's survival?
- How do social interactions in a

preindustrial village differ from those in a modern urban center?
- What are some of the positive and negative consequences of bureaucracy?
- How has the social structure of the United States been affected by the spread of AIDS?

Many of us know or have been visited by someone employed by a direct-selling organization (DSO) such as Amway, Tupperware, Shaklee, or Mary Kay Cosmetics. These salespeople often go door to door or arrange house parties in an attempt to reach potential customers. Involvement in DSO work is an intense experience; the gatherings of DSO employees have been compared to religious revival meetings. After conducting a study of 42 DSOs, sociologist Nicole Woolsey Biggart (1989) characterized DSOs as "charismatic" because of the awe they arouse in employees.

The strong personal appeal of DSO founders accounts in good part for the intense and passionate tone of gatherings. DSO employees speak of their companies' founders in terms not usually applied to corporate chief executive officers (CEOs):

[Shaklee was] a remarkable man. He was far ahead of his time. He developed Vita-Line minerals, the first product, a year before the word "vitamin" was even coined. He's [had] a special place in my heart (Biggart, 1989:142).

Even watching [Mary Kay] on TV is real hard for me. I just get this knot in my stomach whenever I see her or listen to her talk or anything (Biggart, 1989:143).

These founders are successful in promoting organizational ideologies that are missionary in char-

acter. DSO employees genuinely believe that their clients will be better people and enjoy happier lives by using DSO products.

In most DSOs, the sales force is overwhelmingly female, and many of these salespeople are homemakers. Sociologist Paul DiMaggio points out that DSOs provide these homemakers with income, enhance their marital power, and offer a sense of community. Nevertheless, DiMaggio (1990:210) concludes that DSOs are "prefeminist" because their ideologies are supportive of male dominance: "women should view selling as not quite a job, seek husbands' permission to enroll, place family before career, or, when firms recruit spouses as teams, take backstage roles."

People in the United States are joiners, whether they join direct-selling organizations, chamber music groups, street gangs, athletic teams, religious institutions, or professional organizations. Many of us ask, "When is the next meeting?" almost as often as we ask, "What should we have for dinner?" As was pointed out in Chapters 2 and 3, social interaction is necessary for the transmission of a culture and the survival of a society. Sociologists use the term ***social interaction*** to refer to the ways in which people respond to one another. These interactions need not be face to face; friends talking over the telephone and coworkers communicating over a computer are engaged in social interaction.

The concepts of social interaction and social structure are central to sociological inquiry; they focus on how different aspects of behavior are related to one another. *Social structure* refers to the way in which a society is organized into predictable relationships. Culture encompasses the elements of a society, while social structure constrains the ways and processes by which these elements are organized. For example, purchasing food is an aspect of culture, yet the social structure defines how food is distributed and consumed.

This chapter will focus on the four basic elements of social structure: statuses, social roles, groups, and institutions. Since much of our social interaction occurs in groups, the vital part that groups play in society's social structure will be emphasized. Social institutions such as the family, religion, and government are a fundamental aspect of social structure; the functionalist, conflict, and interactionist approaches to the study of social institutions will be contrasted.

In the second half of the chapter, we will examine the comparisons of modern societies with simpler forms of social structure offered by sociologists Émile Durkheim and Ferdinand Tönnies. To better understand the social structures of contemporary societies, we will describe Max Weber's model of the modern bureaucracy. Finally, the social policy section will consider the AIDS crisis and its implications for the social institutions of the United States.

ELEMENTS OF SOCIAL STRUCTURE

Predictable social relationships can be examined in terms of four elements: statuses, social roles, groups, and social institutions. These elements make up social structure just as a foundation, walls, ceilings, and furnishings make up a building's structure. We know that furnishings can vary widely from those of an office building to the elaborate furnishings of a palace. Similarly, the elements of a society's social structure can vary dramatically.

Statuses

When we speak of a person's "status" in casual conversation, the term usually conveys connotations of influence, wealth, and fame. However, sociologists use *status* to refer to any of the full

FIGURE 4-1 Social Statuses

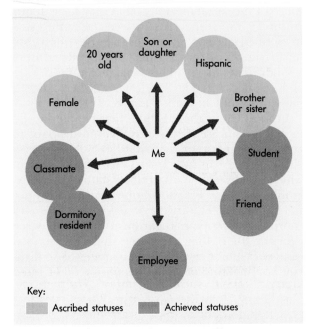

The person in this figure—"me"—occupies many positions in society, each of which involves distinct statuses. The gold circles indicate ascribed statuses; the brown circles represent achieved statuses.

range of socially defined positions within a large group or society—from the lowest to the highest position. Within our society, a person can occupy the status of president of the United States, fruit picker, son or daughter, violinist, teenager, resident of Minneapolis, dental technician, or neighbor. Clearly, a person holds more than one status simultaneously. For example, Alina is an economist, an author, a sister, a resident of Connecticut, and a Puerto Rican at the same time.

Ascribed and Achieved Status Some of the statuses we hold are viewed by sociologists as *ascribed*, while others are categorized as *achieved* (see Figure 4-1). An ***ascribed status*** is "assigned" to a person by society without regard for the person's unique talents or characteristics. Generally, this assignment takes place at birth; thus, a person's racial background, gender, and age are all considered ascribed statuses. These characteristics are biological in origin but are significant mainly because of the social meanings that they have in our culture. Conflict theorists are especially interested in ascribed statuses, since these statuses often confer privileges or reflect a person's membership in a subordinate group. The social meanings of race and ethnicity, gender, and age will be analyzed more fully in Chapters 7 and 8.

In most cases, there is little that people can do to change an ascribed status. We must adapt to any constraints that such statuses hold for us—although we can attempt to change the way in which society views an ascribed status. As an example, the Gray Panthers hope to restructure social reality by modifying society's negative and confining stereotypes regarding older people (see Chapter 8). If they are successful, the ascribed status of "senior citizen" will no longer be so difficult for millions of older people in the United States.

It is important to emphasize that an ascribed status does not necessarily have the same social meaning in every society. In a cross-cultural study, sociologist Gary Huang (1988) confirmed the long-held view that respect for the elderly is an important cultural norm in China. In many cases, the prefix "old" will be used respectfully: calling someone "old teacher" or "old person" has a similar meaning to calling an American judge "your honor." Huang points out that positive age-seniority distinctions in language are absent in the United States; consequently, the term "old man" is viewed as more of an insult than a celebration of seniority and wisdom.

Unlike ascribed statuses, an **achieved status** is attained by a person largely through his or her own effort. Both "bank president" and "burglar" are achieved statuses, as are "lawyer," "pianist," "advertising executive," and "social worker." One must do something to acquire an achieved status—go to school, learn a skill, establish a friendship, or invent a new product.

Master Status Each person holds many different statuses; some may connote higher social positions and some, lower positions. How is one's overall position viewed by others in light of these conflicting statuses? Sociologist Everett Hughes (1945) observed that societies deal with such inconsistencies by agreeing that certain statuses are

Arthur Ashe is shown at a 1992 press conference at which he announced that he had AIDS. Ashe, who died in 1993, had been a remarkable tennis star; but at the end of his life, his status as a person with AIDS may have outweighed his statuses as a retired athlete, an author, and a political activist.

more important than others. A **master status** is a status that dominates others and thereby determines a person's general position within society. For example, Arthur Ashe, who died of AIDS in 1993, had a remarkable career as a tennis star; but at the end of his life, his status as a person with AIDS may have outweighed his statuses as a retired athlete, an author, and a political activist. As we will see in Chapter 13, many people with disabilities find that their status as "disabled" is given undue weight and overshadows their actual ability to perform successfully in meaningful employment.

Race and gender are given such importance in our society that they often dominate one's life. Indeed, such ascribed statuses often influence achieved status. The African American activist Malcolm X (1925–1965), an eloquent and controversial advocate of Black power and Black pride in the early 1960s, recalled that his feelings and perspectives changed dramatically while in eighth grade. His English teacher, a White man, advised him that his goal of becoming a lawyer was "no realistic goal for a nigger" and encouraged him instead to become a carpenter. Malcolm X (1964:37) found that his position as a Black man (ascribed status) was an obstacle to his dream of becoming a lawyer (achieved status). In the United States, ascribed statuses of race and gender can function as master statuses that have an important impact on one's potential to achieve a desired professional and social status.

Social Roles

What Are Social Roles? Throughout our lives, we are acquiring what sociologists call *social roles*. A *social role* is a set of expectations for people who occupy a given social position or status. Thus, in the United States, we expect that cab drivers will know how to get around a city, that secretaries will be reliable in handling phone messages, and that police officers will take action if they see a citizen being threatened. With each distinctive social status—whether ascribed or achieved—come particular role expectations. However, actual performance varies from individual to individual. One secretary may assume extensive administrative responsibilities, while another may focus on clerical duties.

Roles are a significant component of social structure. Viewed from a functionalist perspective, roles contribute to a society's stability by enabling members to anticipate the behavior of others and to pattern their own actions accordingly. Yet social roles can also be dysfunctional by restricting people's relationships with each other. If we view a person *only* as a "police officer" or a "supervisor," it will be difficult to relate to this person as a friend or neighbor. The demands and restrictions of certain roles contribute to the process of disengagement known as *role exit* (see Box 4-1 on page 86).

Role Conflict Imagine the delicate situation of a woman who has worked for a decade on an assembly line in an electrical plant and has recently been named supervisor of the unit she worked in. How is this woman expected to relate to her long-time friends and coworkers? Should she still go out to lunch with them, as she has done almost daily for years? How should she deal with the workers' resentment of an arrogant supervisor who is now her equal and colleague? Is it her responsibility to recommend the firing of an old friend who cannot keep up with the work demands of the assembly line?

Role conflict occurs when incompatible expectations arise from two or more social positions that are held by the same person. Fulfillment of the roles associated with one status may directly violate the roles linked to a second status. In the example above, the newly promoted supervisor will experience a serious conflict between certain social and occupational roles. As a friend, she should try to protect her former coworker; but as a supervisor, she should report an unsatisfactory employee.

Role conflicts call for important ethical choices. In the example just given, the new supervisor has to make a difficult decision about how much allegiance she owes her friend. In the culture of the United States, success is presumably more important than friendship. If our friends are holding us back, we should leave them and pursue our ambitions. Yet, at the same time, we are told that abandoning our friends is contemptible. The supervisor must decide whether she will risk her promotion out of concern for her friend.

In some instances, changing gender roles have contributed to role conflict. Sociologist Tracey Watson (1987) studied the ways in which female athletes in college sports programs resolve the conflicts raised by two traditionally incongruent identities: being a woman and being an athlete. On the basketball court, the identity of "athlete" is clearly dominant for these college students. According to an unwritten norm, no makeup is worn during games, much less jewelry; knee pads and Ace bandages are the more likely attire. By

THE PROCESS OF ROLE EXIT

Often when we think of assuming a social role, we focus on the preparation and anticipatory socialization that a person undergoes in becoming ready for that role. This is true if a person is about to become an attorney, a chef, a spouse, or a parent. Yet, until recently, social scientists have given less attention to the adjustments involved in *leaving* social roles.

Sociologist Helen Rose Fuchs Ebaugh (1988) developed the term **role exit** to describe the process of disengagement from a role that is central to one's self-identity and reestablishment of an identity in a new role. Drawing on interviews with 185 people—among them ex-convicts, divorced men and women, recovering alcoholics, ex-nuns, former doctors, retirees, and transsexuals—Ebaugh studied the process of voluntarily exiting from significant social roles.

Ebaugh's interest in role exit grew out of her own background as an ex-nun. She recalls: "I grew up in a small Catholic, German community in Olfen, Texas, where at 18 women had the choice of getting married or joining the convent. The nuns were unwitting feminists back then in that they were the only educated role models we had." She spent 11 years as Sister Helen Rose, but while working on her doctorate at Columbia University, she began questioning her religious life and realized she felt a strong desire to be married and have children (Bartlett, 1988:C1).

Ebaugh has offered a four-stage model of role exit. The first stage begins with doubt—as the person experiences frustration, burnout, or simply unhappiness with an accustomed status and the roles associated with this social position. This doubt leads to what Ebaugh calls *unconscious cueing*, which was evident in the convent in the hairstyles of nuns. In Ebaugh's view, those nuns who let their hair grow longer and turned to fashionable hairstyles were in the initial stage of role exit.

The second stage involves a search for alternatives. A person unhappy with his or her career may take a leave of absence; an unhappily married couple may begin what they see as a temporary separation. Then comes the third stage of role exit: the action stage or departure. Ebaugh found that the vast majority of her respondents identified a clear turning point which made them feel it was essential to take final action and leave their jobs, end their marriages, or engage in other types of role exit. However, 20 percent of respondents saw their role exits as a gradual, evolutionary process that had no single turning point.

The last stage of role exit involves the creation of a new identity. Ebaugh points out: "It is important to maintain contact with some people in the old role, to keep some bridges. . . . It's also important to be able to talk to someone about who one used to be." Consequently, while she is now a sociologist, wife, and mother of two children, Ebaugh has not blocked out her memories of her years in the convent. In fact, in 1988 she attended what would have been her twenty-fifth anniversary as a nun, had she remained in her religious order. "It was a wonderful kind of closure for me," says Ebaugh (Bartlett, 1988:C1).

contrast, when dressing for a dinner honoring college athletes, these women present a conventional feminine image with notable adornment and makeup.

Clearly, these women resorted to impression management (described by Erving Goffman in Chapter 3) to resolve the role conflicts of women athletes. Nevertheless, as Tracey Watson observed, the general college population took little notice of such impression management and instead stereotyped these athletes as decidedly unfeminine. This stereotyping serves as a reminder that while there has been a significant change in gender roles in the United States—as is evident in the dramatic increase in girls' and women's participation in sports—traditional assumptions about femininity and masculinity remain an influential part of our culture.

©1985 Sarah Leen

People in certain professions— among them, journalism—commonly experience role conflict during disasters, crimes, and other distressing situations. Professional photographer Sarah Leen experienced role conflict as she stopped to change a lens and take this picture of the mugging of an intoxicated man in Los Angeles. At the same moment, Leen felt fear for her own safety and wondered whether she should attempt to stop the crime. Note that other bystanders seem oblivious of the entire event.

Groups

In everyday speech, people use the term *group* for any collection of individuals, whether three strangers sharing an elevator or hundreds at a meeting of the Tupperware sales force. However, in sociological terms a **group** is any number of people with similar norms, values, and expectations who regularly and consciously interact. Sororities and fraternities, dance companies, tenants' associations, and chess clubs are all considered groups. It is important to emphasize that members of a group share some sense of belonging. This distinguishes groups from mere *aggregates* of people, such as passengers who happen to be together on an airplane flight, or from *categories* who share a common feature (such as being retired) but otherwise do not act together.

Groups play a vital part in a society's social structure. Much of our social interaction takes place within groups and is influenced by the norms and sanctions established by groups. Being a teenager or a rock climber takes on special meanings as individuals interact within groups designed for people with that particular status. The expectations associated with many social roles, including those accompanying the statuses of brother, sister, and student, become most clearly defined in the context of a group.

The study of groups has become an important part of sociological investigation because of their importance in the transmission of culture. Sociologists have made a number of useful distinctions between types of groups.

Primary and Secondary Groups A 1979 Hollywood film, *The Warriors*, begins with an outdoor meeting of delegates of numerous New York City street gangs in a playground. Each gang has sent nine members to this unusual convocation. Dressed in colorful garb, these gangs represent various neighborhoods and racial and ethnic groups within New York. There are White gangs, Black gangs, Hispanic gangs, and Asian gangs— all assembled in an explosive mix.

This scene from *The Warriors* can be used to illustrate an important distinction made by sociologist Charles Horton Cooley in categorizing groups. Cooley (1902:23–57) coined the term **primary group** to refer to a small group characterized by intimate, face-to-face association and cooperation. The members of the street gang known as the *Warriors* constitute a primary group. So do members of a family living in the same household as well as "sisters" in a college sorority. Primary groups play a pivotal role both in the socialization process (see Chapter 3) and in the development of roles and statuses.

In the United States, groups take many forms. Shown are World War II veterans who fought together at Pearl Harbor, members of a sorority at Bucknell University, and a crew of construction workers.

TABLE 4-1 Comparison of Primary and Secondary Groups

PRIMARY GROUP	SECONDARY GROUP
Generally small	Usually large
Relatively long period of interaction	Short duration, temporary
Intimate, face-to-face association	Little social intimacy or mutual understanding
Some emotional depth in relationships	Relationships generally superficial
Cooperative, friendly	More formal and impersonal

In distinguishing between types of groups, sociologists have noted the differences between primary and secondary groups.

When we find ourselves identifying closely with a group, it is probably a primary group. However, people in the United States participate in many groups which are not characterized by close bonds of friendship, such as large college classes and business associations. The term **secondary group** refers to a formal, impersonal group in which there is little social intimacy or mutual understanding (see Table 4-1). If the diverse gangs portrayed in *The Warriors* had successfully established a citywide gang organization, it would have been a secondary, rather than primary, group. The distinction between these types of groups is not always clear-cut. Some fraternities or social clubs become so large and impersonal that they no longer function as primary groups.

In-Groups and Out-Groups A group can hold special meaning for members because of its relationship to other groups. People sometimes feel antagonistic to or threatened by another group, especially if the group is perceived as being different culturally or racially. Sociologists identify these "we" and "they" feelings by using two terms first employed by William Graham Sumner (1906:12–13): *in-group* and *out-group*.

An **in-group** can be defined as any group or category to which people feel they belong. Simply put, it comprises everyone who is regarded as "we" or "us." The in-group may be as narrow as one's family or as broad as an entire society. The very existence of an in-group implies that there is an out-group viewed as "they" or "them." More formally, an **out-group** is a group or category to which people feel they do not belong.

People in the United States tend to see the world in terms of in-groups and out-groups, a perception often fostered by the very groups to which we belong. "*Our* generation does not have those sexual hangups." "*We* Christians go to church every week." "*We* have to support *our* troops in the Persian Gulf." Although not explicit, each of these declarations suggests who the in-groups and out-groups are.

One typical consequence of in-group membership is a feeling of distinctiveness and superiority among members, who see themselves as better than people in the out-group. This sense of superiority can be enhanced by a double standard maintained by members of the in-group. Proper behavior for the in-group is simultaneously viewed as unacceptable behavior for the out-group. Sociologist Robert Merton (1968:480–488) describes this process as the conversion of "in-group virtues" into "out-group vices."

Drawing by Weber; © 1979 The New Yorker Magazine, Inc.

"So long, Bill. This is my club. You can't come in."

SOCIAL STRUCTURE, GROUPS, AND ORGANIZATIONS

The attitudes of certain Christians toward Jews illustrate such a double standard. If Christians take their faith seriously, it is seen as "commendable"; if Jews do the same, it is a sign of "backwardness" and a refusal to enter the twentieth century. If Christians prefer other Christians as friends, it is "understandable"; if Jews prefer other Jews as friends, they are attacked for being "clannish." This view of "us and them" can be destructive, as conflict theorists have suggested. At the same time, it promotes in-group solidarity and a sense of belonging (Karlins et al., 1969).

Reference Groups Both in-groups and primary groups can dramatically influence the way an individual thinks and behaves. Sociologists use the term *reference group* when speaking of any group that individuals use as a standard for evaluating themselves and their own behavior. For example, a high school student who aspires to join a social circle of punk rock devotees will pattern his or her behavior after that of the group. The student will begin dressing like these peers, listening to the same record albums, and hanging out at the same stores and clubs.

Reference groups have two basic purposes. First, they serve a normative function by setting and enforcing standards of conduct and belief. Thus, the high school student who wants the approval of the punk rock crowd will have to follow the group's dictates to at least some extent. He or she will be expected to cut classes along with group members and to rebel against parental curfews. Second, reference groups also perform a comparison function by serving as a standard against which people can measure themselves and others. A law student will evaluate himself or herself against a reference group composed of lawyers, law professors, and judges (Merton and Kitt, 1950).

In many cases, people model their behavior after groups to which they do not belong. For example, a college student majoring in finance may read the *Wall Street Journal,* study the annual reports of corporations, and listen to midday stock market news on the radio. The student is engaging in the process of anticipatory socialization (see Chapter 3) by using financial experts as a reference group to which he or she aspires.

It is important to recognize that individuals are often influenced by two or more reference groups at the same time. One's family members, neighbors, and coworkers shape different aspects of a person's self-evaluation. In addition, certain reference group attachments change during the life cycle. A corporate executive who quits the rat race at age 45 to become a social worker will find new reference groups to use as standards for evaluation. We shift reference groups as we take on different statuses during our lives.

Social Networks Groups do not merely serve to define other elements of the social structure, such as roles and statuses; they also are an intermediate link between the individual and the larger society. For example, members of occupational or social groups may be acquaintances rather than close friends; consequently, they are likely to connect other members to people in different social circles. This connection is known as a *social network*—that is, a series of social relationships that link a person directly to others and therefore indirectly to still more people.

Involvement in social networks—commonly known as *networking*—provides a vital social resource in such tasks as finding employment. For example, while looking for a job one year after finishing school, Albert Einstein was successful only when the father of a classmate put him in touch with his future employer. These kinds of contacts, even weak and distant contacts, can be crucial in establishing social networks and facilitating transmission of information. According to one 1989 survey, 70 percent of respondents learned about employment opportunities through personal contacts and social networks, while only 14 percent did so through advertisements. Yet, as conflict theorists have emphasized, networking is not so easy for some individuals or groups as for others. In comparison with women, men tend to have longer job histories, a fact which leads to larger networks which can be used in locating employment opportunities. Men are better able to utilize what is literally an "old boy network" (Carter, 1989; Marsden, 1990).

Sociologist Melvin Oliver (1988) used the concept of *social network* to better understand life in African American urban neighborhoods, which are often stigmatized as chaotic. Oliver interviewed Black adults in three areas of metropolitan Los Angeles to study their friendship and kinfolk

Involvement in social networks— commonly known as networking— *provides a vital social resource in such tasks as finding employment. Shown is a job fair in Philadelphia for African Americans with M.B.A. degrees.*

ties. Respondents were *not* found to be socially isolated; they generally had little difficulty identifying members of their social networks. Oliver's data contradict the stereotype of such neighborhoods as being "disorganized" or even "pathological." Instead, a picture unfolds of an elaborate organization of personal social networks that tie people together within and outside the Black community in bonds of concern and support.

A very different type of African American social network is evident in the United States Army. In 1975, a group of African American senior officers founded Rocks, an association named after Brigadier General Roscoe Cartwright, who had been killed in an airplane crash the year before. Cartwright, better known as "Rock," was an esteemed role model and mentor for many Black officers who entered the Army during the 1960s. Rocks does not view itself as a pressure group; it is dedicated to mentoring junior Black officers. Unlike African American associations outside the military, Rocks and its members tend to distance themselves from any social agenda that views recognition of past discrimination as central to Black achievement. In their political conservatism and discomfort with viewing Blacks as victims, senior African American army officers differ in an important way from the types of mentors and social networks found among Blacks' civilian leadership (Moskos, 1991).

Social Institutions

The mass media, the government, the economy, the family, and the health care system are all examples of social institutions found in the United States. *Social institutions* are organized patterns of beliefs and behavior centered on basic social needs. Institutions are organized in response to particular needs, such as replacing personnel (the family) and preserving order (the government).

By studying social institutions, sociologists gain insight into the structure of a society. For example, the institution of religion adapts to the segment of society that it serves. Church work has a very different meaning for ministers who serve a skid row area, a naval base, and a suburban middle-class community. Religious leaders assigned to a skid row mission will focus on tending to the ill and providing food and shelter. By contrast, clergy in affluent suburbs will be occupied with counseling those considering marriage and divorce, arranging youth activities, and overseeing cultural events.

Functionalist View One way to understand social institutions is to see how they fulfill essential functions. Anthropologist David F. Aberle and his colleagues (1950) and sociologists Raymond Mack and Calvin Bradford (1979:12–22) have identified five major tasks, or functional prerequisites, that a society or relatively permanent group must accomplish if it is to survive.

1 *Replacing personnel.* Any society or group must replace personnel when they die, leave, or become incapacitated. This is accomplished through immigration, annexation of neighboring groups of people, acquisition of slaves, or normal sexual reproduction of members. The Shakers, a religious sect found in the United States, are a conspicuous example of a group that failed to replace personnel. The Shakers' religious doctrines forbade any physical contact between the sexes; therefore, the group's survival depended on recruiting new members. At first, the Shakers proved quite effective in attracting members; however, their recruitment subsequently declined dramatically. Despite this fact, the Shakers maintained their commitment to celibacy, and their numbers have eventually dwindled to only a few members today (Riddle, 1988).

2 *Teaching new recruits.* No group can survive if many of its members reject the established behavior and responsibilities of the group. As a result, finding or producing new members is not sufficient. The group must encourage recruits to learn and accept its values and customs. This learning can take place formally within schools (where learning is a manifest function) or informally through interaction and negotiation in peer groups (where instruction is a latent function).

3 *Producing and distributing goods and services.* Any relatively permanent group or society must provide and distribute desired goods and services for its members. Each society establishes a set of rules for the allocation of financial and other resources. The group must satisfy the needs of most members at least to some extent, or it will risk the possibility of discontent and, ultimately, disorder.

4 *Preserving order.* The native people of Tasmania, a large island just south of Australia, are now extinct. During the 1800s, they were destroyed by the hunting parties of European conquerors, who looked upon the Tasmanians as half-human. This annihilation underscores a critical function of every group or society—preserving order and protecting itself from attack. When faced with the more developed European technology of warfare, the Tasmanians were unable to defend themselves and an entire people was wiped out.

5 *Providing and maintaining a sense of purpose.* People must feel motivated to continue as members of a society in order to fulfill the previous four requirements. The behavior of United States prisoners of war (POWs) while in confinement during the war in Vietnam is a testament to the importance of maintaining a sense of purpose. While in prison camps, some of these men mentally made elaborate plans for marriage, family, children, reunions, and new careers. A few even built houses in their minds—right down to the last doorknob or water faucet. By holding on to a sense of purpose—their intense desire to return to their homeland and live normal lives—the POWs refused to allow the agony of confinement to destroy their mental health.

Many aspects of a society can assist people in developing and maintaining a sense of purpose. For some people, religious values or personal moral codes are most crucial; for others, national or tribal identities are especially meaningful. Whatever these differences, in any society there remains one common and critical reality. If an individual does not have a sense of purpose, he or she has little reason to contribute to a society's survival.

This list of functional prerequisites does not specify how a society will perform each task. For example, one society may protect itself from external attack by maintaining a frightening arsenal of weaponry, while another may make determined efforts to remain neutral in world politics and to promote cooperative relationships with its neighbors. No matter what its particular strategy, any society or relatively permanent group must attempt to satisfy all these functional prerequisites for survival. If it fails on even one condition, as the Tasmanians did, the society runs the risk of extinction.

Conflict View Conflict theorists do not concur with the functionalist approach to social institutions. While both perspectives agree that institutions are organized to meet basic social needs, conflict theorists object to the implication inherent in the functionalist view that the outcome is necessarily efficient and desirable. Conflict theorists concede the presence of a negotiated order, but they add that many segments of our society—among them the homeless, the disabled, and people with AIDS—are not in a position to negotiate effectively, because they lack sufficient power and resources.

From a conflict perspective, the present organization of social institutions is no accident. Major institutions, such as education, help to maintain the privileges of the most powerful individuals and groups within a society, while contributing to the powerlessness of others. As one example, public schools in the United States are financed largely through property taxes. This allows more affluent areas to provide their children with better-equipped schools and better-paid teachers than low-income areas can afford. Children from prosperous communities will therefore be better prepared to compete academically than children from impoverished communities. The structure of the nation's educational system permits and even promotes such unequal treatment of schoolchildren.

Conflict theorists argue that social institutions such as education have an inherently conservative nature. Without question, it has been difficult to implement educational reforms that promote equal opportunity—whether in the area of bilingual education, school desegregation, or mainstreaming of students with disabilities. From a functionalist perspective, social change can be dysfunctional, since it often leads to instability. However, from a conflict view, why should we preserve the existing social structure if it is unfair and discriminatory?

Sociologist D. Stanley Eitzen notes a basic paradox of all institutions: they are absolutely necessary, yet they are a source of social problems. He adds that it has become fashionable to attack social institutions, such as the family and the government, in recent years. In Eitzen's view, we should not forget that people depend on institutions for "stability and guarantees against chaos" (1978:545). We must recognize that social institutions are essential, yet we must not regard permanence as a justification for inequality and injustice.

Interactionist View Social institutions affect our daily lives. Whether we are driving down the street or standing in a long shopping line, our everyday behavior is governed by social institutions. For example, in her fascinating account of behavior within large organizations, *Men and Women of the Corporation*, sociologist Rosabeth Moss Kanter (1977:34–36) describes lunchtime behavior that comes to be routine. If a visitor comes for lunch, a trip to a posh restaurant is typical. At such lunches, a drink is quite common. At one time, people drank martinis, but more recently wine has become customary. Yet, while social drinking is encouraged, heavy drinking can destroy a person's career.

Interactionist theorists emphasize that our social behavior is conditioned by the roles and statuses which we accept, the groups to which we belong, and the institutions within which we function. For example, the social roles associated with being a judge occur within the larger context of the criminal justice system. The status of "judge" stands in relation to other statuses, such as attorney, plaintiff, defendant, and witness, as well as to the social institution of government. While the symbolic aspects of courts and jails, for example, are awesome, the judicial system derives continued significance from the roles people carry out in social interactions (P. Berger and Luckmann, 1966:74–76).

In studying day-to-day behavior in social institutions, interactionists are interested in the informal norms that can shape people's behavior. In Box 4-2 (page 94), we present sociologist William Thompson's research (1983) on the informal norms developed by assembly line workers at a beef processing plant in the midwest.

SOCIAL STRUCTURE AND MODERN SOCIETY

A common feature of modern societies when contrasted with earlier social arrangements is the greater complexity of contemporary life. Sociologists Émile Durkheim and Ferdinand Tönnies examined the contrasts between modern societies and simpler forms of social structure.

Durkheim's Mechanical and Organic Solidarity

In his *Division of Labor* (1933, original edition 1893), Durkheim argued that social structure depends on the level of division of labor in a society—in other words, on the manner in which tasks are performed. Thus, a task such as providing food can be carried out almost totally by one individual or can be divided among many people. The latter pattern typically occurs in modern soci-

BOX 4-2

INFORMAL NORMS AT THE WORKPLACE: HANGING BEEF TONGUES

Drawing on the interactionist perspective, sociologist William Thompson studied the day-to-day activities of assembly line workers by conducting nine weeks of observation research in the slaughter division of a beef processing plant in the midwest. Thompson (1983:215) notes that "working in the beef plant is 'dirty' work, not only in the literal sense of being drenched with perspiration and beef blood, but also in the figurative sense of performing a low status, routine, and demeaning job." In addition to being "dirty," work in this plant is monotonous and exhausting: Thompson and his coworkers had to hang, brand, and bag between 1350 and 1500 beef tongues in an eight-hour shift.

Thompson emphasizes that a subtle sense of unity exists among the "beefers," as they call themselves. It is almost impossible for workers to speak with one another while on the assembly line because of noise, the need for earplugs, and the isolation of certain work

areas. Nevertheless, workers communicated through an extensive system of nonverbal symbols, including exaggerated gestures, shrill whistles, "thumbs up" and "thumbs down," and the clanging of knives against stainless steel tables and tubs. Thompson (1983:233) suggests that "in a setting which would apparently eliminate it, the workers' desire for social interaction won out and interaction flourished."

In order to reduce alienation and retain a sense of humanity, the beefers developed certain coping mechanisms. Importantly, they subverted formal norms of the workplace and established their own informal norms. At times, rather than working at a steady pace consistent with the required line speed, the workers would set a frantic pace and get ahead of the line. This not only added a few precious minutes to their scheduled break time or lunch hour; it symbolically challenged the company's dictates about the speed of the line and

gave the beefers a small measure of control over the work process.

Despite formal norms against sabotage, the informal norms of the workers encouraged certain types of rule breaking. Thompson (1983:231) recalls that the "workers practically made a game out of doing forbidden things simply to see if they could get away with it." At his workstation, despite strict rules to the contrary, workers covered with beef blood commonly washed their hands, arms, and knives in a tub of water supposedly reserved for cleaning of tongues. In addition, workers often cut chunks out of pieces of meat and threw them at other employees. If an inspector or a supervisor did not notice, these chunks of meat might be picked up off the floor and put back on the line—a clear violation of health codes. Thompson (1983:231) concludes that "artful sabotage served as a symbolic way in which workers could express a sense of individuality, and hence, self-worth."

---

eties; cultivation, processing, distribution, and retailing of a single food item are performed by literally hundreds of people.

In societies in which there is minimal division of labor, a collective consciousness develops with an emphasis on group solidarity. Durkheim termed this *mechanical solidarity,* implying that all individuals perform the same tasks. No one needs to ask, "What do your parents do?" since everyone is engaged in similar work. Each person prepares food, hunts, makes clothing, builds homes, and so forth. People have few options regarding what to do with their lives; consequently, there is little

concern for individual needs. Instead, the group will is the dominating force in society. Both social interaction and negotiation are based on close, intimate, face-to-face social contacts. Since there is little specialization, there are few social roles.

As societies become more advanced technologically, greater division of labor takes place. The person who cuts down timber is not the same person who puts up your roof. With increasing specialization, many different tasks must be performed by different individuals—even in manufacturing one item such as a radio or stove.

In general, social interactions become less personal than in societies characterized by mechanical solidarity. We begin relating to others on the basis of their social positions ("butcher," "nurse") rather than their distinctive human qualities. Statuses and social roles are in perpetual flux as the overall social structure of the society continues to change.

In Durkheim's terms, **organic solidarity** involves a collective consciousness resting on the need a society's members have for one another. Once society becomes more complex and there is greater division of labor, no individual can go it alone. In a complex society, dependence on others becomes essential for group survival. Durkheim chose the term *organic solidarity*, since, in his view, individuals become interdependent in much the same way as organs of the human body are interdependent.

Tönnies's *Gemeinschaft* and *Gesellschaft*

Sociologist Ferdinand Tönnies (1855–1936) was appalled by the rise of an industrial city in his native Germany during the late 1800s. In his view, this marked a dramatic change from the ideal type of a close-knit community, which Tönnies (1988, original edition 1887) termed *Gemeinschaft,* to that of an impersonal mass society known as *Gesellschaft.*

The ***Gemeinschaft*** ("guh-MINE-shoft") community is typical of rural life. It is a small community in which people have similar backgrounds and life experiences. Virtually everyone knows everyone else, and social interactions (including negotiations) are intimate and familiar, almost as one might find among kinfolk. There is a commitment to the larger social group and a sense of togetherness among community members. Therefore, in dealing with people, one relates to them not merely as "clerk" or "manager" but, rather, in a more personal way. With this more personal interaction comes less privacy: we know more about everyone.

Social control in the *Gemeinschaft* community is maintained through informal means such as moral persuasion, gossip, and even gestures. These techniques work effectively because people are genuinely concerned about how others feel toward them.

Social change is relatively limited in the *Gemeinschaft;* the lives of members of one generation may be quite similar to the lives of their grandparents.

Drawing by Victor; © 1986 The New Yorker Magazine, Inc.

"I'd like to think of you as a person, David, but it's my job to think of you as personnel."

In a Gesellschaft, *people are likely to relate to one another in terms of their roles rather than their individual backgrounds.*

By contrast, the **Gesellschaft** ("guh-ZELL-shoft") is an ideal type characteristic of modern urban life. Most people are strangers and perceive little sense of commonality with other community residents. Relationships are governed by social roles which grow out of immediate tasks, such as purchasing a product or arranging a business meeting. Self-interests dominate, and there is generally little consensus concerning values or commitment to the group. As a result, social control must rely on more formal techniques, such as laws and legally defined punishments. Social change is an important aspect of life in the *Gesellschaft;* it can be strikingly evident even within a single generation.

Sociologists have used the terms *Gemeinschaft* and *Gesellschaft* to compare social structures stressing close relationships with those that emphasize less personal ties. It is easy to view the *Gemeinschaft* with nostalgia as a far better way of life than the "rat race" of contemporary existence. However, with the more intimate relationships of the *Gemeinschaft* comes a price. The prejudice and discrimination found within the *Gemeinschaft* can be quite confining; more emphasis is placed on such ascribed statuses as family background than on people's unique talents and achievements. In addition, the *Gemeinschaft* tends to be distrustful of the individual who seeks to be creative or just to be different.

The work of Émile Durkheim and Ferdinand Tönnies shows that a major focus of sociology has been to identify changes in social structure and the consequences for human behavior. At the macro level, they both offer descriptions of societies shifting to more advanced forms of technology. In addition, they identify the impact of these societywide changes at the micro level in terms of the nature of social interactions between people. Durkheim emphasizes the degree to which people carry out the same tasks. Tönnies directs our attention to whether people look out for their own interests or for the well-being of the larger group. Nevertheless, there is a great deal of similarity between the analyses of these European sociologists. They agree that as social structure becomes more complex, people's relationships tend to become more impersonal, transient, and fragmented.

FORMAL ORGANIZATIONS AND BUREAUCRACIES

As contemporary societies have shifted to more advanced forms of technology and their social structures have become more complex, our lives have become increasingly dominated by large secondary groups which take the form of formal organizations designed for a specific purpose. A **formal organization** is a special-purpose group designed and structured in the interests of maximum efficiency. Organizations vary in their size, specificity of goals, and degree of efficiency, but are structured in such a way as to facilitate the management of large-scale operations. They also have a bureaucratic form of organization, which will be described in the next section of the chapter. The United States Postal Service, the Boston Pops orchestra, and the college you attend are all examples of formal organizations.

In our society, formal organizations fulfill an enormous variety of personal and societal needs and shape the lives of every person. In fact, formal organizations have become such a dominant force that we must create organizations to supervise other organizations, such as the Securities and Exchange Commission (SEC) and other federal regulatory agencies. It sounds much more exciting to say that we live in the "space age" than that we live in the "age of formal organizations"; however, the latter is probably a more accurate description of the 1990s (Azumi and Hage, 1972:1; Etzioni, 1964:1–2).

Characteristics of a Bureaucracy

When we think of the term *bureaucracy,* a variety of images—mostly unpleasant—come to mind. Rows of desks staffed by seemingly faceless people, endless lines and forms, impossibly complex language, and frustrating encounters with red tape—all these have combined to make *bureaucracy* a dirty word and an easy target in political campaigns. However, for sociologists, a **bureaucracy** is simply a component of formal organization in which rules and hierarchical ranking are used to achieve efficiency. Although few people in this country would want to identify their occupation as "bureaucrat," elements of bureaucracy are found in almost every occupation in an industrial society such as the United States.

TABLE 4-2   Characteristics of a Bureaucracy

CHARACTERISTIC	POSITIVE CONSEQUENCE	NEGATIVE CONSEQUENCE	
		FOR THE INDIVIDUAL	FOR THE ORGANIZATION
Division of labor	Produces efficiency in large-scale corporation	Produces trained incapacity	Produces narrow perspective
Hierarchy of authority	Clarifies who is in command	Deprives employees of a voice in decision making	Permits concealment of mistakes
Written rules and regulations	Let workers know what is expected of them	Stifle initiative and imagination	Lead to goal displacement
Impersonality	Reduces bias	Contributes to feelings of alienation	Discourages loyalty to company
Employment based on technical qualifications	Discourages favoritism and reduces petty rivalries	Discourages ambition to improve oneself elsewhere	Allows Peter principle to operate

In order to develop a better understanding of bureaucracy, we must turn to the writings of Max Weber (1947:333–340, original edition 1922). This pioneer of sociology, who was introduced in Chapter 1, first directed researchers to the significance of bureaucratic structure. In an important sociological advance, Weber emphasized the basic similarity of structure and process found in the otherwise dissimilar enterprises of religion, government, education, and business.

Weber viewed bureaucracy as a form of organization quite different from the family-run business. He developed an ideal type of bureaucracy, which reflects the most characteristic aspects of all human organizations. Since perfect bureaucracies are never achieved, no actual organization will correspond exactly to Weber's ideal type (Blau and Meyer, 1987:19–22). Nevertheless, Weber argued that every bureaucracy—whether its purpose is to run a day care center, corporation, or army—will have five basic characteristics. These characteristics, as well as *dysfunctions* (or potential negative consequences), of bureaucracy are discussed below and summarized in Table 4-2.

1 Division of Labor   Specialized experts are employed in each position to perform specific tasks. The president of the United States need not be a good typist; a lawyer need not be able to complete an income tax form. By working at a specific task, people are more likely to become highly skilled

Max Weber introduced the concept of bureaucracy but tended to emphasize its positive aspects. More recently, social scientists have described the negative consequences (or dysfunctions) of bureaucracy both for the individual within the organization and for the bureaucracy itself.

and carry out a job with maximum efficiency. This emphasis on specialization is so basic a part of our lives that we may not realize that it is a fairly recent development in western culture.

Analysis of division of labor by interactionist researchers has led to scrutiny of how various employees at a workplace interact with one another. For example, after a cardiac patient is brought into a surgical recovery room, nurses and technicians independently make 10 or 20 connections between the patient and various monitoring devices. Later procedures, by contrast, are more likely to involve the cooperative efforts of two or more workers. Through these tasks, medical personnel gain proficiency in delicate and essential procedures (Strauss, 1985:2).

Although division of labor has certainly been beneficial in the performance of many complex bureaucracies, in some cases it can lead to *trained incapacity;* that is, workers become so specialized that they develop blind spots and fail to notice obvious problems. Even worse, such workers may not *care* about, say, what is happening next to

FIGURE 4-2   Organization Chart of a Government Agency

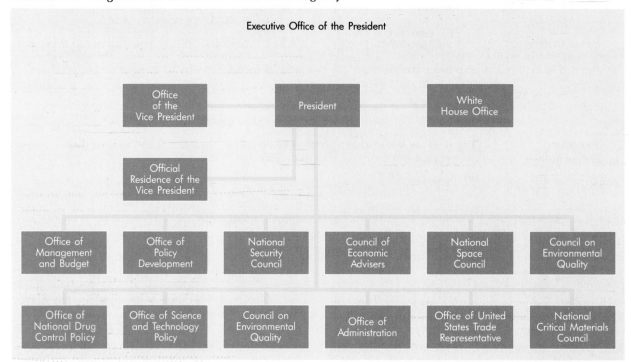

SOURCE: Office of the Federal Register, 1991:88.

The formal structure of a government agency is fairly easy to ascertain. Equally important, but less apparent, is the informal chain of command.

them on the assembly line. Some observers believe that, through such developments, workers in the United States have become much less productive on the job.

Although trained incapacity has negative implications for the smooth running of organizations, it is especially disastrous for the person who loses a job during a layoff. An unemployed worker may have spent years becoming proficient at highly technical work and yet may be totally unsuited for other positions, even those which are directly related to his or her former job. As an example, an automotive machinist who pushes buttons on an automobile assembly line in Michigan will lack the proper training and skill to work as an oil industry machinist in Texas (Wallis, 1981).

In some instances, the division of labor (as reflected in the fragmentation of job titles) may actually contribute to sex discrimination by creating unnecessary and inappropriate distinctions between female and male employees. In a study of 368 businesses in California, sociologists James Baron and William Bielby (1986) found that pro-

liferation of job titles tended to increase as men and women reached parity in their level of employment. Apparently, separate job titles—ostensibly designed to reflect a division of labor—were actually being used to preserve traditional occupational segregation by gender.

2 Hierarchy of Authority   Bureaucracies follow the principle of hierarchy; that is, each position is under the supervision of a higher authority (see Figure 4-2). A professional baseball team is run by an owner, who hires a general manager, who in turn hires a manager. Beneath the manager come the coaches and last the players. In the Roman Catholic church, the pope is the supreme authority; under him are cardinals, bishops, and so forth. Even large medical group practices have boards of directors, executive committees, and administrators (Kralewski et al., 1985).

Social science research suggests that bureaucracies may be a positive environment for women at the lower but not the upper echelons of the hierarchy. Political scientist Kathy Ferguson (1983, 1984) observes that many traits traditionally associated with the feminine gender role—such as valuing warm, supportive, cooperative relationships—are conducive to participation in a bureaucratic organization. However, upwardly mobile women may find their career progress hindered because they function more as facilitators than as innovators, and then are not viewed as aggressive enough to serve in higher management posts. Consequently, although traditional feminine values may be functional for women in the lower levels of bureaucratic structure, they appear to become dysfunctional as women aspire to greater power and prestige.

3 Written Rules and Regulations

Wouldn't it be nice if a bank teller cashed your check for $100 and deliberately handed you six $20 bills, saying: "You have such a friendly smile; here's an extra $20"? It would certainly be a pleasant surprise, but it would also be "against the rules."

Rules and regulations, as we all know, are an important characteristic of bureaucracies. Ideally, through such procedures, a bureaucracy ensures uniform performance of every task. This prohibits us from receiving an extra $20 at the bank, but it also guarantees us that we will receive essentially the same treatment as other customers. If the bank provides them with special services, such as monthly statements or investment advice, it will also provide us with those services.

Through written rules and regulations, bureaucracies generally offer employees clear standards as to what is considered an adequate (or exceptional) performance. In addition, procedures provide a valuable sense of continuity in a bureaucracy. Individual workers will come and go, but the structure and past records give the organization a life of its own that outlives the services of any one bureaucrat. Thus, if you are brought in to work as the new manager of a bookstore, you do not have to start from scratch. Instead, you can study the store's records and accounting books to learn about the payroll, financial dealings with distributors, discount policies on "sale" books, and other procedures.

Of course, rules and regulations can over-shadow the larger goals of an organization and become dysfunctional. If blindly applied, they will no longer serve as a means to achieving an objective but instead will become important (and perhaps too important) in their own right. This would certainly be the case if a hospital emergency room physician failed to treat a seriously injured person because he or she had no valid proof of United States citizenship. Robert Merton (1968:254–256) has used the term **goal displacement** to refer to overzealous conformity to official regulations.

4 Impersonality

Max Weber wrote that in a bureaucracy, work is carried out *sine ira et studio,* "without hatred or passion." Bureaucratic norms dictate that officials perform their duties without the personal consideration of people as individuals. This is intended to guarantee equal treatment for each person; however, it also contributes to the often cold and uncaring feeling associated with modern organizations.

We typically think of big government and big business when we think of impersonal bureaucracies. Interestingly, during the most turbulent years of the 1960s, student activists bitterly protested the bureaucratic nature of the American university. One of the symbols of the free speech movement at the University of California at Berkeley was an IBM computer card which stated: "Student at U.C.: Do not bend, fold, or mutilate." In the view of dissidents, the university had become one more giant, faceless, unfeeling bureaucracy which cared little for the uniqueness of the individual (P. Jacobs and Landau, 1966:216–219).

5 Employment Based on Technical Qualifications

Within a bureaucracy, hiring is based on technical qualifications rather than on favoritism, and performance is measured against specific standards. This is designed to protect bureaucrats against arbitrary dismissal and to provide a measure of security. Promotions are dictated by written personnel policies, and people often have a right to appeal if they believe that particular rules have been violated. Such procedures encourage loyalty to the organization.

In this sense, the "impersonal" bureaucracy can be an improvement over nonbureaucratic organizations. A federal bureaucrat in a civil service position, for example, has ideally been selected on the basis of merit, not because he or she did favors for a political machine. Above all, the bureaucracy is expected to value technical and professional competence, which is essential in the day-to-day functioning of a complex, industrial society such as the United States.

Unfortunately, personnel decisions within a bureaucracy do not always follow this ideal pattern. Dysfunctions within bureaucracy have become well publicized, particularly because of the work of Laurence J. Peter. According to the *Peter principle,* every employee within a hierarchy tends to rise to his or her level of incompetence (Peter and Hull, 1969:25). This hypothesis, which has not been directly or systematically tested, reflects a possible dysfunctional outcome of structuring advancement on the basis of merit. Talented persons receive promotion after promotion until, sadly, they finally achieve positions that they cannot handle (Blau and Meyer, 1987:21; Chinoy, 1954:40–41).

Bureaucratization as a Process

As stated earlier, Weber's characteristics of bureaucracy should be seen as describing an ideal type rather than as offering a precise definition of an actual bureaucracy. Sociologist Alvin Gouldner (1950:53–54) notes that not every formal organization will possess all of Weber's characteristics. In fact, there can be wide variation among actual bureaucratic organizations.

Stanley Udy (1959) compared the structure of formal organizations in 150 nonindustrial societies. Like their counterparts in modern industrial nations, these organizations possessed many of—but not necessarily all—the bureaucratic characteristics identified by Weber. Similarly, Richard Hall (1963) tested Weber's ideal type against 10 formal organizations within the United States, including a hotel and a stock brokerage firm. His findings concurred with those of Udy: bureaucracy must be viewed as a matter of degree, that is, as more, or less, bureaucratic. Therefore, in describing organizations, we need to apply the Weberian model carefully, with the understanding that an organization can be more or less rule-oriented, more or less hierarchical, and so forth.

Sociologists have used the term *bureaucratization* to refer to the process by which a group, organization, or social movement becomes increasingly bureaucratic. Normally, we think of bureaucratization in terms of large organizations. In a typical citizen's nightmare, one may have to speak to 10 or 12 individuals in a corporation or government agency to find out which official has jurisdiction over a particular problem. Callers get transferred from one department to another until they finally hang up in disgust. Interestingly, though, bureaucratization also takes place within small-group settings. Children organizing a school club may elect as many officers as there are club members and may develop various rules for meetings.

As we have seen, bureaucratization is not a finite process, nor does it inevitably lead to a specific structure. For example, sociologists have recognized that organizations may take quite different forms in different cultures. In addition to varying from society to society, bureaucratization also serves as a causal variable affecting social change. Conflict theorists have argued that bureaucratic organizations tend to inhibit change because of their emphasis on regulations and security for officeholders. As one example, some public assistance (or welfare) caseworkers are so preoccupied with the required forms for clients that they forget to see whether people's basic needs are being satisfied. Paper becomes more meaningful than people; numbers take precedence over needs.

Oligarchy: Rule by a Few

The bureaucratizing influence on social movements has also been a concern of conflict theorists. German sociologist Robert Michels (1915), in studying socialist parties and labor unions in Europe before World War I, found that such organizations were becoming increasingly bureaucratic. The emerging leaders of these organizations—even some of the most radical—had a vested interest in clinging to power. If they lost their leadership posts, they would have to return to full-time work as manual laborers.

Similarly, a team of sociologists studied bureaucratization in "crisis centers." These organizations, born in the counterculture of the 1960s (see Chapter 2), were established to offer counseling and support to people experiencing divorce, death of a family member, drug and alcohol problems, and other types of emotional crisis. Despite their initial commitment to less bureaucratic, nonhierarchical structures, crisis centers increasingly turned to written job descriptions, organization charts, and written policies regarding treatment of cases and clients (Senter et al., 1983; for a different view, see Rothschild-Whitt, 1979).

Through his research, Michels originated the idea of the *iron law of oligarchy,* under which even a democratic organization will develop into a bureaucracy ruled by a few (the oligarchy). Why do oligarchies emerge? People who achieve leadership roles usually have the skills, knowledge, or charismatic appeal (as Weber noted) to direct, if not control, others. Michels argues that the rank and file of a movement or organization look to leaders for direction and thereby reinforce the process of rule by a few. In addition, members of an oligarchy are strongly motivated to maintain their leadership roles, privileges, and power.

Michels's insights continue to be relevant in the 1990s. Contemporary labor unions in the United States and western Europe bear little resemblance to those organized after spontaneous activity by exploited workers. Conflict theorists have expressed concern about the longevity of union leaders, who are not always responsive to the needs and demands of membership. As Michels noted in his iron law of oligarchy, leaders may become more concerned with maintaining their own positions and power.

At least one recent study, however, raises questions about Michels's views. On the basis of her research on organizations active in the "pro-choice" social movement, which endorses the right to legal abortions, sociologist Suzanne Staggenborg (1988) disputes the assertion that formal organizations with professional leaders inevitably become conservative and oligarchical. Indeed, she notes that many formal organizations in the pro-choice movement appear to be more democratic than informal groups; the routinized procedures that they follow make it more difficult for leaders to achieve excessive power.

While the "iron law" may sometimes help us to understand the concentration of formal authority within organizations, sociologists recognize that there are a number of checks on leadership. Groups often compete for power within a formal organization, as in an automotive corporation in which divisions manufacturing heavy machinery and passenger cars compete against each other for limited research and development funds. Moreover, informal channels of communication and control can undercut the power of top officials of an organization. This is bureaucracy's "other face."

Bureaucracy's Other Face

How does bureaucratization affect the average individual who works in an organization? The early theorists of formal organizations tended to neglect this question. Max Weber, for example, focused on management personnel within bureaucracies, but he had little to say about workers in industry or clerks in government agencies.

According to the *classical theory* of formal organizations, also known as the *scientific management approach,* workers are motivated almost entirely by economic rewards. This theory stresses that productivity is limited only by the physical constraints of workers. Therefore, workers are treated as a resource, much like the machines that have begun to replace them in the twentieth century. Management attempts to achieve maximum work efficiency through scientific planning, established performance standards, and careful supervision of workers and production. Planning under the scientific management approach involves time and motion studies but not studies of workers' attitudes or feelings of job satisfaction.

It was not until workers organized unions—and forced management to recognize that they were not objects—that theorists of formal organizations began to revise the classical approach. Along with management and administrators, social scientists became aware that informal groups of workers have an important impact on organizations (Perrow, 1986:79–118). One result was an alternative way of considering bureaucratic dynamics, the *human relations approach,* which emphasizes the role of people, communication, and participation within a bureaucracy. This type of analysis reflects the interest of interactionist theorists in small-group behavior. Unlike planning under the scientific management approach, planning based on the human relations perspective focuses on workers' feelings, frustrations, and emotional need for job satisfaction.

The gradual move away from a sole focus on

physical aspects of getting the job done—and toward the concerns and needs of workers—led advocates of the human relations approach to stress the less formal aspects of bureaucratic structure. Informal structures and social networks within organizations develop partly as a result of people's ability to create more direct forms of communication than the formal structures mandate. Charles Page (1946) has used the term *bureaucracy's other face* to refer to the unofficial activities and interactions which are such a basic part of daily organizational life. A classic study of a factory illustrates the value of the human relations approach.

In Chapter 1, we looked at the Hawthorne studies, which alerted sociologists to the fact that research subjects may alter their behavior to match the experimenter's expectations. This methodological finding notwithstanding, the major focus of the Hawthorne studies was the role of social factors in workers' productivity. As one aspect of the research, an investigation was made of the switchboard-bank wiring room, where 14 men were making parts of switches for telephone equipment. These men were found to be producing far below their physical capabilities. This was especially surprising because they would earn more money if they produced more parts.

Why was there such an unexpected restriction of output? According to the classical theory, productivity should be maximized, since workers had been given a financial incentive. However, in practice the men were carefully subverting this scheme to boost productivity. They feared that if they produced switch parts at a faster rate, their pay rate might be reduced or some might lose their jobs.

As a result, this group of workers established their own (unofficial) norm for a proper day's work. They created informal rules, sanctions, and argot terms to enforce this standard. Workers who produced "too much" were called "speed kings" and "rate busters," while those judged to be "too slow" were "chiselers." Those who violated this agreement were "binged" (slugged on the shoulder) by coworkers. Yet management was unaware of such practices and had actually come to believe that the men were working as hard as they could (Etzioni, 1964:33–34; Roethlisberger and Dickson, 1939).

Both the Hawthorne studies and William Thompson's study of a beef processing plant (refer back to Box 4-2) testify to the importance of informal structures within formal organizations. Whenever we examine sufficiently small segments of such organizations, we discover patterns of interaction that cannot be accounted for by the official structure. Thus, while a bureaucracy may establish a clear hierarchy and well-defined rules and standards, people can always get around their superiors. Informal understandings among workers can redefine official policies of a bureaucracy.

SOCIAL POLICY AND SOCIAL STRUCTURE

THE AIDS CRISIS

- How has AIDS affected the normal functioning of social institutions in the United States?
- Why is there such a strong stigma attached to infection with the HIV virus and to AIDS?
- How might sociologists influence research on AIDS and AIDS-related issues?

The first cases of AIDS in the United States were reported in 1981. By 1987, 50,000 cases had been reported; by mid-1989, 100,000 cases. As of September 30, 1992, 242,000 cases of AIDS had been reported in the United States, and more than 160,000 people had died of AIDS-related causes. Around the world, about 350,000 cases had been formally reported as of 1992, but it is estimated that more than one million people actually have AIDS (R. Anderson and May, 1992; Centers for Disease Control, 1992b, 1992c).

AIDS is the acronym for *acquired immune deficiency syndrome*. Rather than being a distinct disease, AIDS is actually a predisposition to disease caused by a virus, the human immunodeficiency virus (HIV), that destroys the body's immune system, thereby leaving the carrier vulnerable to infections such as pneumonia that those with healthy immune systems can generally resist. AIDS is not transmitted through touching, shak-

The best-known and most controversial AIDS activist organization is the AIDS Coalition to Unleash Power (ACT-UP), which has conducted protests and sit-ins in the halls of government, at New York City's St. Patrick's Cathedral, and on Wall Street.

ing hands, sharing meals, drinking from the same cup, or other types of routine, nonintimate contact in the home or the workplace. Transmission from one person to another appears to require either intimate sexual contact or exchange of blood or bodily fluids (whether from contaminated hypodermic needles or syringes, transfusions of infected blood, or transmission from an infected mother to her child before or during birth).

As has been well publicized, the high-risk groups most in danger of contracting AIDS in the United States are homosexual and bisexual men (who account for about 60 percent of all cases), intravenous (IV) drug users (who account for about 30 percent of all cases), and their sexual partners. Recently, there has been increasing evidence that AIDS is a particular danger for the urban poor, in good part because of transmission via IV drug use. Whereas Blacks and Hispanics represent about 20 percent of the nation's population, they constitute 48 percent of all adults in the United States who have been found to have AIDS in the last two years. Around the world, women are becoming infected with HIV about as often as men. According to Dr. Michael Merson, head of the World Health Organization's global program on AIDS, the "AIDS epidemic is becoming heterosexual everywhere" (L. Altman, 1992a:C3; Centers for Disease Control, 1992b; *New York Times*, 1991).

The staggering rise of AIDS cases has affected the United States in a profound way. Harvey Fineberg (1988:128), dean of the Harvard School of Public Health, has observed: "Its reach extends to every social institution, from families, schools, and communi-

ties to businesses, courts of law, the military and Federal, state, and local governments." The strain on the nation's health care system has been increasingly obvious, as hospitals are becoming overwhelmed by the demands of caring for AIDS patients and the desperate need for more beds to meet the rising AIDS caseload.

On the micro level of social interaction, it has been widely forecast that AIDS will lead to a more conservative sexual climate—among both homosexuals and heterosexuals—in which people will be much more cautious about involvement with new partners. Yet it appears that many sexually active people in the United States have not heeded precautions about "safer sex." According to the 1990 nationwide Youth Risk Behavior Survey, only half of males questioned and only 40 percent of females reported that they or their partner used a condom during their last experience of sexual intercourse (Centers for Disease Control, 1992a).

People with AIDS or infected with HIV face a powerful dual stigma. Not only have they acquired a master status associated with a lethal and contagious disease; they have a disease which is disproportionately evident in already stigmatized groups, such as gay males and drug users. This linkage with stigmatized groups delayed recognition of the severity of the AIDS epidemic; the media took little interest in the disease until it seemed to be spreading beyond the gay community. Viewed from a conflict perspective, policymakers have been slow to respond to the AIDS crisis because those in high-risk groups—gay men and IV drug users—are comparatively powerless. As one health care consultant pointedly asked: "Who speaks for the drug abuser in our society? Who's in favor of them?" (J. Gross, 1987:A16; Herek and Glunt, 1988; Shilts, 1987).

Polling data show how the stigma associated with high-risk groups affects people's feelings about AIDS. According to a national survey in 1991, 85 percent of Americans said they had a "lot of sympathy" or "some sympathy" for people with AIDS—an increase from the 75 percent who answered the same question this way in a 1988 survey. Yet only 39 percent of those questioned in 1991 indicated that they had a lot of sympathy or some sympathy for "people who get AIDS from homosexual activity," while only 30 percent expressed such sympathy for "people who get AIDS from sharing needles while using illegal drugs." The discrepancy in these data reflects a tendency to blame members of high-risk groups for contracting AIDS. Indeed, those who got AIDS without engaging in homosexual behavior or drug use, such as teenage hemophiliacs, are often spoken of as "innocent victims"—with the implication that others with AIDS are "blamable victims" (Herek and Glunt, 1988:888; Kagay, 1991:C3).

In this climate of fear and blame, there has been increasing harassment of homosexual males. Gay rights leaders believe that the concept of homosexuals as "disease carriers" has contributed to violent incidents directed at people known or suspected to be gay. "What AIDS has done," argues Kevin Berrill of the National Lesbian and Gay Task Force, "is simply give bigots and bashers the justification to attack gays" (D. Altman, 1986:58–70; D. Johnson, 1987:A12).

Fears about AIDS have led to growing discrimination within major social institutions of the United States. For example, people with AIDS have faced discrimination in employment, housing, and insurance. Yet the legal system has hardly taken the lead in fighting such discrimination. According to a report issued in 1992 by the National AIDS Program Office, which coordinates the work of all federal agencies dealing with the disease, the courts seem guided more by stereotypes and fears than by scientific evidence when they rule on AIDS-related cases. Larry Gostin, a professor of health law and a coauthor of the report, points out that some courts have exacerbated public fears of the disease by placing "Do Not Touch" signs on AIDS-related evidence, by having defendants with HIV wear rubber gloves, and by levying harsh penalties to people with AIDS for biting or spitting at others.

Gostin insists that these situations pose minimal risks of transmission and that the court decisions "fly in the face of all the public health wisdom about AIDS" (Margolick, 1992:16).

Any such dramatic crisis is likely to bring about certain transformations in a society's social structure. From a functionalist perspective, if established social institutions cannot meet a crucial need, new institutions and social networks are likely to emerge to fulfill that function. In the case of AIDS, self-help groups—especially in the gay communities of major cities—have been established to care for the sick, educate the healthy, and lobby for more responsive public policies. By 1990, Gay Men's Health Crisis (GMHC) in New York City had a paid staff of 140 and more than 1600 volunteers typically working in a "buddy system" with those afflicted with AIDS. GMHC counsels about one-third of all New Yorkers with AIDS; as many as 20 percent of the patients it services are heterosexuals. The group operates a telephone hot line, sends advocates to hospitals to insist on better care for patients, and runs legal and financial clinics as well as therapy and support groups for people with AIDS and their loved ones (D. Altman, 1986:84–87; J. Gross, 1987:A16).

GMHC and other groups concerned with AIDS argue that the proper societal response to this deadly disease includes testing of new drugs to combat AIDS, massive public education campaigns regarding the need for "safer sex," wide distribution and proper use of condoms, and effective counseling and support services for those with AIDS and HIV infection. AIDS activist organizations charge that there has been grossly inadequate governmental funding for AIDS-related research and public health efforts. Especially visible and outspoken in this effort is the AIDS Coalition to Unleash Power (ACT-UP), which has conducted controversial protests and sit-ins in the halls of government, at New York City's St. Patrick's Cathedral, and on Wall Street. ACT-UP has popularized the slogan it views as the crucial message of the AIDS crisis: "Silence = Death" (France, 1988; Gamson, 1989; Shilts, 1989).

How can sociologists use their expertise to assist in responding to the AIDS crisis? In an address before the American Sociological Association, Canadian sociologist Barry Adam (1992:5–15) expressed concern that research on AIDS has been largely conducted by biomedical scientists. Adam argued that sociologists can make an important contribution to AIDS-related research; he outlined several directions for such sociological research:

- How is information about AIDS produced and distributed? Is the distribution of information about how to have "safer sex" being limited or even censored?
- How does an AIDS "folklore" emerge, and how does it become integrated into a community? Why do certain communities and individuals resist or ignore scientific information about the dangers of AIDS?

- How are medical and social services made available to people with AIDS? Why are these services often denied to the poorest patients?
- How is *homophobia* (fear of and prejudice against homosexuality) related to fears concerning AIDS? In what ways does homophobia correlate with other forms of bias?

SUMMARY

Social structure refers to the way in which a society is organized into predictable relationships. This chapter examines the basic elements of social structure—statuses, social roles, groups, and institutions—with a special focus on the importance of formal organizations in contemporary societies.

1 An *ascribed status* is generally assigned to a person at birth, whereas an *achieved status* is attained largely through one's own effort.

2 With each distinctive status—whether ascribed or achieved—come particular *social roles*.

3 Much of our patterned behavior takes place within *groups* and is influenced by the norms and sanctions established by groups.

4 When we find ourselves identifying closely with a group, it is probably a *primary group*.

5 *Reference groups* set and enforce standards of conduct and perform a comparison function for people's evaluations of themselves and others.

6 The mass media, the government, the economy, the family, and the health care system are all examples of *social institutions* found in the United States.

7 One way to understand social institutions is to see how they fulfill essential functions, such as replacing personnel, training new recruits, and preserving order.

8 Ferdinand Tönnies distinguished the close-knit community of the *Gemeinschaft* from the impersonal mass society known as the *Gesellschaft*.

9 Max Weber argued that, in its ideal form, every *bureaucracy* will share these five basic characteristics: division of labor, hierarchical authority, written rules and regulations, impersonality, and employment based on technical qualifications.

10 Bureaucracy can be understood as a process and as a matter of degree; thus, an organization is more or less bureaucratic than other organizations.

11 The AIDS crisis has affected every social institution in the United States, including the family, the schools, the health care system, the economy, and government.

CRITICAL THINKING QUESTIONS

1 The functionalist, conflict, and interactionist perspectives can all be used in analyzing social institutions. What are the flaws or weaknesses in each perspective's analysis of social institutions?

2 Within a formal organization, are you likely to find primary groups, secondary groups, in-groups, out-groups, and reference groups? What functions do these groups serve for the formal organization? What dysfunctions might occur as a result of their presence?

3 Max Weber identified five basic characteristics of bureaucracy. Select an actual organization with which you are familiar (for example, your college, a business at which you work, a religious institution or civic association to which you belong) and apply Weber's analysis to that organization. To what degree does it correspond to Weber's ideal type of bureaucracy?

KEY TERMS

Achieved status A social position attained by a person largely through his or her own effort. (page 84)

Ascribed status A social position "assigned" to a person by society without regard for the person's unique talents or characteristics. (83)

Bureaucracy A component of formal organization in which rules and hierarchical ranking are used to achieve efficiency. (96)

Bureaucratization The process by which a group, organization, or social movement becomes increasingly bureaucratic. (100)

Classical theory An approach to the study of formal organizations which views workers as being motivated almost entirely by economic rewards. (101)

Dysfunction An element or a process of society that may disrupt a social system or lead to a decrease in stability. (97)

Formal organization A special-purpose group designed and structured in the interests of maximum efficiency. (96)

Gemeinschaft A term used by Ferdinand Tönnies to describe close-knit communities, often found in rural areas, in which strong personal bonds unite members. (95)

Gesellschaft A term used by Ferdinand Tönnies to describe communities, often urban, that are large and impersonal, with little commitment to the group or consensus on values. (96)

Goal displacement Overzealous conformity to official regulations within a bureaucracy. (99)

Group Any number of people with similar norms, values, and expectations who regularly and consciously interact. (87)

Homophobia Fear of and prejudice against homosexuality. (105)

Human relations approach An approach to the study of formal organizations which emphasizes the role of people, communication, and participation within a bureaucracy and tends to focus on the informal structure of the organization. (101)

In-group Any group or category to which people feel they belong. (89)

Iron law of oligarchy A principle of organizational life developed by Robert Michels under which even democratic organizations will become bureaucracies ruled by a few individuals. (101)

Master status A status that dominates others and thereby determines a person's general position within society. (84)

Mechanical solidarity A term used by Émile Durkheim to describe a society in which people generally all perform the same tasks and in which relationships are close and intimate. (94)

Organic solidarity A term used by Émile Durkheim to describe a society in which members are mutually dependent and in which a complex division of labor exists. (95)

Out-group A group or category to which people feel they do not belong. (89)

Peter principle A principle of organizational life, originated by Laurence J. Peter, according to which each individual within a hierarchy tends to rise to his or her level of incompetence. (100)

Primary group A small group characterized by intimate, face-to-face association and cooperation. (87)

Reference group A term used when speaking of any group that individuals use as a standard in evaluating themselves and their own behavior. (90)

Role conflict Difficulties that occur when incompatible expectations arise from two or more social positions held by the same person. (85)

Role exit The process of disengagement from a role that is central to one's self-identity and reestablishment of an identity in a new role. (86)

Scientific management approach Another name for the *classical theory* of formal organizations. (101)

Secondary group A formal, impersonal group in which there is little social intimacy or mutual understanding. (89)

Social institutions Organized patterns of beliefs and behavior centered on basic social needs. (91)

Social interaction The ways in which people respond to one another. (82)

Social network A series of social relationships that link a person directly to others and therefore indirectly to still more people. (90)

Social role A set of expectations of people who occupy a given social position or status. (85)

Social structure The way in which a society is organized into predictable relationships. (83)

Status A term used by sociologists to refer to any of the full range of socially defined positions within a large group or society. (83)

Trained incapacity The tendency of workers in a bureaucracy to become so specialized that they develop blind spots and cannot notice obvious problems. (97)

What are the four basic elements of social structure?
Statuses, social roles, groups & institutions

Name the 5 social institutions:
Mass media, government, economy, family, health care systems

What are the 5 characteristics of Bureaucracy?
Division of labor, hierachical authority, written rules + regulations, impersonality, and employment based on technical qualifications

ADDITIONAL READINGS

Huber, Joan, and Beth E. Schneider (eds.). *The Social Context of AIDS*. Newbury Park, Calif.: Sage, 1992. This anthology addresses a variety of issues as they relate to AIDS, including race, gender stratification, education, and persistent poverty.

Kephart, William, and William M. Zellner. *Extraordinary Groups: An Examination of Unconventional Lifestyles* (4th ed.). New York: St. Martin's, 1991. Among the groups described in this very readable book are the Amish, the Oneida community, the Shakers, the Mormons, Hasidic Jews, Jehovah's Witnesses, and the Romani (commonly known as *Gypsies*).

Majors, Richard, and Janet Mancini Bellson. *Cool Pose: The Dilemmas of Black Manhood in America*. New York: Lexington, 1992. An African American psychologist and a White sociologist analyze the ways in which African American adolescent males present themselves in everyday life.

Scheff, Thomas J. *Microsociology: Discourse, Emotion, and Structure*. Chicago: University of Chicago Press, 1992. An examination of sociological treatment of self and society.

Tannen, Deborah. *You Just Don't Understand: Women and Men in Conversation*. New York: Ballantine, 1990. A popularly written book that provides an overview of how men and women in the United States differ in their styles of communication.

5

DEVIANCE AND SOCIAL CONTROL

LOOKING AHEAD

- How does a society bring about acceptance of social norms?
- How do sociologists view the creation of laws?
- Can we learn deviant behavior from others?
- Why is certain behavior evaluated as "deviant" while other behavior is not considered deviant?
- Should gambling, prostitution, public drunkenness, and use of marijuana be viewed as "victimless crimes"?
- Should Congress and state legislatures adopt stricter gun control measures?

Life in his hotel room was very secure, for the room was closed off behind three locked and guarded partitions while the windows were blocked out by drapes. He spent his later years alone, reclining naked in a lounge chair and watching old movies. His greatest fear was of being seen; over a period of years, only his most trusted guards saw him. He insisted that communications with business associates be indirect because he feared contracting their germs. Indeed, these associates received numerous memoranda from him on how to reduce the germs on newspapers and canned goods with which he would come into contact.

Despite a lifestyle that deviated dramatically from the social norms of acceptable behavior, billionaire Howard Hughes (1905–1976) remained a man of immense wealth and power. His diverse and lucrative holdings included Trans World Airlines (TWA), RKO Studios, Nevada casinos, and television stations. Unlike most wealthy business leaders, Hughes did not lead a high-profile life or take an active role in civic organizations. Yet, because of his wealth and power, he did not experience personal rejection and abuse for his deviant lifestyle. At worst, when outside his hearing, people might call Hughes "eccentric" or "bizarre" (Barlett and Steele, 1981; Drosnin, 1985).

People maintain distinctive standards regarding the proper appearance and behavior of physicians, military officers, and members of the clergy, among others. During the latter part of his life, Howard Hughes clearly deviated from societal expectations concerning the appearance and behavior of business leaders. However, as we will see in this chapter, conformity, obedience, and deviance can be understood only within a given social context. If people disrobe publicly, they are violating widely held social norms. Yet if the same people disrobe within a "naturist" (or nudist) camp, they are obeying the rules and are conforming to the behavior of peers. Clearly, then, what is deviant in one setting may be common and acceptable in another.

Conformity and deviance are two responses to real or imagined pressures from others. People in the United States are socialized to have mixed feelings about both conformity and nonconforming behavior. The term *conformity* can conjure up images of mindless imitation of one's peer group—whether a circle of teenagers wearing punk rock garb or a group of business people dressed in similar gray suits. Yet the same term can also suggest that a person is cooperative or a "team player." What about those who do not conform? They may be respected as individualists, leaders, or creative thinkers who break new ground. Or they may be labeled as "troublemakers" and "weirdos" (Aronson, 1972:14–15).

This chapter will examine the relationship between conformity, deviance, and social control. It begins by distinguishing between conformity and obedience and then looks at two experiments regarding conforming behavior and obedience to authority. The informal and formal mechanisms used by societies to encourage conformity and

what sanctions are to be applied (Schur, 1968: 39–43).

Sociologists representing varying theoretical perspectives agree that the legal order reflects underlying social values. Therefore, the creation of criminal law can be a most controversial matter. Should it be against the law to employ illegal immigrants in a factory, to have an abortion, or to smoke on an airplane? Such issues have been bitterly debated because they require a choice among competing values. Not surprisingly, laws that are unpopular—such as the prohibition of the manufacture and sale of intoxicating liquors under the Eighteenth Amendment in 1919 and the establishment of a national 55-mile-per-hour speed limit on highways in 1973—become difficult to enforce owing to lack of consensus supporting the norms.

It is important to underscore the fact that socialization is the primary source of conforming and obedient behavior, including obedience to law. Generally, it is not external pressure from a peer group or authority figure that makes us go along with social norms. Rather, we have internalized such norms as valid and desirable and are committed to observing them. In a profound sense, we *want* to see ourselves (and to be seen) as loyal, cooperative, responsible, and respectful of others. In the United States, and in other societies around the world, individuals are socialized both to want to belong and to fear being viewed as different or deviant.

What Is Deviance?

For sociologists, the term *deviance* does not mean perversion or depravity. **Deviance** is behavior that violates the standards of conduct or expectations of a group or society (Wickman, 1991:85). In the United States, alcoholics, people with tattoos, compulsive gamblers, and the mentally ill would all be classified as deviants. Being late for class is categorized as a deviant act; the same is true of dressing too casually for a formal wedding. On the basis of the sociological definition, we are all deviant from time to time. Each of us violates common social norms in certain situations.

Deviance involves the violation of group norms which may or may not be formalized into law. It is a comprehensive concept that includes not only criminal behavior but also many actions not subject to prosecution. The public official who takes a bribe has defied social norms, but so has the high school student who refuses to sit in an assigned seat or cuts class. Of course, deviation from norms is not always negative, let alone criminal. A member of an exclusive social club who speaks out against its traditional policy of excluding women, Blacks, and Jews from admittance is deviating from the club's norms. So is a police officer who "blows the whistle" on corruption or brutality within the department.

As we noted earlier, deviance can be understood only within its social context. A nude photo-

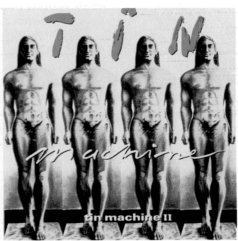

Left, Ted Streshinsky, Photo 20-20; right, courtesy Isolar Enterprises, Inc.

tin machine II

Deviance is often a highly relative matter. People may consider it acceptable to view nude statues in a museum, but are shocked by seeing nude statues on a record album cover. The resulting controversy caused by Tin Machine's album forced their record company to remove the male genitalia from the statues featured on the cover.

graph of a woman or man may be appropriate in an art museum but would be regarded as out of place in an elementary school classroom. A pharmacist is expected to sell prescription drugs only to people who have explicit instructions from medical authorities. If the pharmacist sells the same drugs to a narcotics dealer, he or she has committed deviant (and criminal) behavior.

Deviance, then, is a highly relative matter. People in the United States may consider it strange for a person to fight a bull in an arena, before an audience of screaming fans. Yet we are not nearly so shocked by the practice of two humans' fighting *each other* with boxing gloves in front of a similar audience.

Explaining Deviance

Why do people violate social norms? We have seen that deviant acts are subject to both informal and formal sanctions of social control. The nonconforming or disobedient person may face disapproval, loss of friends, fines, or even imprisonment. Why, then, does deviance occur?

Early explanations for deviance identified supernatural causes or genetic factors (such as "bad blood" or evolutionary throwbacks to primitive ancestors). By the 1800s, there were substantial research efforts to identify biological factors that lead to deviance and especially to criminal activity. While such research has been discredited in the twentieth century, contemporary studies, primarily by biochemists, have sought to isolate genetic factors leading to a likelihood of certain personality traits. Although criminality (much less deviance) is hardly a personality characteristic, researchers have focused on traits that might lead to crime, such as aggression. Of course, aggression can also lead to success in the corporate world, professional sports, or other areas of life.

The contemporary study of possible biological roots of criminality is but one aspect of the larger sociobiology debate discussed in Chapter 3. In general, sociologists reject any emphasis on genetic roots of crime and deviance. The limitations of current knowledge are so significant, the likelihood of reinforcing racist and sexist assumptions so clear, and the implications for rehabilitation of criminals so disturbing that sociologists have largely drawn on other approaches to explain deviance (Sagarin and Sanchez, 1988).

Functionalist Perspective According to functionalists, deviance is a common part of human existence, with positive (as well as negative) consequences for social stability. Deviance helps to define the limits of proper behavior. Children who see one parent scold the other for belching at the dinner table learn about approved conduct. The same is true of the driver who receives a speeding ticket, the department store cashier who is fired for yelling at a customer, and the college student who is penalized for handing in papers weeks overdue.

DURKHEIM'S LEGACY Émile Durkheim (1964:67, original edition 1895) focused his sociological investigations mainly on criminal acts, yet his conclusions have implications for all types of deviant behavior. In Durkheim's view, the punishments established within a culture (including what we have identified as formal and informal mechanisms of social control) help to define acceptable behavior and thus contribute to stability. If improper acts were not committed and then sanctioned, people might extend their standards as to what constitutes appropriate conduct.

Kai Erikson (1966) illustrated this boundary-maintenance function of deviance in his study of the Puritans of seventeenth-century New England. By today's standards, the Puritans placed tremendous emphasis on conventional morals. Their persecution of Quakers and execution of women as witches represented continuing attempts to define and redefine the boundaries of their community. In effect, changing social norms created "crime waves," as people whose behavior was previously acceptable suddenly faced punishment for being deviant (Abrahamson, 1978:78–79; N. Davis, 1975:85–87).

Unexpectedly, boundary maintenance reemerged in the same area some 300 years later. The town of Salem, Massachusetts, draws (and profits from) 1 million visitors per year who come to see the sites of the witch trials and executions. At the urging of descendants of 20 innocent victims who had been executed, a statue was designed to commemorate the slain women. However, protests blocked the public installation of the statue; the protesters were concerned that such a prominent memorial to the *victims* would dampen tourists' interest in witch lore (Driscoll, 1988).

Durkheim (1951, original edition 1897) also introduced the term *anomie* into sociological literature to describe a loss of direction felt in a society when social control of individual behavior has become ineffective. Anomie is a state of normlessness which typically occurs during a period of profound social change and disorder, such as a time of economic collapse. People become more aggressive or depressed, and this results in higher rates of violent crime and suicide. Since there is much less agreement on what constitutes proper behavior during times of revolution, sudden prosperity, or economic depression, conformity and obedience become less significant as social forces. It also becomes much more difficult to state exactly what constitutes deviance.

MERTON'S THEORY OF DEVIANCE A mugger and a secretary do not seem at first to have a great deal in common. Yet, in fact, each is "working" to obtain money which can then be exchanged for desired goods. As this example illustrates, behavior that violates accepted norms (such as mugging) may be performed with the same basic objectives in mind as those of people who pursue more conventional lifestyles.

Using the above analysis, sociologist Robert Merton of Columbia University (1968:185–214) adapted Durkheim's notion of anomie to explain why people accept or reject the goals of a society, the socially approved means to fulfill their aspirations, or both. Merton maintained that one important cultural goal in the United States is success, measured largely in terms of money. In addition to providing this goal for people, our society offers specific instructions on how to pursue success—go to school, work hard, do not quit, take advantage of opportunities, and so forth.

What happens to individuals in a society with a heavy emphasis on wealth as a basic symbol of success? Merton reasoned that people adapt in certain ways, either by conforming to or by deviating from such cultural expectations. Consequently, he developed the *anomie theory of deviance,* which posits five basic forms of adaptation (see Table 5-1 on page 118).

Conformity to social norms, the most common adaptation in Merton's typology, is the opposite of deviance. It involves acceptance of both the overall societal goal ("become affluent") and the approved means ("work hard"). In Merton's view,

The Bettmann Archive

On the basis of his study of the Puritans of seventeenth-century New England, Kai Erikson suggested that the Puritans' persecution of Quakers and execution of women as witches represented continuing attempts to define and redefine the boundaries of their community.

there must be some consensus regarding accepted cultural goals and legitimate means for attaining them. Without such consensus, societies could exist only as collectives of people—rather than as unified cultures—and might function in continual chaos.

Of course, in a society such as the United States, conformity is not universal. For example, the means for realizing objectives are not equally distributed. People in the lower social classes often identify with the same goals as more powerful and affluent citizens yet lack equal access to high-quality education and training for skilled work. Even within a society, institutionalized means for realizing objectives vary. For instance, it is legal to gain money through roulette or poker in Nevada, but not in neighboring California.

TABLE 5-1 Modes of Individual Adaptation

MODE	INSTITUTIONALIZED MEANS (HARD WORK)	SOCIETAL GOAL (ACQUISITION OF WEALTH)
Nondeviant		
Conformity	+	+
Deviant		
Innovation	−	+
Ritualism	+	−
Retreatism	−	−
Rebellion	±	±

NOTE: + indicates acceptance; − indicates rejection; ± indicates replacement with new means and goals.

Robert Merton's typology (1968:194) shows that, in many cases, those whose form of adaptation is deviant still accept either the work ethic or the desire for material wealth widely valued by "conformists."

The other four types of behavior represented in Table 5-1 all involve some departure from conformity. The "innovator" accepts the goals of a society but pursues them with means regarded as improper. For example, Harry King—a professional thief who specialized in safecracking for 40 years—gave a lecture to a sociology class in which he explained that he saw his criminal lifestyle as an adaptation to the goal of material success (Chambliss, 1972:x). According to Merton's anomie theory of deviance, if a society largely denies people the opportunity to achieve success through socially approved avenues, some individuals (like Harry King) will turn to illegitimate paths of upward mobility.

In Merton's typology, the "ritualist" has abandoned the goal of material success and become compulsively committed to the institutional means. Therefore, work becomes a way of life rather than a means to the goal of success. In discussing goal displacement within bureaucracy in Chapter 4, we noted that officials can blindly apply rules and regulations without remembering the larger goals of an organization. Certainly this would be true of a welfare caseworker who refuses to assist a homeless family because their last apartment was in another district. People who overzealously and rigidly enforce bureaucratic regulations can be classified as "ritualists."

The "retreatist," as described by Merton, has basically withdrawn (or "retreated") from both the goals and the means of a society. In the United States, while drug addicts and residents of skid row are typically portrayed as retreatists, there is growing concern about adolescents addicted to alcohol who become retreatists at an early age.

The final adaptation identified by Merton reflects people's attempts to create a new social structure. The "rebel" is assumed to have a sense of alienation from dominant means and goals and to be seeking a dramatically different social order. Members of a revolutionary political organization, such as the Irish Republican Army (IRA) or the Puerto Rican nationalist group Fuerzas Armadas de Liberación Nacional (FALN), can be categorized as rebels according to Merton's model.

Merton has stressed that he was not attempting to describe five types of individuals. Rather, he offered a typology to explain the actions that people *usually* take. Thus, leaders of organized crime syndicates will be categorized as innovators, since they do not pursue success through socially approved means. Yet they may also attend church and send their children to medical school. Conversely, "respectable" people may occasionally cheat on their taxes or violate traffic laws. According to Merton, the same person will move back and forth from one mode of adaptation to another, depending on the demands of a situation.

Despite its popularity, Merton's theory of deviance has had relatively few applications. Little effort has been made to determine how comprehensive the five modes of adaptation are—in other words, to what extent all acts of deviance can be accounted for by innovation, ritualism, retreatism, and rebellion. Moreover, while Merton's theory is useful in examining certain types of behavior, such as illegal gambling by disadvantaged people functioning as innovators, his formulation fails to explain key differences in rates. Why, for example, do some disadvantaged groups have lower rates of reported crime than others? Why is criminal behavior not viewed as a viable alternative by many people faced with adversity? Such questions are not easily answered by Merton's theory of deviance (Cloward, 1959; Hartjen, 1978).

Nevertheless, Merton has made a key contribution to sociological understanding of deviance by pointing out that deviants (such as innovators and ritualists) share a great deal with conforming people. The convicted felon may hold many of the same aspirations that people with no criminal background have. Therefore, deviance can be understood as socially created behavior, rather than as the result of momentary pathological impulses.

Interactionist Perspective: Cultural Transmission

The functionalist approaches to deviance explain why rule violation continues to exist in societies despite pressures to conform and obey. However, functionalists do not indicate how a given person comes to commit a deviant act. The theory of cultural transmission draws on the interactionist perspective to offer just such an explanation.

There is no natural, innate manner in which people interact with one another. Rather, humans *learn* how to behave in social situations—whether properly or improperly. These simple ideas are not disputed today, but this was not the case when sociologist Edwin Sutherland (1883–1950) advanced the argument that an individual undergoes the same basic socialization process whether learning conforming or deviant acts.

Sutherland's ideas have been the dominating force in criminology. He drew on the *cultural transmission* school, which emphasizes that criminal behavior is learned through interactions with others. Such learning includes not only techniques of lawbreaking (for example, how to break into a car quickly and quietly) but also the motives, drives, and rationalizations of criminals. The cultural transmission approach can also be used to explain the behavior of people who engage in habitual—and ultimately life-threatening—use of alcohol or drugs.

Sutherland maintained that through interactions with a primary group and significant others, people acquire definitions of behavior that are deemed proper and improper. He used the term *differential association* to describe the process through which exposure to attitudes favorable to criminal acts leads to violation of rules. Recent research suggests that this view of differential association can be applied to such noncriminal deviant acts as sitting down during the singing of the National Anthem or lying to a spouse or friend (E. Jackson et al., 1986).

To what extent will a given person engage in activity regarded as proper or improper? For each individual, it will depend on the frequency, duration, and importance of two types of social interaction experiences—those which endorse deviant behavior and those which promote acceptance of social norms. Deviant behavior, including criminal activity, is selected by those who acquire more sentiments in favor of violation of norms. People are more likely to engage in norm-defying behavior if they are part of a group or subculture that stresses deviant values.

Sutherland offers the example of a boy who is sociable, outgoing, and athletic and who lives in an area with a high rate of delinquency. The youth is very likely to come into contact with peers who commit acts of vandalism, fail to attend school, and so forth, and may, thus, adopt such behavior. However, an introverted boy living in the same neighborhood may stay away from his peers and avoid delinquency. In another community, an outgoing and athletic boy may join a Little League baseball team or a scout troop because of his interactions with peers. Thus, Sutherland views learning improper behavior as the result of the types of groups to which one belongs and the kinds of friendships one has with others (Sutherland and Cressey, 1978:82).

As another example, differential association theory can be applied to a star high school football player who accepts a bribe from a college recruiter in exchange for a commitment to attend the recruiter's school. Such football stars are typically surrounded by other players, family members, coaches, and recruiters who stress the paramount goals of success in "big-time" football and the money and fame that such success can bring. Consequently, these athletes may be exposed to many people who favor norm-defying behavior and relatively few who oppose the deviant act of accepting a recruiter's bribe.

According to its critics, however, the cultural transmission approach fails to explain the deviant behavior of the first-time impulsive shoplifter or the impoverished person who steals out of necessity. While not a precise statement of the process through which one becomes a criminal, differential association does direct our attention to the paramount role of social interaction in increasing a person's motivation to engage in deviant behavior (Cressey, 1960:53–54; E. Jackson et al., 1986; Sutherland and Cressey, 1978:80–82).

119

DEVIANCE AND SOCIAL CONTROL

Labeling Theory The Saints and Roughnecks were two groups of high school males who were constantly occupied with drinking, wild driving, truancy, petty theft, and vandalism. There the similarity ended. None of the Saints was ever arrested, but every Roughneck was continually in trouble with police and townspeople. Why the disparity in their treatment? On the basis of his observation research in their high school, sociologist William Chambliss (1973) concluded that social class played an important role in the varying fortunes of the two groups.

The Saints effectively produced a facade of respectability. They came from "good families," were active in school organizations, expressed the intention of attending college, and received good grades. Their delinquent acts were generally viewed as a few isolated cases of "sowing wild oats." By contrast, the Roughnecks had no such aura of respectability. They drove around town in beaten-up cars, were generally unsuccessful in school, and were viewed with suspicion no matter what they did.

The Roughnecks were labeled as "troublemakers," whereas the Saints were seen merely as "fun-loving kids." Both groups were gangs of delinquents, yet only one came to be treated that way. More recently, Chambliss's observations concerning juveniles have been confirmed in research using self-reports of delinquents and police records in Seattle, Washington. Sociologist Robert Sampson (1986) found that juveniles from the lower classes who came into contact with the Seattle police because of delinquent behavior were more likely to be arrested and then indicted than were their middle-class counterparts engaged in similar activities.

Such discrepancies can be understood by use of an approach to deviance known as ***labeling theory***. Unlike Sutherland's work, labeling theory does not focus on why some individuals come to commit deviant acts. Instead, it attempts to explain why certain people (such as the Roughnecks) are *viewed* as deviants, delinquents, "bad kids," "losers," and criminals, while others whose behavior is similar (such as the Saints) are not seen in such harsh terms.

Reflecting the contribution of interactionist theorists, labeling theory emphasizes how a person comes to be labeled as deviant or to accept that label. Sociologist Howard Becker (1963:9; 1964), who popularized this approach, summed it up with the statement: "Deviant behavior is behavior that people so label." Labeling theory is also called the ***societal-reaction approach,*** reminding us that it is the *response* to an act and not the behavior that determines deviance. For example, studies have shown that some school personnel and therapists expand educational programs designed for learning-disabled students to include those with behavioral problems. Consequently, a "troublemaker" can be improperly labeled as learning-disabled, and vice versa (Osborne et al., 1985).

Traditionally, research on deviance has focused on people who violate social norms. In contrast, labeling theory focuses on police, probation officers, psychiatrists, judges, teachers, employers, school officials, and other regulators of social control. These agents, it is argued, play a significant role in creating the deviant identity by designating certain people (and not others) as "deviant." An important aspect of labeling theory is the recognition that some individuals or groups have the power to *define* labels and apply them to others. This view recalls the conflict perspective's emphasis on the social significance of power.

The labeling approach does not fully explain why certain people accept a label and others are able to reject it. In fact, this perspective may exaggerate the ease with which our self-images can be altered by societal judgments. Labeling theorists do suggest, however, that differential power is important in determining a person's ability to resist an undesirable label. Competing approaches (including those of both Merton and Sutherland) fail to explain why some deviants continue to be viewed as conformists rather than as violators of rules. According to Howard Becker (1973:179–180), labeling theory was not conceived as the *sole* explanation for deviance; its proponents merely hoped to focus more attention on the undeniably important actions of those people officially in charge of defining deviance (N. Davis, 1975:172; compare with Cullen and Cullen, 1978:36–37).

Conflict Theory Why is certain behavior evaluated as deviant while other behavior is not? According to conflict theorists, it is because people with power protect their own interests and define deviance to suit their own needs. For decades, laws against rape reflected the overwhelmingly male composition of state legislatures. As one consequence, the legal definition of rape pertained only to sexual relations between unmarried people. It was legally acceptable for a husband to have forcible sexual intercourse with his wife—without her consent and against her will. However, repeated protests by feminist organizations finally led to changes in the criminal law. By 1991, husbands in all 50 states could be prosecuted under certain circumstances for the rape of their wives (although 34 states still required a higher standard for conviction if an accused rapist was the victim's husband). In this instance, the rise of the women's liberation movement (see Chapter 8) led to important changes in societal notions of criminality—as it has in educating judges, legislators, and police officers to view wife battering and other forms of domestic violence as serious crimes (National Center on Women and Family Law, 1991).

Sociologist Richard Quinney (1974, 1979, 1980) is a leading exponent of the view that the criminal justice system serves the interests of the powerful. Crime, according to Quinney (1970:15–23), is a definition of conduct created by authorized agents of social control—such as legislators and law enforcement officials—in a politically organized society. He and other conflict theorists argue that lawmaking is often an attempt by the powerful to coerce others into their own morality.

This helps to explain why our society has laws against gambling, drug usage, and prostitution which are violated on a massive scale (we will examine these "victimless crimes" later in the chapter). According to the conflict school, criminal law does not represent a consistent application of societal values, but instead reflects competing values and interests. Thus, marijuana is outlawed in the United States because it is alleged to be harmful to users, yet cigarettes and alcohol are sold legally almost everywhere.

The conflict perspective reminds us that while the basic purpose of law may be to maintain stability and order, this can actually mean perpetuating inequality. For example, researchers have found that African Americans and Hispanics receive stiffer prison sentences and serve longer terms than Whites convicted of similar felonies. A

Historical Pictures Service

Should it be against the law to sell or use marijuana? In the 1930s, the Federal Bureau of Narcotics launched a campaign to have marijuana viewed as a dangerous drug rather than as a pleasure-inducing substance. From a conflict perspective, lawmaking is often an attempt by the powerful to coerce others into their own brand of morality. Marijuana is outlawed because it is alleged to be harmful to users, yet cigarettes and alcohol are sold legally almost everywhere.

1991 study by the United States Sentencing Commission reported that Blacks and Hispanics are more likely than Whites to receive mandatory minimum sentences in federal court. Ironically, Congress had adopted such mandatory minimums for certain federal crimes in order to end discrimination based on gender, race, and age. Yet, whereas 68 percent of African Americans facing mandatory minimum sentences actually get them, the same is true for 57 percent of Hispanics and only 54 percent of Whites. According to the commission, Whites are more likely to enter into plea bargains which lead to the dropping of those charges that require mandatory minimum sentences (Cauchon, 1991:8A).

On the whole, conflict theories contend that the criminal justice system of the United States treats suspects differently on the basis of racial, ethnic, and social class backgrounds. In commenting on the exercise of discretion in the courts, Justice Lois Forer (1984:9) of Philadelphia suggests that there are:

> . . . two separate and unequal systems of justice: one for the rich in which the courts take limitless time to examine, ponder, consider, and deliberate over hundreds of thousands of bits of evidence, . . . and hear elaborate, endless appeals; the other for the poor, in which hasty guilty pleas and brief hearings are the rule and appeals are the exception.

Quinney (1974) argues that, through such differential applications of social control, the criminal justice system helps to keep the poor and oppressed in their deprived position. In his view, disadvantaged individuals and groups who represent a threat to those with power become the primary targets of criminal law. Yet the real criminals in poor neighborhoods are not the people arrested for vandalism and theft, but rather absentee landlords and exploitative store owners. Even if we do not accept this challenging argument, we cannot ignore the role of the powerful in creating a social structure that perpetuates suffering.

The perspective advanced by labeling and conflict theorists forms quite a contrast to the functionalist approach to deviance. Functionalists view standards of deviant behavior as merely reflecting cultural norms, whereas conflict and labeling theorists point out that the most powerful groups in a society can *shape* laws and standards and determine who is (or is not) prosecuted as a criminal. Thus, the label "deviant" is rarely applied to the corporate executive whose decisions lead to large-scale environmental pollution. In the opinion of conflict theorists, agents of social control and powerful groups can generally impose their own self-serving definitions of deviance on the general public.

CRIME

Crime is a violation of criminal law for which formal penalties are applied by some governmental authority. It represents some type of deviation from formal social norms administered by the state. Crimes are divided by law into various categories, depending on the severity of the offense, the age of the offender, the potential punishment that can be levied, and the court which holds jurisdiction over the case.

The term *index crimes* refers to the eight types of crime that are reported annually by the Federal Bureau of Investigation (FBI) in its *Uniform Crime Reports.* This category of criminal behavior generally consists of those serious offenses that people think of when they express concern about the nation's crime problem. Index crimes include murder, rape, robbery, and assault—all of which are violent crimes committed against people—as well as the property crimes of burglary, theft, motor vehicle theft, and arson.

Types of Crime

Rather than relying solely on legal categories, sociologists classify crimes in terms of how they are committed and how the offenses are viewed by society. In this section, we will examine four types of crime as differentiated by sociologists: professional crime, organized crime, white-collar crime, and "victimless crimes."

Professional Crime   Although the adage "crime doesn't pay" is familiar, many people do make a career of illegal activities. A *professional criminal* is a person who pursues crime as a day-to-day occupation, developing skilled techniques and enjoying a certain degree of status among other criminals. Some professional criminals specialize in burglary, safecracking, hijacking of cargo, pickpocketing, and shoplifting. Such people have acquired skills that reduce the likelihood of arrest, conviction, and imprisonment. As a result, they may have long careers in their chosen "professions."

Edwin Sutherland (1937) offered pioneering insights regarding professional criminals by publishing an annotated account written by a professional thief. Unlike the person who engages in crime only once or twice, professional thieves make a business of stealing. These professional criminals devote their entire working time to planning and executing crimes and sometimes travel across the nation to pursue their "professional duties." Like people in regular occupations, professional thieves consult with their colleagues concerning the demands of work, thus becoming part of a subculture of similarly occupied individuals. They exchange information on possible places to burglarize, on outlets for unloading stolen goods, and on ways of securing bail bonds if arrested.

Learning technical skills is an important aspect of working as a professional criminal. Sociologist Peter Letkemann (1973:117–136) makes a distinction between two types of criminal skills: those which are extensions of the legitimate social order but are sharpened and refined (such as the ability to detect when homeowners are away) and those skills not easily available to the average citizen (such as opening a safe). The latter are learned in the manner suggested by Sutherland in his cultural transmission approach. It is a norm among professional criminals that the chief areas for the exchange of criminal skills are the streets and prisons. Although such skills are not *systematically* taught in either place, they are nonetheless communicated effectively (Chambliss and Seidman, 1971:487; McCaghy, 1980:180–192).

Organized Crime The term *organized crime* has many meanings, as is evident from a 1978 government report that uses three pages to define the term. For our purposes, we will consider **organized crime** to be the work of a group that regulates relations between various criminal enterprises involved in smuggling and sale of drugs, prostitution, gambling, and other activities. Organized crime dominates the world of illegal business just as large corporations dominate the conventional business world. It allocates territory, sets prices for illegal goods and services, and acts as an arbitrator in internal disputes (Blakey et al., 1978:107–109).

Organized crime is a secret, conspiratorial activity that generally evades law enforcement. Although precise information is lacking, a presidential commission estimated that organized crime operates in 80 percent of all cities with more than 1 million residents (President's Commission on Law Enforcement and Administration of Justice, 1967:191). Organized crime takes over legitimate businesses, gains influence over labor unions, corrupts public officials, intimidates witnesses in criminal trials, and even "taxes" merchants in exchange for "protection" (National Advisory Commission on Criminal Justice, 1976).

Through its success, organized crime has served as a means of mobility for groups of people struggling to escape poverty. Daniel Bell (1953:127–150) used the term *ethnic succession* to describe the process during which leadership of organized crime, held by Irish Americans in the early part of the twentieth century, was transferred in the 1920s to Jewish Americans. In the early 1930s, Jewish crime leaders were in turn replaced by Italian Americans. More recently, ethnic succession has become more complex, reflecting the diversity of the nation's latest immigrants. Colombian, Mexican, Pakistani, and Nigerian immigrants are among those who have begun to play a significant role in organized crime.

White-Collar Crime Edwin Sutherland, who popularized the differential association theory discussed earlier, noted that certain crimes are committed by affluent, "respectable" people in the course of their daily business activities. Sutherland (1949, 1983) likened these crimes to organized crime because they are often perpetrated through the roles of one's occupation (Hagan and Parker, 1985). In his 1939 presidential address to the American Sociological Society, Sutherland (1940) referred to such offenses as **white-collar crimes.** More recently, the term *white-collar crime* has been broadened to include offenses by businesses and corporations as well as by individuals. A wide variety of offenses are now classified as white-collar crimes, such as income tax evasion, stock manipulation, consumer fraud, bribery and extraction of "kickbacks," embezzlement, and misrepresentation in advertising.

A new type of white-collar crime has emerged since Sutherland first wrote on this topic: computer crime. The use of such "high technology" allows one to carry out embezzlement or electronic fraud without leaving a trace, or to gain access to a company's inventory without leaving one's home. An adept programmer can gain ac-

"HERE WE ARE, CONWAY — THE FINANCIAL DISTRICT. KEEP YOUR EYES OPEN FOR ANY SHADY DEALS AND VIOLATIONS OF THE SECURITIES BUSINESS."

White-collar crime has become a widespread and disturbing reality in the nation's top corporate and financial circles.

cess to a firm's computer by telephone and then copy valuable files. It is virtually impossible to track such people unless they are foolish enough to call from the same phone each time. According to a 1990 estimate, the cost of computer crimes in the United States has reached $3 to $5 billion annually (Conly and McEwen, 1990:2).

White-collar crime has become a widespread and disturbing reality in the United States. In a survey of business practices in the period 1975–1984, sociologist Amitai Etzioni (1990) found that 62 percent of *Fortune*'s 500 largest industrial corporations had been involved in one or more illegal incidents, such as price-fixing, overcharging, fraud, and falsification of tax records. Indeed, the top 100 corporations were guilty of more such crimes than all the other firms combined. Since Etzioni's study was limited to white-collar crimes

detected by the government, his findings must be regarded as an underestimate of the prevalence of white-collar crime in the corporate world (Department of Justice, 1987; Reiman, 1984).

In addition to the financial costs of this form of crime, which run into billions of dollars per year, white-collar crime has distinctive social costs, including a decline in the quality of life and a weakening of the social order (Conklin, 1981:50). If those at the top of the nation's economic and social structure feel free to violate the law, less privileged citizens can certainly be expected to follow suit. Ralph Nader (1985:F3), director of the Corporate Accountability Research Group, suggests that "by almost any measure, crime in the suites takes far more money and produces far more casualties and diseases than crime in the streets— bad as that situation is."

Given the economic and social costs of white-collar crime, one might expect this problem to be taken quite seriously by the criminal justice system of the United States. Yet white-collar offenders are more likely to receive fines than prison sentences. In federal courts—where most white-collar cases are considered—probation is granted to 40 percent of those who have violated antitrust laws, 61 percent of those convicted of fraud, and 70 percent of convicted embezzlers (Gest, 1985). Etzioni (1985, 1990) reported in his study that in 43 percent of the incidents either no penalty was imposed or the company was required merely to cease engaging in the illegal practice and to return any funds gained through illegal means (for a different view, see Manson, 1986).

Moreover, conviction for such illegal acts does not generally harm a person's reputation and career aspirations nearly so much as conviction for an index crime would. Apparently, the label "white-collar criminal" does not carry the stigma of the label "felon convicted of a violent crime." In the view of conflict theorists, such differential labeling and treatment are not surprising. The conflict perspective argues that the criminal justice system largely disregards the white-collar crimes of the affluent, while focusing on index crimes often committed by the poor. Thus, if an offender holds a position of status and influence, his or her crime is treated as less serious and the sanction is much more lenient (Katznelson and Kesselman, 1979:352–355; Maguire, 1988).

BOX 5-1

THE 10 WORST CORPORATIONS OF 1992

Each year, the *Multinational Monitor,* an investigative weekly publication based in Washington, D.C., identifies the global corporations that are the "worst" because they wield vast power, often recklessly and often to the detriment of workers, consumers, governments, and the environment. The actions discussed below do not necessarily constitute white-collar crime, but they may seem criminal even when they do not violate the law.

According to the *Multinational Monitor,* the 10 worst corporations of 1992 are:

- *Absolut Vodka.* This Swedish corporation is viewed as one of the most persistent abusers of alcohol advertising; it bombards young people with colorful and seductive ads to increase alcohol consumption. Absolut Vodka has also threatened legal action to silence *Adbuster Quarterly* for that publication's satires of Absolut Vodka ads.
- *Caterpillar.* The Illinois-based manufacturer of tractors and construction machinery refuses to engage in collective bargaining with 17,000 employees represented by the United Auto Workers and has dramatically reduced traditional health care benefits.
- *Chevron.* This giant oil company has a distressing environmental record. In 1992, it pleaded guilty to 65 violations of the Clean Water Act, admitting that it had illegally discharged oil and grease into the Pacific Ocean. Community activists in San Francisco charge that a Chevron refinery released at least 40 tons of toxic dust into residential neighborhoods in late 1991.
- *Food Lion.* The fastest-growing food chain store in the United States, Food Lion was spotlighted in 1992 in an ABC television exposé for its unsanitary food-handling practices.
- *General Electric (GE).* According to INFACT, a public-interest group in Boston, GE's Knolls Atomic Power Lab in Schenectady, New York, is a serious health hazard. INFACT suggests that thousands of the plant's employees and neighbors have been exposed to radiation because of dangerous operations.
- *General Motors (GM).* In early 1992, the Center for Auto Safety charged that GM has manufactured pickup trucks with hazardous gas tanks that have led to more than 300 deaths. According to the Center, GM covered up the problem of these exploding gas tanks.
- *Martin Marietta.* In 1992, the Department of Labor determined that this defense contractor had retaliated against an employee "whistleblower" by forcing him to do useless work in a room filled with toxic and radioactive chemicals.
- *Mitsubishi.* This Japanese-based multinational corporation is one of the leading importers of timber from tropical rain forests. One of its subsidiaries has nearly destroyed entire regions of the rain forest in Sarawak, Malaysia.
- *Stone Container.* In March 1992, one of the company's mechanics at a Louisiana plant was crushed to death by a paper machine because the machine was not "locked out" so that it could not be turned on during maintenance. The mechanic's death was the third at the plant since 1991 and the third stemming from lock-out failures.
- *Time Warner/Whittle.* In 1992, the media giant Time Warner became majority owner of Whittle Communications, which hopes to establish 200 private "for profit" schools across the United States by 1996. Media critics are troubled by the growing concentration of ownership of newspapers and magazines, radio and television stations, and publishing houses; possible control of local schools by such corporate giants is viewed with serious concern.

SOURCE: Mokhiber et al., 1992:7–16.

Victimless Crimes In white-collar or index crimes, people's economic or personal well-being is endangered against their will (or without their direct knowledge). By contrast, sociologists use the term ***victimless crimes*** to describe the willing exchange among adults of widely desired, but illegal, goods and services (Schur, 1965:169; 1985). Despite the social costs to families and friends of those engaged in such behavior, many people in the United States continue to view gambling, prostitution, public drunkenness, and use of marijuana as victimless crimes, that is, crimes in which there is no "victim" other than the offender. As a result, there has been pressure from some groups to decriminalize various activities which fall into the category of victimless crimes.

Supporters of decriminalization are troubled by the attempt to legislate a moral code of behavior for adults. In their view, it is impossible to prevent prostitution, gambling, and other victimless crimes. The already overburdened criminal justice system should instead devote its resources to "street crimes" and other offenses which have obvious victims. However, opponents of decriminalization insist that such offenses do indeed have victims, in the sense that they bring harm to innocent people. For example, a person with a drinking problem can become abusive to a spouse or children; a compulsive gambler or drug user may steal in order to pursue this obsession. Therefore, according to critics of decriminalization, society must not give tacit approval to conduct which has such harmful consequences (National Advisory Commission on Criminal Justice, 1976:216–248; Schur, 1968, 1985).

The controversy over decriminalization reminds us of the important insights of labeling and conflict theories presented earlier. Underlying this debate are two interesting questions: Who has the power to define gambling, prostitution, and public drunkenness as "crimes"? And who has the power to label such behaviors as "victimless"? It is generally the state legislatures and, in some cases, the police and the courts.

Again, we can see that criminal law is not simply a universal standard of behavior agreed on by all members of society. Rather, it reflects the struggle among competing individuals and groups to gain governmental support for their particular moral and social values. For example, such organizations as Mothers Against Drunk Driving (MADD) and Students Against Drunk Driving (SADD) have had success in recent years in shifting public attitudes toward drunkenness. Rather than being viewed as a "victimless crime," drunkenness is increasingly being associated with the potential dangers of driving while under the influence of alcohol. As a result, the mass media are giving greater (and more critical) attention to people who are guilty of drunk driving, while many states have instituted more severe fines and jail terms for a wide variety of alcohol-related offenses.

Crime Statistics

Crime statistics are among the least reliable social data. However, since they deal with an issue of grave concern to the people of the United States, they are frequently cited as if they are quite accurate. Such statistics do serve as an indicator of police activity, as well as an approximate indication of the level of certain crimes. Yet it would be a mistake to interpret these data as an exact representation of the incidence of crime.

Use and Meaning of Crime Statistics Typically, the crime data used in the United States are based on the index crimes described earlier. The crime index, published annually by the FBI as part of the *Uniform Crime Reports,* includes statistics on murder, rape, robbery, assault, burglary, larceny-theft, motor vehicle theft, and arson (see Table 5-2). Obviously many serious offenses, such as those referred to as *white-collar crimes,* are not included in this index (although they are recorded elsewhere). In addition, the crime index is disproportionately devoted to property crimes, whereas most citizens are more worried about violent crimes against people. Thus, a significant decrease in the number of rapes and robberies could be overshadowed by a slightly larger increase in the number of automobiles stolen, thereby leading to the mistaken impression that *personal* safety is more at risk than before.

The most serious limitation of such official crime statistics is that they include only those crimes actually *reported* to law enforcement agencies. As is clear in Figure 5-1, many crimes are not reported, including about half of all assaults and robberies. In these instances, victims typically feel that the experience has been too personal to reveal to police officers and other strangers or that the crime is "not important enough."

TABLE 5-2 National Crime Rates and Percent Change

CRIME INDEX OFFENSES IN 1991	NUMBER REPORTED	RATE PER 100,000 INHABITANTS	PERCENT CHANGE IN RATE	
			SINCE 1987	SINCE 1982
Violent crime				
Murder	24,700	10	+19	+8
Forcible rape	106,590	42	+13	+24
Robbery	687,730	273	+28	+14
Aggravated assault	1,092,740	433	+23	+50
Total	1,911,770	758	+24	+33
Property crime				
Burglary	3,157,200	1,252	−6	−16
Larceny-theft	8,142,200	3,229	+5	+5
Motor vehicle theft	1,661,700	659	+24	+44
Total	12,961,100	5,140	+4	+2
Total index crime	14,872,900	5,898	+6	+5

NOTE: (1) Arson was designated an index offense beginning in 1979; data on arson are still incomplete as of 1991. (2) Because of rounding, the offenses may not add to totals.
SOURCE: Department of Justice, 1992:58.

The crime index, published annually by the FBI, is the major source of information on crime in the United States (although victimization surveys are increasingly being used).

Use of official police statistics clearly presents major methodological problems for sociologists and other researchers in understanding crime. Partly because of the deficiencies of police data, the *National Crime Survey* was introduced in 1972 as a means of learning how much crime actually takes place in the United States. The Bureau of Justice Statistics, in compiling this report, seeks information from law enforcement agencies but also interviews members of 100,000 households annually and asks if they have been victims of a specific set of crimes during the preceding year. In general, *victimization surveys* question ordinary people, not police officers, to learn how much crime occurs.

The FBI has noted that forcible rape is one of the nation's most underreported crimes, owing primarily to the victims' feelings of fear, embarrassment, or both. Using victimization surveys, we

A large proportion of serious crimes go unreported. Only about one-half of rapes, robberies, and assaults are reported to the police. Larceny—theft without the use of force—is reported even less frequently; the reason primarily given by victims is that they do not consider it important enough.

FIGURE 5-1   Percent of Crime Reported to the Police, 1989

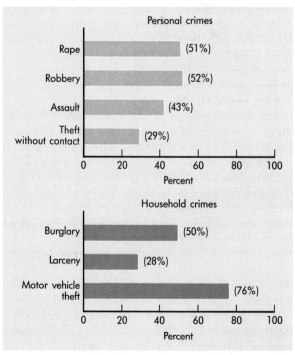

SOURCE: Department of Justice, 1991:101.

David Portnoy/Black Star

In contrast to certain popular misconceptions about crime, minorities and the poor are especially likely to become the victims of serious crimes.

can better assess the underreporting of rape. As we noted earlier, the feminist movement has spoken out strongly regarding the way in which rape reflects men's hatred of women. The media have paid increasing attention to this offense—with a recent focus on date and acquaintance rape (see Chapter 9)—and law enforcement agencies have sensitized their officers to the plight of victims.

Partly as a result, victimization surveys showed an increase in the reporting of rapes from 41 percent in 1980 to 51 percent in 1989 (although the figure had reached as high as 61 percent in 1985). Thus, victimization data show that while many rapes are still not reported, the proportion of rapes that *are* reported is somewhat higher than in the past. Moreover, the data reveal that rape victims most often fail to report this crime because they fear further reprisal from the offender or consider it too personal to bring to the attention of law enforcement officials (Department of Justice, 1991:96–97).

Unfortunately, like other crime data, victimization surveys have particular limitations. They require first that victims understand what has happened to them and also that victims disclose such information to interviewers. Fraud, income tax evasion, and blackmail are examples of crimes that are unlikely to be reported in victimization studies. Nevertheless, virtually all households have been willing to cooperate with investigators for the *National Crime Survey* (see Skogan, 1981, for a detailed analysis of victimization surveys).

Who Commits Index Crimes?

Is the United States currently experiencing a crime wave, or has there actually been an increase in law-abiding behavior? As reported in the FBI's crime index, crime rates rose steadily during the last half of the 1980s (see Table 5-2). These increases may reflect a gradual tendency of the public to report a higher proportion of crimes to the police. At the same time, observers believe that the increases in crime in the late 1980s would have been even higher but for a decline in the number of males in the high-crime age group of 14 to 24 years.

Even with its weaknesses, the *Uniform Crime Reports* offers useful insights into the profile of people convicted of index crimes. Sociologists are especially interested in how gender, age, race, and social class shape the profile of lawbreakers.

BY GENDER Most index crimes are committed by males. This is hardly surprising, since our society has traditionally encouraged boys to become "masculine"—meaning, among other things, physically strong, aggressive, and "tough." Over 87 percent of all people arrested for murder, rape, robbery, and assault in 1989 were male. Among crimes tabulated nationally, females account for the majority of those arrested only in the cases of prostitution and running away from home. However, arrests of females are growing at a somewhat faster rate than arrests of males: In 1989, of those arrested, 19 percent were female, compared with only 13 percent in 1965 (Department of Justice, 1992:218).

BY AGE Index crimes are predominantly an activity of the young. This reflects the strenuous nature of many index crimes and the visibility of juveniles, which makes them more subject to supervision and apprehension and, thus, more likely to be included in crime statistics. About 46 percent of those arrested for index crimes in the United States are under age 25. Young people are less heavily represented among white-collar criminals, since it generally requires time and skill to achieve a white-collar position (Department of Justice, 1992:223–224).

BOX 5-2

INTERNATIONAL CRIME RATES

As we have seen, it is difficult to develop crime data within the United States. Making useful cross-national comparisons is even more difficult. Nevertheless, with some care, we can offer certain preliminary conclusions about how crime rates differ around the world.

During the 1980s, violent crimes were far more common in the United States than in western Europe. Murders, rapes, and robberies were reported to police at rates four to nine times higher in the United States. Rates for other violent crimes were also higher in this country than in western Europe, but the difference in rates of property crimes was not so great. For example, in 1984, the most recent year for which comparative data are available, the burglary rate in the United States was about 20 percent higher than that of western Europe, while rates of automobile theft and larceny in the United States were twice as high.

Rates of violent crime in the United States were also higher than in Canada, Australia, and New Zealand, while rates of bur-

glary and automobile theft were comparable in these four countries. The homicide rate of the United States is fairly similar to that of the former Soviet Union, but the rate of reported rape in the United States is more than five times as high. A 1990 report by the National Center for Health Statistics compared homicide rates for young males in the United States with rates for young males in 21 other countries. The homicide rate for young males in the United States was four times higher than that of any other nation studied, and it was at least 20 times as high as the homicide rate for young males in such diverse nations as France, Poland, and Japan (Clines, 1989; Fingerhut and Kleinman, 1990).

Why are rates of violent crime so much higher in the United States? While there is no simple answer to this question, sociologist Elliot Currie (1985) has suggested that our society places greater emphasis than other societies on individual economic achievement. At the same time, many observers have noted that the culture of the United States has long tolerated, if

not condoned, many forms of violence. When coupled with sharp disparities between poor and affluent citizens, significant unemployment, and substantial alcohol and drug abuse, these factors combine to produce a climate conducive to crime. Finally, the comparatively easy availability of firearms in the United States makes crime relatively more lethal than in other countries (Fingerhut and Kleinman, 1990). The issue of gun control will be examined in the social policy section at the end of the chapter.

Trends in crime also vary from one nation to another. In the period 1980–1984, the rate of crimes reported to the police in the United States fell for each offense studied, with the exception of rape. The decreases in crime ranged from 12 percent for auto theft to 24 percent for burglary. By contrast, the average crime rates in western Europe, Canada, Australia, and New Zealand increased for all crimes except murder—for which there were insufficient data to make reliable comparisons (Department of Justice, 1989:1G).

BY RACE AND CLASS According to the *Uniform Crime Reports,* Blacks account for 29 percent of all arrests even though they represent only about 12 percent of the nation's population. This higher arrest rate is not surprising for a group that is disproportionately poor—and therefore much less able to afford private attorneys who might be able to prevent formal arrests. Even more significantly, the high arrest rate of African Americans reflects the *Uniform Crime Reports'* focus on index

crimes (mainly property crimes), which are the crimes most often committed by low-income people (Department of Justice, 1992:231).

In contrast to certain popular misconceptions about crime, minorities and the poor are especially likely to become the *victims* of serious crimes. According to victimization surveys, Black and Hispanic households are more likely to be touched by crime than are White households; members of families earning less than $7500 per year are more likely to become victims of rape, robbery, or assault than are more affluent people. Perhaps the most telling statistics are lifetime victimization rates. The likelihood that a Black male in the United States will be a homicide victim is 1 out of 30. For Black females, the likelihood of being a homicide victim is 1 out of 132; for White males, the likelihood 1 out of 179; and for White females, the likelihood 1 out of 495 (Department of Justice, 1989:13; 1990).

SOCIAL POLICY AND CRIMINAL JUSTICE
GUN CONTROL

- What are the main approaches open to policymakers who favor some form of gun control legislation?
- How do conflict theorists view the power of the National Rifle Association and other strong lobbying groups?
- In what way has social science research offered some support for gun control advocates?

Firearms have achieved an almost inevitable place in the United States. The right to bear arms stems in part from the nation's gun-ridden frontier heritage. In addition, the Second Amendment to the Constitution guarantees that the "right of the people to keep and bear arms shall not be infringed." Currently, the population of the United States has an estimated arsenal of 60 to 70 million automatic weapons and revolvers (Mackenzie, 1991:25). Clearly, owning a gun is not an act of deviance in our society. Informal gun clubs of both a primary- and secondary-group nature exist across the country, while, as we shall see, formal organizations promoting gun ownership exist on a national basis.

Many index crimes in the United States involve the use of a firearm. According to the FBI, in the year 1989, 24 percent of all reported aggravated assaults, 40 percent of reported robberies, and 66 percent of reported murders involved a firearm. More than 14,000 people died in 1991 through homicides committed with a firearm. Gunshot wounds have become the second-leading cause of death among high school–age youths. Since 1963, there have been more than 400,000 gun-related deaths in the United States, a figure which exceeds the number of the nation's troops who died in World War II (Department of Justice, 1992:17, 29, 32; Hilts, 1992).

These deaths—along with the assassinations of such public figures as President John F. Kennedy, Senator Robert Kennedy, Dr. Martin Luther King, Jr., and singer John Lennon—have forced legislators to consider gun control measures. Although handgun owners frequently insist that they need to own firearms in order to protect themselves and their loved ones from violent criminals, studies have shown that gun owners kill themselves and members of their families 43 times as often as they shoot a criminal who has entered their home. Moreover, in a society where domestic violence is all too common (see Chapter 9), use of firearms in domestic quarrels is 12 times more likely to result in death than use of other weapons (Hilts, 1992).

As noted earlier in the chapter, society's laws are not a static body of rules but reflect changing standards of right and wrong. There are four main approaches open to policymakers who favor some form of gun control legislation:

1 *Requiring registration of handguns.* This option is already in use in states across the nation. However, experts agree that registration of guns has only a limited impact in reducing crime.
2 *Requiring a waiting period before a person can purchase a gun.* As of 1991, 14 states had waiting periods ranging from 48 hours to 15 days (Police Foundation, 1992).
3 *Allowing unrestricted ownership of firearms, but toughening criminal penalties for illegal use of guns.* This approach is favored by opponents of other gun control measures, such as the National Rifle Association (NRA).
4 *Banning handguns altogether.* This could include prohibiting the manufacture, sale, and possession of such weaponry. Yet, even if Congress were to pass such a law, the enormous nationwide reserve of guns would mean that many firearms would still be available illegally, and these could, of course, contribute to many violent crimes.

Social science research offers some support for gun control advocates. According to a study comparing crime rates in Seattle and Vancouver, Canada, gun control measures may reduce a community's homicide rate. A team of researchers studied crime data in the

two cities over the period 1980 to 1986. These port cities are only 140 miles apart, and residents were found to have comparable levels of schooling, median annual incomes, and rates of unemployment. During the period under study, Seattle and Vancouver had similar rates of burglary and robbery, while Seattle's rate of assault was only slightly higher than that of Vancouver. Yet the risk of being killed with a firearm was nearly five times as high in Seattle as in Vancouver—which has more restrictive regulation of handguns (Sloan et al., 1988).

While the people of the United States have consistently favored gun control legislation in recent decades, the nation's major anti-gun control lobbying group, the National Rifle Association (NRA), has wielded impressive power in blocking or diluting such measures. Conflict theorists contend that powerful groups like the NRA can dominate the decision-making process because of their ability to mobilize resources and exert influence—even in opposition to the will of the majority. The National Rifle Association was founded in 1871 and now has 3 million members; in addition, 4 to 5 million members of state rifle associations support many of the NRA's goals. These figures compare with only 350,000 members of Handgun Control, a key organization in the gun control lobby. Whereas the NRA has a formidable war chest, Handgun Control has less than $7 million per year (Mackenzie, 1991; McLean, 1992).

Despite opposition from the NRA and its allies, some communities have passed gun control measures. For example, Morton Grove, a Chicago suburb of 24,000 people, made the mere possession of a handgun a crime beginning in 1982. Violators are subject to up to six months in jail and a $500 fine. This statute, the nation's most stringent gun control law, has had little practical impact, since town police have not launched an enforcement drive. Nevertheless, the Morton Grove law has symbolic value, as was recognized by the NRA, which unsuccessfully attempted to have the statute ruled unconstitutional. Spurred in part by the Morton Grove measure, the city of Chicago passed a law prohibiting the registration of any new handguns. Yet, although four suburbs followed suit, such legislation has not yet been passed by any other city in the United States (McRoberts and Kuczka, 1992; Time, 1982).

The crucial problem in assessing the effectiveness of any state or local gun law is that weapons can be imported from localities in which laws are more lax. Consequently, advocates of handgun control insist that stringent federal gun control legislation is essential. In recent years, congressional debate on this issue has centered on the so-called Brady bill. This bill is named after one of its chief advocates, former White House press secretary James Brady, who was shot and paralyzed in 1981 by John Hinckley during Hinckley's attempt to assassinate President Ronald Reagan.

The Brady bill would impose a compulsory seven-day waiting period on all handgun purchases to allow for background checks of those who wish to buy guns and to permit impulse purchasers to "cool off." While the NRA has predictably opposed this bill—noting that it would not have deterred Hinckley, who obtained his firearm six months before the assassination attempt—a 1991 Gallup poll revealed that 87 percent of Americans favor such a seven-day waiting period. Nevertheless, as of early 1993, Congress had not passed the Brady bill, and its future was in question (Dumas, 1992; Mackenzie, 1991:24; Prud'homme, 1991a).

In the aftermath of the Los Angeles riots in 1992—which erupted after the acquittal of four White police officers charged with the (videotaped) beating of suspect Rodney King—gun control advocates and opponents had still another way of debating this controversial issue. California has a 15-day waiting period for gun purchases, which helped reduce impulse buying during the riots. However, after the disturbances, in the first 11 days of May 1992, gun sales in the state were 50 percent higher than in the same period in 1991. Supporters of gun control argue that, had such

impulse purchases of guns occurred on a large scale *during* the riots, many more people would have died. NRA officials counter that while rioters stole thousands of weapons during the riots, law-abiding citizens were not able to buy guns to protect themselves (Eckholm, 1992).

This debate recalls a controversy that erupted in 1991, when the Chicago Housing Authority began to enforce a 20-year-old rule forbidding tenants to keep guns on the premises. This action was taken primarily because in 1990 alone, 72 murders had occurred in the city's public housing projects. While the Housing Authority's tenants, many of them African American, supported this ban on guns, the National Rifle Association did not. The NRA insisted that the Housing Authority was infringing on the tenants' constitutional right to bear arms and that this action would have disproportionate and unfair impact on the rights of Blacks living in public housing. Critics of the NRA charged that the NRA's sudden concern for the rights of African Americans was rather transparent and added that the ban on guns would disproportionately *save the lives* of Blacks (Prud'homme, 1991b).

SUMMARY

Conformity and deviance are two ways in which people respond to real pressures or to imagined pressures from others. In this chapter, we examine the relationships between conformity, deviance, and mechanisms of social control.

1 A society uses *social control* to bring about acceptance of basic norms.

2 Stanley Milgram defined *conformity* as going along with one's peers; *obedience* is defined as compliance with higher authorities in a hierarchical structure.

3 For functionalist theorists, deviance helps to define the limits of proper behavior.

4 The theory of *differential association* holds that deviance results from exposure to attitudes favorable to criminal acts.

5 An important aspect of *labeling theory* is the recognition that some people are *viewed* as deviant while others engaged in the same behavior are not.

6 The conflict perspective views laws and punishments as reflecting the interests of the powerful.

7 *Crime* represents a deviation from formal social norms administered by the state.

8 The category of *index crimes* includes murder,

rape, assault, and other serious offenses that people think of when they express concern about crime.

9 *White-collar crimes* have serious economic and social costs for the society of the United States.

10 Crime statistics are among the least reliable social data, partly because so many crimes are not reported.

11 The power of the National Rifle Association (NRA) has been a major factor in preventing the passage of strong gun control legislation.

CRITICAL THINKING QUESTIONS

1 What mechanisms of formal and informal social control are evident in your college classes and in day-to-day life and social interactions at your school?

2 Which approach to deviance do you find most persuasive: that of functionalists, conflict theorists, interactionists, or labeling theorists? Why is this approach more convincing than the other three? What are the main weaknesses of each approach?

3 As is discussed in Box 5-2, rates of violent crime are much higher in the United States than in western Europe, Canada, Australia, or New Zealand. Draw on as many of the theories discussed in the chapter as possible to explain why the United States is such a comparatively violent society.

KEY TERMS

Anomie Durkheim's term for the loss of direction felt in a society when social control of individual behavior has become ineffective. (page 117)

Anomie theory of deviance A theory developed by Robert Merton which explains deviance as an adaptation either of socially prescribed goals or of the norms governing their attainment. (117)

Conformity Going along with one's peers, individuals of a person's own status, who have no special right to direct that person's behavior. (111)

Crime A violation of criminal law for which formal penalties are applied by some governmental authority. (122)

Cultural transmission A school of criminology which argues that criminal behavior is learned through social interactions. (119)

Deviance Behavior that violates the standards of conduct or expectations of a group or society. (115)

Differential association A theory of deviance proposed by Edwin Sutherland which holds that violation of rules results from exposure to attitudes favorable to criminal acts. (119)

Formal social control Social control carried out by authorized agents, such as police officers, judges, school administrators, and employers. (114)

Index crimes The eight types of crime reported annually by the FBI in the *Uniform Crime Reports*. These are murder, rape, robbery, assault, burglary, theft, motor vehicle theft, and arson. (122)

Informal social control Social control carried out by people casually through such means as laughter, smiles, and ridicule. (114)

Labeling theory An approach to deviance popularized by Howard S. Becker which attempts to explain why certain people are *viewed* as deviants while others engaging in the same behavior are not. (120)

Law In a political sense, the body of rules made by government for society, interpreted by the courts, and backed by the power of the state. (114)

Obedience Compliance with higher authorities in a hierarchical structure. (111)

Organized crime The work of a group that regulates relations between various criminal enterprises involved in smuggling and sale of drugs, prostitution, gambling, and other activities. (123)

Professional criminal A person who pursues crime as a day-to-day occupation, developing skilled techniques and enjoying a certain degree of status among other criminals. (122)

Sanctions Penalties and rewards for conduct concerning a social norm. (111)

Social control The techniques and strategies for regulating human behavior in any society. (111)

Societal-reaction approach Another name for *labeling theory*. (120)

Victimization surveys Questionnaires or interviews used to determine whether people have been victims of crime. (127)

Victimless crimes A term used by sociologists to describe the willing exchange among adults of widely desired, but illegal, goods and services. (126)

White-collar crimes Crimes committed by affluent individuals or corporations in the course of their daily business activities. (123)

ADDITIONAL READINGS

Erikson, Kai. *Wayward Puritans: A Study in the Sociology of Deviance.* New York: Wiley, 1966. An insightful attempt to extend the functionalist approach to historical materials (in this case, to the Puritan settlers of seventeenth-century Massachusetts).

Miyazawa, Setsuo. *Policing in Japan: A Study on Making Crime.* Albany: State University of New York Press, 1992. A professor of law in Japan reviews the nation's legal environment and criminal justice system in a work translated into English.

Pasternoster, Raymond. *Capital Punishment in America.* New York: Lexington, 1991. A criminologist examines the social implications of replacing the death penalty with life sentences without parole and mandatory financial restitution.

Sanders, Clinton R. *Customizing the Body: The Art and Culture of Tattooing.* Philadelphia: Temple University Press, 1989. Sanders offers a brief history of the practice of tattooing and discusses his observation research of those who work as tattooists.

Schur, Edwin M. *Labeling Women Deviant: Gender, Stigma, and Social Control.* Philadelphia: Temple University Press, 1983. An examination of the criminal justice system in its broadest context as it applies to women. Includes coverage of sexual harassment, rape, family violence, and mental illness.

Weisburd, David, Stanton Wheeler, Elin Waring, and Nancy Bode. *Crimes of the Middle Classes: White-Collar Offenders in the Federal Courts.* New Haven, Conn.: Yale University Press, 1991. An analysis of the handling of cases of securities fraud, antitrust violation, and tax fraud.

6

STRATIFICATION IN THE UNITED STATES AND WORLDWIDE

LOOKING AHEAD

- How are societies organized to deny privileges to some members while extending them to others?
- How did Karl Marx and Max Weber contribute to our understanding of social class?
- How is the ideology of "blaming the victim" used to minimize the problems of poverty in the United States?
- How likely are people in the United

States either to move into or to rise out of poverty?
- What impact do multinational corporations have on the world's developing nations?
- Which nations have the highest and lowest levels of income inequality?
- Should there be major cuts in welfare programs in the United States?

The German air force, the *Luftwaffe,* bombed London for nine months during the Second World War. Hitler's fury was felt first by the working-class East End of London. However, the magnitude of news coverage and international concern increased noticeably when aerial bombs began to strike the upper-class West End and its landmarks. Stratification makes a difference (L. Mosley, 1971:132).

A shocking study released in 1990 by a prestigious medical journal reveals that a man in Harlem, a predominantly Black neighborhood in New York City, is less likely to live to the age of 65 than is a man in Bangladesh, one of the poorest nations of the world. Whereas 55 percent of men in Bangladesh will reach age 65, the same will be true for only 40 percent of men in Harlem. The researchers add that Harlem's high mortality rate is not unique; they have identified 53 other areas, predominantly inner-city neighborhoods with high African American or Hispanic populations, that have age-adjusted mortality rates approximately twice the national average for Whites. Again, stratification makes a difference (McCord and Freeman, 1990).

Ever since people began to speculate about the nature of human society, their attention has been drawn to the differences that can be readily observed between individuals and groups within any society. The term *social inequality* describes a condition in which members of a society have different amounts of wealth, prestige, or power. All societies are characterized by some degree of social inequality.

When a system of social inequality is based on a hierarchy of groups, sociologists refer to it as *stratification:* a structured ranking of entire groups of people that perpetuates unequal economic rewards and power in a society. These unequal rewards are evident not only in the distribution of wealth and income, but even in the distressing mortality rates of impoverished communities such as Harlem. Stratification involves the ways in which social inequalities are passed on from one generation to the next, thereby producing groups of people arranged in rank order from low to high.

Stratification is one of the most important and complex subjects of sociological investigation because of its pervasive influence on human interactions and institutions. Social inequality is an inevitable result of stratification in that certain groups of people stand higher in social rankings, control scarce resources, wield power, and receive special treatment. As we will see in this chapter, the consequences of stratification are evident in the unequal distribution of wealth and income within industrial societies. The term *income* refers to salaries and wages. By contrast, *wealth* is an inclusive term encompassing all of a person's material assets, including land and other types of property.

This chapter will focus on the unequal distribution of socially valued rewards within human societies. First, we will examine four general systems of stratification. We will pay particular attention to Karl Marx's theories of class and to Max Weber's analysis of the components of stratification. In addition, we will consider and compare functionalist and conflict theorists' explanations for the existence of stratification. We will then examine the movement of individuals up and down the social hierarchies of the United States.

Later in the chapter, we will focus on stratification around the world. We will consider the impact of colonialism and neocolonialism on social inequality, as well as world systems theory and the immense power of multinational corporations. After this macro-level examination of the disparity between rich and poor countries, we will focus on stratification *within* the nations of the world through discussions of the distribution of wealth and income and of comparative social mobility. Finally, in the social policy section, we will address the controversy over the welfare system of the United States.

UNDERSTANDING STRATIFICATION

Systems of Stratification

This section will examine four general systems of stratification—systems of slavery, castes, estates, and social classes. These should be viewed as ideal types useful for purposes of analysis. Any stratification system may include elements of more than one type. For example, during the eighteenth century, the southern states of the United States had both social classes dividing Whites and institutionalized enslavement of Blacks.

Slavery The most extreme form of legalized social inequality for individuals or groups is *slavery.* The distinguishing characteristic of this system of stratification is that slaves are owned by other people. These human beings are legally treated as property, as if they were equivalent to household pets or appliances.

Slavery has varied in the way it has been practiced. In ancient Greece, the main source of slaves consisted of captives of war and piracy. Although slave status could be inherited by succeeding gen-

erations, it was not necessarily permanent. A person's status might change depending on which city-state happened to triumph in a military conflict. In effect, all citizens had the potential of becoming slaves or of being granted freedom, depending on the circumstances of history. By contrast, in the United States and Latin America, racial and legal barriers were established to prevent the freeing of slaves. Nevertheless, as we will see in Box 6-1 (page 138), millions of people around the world continue to live as slaves.

Castes *Castes* are hereditary systems of rank, usually religiously dictated, that tend to be fixed and immobile. The caste system is generally associated with Hinduism in India and other countries. In India there are four major castes, called *varnas*. A fifth category of outcastes, referred to as *untouchables*, is considered to be so lowly and unclean as to have no place within this system of stratification. There are also many minor castes. Caste membership is established at birth, since children automatically assume the same position as their parents. Each caste is quite sharply defined, and members are expected to marry within that caste.

Caste membership generally determines one's occupation or role as a religious functionary. An example of a lower caste is the *Dons,* whose main work is the undesirable job of cremating bodies. The caste system promotes a remarkable degree of differentiation. Thus, the single caste of chauffeurs has been split into two separate subcastes: drivers of luxury cars have a higher status than drivers of economy cars.

In recent decades, industrialization and urbanization have taken their toll on India's rigid caste system. Many villagers have moved to urban areas where their low-caste status is unknown. Schools, hospitals, factories, and public transportation facilitate contacts between different castes that were previously avoided at all costs. In addition, there have been governmental efforts to reform the caste system. India's constitution, adopted in 1950, includes a provision abolishing discrimination against untouchables, who had traditionally been excluded from temples, schools, and most forms of employment. Today, untouchables constitute about 15 percent of India's population and are eligible for certain reserved governmental

BOX 6-1

SLAVERY IN THE 1990S

According to estimates, at least 300,000 (and perhaps 1 million) children work as rug weavers in northern India. They work 12 to 16 hours a day, seven days a week, 52 weeks a year, creating carpets sold in the United States and other countries. Many of these children come from Bihar, India's most impoverished state, and are sold by their parents to agents for the loom owners at the going rate of $50 to $66 for an 8-year-old boy. A 10-year-old who escaped with three friends after 18 months working in and confined to a red adobe hut recalls: "No money was paid to me. All day we had to weave, even up until midnight. We were not allowed to rest during the day. If we became slow, . . . we were beaten with sticks" (Gargan, 1992:A8).

According to the 1948 Universal Declaration of Human Rights, which is supposedly binding on all members of the United Nations: "No one shall be held in slavery or servitude; slavery and the slave trade shall be prohibited in all their forms" (Masland, 1992:30, 32). Yet Britain's Anti-Slavery International, the world's oldest human rights organization, estimates that more than 100 million people around the world are still enslaved.

The Islamic Republic of Mauritania, an Arabic state in northwest Africa, is but one country in which slavery is all too common. Although Mauritania outlawed slavery upon achieving independence in 1960 and passed a similar measure in 1980, the government never passed legislation setting punishment for slave owners and never informed most of its population that slavery had become illegal. Consequently, more than 100,000 of Mauritania's residents of African descent are still believed to be living as slaves. Dada Ould Mbarek, a 25-year-old man who lives on a date plantation, declares: "I am a slave, my whole family are slaves." When asked about the emancipation of Mauritania's slaves, he says: "I never heard of it. And what's more, I don't believe it. Slaves free? Never here" (Masland, 1992:32).

The United Nations considers any person a slave who is unable to withdraw his or her labor voluntarily from an employer. Yet, in many parts of the world, "bonded laborers" are imprisoned in virtual lifetime employment as they struggle to repay small debts. As of 1991, India alone had an estimated 5 million bonded laborers working in road-building gangs, in quarries and brickworks, on plantations and in sweatshops. In many cases, bonded laborers endure beatings and torture while repaying debts incurred by their parents or other ancestors. Indeed, the Bonded Labor Liberation Front has found workers paying off debts that are eight centuries old.

Exploitation of children is often an aspect of slavery in the 1990s. On the Indian-Bangladeshi border, girls are commonly sold at an exchange rate of six cows; these girls may later surface as child prostitutes in Calcutta or Bombay. In some parts of Asia, young females are abducted and then sold at auctions reminiscent of the southern United States during the plantation era.

While contemporary slavery may be most obvious in Third World countries, it is also present in industrialized nations of the west. Throughout Europe, guest workers and maids are employed by "masters" who hold their passports, subject them to degrading working conditions, and threaten them with deportation if they protest. In the United States, such exploitation occurs primarily in the agricultural sector of the economy. In 1992, for example, a California rancher was accused of enslaving 300 workers he had smuggled in illegally from Mexico.

SOURCES: *Economist*, 1990a; Gargan, 1992; Masland, 1992; *New York Times*, 1992b; C. Tyler, 1991.

In India's caste system, the lowest caste, referred to as untouchables, is considered to be so lowly and unclean as to have no place within this system of stratification. However, India's constitution, adopted in 1950, includes a provision abolishing discrimination against untouchables.

jobs. This situation has created resentment among people just above the untouchables in the caste system and therefore deemed ineligible for these special jobs (*Economist*, 1991:22–23).

Sociologists have also used the term *caste* to describe stratification systems that emphasize racial distinctions. The type of differential treatment given to White, "Colored," Asian, and Black people in the Republic of South Africa, and to a lesser extent to racial groups in the United States (see Chapter 7), brings to mind certain aspects of India's caste system.

Estates   A third type of stratification system, called *estates*, was associated with feudal societies during the Middle Ages. The ***estate system,*** or feudalism, required peasants to work land leased to them by nobles in exchange for military protection and other services. The basis for the system was the nobles' ownership of land, which was critical to their superior and privileged status. As in systems based on slavery and caste, inheritance of one's position largely defined the estate system. The nobles inherited their titles and property, whereas the peasants were born into a subservient position within an agrarian society.

As the estate system developed, it became more differentiated. Nobles began to achieve varying degrees of authority. By the twelfth century, a priesthood emerged in most of Europe, as did classes of merchants and artisans. For the first time, there were groups of people whose wealth did not depend on land ownership or agriculture. This economic change had profound social consequences as the estate system ended and a class system of stratification came into existence.

Social Classes   A ***class system*** is a social ranking based primarily on economic position in which achieved characteristics can influence mobility. In contrast to slavery, caste, and estate systems, the boundaries between classes are less precisely defined, and there is much greater movement from one stratum, or level, of society to another. Yet class systems maintain stable stratification hierarchies and patterns of class divisions. Consequently, like the other systems of stratification described thus far, class systems are marked by unequal distribution of wealth and power.

Income inequality is also a basic characteristic of a class system. In 1990, the median family income in the United States was $35,353. In other words, half of all families had higher incomes in that year and half had lower incomes. Yet this fact may not fully convey the income disparities in our society. In 1987, about 36,000 tax returns reported incomes in excess of $1 million. At the same time, some 6 million households reported incomes under $5000 (Bureau of the Census, 1990a:320; 1992a:49).

TABLE 6-1 Family Income in the United States, 1990

INCOME LEVEL	PERCENT DISTRIBUTION
$75,000 and over	12.3
$50,000 to $74,999	18.2
$35,000 to $49,999	20.1
$25,000 to $34,999	16.2
$15,000 to $24,999	16.4
$10,000 to $14,999	7.5
Under $10,000	9.4

SOURCE: Bureau of the Census, 1992a:49.

In 1990, half of all families in the United States earned more than $35,353 in income; half of all families earned less than that amount.

There are many ways in which sociologists conceptualize social class; a common method is to look at class in terms of income differences. Table 6-1 offers a picture of the relative number of people in the United States earning various incomes. However, such data do not provide a complete picture of class; among other limitations, they fail to consider sources of wealth apart from income.

Sociologist Daniel Rossides (1990:404–416) has conceptualized the class system of the United States using a five-class model. While the lines separating social classes in his model are not so sharp as the divisions between castes, he shows that members of the five classes differ significantly in ways other than their levels of income.

About 1 to 3 percent of the people of the United States are categorized by Rossides as upper-class, a group limited to the very wealthy. These people form intimate associations with one another in exclusive clubs and social circles. By contrast, the lower class, consisting of approximately 20 percent of the population, is disproportionately populated by Blacks, Hispanics, single mothers with dependent children, and people who cannot find regular work. This class lacks both wealth and income and is too weak politically to exercise significant power.

Both of these classes, at opposite ends of the nation's social hierarchy, reflect the importance of *ascribed status*, which is a social position "assigned" to a person without regard for the person's unique characteristics or talents. The nation's most affluent families generally inherit wealth and status, while many members of racial and ethnic minorities inherit disadvantaged status. Age and gender, as well, are ascribed statuses that influence a person's wealth and status. While privilege and deprivation are not guaranteed in the United States, those born into extreme wealth or poverty will often remain in the same class position they inherited from their parents.

Between the upper and lower classes in Rossides' model are the upper middle class, the lower middle class, and the working class. The upper middle class, numbering about 10 percent of the population, is composed of professionals such as doctors, lawyers, and architects. The lower middle class, which accounts for approximately 30 percent of the population, includes less affluent professionals (such as elementary school teachers and nurses), owners of small businesses, and a sizable number of clerical workers. Rossides describes the working class—about 40 percent of the population—as people holding regular manual or blue-collar jobs.

Social class is one of the independent or explanatory variables most frequently used by social scientists. In later chapters we will analyze the relationships between social class and divorce patterns (Chapter 9), religious behavior (Chapter 10), formal schooling (Chapter 10), and residence and housing (Chapter 12), as well as other relationships in which social class is a variable.

Perspectives on Stratification

As sociologists have examined the subject of stratification and attempted to describe and explain social inequality, they have engaged in heated debates and reached varying conclusions. No theorist stressed the significance of class for society—and for social change—more strongly than Karl Marx. Marx viewed class differentiation as the crucial determinant of social, economic, and political inequality. By contrast, Max Weber questioned Marx's emphasis on the overriding importance of the economic sector and argued that stratification should be viewed as a multidimensional phenomenon.

In his analysis of capitalism, Karl Marx argued that the bourgeoisie owns the means of production, such as factories and machinery; and that in attempting to maximize profit, the bourgeoisie exploits workers, who must exchange their labor for subsistence wages.

Karl Marx's View of Class Differentiation Sociologist Leonard Beeghley (1978:1) aptly noted that "Karl Marx was both a revolutionary and a social scientist." Marx was concerned with stratification in all types of human societies, beginning with primitive agricultural tribes and continuing into feudalism. But his main focus was on the effects of class on all aspects of nineteenth-century Europe. Marx focused on the plight of the working class and felt it imperative to strive for changes in the class structure of society.

In Marx's view, social relations during any period of history depend on who controls the primary mode of economic production. His analysis centered on how the relationships between various groups were shaped by differential access to scarce resources. Thus, under the estate system, most production was agricultural, and the land was owned by the nobility. Peasants had little choice but to work according to terms dictated by those who owned land.

Using this type of analysis, Marx examined social relations within ***capitalism***—an economic system in which the means of production are largely in private hands and the main incentive for economic activity is the accumulation of profits (Rosenberg, 1991). Marx focused on the two classes that began to emerge as the estate system declined—the bourgeoisie and the proletariat. The ***bourgeoisie,*** or capitalist class, owns the means of production, such as factories and machinery, while the ***proletariat*** is the working class. In capitalist societies, the bourgeois maximize profit in competition with other firms. In the process, they exploit workers, who must exchange their labor for subsistence wages.

According to Marx, exploitation of the proletariat will inevitably lead to the destruction of the capitalist system. But, for this to occur, the working class must first develop ***class consciousness***—a subjective awareness held by members of a class regarding their common vested interests and the need for collective political action to bring about social change. Workers must often overcome what Marx termed ***false consciousness,*** or an attitude held by members of a class that does not accurately reflect its objective position. A worker with false consciousness may feel that he or she is being treated fairly by the bourgeoisie or may adopt an individualistic viewpoint toward capitalist exploitation ("*I* am being exploited by *my* boss"). By contrast, the class-conscious worker realizes that *all* workers are being exploited by the bourgeoisie and have a common stake in revolution (Vanneman and Cannon, 1987).

For Karl Marx, the development of class consciousness is part of a collective process whereby the proletariat comes to identify the bourgeoisie as the source of its oppression. Through the guidance of revolutionary leaders, the working class will become committed to class struggle. Ultimately, the proletariat will overthrow the rule of the bourgeoisie and the government (which Marx saw as representing the interests of capitalists) and will eliminate private ownership of the means of production. In his rather utopian view, classes and oppression will cease to exist in the postrevolutionary workers' state.

Many of Marx's predictions regarding the future of capitalism have not been borne out. Marx failed to anticipate the emergence of labor unions, whose power in collective bargaining weakens the stranglehold that capitalists maintain over workers. Moreover, as contemporary conflict theorists note, he did not foresee the extent to which the political liberties present in western democracies and the relative prosperity achieved by the working and middle classes could contribute to what he called *false consciousness*. Many people have come to view themselves as individuals striving for improvement within "free" societies with substantial mobility—rather than as members of social classes facing a collective fate. Finally, Marx did not predict that Communist party rule would be established and later overthrown in the former Soviet Union and throughout eastern Europe. Despite these limitations, the Marxist approach to the study of class is useful in stressing the importance of stratification as a determinant of social behavior and the fundamental separation in many societies between two distinct groups, the rich and the poor.

Max Weber's View of Stratification Unlike Karl Marx, Max Weber insisted that no single characteristic (such as class) totally defines a person's position within the stratification system. Instead, writing in 1916, he identified three analytically distinct components of stratification: class, status, and power (Gerth and Mills, 1958).

Weber used the term *class* to refer to people who have a similar level of wealth and income. For example, certain workers in the United States provide the sole financial support for their families through jobs which pay the federal minimum wage. According to Weber's definition, these wage earners constitute a class, because they have the same economic position and fate. In this conception, Weber agreed with Marx regarding the importance of the economic dimension of stratification. Yet Weber argued that the actions of individuals and groups could not be understood solely in economic terms.

Weber used the term ***status group*** to refer to people who have the same prestige or lifestyle, independent of their class positions. In his analysis, status is a cultural dimension that involves the ranking of groups in terms of the degree of prestige they possess. An individual gains status through membership in a desirable group, such as the medical profession. Weber further suggested that status is subjectively determined by people's lifestyles and therefore can diverge from economic class standing. In our culture, a successful pickpocket may be in the same income class as a college professor. Yet the thief is widely regarded as a member of a low-status group, while the professor holds high status.

For Weber, the third major component of stratification, power, reflects a political dimension. ***Power*** is the ability to exercise one's will over others. In the United States, power stems from membership in particularly influential groups, such as corporate boards of directors, government bodies, and interest groups. As we will explore more fully in Chapter 11, conflict theorists generally agree that two major sources of power—big business and government—are closely interrelated.

In Weber's view, then, each of us has not one rank in society but three. A person's position in a stratification system reflects some combination of his or her class, status, and power. Each factor influences the other two, and in fact the rankings on these three dimensions tend to coincide. Thus, John F. Kennedy came from an extremely wealthy family, attended exclusive preparatory schools, graduated from Harvard University, and went on to become president of the United States. Like Kennedy, many people from affluent backgrounds achieve impressive status and power.

At the same time, these dimensions of stratification may operate somewhat independently in determining a person's position. A widely published poet may achieve high status while earning a relatively modest income. Successful professional athletes have little power but enjoy a relatively high position in terms of class and status. In order to understand the workings of a culture more fully, sociologists must carefully evaluate the ways in which it distributes its most valued rewards, including wealth and income, status, and power (Duberman, 1976:35–40; Gerth and Mills, 1958:180–195).

Is Stratification Universal?

Is it necessary that some members of society receive greater rewards than others? Can social life be organized without structured inequality? Do people need to feel socially and economically superior to others? These questions have been debated by social theorists (and by the "average" woman and man) for centuries. Such issues of stratification have also been of deep concern to political activists. Utopian socialists, religious minorities, and members of recent countercultures have all attempted to establish communities which, to some extent or other, would abolish inequality in social relationships.

Social science research has found that inequality exists in all societies—even the simplest. For example, when anthropologist Gunnar Landtman (1968, original edition 1938) studied the Kiwai Papuans of New Guinea, he initially noticed little differentiation among them. Every man in the village did the same work and lived in similar housing. However, on closer inspection, Landtman observed that certain Papuans—the men who were warriors, harpooners, and sorcerers—were described as "a little more high" than others. By contrast, villagers who were female, unemployed, or unmarried were considered "down a little bit" and were barred from owning land.

Stratification is universal in that all societies maintain some form of differentiation among members. Depending on its values, a society may assign people to distinctive ranks based on their religious knowledge, skill in hunting, beauty, trading expertise, or ability to provide health care. But why has such inequality developed in human societies? How much differentiation among people, if any, is actually essential?

Functionalist and conflict sociologists offer contrasting explanations for the existence and necessity of social stratification. Functionalists maintain that a differential system of rewards and punishments is necessary for the efficient operation of society. Conflict theorists argue that competition for scarce resources results in significant political, economic, and social inequality.

Fashion models are an example of a group that enjoys a relatively high position in terms of class and status but has little power.

The Functionalist Answer Would people go to school for many years to become physicians if they could make as much money and gain as much respect working as street cleaners? Functionalists reply in the negative, which is partly why they believe that a stratified society is universal.

In the view of Kingsley Davis and Wilbert Moore (1945), society must distribute its members among a variety of social positions. It must not only make sure that these positions are filled but also see that they are staffed by people with the appropriate talents and abilities. Thus, rewards, including money and prestige, are based on the importance of a position and the relative scarcity of qualified personnel. Yet this assessment often devalues work performed by certain segments of society, such as women's work as homemakers or in occupations traditionally filled by women.

Davis and Moore argue that stratification is universal and that social inequality is necessary so that people will be motivated to fill functionally important positions. One critique of this functionalist explanation of stratification holds that unequal rewards are not the only means of encouraging people to fill critical positions and occupations. Personal pleasure, intrinsic satisfaction, and value orientations motivate people to enter particular careers. Functionalists agree but note that society must use *some* type of rewards to motivate people to enter unpleasant or dangerous jobs, as well as jobs that require a long training period. However, this response does not justify stratification systems such as slave or caste societies in which status is largely inherited. Similarly, it is difficult to explain the high salaries our society offers to professional athletes or entertainers on the basis of importance of these jobs to the survival of society (R. Collins, 1975; Kerbo, 1991:129–134; Tumin, 1953; 1985:16–17).

Even if stratification is inevitable, the functionalist explanation for differential rewards does not explain the wide disparity between the rich and the poor. Critics of the functionalist approach point out that the richest 10 percent of households account for 21 percent of the nation's income in Sweden, 25 percent in the United States, and 30 percent in Switzerland. In their view, the level of income inequality found in contemporary industrial societies cannot be defended—even though these societies have a legitimate need to fill certain key occupations (World Bank, 1992:277).

The Conflict Response As was noted in Chapter 1, the intellectual tradition at the heart of conflict theory begins principally with the writings of Karl Marx. Marx viewed history as a continuous struggle between the oppressors and the oppressed which would ultimately culminate in an egalitarian, classless society. In terms of stratification, he argued that the dominant class under capitalism—the bourgeoisie—manipulated the economic and political systems in order to maintain control over the exploited proletariat. Marx did not believe that stratification was inevitable, but he did see inequality and oppression as inherent in capitalism (E. Wright et al., 1982).

Contemporary conflict theorists believe that human beings are prone to conflict over such scarce resources as wealth, status, and power. However, where Marx focused primarily on class conflict, more recent theorists have extended this analysis to include conflicts based on gender, race, age, and other dimensions. Sociologist Ralf Dahrendorf, formerly president of the respected London School of Economics and now at Oxford University, is one of the most influential contributors to the conflict approach.

Dahrendorf (1959) has argued that while Marx's analysis of capitalist society was basically correct, it must be modified if it is to be applied to *modern* capitalist societies. For Dahrendorf, social classes are groups of people who share common interests resulting from authority relationships. In identifying the most powerful groups in society, he includes not only the bourgeoisie—the owners of the means of production—but also the managers of industry, legislators, the judiciary, heads of the government bureaucracy, and others. In one respect, Dahrendorf has merged Marx's emphasis on class conflict with Weber's recognition that power is an important element of stratification (Cuff and Payne, 1979:81–84).

Conflict theorists, including Dahrendorf, contend that the powerful of today, like the bourgeois of Marx's time, want society to run smoothly so that they can enjoy their privileged positions. The status quo is satisfactory to those with wealth, status, and power; thus, they have a clear interest in preventing, minimizing, or at least controlling societal conflict.

The powerful, such as leaders of government, use limited social reforms to buy off the oppressed and reduce the danger of challenges to their dominance. For example, minimum wage laws and unemployment compensation unquestionably give some valuable assistance to needy men and women in the United States. Yet these reforms also have the effect of pacifying those who might otherwise become disgruntled and rebellious. Of course, in the view of conflict theorists, such maneuvers can never eliminate conflict, since workers will continue to demand equality and the powerful will not give up their control of society.

Conflict theorists see stratification as a major source of societal tension and conflict. They do not agree with Davis and Moore that stratification is functional for a society or that it serves as a source of stability. Rather, conflict sociologists argue that stratification will inevitably lead to instability and to social change (R. Collins, 1975:62; L. Coser, 1977:580–581).

We now return to the question posed earlier—"Is stratification universal?"—and consider the sociological response. Some form of differentiation is found in every culture, including the advanced industrial societies of our time. As sociologist Gerhard Lenski, Jr. (1966; Lenski et al., 1991), has suggested, as a society advances in terms of technology, it becomes capable of producing a considerable surplus of goods—more than enough to attract members to valued occupations. The allocation of these surplus goods and services—controlled by those with wealth, status, and power—reinforces the social inequality which accompanies stratification systems. While this reward system may once have served the overall purposes of society, as functionalists contend, the same cannot be said for present disparities separating the "haves" of current societies from the "have-nots."

STRATIFICATION BY SOCIAL CLASS IN THE UNITED STATES

Measuring Social Class

In everyday life, people in the United States are continually judging relative amounts of wealth and income by assessing the cars people drive, the neighborhoods in which they live, the clothing they wear, and so forth. Yet it is not so easy to locate an individual within our social hierarchies as it would be in caste or estate systems of stratification, where placement is determined by religious dogma or legal documents. In order to determine someone's class position, sociologists generally rely on the objective method.

The *objective method* of measuring social class views class largely as a statistical category. Individuals are assigned to social classes on the basis of criteria such as occupation, education, income, and residence. The key to the objective method is that the *researcher,* rather than the person being classified, makes a determination about the individual's class position.

The first step in using this method is to decide what indicators or causal factors will be measured objectively, whether wealth, income, education, or occupation. The prestige ranking of occupations has proved to be a useful indicator in determining a person's class position. The term *prestige* refers to the respect and admiration with which an occupation is regarded by society. "My daughter, the physicist" has a very different connotation from "my daughter, the waitress." Prestige is independent of the particular individual who occupies a job, a characteristic which distinguishes it from esteem. *Esteem* refers to the reputation that a specific person has within an occupation. Therefore, one can say that the position of president of the United States has high prestige, even though it has been occupied by people with varying degrees of esteem.

Table 6-2 (page 146) shows the results of an effort to assign prestige to a number of well-known occupations. In a series of national surveys from 1972 to 1991, sociologists drawing on earlier survey responses assigned prestige rankings to about 500 occupations, ranging from surgeon to electrician to panhandler. The highest possible prestige score was 100; the lowest was 0. As the data indicate, surgeon, lawyer, and college professor were among the most highly regarded occupations. Sociologists have used such data to assign prestige rankings to virtually all jobs and have found a stability in rankings from 1925 through 1991. Similar studies in other countries have also developed useful prestige rankings of occupations (Hodge and Rossi, 1964; Lin and Xie, 1988; NORC, 1991; Treiman, 1977).

Sociologists have become increasingly aware that studies of social class tend to neglect the occupations and incomes of women as determinants of social rank. In an exhaustive study of 589 occupations, sociologists Mary Powers and Joan Holmberg (1978) examined the impact of women's participation in the paid labor force on occupational status. Since women tend to dominate the relatively low-paying occupations, such as bookkeepers and secretaries, their participation in the work force leads to a general upgrading of the status of most male-dominated occupations.

The objective method of measuring social class has traditionally focused on the occupation and education of the husband in measuring the class

TABLE 6-2   Prestige Ranking of Occupations

OCCUPATION	SCORE	OCCUPATION	SCORE
Surgeon	88	Nursery school teacher	55
Lawyer	75	Librarian	54
College professor	74	Electrician	51
Airline pilot	73	Funeral director	49
Dentist	72	Cattle rancher	48
Clergy	69	Mail carrier	47
Pharmacist	68	Insurance agent	46
Registered nurse	67	Secretary	46
High school teacher	66	Auto mechanic	40
Professional athlete	65	Salesclerk	36
Accountant	65	Baker	35
Public grade school teacher	64	Bus driver	32
Banker	63	Waiter and waitress	29
Police officer	61	Garbage collector	28
Sociologist	61	Janitor	22
Actor	60	Street corner drug dealer	13
Painter and sculptor	56	Panhandler	11

In a national survey conducted in 1989, occupations were ranked in terms of prestige. The highest possible score was 100, the lowest 0. Some of the results are presented above.

SOURCES: Nakao and Treas, 1990a, 1990b; see also NORC, 1991:827–838.

position of two-income families. With more than half of all married women now working outside the home (see Chapter 8), this represents a serious omission. Furthermore, how is class or status to be judged in dual-career families—by the occupation regarded as having greater prestige, the average, or some other combination of the two occupations?

Drawing by Victor; © 1981 The New Yorker Magazine, Inc.

"And just why do we always call my *income the second income?*"

Studies of social class tend to ignore the occupations and incomes of wives and focus on the incomes of husbands in determining social rank or measuring the class position of two-income families.

Research in the area of women and social class is just beginning, because until recently few sociologists had raised such methodological questions. One study found that over the last 20 years married men have typically used their own occupations to define their class positions—whether or not their wives worked outside the home. By contrast, there has been a noticeable change in how married women define their class positions. Whereas in the 1970s married women tended to attach more weight to their husbands' occupations than to their own in defining their class positions, by the 1980s they began to attach equal weight to their own occupations and those of their husbands (N. Davis and Robinson, 1988).

Consequences of Social Class

Wealth and Income   By all measures, income in the United States is distributed unevenly. Nobel prize–winning economist Paul Samuelson describes the situation as follows: "If we made an income pyramid out of a child's blocks, with each layer portraying $500 of income, the peak would be far higher than Mount Everest, but most people would be within a few feet of the ground" (Samuelson and Nordhaus, 1992:355).

Samuelson's analogy is certainly supported by recent data on incomes. In 1990, the top fifth (or 20 percent) of the nation—earning $61,490 or more—accounted for almost 47 percent of total wages and salaries. By contrast, the bottom fifth of the population—earning $13,264 or less—accounted for less than 4 percent of income (Bureau of the Census, 1991b:58).

As Figure 6-1 shows, there has been modest redistribution of income in the United States over the past 60 years. From 1929 through 1970, the government's economic and tax policies seemed to shift income somewhat to the poor. However, in the last 20 years—especially during the 1980s—federal budgetary policies favored the affluent. Moreover, while the salaries of highly skilled workers and professionals have continued to rise, the wages of less skilled workers have *decreased* when controlled for inflation.

As a result, the income gap between the richest and poorest groups in the United States has increased over the last two decades. According to data compiled by the Congressional Budget Office, the wealthiest 1 percent of families in the United States were the main beneficiaries of the prosperity of the late 1970s and 1980s. In the period 1977 to 1989, about 60 percent of the growth in after-tax income among all families in the na-

FIGURE 6-1   Distribution of Income in the United States, 1929 and 1990

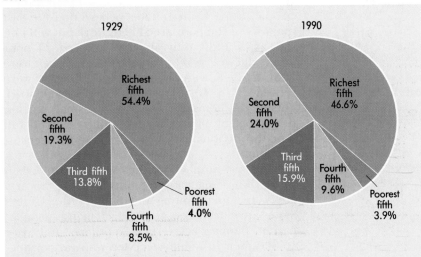

NOTE: 1929 data for the bottom two-fifths are an estimate by the authors based on data from Bureau of the Census, 1975.
SOURCES: Bureau of the Census, 1975:301; 1991b:6.

In the United States from 1929 to 1970, there was some redistribution of income to the less affluent. But over the last 20 years this trend has reversed, with the distribution of income shifting in favor of the most affluent.

FIGURE 6-2 Comparison of Distribution of Income and Wealth in the United States

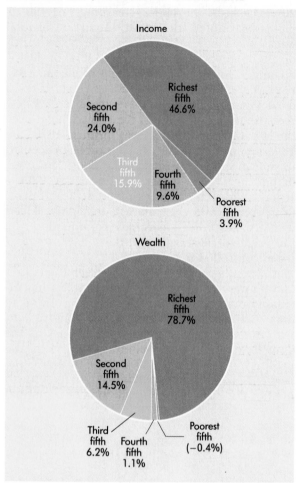

SOURCES: Income data are for 1990 and are from Bureau of the Census, 1991b:6. Data on wealth are for 1983 and are from Kerbo, 1991:40; and J. Smith, 1986.

As these data illustrate, wealth in the United States is distributed much less evenly than income. The richest 20 percent of the population hold close to 80 percent of all wealth. By contrast, the poorest fifth are, as a group, in debt to an amount equivalent to −0.4 percent of the nation's wealth.

tion went to the wealthiest 660,000 families. The average before-tax income of these families rose from $315,000 to $560,000—a staggering 77 percent increase. By contrast, in this same period the bottom 40 percent of families experienced actual declines in income (Nasar, 1992; see also Mishel and Frankel, 1991).

As concentrated as income is in the United States, wealth is much more unevenly distributed. As Figure 6-2 shows, in 1983 (the latest year for which such data are available) the richest fifth of the population held almost 80 percent of the wealth. A study by the Bureau of the Census (1986:10) found that more than 1.6 million households had assets over $500,000, while 9.6 million households were in debt (had a negative net worth).

Poverty   What are the consequences of this uneven distribution of wealth and income? Approximately one out of every nine people in the United States lives below the poverty line established by the federal government. Indeed, in 1991, the number of people living in poverty rose by 2.1 million, to a total of 35.7 million. This represented the highest number of poor people in the United States since 1964, when President Lyndon Johnson declared a national "war on poverty" (Pear, 1992:A1).

However, the category of the "poor" defies any simple definition—and counters common stereotypes about "poor people." For example, many people in the United States believe that the vast majority of the poor are able to work but will not. Yet, as of 1989, only about 60 percent of poor adults did not work, primarily because they were ill or disabled, were maintaining a home, or were retired. Fully 40 percent of the poor did work outside the home, although only a small portion (9 percent of all low-income adults) worked full time throughout the year (Bureau of the Census, 1990b:65).

A sizable number of the poor live in urban slums, but a majority live outside these poverty areas. Included among the poor of the United States are elderly people, children living in single-parent families with their mothers, and over 10,000 men in military service who cannot adequately support their large families. Table 6-3 on the opposite page provides additional statistical information regarding low-income people in the United States.

Since World War II, an increasing proportion of the nation's poor have been women—many of whom are divorced or never-married mothers. Currently, two out of three adults classified as "poor" by the federal government are women. In 1959, female-headed households accounted for 26 percent of the nation's poor; by 1990, that figure had risen to 53 percent (Bureau of the Census, 1991b). This alarming trend, known as the *feminization of poverty*, is evident not only in the United States but also around the world.

About half of all women in the United States living in poverty are in "transition," coping with an economic crisis caused by the departure, disability, or death of a husband. The other half tend to be economically dependent either on the welfare system or on friends and relatives living nearby. A key factor in the feminization of poverty has been the increase in families with women as single heads of the household (see Chapter 9). In the view of conflict theorists, the higher rates of poverty among women can be traced to three distinct causes: the difficulty in finding affordable child care (see Chapter 3), sex discrimination on the job (see Chapter 8), and sexual harassment (see Chapter 11).

THE UNDERCLASS In 1990, 43 percent of poor people in the United States were living in central cities. These urban residents have the greatest visibility among low-income people and are the focus of most governmental efforts to alleviate poverty. According to many observers, the plight of the urban poor is growing worse, owing to the devastating interplay of inadequate education and limited employment prospects. Traditional employment opportunities in the industrial sector are largely closed to the unskilled poor. For low-income urban residents who are Black and Hispanic, these problems have been heightened by past and present discrimination.

Sociologist William Julius Wilson (1980, 1987a, 1987b, 1988:15, 1989, 1991) and other social scientists have used the term *underclass* to describe long-term poor people who lack training and skills. While estimates vary depending on the definition, in 1990 the underclass comprised more than 3 million adults in the United States, not including the elderly. In central cities, about 49 percent of the underclass are African American, 29 percent are Hispanic, 17 percent are White, and 5 percent are "Other" (W. O'Hare and Curry-White, 1992).

Conflict theorists, among others, have expressed alarm at the portion of the nation's popu-

TABLE 6-3 Who Are the Poor in the United States?

GROUP	PERCENT OF THE POPULATION OF THE UNITED STATES	PERCENT OF THE POOR OF THE UNITED STATES
Under 15 years old	22	35
15 to 65 years old	66	54
Over 65 years old	12	11
Whites	84	67
Blacks	12	29
Hispanics	8	18
People in families with male heads of households	84	47
People in families with female heads of households	16	53

NOTE: Percentages in the racial and ethnic category exceed 100 percent, since Hispanic people can be either Black or White.
SOURCE: Adapted from Bureau of the Census, 1991c:4, 15.

In 1991, the poverty level for a family of four was a combined income of $13,924 or less.

lation living on this lower rung of the stratification hierarchy and at society's reluctance to address the lack of economic opportunities for these people. Often portraits of the underclass seem to "blame the victims" for their own plight (this phenomenon will be explored in Box 6-2 later in the chapter; see page 152). Yet Wilson and other scholars insist that the core of the problem is not the antisocial behavior of some members of the underclass, but rather structural factors (such as the loss of manufacturing jobs in cities) which have had a devastating impact on low-income neighborhoods. Moreover, members of the underclass experience social isolation; they lack contact and sustained interaction with individuals and institutions that are part of the legitimate and profit-making economy. In the view of many scholars concerned about the problems of the underclass, it is the economy, not the poor, that needs reforming (Kornblum, 1991; Morris, 1989; Schaefer, 1993:72–75; S. Wright, 1993).

Poverty, of course, is not a new phenomenon. Yet the concept of the underclass describes a chilling development: individuals and families, whether employed or unemployed, who are beyond the reach of any safety net provided by existing social programs. In addition, membership in the underclass is not an intermittent condition but a long-term attribute. The underclass is understandably alienated from the larger society and engages sporadically in illegal behavior. Not surprisingly, these illegal acts hardly encourage society to genuinely address the long-term problems of the underclass.

STUDYING POVERTY The efforts of sociologists and other social scientists to better understand poverty are complicated by the difficulty of developing a satisfactory operational definition of poverty. This problem is evident even in government programs which conceive of poverty in either absolute or relative terms. *Absolute poverty* refers to a minimum level of subsistence below which families should not be expected to exist. This standard theoretically remains unchanged from year to year. Policies concerning minimum wages, housing standards, or school lunch programs for the poor imply a need to bring citizens up to some predetermined level of existence.

By contrast, *relative poverty* is a floating standard of deprivation by which people at the bottom of a society, whatever their lifestyles, are judged to be disadvantaged in comparison with the nation as a whole. Most of our country's current social programs view poverty in relative terms. Therefore, even if the poor of the 1990s are better off in absolute terms than the poor of the 1930s or 1960s, they are still seen as deserving special assistance from government.

One commonly used measure of relative poverty is the federal government's *poverty line,* which serves as an official definition of which people are poor. In 1991, for example, any family of four with a combined income of $13,924 or less fell below the poverty line. This definition determines which individuals and families will be eligible for certain governmental benefits.

Analyses of the poor reveal that they are not a static social class. Instead, the composition of the poor changes continually, with some individuals and families moving above the poverty level after a year or two, while others slip below the level. Depending on definitions, a significant segment of people in the United States are "persistently poor." At any given time, some 40 to 60 percent of the poor can be expected to remain in a state of poverty for at least eight consecutive years. African Americans and Hispanics are more likely than Whites to be found among the persistent poor (Bureau of the Census, 1990c; Ruggles, 1991).

Why does such pervasive poverty continue in a nation of vast wealth? Herbert Gans (1991:263–270) has applied functionalist analysis to the existence of poverty and has identified various social, economic, and political functions that the poor perform for society, among them the following:

- The presence of poor people means that society's "dirty work"—physically dirty or dangerous, dead-end and underpaid, undignified and menial jobs—will be performed at low cost.
- Poverty creates jobs for occupations and professions which "service" the poor. It creates both legal employment (public health experts, welfare caseworkers) and illegal jobs (drug dealers, numbers "runners").
- The identification and punishment of the poor as deviants uphold the legitimacy of conven-

tional social norms regarding hard work, thrift, and honesty (see Chapter 5).

- The poor serve as a measuring rod for status comparisons. Within a relatively hierarchical society, they guarantee the higher status of more affluent people. Indeed, as is described in Box 6-2, the affluent may justify inequality (and gain a measure of satisfaction) by "blaming the victims" of poverty for their disadvantaged conditions.

- Because of their lack of political power, the poor often absorb the costs of social change. Under the policy of deinstitutionalization, released mental patients have been "dumped" primarily into low-income communities and neighborhoods. Urban renewal projects to restore central cities have typically pushed out the poor in the name of "progress."

Consequently, in Gans's view, poverty and the poor actually satisfy positive functions for many nonpoor groups in the United States.

Unemployment As we have seen in our discussion of poverty, a substantial portion of poor people experience intermittent or long-term unemployment. As sociological research points out, unemployment affects the entire society and has far-reaching consequences on both the macro and the micro levels. On the societal, or macro, level, unemployment leads to a reduced demand for goods and services. Sales by retail firms and other businesses are affected adversely, and this can lead to further layoffs. Wage earners must contribute to unemployment insurance and welfare programs that assist those without jobs.

From the micro level, the unemployed person and his or her family must adjust to a loss of spending power. Both marital happiness and family cohesion may suffer as a result. In addition, there is an accompanying loss of self-image and social status, since our society and others view unemployment as a kind of personal failure. According to one estimate, a 1.4 percent increase in the unemployment rate of the United States is associated with a 5.7 percent increase in suicide, a 4.7 percent increase in admissions to state mental hospitals, and an 8.0 percent increase in homicides (Tipps and Gordon, 1983).

The unemployment rate of the United States is traditionally represented as a percentage, such as about 7 percent in 1992. Such statistics can minimize the problem; it is more striking to realize that in 1992, over 8 million people across the nation were unemployed at any one time. But even this latter figure may disguise the severity of unemployment. The federal government's Bureau of Labor Statistics regards as unemployed only those people *actively* seeking employment. Thus, in order to be counted as unemployed, a person must not hold a full-time job, must be registered with a government unemployment agency, and must be engaged in writing job applications and seeking interviews. Quite simply, the official unemployment rate leaves out millions of people who are effectively unemployed but have given up and are not seeking work.

The burden of unemployment in the United States is unevenly distributed throughout the nation's labor force. Women are about 20 percent more likely than men to be unemployed and are less likely to be rehired following layoffs. Racial minorities and teenagers have unemployment rates twice that of adult White males. The unemployment rate for Black teenagers in urban areas is about 43 percent, well above the rate for the nation as a whole during the Depression of the 1930s, which was 25 percent. Again, such statistics do not include those who have dropped out of the system—who are not at school, not at work, and not looking for a job. If we add discouraged job seekers to the official statistics, the rate of unemployment and underemployment for Black teenagers in central-city areas climbs to 90 percent (Gordus and Yamakawa, 1988; Swinton, 1987).

Stratification and Life Chances Poverty and unemployment unquestionably have a marked influence on people's lives. Max Weber saw class as closely related to people's *life chances*—that is, their opportunities to provide themselves with material goods, positive living conditions, and favorable life experiences (Gerth and Mills, 1958:181). Life chances are reflected in such measures as housing, education, and health. Occupying a higher position in a society will improve one's life chances and bring greater access to social rewards. By contrast, people in the lower social classes are forced to devote a larger propor-

BOX 6-2

BLAMING THE VICTIM

*P*sychologist William Ryan struck a vulnerable chord in 1971 when he coined the phrase "blaming the victim" to describe how some people essentially justify inequality by finding defects in the victims rather than examining the social and economic factors that contribute to poverty, racism, and other national problems. In the following selection, Ryan (1976:3–8) explains the generic process of "blaming the victim" and notes that this process is aimed not only at disadvantaged people in the United States but also at residents of the world's less developed nations.

Courtesy William Ryan, photo by Carillo

William Ryan.

. . . Consider some victims. One is the miseducated child in the slum school. He is blamed for his own miseducation. He is said to contain within himself the causes of his inability to read and write well. The shorthand phrase is "cultural deprivation," which, to those in the know, conveys what they allege to be inside information: that the poor child carries a scanty pack of intellectual baggage as he enters school. He doesn't know about books and magazines, they say. . . . They say if he talks at all . . . he certainly doesn't talk correctly. . . . In a word, he is "disadvantaged" and "socially deprived," they say, and this, of course, accounts for his failure (*his* failure, they say) to learn much in school. . . .

What is the culturally deprived child *doing* in the school? What is wrong with the victim? In pursu-

ing this logic, no one remembers to ask questions about the collapsing buildings and torn textbooks; the frightened, insensitive teachers; the six additional desks in the room; the blustering, frightened principals; the relentless segregation; the callous administrator; the irrelevant curriculum; the bigoted or cowardly members of the school board; the insulting history book; the stingy taxpayers; the fairy-tale readers; or the self-serving faculty of the local teachers' college. We are encouraged to confine our attention to the child and to dwell on all his alleged defects. Cultural deprivation becomes an omnibus explanation for the educational disaster area known as the inner-city school. This is Blaming the Victim. . . .

The generic process of Blaming the Victim is applied to almost every American problem. The miserable health care of the poor is explained away on the grounds that the victim has poor motivation and lacks health information. The problems of slum housing are traced to the characteristics of tenants who are labeled as "Southern rural migrants" not yet "acculturated" to life in the big city. . . . It would be possible for me to venture into other areas—one finds a perfect example in literature about the underdeveloped countries of the Third World, in which the lack of prosperity and technological progress is attributed to some aspect of the national character of the people, such as lack of "achievement motivation." . . .

Blaming the Victim is, of course, quite different from old-fashioned conservative ideologies. . . . The new ideology attributes defect and inadequacy to the malignant nature of poverty, injustice, slum life, and racial difficulties. The stigma that marks the victim and accounts for his victimization is an acquired stigma, a stigma of social, rather than genetic, origin. But the stigma, the defect, the fatal difference . . . is still located *within* the victim, inside his skin. . . . It is a brilliant ideology for justifying a perverse form of social action designed to change, not society, as one might expect, but rather society's victim.

tion of their limited resources to the necessities of life.

The affluent and powerful not only have more material possessions than others; they also benefit in many nonmaterial ways. For example, as is shown in Figure 6-3, children from higher-income families in the United States are much more likely to attend college than are children from less affluent families. In 1990, 79 percent of all unmarried high school graduates ages 18 to 24 from families earning $60,388 and over were enrolled in or had attended college. For families earning less than $20,436, the comparable figure was 44 percent. This gap in educational opportu-

nity has remained significant and fairly constant over the last 20 years (Mortenson, 1992).

As is true of educational opportunities, a person's health is affected in important ways by his or her class position (see Chapter 12). The probability of a child's dying during the first year of life is approximately 70 percent higher in poor families than for the middle class. This higher infant mortality rate results in part from the inadequate nutrition received by low-income expectant mothers. Even when they survive infancy, the poor are more likely than the affluent to suffer from serious, chronic illnesses such as arthritis, bronchitis, diabetes, and heart disease. In addition, the poor

FIGURE 6-3 College Participation Rates by Family Income, 1970 to 1990

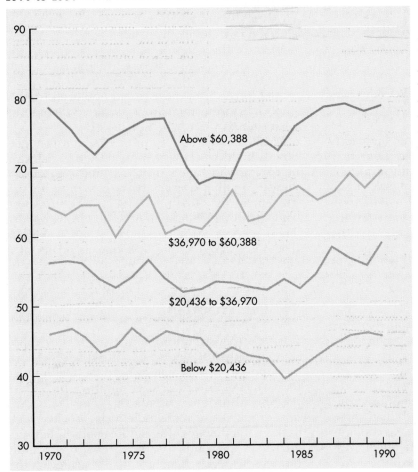

SOURCE: Mortenson, 1992.

This figure shows the college participation rates of unmarried 18- to 24-year-old high school graduates over the last 20 years. Despite the existence of financial aid programs to assist the college-bound from lower-income backgrounds, a poor young person in the United States continues to be much less likely to go to college than a more affluent young person.

AP/Wide World Photos

Although Blacks and Hispanics together constitute only 20 percent of all young adults in the United States, about 36 percent of the nation's military personnel in the Persian Gulf were Black or Hispanic.

are less likely to be protected from the high costs of illness by private health insurance. They may be employed in jobs in which health insurance is not a fringe benefit; may not be employed full time and, thus, may be ineligible for employee health benefits; or may simply be unable to afford the premiums. Moreover, the occupations of the nation's lower classes tend to be more dangerous than those of more affluent citizens (Erickson and Bjerkedal, 1982; Kessler et al., 1989; Paneth, 1982; Szymanski, 1983:301–314).

Research shows that the lower classes are more vulnerable to environmental pollution than the affluent; this is the case not only where the lower classes work but also where they live. Sociologist Timothy Maher (1991) studied this issue by examining the locations of all hazardous waste sites identified by the Indiana Department of Environmental Management. Maher found that these sites are especially likely to be found near communities with many working-class residents or with substantial Black populations. Indeed, the more hazardous the site is, the more likely it is that the nearby community will be less affluent and will

have many residents from racial and ethnic minorities.

Even in the armed forces, social class standing in civilian life can be crucial to determining a person's fortunes. Members of lower classes were more likely to be drafted when the military draft was in operation. Once in the service, people from low- and moderate-income backgrounds are more likely to die in combat. Research indicates that during the wars in Korea and Vietnam, soldiers from the lower social classes suffered a higher casualty rate than the more affluent, who tended to be officers (Peterson, 1987; J. Willis, 1975; Zeitlin et al., 1973:328).

Differences in life chances based on race and ethnicity were evident in 1991 during the war in the Persian Gulf. Only two members of Congress (one of whom was Hispanic) had children serving in Operation Desert Storm. Although Blacks and Hispanics together constitute only 20 percent of all young adults in the United States, about 36 percent of the nation's military personnel in the Gulf were Black or Hispanic. In some respects, these data reflect the irony that the all-volunteer armed forces offer more career options for many minority citizens than are available to them in civilian life (Howlett and Keen, 1991).

Wealth, status, and power may not ensure happiness, but they certainly provide additional ways of coping with one's problems and disappointments. For this reason, the opportunity for advancement is of special significance to those who are on the bottom of society looking up. These people want the rewards and privileges that are granted to high-ranking members of a culture.

SOCIAL MOBILITY

It is clear that stratification matters, that class position quietly influences one's life chances. It can be important for people to have the feeling that they can hold on to or even improve their class position. But how significant—how frequent, how dramatic—is mobility in a class society such as the United States? Ronald Reagan's father was a barber, and Jimmy Carter began as a peanut farmer, yet each man eventually achieved the most powerful and prestigious position in our country.

The rise of a child from a modest background to the presidency—or to some other position of great prestige, power, or financial reward—is an example of social mobility. The term *social mobility* refers to movement of individuals or groups from one position of a society's stratification system to another.

Open versus Closed Class Systems

Sociologists use the terms *open class system* and *closed class system* to distinguish between two ideal types of class system in terms of social mobility. An *open system* implies that the position of each individual is influenced by achieved status. *Achieved status,* as we saw in Chapter 4, is a social position attained by a person largely through his or her own effort. In an open class system, competition between members of society is encouraged. The United States is moving toward this ideal type as it attempts to reduce barriers to mobility faced by women, racial and ethnic minorities, and people born in lower social classes.

At the other extreme is the *closed system,* in which there is little or no possibility of individual social mobility. The slavery and caste systems of stratification, and to a lesser extent the estate system, are examples of closed systems. In such societies, social placement is based on ascribed characteristics, such as race or family background, which cannot easily be changed. As noted earlier, *ascribed status* is a social position "assigned" to a person by society without regard for the person's unique characteristics or talents.

Types of Social Mobility

Following the lead of Pitirim Sorokin (1959, original edition 1927), contemporary sociologists distinguish between horizontal and vertical mobility. *Horizontal mobility* refers to the movement of a person from one social position to another of the same rank. If we use the prestige rankings presented earlier in Table 6-2, a professional athlete who becomes an accountant would be experiencing horizontal mobility. Each occupation has the same prestige ranking: 65 on a scale ranging from a low of 0 to a high of 100. If the accountant later leaves a Los Angeles firm for a similar job at an accounting firm in New York, he or she would once again experience horizontal mobility.

Most sociological analysis, however, focuses on vertical rather than horizontal mobility. *Vertical mobility* refers to the movement of a person from one social position to another of a different rank. A professional athlete who becomes a lawyer (prestige ranking of 75) would experience vertical mobility. So, too, would an athlete who becomes a sales clerk (prestige ranking of 36). Thus, vertical mobility can involve moving upward or downward in a society's stratification system.

One way of examining vertical social mobility is to contrast intergenerational and intragenerational mobility. *Intergenerational mobility* involves changes in the social position of children relative to their parents. Thus, a plumber whose father was a physician provides an example of downward intergenerational mobility. A film star whose parents were both factory workers illustrates upward intergenerational mobility.

Intragenerational mobility involves changes in a person's social position within his or her adult life. A woman who enters the paid labor force as a teacher's aide and eventually becomes superintendent of the school district has experienced upward intragenerational mobility. A man who becomes a taxicab driver after his accounting firm goes bankrupt has undergone downward intragenerational mobility.

Social Mobility in the United States

The belief in upward mobility is an important aspect of our society. Does this mean that the United States is indeed the land of opportunity? Not if the phrase "land of opportunity" implies that such ascriptive characteristics as race, gender, and family background have ceased to be significant in determining one's future prospects.

Two sociological studies conducted a decade apart offer insight into the degree of mobility in the nation's occupational structure. The highly regarded work of Peter Blau and Otis Duncan (1967) was followed by the research of David Featherman and Robert Hauser (1978), two of Duncan's students, who replicated the earlier study. Taken together, these investigations led to several noteworthy conclusions. First, occupational mobility (which can be intergenerational or intragenerational) has been common among males. Approximately 60 to 70 percent of sons

Larry Kolvoord/The Image Works

Shown is Sharon Howell, who started a baby shoe business in her home in Austin, Texas. On the whole, self-employment as shopkeepers, entrepreneurs, independent professionals, and the like—an important road to upward mobility for men—has often been closed to women.

are employed in different and higher-ranked occupations than their fathers.

Second, although there is a great deal of mobility in the United States, much of it covers a very "short distance." By this, researchers mean that people who reach an occupational level different from that of their parents usually advance or fall back only one or two out of a possible eight occupational levels. Thus, the child of a laborer may become an artisan or a technician, but he or she is less likely to become a manager or professional. The odds against reaching the top, then, are extremely high unless one begins from a relatively privileged position.

Third, as the later study by Featherman and Hauser (1978:381–384) documents, occupational mobility among African Americans remains sharply limited by racial discrimination (see Chapter 7). Even when the researchers compared Black and White males who had similar levels of schooling, parental background, and early career experience, the achievement levels of Blacks were less than those of Whites. The researchers have also noted that Blacks are more likely than Whites to be downwardly mobile and less likely to be upwardly mobile. Featherman and Hauser offer evidence that there is a modest decline in the significance of race; yet, their conclusions must be regarded with some caution, since they did not consider households with no adult male present or individuals who were not counted in the labor force.

A final conclusion of both studies is that education plays a critical role in social mobility. The impact of formal schooling on adult status is even greater than that of family background (although, as we saw in our discussion of stratification and life chances, family background influences the likelihood that one will receive higher education). Furthermore, education represents an important way of effecting intergenerational mobility. Three-fourths of college-educated men achieved some upward mobility, compared with only 12 percent of those who received no schooling (see also J. Davis, 1982).

It should be noted, however, that the impact of education on mobility has diminished somewhat in the last decade. While completing a college education remains essential for occupational success, an undergraduate degree—a B.A. or B.S.—serves less as a guarantee of upward mobility than it did in the past—simply because more and more entrants into the job market now hold such a degree. Moreover, intergenerational mobility is declining, since there is no longer such a stark difference between generations. Whereas in earlier decades many high school–educated parents successfully sent their children to college, today's college students are increasingly likely to have college-educated parents (Hout, 1988).

Thus far, although we have given some consideration to the impact of race on mobility, we have dealt primarily with social mobility as a monolithic phenomenon. However, gender, like race, is an important factor in one's mobility. Earlier we noted that studies of class have only recently given serious consideration to the occupations and incomes of women as determinants of social rank. Studies of mobility, even more than those of class, have traditionally ignored the significance of gender, but some research findings are now available which explore the relationship between gender and mobility.

As we will discuss in more detail in Chapter 8, women's employment opportunities are much more limited than men's. According to recent research, women are more likely than men to withdraw entirely from the paid labor force when faced with downward mobility because of a substantial gap between their employment skills and the jobs being offered them. This withdrawal violates an assumption common to traditional mobility studies: that most people will aspire to upward mobility and seek to make the most of their opportunities.

In contrast to men, women have a rather large range of clerical occupations open to them. Yet many of these positions have modest salary ranges and limited prospects for advancement, thereby severely restricting the possibility of upward mobility. Moreover, self-employment as shopkeepers, entrepreneurs, independent professionals, and the like—an important road to upward mobility for men—has often been closed to women. Although sons commonly follow in the footsteps of their fathers, women are unlikely to move into these areas even when their fathers held such positions. Consequently, gender remains an important factor in shaping social mobility within the United States. Moreover, women in the United States (and in other parts of the world) are especially likely to be trapped in poverty and unable to rise out of their low-income status.

In the next section, we will broaden our focus to consider stratification from a global perspective.

STRATIFICATION IN THE WORLD SYSTEM: A GLOBAL PERSPECTIVE

While the marketplace is gradually being unified in terms of space and taste, the profits of business are not equally shared. There remains a substantial disparity between the world's "have" and "have-not" nations.

For example, in 1990 the average value of goods and services produced per citizen (per capita gross national product) in the United States, Canada, Switzerland, and Norway was more than $20,450. By contrast, the figure was $400 in several poorer countries. The 140 developing nations accounted for 75 percent of the world's population but possessed only 20 percent of all wealth (Haub and Yanagishita, 1992; Strasser et al., 1981). These contrasts are vividly illustrated in Figure 6-4 (page 158). Two forces discussed below are particularly responsible for the domination of the world marketplace by a few nations: the legacy of colonialism and the advent of multinational corporations.

Colonialism, Neocolonialism, and World Systems Theory

Colonialism is the maintenance of political, social, economic, and cultural domination over a people by a foreign power for an extended period of time (W. Bell, 1981b). In simple terms, it is rule by outsiders. The long reign of the British Empire over much of North America, parts of Africa, and India is an example of colonial domination. The same can be said of French rule over Algeria, Tunisia, and other parts of North Africa. Relations between the colonial nation and the colonized people are similar to those between the dominant capitalist class and the proletariat as described by Karl Marx.

By the 1980s, colonialism had largely become a phenomenon of the past; most of the world's nations that were colonies before World War I had achieved political independence and established their own governments. However, for many of these countries, the transition to genuine self-rule was not yet complete. Colonial domination had established patterns of economic exploitation that continued even after nationhood was achieved—in part because former colonies were unable to develop their own industry and technology. Their dependence on more industrialized nations, including their former colonial masters, for managerial and technical expertise, investment capital, and manufactured goods kept former colonies in a subservient position. Such continuing dependence and foreign domination is known as *neocolonialism.*

FIGURE 6-4 Worldwide Gross National Product Per Capita

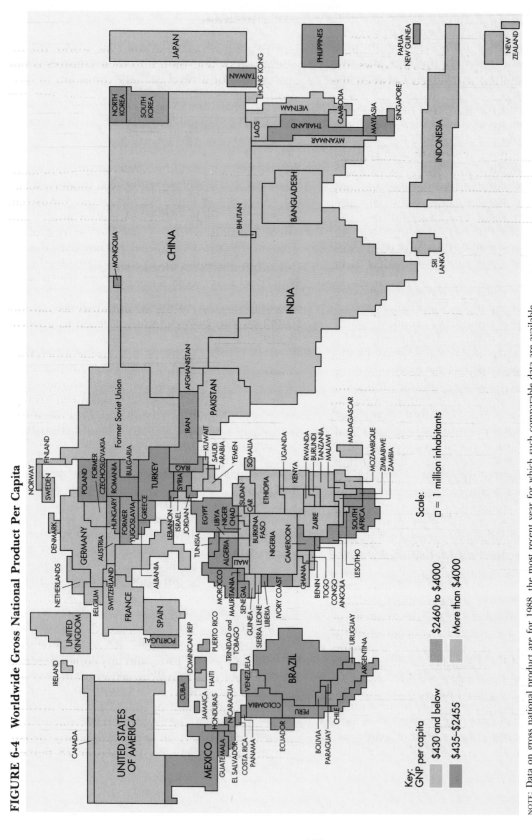

NOTE: Data on gross national product are for 1988, the most recent year for which such comparable data are available.
SOURCES: Crow and Thomas, 1983:14; Haub et al., 1990.

This stylized map reflects the different sizes in population of the world's nations. The color for each country shows the gross national product (the total value of goods and services produced by that nation in a given year) per capita. As the map shows, some of the world's most populous nations—such as the People's Republic of China, India, Indonesia, Bangladesh, and Pakistan—are among the countries with the lowest standard of living as measured by per capita gross national product.

158

The economic and political consequences of colonialism and neocolonialism are quite evident. Drawing on the conflict perspective, sociologist Immanuel Wallerstein (1974, 1979) views the global economic system as divided between nations who control wealth and those from whom capital is taken. Neocolonialism is one means by which industrialized societies accumulate even more capital.

Wallerstein has advanced a *world systems theory* of unequal economic and political relationships in which certain industrialized nations (among them, the United States, Japan, and Germany) and their multinational corporations are in a dominant position at the *core* of the system. Found at the *semiperiphery* of the system are countries with marginal economic status, such as Israel, Ireland, and South Korea. Wallerstein suggests that the poor developing countries of Asia, Africa, and Latin America are on the *periphery* of the world economic system. Their economies are controlled and exploited by core nations and corporations much as the old colonial empires ruled their colonies (Kerbo, 1991:495–498).

In addition to their political and economic impact, colonialism and neocolonialism have an important cultural component. The colonized people lose their native values and begin to identify with the culture of the colonial power. The native language of the country is discarded and even hidden as people attempt to emulate the colonizers.

Therefore, in the view of opponents of contemporary neocolonialism, every consumer product, every film, or every television program exported or designed by a colonial nation is an attack on the traditions and cultural autonomy of the dependent people. Even the popularity of *Batman* or *Dallas* may be viewed as a threat to native cultures when such programs dominate their media at the expense of local art forms. In reflecting on the dangers posed by television, Sembene Ousmane, one of Africa's most prominent writers and filmmakers, noted: "[Today] we are more familiar with European fairy tales than with our own traditional stories" (Emerson, 1968; T. McPhail, 1981:244–245; Memmi, 1967:105–108; Schramm et al., 1981; *World Development Forum*, 1990:4).

Modernization

For millions of people around the world, the introduction of television into their cultures is but one symbol of a revolutionary transition in day-to-day life. Contemporary sociologists use the term **modernization** to describe the far-reaching process by which a society moves from traditional or less developed institutions to those characteristic of more developed societies.

Wendell Bell (1981a), whose definition of modernization we are using, notes that modern societies tend to be urban, literate, and industrial. They have sophisticated transportation and media systems. Families tend to be organized within the nuclear family unit rather than the extended-family model (see Chapter 9). On the individual level, members of societies which have undergone modernization shift allegiance from such traditional sources of authority as parents and priests to newer authorities such as government officials.

Historian C. E. Black (1966) has identified four cultural phases common to all modernizing societies, which we can apply to a case study of the Republic of Kenya, an African nation of 26 million people. Black's first stage involves the introduction of modern ideas and social institutions. Initially, the impact of technological and institutional changes can be quite unsettling. The introduction of improved health measures in Kenya led to a rise in the birthrate, a decline in the death rate, and an overall increase in population growth; yet, at first, there were not adequate food supplies or school facilities to cope with the larger population.

The next stage of modernization is marked by the transfer of power from traditional to modernizing leaders. For Kenya and most other developing nations, colonialism stimulated the initial use of modern technology, but it also delayed the development of new leaders. Kenya remained a British colony until 1962, and its people exercised little authority, as European settlers clung to their privileges and power.

Black's third phase of modernization involves economic and social transformation from a rural, horticultural society to a predominantly urban, industrialized society. Kenya is over 78 percent

Mary M. Thacher/Photo Researchers

Although Kenya is over 78 percent rural, modernization is clearly underway in its cities.

rural; at least one-third of its labor force is still engaged in subsistence agriculture or bartering of goods. Therefore, the nation has not completed this phase of modernization. Nevertheless, urbanization is clearly under way. Nairobi, the nation's capital and largest city, has grown twice as fast as the country as a whole.

The final stage of Black's model is the cultural integration of society, which involves bringing together conflicting cultural elements to develop a harmonious and cohesive society. This process requires fundamental reorganization of the social structure. For example, ascribed characteristics such as gender and race become less important in individual attempts to gain power. In Kenya, the 2 percent of the population descended from early European and Asian immigrants still play a dominant role in commerce and industry. However, their dominance has decreased somewhat since the nation achieved independence.

Upon independence in 1962, Kenyans turned to the charismatic Jomo Kenyatta, longtime organizer against colonial rule, for political leadership. Popularly elected and in office until his death in 1978, Kenyatta maintained a model of *harambee,* Swahili for "let us all pull together." This motto symbolized his effort to bring together Kenyans—rural and urban, Black and White, of various tribes and groups. As one indicator of Kenyatta's effectiveness, presidential succession occurred peacefully after his death.

However, social inequality and ethnic unrest persist in contemporary Kenya. While a small, privileged African elite holds disproportionate wealth and power, the World Bank has estimated per capita annual income at $370. According to United Nations studies, about 30 percent of the nation's population is malnourished. The political situation in Kenya had been characterized as a retreat from democracy until multiparty elections were held at the end of 1992. The situation remained unsettled, as the president quickly adjourned the parliament temporarily to quiet the opposition. (Barnet, 1990; Perlez, 1991).

From a conflict perspective, modernization in developing countries such as Kenya often perpetuates their dependence on more industrialized nations. For example, Kenya is the second-largest recipient of American assistance in sub-Saharan Africa, owing in good part to Kenya's anticommunist posture when this was a factor and to a 1980 defense agreement that gives the United States access to its airports and seaports. Conflict theorists view such continuing dependence on foreign powers as an example of neocolonialism.

Sociologist York Bradshaw (1988) has modified Immanuel Wallerstein's world systems analysis as it relates to Kenya. After examining changes in the economy and the role of foreign capital since 1963, Bradshaw concluded that while multinational corporations obviously find it profitable to invest in Kenya, they do not completely dominate the nation's economy. These corporations are heavily taxed and are required by law to form joint ventures with local business people. However, as noted earlier, a small, privileged elite benefits from such foreign investment—while most Kenyans gain little from economic development.

Multinational Corporations

A key role in the neocolonialism of the 1990s is played by worldwide corporate giants. The term *multinational corporations* refers to commercial organizations which, while headquartered in one country, own or control other corporations and subsidiaries throughout the world. Such private trade and lending relationships are not new; merchants have conducted business abroad for hundreds of years, trading gems, spices, garments, and other goods. However, today's multinational giants are not merely buying and selling overseas; they are also *producing* goods all over the world (I. Wallerstein, 1974).

Moreover, today's "global factory" (the factories throughout the developing world run by multinational corporations) now has alongside it the "global office." Multinationals based in core countries are beginning to establish reservations services, centers to process insurance claims, and data processing centers in the periphery nations. As service industries become a more important

part of the international marketplace, many companies have concluded that the low costs of overseas operations more than offset the expense of transmitting information around the world (J. Burgess, 1989).

Traditionally, a high percentage of multinationals have been based in the United States, but this pattern has changed somewhat in recent decades. The size of these global corporations should not be underestimated. For example, Samsung, only the twentieth-largest multinational, had 1989 sales of $35.2 billion—a figure which exceeded the final value of goods and services of Nigeria and Sri Lanka combined for the year. Even more striking is the fact that the sales of the top 200 multinational corporations account for almost 30 percent of the gross *world* product (George, 1988:12; World Bank, 1990:182).

Foreign sales represent an important source of profit for multinational corporations. For example, foreign subsidiaries account for about 40 percent of all sales of larger multinationals headquartered in the United States. In general, foreign sales have grown more rapidly than domestic sales for such corporations, a fact which encourages them to expand into other countries (in many cases, the developing nations). The economy of the United States is heavily dependent on foreign commerce, much of which is conducted by multinationals. According to a 1991 report by

Many multinational corporations based in the United States have opened factories in the developing world to take advantage of the pool of cheap labor. This photograph shows workers in an assembly plant in Mexico owned by a company from the United States.

the Bureau of the Census (1991a), one out of seven manufacturing jobs in the United States had to do with the export of goods to foreign countries.

Multinational corporations can have a positive impact on the developing nations of the world. They bring jobs and industry to areas where subsistence agriculture previously served as the only means of survival. Viewed from a functionalist perspective, the combination of skilled technology and management provided by multinationals and the relatively cheap labor available in developing nations is ideal for a global enterprise. The international ties of multinational corporations also facilitate the exchange of ideas and technology around the world. Their worldwide influence contributes to interdependence among nations, which may prevent certain disputes from reaching the point of serious conflict.

Conflict theorists challenge this favorable evaluation of the impact of multinational corporations and emphasize that multinationals exploit local workers to maximize profits. They point out that when business firms build plants in places such as South Korea, residents (including those as young as 13 years old) may work seven days a week, 10 hours a day, for as little as 62 cents an hour. More than 80 percent of the low-skilled assembly jobs in these plants are held by women. Because there is a pool of cheap labor available in the developing world, multinationals are able to move factories out of countries such as the United States, thereby increasing unemployment in core nations. Moreover, governments in the developing world seeking to attract or keep multinationals may develop a "climate for investment" which includes repressive labor laws restricting union activity and collective bargaining. Conflict theorists therefore conclude that, on the whole, multinational corporations have a negative social impact on workers in both industrialized and developing nations (Bluestone and Harrison, 1982; Ehrenreich and Fuentes, 1981; Gittelsohn, 1987; Harrison and Bluestone, 1988).

Several sociologists have surveyed the effects of foreign investment and concluded that although it may initially contribute to a host nation's wealth, it eventually increases economic inequality within developing nations. This is true in terms of both income and ownership of land. Multinationals invest in limited areas of an economy and in restricted regions of a nation. Although certain sectors of the host nation's economy then expand—hotels and expensive restaurants, for example—this very expansion appears to retard growth in agriculture and in other economic sectors. Recent studies suggest that multinationals tend to generate income for a developing nation's elite, while at the same time undermining the market for goods produced by the poor (Bornschier et al., 1978; Moran, 1978; I. Wallerstein, 1979).

In many respects, the rise of multinational corporations has become a threat to national sovereignty. One of the most flagrant illustrations of the power of multinationals took place in Chile. In 1970, International Telephone and Telegraph (ITT) attempted to stop a Marxist politician, Salvador Allende, from coming to power—even though he was running for the Chilean presidency in a free and democratic election. After Allende was victorious, ITT and the Central Intelligence Agency (CIA) participated in the overthrow of the legally constituted government. In 1973, Allende and many of his supporters died during a bloody military coup. The elected regime was then replaced by a military dictatorship which was widely denounced for its violations of human rights (A. Sampson, 1973; see also Barnet and Müller, 1974; Michalowski and Kramer, 1987; R. Vernon, 1977).

Consequences of Stratification for Developing Nations

As discussed above, colonialism, neocolonialism, and foreign investment by multinationals have often had unfortunate consequences for residents of developing nations. From 1950 to 1980, the gap between the world's rich and poor nations continued to grow, primarily because the rich nations got even richer. As for the decade of the 1980s, it is estimated that more than 40 Third World countries finished the decade poorer in per capita terms than they started it. The world's 14 most-devastated nations—including Zambia, Bolivia, and Nigeria—saw per capita income plummet as dramatically as it did in the United States during the Great Depression of the 1930s. With these trends in mind, researcher Alan Durning (1990:26) observed that the term "developing nation" has become a cruel misnomer; many of the world's less affluent nations are disintegrating rather than developing.

The day-to-day impact of the economic backslide in Africa, Latin America, and parts of Asia during the 1980s has been tragic. Malnutrition has risen in Burma, Burundi, the Gambia, Guinea-Bissau, Jamaica, Niger, Nigeria, Paraguay, the Philippines, Nicaragua, El Salvador, and Peru. According to the World Bank, life expectancy declined in nine African countries over the period 1979–1983. Today, more than 100 million Africans are believed to lack sufficient food to sustain themselves in good health (Durning, 1990:26; World Bank, 1990).

The 1980s were a particularly cruel decade for Latin America. El Salvador, Nicaragua, and Peru, all torn by war, went into economic tailspins. According to Peru's government, one-third of the country's children are malnourished to the extent that they have stunted growth. The per capita income of the average Latin American—only about $3500 in 1980—declined by 9 percent over the next eight years (Durning, 1990:26–27).

What factors have contributed to the recent difficulties of developing nations? Certainly runaway population growth—which will be discussed in detail in Chapter 12—has hurt the standard of living of many Third World peoples. So, too, has the accelerating environmental decline evident in the quality of air, water, and other natural resources. Still another factor has been the developing nations' collective debt of $1.3 trillion, which has the ironic effect of prolonging their dependence on industrialized nations.

Today, poor nations are paying rich countries $50 billion each year in debt and interest payments beyond what they receive in new loans. If we add to this figure the estimates of capital flight involving wealthy citizens of poor nations, the annual outflow of funds may reach $100 billion. As viewed from a world systems approach, a growing share of the human and natural resources of developing countries is being redistributed to the core industrial nations (Durning, 1990:25–26; Kerbo, 1991:498).

Unfortunately, the massive exodus of money from poorer regions of the world only intensifies their destruction of natural resources. From a conflict view, less affluent nations are being forced to exploit their mineral deposits, forests, and fisheries in order to meet their debt obligations while offering subsistence labor to local workers. The poor turn to the only means of survival available to them: marginal lands. They plow mountain slopes, burn plots in tropical forests, and overgraze grasslands—often knowing that their actions are destructive to the environment. But they see no alternative in their agonizing fight for simple survival (Durning, 1990:26; Waring, 1988).

STRATIFICATION WITHIN NATIONS: A COMPARATIVE PERSPECTIVE

The world marketplace is highly stratified, with affluent, industrialized nations well in control while poorer developing countries face desperate problems. Worldwide stratification is evident not only in the disparity between rich and poor nations (in Wallerstein's terms, between countries at the core and at the periphery of the world economic system) but also *within* nations in the substantial gap between rich and poor citizens.

Stratification in developing nations is closely related to their relatively weak and dependent position in the world economic system. As discussed earlier, local elites work hand in hand with multinational corporations and prosper from such alliances, while the exploitation of industrial and agricultural workers is created and perpetuated by the economic system and prevailing developmental values. Consequently, foreign investment in developing countries tends to increase economic inequality (Bornschier et al., 1978; Kerbo, 1991:507–511).

Distribution of Wealth and Income

Earlier, we noted that in 1990, the top fifth (or 20 percent) of the United States population—earning $61,490 or more—accounted for almost 47 percent of total wages and salaries in the nation (Bureau of the Census, 1991b:58).

As Figure 6-5 (below) shows, the degree of income inequality varies markedly around the world. Of the seven nations that are contrasted in Figure 6-5 Brazil had the greatest gap between its most affluent and least affluent residents. The top fifth in Brazil received 63 percent of total wages and salaries, while the bottom fifth accounted for only 2 percent of income. Similar disparities are found in many developing countries, where small elites control a large portion of the nation's income. There are 10 countries around the globe in which the most affluent 10 percent receive at least 40 percent of income, and they are all developing countries: Brazil (the leader at 46 percent), Kenya, Sri Lanka, Botswana, Guatemala, Mauritius, Mexico, Panama, Turkey, and Zambia.

In examining the world's advanced industrial economies, researchers have found the *least* income inequality in Sweden, Japan, Norway, and Belgium. By contrast, the *highest* income inequality is found in the United States, Canada, Great Britain, France, and Australia (World Bank, 1992:262–263). Redistributive tax policies have reduced income inequality in many European nations.

As we saw earlier, wealth in the United States is much more unevenly distributed than income. The richest fifth of the population holds almost 80 percent of the nation's wealth (refer back to Figure 6-2). This extreme concentration of wealth is evident in most industrial societies. In the United Kingdom, for example, the distribution of wealth is even more lopsided than in the United States. In good part, this is because in the United States many people with rather modest incomes own automobiles and homes, whereas ownership of automobiles or homes is less common among poorer residents of Great Britain (Samuelson and Nordhaus, 1992:355–358).

Social Mobility

Social mobility—both upward and downward—is rather limited in societies characterized by slavery, caste, and estate systems of stratification. For example, a study of agricultural households in central India between 1975 and 1983 found that, on average, 84 percent of those who were poor in any year had been poor in the previous year. Over the nine-year period of study, 44 percent of households had been poor for six or more years,

FIGURE 6-5 Distribution of Income in Seven Nations

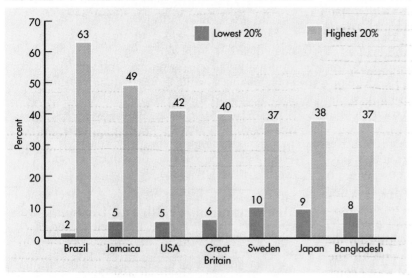

This figure shows the distribution of household income by population fifths in seven countries. Data were collected by the World Bank and by United Nations agencies. As the figure shows, the proportion of income held by the most affluent 20 percent of the population is highest in Brazil (63 percent) and Jamaica (49 percent) and lowest in Sweden (37 percent). By comparing the bars for the poorest and richest quintiles (a quintile is 20 percent of the population), we can see that the gap between the highest and lowest quintiles is smallest in Japan and Bangladesh. Consequently, of the seven countries pictured, these two nations have the lowest level of income inequality.

NOTE: Data are considered comparable although based on statistics covering 1979 to 1988.
SOURCE: World Bank, 1992:276–277.

Haitian immigrants are shown working in a potato field in New York State. Sociological research suggests that high rates of immigration contribute to an expansion of job opportunities and therefore facilitate social mobility.

and 19 percent were poor in all nine years (World Bank, 1990:135).

Studies of intergenerational mobility in industrialized nations have found that (1) there are substantial similarities in the ways that parents' positions are transmitted to their children; (2) as in the United States, opportunities for mobility in other nations have been influenced by structural factors, such as labor market changes, which lead to the rise or decline of an occupational group within the social hierarchy; (3) immigration continues to be a significant factor in a society's level of intergenerational mobility (Ganzeboom et al., 1991; Grusky and Hauser, 1984; Haller et al., 1990; Hauser and Grusky, 1988; Kalleberg, 1988:208).

Cross-cultural studies suggest that intergenerational mobility has been increasing in recent decades, at least among men. Dutch sociologists Harry Ganzeboom and Ruud Luijkx joined by sociologist Donald Treiman of the United States (1989) examined surveys of mobility in 35 industrial and developing nations; they found that almost all the countries studied had witnessed increased intergenerational mobility between the 1950s and 1980s. In particular, there was a common pattern of movement away from agriculture-based occupations.

How extensive was mobility within Europe's socialist countries? Although studies of nations with centrally planned economies, such as Hungary and Poland, revealed little inheritance of wealth, there was no evidence of any substantial level of mobility. It will be interesting to study these countries in the 1990s to see if the growth of privately owned businesses leads to sharp increases in social mobility (Dahrendorf, 1990; Wong, 1990).

Only recently have researchers begun to investigate the impact of gender differences on the mobility patterns of developing nations. Many aspects of the development process—especially modernization in rural areas and the rural-to-urban migration described above—may result in the modification or abandonment of traditional cultural practices and even marital systems. The effects on women's social standing and mobility are not necessarily positive. Through development and modernization, women's vital role in food production deteriorates, thereby jeopardizing both their autonomy and their material well-being. The movement of families to the cities weakens women's ties to relatives who can provide them with food, financial assistance, and social support (Alam, 1985; Boserup, 1977; Tiano, 1987).

- How does the level of spending for social services in the United States compare with that of European countries?
- How do conflict theorists view the backlash against welfare recipients in the United States?
- How do welfare mothers draw on social networks to supplement their incomes?

While stratification is evident around the world, countries differ substantially in their commitment to social service programs that will assist the needy. It is difficult to develop cross-national comparisons of welfare programs, since there is such variance from nation to nation. Nevertheless, the World Bank (1992:238–239) has calculated the proportion of central-government expenditures in various countries that are devoted to housing, Social Security, welfare, and unemployment compensation. In 1990, the figure for the United States stood at 28 percent, but no European nation had a proportion that low. In Great Britain, 35 percent of central-government spending went to these social service areas; in Spain, 38 percent; in France, 46 percent. In good part, this is because the United States has such a comparatively high level of military spending. In 1990, the United States spent 23 percent of its central budget on defense, as compared with 12 percent in Britain, 7 percent in France, and only 6 percent in Spain.

As noted earlier in the chapter, fully 40 percent of poor adults in the United States work outside the home. The 60 percent of poor adults who do not work outside the home include many who are ill or disabled, are taking care of young children, or are retired. Despite such data, in 1992, many political candidates reflected the public mood by offering "tough talk" commercials concerning welfare. President George Bush used advertisements pledging that he would "change welfare and make the able-bodied work," while Governor Bill Clinton's commercials showed him insisting that "those on welfare move into the workplace." Such "welfare scapegoating," as it has been labeled by Governor Mario Cuomo of New York, unfairly blames the nation's serious economic problems on welfare spending and the poor. Viewed from a conflict perspective, this backlash against welfare recipients reflects deep fears and hostility toward the nation's urban, and predominantly Black and His-panic, underclass (Bureau of the Census, 1990b:65; Sack, 1992:24).

Stereotypes about lavish welfare spending mask well-documented realities. The average state in the United States spends only 3.4 percent of its budget on welfare programs. Moreover, such spending is being cut by federal, state, and local governments. According to a report by the Center on Budget and Policy Priorities, states slashed welfare programs more extensively in 1991 than at any time since 1901. In 1991, 40 states froze or cut funds for families with children, 27 of the 30 states with welfare for single adults and childless couples cut or froze such benefits, 12 states cut emergency aid to prevent homelessness, and 9 states decreased funding for those already homeless (DeParle, 1992a; A. Stone, 1991).

The best-publicized and most controversial part of the welfare system is Aid to Families with Dependent Children (AFDC), a public assistance program which provides aid to low-income families with children. Currently, about 13.2 million people in the United States receive AFDC benefits, of whom about 9 million are children. (In contrast to stereotypes, the size of the average welfare family has decreased substantially in the last 20 years, and only 10 percent of such families have three or more children.) Overall, the number of AFDC recipients in the United States increased by more than 20 percent in the early 1990s—a sharp increase undoubtedly fueled by the nation's economic recession and the rise in families headed by single mothers (DeParle, 1992a; 1992b:A11).

Of families that receive AFDC assistance, 40 percent are Black, while 38 percent are White, and 16 percent are of Hispanic descent. More than half the women who enter the welfare system stay on the rolls for less than four years and do not return once they leave welfare. However, one-fourth of welfare recipients remain on the rolls for more than 10 years; it is this minority of recipients that most closely fits the picture of a permanent underclass trapped in persistent poverty (DeParle, 1992a; Sack, 1992).

Many states have instituted welfare reform programs in recent years, often with the stated goal of "cracking down" on abuses of the system. Some reform proposals assume that small incentives, such as cuts or bonuses of $50 or $100 per month, will lead recipients to make major behavioral changes. The state of Ohio offers a $62-per-month bonus to teenage parents who continue in school, while Wisconsin's Learnfare program has cut aid to hundreds of families when their teenage children miss too many school days. In Maryland, families can lose their AFDC benefits if they fail to see a doctor regularly or fail to pay the rent on time. Yet, after studying such welfare reform experiments, David Ellwood, a professor of public policy, concludes: "There's absolutely no evidence that small changes have more than a tiny, tiny impact" (Conniff, 1992; DeParle, 1992a:E3).

On the federal level, the Family Support Act, passed by Congress in 1988, was hailed as the most sweeping welfare reform in 50 years. Under this law, states must require some welfare recipients to look for jobs or enter educational and training programs. However, about half the women on welfare are exempt from the provisions of this measure because their children are too young or because they lack transportation and child care. A federal study released in 1992 found that the Family Support Act had not succeeded in spurring states to make a strong commitment to welfare reform. While a more recent report showed that the law had raised the earnings of people on welfare in California and had reduced the amount they received in public assistance, analysts disagree on whether the California data suggest that the program has made a significant contribution in reducing welfare dependency (DeParle, 1992a, 1992b, 1992c).

It is important to emphasize that inflation has substantially eroded the purchasing power of welfare payments. As of early 1992, the average monthly payment for a family of three was only $402; even adding in the value of food stamps, the monthly average rose to only $623. These combined payments will allow the typical welfare family to buy 27 percent less (in terms of value of goods) than the average grant did in 1972. Thus, welfare does not encourage dependency, simply because welfare benefits are too low to live on (DeParle, 1992a).

Kathryn Edin (1991) of the Russell Sage Foundation conducted in-depth interviews with 50 welfare mothers in the Chicago area and questioned them intensively about their family finances. She reports that the total income of the women in her sample averaged $897 per month, of which 58 percent ($521) came from AFDC benefits and food stamps. About half of the remaining 42 percent came from unreported work in regular or illegal jobs, while the other half (also unreported) came from social networks consisting of family members, friends, boyfriends, absent fathers, churches, and community organizations. Although

Reprinted by permission of Mike Luckovich and Creators Syndicate

The majority of people in the United States below the government's poverty line are under 18 years of age. In 1992, of the more than 13 million people receiving benefits from Aid to Families with Dependent Children (AFDC), about 9 million were children.

these welfare recipients generally felt guilty about concealing this additional income from caseworkers, they did conceal it because they needed the income to survive and would lose their benefits if they reported the extra income.

On the basis of her research, Edin challenges the stereotypes that welfare mothers do not work, do not want to work, and hold values different from those of mainstream society. Indeed, many of her interview subjects wanted to work outside the home but could not find jobs that would pay them more than welfare did—especially when the added costs of child care, clothing, and transportation were considered. Edin (1991:472) concludes:

In a society where single mothers must provide financially for their children, where women are economically marginalized into unreliable jobs that pay little more than the minimum wage, where child-support is inadequate or nonexistent, and where day care costs and health insurance (usually not provided by employers) are unaffordable for most, it should surprise no one that half the mothers supporting children on their own choose welfare over reported work.

SUMMARY

Stratification is the structured ranking of entire groups of people that perpetuates unequal economic rewards and power in a society. In this chapter, we examine four general systems of stratification, the explanations offered by functionalist and conflict theorists for the existence of social inequality, the relationship between stratification and social mobility, and stratification within the world economic system.

1 All cultures are characterized by some degree of ***social inequality.***

2 In contrast to other systems of stratification, the boundaries between social classes are less precisely defined.

3 Karl Marx viewed class differentiation as the crucial determinant of social, economic, and political inequality.

4 Max Weber identified three analytically distinct components of stratification: class, status, and power.

5 Functionalists argue that stratification is necessary so that people will be motivated to fill society's important positions; conflict theorists see stratification as a major source of societal tension and conflict.

6 The category of the "poor" defies any simple definition and counters common stereotypes about "poor people."

7 ***Social mobility*** is more likely to be found in an ***open system*** that emphasizes ***achieved status*** than in a ***closed system*** that focuses on ascribed characteristics.

8 Drawing on the conflict perspective, sociologist Immanuel Wallerstein views the global economic system as divided between nations who control wealth *(core nations)* and those from whom capital is taken *(periphery nations)*.

9 Historian C. E. Black has identified four cultural phases common to all societies undergoing the process of ***modernization.***

10 Conflict theorists argue that ***multinational corporations*** have a negative social impact on workers in both industrialized and developing nations.

11 Much of the debate over the welfare system of the United States has focused on Aid to Families with Dependent Children (AFDC), a public assistance program that provides aid for low-income families with children.

CRITICAL THINKING QUESTIONS

1 Sociologist Daniel Rossides has conceptualized the class system of the United States using a five-class model. According to Rossides, the upper middle class and the lower middle class together account for about 40 percent of the nation's population. Yet studies suggest that a higher proportion of respondents identify themselves as "middle class." Drawing on the model presented by Rossides, suggest why members of the upper class and the working class might prefer to identify themselves as "middle class."

2 Sociological study of stratification generally is conducted at the macro level and draws most heavily on the functionalist and conflict perspectives. How might sociologists use the interactionist perspective to examine social class inequalities within a college community?

3 Analyze the recent war in the Persian Gulf, drawing on the concepts and issues in the chapter (especially colonialism, neocolonialism, world systems theory, modernization, and multinational corporations).

KEY TERMS

Absolute poverty A standard of poverty based on a minimum level of subsistence below which families should not be expected to exist. (page 150)

Achieved status A social position attained by a person largely through his or her own effort. (155)

Ascribed status A social position "assigned" to a person by society without regard for the person's unique talents or characteristics. (140)

Bourgeoisie Karl Marx's term for the capitalist class, comprising the owners of the means of production. (141)

Capitalism An economic system in which the means of production are largely in private hands, and the main incentive for economic activity is the accumulation of profits. (141)

Castes Hereditary systems of rank, usually religiously dictated, that tend to be fixed and immobile. (137)

Class A term used by Max Weber to refer to people who have a similar level of wealth and income. (142)

Class consciousness In Karl Marx's view, a subjective awareness held by members of a class regarding their common vested interests and need for collective political action to bring about social change. (141)

Class system A social ranking based primarily on economic position in which achieved characteristics can influence mobility. (139)

Closed system A social system in which there is little or no possibility of individual mobility. (155)

Colonialism The maintenance of political, social, economic, and cultural dominance over a people by a foreign power for an extended period of time. (157)

Estate system A system of stratification under which peasants were required to work land leased to them by nobles in exchange for military protection and other services. Also known as *feudalism.* (139)

Esteem The reputation that a particular individual has within an occupation. (145)

False consciousness A term used by Karl Marx to describe an attitude held by members of a class that does not accurately reflect its objective position. (141)

Horizontal mobility The movement of an individual from one social position to another of the same rank. (155)

Income Salaries and wages. (136)

Intergenerational mobility Changes in the social position of children relative to their parents. (155)

Intragenerational mobility Changes in a person's social position within his or her adult life. (155)

Life chances Max Weber's term for people's opportunities to provide themselves with material goods, positive living conditions, and favorable life experiences. (151)

Modernization The far-reaching process by which a society moves from traditional or less developed institutions to those characteristic of more developed societies. (159)

Multinational corporations Commercial organizations which, while headquartered in one country, own or control other corporations and subsidiaries throughout the world. (161)

Neocolonialism Continuing dependence of former colonies on foreign countries. (157)

Objective method A technique for measuring social class that assigns individuals to classes on the basis of criteria such as occupation, education, income, and place of residence. (145)

Open system A social system in which the position of each individual is influenced by his or her achieved status. (155)

Power The ability to exercise one's will over others. (142)

Prestige The respect and admiration with which an occupation is regarded by society. (145)

Proletariat Karl Marx's term for the working class in a capitalist society. (141)

Relative poverty A floating standard of deprivation by which people at the bottom of a society, whatever their lifestyles, are judged to be disadvantaged in comparison with the nation as a whole. (150)

Slavery A system of enforced servitude in which people are legally owned by others and in which enslaved status is transferred from parents to children. (137)

Social inequality A condition in which members of a society have different amounts of wealth, prestige, or power. (136)

Social mobility Movement of individuals or groups from one position of a society's stratification system to another. (155)

Status group A term used by Max Weber to refer to people who have the same prestige or lifestyle, independent of their class positions. (142)

Stratification A structured ranking of entire groups of people that perpetuates unequal economic rewards and power in a society. (136)

Underclass Long-term poor people who lack training and skills. (149)

Vertical mobility The movement of a person from one social position to another of a different rank. (155)

Wealth An inclusive term encompassing all of a person's material assets, including land and other types of property. (136)

World systems theory Immanuel Wallerstein's view of the global economic system as divided between certain industrialized nations who control wealth and developing countries who are controlled and exploited. (159)

ADDITIONAL READINGS

Braun, Denny. *The Rich Get Richer*. Chicago: Nelson-Hall, 1991. A sociologist looks at growing inequality within the United States, as well as throughout the world, with a special focus on the rise of multinational corporations.

Lamont, Michèle, and Marcel Fournier. *Cultivating Differences: Symbolic Boundaries and the Making of Inequality.* Chicago: University of Chicago Press, 1993. A sociological analysis of how cultural tastes and practices vary according to social class.

McGuire, Randall M., and Robert Paynter (eds.). *The Archaeology of Inequality.* Oxford, Eng.: Basil Blackwell, 1991. An archeologist draws on primary sources to examine racial, gender, and class-based inequality both among and within Native American, African American, and European peoples living on the North American continent.

Simon, John L. *Population and Development in Poor Countries.* Princeton, N.J.: Princeton University Press, 1992. A collection of essays by a well-known economist, including both theoretical treatments and empirical studies.

Tinker, Irene (ed.). *Persistent Inequalities: Women and World Development.* New York: Oxford University Press, 1990. Tinker's anthology offers an overview of the past and current debates regarding the role of women in world development and the impact of development of women.

Weigard, Bruce. *Off the Books: A Theory and Critique of the Underground Economy.* Dix Hills, N.Y.: General Hall, 1992. An examination of the social consequences of people's participation in activities outside the mainstream economy.

7

RACIAL AND ETHNIC INEQUALITY

LOOKING AHEAD

- In sociological terms, why are Blacks, Native Americans, and Jews considered minority groups?
- Why are stereotypes harmful to members of racial and ethnic minorities?
- How does the Marxist perspective view race relations?
- What types of interracial contact can

foster tolerance between dominant and subordinate groups?
- Is it harmful to Asian Americans to view them as a "model minority"?
- Have affirmative action programs gone too far—or not far enough—in an effort to combat discrimination against women and minorities?

In 1991, Rodney King, a Black construction worker, was beaten by Los Angeles Police Department officers after a high-speed car chase. A shocking videotape, shown repeatedly on television in subsequent months, captured the police administering 56 blows to King in 81 seconds as he lay on the ground. A year later, four White officers were charged in connection with the beatings, but they were found not guilty by a jury of 10 Whites, one Hispanic, and one Asian American. For many Blacks, the acquittal of these officers was an outrageous reminder of the historic persecution of African Americans. Even though White officers had been shown on videotape repeatedly beating a defenseless Black man, they were not convicted of any crime.

The jury's verdict touched off rioting in Los Angeles and other cities across the United States. The Los Angeles riots became the nation's worst in the twentieth century, leading to 58 deaths, 2283 injuries, 13,505 arrests, and about 1 billion dollars in property damage. Ironically, the South-Central neighborhood where the most serious disturbances took place borders Watts, the area where rioting had occurred in 1965. As in Watts 27 years earlier, South-Central was shattered by fires and looting. Small businesses owned by Koreans were a particular target, reflecting continuing anger about a light sentence given in 1991 to a Korean grocer who had shot and killed a 15-year-old Black woman in a dispute over a bottle of orange juice (M. Davis, 1992; Kwong, 1992; *Los Angeles Times*, 1992).

Media coverage of the riots was typified by a cover story in *U.S. News and World Report* entitled

"Black vs. White." As journalist Peter Kwong (1992:29–32) points out, this overly simplistic view ignores the important role of Koreans and Hispanics in the events in Los Angeles. Hispanics constitute about half the population of south Los Angeles—although there are no Hispanic elected officials from this area. At least 1000 of those arrested during the disturbances (primarily for violating curfew) were undocumented Hispanic immigrants who were turned over to the Immigration and Naturalization Service for immediate deportation. As for the victims of the riots, more than one-third of those killed were Hispanic. More than 1800 Korean businesses—many of them groceries and liquor stores—were looted or burned. Together, Korean establishments suffered $347 million in property damage—more than one-third of all such losses from the riots. In addition, between 30 and 40 percent of businesses wiped out during the riots were owned by Hispanics, mostly Mexican Americans and Cuban Americans.

African Americans, Hispanic Americans, Asian Americans, and many other racial and ethnic minorities in the United States have experienced the often bitter contrast between the "American dream" of freedom, equality, and success and the grim realities of poverty, prejudice, and discrimination. The social definitions of race and ethnicity—like class—affect people's place and status in a stratification system. This is true not only in this country but throughout the world.

By the 1990s, as one result of the successful revolts against communist rule in the Soviet Union and eastern Europe, traditional and long-suppressed ethnic rivalries had once again erupted into open conflict in many areas. The Soviet Union officially dissolved in 1991 along boundaries reflecting its many nationalities, while Yugoslavia's republics entered into a long and bloody civil war. Protests against mistreatment by dominant groups came from national, racial, and ethnic minorities throughout the region—among them, Hungarians living in Rumania, Turks living in Bulgaria, and Slovaks living in the former Czechoslovakia. Moreover, long-standing prejudices against Jews and Romani (better known as Gypsies) were being expressed more openly in many of these nations.

This chapter will focus primarily on the meaning of race and ethnicity in the United States. It will begin by identifying the basic characteristics of a minority group and distinguishing between racial and ethnic groups; then it will consider the functionalist, conflict, and interactionist perspectives on race and ethnicity. Next, it will examine the dynamics of prejudice and discrimination and their impact on intergroup relations. Particular attention will then be given to the experiences of racial and ethnic minorities in the United States. Finally, the social policy section will explore the controversy over affirmative action.

MINORITY, RACIAL, AND ETHNIC GROUPS

Sociologists frequently distinguish between racial and ethnic groups. The term *racial group* is used to describe a group which is set apart from others because of obvious physical differences. Whites, Blacks, and Asian Americans are all considered racial groups in the United States. Unlike racial groups, an *ethnic group* is set apart from others primarily because of its national origin or distinctive cultural patterns. In the United States, Puerto Ricans, Jews, and Polish Americans are all categorized as ethnic groups.

Minority Groups

A numerical minority is a group that makes up less than half of some larger population. The population of the United States includes thousands of numerical minorities, including television actors, green-eyed people, tax lawyers, and descendants of the Pilgrims who arrived on the *Mayflower*. However, these numerical minorities are not considered to be minorities in the sociological sense; in fact, the number of people in a group does not necessarily determine its status as a social minority (or dominant group). When sociologists define a minority group, they are primarily concerned with the economic and political power, or powerlessness, of that group. A *minority group* is a subordinate group whose members have significantly less control or power over their own lives than the members of a dominant or majority group have over theirs.

Sociologists have identified five basic properties of a minority group—physical or cultural traits, unequal treatment, ascribed status, solidarity, and in-group marriage (M. Harris, 1958:4–11):

1 Members of a minority group share physical or cultural characteristics that distinguish them from the dominant group. Each society has its own arbitrary standard for determining which characteristics are most important in defining dominant and minority groups.

2 Members of a minority experience unequal treatment and have less power over their lives than members of a dominant group have over theirs. For example, the management of an apartment complex may refuse to rent to African Americans, Hispanics, or Jews. Social inequality may be created or maintained by prejudice, discrimination, segregation, or even extermination.

3 Membership in a minority (or dominant) group is not voluntary; people are born into the group. Thus, race and ethnicity are considered *ascribed* statuses (see Chapter 4).

4 Minority group members have a strong sense of group solidarity. William Graham Sumner, writing in 1906, noted that people make distinctions between members of their own group (the *in-group*) and everyone else (the *out-group*). In-groups and out-groups were discussed in Chapter 4. When a group is the object of long-term prejudice and discrimination, the feeling of "us versus them" can and often does become extremely intense.

5 Members of a minority generally marry others from the same group. A member of a dominant group is often unwilling to join a supposedly inferior minority by marrying one of its members. In addition, the minority group's sense of solidarity encourages marriages within the group and discourages marriages to outsiders.

David Butow/Black Star

Members of a minority group have a strong sense of group solidarity, which develops partly as a result of the prejudice and discrimination they experience. Korean Americans are shown demonstrating after the 1992 riots in Los Angeles.

Race

As we have already suggested, the term *racial group* is reserved for those minorities (and the corresponding dominant groups) set apart from others by obvious physical differences. But what is an "obvious" physical difference? Each society determines which differences are important while ignoring other characteristics that could serve as a basis for social differentiation. In the United States, differences in both skin color and hair color are generally quite obvious. Yet people learn informally that differences in skin color have a dramatic social and political meaning, while differences in hair color are not nearly so socially significant.

The largest racial minorities in the United States are Blacks (or African Americans), Native Americans (or American Indians), Japanese Americans, Chinese Americans, and other Asian peoples. Information about the population and distribution of racial and ethnic groups in this country is presented in Table 7-1 on the opposite page.

Biological Significance of Race

Viewed from a biological perspective, the term *race* would refer to a genetically isolated group with distinctive gene frequencies. It is impossible to scientifically define or identify such a group. Consequently, contrary to popular belief, there are no "pure races." Nor are there physical traits—whether skin color or baldness—that can be used to describe one group to the exclusion of all others. If scientists examine a smear of human blood under a microscope, they cannot tell whether it came from a Chinese or a Navajo, a Hawaiian or an African American.

Migration, exploration, and invasion have further compromised racial purity and have led to increased intermingling of races. Scientific investigations suggest that the percentage of North American Blacks with White ancestry ranges from 20 percent to as much as 75 percent. Such statistics undermine a fundamental assumption of life in the United States: the assumption that we can accurately categorize individuals as "Black" or "White" (Herskovits, 1930:15; D. Roberts, 1975).

Some people would like to find biological explanations which could help us to understand why certain peoples of the world have come to dominate others (refer back to the discussion of sociobiology in Chapter 3). Given the absence of pure racial groups, there can be no satisfactory biological answers for such social and political questions.

Social Significance of Race One of the most crucial aspects of the relationship between dominant and subordinate groups is the ability of the dominant groups or majority groups to define a society's values.

Sociologist William I. Thomas (1923:41–44), an early critic of theories of racial and gender differences, saw that the "definition of the situation" could mold the personality of the individual. To put it another way, Thomas, writing from the interactionist perspective, observed that people respond not only to the objective features of a situation or person but also to the meaning that situation or person has for them. Thus we can create false images or stereotypes that become real in their consequences. *Stereotypes* are unreliable generalizations about all members of a group which do not recognize individual differences within the group.

In the last 25 years, there has been growing awareness of the power of the mass media to introduce stereotypes into everyday life. As one result, stereotyping of racial and ethnic minorities in Hollywood films, on television, and in Broadway shows has come under increasing fire. For example, in 1991, Asian American groups in New York City picketed the opening of the musical *Miss Saigon*. One of their charges was that the show reinforced the traditional stereotype of Asian women as either prostitutes or exotics. Hispanics note that Hollywood has traditionally presented them as vicious bandits, lazy peasants, or humorous buffoons. In a striking example of stereotyping in the print media, *Newsweek* used two photos of African American robbers to illustrate a 1991 article entitled "The Bank Robbery Boom"—even though the article stated that the modern bank robber is "usually White." While the use of stereotyping can promote in-group solidarity, conflict theorists point out that stereotypes contribute to prejudice and thereby assist the subordination of minority groups (Kaplan, 1991:63; Schaefer, 1993:46–49).

In certain situations, we may respond to stereotypes and act on them, with the result that false definitions become accurate. This is known as the *self-fulfilling prophecy*. A person or group is desired as having particular characteristics and then begins to display the very traits that were said to exist. In assessing the impact of self-fulfilling

TABLE 7-1 Racial and Ethnic Groups in the United States, 1990

CLASSIFICATION	NUMBER, IN THOUSANDS	PERCENT OF TOTAL POPULATION
Racial groups		
Whites	199,686	80.3
Blacks	29,986	12.1
Native Americans, Eskimos, Aleuts	1,959	0.8
Chinese	1,645	0.7
Filipinos	1,407	0.6
Japanese	848	0.3
Asian Indians	815	0.3
Koreans	799	0.3
Vietnamese	615	0.2
Laotians	149	0.1
Cambodians	147	0.1
Ethnic groups		
White ancestry (single or mixed)		
Germans	57,986	23.3
Irish	38,740	15.6
English	32,656	13.1
Italians	14,715	5.9
French	10,321	4.1
Poles	9,366	3.8
Jews	5,935	2.6
Hispanics (or Latinos)	22,354	9.0
Mexican Americans	13,496	5.4
Puerto Ricans	2,728	1.0
Cubans	1,044	0.4
Other	5,086	2.2
Total (all groups)	248,710	

NOTE: Percentages do not total 100 percent, and subheads do not add up to figures in major heads, since overlap between groups exists (e.g., Polish American Jews or people of mixed ancestry, such as Irish and Italian). Therefore, numbers and percentages should be considered approximations. Data on Jews are for 1989.
SOURCE: Bureau of the Census, 1992a:24–25, 43.

prophecies, we can refer back to labeling theory (see Chapter 5), which emphasizes how a person comes to be labeled as deviant and even to accept a self-image of deviance.

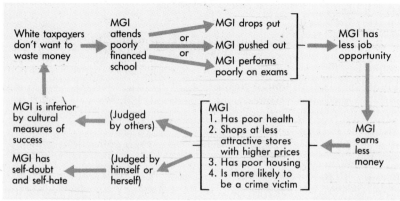

NOTE: MGI stands for "minority group individual." Arrows represent direction of negative cumulative effect.
SOURCE: Schaefer, 1993:19.

The self-validating effects of definitions made by the dominant group are shown in this figure. A minority group person attends a poorly financed school and is left unequipped to perform jobs which offer high status and high pay. He or she then gets a low-paying job and must settle for a lifestyle far short of society's standards. Since the person shares these standards, he or she may begin to feel self-doubt and self-hatred. This last phase of the cycle has been called into question in recent research.

Self-fulfilling prophecies can be especially devastating for minority groups (see Figure 7-1). Such groups often find that they are allowed to hold only low-paying jobs with little prestige or opportunity for advancement. The rationale of the dominant society is that these members of a minority lack the ability to perform in more important and lucrative positions. Minority group members are then denied the training needed to become scientists, executives, or physicians and are locked into society's inferior jobs. As a result, the false definition has become real: in terms of employment, the minority has become inferior because it was originally defined as inferior and was prevented from achieving equality.

Because of this vicious circle, talented people from minority groups may come to see the worlds of entertainment and professional sports as their only hope for achieving wealth and fame. Thus, it is no accident that successive waves of Irish, Jewish, Italian, Black, and Hispanic performers and athletes have made their mark on our society. Unfortunately, these very successes may convince the dominant group that its original stereotypes are valid—that these are the only areas of society in which minorities can excel. Furthermore, athletics and the arts are well known in the United States as highly competitive arenas. For every Gloria Estefan, Michael Jordan, Jose Canseco, or Oprah Winfrey who "makes it," many, many more will end up disappointed (Allport, 1979: 189–205; Merton, 1968:475–490).

Sociologist Harry Edwards (1984:8–13) agrees that the self-fulfilling prophecy of "innate Black athletic superiority" can have damaging consequences. Edwards points out that although this perception of athletic prowess may cause many African Americans to be channeled into sports, at best, only about 2500 of them currently make a living in professional sports as players, coaches, trainers, team doctors, and executives. In his view, Blacks should no longer put football playbooks ahead of textbooks, and the Black community should abandon its "blind belief in sport as an extraordinary route to social and economic salvation" (see also Gates, 1991).

African Americans and other minorities do not always passively accept harmful stereotypes and self-fulfilling prophecies. In the 1960s and 1970s, many subordinate minorities in the United States rejected traditional definitions and replaced them with feelings of pride, power, and strength. "Black is beautiful" and "Red power" movements among Blacks and Native Americans respectively were efforts to take control of their own lives and self-images.

However, although a minority can make a determined effort to redefine a situation and resist stereotypes, the definition that remains most important is the one used by a society's most powerful groups. In this sense, the historic White, Anglo-Saxon, Protestant norms of the United States still shape the definitions and stereotypes of racial and ethnic minorities.

Ethnicity

An ethnic group, unlike a racial group, is set apart from others because of its national origin or distinctive cultural patterns. Among the ethnic groups in the United States are peoples referred to collectively as *Hispanics* (or *Latinos*), such as Puerto Ricans, Mexican Americans, Cubans, and other Latin Americans (refer back to Table 7-1); other ethnic groups include Jewish, Irish, Polish, Italian, and Norwegian Americans.

The distinction between racial and ethnic minorities is not always clear-cut. Some racial minorities, such as Asian Americans, may have significant cultural differences from other groups. Certain ethnic minorities, such as Hispanics, may have obvious physical differences which set them apart from other people in the United States.

Despite such problems of categorization, sociologists continue to feel that the distinction between racial groups and ethnic groups is socially significant. In most societies, including the United States, physical differences tend to be more visible than ethnic differences. Partly as a result, stratification along racial lines is less subject to change than stratification along ethnic lines. Members of an ethnic minority sometimes can, over time, become indistinguishable from the majority—although this process may take generations and may never include all members of the group. By contrast, members of a racial minority find it much more difficult to blend in with the larger society and to gain acceptance from the majority.

STUDYING RACE AND ETHNICITY

Relations among racial and ethnic groups have lent themselves to analysis from the three major perspectives of sociology. Viewing race from the macro level, functionalists observe that racial prejudice and discrimination serve positive functions for dominant groups. Conflict theorists, on the other hand, see the economic structure as a central factor in the exploitation of minorities. The micro-level analysis of interactionist researchers stresses the manner in which everyday contact between people from different racial and ethnic backgrounds contributes to tolerance or leads to hostility.

Functionalist Perspective

It would seem reasonable to assume that racial bigotry offers no essential benefits for society. Why, then, does it exist? Functionalist theorists, although they agree that racial hostility is hardly to be admired, point out that it does indeed serve positive functions for those practicing discrimination.

Anthropologist Manning Nash (1962) has identified three functions that racially prejudiced beliefs have for the dominant group. First, such views provide a moral justification for maintaining an unequal society that routinely deprives a minority of its rights and privileges. Southern

Dennis MacDonald/The Picture Cube

"Street scrubbing" is one of the traditions of the annual Tulip Festival in Holland, Michigan. This festival celebrates the ethnic heritage of Dutch Americans.

Whites justified slavery by believing that Africans were physically and spiritually subhuman and devoid of souls (Hoebel, 1949:85–86). Second, racist beliefs discourage the subordinate minority from questioning its lowly status, since to do so is to question the very foundations of society. Finally, racial myths encourage support for the existing order by introducing the argument that if there were any major societal change (such as an end to discrimination), the minority would experience greater poverty and the majority would see its standard of living lowered. As a result, Nash suggests, racial prejudice grows when a society's value system (for example, that underlying a colonial empire or a regime perpetuating slavery) is being threatened.

Although racial prejudice and discrimination may serve the interests of the powerful, such unequal treatment can also be dysfunctional to a society as a whole and even to its dominant group. Sociologist Arnold Rose (1951:19–24) has outlined four dysfunctions associated with racism; they are as follows:

1 A society which practices discrimination fails to use the resources of all individuals. Discrimination limits the search for talent and leadership to the dominant group.

2 Discrimination aggravates social problems such as poverty, delinquency, and crime and places the financial burden to alleviate these problems on the dominant group.

3 Society must invest a good deal of time and money to defend its barriers to full participation of all members.

4 Goodwill and friendly diplomatic relations between nations are often undercut by racial prejudice and discrimination.

Conflict Perspective

Conflict theorists would certainly agree with Arnold Rose that racial prejudice and discrimination have many harmful consequences for society. Sociologists such as Oliver Cox (1948) and Robert Blauner (1972) have used the *exploitation theory* (or Marxist class theory) to explain the basis of racial subordination in the United States. As we saw in Chapter 6, Karl Marx viewed the exploitation of the lower class as a basic part of the capitalist economic system. Under a Marxist approach,

racism keeps minorities in low-paying jobs, thereby supplying the capitalist ruling class with a pool of cheap labor. Moreover, by forcing racial minorities to accept low wages, capitalists can restrict the wages of *all* members of the proletariat. Workers from the dominant group who demand higher wages can always be replaced by minorities who have no choice but to accept low-paying jobs (O. Cox, 1976; H. Hunter and Abraham, 1987; C. Johnson, 1939).

This Marxist perspective seems persuasive in a number of instances. Japanese Americans were the object of little prejudice until they began to enter jobs that brought them into competition with Whites. The movement to keep Chinese immigrants out of the United States became most fervent during the latter half of the nineteenth century, when Chinese and Whites fought over dwindling work opportunities. Both the enslavement of Blacks and the removal westward of Native Americans were, to a significant extent, economically motivated (McWilliams, 1951:144–150).

However, though some examples support the exploitation theory of race relations, this theory is too limited to explain prejudice in its many forms. Not all minority groups have been economically exploited to the same extent. In addition, many groups (among them the Quakers and the Mormons, for example) have been victimized by prejudice for reasons other than economic ones. Still, as Gordon Allport (1979:210) concludes, the exploitation theory correctly "points a sure finger at one of the factors involved in prejudice, . . . rationalized self-interest of the upper classes."

Interactionist Perspective

A Black woman is transferred from a job on an assembly line to a similar position working next to a White man. At first, the White man is patronizing, assuming that she must be incompetent. She is cold and resentful; even when she needs assistance, she refuses to admit it. After a week, the growing tension between the two leads to a bitter quarrel. Yet, over time, each slowly comes to appreciate the other's strengths and talents. A year after they begin working together, these two workers become respectful friends. This is an example of what interactionists call the *contact hypothesis* in action.

Bob Daemmrich/Stock, Boston

✳ *The* contact hypothesis *states that interracial contact of people with equal status in cooperative circumstances will cause them to become less prejudiced and to abandon previous stereotypes.*

✳ The ***contact hypothesis*** states that interracial contact of people with equal status in cooperative circumstances will cause them to become less prejudiced and to abandon previous stereotypes. The factors of *equal status* and a *pleasant, noncompetitive* ✳ *atmosphere* must be underscored. In the example above, if the two workers had been competing for one vacancy as a supervisor, the racial hostility between them might have worsened (Allport, 1979:261–282; Schaefer, 1993:63–64).

As African Americans and other minorities slowly gain access to better-paying and more responsible jobs in the United States, the contact hypothesis may take on even greater significance. The trend in our society is toward increasing con-✳ tact between individuals from dominant and subordinate groups. This may be one hope of eliminating—or at least reducing—racial and ethnic stereotyping and prejudice.

PREJUDICE AND DISCRIMINATION

False definitions of individuals and groups are perpetuated by prejudice. ***Prejudice*** is a negative ✳ attitude toward an entire category of people, often an ethnic or racial minority. If you resent your roommate because he or she is sloppy, you are not necessarily guilty of prejudice. However, if you immediately stereotype your roommate on the basis of such characteristics as race, ethnicity, or religion, that is a form of prejudice.

In recent years, college campuses across the United States have been the scene of bias-related incidents. Student-run newspapers and radio stations have ridiculed racial and ethnic minorities; threatening literature has been stuffed under the doors of minority students; graffiti endorsing the views of White supremacist organizations such as the Ku Klux Klan have been scrawled on university walls. In some cases, there have even been violent clashes between groups of White and Black students. These distressing incidents serve as a reminder that prejudice is evident among both educated and uneducated members of our society (Hively, 1990).

✳ Prejudice can result from ***ethnocentrism***—the tendency to assume that one's culture and way of life are superior to all others (see Chapter 2). Ethnocentric people judge other cultures by the standards of their own group, which leads quite easily to prejudice against cultures viewed as inferior.

One important and widespread form of preju-✳ dice is ***racism,*** the belief that one race is supreme and all others are innately inferior. When racism prevails in a society, members of subordinate groups generally experience prejudice, discrimination, and exploitation. In 1990, as concern mounted about racist attacks in the United States, Congress passed and President George Bush signed into law the Hate Crimes Statistics Act. This law directs the Department of Justice to gather data on crimes motivated by the victim's race, religion, ethnicity, or sexual orientation.

179
RACIAL AND ETHNIC INEQUALITY

In recent years, college campuses across the United States have been the scene of bias-related incidents. Columbia University students are shown in a rally against racism in the United States and South Africa.

Discriminatory Behavior

The biased attitudes of the prejudiced person often lead to discriminatory behavior. ***Discrimination*** is the process of denying opportunities and equal rights to individuals and groups because of prejudice or other arbitrary reasons. Imagine that a White corporate president with a stereotyped view of Asian Americans has an executive position to fill. The most qualified candidate for the job is a Korean American. If the president refuses to hire this candidate and instead selects an inferior White candidate, he or she is engaging in an act of racial discrimination.

Prejudiced *attitudes* should not be equated with discriminatory *behavior*. Although the two are generally related, they are not identical, and either condition can be present without the other. For example, a prejudiced person does not always act on his or her biases. In the situation described above, the White president might choose—despite his or her stereotypes—to hire the Korean American. This would be prejudice without discrimination. On the other hand, a White corporate president with a completely respectful view of Korean Americans might refuse to hire them for executive posts out of fear that biased clients would take their business elsewhere. In this case, the president's action would constitute discrimination without prejudice.

Institutional Discrimination

Discrimination is practiced not only by individuals in one-to-one encounters but also by institutions in their daily operations. Social scientists are particularly concerned with the ways in which structural factors such as employment, housing, health care, and government operations maintain the social significance of race and ethnicity. ***Institutional discrimination*** refers to the denial of opportunities and equal rights to individuals and groups which results from the normal operations of a society.

Institutional discrimination continuously imposes more hindrances on—and awards fewer benefits to—certain racial and ethnic groups than it does others. In some cases, even ostensibly neutral institutional standards can turn out to have discriminatory effects. In 1992, African American students at a midwestern state university protested a policy under which fraternities and sororities who wished to use campus facilities for a dance were required to post $150 security deposits to cover possible damages. The Black students complained that this policy had a discriminatory impact on minority student organizations. Campus police countered that the university's policy applied to *all* student groups interested in using these facilities. However, since overwhelmingly White fraternities and sororities at the school had their own houses that they used for dances, the policy indeed affected only African American and other minority organizations.

The U.S. Commission on Civil Rights (1981:9–10) has identified various forms of institutional discrimination, including:

- Rules requiring that only English be spoken at a place of work, even when it is not a business necessity to restrict the use of other languages
- Preferences shown by law schools and medical schools in the admission of children of wealthy and influential alumni, nearly all of whom are White
- Restrictive employment-leave policies, coupled with prohibitions on part-time work, that make it difficult for the heads of single-parent families (most of whom are women) to obtain and keep jobs

The social policy section on affirmative action at the end of the chapter will examine legal prohibitions against institutional discrimination.

Discrimination in the United States has proved difficult to eradicate. The 1960s saw the passage of many pioneering civil rights laws, including the landmark 1964 Civil Rights Act (which prohibits discrimination in public accommodations and publicly owned facilities on the basis of race, color, creed, national origin, and gender). In two important rulings in 1987, the Supreme Court held that federal prohibitions against racial discrimination protect members of all ethnic minorities—including Hispanics, Jews, and Arab Americans—even though they may be considered White. Yet discriminatory practices continue to pervade nearly all areas of life in the United States today.

In part, this is because—as Manning Nash's functionalist analysis suggests—various individuals and groups actually *benefit* from racial and ethnic discrimination in terms of money, status, and influence. Discrimination permits members of the majority to enhance their wealth, power, and prestige at the expense of others. Less qualified people are hired and promoted simply because they are members of the dominant group. Such individuals and groups will not surrender these advantages easily.

A member of a racial or ethnic minority in the United States is likely to face various forms of prejudice and discrimination from dominant group members and from important institutions of our society. This is the underlying and painful context of intergroup relations in this country.

PATTERNS OF INTERGROUP RELATIONS

Racial and ethnic groups can relate to one another in a wide variety of desirable and undesirable ways, ranging from friendships and intermarriages that require mutual approval to behaviors imposed on the subordinate group by the dominant group.

Undesirable patterns include *genocide*—the deliberate, systematic killing of an entire people or nation. This term has been used in reference to the killing of 1 million Armenians by Turkey beginning in 1915 (Melson, 1986:64–66). It is most commonly applied to Nazi Germany's extermination of 6 million European Jews, as well as members of other ethnic minorities, during World War II. However, the term *genocide* is also appropriate in describing the United States' policies toward Native Americans in the nineteenth century. In 1800, the Native American (or American Indian) population of the United States was about 600,000; by 1850, it had been reduced to 250,000 through warfare with the cavalry, disease, and forced relocation to inhospitable environments.

The *expulsion* of a people is another extreme means of acting out racial or ethnic prejudice. In 1979, Vietnam expelled nearly 1 million ethnic Chinese, partly as a result of centuries of hostility between Vietnam and neighboring China. These Chinese "boat people" were abruptly eliminated as a minority within Vietnamese society. In a more recent example of expulsion (which had aspects of genocide), Serbian forces began a program of "ethnic cleansing" in 1991 in the newly independent states of Bosnia and Herzegovina. Throughout the former nation of Yugoslavia, the Serbs drove more than 1 million Croats and Muslims from their homes. Some were tortured and killed, others abused and terrorized, in an attempt to "purify" the land for the remaining ethnic Serbs.

There are four identifiable patterns that describe typical intergroup relations as they occur in North America and throughout the world: (1) amalgamation, (2) assimilation, (3) segregation, and (4) pluralism. Each pattern defines the dominant group's actions and the minority group's responses. Intergroup relations are rarely restricted to only one of the four patterns, although invariably one does tend to dominate. Therefore, these patterns should be viewed primarily as ideal types.

Amalgamation

Amalgamation describes the end result when a majority group and a minority group combine to form a new group. Through intermarriage over several generations, various groups in the society combine to form a new group. This can be expressed as A + B + C = D, where A, B, and C represent different groups present in a society, and D signifies the end result, a unique cultural-racial group unlike any of the initial groups (Newman, 1973).

The belief in the United States as a "melting pot" became very compelling in the first part of the twentieth century, particularly since it suggested that the nation had an almost divine mission to amalgamate various groups into one people. However, in actuality many residents were not willing to have Native Americans, Jews, African Americans, Asian Americans, and Irish Roman Catholics as a part of the melting pot. Therefore, this pattern does not adequately describe dominant-subordinate relations existing in the United States.

Assimilation

Many Hindus in India complain about Indian citizens who copy the traditions and customs of the British. In Australia, Aborigines who have become part of the dominant society refuse to acknowledge their darker-skinned grandparents on the street. In the United States, there are Italian Americans, Polish Americans, Hispanics, and Jews who have changed their ethnic-sounding family names to names typically found among White, Protestant families.

Assimilation is the process by which a person forsakes his or her own cultural tradition to become part of a different culture. Generally, it is practiced by a minority group member who wants to conform to the standards of the dominant group. Assimilation can be described as an ideology in which A + B + C = A. The majority A dominates in such a way that members of minorities B and C imitate A and attempt to become indistinguishable from the dominant group (Newman, 1973).

Assimilation can strike at the very roots of a person's identity as he or she seeks to gain full acceptance as an "American." Hence, Nathan Birnbaum changed his name to George Burns, and Joseph Levitch became Jerry Lewis. Despite such efforts, assimilation does not necessarily bring acceptance for the minority group individual. A Chinese American may speak flawless English, go faithfully to a Protestant church, and know the names of all members of the Baseball Hall of Fame. Yet he or she is still *seen* as different and may therefore be rejected as a business associate, a neighbor, or a marriage partner.

Segregation

Segregation refers to the physical separation of two groups of people in terms of residence, workplace, and social functions. Generally, it is imposed by a dominant group on a minority group. However, segregation is rarely complete; intergroup contact inevitably occurs even in the most segregated societies.

In the 1990s, the Republic of South Africa finally began to lift the severe restrictions on the movement of Blacks and other non-Whites that had been historically enforced through a wide-ranging system of segregation known as *apartheid*. Apartheid has involved many forms of segregation, including the creation of homelands where Blacks are expected to live. Moreover, as of 1993, Blacks were still not allowed to vote in elections for the South African parliament. From a conflict perspective, apartheid can perhaps best be understood as a twentieth-century effort to reestablish the form of race relations typified by the master-slave relationship.

South Africa is far from the only country in which segregation is common. Housing practices

When segregation was common in the southern states, "Jim Crow" laws enforced official segregation of the races. In a blatant example of institutional discrimination, photographed by Elliott Erwitt in North Carolina in 1950, Blacks were not allowed to use a water fountain reserved for Whites. Instead, Blacks had to drink out of a nearby sink.

in the United States have often forced subordinate racial and ethnic groups into certain neighborhoods, usually undesirable ones. In addition, members of a minority group may voluntarily seek to separate themselves from the dominant majority because they fear reprisals. This is not, however, the primary factor contributing to segregation. The central causes of residential segregation in the United States appear to be the prejudices of Whites and the resulting discriminatory practices in the housing and lending markets. Data consistently show that Blacks, Hispanics, and (to a somewhat lesser extent) Asians face segregation in the nation's metropolitan areas. Such housing segregation is evident around the world: studies in Sweden, for example, document that migrants from Chile, Greece, and Turkey are confined to segregated areas of Swedish cities (Andersson-Brolin, 1988; Massey and Denton, 1989a, 1989b).

Pluralism

In a pluralistic society, a subordinate group will not have to forsake its lifestyle and traditions. ***Pluralism is based on mutual respect between various groups in a society for one another's cultures. It allows a minority group to express its own culture and still to participate without prejudice in the larger society.*** Earlier, amalgamation was described as A + B + C = D, and assimilation as A + B + C = A. Using this same approach, we can conceive of pluralism as A + B + C = A + B + C. All the groups are able to coexist in the same society (Newman, 1973).

In the United States, pluralism is more of an ideal than a reality. There are distinct instances of pluralism: the ethnic neighborhoods in major cities, such as Koreatown, Little Tokyo, Andersonville (Swedish Americans), and Spanish Harlem. Yet there are also limits to such cultural freedom. In order to survive, a society must promote a certain consensus among its members regarding basic ideals, values, and beliefs. Thus, if a Rumanian migrating to the United States wants to move up the occupational ladder, he or she cannot avoid learning the English language.

Several authors argue persuasively that Switzerland exemplifies a modern pluralistic state. The absence both of a national language and of a dominant religious faith leads to a tolerance for cultural diversity. In addition, various political devices have been adopted to safeguard the interests of ethnic groups in a way that has no parallel in the United States. By contrast, Great Britain has found it difficult to achieve cultural pluralism in a multiracial society. East Indians, Pakistanis, and Blacks from the Caribbean and Africa are experiencing prejudice and discrimination within the dominant White British society. There is increasing pressure to cut off all Asian and Black immigration and to expel non-Whites currently living in Britain. Race relations in contemporary Brazil are examined in Box 7-1 (page 184).

BOX 7-1

RACE RELATIONS IN BRAZIL: THE LEGACY OF SLAVERY

To someone knowledgeable in racial and ethnic relations in the United States, Brazil seems familiar in a number of respects. Like the United States, Brazil was colonized by Europeans (in Brazil's case, the Portuguese) who overwhelmed the native population. Like the United States, Brazil imported Black Africans as slaves to meet the demand for laborers. Even today, excluding nations on the African continent, Brazil is second only to the United States in number of people of African descent.

Brazil depended much more on slave trade than the United States did, even though at the height of slavery each nation had approximately 4 to 4.5 million slaves. Brazil's reliance on a continual influx of slaves from Africa meant that typical Brazilian slaves had closer ties to Africa than did their counterparts in the United States. Revolts and escapes were more common among slaves in Brazil. The most dramatic example was the slave *quilombo (or hideaway)* of Palmores, where 20,000 inhabitants repeatedly fought off Portuguese assaults until 1698 (Degler, 1971:7–8, 47–52).

Today, rather than being classified simply as "Black" or "White" (as is typical in the United States), Brazil's racial groupings constitute a type of color gradient on a continuum from light to dark skin color. Consequently, Mulattos (people of mixed racial ancestry) are viewed as an identifiable social group. According to the 1980 census, Brazil's population was 55 percent *Branco* (White), 38 percent Mulatto, 6 percent *Preto* (Black), and 1 percent other. Over the last 50 years, the proportion of Mulattos has grown, while the proportion of both *Brancos* and *Pretos* has declined (Brazil, 1981; C. Wood and de Carvalho, 1988:135–153).

Historian Carl Degler (1971) has suggested that the key difference between race relations in Brazil and race relations in the United States is Brazil's "Mulatto escape hatch," under which Mulattos are not classified with Blacks. But, while lighter skin color does appear to enhance status in Brazil, the impact of this escape hatch has been exaggerated. Recent income data show that Mulattos earn 42 percent more income than Blacks, but this difference is not especially remarkable, given that Mulattos have more formal schooling. More striking is the finding that Whites earn 98 percent more income than Mulattos. As a result, the most significant distinction appears to be that between Whites and all Brazilian "people of color," rather than that between the country's Blacks and Mulattos (Dzidzienyo, 1987; Silva, 1985).

In 1988, Brazil marked as a national holiday the hundredth anniversary of the abolition of slavery, but for 40 to 50 percent of Brazil's people of color there was little rejoicing. Zézé Motta, Brazil's leading Black actress and a longtime campaigner for Black civil rights, observed: "We have gone from the hold of the ship to the basements of society." Of 559 members of the nation's Congress, only 7 were Black. Whites are still seven times more likely to graduate from college, while job advertisements continue to seek individuals of "good appearance" (a euphemism for light skin). Even Black professionals such as physicians, teachers, and engineers earn 20 to 25 percent less than their lighter-skinned counterparts (T. Robinson, 1989; Simons, 1988:1; Webster and Dwyer, 1988).

RACE AND ETHNICITY IN THE UNITED STATES

Few societies have a more diverse population than the United States does; the nation is truly a multiracial, multiethnic society. Of course, this has not always been true. The different groups listed in Table 7-1 have come to the United States as a result of immigration, colonialism, and, in the case of Blacks, the institution of slavery.

Racial Groups

The largest racial minorities in the United States include Black Americans, Native Americans, Chinese Americans, Japanese Americans, and Indochinese Americans.

Black Americans "I am an invisible man," wrote Black author Ralph Ellison in his novel _Invisible Man_ (1952:3). "I am a man of substance, of flesh and bone, fiber and liquids—and I might even be said to possess a mind. I am invisible, understand, simply because people refuse to see me." Over four decades later, many Blacks (or African Americans) still feel invisible. Despite their large numbers, African Americans have long been treated as second-class citizens. Currently, by the standards of the federal government, nearly 1 out of every 3 Blacks—as opposed to 1 out of every 10 Whites—is poor (Bureau of the Census, 1991a).

Contemporary institutional discrimination and individual prejudice against African Americans are rooted in the history of slavery in the United States. Even in bondage, the Africans were forced to assimilate and were stripped of much of their African tribal heritage. Yet the destruction of African cultures was not complete; some aspects survived in oral literature, religious customs, and music. Black resistance to slavery included many slave revolts, such as those led by Denmark Vesey in South Carolina in 1822 and Nat Turner in Virginia in 1831. Still, most Blacks remained subject to the arbitrary and often cruel actions of their White owners (Du Bois, 1909; Herskovits, 1941, 1943).

The end of the Civil War did not bring genuine freedom and equality for Blacks. The "Jim Crow" laws of the south, which were designed to enforce

OH, IT'S YOU AGAIN

WASSERMAN
©'92 BOSTON GLOBE
DIST. BY L.A. TIMES SYND.

By Daniel M. Wasserman. © 1992 Boston Globe. Distributed by Los Angeles Times Syndicate. Reprinted with permission.

The riots in Los Angeles and other cities in 1992 following the acquittal of four White police officers in the videotaped beating of Black construction worker Rodney King reminded people that the historic racial problems of the United States have not been resolved.

official segregation, were upheld as constitutional by the Supreme Court in 1896. In addition, Blacks faced the danger of lynching campaigns, often led by the Ku Klux Klan, during the late nineteenth and early twentieth centuries. From a conflict perspective, the dominance of Whites was maintained formally through legalized segregation and maintained informally by means of vigilante terror and violence (J. Franklin and Moss, 1988).

A turning point in the struggle for Black equality came in the unanimous Supreme Court decision in the 1954 case of _Brown v. Board of Education of Topeka, Kansas._ The Court outlawed segregation of public school students, ruling that "separate educational facilities are inherently unequal." In the wake of the _Brown_ decision, there was a surge of activism on behalf of Black civil rights, including boycotts of segregated bus companies and sit-ins at restaurants and lunch counters which refused to serve Blacks.

During the decade of the 1960s, a vast civil rights movement emerged, with many competing factions and strategies for change. The Southern Christian Leadership Conference (SCLC),

TABLE 7-2 Relative Economic Positions of Blacks and Whites, 1991

CHARACTERISTIC	BLACKS	WHITES	RATIO, BLACK TO WHITE
Four-year college education, people 25 and over	11.5%	22.5%	0.51
Median family money income	$21,423	$36,915	0.58
Unemployment rate	12.4%	6.0%	2.06
Persons below the poverty level	31.9%	10.7%	2.98

SOURCE: Bureau of the Census, 1992a:39.

Despite some progress among Blacks in the 1960s and 1970s, there remains a wide gap in the economic positions of African Americans and Whites in the United States.

founded by Dr. Martin Luther King, Jr., used nonviolent civil disobedience to oppose segregation. The National Association for the Advancement of Colored People (NAACP) favored use of the courts to press for equality for African Americans. But many younger Black leaders, most notably Malcolm X, turned toward an ideology of Black power. Proponents of ***Black power*** rejected the goal of assimilation into White, middle-class society. They defended the beauty and dignity of Black and African cultures and supported the creation of Black-controlled political and economic institutions (Carmichael and Hamilton, 1967).

Although numerous courageous actions have taken place to achieve Black civil rights, Black and White America are still separate, still unequal. From birth to death, Blacks suffer in terms of the life chances described in Chapter 6. Life remains quite difficult for millions of poor Blacks, who must attempt to survive in ghetto areas shattered by high unemployment and abandoned housing. The economic position of Blacks is shown in Table 7-2. As the table illustrates, the median income of Blacks is only 58 percent that of Whites, and the unemployment rate among Blacks is more than twice that of Whites (Bureau of the Census, 1992a:39).

The economic position of African American women and their children is particularly critical. A 1988 survey of Black female heads of households showed that only 34 percent of them worked full time; the poverty rate for Black, single mothers with children was 83 percent. Economist Bernard Anderson of the Rockefeller Foun-

dation observes: "You cannot discuss Black poverty without discussing the dreadful condition of life and opportunity among Black women who are poor and raising children" (Bureau of the Census, 1992a:457; Noble, 1984:E20; Rawlings, 1989:23).

There have been economic gains for *some* Blacks—especially middle-class Blacks—over the last 35 years. For example, data compiled by the Department of Labor show that Blacks in management areas of the labor market increased nationally from 2.4 percent of the total in 1958 to 6.3 percent in 1991. Yet African Americans still represent only 4 percent or less of all physicians, engineers, scientists, lawyers, judges, and marketing and financial managers. Moreover, with regard to an area that is especially important for developing role models, Blacks and Hispanics together account for less than 7.3 percent of all editors and reporters in the United States (Bureau of the Census, 1992a:392).

In many respects, the civil rights movement of the 1960s left institutionalized discrimination against Blacks untouched. Consequently, in the 1980s, Black leaders worked to mobilize Black political power as a force for social change. Between 1969 and 1986, the number of African American elected officials increased by more than fivefold. By 1991, there were 314 Black mayors in the United States, more than two-thirds from cities in the south. African American mayors held office in many of the nation's largest cities, including New York, Philadelphia, Detroit, Atlanta, Los Angeles, and New Orleans (Joint Center for Political Studies, 1992).

Native Americans There are approximately 2 million Native Americans (or American Indians). They represent a diverse array of cultures, distinguishable by language, family organization, religion, and livelihood.

To the outsiders who came to the United States—European settlers and their descendants—the native people came to be known as "American Indians." By the time that the Bureau of Indian Affairs (BIA) was organized as part of the *War* Department in 1824, Indian-White relations had already included three centuries of mutual misunderstanding (Berg, 1975). As we saw earlier, many bloody wars took place during the nineteenth century in which a significant part of the nation's Indian population was wiped out. By the end of the nineteenth century, schools for Indians operated by the BIA or church missions prohibited the practice of Native American cultures. Yet such schools did little to make the children effective competitors in White society.

Today, Native Americans are an impoverished people; life is difficult, whether they live in cities or on the reservations. For example, the death rate of Navajo babies over 18 weeks old is 2½ times that of the overall population of the United States. One Native American teenager in six has attempted suicide—a rate four times higher than the rate for other teenagers. In 1987, the National Urban Indian Council estimated that 60 to 80 percent of Native Americans living in cities are unemployed (Giago and Illoway, 1982; D. Martin, 1987:46; *New York Times*, 1992c:D24).

In 1972, a regional director of the Commission on Civil Rights characterized government policy toward American Indians as "assimilate—or starve!" Native Americans who choose to abandon all vestiges of their tribal cultures may escape certain forms of prejudice. Native Americans who remain on the reservation and cherish their cultural heritage will suffer the consequences of their choice (Muskrat, 1972).

Nevertheless, an increasing number of people in the United States are openly claiming an identity as Native American. Since 1960, the federal government's count of Native Americans has tripled, to an estimated 1.8 million. According to the 1990 census, there has been a 38 percent increase in Native Americans over the last 10 years. Demographers believe that more and more Native

Americans who previously concealed their identity are no longer pretending to be White. Russell Thornton, a sociologist and member of the Cherokee nation of Oklahoma, notes: "There were many people who were ashamed of their Indian past, so they hid it." But, today, many Indian tribes have reported sharp increases in applications for membership, and there has been a noticeable rise in participation in Native American cultural events (D. Johnson, 1991).

Native American activists have bitterly protested the mistreatment of their people in the United States. The latest battleground—not only in the United States, but also in Brazil and other societies—has been land and natural resources. Reservations typically contain a wealth of resources. In the past, Indian tribes have lacked the technical knowledge to negotiate beneficial agreements successfully with private corporations; when they had such ability, the federal government often stepped in and made the final agreements more favorable to corporations than to residents of the reservations. More recently, however, a coalition of Native American tribes has had impressive results in its bargaining efforts. An Atlantic Richfield Company (ARCO) offer of $300,000 for an oil pipeline right-of-way on a Navajo reservation was converted through skillful negotiating into a contract that will bring the tribe $78 million over 20 years (Schaefer, 1993:179–181).

Chinese Americans Unlike African slaves and Native Americans, the Chinese were initially encouraged to immigrate to the United States. From 1850 to 1880, over 200,000 Chinese immigrated to this country, lured by job opportunities created by the discovery of gold. However, as employment possibilities decreased and competition for mining grew, the Chinese became the target of a bitter campaign to limit their numbers and restrict their rights. Chinese laborers were exploited, then discarded.

In 1882 Congress enacted the Chinese Exclusion Act, which prevented Chinese immigration and even forbade Chinese in America from sending for their families. As a result, there was a steady decline in the Chinese population until after World War II. More recently, the descendants of the nineteenth-century immigrants have

BOX 7-2
ASIAN AMERICANS AND THE "MODEL MINORITY" STEREOTYPE

It is commonly believed that Asian Americans constitute a model or ideal minority group, supposedly because, despite past suffering from prejudice and discrimination, they have succeeded economically, socially, and educationally without resorting to political and violent confrontations with Whites. Some observers see the existence of a model minority as a reaffirmation that anyone can get ahead in the United States with talent and hard work.

Indeed, there is an implicit critique of Blacks, Hispanics, and others for failing to succeed as well as the model minority has. Viewed from a conflict perspective, this becomes yet another instance of "blaming the victim" (refer back to Box 6-2 on page 152), for the hidden allegation is that any minorities who have been less successful than Asian Americans are completely responsible for their own failures. Proponents of the model minority view add that because Asian Americans have achieved success, they have ceased to be a disadvantaged minority (Hurh and Kim, 1989).

The concept of a model minority ignores the diversity among Asian Americans: there are rich and poor Japanese Americans, rich and poor Filipino Americans, and so forth. Moreover, even when certain Asian Americans are clustered at the higher-paying end of the stratification system, there may nevertheless be limits on how far they can advance. A study conducted in 1988 showed that only 8 percent of Asian Americans were classified as "officials" and "managers," compared with 12 percent for all groups (Takaki, 1990).

The dramatic success of Asian Americans in the educational system has undoubtedly contributed to the model minority stereotype.

In comparison with their numbers in the population of the United States, Asian Americans are overrepresented by far as students in the nation's most prestigious public and private universities. Their success can be attributed, in part, to the belief in many Asian cultures in the value of education, family pressures to succeed, and the desire to use academic achievement as a means of escaping discrimination.

Even the positive stereotype of Asian American students as "academic stars" can be dysfunctional. Asian Americans who do only modestly well in school may face criticism from parents or teachers for their failure to conform to the "whiz kid" image. In fact, despite the model minority label, the high school dropout rate for Asian Americans is increasing rapidly. California's special program for low-income, academically disadvantaged students has a 30 percent Asian American clientele, and the proportion of Asian students in the program is on the rise (Tachibana, 1990).

A study of the California state university system, released in 1991, casts further doubt on the model minority stereotype of Asian Americans. According to the report, while Asian Americans are often viewed as successful overachievers, they suffer from unrecognized and overlooked needs, discomfort, and harassment on campus—as well as from a shortage of Asian faculty and staff members to whom they can turn for support. The report noted that an "alarming number" of Asian-American students appear to be experiencing intense stress and alienation—problems which have often been "exacerbated by racial harassment" (Ohnuma, 1991:5).

Ben Fong-Torres (1986:7) worries that while reports of successes achieved by Asian Americans may inspire pride within this minority, they may also intensify fear and envy in the dominant White majority and even in other minorities. Combined with resentment about the growing economic dominance of Japan, such jealousy may contribute not only to racial slurs and biases against Asian Americans but to violent attacks as well. In 1982, two White males began arguing with a Chinese American, Vincent Chin, whom they mistook for being of Japanese descent and blamed for the dire straits of the United States' automobile industry. The Whites chased Chin into a parking lot and repeatedly beat him with a baseball bat; he died four days later. Much to the shock of the local Asian American community, Chin's accused killers were allowed to make a plea-bargaining agreement whereby they were sentenced to only three years' probation and were given fines of $3700 each.

Viewed from a conflict perspective, the model minority stereotype is likely to provoke further prejudice and discrimination against a racial minority that is quite easily viewed as "different." Full social acceptance of Asian Americans may be hindered if they are resented for becoming "too successful too fast." Ginger Lew, a Washington attorney and former State Department official, concludes that the "'model minority' myth is just that. It's not true in terms of income or status. Stereotypes, whether positive or negative, are a disservice to the community" (Commission on Civil Rights, 1992; Oxnam, 1986:89, 92; Schaefer, 1993:340–350).

Shown is Gene Sogioka's watercolor, "FBI Takes Father Away." Born in California, Sogioka worked as a background artist for Walt Disney studios and taught art part time. During World War II, he was taken (along with his wife Mini and their very young daughter) to an evacuation camp for Japanese Americans in Poston, Arizona. The camp was located on a deserted Indian reservation near the Colorado River. Sogioka was later hired by the wartime Bureau of Sociological Research to document the lives of the confined Japanese Americans through his artwork (Gesensway and Roseman, 1987:166).

been joined by a new influx from Hong Kong and Taiwan. The groups of immigrants sometimes form sharp contrasts in their degree of assimilation, desire to live in Chinatowns, and feelings about this country's relations with the People's Republic of China (Kwong and Lum, 1988).

There are currently about 1.65 million Chinese Americans in the United States. Some Chinese Americans have entered lucrative occupations. This has led to the popular concept that the strides made by Chinese Americans (and other Asian Americans) constitute a success story. We examine the consequences of this "model minority" image in Box 7-2.

Many Chinese immigrants struggle to survive under living and working conditions that belie the "model minority" stereotype. New York City's Chinatown district is filled with illegal sweatshops in which recent immigrants—many of them Chinese women—work for minimal wages. Even in "legal" factories in the garment industry, hours are long and rewards are limited. A seamstress typically works 11 hours per day, six days a week, and earns about $10,000 a year. Other workers, such as hemmers and cutters, earn only $5000 per year (Lum and Kwong, 1989).

Japanese Americans   There are approximately 800,000 Japanese Americans in the United States. As a people, they are relatively recent arrivals to this nation. In 1880 there were only 148 Japanese in the United States, but by 1920 there were over 110,000. The early Japanese immigrants—who are called the **Issei**—were usually males seeking employment opportunities. Along with Chinese immigrants, they were seen as a "yellow peril" by many Whites, and they were subjected to widespread prejudice and discrimination.

In 1941, the attack on Pearl Harbor by Japan—by then allied with Hitler's Germany—had severe repercussions for Japanese Americans. The federal government decreed that all Japanese Americans on the west coast must leave their homes and report to "evacuation camps." They became, in effect, scapegoats for the anger that other people in the United States felt concerning Japan's role in World War II. By August 1943, in an unprecedented application of guilt by virtue of ancestry, 113,000 Japanese Americans were forced to live in hastily built camps (Hosokawa, 1969).

Financially, the Federal Reserve Board placed the losses entailed by evacuation for Japanese Americans at nearly half a billion dollars, or more than $4500 per person. Accounting for inflation, this figure represents a loss of about $27,000 per person today. Moreover, the psychological effect on these citizens—including the humiliation of being labeled as "disloyal"—was immeasurable. Eventually, the Japanese born in the United States, the *Nisei,* were allowed to enlist in the Army and serve in a segregated combat unit in Europe. Others resettled in the east and midwest to work in factories.

In 1983, the federal Commission on Wartime Relocation and Internment of Civilians recommended government payments to all surviving Japanese Americans held in detention camps during World War II. The commission reported that the detention was motivated by "race prejudice, war hysteria, and a failure of political leadership." It added that "no documented acts of espionage, sabotage, or fifth-column activity were shown to have been committed" by Japanese Americans (Pear, 1983).

In 1988, President Ronald Reagan signed unprecedented legislation, entitled the Civil Liberties Act, in which the United States government apologized for the forced relocation of 120,000 Japanese Americans and established a $1.25 billion trust fund to pay reparations to those placed in detention camps. Under the new law, the federal government was to issue individual apologies for all violations of Japanese Americans' constitutional rights. Beginning in 1990, awards of $20,000 were to be given to each of the approximately 77,500 surviving Japanese Americans who had been interned by the federal government.

Indochinese Americans The problems of the United States government's involvement in Vietnam did not end with the withdrawal of all military assistance, or even with the evacuation of all the United States' personnel from South Vietnam. A subsequent tragedy was the reluctant welcome given to the refugees from Vietnam, Cambodia, and Laos by people of the United States and other nations. One week after the evacuation of Vietnam in April 1975, a Gallup poll reported that 52 percent of people in the United States were against giving any sanctuary to the Asian refugees, 36 percent were in favor, and 12 percent were undecided. The primary objection to Vietnamese immigration was that it would further increase unemployment (Gallup Opinion Index, 1975; Schaefer and Schaefer, 1975).

The initial 135,000 Vietnamese refugees who fled in 1975 were joined by another 800,000 fleeing later fighting that plagued Indochina. The United States eventually accepted about 250,000 Asian refugees for political settlement. Numerous others were stranded in overcrowded refugee camps administered by the United States. Yet, in a sense, those who reached the refugee camps were the lucky ones. It is estimated that 30 to 35 percent of those who left Vietnam in rickety boats did not survive (Haupt, 1979).

Most Indochinese refugees faced problems similar to those experienced by earlier immigrants to the United States. Generally, they had to accept jobs which were well below their occupational positions in southeast Asia; with geographical mobility came downward social mobility. Like European immigrants before them, the Indochinese refugees coming to a new land sought out their compatriots. As a result, Indochinese communities and neighborhoods have begun to emerge, especially in California, Texas, and New York. In such areas, where Indochinese Americans have been able to reestablish some of the distinctive cultural practices of their homelands, the outlook is for a more pluralistic period in their adjustment, rather than adjustment involving complete assimilation.

Ethnic Groups

Unlike racial minorities, members of subordinate ethnic groups are generally not hindered by physical differences from assimilating into the dominant culture of the United States. However, members of ethnic minority groups still face many forms of prejudice and discrimination. This will be apparent as we examine the situations of the country's largest ethnic groups—Hispanics, Jews, and White ethnics.

Hispanics: Mexican Americans and Puerto Ricans
Taken together, the various groups which are included under the general terms *Hispanics* and *Latinos* represent the largest ethnic minority in the United States. It is estimated that there are more than 20 million Hispanics in this country, including 13 million Mexican Americans, over 2 million Puerto Ricans, and smaller numbers of Cubans and people of Central or South American origin.

The various Hispanic groups share a heritage of Spanish language and culture. Yet people whose first language is Spanish have serious problems with assimilation in the United States. An intelligent student for whom English is a second language may be presumed slow or even unruly by English-speaking schoolchildren, and frequently by English-speaking teachers as well. This self-fulfilling prophecy can lead to the immediate labeling of Hispanic children as being underachievers, as having learning disabilities, or as suffering from emotional problems—all labels which some of the children may then fulfill. Bilingual education has been introduced in many school districts as a means of easing the educational difficulties experienced by Hispanic children and others whose first language is not English.

The educational difficulties of Hispanic students certainly contribute to the generally low economic status of Hispanics. By 1991, only 10 percent of Hispanic adults had completed college, compared with 22 percent of Whites. At the same time, the median family income of Hispanics was only 63 percent that of Whites. In 1991, 5.6 million Hispanics (or 28 percent of all Hispanics in the United States) lived below the poverty line (Bureau of the Census, 1992a:39, 41).

Despite common problems, there is considerable diversity among the various Hispanic groups found in the United States. The largest Hispanic population comprises Mexican Americans, who can be further subdivided into those descended from the residents of the territories annexed after the Mexican-American War of 1848 and those who have immigrated from Mexico to the United States. The opportunity for a Mexican to earn in 1 hour what it would take an entire day to earn in Mexico has motivated millions of legal and illegal immigrants to come north.

The second-largest segment of Hispanics in the United States is composed of Puerto Ricans. Since 1917, residents of Puerto Rico have held the status of American citizens. Many have migrated to New York and other eastern cities. Unfortunately, Puerto Ricans experience serious poverty both in the United States and on the island. Those living in the continental United States have barely half the family income of Whites. As a result, a reverse migration began in the 1970s; more Puerto Ricans began leaving for the island than were coming to the mainland (Lemann, 1991).

Politically, Puerto Ricans in the United States have not been so successful as Mexican Americans in organizing for their rights. For many mainland Puerto Ricans—as for many residents of the island—the paramount political issue is the destiny of Puerto Rico itself. Should it continue in its present commonwealth status, petition for admission to the United States as the fifty-first state, or attempt to become an independent nation? This question has divided Puerto Rico for decades and remains a central issue in Puerto Rican elections. As of 1993, a referendum was under consideration in which Puerto Ricans could express their preferences regarding the future status of their homeland.

The fastest-growing segment, by far, of the Hispanic community consists of people from Central or South America. Until recently, this group has not been closely studied; government data have rarely differentiated these people by nationality and have instead lumped them together as "other." Yet people from Chile and Costa Rica may have little in common except their hemisphere of origin and the Spanish language. Moreover, immigrants from Brazil speak Portuguese, those from Surinam speak Dutch, and those from French Guiana speak French. In recent years, increasing numbers of Central Americans and South Americans have fled to the United States to escape political unrest. Many of them have had difficulty gaining official status as refugees. The arrival of immigrants and refugees from countries in Central and South America has contributed to changes in the racial and ethnic balance of the population of the United States.

Jewish Americans Jews constitute almost 3 percent of the population of the United States. They play a prominent role in the worldwide Jewish community because the United States has the world's largest concentration of Jews. Like the Japanese, many Jewish immigrants came to this country and became white-collar professionals. But again, as in the case of the Japanese, Jewish achievements have come despite prejudice and discrimination.

Anti-Semitism—that is, anti-Jewish prejudice—in the United States has often been vicious, although rarely so widespread and never so formalized as in Europe. In many cases, Jews have been

Steve Shay/Photography

Many racial and ethnic minorities in the United States attempt to strike a balance between emulating the values of the dominant culture (assimilation) and preserving their own distinctive heritages (pluralism). In this photograph, a young Orthodox Jew in Chicago adheres to Jewish law by wearing the traditional yarmulke on his head—but it is a yarmulke with the emblem of the National Basketball Association's Chicago Bulls.

used as scapegoats for other people's failures. This was clearly indicated in a study of World War II veterans conducted by Bettelheim and Janowitz (1964). The researchers found that men who had experienced downward mobility (for example, job failure) were more likely to blame their setbacks on Jewish Americans than on their own shortcomings.

Jews have not achieved equality in the United States. Despite high levels of education and professional training, they are still conspicuously absent from the top management of large corporations (except for the few firms founded by Jews). However, anti-Semitism in the corporate world may be on the decline. In 1985 and 1986, sociologist Samuel Klausner (1988) and his colleagues questioned 444 people with master of business administration (M.B.A.) degrees from three business schools. Researchers tested seven indicators of discrimination and, in each case, *failed* to find evidence of discrimination against Jewish executives. (The same study, however, did detect substantial discrimination against Black and female executives.)

As is true for other minorities discussed in this chapter, Jewish Americans face the choice of maintaining ties to their long religious and cultural heritage or becoming as indistinguishable as possible from gentiles. Many Jews have tended to assimilate, as is evident from the rise in marriages between Jews and Christians. This trend worries Jewish religious leaders, some of whom fear that the long-term future of the Jewish faith is in jeopardy. While studies show that 78 percent of Jews who intermarry maintain their self-identification as "Jewish" after their marriages, other research indicates that children in these interfaith marriages do not identify as Jewish if the gentile parent does not convert—which is the case in the majority of Jewish-Christian marriages (E. Mayer, 1983, 1985).

In the 1980s, there were disturbing increases in acts of violence against Jews and against Jewish institutions. This same period was marked by a wave of cross burnings and bombings directed at Blacks who were living in predominantly White neighborhoods. These actions seemed to coincide with renewed activity among anti-Semitic White supremacist groups such as the Ku Klux Klan and the Aryan Nation. The Anti-Defamation League of B'nai B'rith (1992) reported that in 1991 anti-Semitic incidents reached the highest level they had been at since the organization began collecting statistics 13 years earlier. Such threatening behavior only underscores the fears of many Jewish Americans, who find it difficult to forget the Holocaust—the extermination of 6 million Jews by the Nazi Third Reich during the late 1930s and 1940s.

TABLE 7-3   Representation of Minorities in the Elite of the United States

	WHITE ANGLO-SAXON PROTESTANTS, %	OTHER WHITE PROTES-TANTS, %	IRISH CATHOLICS, %	OTHER WHITE CATHOLICS, %	JEWS, %	BLACKS, HISPANICS, ASIANS, NATIVE AMERICANS, %
National population Men born before 1932	22.9	22.5	4.2	17.2	2.9	14.4
College-educated men born before 1932	31.0	19.8	6.0	15.5	8.9	5.2
Overall elite	43.0	19.5	8.5	8.7	11.3	3.9
Business	57.3	22.1	5.3	6.1	6.9	0.0
Labor	23.9	15.2	37.0	13.0	4.3	2.2
Political parties	44.0	18.0	14.0	4.0	8.0	4.0
Voluntary associations	32.7	13.5	1.9	7.7	17.3	19.2
Mass media	37.1	11.3	4.8	9.7	25.8	0.0
Congress	53.4	19.0	6.9	8.6	3.4	3.4
Political appointees	39.4	28.8	1.5	13.6	10.6	3.0
Civil servants	35.8	22.6	9.4	9.4	15.1	3.8

SOURCE: Alba and Moore, 1982.

This table shows the representation of White Anglo-Saxon Protestants, Irish Catholics, and others among the leaders of powerful social, economic, and political institutions of the United States. The representation of each group within the nation's overall elite and within particular types of positions is compared with the percentage of group members who are men born before 1932 or college-educated men born before 1932. These comparative data are offered because older males and college-educated males have traditionally been the groups from which members of the elite emerge.

White Ethnics   A significant segment of the population of the United States is made up of White ethnics whose ancestors have emigrated from Europe within the last 100 years. In terms of ancestry, the nation's White ethnic population includes about 58 million people who claim at least partial German ancestry, 39 million Irish Americans, 15 million Italian Americans, and 9 million Polish Americans, as well as immigrants from other European nations. Some of these people continue to live in close-knit ethnic neighborhoods, while others have largely assimilated and have left the "old ways" behind (Bureau of the Census, 1992a:43).

To what extent are White ethnics found among the nation's top decision makers? Sociologists Richard Alba and Gwen Moore (1982) conducted interviews with 545 people who held important positions in powerful social, economic, and political institutions. Table 7-3 compares the representation of White Anglo-Saxon Protestants in these positions with that of certain minorities. It shows that White Anglo-Saxon Protestants are overrepresented among the nation's elite, while White ethnics are underrepresented (although not so dramatically as are Blacks, Hispanics, Asians, and Native Americans). Some ethnic minorities appear to have risen to key positions in particular areas of the elite structure. Irish Catholics are well represented among labor leaders; Jews and racial minorities compare favorably among leaders of voluntary associations (organizations established on the basis of common interest, whose members volunteer or even pay to participate).

White ethnics and racial minorities have often been antagonistic to one another because of economic competition—an interpretation that is in line with the conflict approach to sociology. As Blacks, Hispanics, and Native Americans emerge from the lower class, they will initially be competing with working-class Whites for jobs, housing, and educational opportunities. In times of high unemployment or inflation, any such competition can easily generate intense intergroup conflict.

In many respects, the plight of White ethnics raises the same basic issues as that of other subordinate people in the United States. How ethnic can people be—how much can they deviate from an essentially White, Anglo-Saxon, Protestant norm—before society punishes them for a willingness to be different? Our society does seem to reward people for assimilating. Yet, as we have seen, assimilation is no guarantee of equality or freedom from discrimination. In the social policy section that follows, we examine the controversy surrounding affirmative action programs and their efforts to address discrimination in hiring practices.

AFFIRMATIVE ACTION

- How has the Supreme Court ruled regarding the constitutionality of affirmative action programs adopted by local governments and universities?
- How do the people of the United States view preferential treatment for women and members of racial minorities?
- What does sociological research reveal regarding the impact of affirmative action programs?

The term *affirmative action* first appeared in an executive order issued by President John F. Kennedy in 1963. That order called for contractors to "take affirmative action to ensure that applicants are employed, and that employees are treated during employment, without regard to their race, creed, color, or national origin." Four years later, the order was amended to prohibit discrimination on the basis of sex, but affirmative action remained a vague concept. Currently, *affirmative action* refers to positive efforts to recruit minority group members or women for jobs, promotions, and educational opportunities.

A variety of court decisions and executive branch statements have outlawed certain forms of job discrimination based on race, sex, or both, including (1) word-of-mouth recruitment among all-White or all-male work forces, (2) recruitment exclusively in schools or colleges that are limited to one sex or are predominantly White, (3) discrimination against married women or forced retirement of pregnant women, (4) advertising in male and female "help wanted" columns when gender is not a legitimate occupational qualification, and (5) job qualifications and tests that are not substantially related to the job. Also, the lack of minority (Black, Asian, American Indian, or Hispanic) or female employees may in itself represent evidence of unlawful exclusion (Commission on Civil Rights, 1981).

In the late 1970s, a number of bitterly debated cases on affirmative action reached the Supreme Court. In 1978, in the *Bakke* case, by a narrow 5–4 vote, the Supreme Court ordered the medical school of the University of California at Davis to admit Allen Bakke, a White engineer who originally had been denied admission. The justices ruled that the school had violated Bakke's constitutional rights by establishing a fixed quota system for minority students. The Court added, however, that it was constitutional for universities to adopt flexible admissions programs that use race as *one* factor in decision making.

FIGURE 7-2 Median Income by Race, Ethnicity, and Gender, 1990

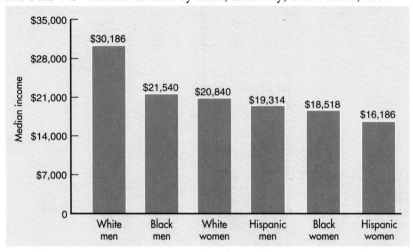

NOTE: Median income is from all sources and is limited to year-round, full-time workers over 15 years of age.
SOURCE: Bureau of the Census, 1992a:452.

Even a casual analysis reveals striking differences in earning power between White men and other groups.

Defenders of affirmative action insist that it is needed to counter continuing discrimination against women and minorities. White males still hold the overwhelming majority of prestigious and high-paying jobs. In fact, despite affirmative action, the gap in earning power between White males and others has remained unchanged over the last 20 years. The contemporary earnings gap is illustrated in Figure 7-2.

Even if they acknowledge the disparity in earnings between White males and others, the majority of people in the United States doubt that everything done in the name of affirmative action is desirable. Public opinion appears united against hiring or admissions programs that offer preferential treatment to women and racial minorities. Surveys conducted throughout the 1980s consistently showed that very few people favored such preferential efforts. Many respondents insisted that these programs unfairly penalize White males and should properly be viewed as "reverse discrimination" (Colasanto, 1989; L. Harris, 1987:188–193).

In recent years, the Supreme Court, increasingly dominated by a conservative majority, has issued many critical rulings concerning affirmative action programs. In a key case in 1989, the Court invalidated, by a 6–3 vote, a Richmond, Virginia, law that had guaranteed 30 percent of public works funds to construction companies owned by minorities. In ruling that the Richmond statute violated the constitutional right of White contractors to equal protection under the law, the Court held that affirmative action programs are constitutional only when they serve the "compelling state interest" of redressing "identified discrimination" by the government or private parties.

Has affirmative action actually helped to alleviate employment inequality on the basis of race and gender? Sociologist Dula Espinosa (1987) studied the impact of affirmative action on a California municipal work force whose hiring practices were traced from 1975 through 1985. As a federal contractor, the city was required to comply with federal guidelines regarding employment practices, including making "good faith efforts" to increase employment opportunities for women and minorities. Espinosa found that employment inequality by gender and ethnicity did indeed decrease during the 10-year period studied.

Espinosa adds, however, that most of the reduction in the city's level of employment inequality occurred just after the affirmative action policy was introduced. In Espinosa's view, once immediate progress can be seen, an organization may then become less inclined to continue to implement an affirmative action policy. Moreover, while high levels of inequality may be relatively easy to address initially, sustaining positive results may take longer because of institutional discrimination. Espinosa concludes that affirmative action was

successful to some degree in reducing employment inequality in the city studied, but clearly had its limitations as well.

Sociologists In Soo Son, Suzanne Model, and Gene Fisher (1989) studied income data and occupational mobility among Black male and White male workers in the period 1974 to 1981 to examine possible class polarization among Blacks. The researchers found that while Black college graduates made substantial gains as a result of affirmative action, less advantaged Blacks apparently did not benefit from it. The researchers (1989:325) conclude that the "racial parity achieved by young college-educated blacks in the 1970s will be maintained only if the government's commitment to affirmative action does not slacken."

In the early 1990s, affirmative action emerged as an increasingly important issue in state and national political campaigns. Generally, discussion focused on the use of quotas (or the "Q word," as it came to be known) in hiring practices. Supporters of affirmative action argue that hiring goals establish "floors" for minority inclusion but do not exclude truly qualified candidates from any group. Opponents insist that these "targets" are, in fact, quotas that lead to reverse discrimination. However, research efforts do not show that any significant reverse discrimination actually occurs. For example, a 1991 survey of employers in Chicago and Washington, D.C.—using similarly skilled African American and White applicants—found that 15 percent of the Whites and only 5 percent of the Blacks received job offers. Despite such studies, confusion continues about the merits of affirmative action—owing in part to the bewildering array of Supreme Court decisions and the often contradictory pronouncements of various administrations (B. Cohn, 1991; M. Turner et al., 1991).

SUMMARY

The social dimensions of race and ethnicity are important factors in shaping people's lives in the United States and other countries. In this chapter, we examine the meaning of race and ethnicity and study the major racial and ethnic minorities of the United States.

1 A *racial group* is set apart from others by obvious physical differences, whereas an *ethnic group* is set apart primarily because of national origin or distinctive cultural patterns.

2 When sociologists define a *minority group,* they are primarily concerned with the economic and political power, or powerlessness, of the group.

3 *Prejudice* is a negative attitude toward an entire category of people, often an ethnic or racial minority.

4 Prejudiced attitudes often lead to *discrimination,* but the two are not identical, and each can be present without the other.

5 *Institutional discrimination* results from the normal operations of a society.

6 Four patterns describe typical intergroup relations in North America and elsewhere: *amalgamation, assimilation, segregation,* and *pluralism.*

7 Contemporary prejudice and discrimination against African Americans are rooted in the history of slavery in the United States.

8 Asian Americans are commonly viewed as a "model minority," a stereotype not necessarily beneficial to members of this group.

9 The various groups included under the general term *Hispanics* represent the largest ethnic minority in the United States.

10 Despite recent *affirmative action* programs, White males continue to hold the overwhelming majority of prestigious and high-paying jobs in the United States.

CRITICAL THINKING QUESTIONS

1. Which sociological perspective would be most helpful in discussing the riots in Los Angeles in 1992? Apply this perspective in exploring the causes of the rioting and the implications of these events for racial and ethnic relations in the United States.

2. The text states that "in the United States, pluralism is more of an ideal than a reality." Can the community in which you grew up and the college you attend be viewed as genuine examples of pluralism? Examine the relations between dominant and subordinate racial and ethnic groups in your hometown and your college.

3. What are some of the similarities and differences in the position of African Americans and Hispanics as minorities in the United States? What are some of the similarities and differences in the position of Asian Americans and Jewish Americans?

KEY TERMS

Affirmative action Positive efforts to recruit minority group members or women for jobs, promotions, and educational opportunities. (page 194)

Amalgamation The process by which a majority group and a minority group combine through intermarriage to form a new group. (182)

Anti-Semitism Anti-Jewish prejudice. (191)

Apartheid The policy of the South African government designed to maintain the separation of Blacks, Coloureds, and Asians from the dominant Whites. (182)

Assimilation The process by which a person forsakes his or her own cultural tradition to become part of a different culture. (182)

Black power A political philosophy promoted by many younger Blacks in the 1960s which supported the creation of Black-controlled political and economic institutions. (186)

Contact hypothesis An interactionist perspective which states that interracial contact of people with equal status in noncompetitive circumstances will reduce prejudice. (179)

Discrimination The process of denying opportunities and equal rights to individuals and groups because of prejudice or for other arbitrary reasons. (180)

Ethnic group A group which is set apart from others because of its national origin or distinctive cultural patterns. (173)

Ethnocentrism The tendency to assume that one's own culture and way of life are superior to all others. (179)

Exploitation theory A Marxist theory which views racial subordination in the United States as a manifestation of the class system inherent in capitalism. (178)

Genocide The deliberate, systematic killing of an entire people or nation. (181)

Institutional discrimination The denial of opportunities and equal rights to individuals or groups which results from the normal operations of a society. (180)

Issei The early Japanese immigrants to the United States. (189)

Minority group A subordinate group whose members have significantly less control or power over their own lives than the members of a dominant or majority group have over theirs. (173)

Nisei Japanese born in the United States who were descendants of the Issei. (190)

Pluralism Mutual respect between the various groups in a society for one another's cultures, which allows minorities to express their own cultures without experiencing prejudice. (183)

Prejudice A negative attitude toward an entire category of people, such as a racial or ethnic minority. (179)

Racial group A group which is set apart from others because of obvious physical differences. (173)

Racism The belief that one race is supreme and all others are innately inferior. (179)

Segregation The act of physically separating two groups; often imposed on a minority group by a dominant group. (182)

Self-fulfilling prophecy The tendency of people to respond to and act on the basis of stereotypes, a predisposition which can lead to validation of false definitions. (175)

Stereotypes Unreliable generalizations about all members of a group that do not recognize individual differences within the group. (175)

ADDITIONAL READINGS

Alba, Richard D. *Ethnic Identity: The Transformation of White America.* New Haven, Conn.: Yale University Press, 1990. A sociologist looks at the changing patterns of ethnic identity in the United States and focuses on the myths that today's White ethnics hold about their place in the history of the United States.

Cowan, Neil M., and Ruth Schwartz Cowan. *Our Parents' Lives: The Americanization of Eastern European Jews.* New York: Basic Books, 1989. Drawing on oral histories, the authors explore the assimilation of eastern European Jews and the implications this had for Jewish identity.

Hacker, Andrew. *Two Nations: Black and White, Separate, Hostile, Unequal.* New York: Scribner, 1992. A political scientist analyzes the relative status of African Americans in terms of family, income, employment, education, criminal justice, and government.

Jaimes, M. Annette (ed.). *The State of Native America.* Boston: South End, 1992. Drawing mostly on Native American writers, Jaimes—a member of the Juaneño and Yaqui Indian tribes—explores the various circumstances confronted by Native Americans in the United States.

Moore, Joan, and Harry Pachon. *Hispanics in the United States.* Englewood Cliffs, N.J.: Prentice-Hall, 1985. A concise sociological examination of Hispanics in the United States.

Pieterse, Jan Nederveen. *White on Black: Images of Africa and Blacks in Western Populous Culture.* New Haven, Conn.: Yale University Press, 1992. A heavily illustrated book that documents the depth of racial stereotyping in the mass media.

Schaefer, Richard T. *Racial and Ethnic Groups* (5th ed.). New York: Harper Collins, 1993. Comprehensive in its coverage of race and ethnicity, this text also discusses women as a social minority and examines minority relations in Great Britain, Northern Ireland, Israeli-occupied territories, Brazil, and South Africa.

Takaki, Ronald. *Strangers from a Different Shore: A History of Asian Americans.* Boston: Little, Brown, 1989. An overview of the historical experiences of diverse groups of Asian Americans.

8

STRATIFICATION
BY GENDER
AND AGE

STRATIFICATION BY GENDER AND AGE

At age 76, Sophie Dickson celebrated her fifty-sixth consecutive season as a player in the North Jersey Field Hockey Association. Once a forward, Dickson subsequently became a skilled defender known for her frequent interceptions and clever stickwork. "Some of our high school players saw her, . . . and the kids couldn't get over how well she anticipated the play," noted a league official. By contrast, old age has been much less satisfying for Rayna Landry. She remarks: "When I run out of money, I beg a coffee and a bagel and live off that, but I don't like to beg much. . . . When you lose your pride, it's the worst thing." Dickson and Landry display the diversity of lifestyles experienced by older women in the United States. At the same time, they are both members of two groups—females and the elderly—that are commonly subjected to second-class treatment (Mifflin, 1984:B11; Rousseau, 1981:43).

Gender and age are ascribed statuses that form a basis for social differentiation. Our society continues to view many types of work as "women's work" or "men's work," thinking in terms of sexual stereotypes. Indeed, differentiation based on gender is evident in virtually every human society about which we have information. Similarly, the ascribed status of "older person" frequently dominates our perceptions of others. Rather than simply suggesting that a particular driver is not competent, people may say, "Those old codgers shouldn't be on the road." In such instances, elderly people are categorized by age in a way that obscures individual differences.

We saw in Chapters 6 and 7 that most societies establish hierarchies based on social class, race, and ethnicity. This chapter will examine the ways in which societies stratify their members on the basis of gender and age. It will begin by looking at how various cultures, including our own, assign women and men to particular social roles. Then it will consider sociological explanations for gender stratification. Next, it will focus on the unique situation of women as an oppressed majority within the United States. Particular attention will be given to the social, economic, and political aspects of women's subordinate position and to the consequences of gender stratification for men.

The second half of the chapter will focus primarily on the position of older people within the age-stratification system of the United States. It will examine various theories developed to explain the impact of aging on the individual and society. The effects of prejudice and discrimination on older people and the growing political consciousness among the elderly will be discussed. Finally, the social policy section will analyze the intense and continuing controversy over abortion.

GENDER IDENTITY AND GENDER ROLES

There are obvious biological differences between the sexes. Most important, women have the capacity to bear children, whereas men do not. These biological differences contribute to the development of **gender identity,** the self-concept of a person as being male or female. Gender identity is one of the first and most far-reaching identities that a human being learns. Typically, a child learns that she is a girl or he is a boy between the ages of 18 months and 3 years (Cahill, 1986).

Many societies have established social distinctions between the sexes which do not inevitably result from biological differences. This largely reflects the impact of conventional gender-role socialization. In Chapter 3, **gender roles** were defined as expectations regarding the proper behavior, attitudes, and activities of males and females. The application of traditional gender roles leads to many forms of differentiation between women and men. Both sexes are physically capable of learning to cook and type, yet most western societies determine that these tasks should be performed by women. Both men and women are capable of learning to weld metal and fly airplanes, but these functions are generally assigned to males.

It is important to stress that gender identity and gender roles are distinct concepts. Gender identity is based on a sense of oneself as male or female; gender roles involve socialization into norms regarding masculinity and femininity. Yet being male does not necessarily mean being "masculine" in a traditional sense; being female does not necessarily mean being "feminine." Thus, a woman who enters a historically male occupation such as welding, and who displays such traditionally masculine qualities as physical strength and assertiveness, may have a positive and highly secure gender identity. She may feel quite comfortable about being female—and, in fact, proud to be a woman—without feeling feminine as femininity has conventionally been defined. Similarly, a gentle, sensitive man who rejects the traditional view of masculinity may be quite secure in his gender identity as a man (Bem, 1978:20–21; Hoffman, 1977; West and Zimmerman, 1987).

Gender Roles in the United States

Gender-Role Socialization All of us can describe the traditional gender-role patterns which have been influential in the socialization of children in the United States. Male babies get blue blankets, while females get pink ones. Boys are expected to play with trucks, blocks, and toy soldiers; girls are given dolls and kitchen goods. Boys must be masculine—active, aggressive, tough, daring, and dominant—whereas girls must be feminine—soft, emotional, sweet, and submissive.

It is *adults,* of course, who play a critical role in guiding children into those gender roles deemed appropriate in a society. Parents are normally the first and most crucial agents of socialization (see Chapter 3). But other adults, older siblings, the mass media, and religious and educational institutions also exert an important influence on gender-role socialization in the United States.

Psychologist Shirley Weitz (1977:60–110) has pointed to two mechanisms which are primarily responsible for gender-role socialization: differential treatment and identification. In an illuminating study of differential treatment, a baby was sometimes dressed in pink and called "Beth" and at other times dressed in blue and called "Adam." Adults who played with the baby indicated that, without question, they *knew* whether the child was male or female from its behavior. They remarked on how sweet and feminine *she* had been, and on how sturdy and vigorous *he* had been. Clearly, these adults perceived the baby's behavior on the basis of their understanding of its sex. Such gender-related assumptions commonly lead to differential treatment of girls and boys (J. Will et al., 1976).

The process of identification noted by Weitz is more complex. How does a boy come to develop a masculine self-image whereas a girl develops one that is feminine? In part, they do so by identifying with females and males in their families and neighborhoods and in the media. If a young girl regularly sees female characters on television working as defense attorneys and judges, she may believe that she herself can become a lawyer. And it will not hurt if women that she knows—her mother, sister, parents' friends, or neighbors—are lawyers. By contrast, if this young girl sees women portrayed in the media only as models,

cathy® by Cathy Guisewite

nurses, and secretaries, her identification and self-image will be quite different.

The portrayal of women and men on television has tended to reinforce conventional gender roles. A cross-cultural content analysis of television advertising in the United States, Mexico, and Australia found sexual stereotyping common in all three countries. Australia had the lowest level of stereotyping, but even in that country, feminist groups were working to eliminate the "use of the woman's body to sell products" (Courtney and Whipple, 1983:183; Gilly, 1988).

Females have been most severely restricted by traditional gender roles. Throughout this chapter, we will see how women have been confined to subordinate roles within the political and economic institutions of the United States. Yet it is also true that gender roles have restricted males.

Men's Gender Role Boys are socialized to think that they should be invulnerable, fearless, decisive, and even emotionless in some situations (Cicone and Ruble, 1978). These are difficult standards to meet, and for boys who do not "measure up," life can be trying. This is especially true for boys who show an interest in activities thought of as feminine (such as cooking) or for boys who do not enjoy traditional masculine activities (such as competitive sports). Following are one man's recollections of his childhood, when he disliked sports, dreaded gym classes, and had particular problems with baseball:

During the game I always played the outfield. Right field. Far right field. And there I would stand in the hot sun wishing I was anyplace else in the world. Every so often a ball looked like it was coming up in my direction and I prayed to God that it wouldn't happen. If it did come, I promised God to be good for the next 37 years if he let me catch it—especially if it was a fly ball (Fager et al., 1971:36).

Boys who do not conform to the male gender role, like the right fielder quoted above, face constant criticism and even humiliation both from other children and from adults. It can be agonizing to be treated as a "chicken" or a "sissy"—particularly if such remarks come from one's father or brothers. At the same time, boys who successfully adapt to cultural standards of masculinity may grow up to be inexpressive men who cannot share their feelings with others. They remain forceful and tough—but as a result they are closed and isolated (Balswick and Peek, 1971).

In the last 25 years, inspired in good part by the contemporary feminist movement (which will be examined later in the chapter), increasing numbers of men in the United States have criticized the restrictive aspects of the traditional male gender role. Some men have taken strong public positions in support of women's struggle for full equality. Nevertheless, the traditional male gender role remains well entrenched as an influential element of our culture (see also Kimmel, 1987; Lamm, 1977; Pleck, 1981, 1985).

Cross-Cultural Perspective

To what extent do actual biological differences between the sexes contribute to the cultural differences associated with gender? This question brings us back to the debate over "nature versus nurture" presented in Chapter 3. In assessing the alleged and real differences between men and women, it is useful to examine cross-cultural data.

The research of anthropologist Margaret Mead points to the importance of cultural conditioning— as opposed to biology—in defining the social roles of males and females. In *Sex and Temperament,* Mead (1963, original edition 1935; 1973) describes typical behaviors of each sex in three different cultures in New Guinea:

> In one [the Arapesh], both men and women act as we expect women to act—in a mild parental responsive way; in the second [the Mundugumor], both act as we expect men to act—in a fierce initiating fashion; and in the third [the Tchambuli], the men act according to our stereotypes for women—are catty, wear curls, and go shopping—while the women are energetic, managerial, unadorned partners (Mead, 1963: preface to 1950 ed.).

If all differences between the sexes were determined by biology, then cross-cultural differences, such as those described by Mead, would not exist. Her findings therefore confirm the influential role of culture and socialization in gender-role differentiation. There appears to be no innate or biological reason to designate completely different gender roles for men and women.

In any society, gender stratification requires not only individual socialization into traditional gender roles within the family, but also the promotion and support of these traditional roles by other social institutions such as religion and education. Moreover, even with all major institutions socializing the young into conventional gender roles, every society has women and men who resist and successfully oppose these stereotypes: strong women who become leaders or professionals, gentle men who care for children, and so forth. With these realities in mind, it seems clear that differences between the sexes are not dictated by biology. Indeed, the maintenance of traditional gender roles requires constant social controls—and these controls are not always effective.

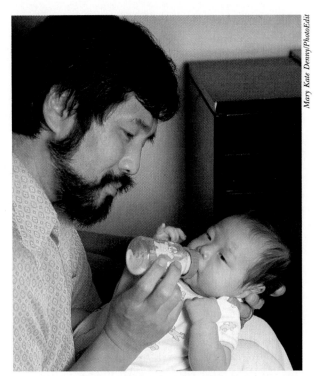

Mary Kate Denny/PhotoEdit

Although major institutions socialize youngsters into conventional gender roles, every society has women and men who resist and successfully oppose traditional gender stereotypes: strong women who become leaders or professionals, gentle men who care for children, and so forth.

EXPLAINING STRATIFICATION BY GENDER

As we will consider further in Chapter 9, cross-cultural studies indicate that societies dominated by men are much more common than those in which women play the decisive role. Sociologists have turned to all the major theoretical perspectives to understand how and why social distinctions between males and females are established. Each approach focuses on culture, rather than biology, as the primary determinant of gender differences. Yet, in other respects, there are wide disagreements between advocates of these sociological perspectives.

The Functionalist View

Within the general framework of their theory, functionalists maintain that gender differentiation has contributed to overall social stability. Sociologists Talcott Parsons and Robert Bales (1955:13–15, 22–26) argue that in order to function most efficiently, the family requires adults who will specialize in particular roles. They view the current arrangement of gender roles as arising out of this earlier need to establish a division of labor between marital partners.

Parsons and Bales contend that women take the expressive, emotionally supportive role and men the instrumental, practical role, with the two complementing each other. *Instrumentality* refers to emphasis on tasks, focus on more distant goals, and a concern for the external relationship between one's family and other social institutions. *Expressiveness* denotes concern for maintenance of harmony and the internal emotional affairs of the family. According to this theory, women's interest in expressive goals frees men for instrumental tasks, and vice versa. Women become "anchored" in the family as wives, mothers, and household managers; men are anchored in the occupational world outside the home. Parsons and Bales do not explicitly endorse traditional gender roles, but they imply that dividing tasks between spouses is functional for the family unit.

Given the typical socialization of women and men in the United States, the functionalist view is initially persuasive. However, it would lead us to expect girls and women with no interest in children to become baby-sitters and mothers. Similarly, males who love spending time with children might be "programmed" into careers in the business world. Clearly, such differentiation between the sexes can have harmful consequences for the individual who does not fit into prescribed roles, while also depriving society of the contributions of many talented people who are confined owing to stereotyping by gender. Even if it were considered ideal for one marital partner to play an instrumental role and the other an expressive role, the functionalist approach does not convincingly explain why men should be categorically assigned to the instrumental role and women to the expressive role.

Viewed from a conflict perspective, this functionalist approach masks underlying power relations between men and women. Parsons and Bales never explicitly present the expressive and instrumental tasks as unequally valued by society, yet this inequality is quite evident. Although social institutions may pay lip service to women's expressive skills, it is men's instrumental skills that are most highly rewarded—whether in terms of money or prestige. Consequently, according to feminists and conflict theorists, any division of labor by gender into instrumental and expressive tasks is far from neutral in its impact on women.

The Conflict Response

Conflict theorists contend that the relationship between females and males has been one of unequal power, with men in a dominant position over women. Men may originally have become powerful in preindustrial times because their size, physical strength, and freedom from childbearing duties allowed them to dominate women physically. In contemporary societies, such considerations are not so important, yet cultural beliefs about the sexes are long established. Such beliefs support a social structure which places males in controlling positions.

In this sense, traditional gender roles do not simply assign various qualities and behaviors to females and males. Feminist author Letty Cottin Pogrebin (1981:40) suggests that the two crucial messages of gender-role stereotypes are that "boys are better" and "girls are meant to be mothers." In order for a system of male dominance to maintain itself, she argues, children must be socialized to accept traditional gender-role divisions as natural and just. Sociologist Barbara Bovee Polk (1974:418), in describing the "conflicting cultures approach" to gender differences, observes that "masculine values have higher status and constitute the dominant and visible culture of the society. They . . . provide the standard for adulthood and normality." According to this view, women are oppressed because they constitute an alternative subculture which deviates from the prevailing masculine value system.

Thus, conflict theorists see gender differences

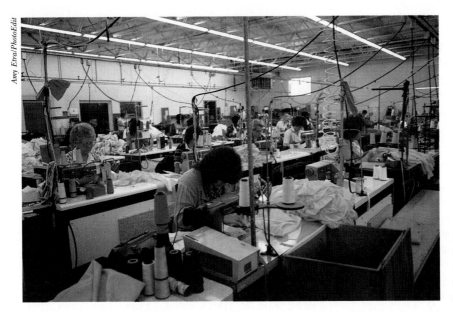

Conflict theorists emphasize that men's work is uniformly valued, while women's work (whether unpaid labor in the home or wage labor) is devalued.

as a reflection of the subjugation of one group (women) by another group (men). If we use an analogy to Marx's analysis of class conflict (see Chapters 1 and 6), we can say that males are like the bourgeois, or capitalists; they control most of the society's wealth, prestige, and power. Females are like the proletarians, or workers; they can acquire valuable resources only by following the dictates of their "bosses." Men's work is uniformly valued, while women's work (whether unpaid labor in the home or wage labor) is devalued.

Admittedly, the issue of women's economic and social subordination was relatively marginal in Marxist theory, which saw class oppression as paramount. However, the plight of women was not entirely ignored. Friedrich Engels, a close associate of Karl Marx, argued that women's subjugation coincided with the rise of private property during industrialization (Feuer, 1959:393–394). Only when people moved beyond an agrarian economy could males "enjoy" the luxury of leisure and withhold rewards and privileges from women. Women, in effect, became the sexual property of men. As Engels suggested, political and economic power in western industrial societies is concentrated in male hands, and there is significant social differentiation between the sexes.

From a conflict perspective, male dominance of our society goes far beyond the economic sphere. Throughout this textbook, we have discussed disturbing aspects of men's behavior toward women. The ugly realities of rape (refer back to Chapter 5), wife battering (see Chapter 9), sexual harassment (see Chapter 11), and street harassment all illustrate and intensify women's subordinate position. Even if women reach economic parity with men, even if women win equal representation in government, genuine equality between the sexes cannot be achieved if these attacks remain as common as they are today.

Both functionalist and conflict theorists acknowledge that it is not possible to change gender roles drastically without dramatic revisions in a culture's social structure. For functionalists, there is potential for social disorder, or at least unknown social consequences, if all aspects of traditional gender stratification are disturbed. Yet, for conflict theorists, no social structure is ultimately desirable if it is maintained by oppressing a majority of its citizens. These theorists argue that gender stratification may be functional for men—who hold power and privilege—but it is hardly in the interests of women (R. Collins, 1975:228–259; N. Goodman and Marx, 1978:312–315; Polk, 1974; Schmid, 1980).

The Interactionist Approach

Sociologists who are associated with the interactionist perspective generally agree with conflict theorists that men hold a dominant position over women. For example, recalling the Marxist view that within the home the man is the counterpart of the bourgeoisie whereas the woman is the counterpart of the proletariat, Erving Goffman (1977:315) has observed:

> A man may spend his day suffering under those who have power over him . . . and yet on returning home each night regain a sphere in which he dominates. . . . Wherever the male goes, apparently, he can carry a sexual division of labor with him.

While conflict theorists studying gender stratification typically focus on macro-level social forces and institutions, interactionist researchers often examine gender stratification on the micro level of everyday behavior.

As an example, studies show that as much as 96 percent of all interruptions in cross-sex (male-female) conversations are initiated by men. Men are also more likely than women to change topics of conversation, to ignore topics chosen by members of the opposite sex, to minimize the contributions and ideas of members of the opposite sex, and to validate their own contributions. These patterns reflect the conversational (and, in a sense, political) dominance of males. Moreover, even when women occupy a prestigious position, such as that of physician, they are more likely to be interrupted than their male counterparts are (A. Kohn, 1988; West, 1984; West and Zimmerman, 1983).

These findings regarding cross-sex conversations have been frequently replicated. They have striking implications when one considers the power dynamics underlying likely cross-sex interactions—employer and job seeker, college professor and student, husband and wife, to name only a few. From an interactionist perspective, these simple, day-to-day exchanges are one more battleground in the struggle for sexual equality—as women try to "get a word in edgewise" in the midst of men's interruptions and verbal dominance.

WOMEN: THE OPPRESSED MAJORITY

Many people—both male and female—find it difficult to conceive of women as a subordinate and oppressed group. Yet, when one looks at the political structure of the United States, one has to look hard to find many women. In the 103rd Congress, which took office in January 1993, there were only 53 women. They accounted for 47 of the 435 members of the House of Representatives and 6 of the 100 members of the Senate.

Other statistics reveal a similar picture. In 1993, only 3 of the nation's 50 states had female governors. In October 1981, Justice Sandra Day O'Connor of the Arizona Court of Appeals was sworn in as the nation's first female Supreme Court justice. But no woman has ever served as president of the United States, vice president, speaker of the House of Representatives, or chief justice of the Supreme Court.

This lack of women in decision-making positions is evidence of women's powerlessness in the United States. In Chapter 7, five basic properties which define a minority or subordinate group were identified. If we apply this model to the situation of women in this country, we find that a group comprising a numerical majority fits our definition of a subordinate minority (Dworkin, 1982):

1 Women obviously share physical and cultural characteristics that distinguish them from the dominant group (men).
2 Women experience unequal treatment. In the year 1990, the median income for year-round, male workers was $29,172; for comparable female workers, it was only $20,586 (Bureau of the Census, 1992a:452). Though they are not segregated from men, women are the victims of prejudice and discrimination in the labor force, in the legal system, and in other areas of society. Moreover, as we saw in Chapter 6, women are increasingly dominating the ranks of the impoverished, leading to what has been called the *feminization of poverty*.
3 Membership in this subordinate group is involuntary.

After the 1992 elections, women held six seats in the United States Senate—an all-time high. Among the new senators is Carol Moseley Braun, Democrat of Illinois, who became the first African American woman ever elected to the Senate.

4 Through the rise of contemporary feminism, women are developing a greater sense of group solidarity. (The women's movement will be studied later in the chapter.)
5 Women are not forced to marry within the group, yet many women feel that their subordinate status is most irrevocably defined within the institution of marriage (Bernard, 1972).

Just as African Americans are victimized by racism, women suffer from the sexism of American society. *Sexism* is the ideology that one sex is superior to the other. The term is generally used to refer to male prejudice and discrimination against women. In Chapter 7, it was noted that Blacks can suffer from both individual acts of racism and institutional discrimination. *Institutional discrimination* was defined as the denial of opportunities and equal rights to individuals or groups which results from the normal operations of a society. In the same sense, women can be said to suffer both from individual acts of sexism (such as sexist remarks and acts of violence) and from institutional sexism.

It is not simply that particular men in the United States are biased in their treatment of women. All the major institutions of our society—including the armed forces, large corporations, the media, the universities, and the medical establishment—are controlled by men. These institutions, in their "normal," day-to-day operations, often discriminate against women and perpetuate sexism. Consequently, if the central office of a nationwide bank sets a policy that single women are a bad risk for loans—regardless of their incomes and investments—the *institution* will discriminate against women in state after state. It will do so even at bank branches in which loan officers hold no personal biases concerning women, but are merely "following orders." We will examine institutional discrimination against women within the educational system in Chapter 10.

Our society is run by male-dominated institutions, yet with the power that comes to men come responsibility and stress. Men have higher reported rates of certain types of mental illness than women do and greater likelihood of death due to heart attack or strokes (see Chapter 12). The pressure on men to succeed—and then to remain on top in a competitive world of work—can be especially intense. This is not to suggest that gender stratification is as damaging to men as it is to women. But it is clear that the power and privilege which men enjoy are no guarantee of mental or physical well-being. Jimmy Carter, shortly after becoming president of the United States,

BOX 8-1

THE STATUS OF WOMEN WORLDWIDE

Women experience second-class status throughout the world. It is estimated that women grow half the world's food, but they rarely own land. They constitute one-third of the world's paid labor force but are generally found in the lowest-paying jobs. Single-parent households headed by women—which appear to be on the increase in many nations—are typically found in the poorest sections of the population. Indeed, the feminization of poverty has become a global phenomenon.

According to a United Nations report on women's lives around the world, the majority of women still lag far behind men in terms of wealth, power, and opportunity. A 120-page book, entitled *The World's Women, 1970–1990,* was released by the U.N. in 1991. This report represents the first global attempt to evaluate women's place statistically.

An analysis of the report in the *New York Times* stated:

• "... The workplace almost everywhere is segregated by sex, with women generally in less prestigious and lower-paid jobs. Japan, South Korea, and Cyprus

were among the countries with the lowest women's wages, about half those of men. . . .
• "The report's findings on leadership show that women are poorly represented in the ranks of power, policy, and decision-making, although they are found in large numbers in low-level positions of public administration, political parties, unions and business. . . .
• "While women have progressed toward equal access to education, huge gaps persist. In 1985, there were 597 million illiterate women, compared with 352 million illiterate men" (M. Howe, 1991:7).

A study by the Population Crisis Committee (1988), a nonprofit group which promotes international family planning programs, attempted to assess and compare the status of women in five major areas: health, control over childbearing, education, employment, and legal protection. In general, the richer the country, the greater the measure of women's equality found by researchers. Western industrialized countries tended to rank high: Sweden scored 87 points (this was the highest score)

out of a possible 100, while the United States ranked third with 82.5 points. By contrast, African, middle eastern, and south Asian countries clustered at the bottom of the list, with Bangladesh ranking last at 21.5 points.

In reviewing the global perspective on women's equality, two conclusions can be offered. First, as anthropologist Laura Nader (1986:383) has observed, even in the relatively more egalitarian nations of the west, women's subordination is "institutionally structured and culturally rationalized, exposing them to conditions of deference, dependency, powerlessness, and poverty." While the situation of women in Sweden and the United States is significantly better than in Saudi Arabia and Bangladesh, women nevertheless remain in a second-class position in the world's most affluent and developed countries.

Second, as was discussed in Chapter 6, on stratification, there is a link between the wealth of industrialized nations and the poverty of the developing countries. Consequently, the affluence of western nations has come, in part, at the expense of women in Third World countries.

---

summed up the potential problems of the male role: "If you're a woman doing more than your mother did, you feel successful. If you're a man and you're not president, you feel like a failure" (E. Goodman, 1977; Pogrebin, 1981:63–64).

Thus far, we have focused primarily on the social and political aspects of women's subordinate position in the United States. In Box 8-1 (above), we look briefly at the situation of women around the world.

Women in the Work Force of the United States

"Does your mother work?" "No, she's just a housewife." This familiar exchange reminds us of women's traditional role in the United States, and it reminds us that women's work has generally been viewed as unimportant. The United States Commission on Civil Rights (1976:1) concluded that the passage in the Declaration of Independence proclaiming that "all men are created equal" has been taken too literally for too long. This is especially true with respect to employment.

A Statistical Overview Women's participation in the paid labor force of the United States has been increasing steadily throughout the twentieth century (see Figure 8-1 below). No longer is the adult woman associated solely with the role of homemaker. Instead, millions of women—married women and single women, with and without children—are working outside the home. In 1989, more than 58 percent of adult women in the United States held jobs outside the home, as compared with 43 percent in 1970. Thus a majority of women are now members of the paid labor force

rather than full-time homemakers (Bureau of the Census, 1991a).

Unfortunately, women entering the job market find their options restricted in important ways. Particularly damaging to women workers is occupational segregation, or confinement to sex-typed "women's jobs." For example, in 1989 women accounted for 99 percent of all secretaries, 96 percent of all private household workers, and 94 percent of all registered nurses. Entering such sex-typed occupations places women in "service" roles which parallel the traditional gender-role standard under which housewives "serve" their husbands and children.

By contrast, women are not found in occupations historically defined as "men's jobs," which often carry much greater financial rewards and much higher prestige than women's jobs do. For example, in 1991 women accounted for approximately 45 percent of the nation's paid labor force. Yet they represented only 8 percent of all engineers, 10 percent of all dentists, 20 percent of all physicians, and 19 percent of all lawyers and judges (Bureau of the Census, 1992a:392). A general picture of women's employment in various occupations appears in Table 8-1 (on page 212).

FIGURE 8-1 Trends in Women's Participation in the Paid Labor Force, 1890–1991

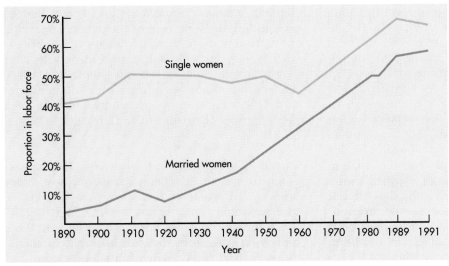

SOURCES: Bureau of the Census, 1975:132–133; 1992a:387.

In 1991, 67 percent of single women and 59 percent of married women were in the paid labor force of the United States.

TABLE 8-1   Employment of Women in Selected Occupations, 1950 and 1991

OCCUPATION	WOMEN AS PERCENT OF ALL WORKERS IN THE OCCUPATION	
	1950	1991
Professional workers	40	52
Engineers	1	8
Lawyers and judges	4	19
Physicians	7	20
Registered nurses	98	95
College teachers	23	41
Other teachers	75	74
Managers	14	41
Sales workers	35	49
Clerical workers	62	80
Machine operators	34	40
Transport operatives	1	9
Service workers	57	60

SOURCES: Bureau of the Census, 1992a:392–394; Department of Labor, 1980:10–11.

Although strides have been made in some areas, many occupations continue to be filled routinely by members of one sex.

According to a study released in 1991 by the Feminist Majority Foundation, women continue to be dramatically underrepresented in top positions at Fortune 500 companies. As of 1990, of 6502 jobs at the vice presidential level or higher in these corporations, only 175 (or 2.6 percent) were held by women. Only five women were chief executives at Fortune 500 companies. However, women appear to be making progress in gaining middle-management jobs. In 1990, women held 40 percent of all executive, management, and administrative positions at Fortune 500 companies—compared with 24 percent in 1976 (*USA Today*, 1991b).

How pervasive is sex-typing of occupations? In one study, researchers compiled a "segregation index" to estimate the percentage of women who would have to change their jobs to make the distribution of men and women in each occupation mirror the relative percentage of each sex in the adult working population. This study showed that 58 percent of women workers would need to switch jobs in order to create a labor force without sex segregation (J. Jacobs, 1990; Reskin and Blau, 1990).

The result of the workplace patterns described throughout this section is that women earn much less money than men do in the paid labor force of the United States. In 1990, the median income of full-time female workers was 71 percent that of full-time male workers. Given these data, it is hardly surprising to learn that many women are living in poverty, particularly when they must function as heads of households. In the discussion of poverty in Chapter 6, it was noted that by 1990 female heads of households and their children accounted for 53 percent of the nation's poor. Yet not all women are in equal danger of experiencing poverty. As will be discussed more fully later in the chapter, women who are members of racial and ethnic minorities suffer from "double jeopardy": stratification by race and ethnicity as well as by gender (Bureau of the Census, 1992a:452, 458).

Social Consequences of Women's Employment
There have already been many obvious consequences of women's increasing involvement in the paid labor force. As was seen in Chapter 3, the need for child care facilities has grown, and there have been pressures for greater public financing of day care. Even the rise of fast-food chains partially reflects the fact that many women are no longer home and cooking during the day.

In theory at least, women should gain in self-esteem and power within the family as they move outside the home and function as productive wage earners. In an ongoing study of women between the ages of 35 and 55, researchers have found that "for employed women, a high-prestige job, rather than a husband, is the best predictor of well-being" (Baruch et al., 1980:199; 1983). Holding this type of position appears to be the factor most influential in a woman's self-esteem. Of course, as we have seen in this chapter, the number of women employed in high-prestige jobs is rather small.

In terms of power dynamics, women clearly gain some degree of power by earning their own incomes. Studies indicate that when a woman provides sole support for her family, employment even in a low-status occupation has a positive effect on her self-esteem (Hoffman and Nye, 1975). For married women, such income from employment can be effective security in case of separation or divorce. In the past, many full-time homemakers had little confidence in their ability to make a living. As a result, some remained in unsatisfying marriages, believing that they had no alternative way to survive. This is still the case for a considerable number of women in the United States and around the world.

As women become increasingly involved in employment outside the home, men will have an opportunity to become more involved in the care and socialization of children. In industrial societies, the demands on men as primary wage earners have traditionally contributed to a deemphasis on the social roles of being a father. Freda Rebelsky and Cheryl Hanks (1973) examined interactions between fathers and babies and found that the longest time period any father in the sample devoted to his infant was 10 minutes 26 seconds. The average period of verbal interaction between father and baby was only *38 seconds per day*. More recently, psychologist Wade Mackey (1987) conducted a cross-cultural study of 17 societies—including Morocco, Hong Kong, Ireland, and Mexico—and found that the limited father-child interactions in the United States were typical of all the societies surveyed.

Studies indicate that there is a clear gender gap in the performance of housework. Drawing on data from a 1985 national survey, sociologist John

Women are not only moving into professions traditionally viewed as "men's jobs"; they are also moving successfully into such nontraditional areas as rap music. Shown is Queen Latifah, a popular rap singer.

Robinson (1988) reports that while men have increased their share of household duties—among them, caring for pets and paying bills—women in the United States continue to perform 2 hours of housework for each hour done by men. In 1985, not including time spent on child care, women averaged 19.5 hours of housework each week, compared with only 9.8 hours for men. Data from a 1989 national survey underscore the common sex segregation evident in the performance of household tasks (see Figure 8-2). For example, 78 percent of women report that they do all or most of their families' meal preparation, and 72 percent say they do all or most of the child

FIGURE 8-2 Division of Household Tasks by Gender

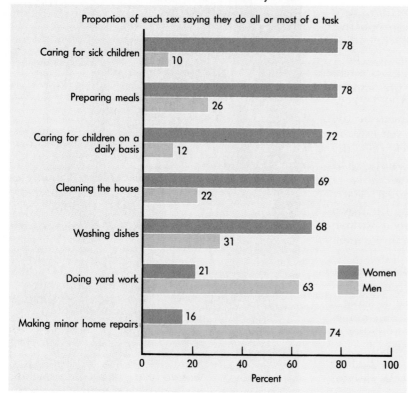

Proportion of each sex saying they do all or most of a task

Task	Women	Men
Caring for sick children	78	10
Preparing meals	78	26
Caring for children on a daily basis	72	12
Cleaning the house	69	22
Washing dishes	68	31
Doing yard work	21	63
Making minor home repairs	16	74

NOTE: Questions regarding child care were asked only of respondents with children living at home.

SOURCE: DeStefano and Colasanto, 1990:31.

In a national survey conducted in 1989, men and women in the United States indicated who they felt did all or most of a variety of household tasks. Segregation of housework and child care was evident, and other studies indicate that women spend more than twice as much time on housework than men—even when child care is not included.

care. By contrast, 74 percent of men indicate that they do all or most of the minor home repairs (DeStefano and Colasanto, 1990:28–29, 31).

A study of Canadian married couples by sociologist Susan Shaw (1988) offers insight into the rather different ways in which men and women view housework. Specifically, men are more likely than women to view these activities as "leisure"—and are less likely to see them as "work." The reason for this is that these tasks continue to be seen as women's work. Consequently, men perceive themselves as having more freedom of choice in engaging in housework and child care; they are more likely than women to report that cooking, home chores, shopping, and child care are, in fact, leisure. Confirming earlier research, Shaw found that the employment status of women had little effect on this gender difference.

The continuing disparity in household labor

has a rather striking meaning in terms of power relationships within the family (a subject which will be examined more fully in Chapter 9). As married women have taken on more and more hours of paid employment, they have been only partially successful in getting their husbands to assume a greater role in needed homemaking duties, including child care. Sociologist Arlie Hochschild (1989, 1990) has used the phrase "second shift" to describe the double burden—work outside the home followed by child care and housework—that many women face and few men share equitably.

On the basis of interviews with and observations of 52 couples over an eight-year period, Hochschild reports that the wives (and not their husbands) drive home from the office while planning domestic schedules and play dates for children—and then begin their second shift. Drawing on national studies, she concludes that women spend 15 fewer hours in leisure activities each week than their husbands do. In a year, these women work an extra month of 24-hour days because of the "second shift"; over a dozen years, they work an extra year of 24-hour days. Hochschild found that the married couples she studied were fraying at the edges, and so were their careers and their marriages. With such reports in mind, many feminists have advocated greater governmental and corporate support for child care (refer back to Chapter 3), more flexible family leave policies, and other reforms designed to ease the burden on the nation's families.

Women: Emergence of a Collective Consciousness

In a formal sense, the feminist movement of the United States was born in upstate New York, in a town called Seneca Falls, in the summer of 1848. On July 19, the first women's rights convention began, attended by Elizabeth Cady Stanton, Lucretia Mott, and other pioneers in the struggle for women's rights. This first wave of *feminists*, as they are currently known, battled ridicule and scorn as they fought for legal and political equality for women. They were not afraid to risk controversy on behalf of their cause; in 1872 Susan B. Anthony was arrested for attempting to vote in that year's presidential election.

Ultimately, the early feminists won many victories, among them the passage and ratification of the Nineteenth Amendment to the Constitution, which granted women the right to vote in national elections beginning in 1920. But suffrage did not lead to other reforms in women's social and economic position, and the women's movement became a much less powerful force in the early and middle twentieth century.

The second wave of feminism in the United States emerged in the 1960s and came into full force in the 1970s. In part, the movement was inspired by three pioneering books arguing for women's rights: Simone de Beauvoir's *The Second Sex*, Betty Friedan's *The Feminine Mystique*, and Kate Millett's *Sexual Politics*. In addition, the general political activism of the 1960s led women—many of whom were working for Black civil rights or against the war in Vietnam—to reexamine their own powerlessness as women. The sexism often found within allegedly progressive and radical political circles made many women decide that they needed to establish their own movement for "women's liberation" (S. Evans, 1980; Firestone, 1970:15–40; J. Freeman, 1973, 1975).

More and more women became aware of sexist attitudes and practices—including attitudes they themselves had accepted through socialization into traditional gender roles—and began to challenge male dominance. A sense of "sisterhood," much like the class consciousness that Marx hoped would emerge in the proletariat (see Chapter 6), became evident. Individual women identified their interests with those of the collectivity *women*. No longer were they "happy" in submissive, subordinate roles ("false consciousness" in Marxist terms).

The women's movement has undertaken public protests on a wide range of issues. Feminists have endorsed passage of the equal rights amendment, government subsidies for child care (see Chapter 3), affirmative action for women and minorities (see Chapter 7), federal legislation outlawing sex discrimination in education (see Chapter 10), greater representation of women in government (see Chapter 11), and the right to legal abortions (which will be discussed later in this chapter). Feminists have condemned violence against women in the family (see Chapter 9), sexual harassment in organizations (see Chapter 11), forced sterilization of poor and minority women, sexist advertising and pornography, and discrimination against lesbians and gay men.

Minority Women: Double Jeopardy

We have seen that the historical oppression of women limits them by tradition and law to specific roles. Many women experience differential treatment not only because of gender but because of race and ethnicity as well. They face a "double jeopardy"—subordinate status twice defined. A disproportionate share of this low-status group are also impoverished, so that the double jeopardy effectively becomes a triple jeopardy. The litany of social ills continues for many if we consider old age, illness, disabilities, and the like.

Feminists have addressed themselves to the particular needs of minority women, but overshadowing the oppression of these women because of gender is the subordinate status imposed because of race and ethnicity. The question for African American women, Chicanas (Mexican American women), Asian American women, and others appears to be whether they should unify with their "brothers" against racism or challenge them for their sexism. One answer is that, in a truly just society, both sexism and racism must be eradicated.

The discussion of gender roles among Blacks has always provoked controversy. Advocates of Black nationalism contend that feminism only distracts women from full participation in the Black struggle. The existence of feminist groups among Blacks, in their view, is simply a divide-and-conquer strategy that serves the dominant White society. By contrast, Black feminists such as Florynce Kennedy argue that little is to be gained by adopting or maintaining the gender-role divisions of the dominant society that place women in a subservient position. Historically, Black women have been more likely than White women to suffer from unemployment; Black women clearly stand to gain from increased employment and educational opportunities (Giddings, 1984; Ladner, 1986; Rothenberg, 1988).

The plight of Chicanas is usually considered part of either the Chicano or the feminist movement, ignoring the distinctive experience of Chicanas. In the past, these women have been excluded from decision making in the two institutions that most directly affect their daily lives: the family and the church. The Mexican American family, especially in the lower class, feels the pervasive tradition of male domination. The Roman Catholic church relegates women to supportive roles while reserving the leadership positions for men (Burciaga et al., 1977; Rosaldo, 1985:415).

We can see that activists among minority women do not agree on whether priority should be granted to fighting for sexual equality or to eliminating inequality among racial and ethnic groups. Perhaps it would be most useful to conclude that neither component of inequality can be ignored. Helen Mayer Hacker (1973:11), who pioneered research on both Blacks and women, stated before the American Sociological Association: "As a partisan observer, it is my fervent hope that in fighting the twin battles of sexism and racism, Black women and Black men will [create] the outlines of the good society for all Americans."

AGING AND SOCIETY

Like gender stratification, age stratification varies from culture to culture. One society may treat older people with great reverence, while another sees them as "unproductive" and "difficult." Societies differ, as well, in their commitment to providing social services for older citizens. Sweden, Denmark, and Finland have pioneered an approach to aging known as "open old-age care," under which older citizens are encouraged and helped to live their later years in dignity in their own homes. "Home helpers" paid by local governments visit the elderly and perform such chores as housekeeping, cleaning, shopping, and cooking. But while Sweden had 1500 home helpers per 100,000 older people in need of such aid in 1987, the United States had only 66 helpers per 100,000 older people (Szulc, 1988).

The elderly were highly regarded in the culture of traditional China. The period beginning at about age 55 was probably the most secure and comfortable time for men and women. As the closest living contact with people's ancestors, older family members received deference from younger kin and had first claim on all family resources. As China has become more urbanized and less traditional, older people without children have been given special assistance by trade unions and have also been granted limited welfare benefits (Foner, 1984; P. Olson, 1987, 1988).

Not all societies have traditions of caring for the elderly. Among the Fulani of Africa, older men and women move to the edge of the family homestead. Since this is where people are buried, the elderly sleep over their own graves, for they are already viewed as socially dead. Among the Mardudjara, a hunting-and-gathering culture of Australia, disabled older members are given food; however, when frequent travel becomes unavoidable, some are left behind to perish (Stenning, 1958; Tonkinson, 1978:83). In Box 8-2 on the opposite page, we look at the aging of the world's populations.

It is understandable that all societies have some system of age stratification and associate certain social roles with distinct periods in one's life. Some of this age differentiation seems inevitable; it would make little sense to send young children off to war or to expect most older people to han-

BOX 8-2

AGING WORLDWIDE

In an important sense, the aging of the world's populations represents a major success story which has unfolded during the later stages of the twentieth century. Through the efforts of both national governments and international agencies, many societies have drastically reduced the incidence of diseases and their rates of death. Consequently, these nations—especially the industrialized countries of Europe and North America—have increasingly high proportions of older members. This does not mean, however, that such nations have aged gracefully. Belated recognition of the demographic and socioeconomic changes associated with aging has often resulted in suffering (Kinsella, 1988).

When compared with other industrialized nations, Japan has a relatively youthful population; only 10 percent of the nation's people are over 65 years of age. However, Japan's population is aging faster than that of any other country as a result of falling birth- and death rates. Japan has traditionally honored its older citizens and even has a national holiday, Respect for the Aged Day, on September 15. Yet the proportion of elderly people living with adult children has decreased substantially in recent decades. Changing attitudes in Japanese culture seem to include a decline in the belief that children are obligated to support their aging parents. Policymakers are clearly worried that the Japanese government will be expected to fill this vacuum and provide financial and emotional support for the nation's rapidly growing elderly population (L. Martin, 1989).

In most developing countries, aging has not yet emerged as a dominant social phenomenon. Rarely are special resources directed to meet the needs of people over 60, even though they are likely to be in poorer health than their counterparts in industrialized nations. Since many younger adults in developing nations immigrate to the cities, rural areas have higher proportions of older people. Formal social support mechanisms are less likely to exist in rural areas, yet at least family caregivers are present. In the cities, these caregivers enter and remain in the work force, which makes it more difficult for them to care for elderly family members. At the same time, urban housing in developing countries is often poorly suited to traditional extended-family arrangements (Kinsella, 1988; Neysmith and Edward, 1984).

In industrialized nations, governmental social programs, such as Social Security, are the primary source of income for older citizens. However, given the economic difficulties of developing countries (refer back to Chapter 6), few of these nations are in a position to offer extensive financial support to the elderly. Regionally, South American countries provide the most substantial benefits, often assisting older people in both urban and rural areas. By contrast, such government support is nonexistent in many African states (Heisel, 1985; Kinsella, 1988).

Ironically, modernization in the developing world, while bringing with it many social and economic advances, has at the same time undercut the traditionally high status of the elderly. In many cultures, the earning power of younger adults now exceeds that of older family members. Consequently, the leadership role of the elderly has come into question, just as the notion of retirement has been introduced in the cultures of developing nations (Cowgill, 1986).

---

dle physically demanding tasks such as loading goods at shipyards. However, as is the case with stratification by gender, age stratification in the United States goes far beyond the physical constraints of human beings at different ages (Babbie, 1980:299–300).

"Being old," in particular, is a master status that commonly overshadows all others in the United States. Moreover, this status is generally viewed in negative terms. In one experiment, college students from three states were shown photographs of men who appeared to be 25, 52, and 73 years old and were asked to evaluate these men for a job. Unbeknownst to the students, the photographs were all of the same person, who had used disguise and makeup to alter his appearance. The results of the study revealed significantly more negative evaluations for the (apparently) older job applicant than for the other applicants. The "older" person was viewed as less competent, less intelligent, less reliable, and less attractive (W. Levin, 1988).

We can draw on the insights of labeling theory (see Chapter 5) in sociological analysis of the consequences of aging. Once people are labeled "old" in the United States, this designation will have a major impact on how they are perceived and even on how they view themselves. As will be discussed more fully later in the chapter, negative stereotypes of the elderly contribute to their position as a minority group subject to discrimination.

Chapter 7 introduced five basic properties of a minority group. This model may be applied to older people in order to clarify the subordinate status of the elderly (M. Harris, 1958:4–11; J. Levin and Levin, 1980):

1 The elderly share physical characteristics that distinguish them from younger people. In addition, their cultural preferences and leisure-time activities are often at variance with those of the rest of society.
2 The elderly experience unequal treatment in employment and may face prejudice and discrimination.
3 Membership in this disadvantaged group is involuntary.
4 Older people have a strong sense of group solidarity, as is reflected in the growth of senior citizens' centers, housing projects, and advocacy organizations.
5 Although the elderly may be single, divorced, or widowed, many older couples share their minority status.

In analyzing the elderly as a minority, we find one crucial difference between older people and other subordinate groups such as Blacks and women. All of us who live long enough will eventually assume the ascribed status of being an older person.

EXPLAINING THE AGING PROCESS

Aging is one important aspect of socialization—the lifelong process through which an individual learns the cultural norms and values of a particular society. As we saw in Chapter 3, there are no clear-cut definitions for different periods of the aging cycle in the United States. The term **age grades** refers to cultural categories that identify the stages of biological maturation. The ambiguity found in our culture about exactly when these age grades begin and end reflects the ambivalence with which we approach the aging process, especially at its end point. Thus, while *old age* has typically been regarded as beginning at 65, which corresponds to the retirement age for many workers, this definition of old age is not universally accepted in our society.

The particular problems of the aged have become the focus for a specialized area of research and inquiry, known as *gerontology*. **Gerontology** is the scientific study of the sociological and psychological aspects of aging and the problems of the aged. It originally developed in the 1930s, as an increasing number of social scientists became aware of the plight of the elderly.

Gerontologists rely heavily on sociological principles and theories to explain the impact of aging on the individual and society. They also draw on the disciplines of psychology, anthropology, physical education, counseling, and medicine in their study of the aging process. Two influential views of aging—disengagement theory and activity theory—can be best understood in terms of the sociological perspectives of functionalism and interactionism, respectively. The conflict perspective can also contribute to our sociological understanding of aging.

Functionalist Approach: Disengagement Theory

Elaine Cumming and William Henry (1961) introduced an explanation of the impact of aging known as **disengagement theory**. This theory, based on a study of elderly people in good health and relatively comfortable economic circumstances, contends that society and the aging individual mutually sever many of their relationships. In keeping with the functionalist perspective, disengagement theory emphasizes that a society's stability is ensured when social roles are passed on from one generation to another.

According to this theory, the approach of death forces people to drop most of their social roles—including those of worker, volunteer, spouse, hobby enthusiast, and even reader. These functions are then undertaken by younger members of society. The aging person, it is held, withdraws into an increasing state of inactivity while preparing for death. At the same time, society withdraws from the elderly by segregating them residentially (in retirement homes and communities), educationally (in programs designed solely for senior citizens), and recreationally (in senior citizens' social centers). Implicit in disengagement theory is the view that society should *help* older people to withdraw from their accustomed social roles.

Since it was first outlined three decades ago, disengagement theory has generated considerable controversy. Some gerontologists have objected to the implication that older people want to be ignored and "put away"—and even more to the idea that they should be encouraged to withdraw from meaningful social roles. Critics of disengagement theory insist that society forces the elderly into an involuntary and painful withdrawal from the paid labor force and from meaningful social relationships. Currently, sociologists agree with the assumption implicit in disengagement theory that aging should not be viewed simply as a personal process, but rather as a social phenomenon interrelated with the social structure and institutions of any particular society. Nevertheless, most sociologists and gerontologists do not regard disengagement theory as a valid explanation of aging (Riley, 1987).

Interactionist Approach: Activity Theory

Often seen as an opposing approach to disengagement theory, *activity theory* argues that the elderly person who remains active will be best-adjusted. Proponents of this perspective acknowledge that a 70-year-old person may not have the ability or desire to perform various social roles that he or she had at age 40. Yet they contend that old people have essentially the same need for social interaction as any other age group.

Many activities open to the elderly involve unpaid labor—even though younger adults may receive salaries for comparable work. Shown is an Emergency Medical Service volunteer in rural Texas.

Research findings have consistently supported the principal arguments of activity theory and have failed to confirm key contentions of disengagement theory. Unfortunately, the substitutions recommended for older people by activity theorists have not been readily available in the United States. The labor force has not traditionally been predisposed to welcome retired workers to new careers, and the economy has not been structured to offer paying positions to older citizens. However, some companies have recently initiated programs to hire retirees for full-time or part-time work. For example, about 130 of the

600 reservationists for the Days Inn motel chain are over 60 years of age. As many firms find a shortage of qualified workers who can fill positions, they are turning to older people who still want to work (Lewin, 1990b).

Admittedly, many activities open to the elderly involve unpaid labor—even though younger adults may receive salaries for comparable work. Such unpaid workers include hospital volunteers (versus aides and orderlies), drivers for charities such as the Red Cross (versus chauffeurs), tutors (as opposed to teachers), and craftspeople for charity bazaars (as opposed to carpenters and dressmakers). Robert Butler (1980:9) of the National Institute of Aging recalls a 1929 cartoon that aptly described the activities open to the elderly. It showed an old man sitting outside an antique store. The caption read: "Some antiques have a market value; others haven't."

Disengagement theory suggests that older people find satisfaction in withdrawal from society. Functionally speaking, they conveniently recede into the background and allow the next generation to take over. Proponents of activity theory view such withdrawal as harmful for both the elderly and society and focus on the potential contributions of older people to the maintenance of society. In their opinion, aging citizens will feel satisfied only when they can be useful and productive in *society's* terms—primarily by working for wages (Dowd, 1980:6–7; Quadagno, 1980:70–71).

The Conflict Response

Conflict theorists have criticized both disengagement theory and activity theory for failing to consider the impact of social structure on patterns of aging. Neither approach, they say, attempts to question why social interaction "must" change or decrease in old age. In addition, these perspectives, in contrast to the conflict perspective, often ignore the impact of social class in the lives of the elderly.

The privileged position of the upper class generally leads to better health and vigor and to less likelihood of dependency in old age. Affluence cannot forestall aging indefinitely, but it can soften the economic hardships faced in later years. By contrast, working-class jobs often carry greater hazards to health and a greater risk of dis-

ability; aging will be particularly difficult for those who suffer job-related injuries or illnesses. Working-class people also depend more heavily on Social Security benefits and private pension programs. During inflationary times, their relatively fixed incomes from these sources hardly keep pace with escalating costs of food, housing, utilities, and other necessities (Atchley, 1985).

Conflict theorists have noted that the transition from agricultural economies to industrialization and capitalism has not always been beneficial for the elderly. As a society's production methods change, the traditionally valued role of older people within the economy tends to erode. Although pension plans, retirement packages, and insurance benefits may be developed to assist older people, those whose wealth allows them access to investment funds can generate the greatest income for their later years (Dowd, 1980:75; Hendricks, 1982; L. Olson, 1982).

The conflict approach views the treatment of older people in the United States as reflective of the many divisions in our society. From a conflict perspective, the low status of older people is reflected in prejudice and discrimination against them, age segregation, and unfair job practices—none of which are directly addressed by either disengagement or activity theory.

AGE STRATIFICATION IN THE UNITED STATES

The "Graying of America"

As is evident in Figure 8-3, an increasing proportion of the population of the United States is composed of older citizens. Men and women aged 65 years and over constituted only 4 percent of the nation's population in the year 1900, but by 1991 this figure had reached 13 percent. It is currently projected that by the year 2030, almost 22 percent of people in the United States will be 65 and older. Moreover, while the proportion of elderly people continues to rise, the "old old" segment of the population (that is, people 85 years old and over) is growing at an ever faster rate. By 2030, the proportion of the population 85 and over will reach 2.7 percent (Bureau of the Census, 1992a:14; Gelman, 1985:62; Spencer, 1989:8).

While the United States is noticeably graying, the nation's older citizens are in a sense getting

FIGURE 8-3 Actual and Projected Growth of the Elderly Population

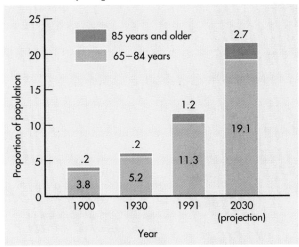

SOURCES: Census data in Bureau of the Census, 1992a:14; Gelman, 1985:62; and Spencer, 1989:8.

An increasing proportion of the population of the United States is aged 65 and over. It is projected that by the year 2030, this group will constitute almost 22 percent of the nation's population. Moreover, projections point to a dramatic rise in the proportion of the "old old" (people aged 85 and over).

younger, owing to improved health and nutrition. As psychologist Sylvia Mertz told a symposium on aging in 1986, the activities of a contemporary 70-year-old "are equivalent to those of a 50-year-old a decade or two ago" (Horn and Meer, 1987:76). From the perspective of activity theory, this is obviously a welcome change which should be encouraged.

In the United States, women account for 60 percent of people 65 years old and over. Older women experience a double burden: they are female in a society which favors males, and they are elderly in a society which values youth. The social inequities that women experience throughout their lifetimes—whether in terms of wealth, status, or power—only intensify as they age. As a result, in 1987 some 25 percent of elderly women living alone were below the poverty line (Bureau of the Census, 1992a:38; see also Duncan and Smith, 1989; Levy, 1988).

According to a report released in 1991 by the Older Women's League, middle-aged and older women face discrimination in the workplace. In 1989, the median annual earnings of women 45 to 54 years of age were $20,466, compared with $34,684 for men of that age. Women 55 to 64 yeas of age had median annual earnings of $18,727, compared with $32,476 for men in this age group. According to the report, less than half these wage differentials result from differences in education or work experience. Segregation of the work force by gender is viewed as a key factor in earning differentials; such segregation is particularly severe among older women. For example, 62 percent of working women over age 55 are found in low-paying sales, clerical, and service jobs (Lewin, 1991b:8).

Viewed from a conflict perspective, it is not surprising that older women experience a double burden; the same is true of elderly members of racial and ethnic minorities. For example, in 1987 the proportion of older Hispanics with incomes below the poverty line (27 percent) was almost three times as large as the proportion of older Whites (10 percent) in this condition. The median household income of older Blacks was about $12,000; for older Hispanics, it was $15,300; for older Whites, it was $21,000. With such data in mind, Lou Glasse, president of the Older Women's League, noted that life is especially difficult for older women from minority groups: "In virtually every aspect of their lives, from income to housing, minority women will be forced to struggle harder to achieve a smaller piece of the pie" (Bureau of the Census, 1990a:446, 460; L. Williams, 1986:A21).

Clearly, the graying of the United States is a phenomenon that can no longer be ignored—either by social scientists or by government policymakers. Advocacy groups on behalf of the elderly have emerged and spoken out on a wide range of issues (as we will see later in the chapter). Politicians are often found courting older citizens who constitute a powerful and growing voting bloc. The elderly are much more likely to vote than younger age groups, a fact which tends to enhance their political clout. In 1988, 69 percent of people 65 years old and over reported voting, compared with 57 percent of the total population and only 33 percent of people ages 18 to 20 (Bureau of the Census, 1990a:262).

Viewed from a conflict perspective, older women experience a double burden. A 60-year-old woman hoping to reenter the job market is shown during an employment interview.

Ageism

Physician Robert Butler (1975, 1989), the founding director of the National Institute on Aging, coined the term *ageism* to refer to prejudice and discrimination against the elderly. Ageism reflects a deep uneasiness among young and middle-aged people about growing old. For many, old age symbolizes disease, disability, and death; seeing the elderly serves as a reminder that *they* may become old and infirm.

For Butler, hostility toward the elderly was apparent when plans were revealed to build a high-rise apartment building for senior citizens in a suburb of Washington, D.C. Young residents of the community were irritated by the inclusion of various luxuries for the elderly, such as a swimming pool. Most basic to their objections was a distaste for the kinds of people who would live in the building—they would be old. "Who wants all those old people around?" asked one community resident.

Even trained professionals are guilty of ageism, as in the case of medical personnel who too quickly diagnose patients as senile or view their ailments as imaginary or "nothing but old age." The consequences of ageism among physicians and other health care professionals can be especially serious. For example, a 1987 study revealed that older women with breast cancer frequently receive less medical treatment than they should, because of their age (Greenfield et al., 1987).

As one reflection of ageism, many people in the United States hold negative stereotypes of the elderly. Studies of college undergraduates and graduates report widespread perceptions of older citizens as stubborn, touchy, quarrelsome, bossy, and meddlesome. Even less judgmental feelings can reflect a belief in the superiority of the young. A typical comment is: "When an older person is walking very slowly right in front of me, I feel pity" (B. Hess and Markson, 1980:65).

In contrast to negative stereotypes, researchers have found that older workers can be an asset for employers. According to a study issued in 1991, older workers can be retrained in new technologies, have lower rates of absenteeism than younger employees, and are often more effective salespeople. The study focused on two corporations based in the United States (the hotel chain Days Inns of America and the holding company Travelers Corporation of Hartford) and a British retail chain—all of which have long-term experience in hiring workers age 50 and over. Thomas Moloney, senior vice president of the Commonwealth Fund, a private foundation which commissioned the study, concluded: "We have here the first systematic hard-nosed economic analysis showing older workers are good investments" (Telsch, 1991:A16).

Age Segregation

Age segregation is an important feature of the landscape of the United States. This form of segregation, every bit as evident as racial segregation, occurs when people at similar points in the life cycle cluster together. As we have seen, some people like residents of the Washington suburb discussed earlier, prefer that the elderly and their problems be kept away from them—isolated in retirement communities and special housing projects. Neighborhoods have also opposed the conversion of single-family homes into apartments for students or fraternity and sorority houses.

For the older person in the United States, age segregation is most obvious in nursing homes. Currently, 5 percent of people over 65 years old live in nursing homes. Entering a nursing home means becoming part of a total institution (see Chapter 3). Activities are determined by the institution and are rarely tailored to the individual preferences of residents. Most of one's personal possessions must be left behind, since available space is limited. Of those who enter such institutions, the majority enter in their late seventies or early eighties, when their health is failing or they lack financial resources needed to live on their own (Lewin, 1990a:A22).

Elderly people who are relatively healthy and financially secure have a greater range of housing options. Studies have not firmly established how such people feel about living in residential communities for the retired, condominiums, hotels catering to the aged, and "seniors'" housing projects. Apparently, older people living in planned communities score higher on life satisfaction scales than retirees in age-integrated communities do. However, these findings must be assessed with caution. Residents of retirement communities also tend to have higher incomes than most elderly people and describe themselves as in better health. Older people who are concentrated (or perhaps one might say "trapped") in inner-city neighborhoods tend to be less happy than those living in more affluent and heterogeneous areas (D. Harris and Cole, 1980:168–172; La Gory et al., 1980, 1981, 1985).

Age segregation has at least one distinct advantage for the elderly; it helps them to organize politically and to wield influence within government circles. It is undoubtedly no coincidence that the chief congressional advocate for older citizens in recent decades—the late U.S. representative Claude Pepper of Miami—represented the retirement area of southern Florida. Nevertheless, such patterns of age segregation are hardly likely to promote mutual understanding among people of differing age groups.

The Elderly: Emergence of a Collective Consciousness

During the 1960s, students at colleges and universities across the country became concerned about "student power" and demanded a role in the governance of educational institutions. In the following decade, the 1970s, many older people became aware that they were being treated as second-class citizens. Just as the National Organization for Women (NOW) had been established to bring about equal rights for women, the Gray Panthers organization was founded in 1971 to work for the rights of the elderly. Moreover, as NOW has enlisted the aid of male allies, the Gray Panthers have actively sought and received aid from younger generations.

In order to combat prejudice and discrimination against older people, the Gray Panthers issue publications and monitor industries particularly important to the elderly, such as health care and housing. For example, the condition of nursing homes in the United States prompted Gray Panther leader Maggie Kuhn to declare: "We throw away people, and before we throw them away, we warehouse them in institutions. We make them vegetables. . . ." Currently, the group has about 40,000 dues-paying members dedicated to the fight against ageism (G. Collins, 1987:C8).

The growing collective consciousness among older people also contributed to the establishment of the Older Women's League (OWL) in 1980. OWL focuses on access to health insurance, Social Security benefits, and pension reform. OWL leaders and the group's 20,000 members hope that the organization will serve as a critical link between the feminist movement and activists for "gray power" (Hillebrand, 1992).

The largest organization representing the nation's elderly is the American Association of Retired Persons (AARP). AARP was founded in 1958 by a retired school principal who was having

Members of the powerful American Association of Retired Persons (AARP) are shown on the telephone trying to "get out the vote."

difficulty getting insurance because of age prejudice. Many of AARP's services involve discounts and insurance for its 33 million members, but the organization also functions as a powerful lobbying group which works for legislation that will benefit the elderly. For example, AARP has backed passage of a uniform mandatory-reporting law for cases of abuse of the elderly, which would be accompanied by enough federal funds to guarantee enforcement and support services.

The potential power of AARP is enormous: it is the second-largest voluntary association in the United States (behind only the Roman Catholic church) and represents one out of every four registered voters in the United States. While criticized for its lack of minority membership (the group is 97 percent White), AARP has endorsed voter registration campaigns, nursing home reforms, and pension reforms (Georges, 1992; Hornblower, 1988; Ornstein and Schmitt, 1990).

SOCIAL POLICY AND GENDER STRATIFICATION

THE BATTLE OVER ABORTION

- From a conflict perspective, how are the factors of race, class, and ethnicity an important part of the controversy over abortion?

- Why have parental notification and parental consent become especially sensitive issues in the debate over abortion?

- Why do rural women find it particularly difficult to exercise their legal right to have abortions?

Few issues seem to stir as much intense conflict as abortion. Until about 20 years ago, it was very difficult for a woman to terminate a pregnancy legally in the United States and most other industrial nations.

Beginning in the late 1960s, a few state governments began to reform statutes and make it easier for a woman to obtain a legal abortion. However, with abortion permissible only in a small minority of states, and only under certain conditions, a large number of women continued to have illegal abortions (Conover and Gray, 1983).

The fight for the right to safe, inexpensive, and legal abortions was a key priority of the feminist movement of the late 1960s and early 1970s. Feminists argued that the right to abortion was fundamental to women's sexual and reproductive freedom. In their view, women—not legislators or judges—should have an unconditional right to decide whether, and under what circumstances, they would bear children. Feminists further insisted that no law would ever prevent women from obtaining abortions. The issue was simply whether these abortions would be performed safely by doctors, or dangerously by "back room" abortionists or by the pregnant women themselves (Petchesky, 1990; E. Willis, 1980).

The critical victory in the struggle for legalized abortion came in the 1973 Supreme Court decision of *Roe v. Wade.* The justices held, by a 7–2 margin, that the "right to privacy . . . founded in the Fourteenth Amendment's concept of personal liberty . . . is broad enough to encompass a woman's decision whether or not to terminate a pregnancy." However, the Court did set certain limits on a woman's right to abortion. During the last three months of pregnancy, the fetus was ruled capable of life outside the womb. Therefore, states were granted the right to prohibit all abortions in the third trimester except those needed to preserve the life, physical health, or mental health of the mother. In subsequent decisions in the 1970s, the Supreme Court upheld the right of a woman to terminate pregnancy without the consent of her husband or (in the case of younger, unmarried women) her parents.

The Court's decision in *Roe v. Wade,* while generally applauded by "pro-choice" groups, which support the right to legal abortions, was bitterly condemned by those opposed to abortion. For people who call themselves "pro-life," abortion is a moral and often a religious issue. In their view, human life actually begins at the moment of conception rather than at the moment of a baby's delivery. On the basis of this judgment, the fetus is a human life, not a potential person. Termination of this life, even before it has left the womb, is viewed as essentially an act of murder. Consequently, antiabortion activists were alarmed by the fact that by 1989, over 22 million legal abortions had taken place in the United States in the years since the Supreme Court decision in *Roe v. Wade* (Bureau of the Census, 1992a:74; Luker, 1984:126–157).

In the mid-1970s, the antiabortion movement focused not only on legislative initiatives to prevent abortions but also on termination of government funding of abortions. In 1976, Congress passed the Hyde amendment, which prohibited use of Medicaid funds to pay for abortions except when the woman's life was in danger or when she was the victim of rape or incest. The effects of the Hyde amendment were dramatic: federally funded abortions were reduced by 99 percent. Moreover, as of 1992, only 13 states paid for abortions for low-income women. Consequently, for 3 million women of childbearing age relying on Medicaid, many of them teenagers, it became much more difficult to exercise the right to a legal abortion (Lewin, 1992; Schultz, 1977).

FIRST TRIMESTER
SECOND TRIMESTER

THIRD TRIMESTER
FOURTH TRIMESTER

Feminists and other "pro-choice" activists argue that the movement opposed to legal abortion is not genuinely "pro-life." These critics charge that "right-to-lifers" care about needy women only when they are pregnant and fail to support government programs to aid women who do choose to bear children.

For at least some low-income women, the results of these policies have been fatal. In 1977, Rosaura Jimenez of Texas became the first woman known to die of complications following an illegal abortion after implementation of the Hyde amendment. Viewing the issue from a conflict perspective, it was not surprising that the first group to lose access to legal abortions comprised poor women, of whom a significant number are Black and Hispanic (*Washington Post,* 1984).

In recent years, influenced by the votes of conservative justices appointed by Ronald Reagan and George Bush, the Supreme Court has increasingly restricted the right to an abortion. In the 1989 case of *Webster v. Reproductive Health Services,* the Court upheld, by a 5–4 vote, the state of Missouri's right to prohibit public hospitals from performing abortions and to prohibit public employees from performing or assisting in abortions not necessary to save a pregnant woman's life. In 1992, in the case of *Planned Parenthood v. Casey,* a 5–4 majority upheld the state of Pennsylvania's right to require a woman to wait 24 hours before having an abortion and to first hear a presentation intended to persuade her to change her mind. The majority also upheld Pennsylvania's right to require a teenager seeking an abortion to get the consent of one parent or a judge. These restrictions appeared likely to make access to abortion extremely difficult for low-income women and teenagers.

Parental notification and parental consent have become especially sensitive issues in the debate over abortion. The respected Alan Guttmacher Institute estimates that over 1 million teenagers in the United States become pregnant each year and that 42 percent of them decide to have abortions. Pro-life activists argue that the parents of these teenagers should have the right to be notified about—and to permit or prohibit—these abortions. In their view, parental authority deserves full support at a time when the traditional nuclear family is embattled. However, pro-choice activists counter that many pregnant teenagers come from troubled families where they have been abused. These young women may have good reason to avoid discussing such explosive issues with their parents (Salholz, 1990).

In 1991, in another controversial ruling that pleased pro-life activists, the Supreme Court upheld federal regulations that prohibited employees of federally funded family planning clinics from discussing abortion with their patients. Under these regulations, 4500 clinics serving almost 4 million women each year were not permitted to offer basic medical information about abortion. The clinics were prohibited from assisting women to find doctors who would perform abortions (Greenhouse, 1991).

However, the election of Bill Clinton as president in 1992 delighted pro-choice activists and led to an immediate and dramatic change in federal policies concerning abortion. In early 1993, only days after his inauguration, and on the twentieth anniversary of the landmark *Roe v. Wade* ruling, President Clinton issued a series of memorandums which reversed the pro-life policies of the Reagan and Bush administrations. The president lifted the ban on abortion counseling at federally funded clinics, eased government policy concerning abortions in military hospitals, and ended a prohibition on aid to international family planning programs involved in abortion-related activities.

As of 1992, the people of the United States appeared to support the right to legal abortion in principle, but some were ambivalent concerning certain applications of that right. In a national survey, 57 percent of respondents stated that abortion should remain legal in all cases, while 16 percent said that it should be legal only in some cases or said that they were unsure. Only 27 percent of respondents stated that abortion should be illegal in all cases (Baumann, 1992).

By the 1990s, abortion had also become a controversial issue in western Europe. As in the United States, many European nations bowed to public opinion and liberalized abortion laws in the 1970s. While Ireland, Belgium, and Malta continue to prohibit abortion, it is legal in other western European countries. Austria, Denmark, Greece, the Netherlands, Norway, and Sweden have laws that allow a woman to have an abortion on request. Other countries have more restrictive legislation, especially concerning abortions in the later stages of pregnancy. Inspired by their counterparts in the United States, antiabortion activists have become more outspoken in Great Britain, France, Spain, Italy, and Germany (Simons, 1989).

In both western Europe and the United States, rural women experience difficulty in finding a physician who will perform an abortion. According to a survey by the Alan Guttmacher Institute, the number of abortion providers in rural areas of the United States declined significantly in the period 1985 to 1988, as did the number of hospitals in the nation that would perform abortions. The inability to find a physician, clinic, or hospital that will perform an abortion forces rural women in the United States and Europe to travel long distances to get an abortion. Viewed from a conflict perspective, this is one more financial and emotional burden that falls especially heavily on low-income women (Lewin, 1990c, 1992).

The intense conflict over abortion reflects broader differences over women's position in society. Sociologist Kristin Luker (1984:158–191) has offered a detailed study of activists in the pro-choice and pro-life movements. Luker interviewed 212 activists in California, overwhelmingly women, who spent at least five hours a week working for one of these movements. According to Luker, each group has a "consistent,

coherent view of the world." Feminists involved in defending abortion rights typically believe that men and women are essentially similar; they support women's full participation in work outside the home and oppose all forms of sex discrimination. By contrast, most antiabortion activists believe that men and women are fundamentally different. In their view, men are best-suited for the public world of work, whereas women are best-suited for the demanding and crucial task of rearing children. These activists are troubled by women's growing participation in work outside the home, which they view as destructive to the family and ultimately to society as a whole.

SUMMARY

Gender and age are ascribed statuses that form the basis for social differentiation. This chapter examines theories regarding gender and age stratification, women as an oppressed majority group, and the "graying of America."

1 *Gender identity* is one of the first and most far-reaching identities that a human being holds.
2 Females have been more severely restricted by traditional gender roles, but these roles have also restricted males.
3 Functionalists maintain that sex differentiation contributes to overall social stability, whereas conflict theorists contend that the relationship between females and males has been one of unequal power, with men in a dominant position over women.
4 Although numerically a majority, in many respects women fit the definition of a subordinate minority group within the United States.
5 In terms of power dynamics, women clearly gain some additional degree of power by earning their own incomes.
6 Minority women experience double jeopardy through differential treatment based not only on gender but also on race and ethnicity.
7 "Being old" is a master status that seems to overshadow all others in the United States.
8 The particular problems of the elderly have become the focus for a specialized area of research and inquiry known as *gerontology.*

9 *Disengagement theory* implicitly suggests that society should help older people to withdraw from their accustomed social roles; *activity theory* argues that elderly people who remain active will be best-adjusted.
10 An increasing proportion of the population of the United States is composed of older citizens.
11 The issue of abortion has bitterly divided the United States and pitted pro-choice activists against pro-life activists.

CRITICAL THINKING QUESTIONS

1 Sociologist Barbara Bovee Polk suggests that women are oppressed because they constitute an alternative subculture which deviates from the prevailing masculine value system. Does it seem valid to view women as an "alternative subculture"? In what ways do women support and deviate from the prevailing masculine value system evident in the United States?
2 In what ways is the social position of White women in the United States similar to that of African American women, Hispanic women, and Asian American women? In what ways is a woman's social position markedly different, given her racial and ethnic status?
3 Is age segregation functional or dysfunctional for older people in the United States? Is it functional or dysfunctional for society as a whole? What are the manifest functions, the latent functions, and the dysfunctions of age segregation?

KEY TERMS

Activity theory   An interactionist theory of aging which argues that elderly people who remain active will be best-adjusted. (page 219)

Age grades   Cultural categories that identify the states of biological maturation. (218)

Ageism   A term coined by Robert N. Butler to refer to prejudice and discrimination against the elderly. (222)

Disengagement theory   A functionalist theory of aging introduced by Cumming and Henry which contends that society and the aging individual mutually sever many of their relationships. (218)

Expressiveness   A term used by Parsons and Bales to refer to concern for maintenance of harmony and the internal emotional affairs of the family. (206)

Gender identity   The self-concept of a person as being male or female. (203).

Gender roles   Expectations regarding the proper behavior, attitudes, and activities of males and females. (203)

Gerontology   The scientific study of the sociological and psychological aspects of aging and the problems of the aged. (218)

Institutional discrimination   The denial of opportunities and equal rights to individuals and groups which results from the normal operations of a society. (209)

Instrumentality   A term used by Parsons and Bales to refer to emphasis on tasks, focus on more distant goals, and a concern for the external relationship between one's family and other social institutions. (206)

Sexism   The ideology that one sex is superior to the other. (209)

ADDITIONAL READINGS

Brinton, Mary C. *Women and the Economic Miracle: Gender and Work in Postwar Japan.* Berkeley: University of California Press, 1992. A sociological analysis of women's education and employment in contemporary Japan.

Butler, Robert N. *Why Survive? Being Old in America.* New York: Harper and Row, 1975. This is the now-classic, Pulitzer prize–winning study that introduced the term *ageism* to our understanding of older people.

Chudacoff, Howard P. *How Old Are You?* Princeton, N.J.: Princeton University Press, 1989. A historian examines how age became such a dominant status in the United States.

Craig, Steve (ed.). *Men, Masculinity, and the Media.* Newbury Park, Calif.: Sage, 1992. An overview of men's roles as portrayed in music, advertisements, films, and television.

Faludi, Susan. *Backlash: The Undeclared War against Women.* New York: Crown, 1991. A Pulitzer prize–winning journalist examines the growing backlash against women and against feminism, with a special focus on how the media have spread the backlash message.

Hochschild, Arlie Russell, with Anne Machung. *The Second Shift: Working Parents and the Revolution at Home.* New York: Viking Penguin, 1989. A critical look at housework in dual-career couples, in which Hochschild observes that women's duties at home constitute a "second shift" after their work in the paid labor force.

9

THE FAMILY

9

THE FAMILY

LOOKING AHEAD

- Are all families necessarily composed of a husband, a wife, and their children?
- What functions does the family perform for society?
- Do married women who work outside the home have greater marital power than full-time homemakers?
- What factors influence our selection of a mate?

- Does divorce have a more detrimental effect on boys than on girls?
- Should gay couples and unmarried heterosexual couples have the same legal protections and benefits as married couples?
- What can be done to prevent violence between family members?

Marina, 33 years old, unmarried, and a member of a French theatrical troupe, is the mother of 5-year-old Sarah and is expecting a baby boy. When her company goes on tour, Marina leaves Sarah either with Michel (Sarah's father) or with Jean (Marina's lover and the father of the baby she is expecting). The friendship between Marina and Michel has survived not only the end of their romance and the breakup of the home they shared but also her new liaison with Jean. In fact, there is no jealousy between the two men; they take turns looking after Sarah during Marina's absences. These three adults have been successful in finding fulfillment while departing from traditional social norms regarding marriage and parenthood (Michel, 1989).

In this chapter, we will see how family patterns differ from one culture to another and even within the same culture. In the Toda culture of southern India, a woman may be simultaneously married to several men. Fatherhood is not always connected with biology: any husband may establish paternity by presenting a pregnant woman with a toy bow and arrow. The Balinese of Indonesia permit twins to marry each other because they believe that twins have already been intimate in the womb. In the Banaro culture of New Guinea, the husband is forbidden to have intercourse with his wife until she has first borne a child by another man chosen for that purpose. Once the wife has proved that she can bear children, the husband is allowed to have sexual relations with her (Leslie and Korman, 1989:15, 30, 39).

As these examples illustrate, there are many variations in "the family" from culture to culture. What do *you* consider a family? A 1987 national survey in the United States asked adults if they would regard certain living arrangements as a "true family" (Kalette et al., 1987). The percentages of those responding affirmatively were as follows:

Married couple, at least one child	99%
Married couple, no children	95%
Single parent, living with children	91%
Unmarried couple living together	45%
Homosexual couple rearing children	33%
Two homosexuals living together	20%

Clearly, even within the United States, people cannot agree on a definition of a family. Consequently, when someone speaks of his or her family, we cannot assume that this family resembles ours in form and structure. For some, the family may consist of only a handful of people; for others, it may involve hundreds. For some, the family may represent a hope for the future; for others, it may seem an outmoded barrier to personal growth.

A *family* can be defined as a set of people related by blood, marriage (or some other agreed-upon relationship), or adoption who share the primary responsibility for reproduction and caring for members of society. In this chapter, we will see that the family is universal—found in every culture—though varied in its organization. We will look at the primary functions of the family and the variations in marital patterns and family life in the United States. Particular attention will be given to the increasing number of people who are living in dual-career or single-parent families. The social policy section will examine the distressing prevalence of domestic violence in the United States.

THE FAMILY: UNIVERSAL BUT VARIED

The family as a social institution is present in all cultures. Although the organization of the family can vary greatly, there are certain general principles concerning its composition, descent patterns, residence patterns, and authority patterns.

Composition: What Is the Family?

In the United States, the family has traditionally been viewed in very narrow terms—as a married couple and their unmarried children living together. However, this is but one type of family, what sociologists refer to as a **nuclear family.** The term *nuclear family* is well chosen, since this type of family serves as the nucleus, or core, upon which larger family groups are built.

As we saw in the survey data presented above, people in the United States see the nuclear family as the preferred family arrangement. Yet, as is shown in Figure 9-1, by 1990 only about one-quarter of the nation's households fit this model. (The term *household* is used by the Bureau of the Census to refer to related or unrelated people sharing a residence as well as to people who live alone.)

FIGURE 9-1   Types of Households in the United States, 1970, 1980, and 1990

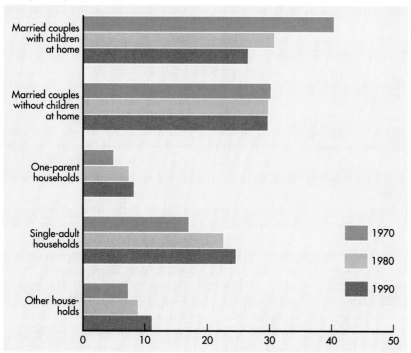

NOTE: "Children" refers to children under 18. "Other households" includes persons living together who may be related (but not married) or unrelated with no children present. Because of rounding, numbers may not total 100 percent.
SOURCE: Bureau of the Census, 1990d:2.

The proportion of households in the United States composed of married couples continues to decline, and the proportion of single-adult households rose from about 17 percent in 1970 to almost 25 percent in 1990.

FIGURE 9-2 Married-Couple Households with Children in Industrialized Nations, 1960 and 1990

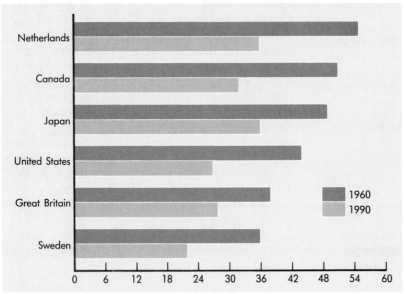

Legend:
- 1960
- 1990

Countries (top to bottom): Netherlands, Canada, Japan, United States, Great Britain, Sweden

Scale: 0, 6, 12, 18, 24, 30, 36, 42, 48, 54, 60

SOURCES: Bureau of Labor Statistics data in Sorrentino, 1990:46–47; and authors' estimates.

As in the United States, the proportion of all households consisting of a married couple with children is declining in many other industrialized nations.

As Figure 9-1 illustrates, the proportion of households in the United States composed of married couples with children at home has decreased steadily over the last 30 years. At the same time, there have been substantial increases in the number of single-person and single-parent households. Similar trends are evident in other industrialized nations, including Canada, Great Britain, and Japan (see Figure 9-2).

A family in which relatives in addition to parents and children—such as grandparents, aunts, or uncles—live in the same home is known as an ***extended family.*** While not common, such living arrangements do exist in the United States. The structure of the extended family offers certain advantages over that of the nuclear family. Crises such as death, divorce, and illness involve less strain for family members, since there are more people who can provide assistance and emotional support. In addition, the extended family constitutes a larger economic unit than the nuclear family. If the family is engaged in a common enterprise—for example, a farm or a small business—the additional family members may represent the difference between prosperity and failure.

In considering these differing family types, we have limited ourselves to the form of marriage that is characteristic of the United States—monogamy. The term ***monogamy*** describes a form of marriage in which one woman and one man are married only to each other. Some observers, noting the high rate of divorce in the United States, have suggested that "serial monogamy" is a more accurate description of the form that monogamy takes in the United States. Under ***serial monogamy,*** a person is allowed to have several spouses in his or her life but can have only one spouse at a time.

Some cultures allow an individual to have several husbands or several wives simultaneously. This form of marriage is known as ***polygamy.*** You may be surprised to learn that most societies throughout the world, past and present, have preferred polygamy, not monogamy. Anthropologist George Murdock (1949, 1957) sampled 565 societies and found that over 80 percent of them practiced some type of polygamy as their preferred form.

There are two basic types of polygamy. According to Murdock, the most common—endorsed by the majority of cultures he sampled—was polygyny. *Polygyny* refers to the marriage of a man to more than one woman at the same time. The various wives are often sisters, who are expected to hold similar values and have already had experience sharing a household. In polygynous societies, relatively few men actually have multiple spouses. Most live in typical monogamous families; having multiple wives is viewed as a mark of status.

The other principal variation of polygamy is **polyandry,** under which a woman can have several husbands at the same time. As we saw earlier in the chapter, this was the case in the culture of the Todas of southern India. Yet, despite such examples, polyandry tends to be exceedingly rare. It has been accepted by some extremely poor societies which practice female infanticide (the killing of baby girls) and thus have a relatively small number of women. Like many other societies, polyandrous cultures devalue the social worth of women.

Descent Patterns:
To Whom Are We Related?

In the late 1970s, many Americans were deeply moved by Alex Haley's successful quest for his family tree, which was documented in his book *Roots* and later popularized on network television.

Beginning with stories passed down by his grandmother, Haley was able to trace his heritage back to a man named Kunta Kinte who lived in The Gambia, West Africa, and was brought to the United States in chains by slave traders.

Many of us, like Haley, have traced our roots by listening to elderly relatives tell us about their lives—and about the lives of ancestors who died long before we were born. Yet a person's lineage is more than simply a personal history; it also reflects societal patterns that govern descent. In every culture, children are introduced to relatives to whom they are expected to show emotional attachment. The state of being related to others is called **kinship.** Kinship is culturally learned and is not totally determined by biological or marital ties. For example, adoption creates a kinship tie which is legally and socially acknowledged.

The family and the kin group are not necessarily the same. While the family is a household unit, kin do not always live together or function as a collective body on a daily basis. Kin groups include aunts, uncles, cousins, in-laws, and so forth. In a society such as the United States, the kinship group may come together only rarely, as for a marriage or funeral. However, kinship ties frequently create obligations and responsibilities. We may feel compelled to assist our kin and feel free to call upon relatives for many types of aid, including loans and baby-sitting.

The state of being related to others is called kinship. *Kin groups include aunts, uncles, cousins, in-laws, and so forth.*

How are kinship groups identified? The principle of descent assigns people to kinship groups according to their relationship to an individual's mother or father. There are three principal ways of determining descent. In the United States, the system of **bilateral descent** is followed, which means that both sides of a person's family are regarded as equally important. No higher value is given to the brothers of one's father as opposed to the brothers of one's mother.

Most societies—according to Murdock, 64 percent—give preference to one side of the family or the other in tracing descent. **Patrilineal** (from Latin *pater*, "father") **descent** indicates that only the father's relatives are important in terms of property, inheritance, and the establishment of emotional ties. Conversely, in societies which favor **matrilineal** (from Latin *mater*, "mother") **descent,** only the mother's relatives are significant; the relatives of the father are considered unimportant.

Family Residence: Where Do We Live?

In every society, there are social norms concerning the appropriate residence of a newly created family. Under the **neolocal** pattern of residence, which is prevalent in the United States, a married couple is expected to establish a separate household. However, if we take a cross-cultural view, it becomes clear that the ideal type of neolocal residence is relatively uncommon. In many societies, the bride and groom live either with his parents (the **patrilocal** pattern) or with her parents (the **matrilocal** pattern). Members of such cultures believe that the new couples need the emotional support and especially the economic support of kinfolk.

Authority Patterns: Who Rules?

Imagine that you have recently married and must begin to make decisions about the future of your new family. You and your spouse face many questions. Where will you live? How will you furnish your place of residence? Who will do the cooking, the shopping, the cleaning? Whose friends will be invited to dinner?

A married couple must face many questions, among them who will do the cooking, the shopping, and the cleaning. Each time a decision must be made, an issue is raised: "Who has the power to make the decision?"

Each time a decision must be made, an issue is raised: "Who has the power to make the decision?" In simple terms, who rules the family? From a conflict perspective, these questions must be examined in light of traditional gender stratification (see Chapter 8), under which men have held a dominant position over women.

Societies vary in the way that power within the family is distributed. If a society expects males to dominate in all family decision making, it is termed a **patriarchy.** Frequently, in patriarchal societies, the eldest male wields the greatest power. Women hold low status in such societies and rarely are granted full and equal rights within the legal system. It may be more difficult, for example, for a woman to obtain a divorce than it is for a man. By contrast, in a **matriarchy,** women have greater authority than men. Matriarchies may have emerged among Native American tribal societies and in nations in which men were absent for long periods of time for warfare or food gathering.

BOX 9-1

MARITAL POWER

Sociologists Robert Blood, Jr., and Donald Wolfe (1960) developed the concept of *marital power* to describe the manner in which decision making is distributed within families. They defined power by examining who makes the final decision in each of eight important areas that, the researchers argue, traditionally have been reserved entirely for the husband or for the wife. These areas include what job the husband should take, what house or apartment to live in, where to go on vacation, and which doctor to use if there is an illness in the family. Using this technique, Blood and Wolfe (1960:22–23) surveyed families in the Detroit area and concluded that the "aggregate balance of power falls slightly in the husband's direction." They added that, in general, it seemed appropriate to "label these as relatively egalitarian couples."

Recent research suggests that money plays a central role in determining marital power. Money has different meanings for members of each sex: for men it typically represents identity and power; for women, security and autonomy. Apparently, money establishes the balance of power not only for married couples but also for unmarried heterosexual couples who are living together. Married women with paying work outside the home enjoy greater marital power than full-time homemakers do (Blumstein and Schwartz, 1983; Godwin and Scanzoni, 1989; Kaufman, 1985).

Labor not only enhances women's self-esteem but also increases their marital power, because some men have greater respect for women who work at paying jobs. Sociologist Isik Aytac (1987) studied a national sample of households in the United States and found that husbands of women holding management positions share more of the domestic chores than other husbands. In addition, as a wife's proportional contribution to the family income increases, her husband's share of meal preparation increases. Aytac's research supports the contention that the traditional division of labor at home can change as women's position in the labor force improves and women gain greater marital power.

Comparative studies have revealed the complexity of marital power issues in other cultures. For example, anthropologist David Gilmore (1990) examined decision making in two rural towns in southern Spain. These communities—one with 8000 residents and the other with 4000—have an agricultural economy based on olives, wheat, and sunflowers. Gilmore studied a variety of decision-making situations, including prenuptial decisions over household location, administration of domestic finances, and major household purchases. He found that working-class women in these communities—often united with their mothers—are able to prevail in many decisions despite opposition from their husbands.

Interestingly, wives' control over finances in these towns appears to lessen with affluence. Among the wealthier peasants, husbands retain more rights over the family purse strings, especially in terms of bank accounts and investments. In some cases, they make investments without their wives' knowledge. By contrast, in the working class—where surplus cash is uncommon and household finances are often based on borrowing and buying on credit because of the uncertainties of household employment—it is the wife who "rules" the household economy, and the husband accepts her rule.

Some marital relationships may be neither male-dominated nor female-dominated. The third type of authority pattern, the *egalitarian family,* is one in which spouses are regarded as equals. This does not mean, however, that each decision is shared in such families. Mothers may hold authority in some spheres, fathers in others. In the view of many sociologists, the egalitarian family has begun to replace the patriarchal family as the social norm. A study of Detroit families by Robert Blood, Jr., and Donald Wolfe (1960) supports this contention (see Box 9-1).

FUNCTIONS OF THE FAMILY

Do we really need the family? A century ago, Friedrich Engels (1884), a colleague of Karl Marx, described the family as the ultimate source of social inequality because of its role in the transfer of power, property, and privilege. More recently, conflict theorists have argued that the family contributes to societal injustice, denies opportunities to women that are extended to men, and limits freedom in sexual expression and selection of a mate.

In order to evaluate such issues, it is helpful to use the tools provided by the functionalist perspective, which encourages us to examine the ways in which an institution gratifies the needs of its members and contributes to the stability of society. The family fulfills a number of functions, such as providing religious training, education, and recreational outlets. Yet there are six paramount functions performed by the family; these functions were first outlined 60 years ago by sociologist William F. Ogburn (Ogburn and Tibbits, 1934):

1 *Reproduction.* For a society to maintain itself, it must replace dying members. In this sense, the family contributes to human survival through its function of reproduction.

2 *Protection.* Unlike the young of animal species, human infants need constant care and economic security. Infants and children experience an extremely long period of dependency, which places special demands on older family members. In all cultures, it is the family that assumes ultimate responsibility for the protection and upbringing of children.

3 *Socialization.* Parents and other kin monitor a child's behavior and transmit the norms, values, and language of a culture to the child (see Chapters 2 and 3). Of course, as conflict theorists point out, the social class of couples and their children significantly influences the socialization experiences to which they are exposed and the protection they receive.

4 *Regulation of sexual behavior.* Sexual norms are subject to change over time (for instance, there have been changes in customs for dating) and across cultures (Islamic Saudi Arabia, for example, can be compared with more permissive Denmark). However, whatever the time period or cultural values in a society, standards of sexual behavior are most clearly defined within the family circle. The structure of society influences these standards so that, characteristically in male-dominated societies, formal and informal norms permit men to express and enjoy their sexual desires more freely than women may.

5 *Affection and companionship.* Ideally, the family provides members with warm and intimate relationships and helps them feel satisfied and secure. Of course, a family member may find such rewards outside the family—from peers, in school, at work—and may perceive the home as an unpleasant place. Nevertheless, unlike other institutions, the family is obligated to serve the emotional needs of its members. We *expect* our relatives to understand us, to care for us, and to be there for us when we need them.

6 *Providing of social status.* We inherit a social position because of the "family background" and reputation of our parents and siblings. The family unit presents the newborn child with an ascribed status of race and ethnicity that is a factor in determining his or her place within a society's stratification system. Moreover, family resources affect children's ability to pursue certain opportunities such as higher education and specialized lessons.

It is apparent, then, that the family has been assigned at least six vital functions in human societies. However, one might ask if the family can effectively fulfill these weighty responsibilities. To answer this question, we must begin a more detailed examination of marital and family life in the United States of the 1990s.

MARRIAGE AND FAMILY IN THE UNITED STATES

Currently, close to 90 percent of all men and women in the United States marry at least once during their lifetimes. Historically, the most consistent aspect of family life in the United States has been the nation's high rate of marriage. In this part of the chapter, we will examine various aspects of love, marriage, and parenthood in the United States.

The process of courtship is clearly influenced by the values of the particular society in which we live. In many South American cultures, teenagers typically get together in group settings rather than as couples on dates.

Courtship and Mate Selection

In certain traditional cultures, arranged marriages are common, and courtship practices are severely restricted. For example, some Japanese traditionalists favor arranged marriages for their children. A go-between will often take a young man to a public place for a *kagemi* (a hidden look) at a young woman viewed as a likely candidate for marriage. The woman is unaware that her appearance is being evaluated (Hendry, 1981:116–123). Similarly, "secret looks" are common in rural Egypt. A boy from a village observes:

> One favorite place for us to get a glimpse of girls is at the village water source. The girls know that and like to linger there. If we see one we like and think she might be suitable, we ask our parents to try to arrange a marriage, but usually not before we have some sign from the girl that she might be interested (Rugh, 1984:137).

As is true in this Egyptian village, courtship in the United States requires people to rely heavily on intricate games, gestures, and signals. For example, how do you act when you have just met an attractive stranger in a bookstore, in a supermarket, or at a party? Do you come right out and say, "I'd really like to see you again," after just meeting the person? Or do you find elaborate and slightly disguised ways of showing your interest and testing how the other person feels about you?

An important aspect of the courtship process is labeling. Sociologist Robert Lewis (1973) reports that early labeling as a couple by family and friends results in a greater likelihood that the relationship will be maintained over time. By contrast, the absence of such labeling—or a negative reaction from people termed *significant others* by George Herbert Mead (see Chapter 3)—can weaken the couple's relationship.

Courtship is clearly influenced by the values of our society. But what about our *choice* of a mate? Why are we drawn to a particular person in the first place? To what extent are such judgments shaped by the society around us?

Theories of Mate Selection Many societies have explicit or unstated rules which define potential mates as acceptable or unacceptable. These norms can be distinguished in terms of endogamy and exogamy. ***Endogamy*** (from the Greek *endon,* "within") specifies the groups within which a spouse must be found and prohibits marriage with others. For example, in the United States, many people are expected to marry within their own racial, ethnic, or religious group and are prohibited from marrying outside the group. Endogamy is intended to reinforce the cohesiveness of the group by suggesting to the young that they should marry someone "of our own kind."

By contrast, **exogamy** (from the Greek *exō,* "outside") requires mate selection outside certain groups, usually one's own family or certain kinfolk. The **incest taboo,** a social norm common to virtually all societies, prohibits sexual relationships between certain culturally specified relatives. For people in the United States, this taboo means that we must marry outside the nuclear family. We cannot marry our siblings, and in most states we cannot marry our first cousins.

Endogamous restrictions may be seen as preferences for one group over another. In the United States, such preferences are most obvious in racial barriers. Until the 1960s, some states outlawed interracial marriages. This practice was challenged by Richard Loving (a White man) and Mildred Jeter Loving (a part-Black, part-Native American woman), who married in 1958. Eventually, in 1967, the Supreme Court ruled that it was unconstitutional to prohibit marriage solely on the basis of race. The decision struck down statutes in Virginia and 16 other states.

According to the Bureau of the Census, the number of marriages between Blacks and Whites in the United States has more than tripled in recent decades, jumping from 65,000 in 1970 to 231,000 in 1991. One of the nation's interracial couples, Tom and Yvette Weatherly, grew up in different parts of Atlanta and first met when she was bused to his overwhelmingly White high school and sat behind him in English class. "We are a segregationist's worst nightmare," notes Tom Weatherly. "But, to other people, we're the perfect example" (Wilkerson, 1991:B6).

Survey data show that many Whites still oppose interracial marriages. According to the General Social Survey, an annual poll of 1500 people in the United States, 66 percent of Whites state that they would oppose a close relative's marrying a Black person. About 45 percent would oppose such a marriage to an Asian or Hispanic person. Moreover, one in five Whites believes that interracial marriage should be illegal (as it was in some states until the Supreme Court's 1967 ruling). By contrast, Blacks were found to be indifferent on the subject of intermarriage; nearly two-thirds of respondents stated that they would neither favor nor oppose a close relative's marrying someone from another race (Wilkerson, 1991).

The Love Relationship Love and mate selection do not necessarily coincide. For example, feelings of love are not a prerequisite for marriage among the Yaruros of inland Venezuela or in other cultures where there is little freedom for mate selection. As Linton Freeman (1958:27–30) has shown, the Yaruro male of marriageable age does not engage in the kind of dating behavior so typical of young people in the United States. Rather, he knows that, under the traditions of his culture, he must marry one of his mother's brothers' daughters or one of his father's sisters' daughters. The young man's choice is further limited because one of his uncles selects the eligible cousin that he must marry.

Many of the world's cultures give priority in mate selection to factors other than romantic feelings. In some societies, marriages are arranged, often by parents or religious authorities. The newly married couple is expected to develop a feeling of love *after* the legal union is formalized. Economic considerations also play a significant role in mate selection in certain societies.

In the United States, love is important in the courtship process. Neolocal residence places added importance on the affectional bond between husband and wife. The couple is able to develop its own emotional ties, free of the demands of other household members for affection. Sociologist William Goode (1959) observed that spouses in a nuclear family have to rely heavily on each other for the companionship and support that might be provided by other relatives in an extended-family situation.

Parents in the United States value love highly as a rationale for marriage, and they encourage love to develop between young people. In addition, the theme of romantic love is reinforced in songs, films, books, magazines, television shows, and even cartoons and comic books. At the same time, our society expects parents and peers to help a person confine his or her search for a mate to "socially acceptable" members of the opposite sex.

Traditional gender-role socialization has made it easier for women to express love and other feelings of social intimacy than it is for men. The qualities identified with intimacy—emotional warmth, expressiveness, vulnerability, and sensitivity—are associated with the female but not the male gender role. Studies show that men are more likely than women to base their perceptions of love and intimacy on sex, on providing practical help, and on simply being in the presence of a loved one. One husband attempted to demonstrate his affection for his wife by washing her car; he was bewildered when she failed to understand the intended message of his assistance (Cancian, 1986; L. Thompson and Walker, 1989:847).

Parenthood and Child Care

Caring for children is a universal function of the family, yet societies vary in assigning this function to family members. Among the Nayars of southern India, the biological role of fathers is acknowledged, but the mother's eldest brother is responsible for her children (Gough, 1974). By contrast, uncles play only a peripheral role in child care in the United States.

Despite such differences, the socialization of children is essential to the maintenance of any culture. Consequently, as we saw in Chapter 3, parenthood is one of the most important (and most demanding) social roles in the United States. Sociologist Alice Rossi (1968, 1984:5–10) has pointed to four factors related to socialization that complicate the transition to parenthood. First, there is little anticipatory socialization for the social roles of caregiver. Subjects most relevant to successful family life—such as child care and home maintenance—are given little attention in the normal school curriculum. Second, only limited learning occurs during the period of pregnancy itself. Third, the transition to parenthood is quite abrupt. Unlike adolescence, it is not prolonged; unlike socialization for work, one cannot gradually take on the duties of care-giving. Finally, in Rossi's view, our society lacks clear and helpful guidelines concerning successful parenthood. There is little consensus on how parents can produce happy and well-adjusted offspring— or even on what it means to be "well-adjusted." For these reasons, socialization for parenthood involves difficult challenges for most men and women in the United States.

One recent development in family life in the United States has been the extension of parenthood, as adult children continue to (or return to) live at home. Currently, more than half of all children ages 20 to 24 and one out of four of those ages 25 to 34 live with their parents. Some of these adult children are still pursuing an educa-

tion, but in many instances financial difficulties are at the heart of these living arrangements. While rents and real estate prices skyrocketed in the 1980s, salaries for younger workers did not keep pace and many found themselves unable to afford their own homes. Moreover, with many marriages now ending in divorce, divorced sons and daughters are now returning to live with their parents, sometimes with their own children (Bureau of the Census, 1992a:51).

Is this living arrangement a positive development for family members? Social scientists have just begun to examine this phenomenon, sometimes called the "boomerang generation" in the popular press. One survey in Virginia seemed to show that neither the parents nor their adult children were happy about continuing to live together. The children often felt resentful and isolated, but the parents also suffered, since learning to live without children in the home can be viewed as an essential stage of adult life and indeed may be a significant turning point for a marriage (*Berkeley Wellness Letter*, 1990:1–2).

Adoption

In a legal sense, *adoption* is a "process that allows for the transfer of the legal rights, responsibilities, and privileges of parenting from legal parents to new legal parents" (E. Cole, 1985:638). In many cases, these rights are transferred from biological parents (often called *birth parents*) to adoptive parents. Viewed from a functionalist perspective, government has a strong interest in encouraging adoption. Kenneth Watson (1986:5) of the Chicago Child Care Society notes: "Adoption is seen as a neat solution to three of society's vexing problems: unplanned pregnancy outside of marriage, children in need of families to rear them, and infertile couples unable to have children."

Policymakers have both a humanitarian and a financial stake in promoting adoption. In theory, adoption offers a stable family environment for children who otherwise might not receive satisfactory care. Moreover, government data show that unwed mothers who keep their babies tend to be of lower socioeconomic status and often require public assistance to support their children (C. Bachrach, 1986). Consequently, various levels of government may lower their social welfare expenses if children are transferred to economi-

Parenthood is one of the most important social roles.

cally self-sufficient families. From a conflict perspective, such financial considerations raise the ugly specter of adoption's serving as a means whereby affluent (often infertile) couples are allowed to "buy" the children of the poor.

The largest single category of adoption in the United States is adoption by relatives. In most cases, a stepparent adopts the children of a spouse. There are two legal methods of adopting an unrelated person: adoptions arranged by licensed agencies and private agreements sanctioned by the courts (E. Cole, 1985:639–640, 662–663; Salvatore, 1986:60).

According to the National Committee for Adoption, an association of private adoption agencies, the number of adoptions between unrelated people in the United States decreased from 82,800 in 1971 to 51,157 in 1986 (the last year for which complete data are available). This change was due largely to a decline in the number of children available for adoption. Key factors contributing to this diminishing pool of children include wider use of contraceptives, an increase in the number of abortions (see Chapter 8), and a lessening of the social stigma faced by single parents who keep their babies (Lawson, 1991:Cl; Lindsey, 1987:30).

According to a study by the National Center for Health Statistics, about 200,000 women in the United States sought to adopt children in 1988. The alleged "parent surplus" often described in the mass media reflects an abundance of childless couples who are anxious to adopt White, nondisabled babies. Ironically, at the same time that these parents wait for babies, many children and adolescents from minority group backgrounds or with disabilities live in group homes or in foster-care situations (M. Harris, 1988; Hilts, 1990).

Dual-Career Families

In the traditional nuclear family, the husband serves as the sole breadwinner, while the wife fills the roles of mother and homemaker. However, an increasing proportion of couples in the United States today are rejecting this traditional model for a "dual-career" lifestyle. Currently, the majority of all married couples have two partners active in the paid labor force. In one-fourth of couples, both partners are "permanently committed" to their careers in that they have worked for at least five years.

Why has there been such a rise in the number of dual-career couples? A major factor, especially among less affluent families, is economic need. In 1990, the median income for married-couple families with both partners employed was $46,777, compared with $30,265 (or 35 percent less) in families in which only the husband was working outside the home. (Sociologists have noted, however, that not all of a family's second wage is genuine additional income because of such work-related costs as child care.) Other factors contributing to the rise of the dual-career model include the nation's declining birthrate (see Chapter 12), the increase in the proportion of women with a college education, the shift in the economy of the United States from manufacturing to service industries, and the impact of the feminist movement in changing women's consciousness (Bureau of the Census, 1992a:452; Hanson and Ooms, 1991).

In a sense, members of dual-career couples must undergo a process of resocialization (see Chapter 3). A newly married couple may intend to have a "two-career household" and share child care in an egalitarian manner. Their parents, however, may have followed the conventional nuclear family pattern described earlier. Thus, neither of the newlyweds may have had useful role models for a dual-career lifestyle. Each may have had to overcome previous socialization into traditional expectations regarding marriage and the "proper" roles of husbands and wives. As was discussed in Chapter 8, sociologist Arlie Hochschild (1989, 1990) has used the phrase "second shift" to describe the double burden—work outside the home followed by child care and housework—that many women carry and few men share equitably.

Some dual-career couples actually come to resemble single-parent families because of their reliance on jobs with evening or weekend hours. These couples split work and parenthood shifts as a means of coping with the pressures of the dual-career lifestyle. Approximately one out of every six dual-income couples with children under the age of 6 has work hours that do not overlap at all (McEnroe, 1991).

Variations in Family Life

Within the United States, there are many variations in family life associated with distinctions of social class, race, and ethnicity. An examination of such variations will give us a more sophisticated understanding of contemporary family styles in our country.

Social Class Differences   Various studies have documented the differences in family organization among social classes in the United States. In the upper class, there is a particular emphasis on lineage and maintenance of family position. One is considered not simply a member of a nuclear family but rather a member of a larger family tradition ("the Rockefellers" or "the Kennedys"). As a result, upper-class families are quite concerned about what they see as "proper training" for children.

Lower-class families do not often have the luxury of worrying about the "family name"; they must first struggle to pay their bills and survive the crises often associated with life in poverty. Such families are more likely to have only one parent in the home, a situation which presents special challenges in terms of child care and financial needs. Children in lower-class families typically assume adult responsibilities—including marriage and parenthood—at an earlier age than children of affluent homes. In part, this is because they may lack the money needed to remain in school.

Social class differences in family life may not be as striking as they once were. In the past, family specialists agreed that there were pronounced contrasts in child-rearing practices. Lower-class families were found to be more authoritarian in rearing children and more inclined to use physical punishment. Middle-class families were more permissive and more restrained in punishing their children. However, these differences may have narrowed as more and more families from all social classes have turned to the same books, magazines, and even television talk shows for advice on rearing children (M. Kohn, 1970; Luster et al., 1989).

Among the poor, women often play a significant role in the economic support of the family. Men may earn low wages, may be unemployed, or may be absent from the family. In 1990, 44 percent of all families headed by women with no husband present were below the government poverty line. This compared with only 7 percent for all traditional dual-parent families (Bureau of the Census, 1992a:460).

Many racial and ethnic groups appear to have distinctive family characteristics. However, racial and class factors are often closely related. In examining family life among racial and ethnic minorities, we must remember that certain patterns may result from class as well as cultural factors.

Racial and Ethnic Differences   It is often assumed that racial and ethnic minorities in the United States find it difficult to maintain healthy family lives because of prejudice and discrimination (see Chapter 7). However, half of Black families have maintained two-parent family environments.

There are many negative and inaccurate stereotypes in the United States regarding the African American family. It is true that a significantly higher proportion of Black than of White families have no husband present in the home (see Figure 9-3). Yet Black single mothers are often part of stable, functioning kin networks, despite the pressures of sexism and racism. Members of these networks—predominantly female kin such as mothers, grandmothers, and aunts—share goods and services and thereby ease financial strains. In addition to these strong kinship bonds, Black family life has emphasized deep religious commitment and high aspirations for achievement. The strengths of the Black family were evident during slavery, when Blacks demonstrated a remarkable ability to maintain family ties despite the fact that the slave enjoyed no legal protections (Gimenez, 1987; R. Hill, 1972, 1987).

Sociologists have also taken note of differences in family patterns between other racial and ethnic groups. For example, Mexican American men have been described as exhibiting a sense of virility, of personal worth, and of pride in their maleness that is called *machismo.* Mexican Americans are also described as being more familistic than many other subcultures. *Familism* refers to pride in the extended family expressed through the maintenance of close ties and strong obligations to kinfolk outside the immediate family (S. Wallace, 1984).

Research indicates that machismo and familism are declining among Mexican Americans. Various factors, including feminism, urbanization, upward mobility, and assimilation, make machismo and familism more of a historical footnote with each new generation. Like earlier immigrants from Europe and Asia, Mexican Americans are likely to gradually adopt the norms of the dominant culture for family life (J. Moore and Pachon, 1985:96–98; E. Stevens, 1973).

DIVORCE IN THE UNITED STATES

"Do you promise to love, honor, and cherish . . . until death do you part?" Every year, people of all social classes and racial and ethnic groups make such legally binding agreements. Yet an increasing number of these promises are apparently not realistic, given our rising divorce rate.

Statistical Trends in Divorce

How common is divorce? Surprisingly, this is not a simple question. Statistics on divorce are difficult to collect and even more difficult to interpret.

The media frequently report that one out of every two marriages ends in divorce. However, this figure is misleading, since it is based on a comparison of all divorces which occur in a single year (regardless of when the couples were married) against the number of new marriages in the same year. As the middle column of Table 9-1 (page 246) indicates, there were 51 divorces in 1992 for every 100 new marriages. But that could, in fact, represent 51 divorces for every 3000 marriages that occurred in the decades leading up to 1992.

A more accurate perspective on divorce can be obtained if we examine the number of divorces per 1000 married women (see the right column in Table 9-1). In the early 1970s, the divorce rate per 1000 married women exceeded the all-time high set in 1946. Using these statistics, we can see that the number of divorces per 1000 married women has more than doubled over the last 30 years. Nevertheless, about half of couples remain married; about 70 percent of those who obtain a divorce before age 35 later remarry, half of those within three years after a first divorce (Bumpass et al., 1990; Sweet and Bumpass, 1987).

FIGURE 9-3   One-Parent Families among Blacks, Hispanics, and Whites, 1970 and 1991

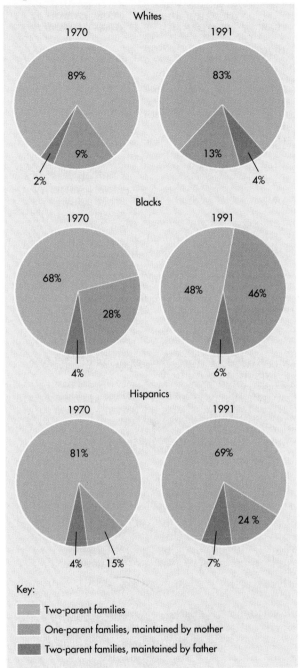

Key:

■ Two-parent families

■ One-parent families, maintained by mother

■ Two-parent families, maintained by father

SOURCE: Bureau of the Census, 1992a:47.

In 1991, 46 percent of Black families, 24 percent of Hispanic families, but only 13 percent of White families were maintained by the mother with no husband in the home.

TABLE 9-1 Divorce Rates in the United States

YEAR	DIVORCES PER 100 MARRIAGES PERFORMED	DIVORCES PER 1000 MARRIED WOMEN, 15 YEARS OLD AND OVER
1920	13.4	8.0
1930	17.0	7.5
1940	16.9	8.8
1946	26.6	17.8
1950	23.1	10.3
1960	25.8	9.2
1970	32.8	14.9
1980	49.7	22.6
1992	51.0	24.2[a]

[a]Data for 1989.
SOURCES: National Center for Health Statistics, 1974, 1990, 1992b; authors' estimates.

Divorce rates have fluctuated since World War II, but represent a two- to threefold increase from pre-1940 levels.

FIGURE 9-4 Living Arrangements of Children by Type of Family, 1990

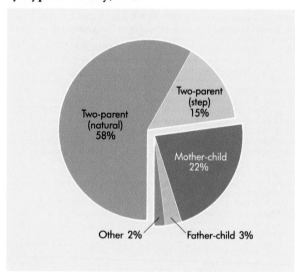

SOURCES: Bureau of the Census, 1991f; and authors' estimates.

As of 1990, less than 60 percent of children under 18 years old in the United States lived in two-parent families with both biological parents.

While the nation's high rate of remarriage is regarded as an endorsement of the institution of marriage, it does lead to the new challenges of a remarriage kin network composed of current and prior marital relationships. This network can be particularly complex if children are involved or if an ex-spouse remarries. As is shown in Figure 9-4, by 1990 about 15 percent of children in the United States lived with a parent and a stepparent.

A study published in 1989 predicts that about two-thirds of all first marriages in the United States are likely to end in separation or divorce. In the view of Teresa Castro Martin and Larry L. Bumpass of the Center for Demography and Ecology, University of Wisconsin, the decline in divorces in the United States between 1980 and 1990 does not mean that a long-term return to more stable family life is under way. The researchers (1989:49) conclude that the "diversity in family life created by patterns of divorce and remarriage is likely an intrinsic feature of modern family life rather than a temporary aberration" (see also Darnton, 1992).

The current high divorce rate of the United States is not the result of a sudden explosion; rather, signs of such a tendency can be seen early in the nation's history. Residents of colonial America could receive divorces more easily than their counterparts anywhere in the western world. The divorce rate in the United States doubled between 1900 and 1920 and rose steadily until 1980, when it began to level off. Furthermore, the country's *teenage* divorce rate is more than twice the overall national average (Bureau of the Census, 1992a:92).

Divorce is a complex and difficult experience for all family members. Anthropologist Paul Bohannan (1970) has identified six overlapping experiences which arise from divorce and which vary in intensity depending on the couple. The "six stations of divorce," as Bohannan calls them, include:

1 *Emotional divorce,* which represents the problem of the deteriorating marriage
2 *Legal divorce,* based on the grounds on which the marriage will be dissolved
3 *Economic divorce,* which deals with the division of money and property

BOX 9-2

THE EFFECTS OF DIVORCE ON FEMALE AND MALE CHILDREN

Traditionally, family researchers have suggested that divorce has a more detrimental effect on boys than on girls. These researchers have often written that the absence of fathers is more harmful for the development of boys than for girls and that girls receive greater emotional support from custodial mothers. However, more recent studies have led to a reexamination of these long-held assumptions (Hetherington, 1979; Zaslow, 1988, 1989).

Psychologist Neil Kalter (1989) and his associates supervised clinical work with more than 600 children of divorce over a 10-year period. In addition, they interviewed and tested about 500 research subjects and conducted preventive intervention programs for about 2000 children in public schools. Kalter's work shows that boys and girls react differently to divorce, but that traditional views concerning their reactions are not necessarily accurate.

Boys from divorced families are often angry and combative and may develop delinquent behavior. They frequently resist the authority of their mothers and teachers, become involved in fights at school or in the neighborhood, and underachieve at school relative to their abilities. The reduced interaction with their fathers which typically results from divorce has a clear and negative impact on sons.

For girls, the harmful effects of divorce emerge somewhat later than for boys, sometimes only in adolescence or even in adulthood. When compared with daughters from intact families, daughters of divorce are more likely to have feelings of lowered self-worth. The absence of a caring father leads many daughters to wonder if they can be loved by a man; indeed, these girls may believe that their fathers left home because their daughters were not attractive or lovable enough.

In suggesting that divorce has a more detrimental impact on boys than on girls, many researchers maintained that custodial mothers develop closer relationships with their daughters than with their sons. However, for the adolescent female, this may be a mixed blessing. A daughter of divorce may find it difficult to achieve a healthy separation and independence from her mother. Moreover, as she struggles with her emerging sexuality during her adolescence, a young woman may face additional complications if she is sharing a home with a stepfather or a close male friend of her mother.

Kalter's studies show that the detrimental effect of divorce often appears *earlier* in boys than in girls—and that this detrimental effect is sometimes more obvious and more dramatic in boys because of their greater tendency toward aggressiveness and antisocial behavior. Nevertheless, these studies remind us that we should not underestimate the harmful impact of divorce on girls.

4 *Coparental divorce*, which includes decisions having to do with child custody and visitation rights
5 *Community divorce*, or the changes in friendships and institutional ties that a divorced person experiences
6 *Psychic divorce*, focused on the person's attempt to regain autonomy and self-esteem

As Bohannan has observed, "undivorced" people rarely appreciate the difficulties that the divorced person experiences in mastering these "stations of divorce" (Gerstel, 1987). The impact of divorce on girls and boys is examined in Box 9-2 above.

An increasing number of families in the United States are coping with the traumas of divorce by experimenting with joint or shared custody arrangements. Joint custody has become popular, since it allows each parent meaningful time with children and promotes an egalitarian sharing of decision-making authority. However, adults unable to live together as husband and wife may find it difficult to cooperate in resolving important issues of parenthood. Three studies by psychologist Judith Wallerstein and her colleagues suggest that joint custody arrangements do not benefit all children whose parents have separated or divorced and, in certain instances, may be harmful for these children (J. Wallerstein and Blakeslee, 1989).

TABLE 9-2 Likelihood of Divorce

FACTORS ASSOCIATED WITH HIGHER PROBABILITY OF DIVORCE
Marriage at a very young age (15 to 19 years old)
Short acquaintanceship before marriage
Short engagement or no engagement
Parents with unhappy marriages
Disapproval of marriage expressed by kin and friends
General dissimilarity in background
Membership in different religious faiths
Failure to attend religious services
Disagreement of husband and wife on role obligations
Urban background

FACTORS ASSOCIATED WITH LOWER PROBABILITY OF DIVORCE
Marriage at or above the average ages 26 years old for males, 24 years old for females
Acquaintanceship of two years or more before marriage
Engagement of six months or more
Parents with happy marriage
Approval of marriage expressed by kin and friends
Similarity of background
Membership in same religious faith
Regular attendance at religious services
Agreement of husband and wife on role obligations
Rural background

SOURCES: Adapted from Goode, 1976:537–538. See also Fergusson et al., 1984. Median age of marriage from Bureau of the Census, 1992a:91.

Research has shown that many factors are associated with greater or lesser probability of divorce.

Factors Associated with Divorce

Why does the United States have such a high frequency of divorce? There is no fully satisfactory answer to this question. Table 9-2 indicates factors which are associated with a higher probability of divorce among married couples. In addition to these strains in each individual relationship, however, there are overall social changes which contribute to the nation's rising divorce rate.

Perhaps the most important factor in the increase in divorce throughout the twentieth century has been the greater social acceptance of divorce. In particular, this increased tolerance has resulted from a relaxation of negative attitudes toward divorce among various religious denominations. Although divorce is still seen as unfortunate, it is no longer treated as a sin by most religious leaders (Gerstel, 1987; Thornton, 1985).

A few other factors deserve mention. Many states have adopted more liberal divorce laws in the last two decades. Divorce has become a more practical option in newly formed families, since they now tend to have fewer children than in the past. A general increase in family incomes, coupled with the availability of free legal aid for some poor people, has meant that more couples can afford the traditionally high legal costs of divorce proceedings. Finally, as society provides greater opportunities for women, more and more wives are becoming less dependent on their husbands—both economically and emotionally. They may then feel more able to leave if the marriage seems hopeless.

The most extreme cause of marital breakdown is domestic violence—an issue that will be discussed in the social policy section at the end of the chapter.

ALTERNATIVE LIFESTYLES

In the 1990s, it is clear that family life in the United States has undergone many changes. Teenagers have babies, children return home as adults, and some parents value their foreign sports cars more than they value their children (Footlick, 1990:16). As we will see in the following discussions, many people have chosen alternative lifestyles rather than the traditional nuclear family.

Cohabitation

Saint Paul once wrote: "It is better to marry than to burn." However, as journalist Tom Ferrell (1979) has suggested, more people than ever "prefer combustible to connubial bliss." One of the most dramatic trends of recent years has been the tremendous increase in male-female couples who choose to live together without marrying, thereby engaging in what is commonly called *cohabitation.*

The number of such households in the United States rose sixfold in the 1960s and increased another sixfold between 1970 and 1991. The dramatic rise in cohabitation has been linked to greater acceptance of premarital sex and delayed entry into marriage. According to a 1988 national survey, 11 percent of women who had never married were cohabiting while 44 percent of women who had married in the early 1980s had cohabited at some time (Bouvier and De Vita, 1991:18; Thomson and Colella, 1992).

Increases in cohabitation have also been found in Canada, France, Sweden, Denmark, and Australia. One report notes that in Sweden it is almost universal for couples to live together before marriage. Demographers in Denmark call the practice of living together *marriage without papers.* In Australia, these couples are known as *de factos* (Blanc, 1984; A. Levinson, 1984; Thomson and Colella, 1992).

For some people in the United States, living together may represent a kind of trial marriage that will eventually lead to a traditional marriage with their current partner (or some other person). Margaret Mead (1966) gave the idea of trial marriage her support when she suggested that mar-

riage be contracted in two stages. The *individual marriage* would involve a minimal legal commitment but would become a legally binding *parental marriage* once a child was expected. Mead's formulation has not yet won wide acceptance. However, in many instances, a couple engaged in extended cohabitation comes to view the relationship as a partnership somewhat like marriage—but with unresolved legal implications.

It would be incorrect, however, to associate cohabitation only with college campuses, sexual experimentation, or trial marriages. According to a study in Los Angeles, working couples are almost twice as likely to cohabit as college students are. At the same time, census data show that 28 percent of unmarried couples have one or more children present in the household. These cohabitants can be regarded as more similar to spouses than to dating partners. Moreover, in contrast to the common perception that people engaged in cohabitation have never married, researchers report that about half of all people involved in cohabitation in the United States have been previously married. Indeed, cohabitation serves as a temporary or permanent alternative to matrimony for many men and women who have experienced marital disruption. Clearly, cohabitation should not be regarded as a pastime limited to the unmarried and the inexperienced (London, 1991; Spanier, 1983).

Remaining Single

Current data indicate that more people in the United States are postponing entry into first marriages than was true in the past. In 1990, 63 percent of all women 20 to 24 years of age had never married, compared with only 28 percent in 1960. Still, less than 10 percent of women and men are likely to remain single throughout their lives (Bureau of the Census, 1991g).

The trend toward maintaining an unmarried lifestyle is related to the growing economic independence of young people. This is especially significant for women. In 1890, women accounted for only one-sixth of the paid labor force; they are now approximately half of it (see Chapter 8). From a financial point of view, it is often no longer necessary for a woman to marry in order to enjoy a satisfying life.

TABLE 9-3 Singleness: An Alternative to Marriage

ATTRACTIONS OF BEING SINGLE	ATTRACTIONS OF BEING MARRIED
Career opportunities	Economic security
Sexual availability	Regular sex
Exciting lifestyle	Desire for family
Self-sufficiency	Sustained love
Freedom to change and experiment	Security in personal relationships

SOURCE: Adapted from P. Stein, 1975. Also appears in P. Stein, 1981:18.

More people in the United States are making a conscious choice to remain single. As the balance sheet above indicates, there are attractions to being single as well as to being married.

There are many reasons why a person may choose not to marry (see Table 9-3). Singleness is an attractive option for those who do not want to limit their sexual intimacy to one lifetime partner. Also, some men and women do not want to become highly dependent on any one person—and do not want anyone depending heavily on them. In a society which values individuality and self-fulfillment, the single lifestyle can offer certain freedoms that married couples may not enjoy.

Remaining single represents a clear departure from societal expectations; indeed, it has been likened to "being single on Noah's Ark." A single adult must confront the inaccurate view that he or she is always lonely, is a workaholic, is immature, and is automatically affluent. These stereotypes help support the traditional assumption in the United States and most other societies that to be truly happy and fulfilled, a person must get married and raise a family (Cargan and Melko, 1991).

Gay Relationships

According to estimates, lesbians and gay men together constitute perhaps 10 percent of the nation's population. Their lifestyles vary greatly. Some live alone, others with roommates. Some live in long-term, monogamous relationships with a lover and with children from former marriages. Others remain married and have not publicly acknowledged their homosexuality.

The contemporary gay liberation movement has given an increasing number of lesbians and gay males the support to proclaim their sexual and affectional preferences. Gay activists were distressed in 1986 when a divided Supreme Court ruled, by a 5–4 vote, that the Constitution does not protect homosexual relations between consenting adults, even within the privacy of their own homes. Nevertheless, as of 1992, the states of California, Wisconsin, Vermont, New Jersey, Hawaii, Massachusetts, and Connecticut; the District of Columbia; and more than 85 municipalities had enacted gay civil rights protections (B. Noble, 1992).

Gay activist organizations emphasize that lesbian and gay male couples are prohibited from marrying—and therefore from gaining traditional partnership benefits—in all 50 states. Consequently, with such inequities in mind, certain municipalities have been encouraged to pass legislation or adopt executive orders to provide benefits to "domestic partners." Under such policies, a *domestic partnership* may be defined as "two unrelated adults who have chosen to share one another's lives in a relationship of mutual caring, who reside together, and agree to be jointly responsible for their dependents, basic living expenses, and other common necessities." While the most passionate support for domestic partnership legislation has come from gay activists, only about 40 percent of those whose long-term relationships would qualify them as domestic partners are gay. The vast majority of those eligible for such benefits would be cohabiting heterosexual couples (Dittersdorf, 1990:6; Isaacson, 1989).

While various municipalities have passed domestic partnership legislation, such proposals continue to face strong opposition from conservative religious and political groups. In the view of opponents, support for domestic partnership undermines the historic societal preference for the nuclear family. Advocates of domestic partnership counter that such relationships fulfill the same functions for the individuals involved and for society as the traditional family and should enjoy the same legal protections and benefits. As one measure of the continuing controversy, a domestic partnership ordinance passed in San Francisco in 1989 was narrowly overturned by voters in a referendum later that year.

Some lesbian and gay couples have joined in formal "commitment ceremonies." Elaine Askari and Galen Ellis, shown together in this photograph, exchanged vows and rings and cut a wedding cake before 100 friends and family members in a park in Oakland, California.

Marriage without Children

There has been a modest increase in childlessness in the United States. According to data from the 1990 census, about 16 percent of women in their 40s will complete their childbearing years without having borne any children. As many as 20 percent of women in their thirties expect to remain childless (Bureau of the Census, 1991g:12).

Childlessness within marriage has generally been viewed as a problem that can be solved through such means as adoption and artificial insemination. Some couples, however, *choose* not to have children and regard themselves as childfree, not childless. They do not believe that having children automatically follows from marriage, nor do they feel that reproduction is the duty of all married couples.

Economic considerations have contributed to this shift in attitudes; having children has become quite expensive. According to a government estimate, the average cost of rearing a child from birth through age 17 for a two-parent family with no more than five children living in the urban midwest will be $122,760 (refer back to Box 3-2 on page 70). If the child attends college, that amount will rise substantially, depending on the college chosen. With such financial pressures in mind, some couples are having fewer children

than they otherwise might, and others are weighing the advantages of a child-free marriage (*Education Week*, 1991; Family Economics Research Group, 1992).

Single-Parent Families

Single-parent families, in which there is only one parent present to care for the children, can hardly be viewed as a rarity in the United States. Because of continuing increases in the nation's rates of divorce and unwed motherhood, 42 percent of White children living today and 86 percent of Black children will spend a significant portion of their adolescence in one-parent homes (Kotulak, 1986).

Whether judged in economic or emotional terms, the lives of single parents and their children are not inevitably more difficult than life in a traditional nuclear family. It is as inaccurate to assume that a single-parent family is necessarily "deprived" as it is to assume that a two-parent family is always secure and happy. Nevertheless, life in a single-parent family can be extremely stressful. Ronald Haskins, director of the Child Development Institute at the University of North Carolina, observes: "It's a big and risky undertaking when so many parents try to raise so many children alone" (Mann, 1983:62).

There is a clear association between the increase in families headed by single mothers and the feminization of poverty (see Chapter 6). Families headed by divorced or never-married mothers represent the fastest-growing segment of the female poor. The economic problems of single mothers result from such factors as sex discrimination in the paid labor force, the high costs of child care, inadequate welfare benefits, and fathers' failure to pay court-ordered child support.

A family headed by a single mother faces especially difficult problems when the mother is a teenager. According to a study released in 1985 and updated in 1989 by the Alan Guttmacher Institute, teenagers in the United States become pregnant, give birth, and have abortions at much higher rates than adolescents in almost any other industrialized nation. And the United States is the only developed country in which pregnancy among teenagers has been on the rise in recent years. Many adults with traditional attitudes toward sexuality and family life have suspected that the availability of birth control and sex education in the United States and other developed countries leads to increases in pregnancy among teenagers. However, the researchers point out that the *lowest* rates of pregnancy among teenagers are found in countries with liberal attitudes toward sex, easily accessible birth control services for young people, and comprehensive sex education programs (Brozan, 1985; Henshaw and Van Vort, 1989; E. Jones et al., 1985, 1986).

Why might low-income teenage women wish to have children and face the obvious financial difficulties of motherhood? Viewed from an interactionist perspective, these women tend to have low self-esteem and limited options; a child may provide a sense of motivation and purpose for a teenager whose economic worth in our society is limited at best. Given the barriers that many young women face because of their gender, race, ethnicity, and class, many teenagers may believe that they have little to lose and much to gain by having a child. In a 1988 survey of 13,000 high school sophomores from varied economic backgrounds, one out of four said that she would consider having a child if she became pregnant while unmarried. A follow-up study showed that these respondents were two to three times more likely than their reluctant peers to actually have become mothers (Abrahamse et al., 1988; V. Alexander et al., 1987; Gimenez, 1987; Zelnick and Young, 1982).

Communal Living

Some people are not satisfied with traditional marriage and family arrangements and prefer to live in some form of community with others. In a sense, they wish to create entirely new families, not necessarily including blood relatives or a spouse, with which they will live. Two such experiments in cooperative living are the Israeli kibbutz and the commune.

The first kibbutzim were founded in 1910, long before the modern state of Israel was established. A *kibbutz* is a group of individuals and families joined together to constitute an economic and social community. Although conscious Marxist thinking is no longer a dominant part of kibbutz life, it was fundamental to the socialist pioneers who founded the kibbutz movement. Most kibbutzim began as collective farming enterprises, growing vegetables and fruits, but many have expanded into industrial production in recent decades.

Kibbutz life in Israel has attracted great interest because it represents an attempt to transform socialist ideology into day-to-day living. The kibbutz owns all assets of the community, and individual property ownership is discouraged. All members are involved in governance, which is typically handled through committee work and community meetings. Child care is considered a responsibility of the entire community rather than being totally delegated to the family. On many kibbutzim, children do not live in homes with their parents. Instead, they reside in special "children's houses."

Like the kibbutz, the *commune* involves a form of cooperative living. Communes are perhaps the best known and least understood of alternative lifestyles. They are often incorrectly associated with the rebellious 1960s. Few people in the United States are aware that some of the nation's most influential communes existed in colonial and nineteenth-century America. One such group was the Oneida community of New York State, founded in 1848 by a religious leader

The Israeli kibbutz *represents one of the world's best-known experiments in collective living.*

named John Noyes. In this community, not only private property but also exclusive sexual relationships were informally outlawed (Kephart and Zellner, 1991).

As of 1991, there were an estimated 3000 communes in the United States. They are found primarily in rural areas, though they are occasionally established in urban centers. Many people join such communes in order to escape the sense of alienation and isolation that they encounter in the "straight" (conventional) world. Often they live in communes for a few months or years and then return to more traditional living arrangements. Some communes have strict moral codes which sharply restrict sexual behavior and prohibit the use of drugs. Others have few rules; each member is free to do whatever he or she pleases within general standards established by the group (B. Berger, 1981; C. Wilson, 1991; Zablocki, 1980).

The emergence of alternative lifestyles is not a sign of basic changes in the family structure of the United States. Men, women, and children involved in communes and other experimental living arrangements still constitute a very small minority of the nation's people.

Still, in view of the rising divorce rate in the United States, is the traditional family in danger of disappearing? As long ago as 1859, a contributor to the *Boston Quarterly Review* declared that the "family, in its old sense, is disappearing from our land, and not only our free institutions are threatened but the very existence of our society is endangered." Obviously, fears concerning the collapse of the family are not new. Yet, even though we must remain skeptical of sweeping predictions, we have seen throughout this chapter that major shifts *are* occurring in family life in the United States (Giddens, 1991:506; Lantz et al., 1977:413).

- Why is it difficult to measure precisely the prevalence of domestic violence in the United States?
- How do conflict theorists view domestic violence?
- In what ways may intervention in cases of domestic violence draw on an interactionist approach?

A television reporter wears long-sleeved, high-collared blouses to hide her bruises. Her husband, a businessman, frequently batters her body but never touches her face. The reporter once filed charges against him but later dropped them out of fear that the beating might become public knowledge.

Deidre still has painful flashbacks about her abusive stepfather. The smell of a country barn or the scent of the after-shave he used to wear brings it all back: how he forced her to have sex with him at the family's rural home. Deidre's mother was sick; her stepfather made the child believe that her mother would die if she told her the truth (*Changing Times*, 1981; R. Watson, 1984:32).

Wife battering, child abuse, abuse of the elderly, and other forms of domestic violence are an ugly reality of family life in the United States. In a sense, domestic violence begins even before marriage in the form of violent behavior within dating and courtship relationships. According to a 1990 review of recent research, while there has been great variance from survey to survey, as many as 67 percent of high school and college students have reported that they have been the victims of such attacks. As with other forms of abuse, victims of courtship violence are reluctant to tell others about their experiences; if they do, they typically tell their peers rather than their parents or teachers. This lack of early intervention is especially regrettable, since studies of battered women in shelters indicate that 51 percent have been physically abused in earlier dating relationships (Gelles and Cornell, 1990:65–66).

Violence during dating resembles other assaults in that it may involve pushing, slapping, punching, hitting with a weapon, and choking. Yet its consequences differ in one important respect: assaults or rapes by strangers leave victims wary of being alone, but rape by an acquaintance often causes the victim to become fearful of trusting someone again or forming close relationships. According to victimization surveys, one-third of victims of reported rapes identify the attacker as an acquaintance or date (Makepeace, 1986).

It is difficult to measure precisely the prevalence of domestic violence, since many victims are reluctant to call the police or bring charges against family members. With so many cases remaining unreported, researchers find it difficult to determine whether the level of domestic violence in the United States is increasing or decreasing. Studies find that 20 to 40 percent of couples seeking divorce cite "physical abuse" as their major complaint, while married couples who are not contemplating divorce report a similar incidence of violence. Moreover, consistently throughout the 1970s and 1980s, 34 percent of all female murder victims in the United States—more than 2800 a year—were killed by members of their own families. Family violence, of course, is a worldwide problem; it can be especially harsh in societies that devalue particular members of the family circle, such as children born outside of marriage, stepchildren, disabled children, female babies, or wives in general (Gelles and Cornell, 1990:28–31, 67–68; Gelles et al., 1988; T. Randall, 1990b:940; Stocks, 1988).

As of 1992, researchers have offered the following generalizations concerning domestic violence in the United States (*Psychology Today*, 1992:22):

- Domestic violence is evident among every racial and ethnic group and socioeconomic class.
- Physical abuse is the leading cause of injury to women.
- One out of every two women will find herself in a battering relationship at some time in her life.
- In 70 percent of cases involving wife battering, it is the abuser—the husband—who is granted custody of the children.
- A person is nine times more likely to be killed in a family relationship than on the streets.

In the United States, the family can be a dangerous place not only for women but also for children and the elderly. In 1987, 2.2 million cases of child abuse were reported to state and local authorities. According to the National Committee for the Prevention of Child

In an effort to combat rape on college campuses, administrators often attempt to heighten awareness through training manuals, videos, pamphlets, and counseling sessions. Male students at Hobart College in Geneva, New York, are shown attending a rape-prevention workshop.

Abuse, about 1300 children in the United States died in 1988 alone as a result of abuse or neglect (Gelles and Cornell, 1990:47, 50).

It is estimated that between 4 and 10 percent of older people have suffered from physical abuse, verbal abuse, or neglect. If these findings are generalized across the nation, by 1995 there will be about 1.3 to 3.4 million abused elderly people in the United States. In general, as is true of wife beating and child abuse, the number of reported cases of abuse of the elderly is undoubtedly well below the actual incidence. As a result of growing public concern, legislation in many states has redefined the concept of "domestic violence" to include abuse of the elderly as well as child abuse and violence between spouses (Bureau of the Census, 1991a:16; Gelles and Cornell, 1990:102).

Viewed from a conflict perspective, domestic violence should be seen in terms of dominance and control. It is one means by which men reinforce their power over women and adults reinforce their power over children. Nevertheless, despite the obvious inequities in domestic violence cases, victims of such assaults are often accused of "asking for" or provoking the abusive behavior. This is a classic example of "blaming the victim" for the misdeeds of others (refer back to Box 6-2 on page 52). In the case of wife beating, for example, feminists and conflict theorists emphasize that blaming the victim is but another reflection of men's power over women (K. Quinn et al., 1984:2; Stets and Pirog-Good, 1987).

Intervention in cases of domestic violence may draw on an interactionist approach by attempting to bolster the self-esteem of victims. Existing programs dealing with wife beating avoid telling the women what to do; instead, they help them to assess their internal strengths, and they provide information about available resources. Counselors typically believe that the female victim should not blame herself or excuse the offender. When working with men who are batterers, counselors encourage them to accept responsibility for their violent behavior and to learn other, nonabusive ways of communicating their feelings (C. Anderson and Rouse, 1988:139).

What can be done to prevent domestic violence? Some sociologists argue that a basic attack on courtship and family violence must involve a challenge to the glorification of violence which pervades our society. This could include reducing the number of television programs and motion pictures with "macho" themes, as well as outlawing use of corporal punishment in schools (Jaffe et al., 1990; McCormick, 1992).

Numerous decisions by federal courts have held that the domestic relations of husband and wife, as well as parent and child, are not a matter of federal jurisdiction. Consequently, in terms of social policy, domestic violence has been addressed primarily on the state and local levels. Over the past 20 years, spurred in good part by the activism of the feminist movement, there has been increasing pressure on police officers, judges, and other criminal justice officials to treat domestic violence as a serious crime. Many state and local governments have increased funding for shelters for battered women, telephone "hot lines" to assist victims of rape and domestic violence, and other social services that will reduce assaults within the family (Malinowski, 1990).

Despite such advances, the magnitude of the problem remains distressing. Sociologist Murray Straus has estimated that at least 8 million people in the United States are assaulted every year by family members. Some form of violence occurs in 25 percent of all marriages. Of those women needing emergency surgery procedures, at least one in every five—and per- haps one in every three—is a victim of domestic violence (Kantrowitz, 1988:59; T. Randall, 1990a:939; see also M. Straus and Gelles, 1990).

With such data in mind, in mid-1992 the American Medical Association (1992) recommended that physicians routinely screen their female patients for indications of domestic violence. Noting that there is widespread denial and apathy concerning assaults within the family, Dr. Antonia Novello, then Surgeon General of the United States, stated: "I think the time has come to take the issue of domestic violence out of the shadows and out of the closet" (New York Times, 1992e:A26).

SUMMARY

The *family,* although it has many varying forms, is present in all human cultures. This chapter examines the state of marriage and the family in the United States and considers alternatives to the traditional nuclear family.

1 There are many variations in the family from culture to culture and even within the same culture.
2 The structure of the *extended family* can offer certain advantages over that of the *nuclear family.*
3 Sociologists are not agreed on whether the *egalitarian family* has replaced the *patriarchal family* as the social norm in the United States.
4 Sociologists have identified six basic functions of the family: reproduction, protection, socialization, regulation of sexual behavior, companionship, and the providing of social status.
5 Currently, the majority of all married couples in the United States have two partners active in the paid labor force.
6 In the United States, there is considerable variation in family life associated with social class, racial, and ethnic differences.
7 Among the factors which contribute to the rising divorce rate in the United States are the greater social acceptance of divorce and the liberalization of divorce laws in many states.
8 More and more people are living together without marrying, thereby engaging in what is called *cohabitation.*
9 It is difficult to measure precisely the prevalence of domestic violence, since many victims are reluctant to call police or bring charges against family members.

CRITICAL THINKING QUESTIONS

1 An increasing proportion of couples in the United States are adopting a dual-career lifestyle. What are the advantages and disadvantages of the dual-career model for women, for men, for children, and for the society as a whole?
2 Given the high rate of divorce in the United States, is it more appropriate to view divorce as dysfunctional or as a "normal" part of our marriage system? What are the implications of viewing divorce as normal rather than as dysfunctional?
3 During the 1992 presidential campaign, there was substantial discussion of "family values." What does this term mean to you? Why was it used by candidates during an election year? Are there ways in which government should act to strengthen family life in the United States? Should government act to promote the traditional nuclear family model? Or should it give equal support to all types of families, including single-parent households and families headed by gay and lesbian parents?

KEY TERMS

Adoption In a legal sense, a process that allows for the transfer of the legal rights, responsibilities, and privileges of parenthood from legal parents to new legal parents. (page 241)
Bilateral descent A kinship system in which both sides of a person's family are regarded as equally important. (236)
Cohabitation The practice of living together as a male-female couple without marrying. (249)

Commune A small, self-supporting community joined voluntarily by people dedicated to cooperative living. (252)

Egalitarian family An authority pattern in which the adult members of the family are regarded as equals. (237)

Endogamy The restriction of mate selection to people within the same group. (239)

Exogamy The requirement that people select mates outside certain groups. (240)

Extended family A family in which relatives in addition to parents and children—such as grandparents, aunts, or uncles—live in the same home. (234)

Familism Pride in the extended family expressed through the maintenance of close ties and strong obligations to kinfolk. (244)

Family A set of people related by blood, marriage (or some other agreed-upon relationship), or adoption who share the responsibility for reproducing and caring for members of society. (232)

Incest taboo The prohibition of sexual relationships between certain culturally specified relatives. (240)

Kibbutz A collective society in Israel in which individuals and groups join together in an economic and social community. (252)

Kinship The state of being related to others. (235)

Machismo A sense of virility, personal worth, and pride in one's maleness. (244)

Marital power A term used by Blood and Wolfe to describe the manner in which decision making is distributed within families. (237)

Matriarchy A society in which women dominate in family decision making. (236)

Matrilineal descent A kinship system which favors the relatives of the mother. (236)

Matrilocal A pattern of residence in which a married couple lives with the wife's parents. (236)

Monogamy A form of marriage in which one woman and one man are married only to each other. (234)

Neolocal A pattern of residence in which a married couple establishes a separate residence. (236)

Nuclear family A married couple and their unmarried children living together. (233)

Patriarchy A society in which men are expected to dominate family decision making. (236)

Patrilineal descent A kinship system which favors the relatives of the father. (236)

Patrilocal A pattern of residence in which a married couple lives with the husband's parents. (236)

Polyandry A form of polygamy in which a woman can have several husbands at the same time. (235)

Polygamy A form of marriage in which an individual can have several husbands or wives simultaneously. (234)

Polygyny A form of polygamy in which a husband can have several wives at the same time. (235)

Serial monogamy A form of marriage in which a person can have several spouses in his or her lifetime but can have only one spouse at a time. (234)

Single-parent families Families in which there is only one parent present to care for children. (251)

ADDITIONAL READINGS

Cherlin, Andrew S. (ed.). *The Changing American Family and Public Policy.* Washington, D.C.: Urban Institute Press, 1988. A collection of articles considering the link between public policy and family-related issues in the United States.

Lewis, Suzan, Dafna N. Izraeli, and Helen Hootsmans. *Dual-Earner Families: International Perspectives.* Newbury Park, Calif.: Sage, 1991. A concise examination of dual-earner families in the United States, Great Britain, the Netherlands, and Japan.

Mindel, Charles H., Robert W. Habenstein, and Roosevelt Wright, Jr. (eds.). *Ethnic Families in America: Patterns and Variations* (3d ed.). New York: Elsevier, 1988. A collection of articles on the family lives of various racial and ethnic groups in the United States, including Italian Americans, Greek Americans, and Irish Americans.

Mintz, Steven, and Susan Kellogg. *Domestic Revolutions: A Social History of American Family Life.* New York: Free Press, 1988. A historian and an anthropologist look at changes in family life in the United States over the last four centuries; they conclude that this social institution has changed dramatically in its structure, role, and conception.

Oved, Yaacov. *Two Hundred Years of American Communes.* Rutgers, N.J.: Transaction, 1992. A study of the founding, growth, and development of alternative societies in the United States.

Sherman, Lawrence W. *Policing Domestic Violence.* New York: Free Press, 1992. A criminologist critically examines the available research on how policy should respond to the millions of domestic violence cases they confront each year.

10

RELIGION AND EDUCATION

LOOKING AHEAD

- What are the manifest and latent functions of religion?
- Why did Karl Marx view religion as a form of social control within an oppressive society?
- What are the basic forms of religious organization?
- How does education transmit the norms and values of a culture?

- In what ways do schools function as agents of social control?
- Does tracking of students serve to maintain social class differences across generations?
- How has the Supreme Court ruled regarding religion in the nation's public schools?

A t noon, the school day comes to a temporary halt at the Clara Muhammad School in Corona, a neighborhood in New York City. The loudspeaker announces: "Allah is great. . . . Come to prayer." All classwork stops, books and pencils are put away, and students and teachers walk silently in their stocking feet to the second-floor mosque. There they face east, fall on bended knees, put their heads to the ground, and pray to Allah.

Across the United States, there are now more than 60 Muslim day schools, in such cities as New York, Boston, Philadelphia, Atlanta, Chicago, Detroit, and Los Angeles. These full-day private schools teach required subjects such as English, history, science, and mathematics—but they also teach the Arabic language and offer religious instruction. The Muslim schools serve a mosaic of students, including African American children and immigrant children from such countries as Egypt, Uganda, Bermuda, Pakistan, Turkey, and Yugoslavia. A significant number of teachers are immigrants who previously worked as engineers, technicians, or college instructors in their native lands.

Many parents send their children to Muslim schools because they view the order and discipline preached in these schools as an important alternative to the drugs, alcohol, and violence found in troubled urban neighborhoods. Moreover, like earlier generations of Catholic and Jewish immigrants to the United States, Islamic parents hope that religious day schools will help to preserve their cherished traditions. "We want to keep Islam alive for us and our children," notes Imam Quasim Bakiridin, the religious director of the Clara Muhammad School (Goldman, 1992:26).

In Chapter 2, various *cultural universals* were identified—general practices found in every culture—such as dancing, food preparation, the family, and personal names. Religion is clearly such a cultural universal; religious institutions are evident in all societies. At present, an estimated 4 billion people belong to the world's many religious faiths (see Figure 10-1).

In contemporary industrial societies, scientific and technological advances have increasingly affected all aspects of life, including the social institution of religion. The term *secularization* refers to the process through which religion's influence on other social institutions diminishes. When this process occurs, religion will survive in the private sphere of individual and family life (as it does in Islamic immigrant communities); indeed, it may thrive on a personal level. At the same time, other social institutions—such as the economy, politics, and education—maintain their own sets of norms independent of religious guidance (McNamara, 1984:345–347; Shupe and Bromley, 1985:58).

Like religion, education is a cultural universal. In a sense, education is an important aspect of *socialization*—the lifelong process of learning the attitudes, values, and behavior appropriate to individuals as members of a particular culture. As the Islamic parents in New York City were well-aware, socialization may occur in a classroom. However, as we learned in Chapter 3, socialization may also take place through interactions with parents, friends, and even strangers. Socialization results as well from exposure to books, films, television, and other forms of communication. When such learning is explicit and formalized—when people consciously teach while others adopt the social role of learner—this process is called ***education***.

This chapter will focus on religion and education as they have emerged in modern industrial societies. It will begin with a brief overview of the approaches that Émile Durkheim first introduced and those that later sociologists have used in studying religion. The basic functions of religion as a source of societal integration and social control and as a means of providing social support will be explored. Particular attention will be given to the insights of Karl Marx and Max Weber regarding the relationship between religion and social change. Three important dimensions of religious behavior—belief, ritual, and experience—will be examined, as will the basic forms of religious organization.

In the second half of the chapter, we will contrast the functionalist and conflict analyses of the educational system of the United States. Functionalists stress the importance of education in transmitting culture, promoting social and political integration, maintaining social control, and promoting social change. To conflict theorists, however, education preserves distinctions based on social class, race, ethnicity, and gender instead of promoting equality. Interactionists generally focus on micro-level classroom dynamics, such as how teachers' expectations about students affect the students' actual achievements. This chapter also analyzes schools as formal organizations, with special focus on the bureaucratization of schools, the role of teachers as employees, and the student subculture. Finally, the social policy section examines the controversy over religion in the public schools of the United States.

FIGURE 10-1 Proportion of the World Population by Religion

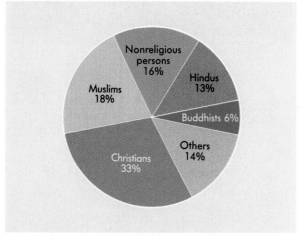

NOTE: The category "nonreligious persons" includes atheists and others who profess no religion.
SOURCE: Based on data from *Encyclopedia Britannica Book of the Year,* 1992:269.

The world's two largest religious faiths are Christianity (accounting for 33 percent of the world population) and Islam (18 percent).

DURKHEIM AND THE SOCIOLOGICAL APPROACH TO RELIGION

Sociologists are interested in the social impact of religion on individuals and institutions. Consequently, if a group believes that it is being directed by a "vision from God," a sociologist will not attempt to prove or disprove this "revelation." Instead, he or she will assess the effects of the religious experience on the group (M. McGuire, 1981:1–2).

Émile Durkheim was perhaps the first sociologist to recognize the critical importance of religion in human societies. He saw its appeal for the individual, but—more important—he stressed the *social* impact of religion. In Durkheim's view, religion is a collective act and includes many forms of behavior in which people interact with others. As in his work on suicide (see Chapter 1), Durkheim was not so interested in the personalities of religious believers as he was in understanding religious behavior within a social context.

カサねガサねの神だのみ。

ご注意ください、傘の置き忘れ。

Émile Durkheim's distinction between the sacred and the profane is evident in this poster distributed by the Tokyo subway system. A sorrowful figure of Jesus urges absent-minded riders not to leave umbrellas in subway cars. While an image of Jesus is sacred for Christians, it is used in a profane manner in Japan—a nation whose dominant faiths are Shintō and Buddhism.

Durkheim initiated sociological analysis of religion by defining **religion** as a "unified system of beliefs and practices relative to sacred things." In his formulation, religion involves a set of beliefs and practices that are uniquely the property of religion—as opposed to other social institutions and ways of thinking. Durkheim (1947:37, original edition 1912) argued that religious faiths distinguish between the everyday world and certain events that transcend the ordinary. He referred to these realms as the *sacred* and the *profane*.

The **sacred** encompasses elements beyond everyday life which inspire awe, respect, and even fear. People become a part of the sacred realm only by completing some ritual, such as prayer or sacrifice. Believers have faith in the sacred; this faith allows them to accept what they cannot understand. By contrast, the **profane** includes the ordinary and commonplace. Interestingly, the same object can be either sacred or profane depending on how it is viewed. A normal dining room table is profane, but it becomes sacred to Christians if it bears the elements of a communion. For Confucians and Taoists, incense sticks are not mere decorative items; they are highly valued offerings to the gods in religious ceremonies marking new and full moons.

Following the direction established by Durkheim almost a century ago, contemporary sociologists evaluate religions in two different ways. The norms and values of religious faiths can be studied through examination of their substantive religious beliefs. For example, we can compare the degree to which Christian faiths literally interpret the Bible, or Muslim groups follow the Qur'an (or Koran), the sacred book of Islam. At the same time, religions can be evaluated in terms of the social functions they fulfill, such as providing social support or reinforcing the social norms. By exploring both the beliefs and the functions of religion, we can better understand its impact on the individual, on groups, and on society as a whole.

FUNCTIONS OF RELIGION

Since religion is a cultural universal, it is not surprising that it fulfills several basic functions within human societies. In sociological terms, these include both manifest and latent functions (see Chapter 1). Among the manifest (open and stated) functions of religion are defining the spiritual world and giving meaning to the divine. Because of its beliefs concerning people's relationships to a beyond, religion provides an explanation for events that seem difficult to understand.

By contrast, latent functions of religion are unintended, covert, or hidden. Church services provide a manifest function by offering a forum for religious worship; at the same time, they fulfill a latent function as a meeting ground for unattached members.

In viewing religion as a social institution, functionalists evaluate its impact on human societies. The first two functions of religion that will be discussed in this section—integration and social control—are oriented toward the larger society. Thus, they are best understood from a macro-level viewpoint in terms of the relationship between religion and society as a whole. The third function—providing social support—is more oriented toward the individual and can be understood more effectively from a micro-level viewpoint. The fourth function, promoting social change, is illustrated using Max Weber's macro-level concept of the Protestant ethic.

The Integrative Function of Religion

Émile Durkheim viewed religion as an integrative power in human society—a perspective reflected in functionalist thought today. Durkheim was concerned with a perplexing question: "How can human societies be held together when they are generally composed of individuals and social groups with diverse interests and aspirations?" In his view, religious bonds often transcend these personal and divisive forces. Durkheim acknowledged that religion is not the only integrative force—nationalism or patriotism may serve the same end.

Why should religion provide this "societal glue"? Religion, whether it be Buddhism, Christianity, or Judaism, offers people meaning and purpose for their lives. It gives them certain ultimate values and ends to hold in common. Although subjective and not always fully accepted, these values and ends help a society to function as an integrated social system. For example, the Christian ritual of communion not only celebrates a historical event in the life of Jesus (the last supper) but also represents a participation in the group of believers. Similarly, funerals, weddings, bar and bat mitzvahs, and confirmations serve to integrate people into larger communities by providing shared beliefs and values about the ultimate questions of life.

Although the integrative impact of religion has been emphasized here, it should be noted that religion is not the *dominant* force maintaining social cohesion in contemporary industrial societies. People are also bound together by patterns of consumption, laws, nationalistic feelings, and other forces. Moreover, in some instances religious loyalties are dysfunctional; they contribute to tension and even conflict between groups or nations. During the Second World War, the Nazis attempted to exterminate the Jewish people, and approximately 6 million European Jews were killed. In modern times, nations such as Lebanon (Muslims versus Christians), Northern Ireland (Roman Catholics versus Protestants), and India (Hindus versus Muslims and, more recently, Sikhs) have been torn by clashes that are in part based on religion.

Religion and Social Control: The Marxist Critique

Karl Marx described religion as an "opiate" particularly harmful to oppressed peoples. In his view, religion often drugged the masses into submission by offering a consolation for their harsh lives on earth: the hope of salvation in an ideal afterlife. For example, during the period of slavery in the United States, White masters forbade Blacks to practice native African religions, while encouraging them to adopt the Christian religion. Through Christianity, slaves were prodded to obey their masters; they were told that obedience would lead to salvation and eternal happiness in the hereafter. Viewed from a conflict perspective, Christianity may have pacified certain slaves and blunted the rage that often fuels rebellion (M. McGuire, 1981:186; Yinger, 1970:598).

Marx acknowledged that religion plays an important role in legitimating the existing social structure. The values of religion, as already noted, reinforce other social institutions and the social order as a whole. From Marx's perspective, religion promotes stability within society and therefore helps to perpetuate patterns of social inequality. In a society with several religious faiths, the dominant religion will represent the ruling economic and political class.

Marx concurred with Durkheim's emphasis on the collective and socially shared nature of religious behavior. At the same time, he was concerned that religion would reinforce social control within an oppressive society. Marx argued that religion's focus on otherworldly concerns diverted attention from earthly problems and from needless suffering created by unequal distribution of valued resources (Harap, 1982).

Religion reinforces the interests of those in power. For example, India's traditional caste system defined the social structure of that society, at least among the Hindu majority (see Chapter 6). The caste system was almost certainly the creation of the priesthood, but it also served the interests of India's political rulers by granting a certain religious legitimacy to social inequality.

In the view of Karl Marx and later conflict theorists, religion is not necessarily a beneficial or admirable force for social control. For example, contemporary Christianity, like the Hindu faith, reinforces traditional patterns of behavior that call for the subordination of the powerless. Assumptions about gender roles leave women in a subservient position both within Christian churches and at home. In fact, women find it as difficult to achieve leadership positions in many churches as they do in large corporations. In 1991, 91 percent of all clergy in the United States were male. While women play a significant role as volunteers in community churches, men continue to make the major theological and financial judgments for nationwide church organizations. Conflict theorists argue that to whatever extent religion actually does influence social behavior, it reinforces existing patterns of dominance and inequality (Bureau of the Census, 1992a:392).

From a Marxist perspective, religion functions as an "agent of de-politicization" (J. Wilson, 1978:355–356). In simpler terms, religion keeps people from seeing their lives and societal conditions in political terms—for example, by obscuring the overriding significance of conflicting economic interests. Marxists suggest that by inducing a "false consciousness" among the disadvantaged (see Chapter 6), religion lessens the possibility of collective political action that can end capitalist oppression and transform society.

It should be noted, however, that religious leaders have sometimes been in the forefront of movements for social change. During the 1960s, Dr. Martin Luther King, Jr., supported by numerous ministers, priests, and rabbis, fought for civil rights for Blacks. In the 1980s, many religious groups spoke out against the involvement of the United States in the arms race. The efforts of religious groups to promote social change extend beyond the United States; in Box 10-1 we focus on religious activism in Latin America.

Religion and Social Support

Most of us find it difficult to accept the stressful events of life—death of a loved one, serious injury, bankruptcy, divorce, and so forth. This is especially true when something "senseless" happens. How can family and friends come to terms with the death of a talented college student, not even 20 years old, from a terminal disease?

Through its emphasis on the divine and the supernatural, religion allows us to "do something" about the calamities we face. In some faiths, one can offer sacrifices or pray to a deity in the belief that such acts will change one's earthly condition. At a more basic level, religion encourages us to view our personal misfortunes as relatively unimportant in the broader perspective of human history—or even as part of an undisclosed divine purpose. Friends and relatives of the deceased college student may see this death as being "God's will" and as having some ultimate benefit that we cannot understand. This perspective may be much more comforting than the terrifying feeling that any of us can die senselessly at any moment—and that there is no divine "answer" as to why one person lives a long and full life whereas another dies tragically at a relatively early age.

As we saw earlier, religion offers consolation to oppressed peoples by giving them hope that they can achieve salvation and eternal happiness in an afterlife. Similarly, during times of national tragedy (assassinations, invasions, and natural disasters), people attend religious services as a means of coping with problems that demand political and technological as well as spiritual solutions. On a more micro level, clergy are often the first source of aid sought out by people faced with a crisis. In a 1990 survey in Texas, respondents were asked to whom they would go first to discuss personal problems. The highest percentage, 41 percent, stated that they would turn to the clergy, as contrasted with 29 percent who would choose medical doctors and 21 percent who would go to psychiatrists or psychologists (Chalfant et al., 1990; McGuire, 1981:186; Yinger, 1970:598).

BOX 10-1

LIBERATION THEOLOGY

Many religious activists, especially in Latin America, support *liberation theology,* a term which refers to use of a church in a political effort to eliminate poverty, discrimination, and other forms of injustice evident in secular society. Advocates of this religious movement sometimes display a sympathy for Marxism. Many believe that radical liberation, rather than economic development in itself, is the only acceptable solution to the desperation of the masses in impoverished developing countries. Despite resistance from Pope John Paul II and others in the Catholic hierarchy—who insist that the clergy should adhere to traditional pastoral duties and keep a distance from radical politics—activists associated with liberation theology believe that organized religion has a moral responsibility to take a strong public stand against the oppression of the poor, of racial and ethnic minorities, and of women (C. Smith, 1991).

The term *liberation theology* has a recent origin, dating back to the 1973 publication of the English translation of *A Theology of Liberation.* This book was written by a Peruvian priest, Gustavo Gutiér-rez, who lived in a slum area of Lima during the early 1960s. After years of exposure to the vast poverty around him, Gutiérrez concluded: "The poverty was a destructive thing, something to be fought against and destroyed. . . . It became crystal clear that in order to serve the poor, one had to move into political action" (R. Brown, 1980:23).

Gutiérrez's discoveries took place during a time of increasing radicalization among Latin American intellectuals and students. An important element in their radicalization was the theory of *dependencia,* developed by Brazilian and Chilean social scientists. According to this theory, the reason for Latin America's continued underdevelopment was its dependence on industrialized nations (first Spain, then Great Britain, and, most recently, the United States). A related approach shared by most social scientists in Latin America was a Marxist-influenced class analysis that viewed the domination of capitalism and multinational corporations as central to the problems of the hemisphere. As these perspectives became more influential, a social network emerged among politically com-mitted Latin American theologians who shared experiences and insights. One result was a new approach to theology which rejected the models developed in Europe and the United States and instead built on the cultural and religious traditions of Latin America (Sigmund, 1990:32).

In the 1970s, many advocates of liberation theology expressed strong Marxist views and saw revolutionary struggle to overthrow capitalism as essential to ending the suffering of Latin America's poor. More recently, liberation theology seems to have moved away from orthodox Marxism and away from endorsement of armed struggle. As an example, Gutiérrez (1990:214, 222) has written that one does not need to accept Marxism as an "all-embracing view of life and thus exclude the Christian faith and its requirements." Gutiérrez adds that the proper concerns of a theology of liberation are not simply the world's "exploited classes," but also "races discriminated against," "despised cultures," and the "condition of women, especially in those sectors of society where women are doubly oppressed and marginalized."

Religion and Social Change: The Weberian Thesis

For Karl Marx, the relationship between religion and social change was clear: religion impeded change by encouraging oppressed people to focus on otherworldly concerns rather than on their immediate poverty or exploitation. However, Max Weber (1958a, original edition 1904) was unconvinced by Marx's argument and carefully examined the connection between religious allegiance and capitalist development. His findings appeared in his pioneering work *The Protestant Ethic and the Spirit of Capitalism,* first published in 1904.

Weber noted that in European nations with both Protestant and Catholic citizens, an overwhelming number of business leaders, owners of capital, and skilled workers were Protestant. In his view, this was no mere coincidence. Weber

Mimi Forsyth/Monkmeyer Press

Shown is a religious ritual in Thailand. From an interactionist perspective, religious rituals serve as important face-to-face encounters in which people reinforce their religious beliefs and their commitment to their faith.

pointed out that the followers of John Calvin (1509–1564), a leader of the Protestant Reformation, emphasized a disciplined work ethic, this-worldly concern, and rational orientation to life that have become known as the **Protestant ethic.** One by-product of the Protestant ethic was a drive to accumulate savings that could be used for future investment. This "spirit of capitalism," to use Weber's phrase, contrasted with the moderate work hours, leisurely work habits, and lack of ambition that he saw as typical of the times (Winter, 1977; Yinger, 1974).

Few books in the sociology of religion have aroused as much commentary and criticism as *The*

Protestant Ethic and the Spirit of Capitalism. It has been hailed as one of the most important theoretical works in the field and as an excellent example of macro-level analysis. Like Durkheim, Weber demonstrated that religion is not solely a matter of intimate personal beliefs. He stressed that the collective nature of religion has social consequences for society as a whole.

Conflict theorists caution that Weber's theory—even if it is accepted—should not be regarded as an analysis of mature capitalism as reflected in the rise of large corporations which transcend national boundaries (see Chapter 6). The primary disagreement between Karl Marx and Max Weber concerned not the origins of capitalism, but rather its future. Unlike Marx, Weber believed that capitalism could endure indefinitely as an economic system. He added, however, that the decline of religion as an overriding force in society opened the way for workers to express their discontent more vocally (R. Collins, 1980).

We can conclude that, although Weber provides a convincing description of the origins of European capitalism, this economic system has subsequently been adopted by non-Calvinists in many parts of the world. Contemporary studies in the United States show little or no difference in achievement orientation between Roman Catholics and Protestants. Apparently, the "spirit of capitalism" has become a generalized cultural trait rather than a specific religious tenet (Greeley, 1989).

RELIGIOUS BEHAVIOR

All religions have certain elements in common, yet these elements are expressed in the distinctive manner of each faith. The patterns of religious behavior, like other patterns of social behavior, are of great interest to sociologists, since they underscore the relationship between religion and society.

Dimensions of Religious Behavior

Religious beliefs, religious rituals, and religious experience all help to define what is sacred and to differentiate the sacred from the profane. Let us now examine these three dimensions of religious behavior.

Belief Some people believe in life after death, in supreme beings with unlimited powers, or in supernatural forces. **Religious beliefs** are statements to which members of a particular religion adhere. These views vary dramatically from religion to religion.

The account of the creation found in Genesis, the first book of the Old Testament, is an example of a religious belief. Many people in the United States strongly adhere to the biblical explanation of creation and insist that this view be taught in public schools. These people, known as **creationists,** are worried by the secularization of society and oppose educational curricula which directly or indirectly question biblical scripture. The efforts of creationists will be examined more fully in the social policy section at the end of the chapter.

Ritual **Religious rituals** are practices required or expected of members of a faith. Rituals usually honor the divine power (or powers) worshipped by believers; they also remind adherents of their religious duties and responsibilities. Rituals and beliefs can be interdependent; rituals generally involve the affirmation of beliefs, as in a public or private statement confessing a sin (K. Roberts, 1984:96–107). Like any social institution, religion develops distinctive normative patterns to structure people's behavior. Moreover, there are sanctions attached to religious rituals, whether rewards (pins for excellence at church schools) or penalties (expulsion from a religious institution for violation of norms).

In the United States, rituals may be very simple, such as saying grace at a meal and observing a moment of silence to commemorate someone's death. Yet certain rituals, such as the process of canonizing a saint, are quite elaborate. Most religious rituals in our culture focus on services conducted at houses of worship. Thus, attendance at a service, silent and spoken reading of prayers, and singing of spiritual hymns and chants are common forms of ritual behavior that generally take place in group settings. From an interactionist perspective, these rituals serve as important face-to-face encounters in which people reinforce their religious beliefs and their commitment to their faith.

Some rituals actually induce an almost trance-like state. The Plains Indians eat or drink peyote, a cactus containing the powerful hallucinogenic drug mescaline. Similarly, the ancient Greek followers of the god Pan chewed intoxicating leaves of ivy in order to become more ecstatic during their celebrations. Of course, artificial stimulants are not necessary to achieve a religious "high." Devout believers, such as those who practice the pentecostal Christian ritual of "speaking in tongues," can reach a state of ecstasy simply through spiritual passion.

Experience In sociological study of religion, the term **religious experience** refers to the feeling or perception of being in direct contact with the ultimate reality, such as a divine being, or of being overcome with religious emotion. A religious experience may be rather slight, such as the feeling of exaltation a person receives from hearing a choir sing Handel's "Hallelujah Chorus." But many religious experiences are more profound, among them being "born again"—that is, having a turning point in life during which one makes a personal commitment to Jesus.

According to a 1990 national survey, 38 percent of people in the United States claimed that they had had a born-again Christian experience at some time in their lives—a figure which translates into nearly 70 million adults. An earlier survey found that Baptists (61 percent) were the most likely to report such experiences; by contrast, only 18 percent of Catholics and 11 percent of Episcopalians stated that they had been born again. The collective nature of religion, as emphasized by Durkheim, is evident in these statistics. The beliefs and rituals of a particular faith can create an atmosphere either friendly or hostile to this type of religious experience. Thus, a Baptist would be encouraged to come forward and share such experiences with others, whereas an Episcopalian would receive much less support if he or she claimed to have been born again (Gallup Opinion Index, 1978; Princeton Religion Research Center, 1990b).

Organization of Religious Behavior

The collective nature of religion has led to many forms of religious association. In modern societies, religion has become increasingly formalized. Specific structures such as churches and synagogues are constructed for religious worship; individuals are trained for occupational roles within various fields. These developments make it possible to distinguish between the sacred and secular parts of one's life—a distinction that could not be made in earlier societies in which religion was largely a family activity carried out in the home.

Sociologists find it useful to distinguish between four basic forms of organization: the ecclesia, the denomination, the sect, and the cult. As is the case with other typologies used by social scientists, this system of classification can help us to appreciate the variety of organizational forms found among religious faiths. Distinctions are made between these types of organizations on the basis of such factors as size, power, degree of commitment expected from members, and historical ties to other faiths.

Ecclesiae An *ecclesia* (plural, *ecclesiae*) is a religious organization that claims to include most or all of the members of a society and is recognized as the national or official religion. Since virtually everyone belongs to the faith, membership is by birth rather than conscious decision. Examples of ecclesiae include the Lutheran church in Sweden, the Catholic church in Spain, Islam in Saudi Arabia, and Buddhism in Thailand. However, there can be significant differences even within the category of *ecclesia*. In Saudi Arabia's Islamic regime, leaders of the ecclesia hold vast power over actions of the state. By contrast, the Lutheran church in contemporary Sweden has no such power over the Riksdag (parliament) or the prime minister.

Generally, ecclesiae are conservative in that they do not challenge the leaders or policies of a secular government. In a society with an ecclesia, the political and religious institutions often act in harmony and mutually reinforce each other's power over their relative spheres of influence. Within the modern world, ecclesiae tend to be declining in power.

Denominations A *denomination* is a large, organized religion that is not officially linked with the state or government. Like an ecclesia, it tends to have an explicit set of beliefs, a defined system of authority, and a generally respected position in society (Doress and Porter, 1977). Denominations count among their members large segments of a population. Generally, children accept the denomination of their parents and give little thought to membership in other faiths. Denominations also resemble ecclesiae in that few demands are made on members. However, there is a critical difference between these two forms of religious organization. Although the denomination is considered respectable and is not viewed as a challenge to the secular government, it lacks the official recognition and power held by an ecclesia.

No nation of the world has more denominations than the United States. In good measure, this is a result of our nation's immigrant heritage. Many settlers in the "new world" brought with them the religious commitments native to their homelands. Denominations of Christianity found in the United States, such as those of the Roman Catholics, Episcopalians, and Lutherans, were the outgrowth of ecclesiae established in Europe. In addition, new Christian denominations emerged, including the Mormons and Christian Scientists. The vast array of Christian denominations in the United States is shown in Figure 10-2.

Although by far the largest single denomination in the United States is Roman Catholicism, at least 23 other religious faiths have 1 million or more members. And these figures are conservative, since other faiths are growing in size. For example, there are close to 5 million Muslims in the United States. Protestants collectively accounted for about 56 percent of the nation's adult population in 1990, compared with 28 percent for Roman Catholics and almost 3 percent for Jews (Princeton Religion Research Center, 1990a:29). The United States also includes a smaller number of people who adhere to such eastern faiths as Hinduism, Confucianism, and Taoism. Certain faiths, such as Episcopalianism, Judaism, and Lutheranism, have a higher proportion of affluent members. Adherents of other faiths, including Baptists and Evangelicals, are comparatively poor.

Sects In contrast to the denomination is the sect, which Max Weber (1958b:114, original edition 1916) termed a "believer's church," because affiliation is based on conscious acceptance of a specific religious dogma. A *sect* can be defined as a relatively small religious group that has broken away from some other religious organization to

FIGURE 10-2   Predominant Christian Faiths by Counties of the United States

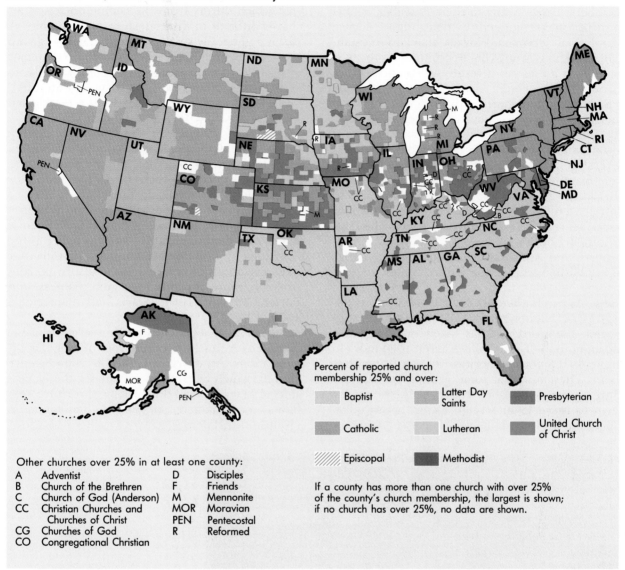

Percent of reported church
membership 25% and over:

- Baptist
- Catholic
- Episcopal
- Latter Day Saints
- Lutheran
- Methodist
- Presbyterian
- United Church of Christ

If a county has more than one church with over 25%
of the county's church membership, the largest is shown;
if no church has over 25%, no data are shown.

Other churches over 25% in at least one county:
A   Adventist
B   Church of the Brethren
C   Church of God (Anderson)
CC   Christian Churches and
        Churches of Christ
CG   Churches of God
CO   Congregational Christian

D   Disciples
F   Friends
M   Mennonite
MOR Moravian
PEN Pentecostal
R   Reformed

SOURCE: B. Quinn et al., 1982.

renew what it views as the original vision of the faith. Many sects, such as that led by Martin Luther during the Reformation, claim to be the "true church" because they seek to cleanse the established faith of what they regard as innovative beliefs and rituals (Stark and Bainbridge, 1985).

Sects are fundamentally at odds with society and do not seek to become established national religions. Unlike ecclesiae, sects require intensive

The diversity of Christian religious life in the United States is apparent here. Typically, many different Christian faiths account for 25 percent or more of the church members in a county. Among non-Christian faiths, only Judaism may figure so significantly—in New York County (Manhattan) of New York City and in Dade County, Florida (which includes Miami Beach).

commitments and demonstrations of belief by members. Partly owing to their "outsider" status in society, sects frequently exhibit a higher degree of religious fervor and loyalty than more established religious groups do. Recruitment is focused mainly on adults; as a result, acceptance comes through conversion.

Sects are often short-lived; however, if able to survive, they may become less antagonistic to society and begin to resemble denominations. In a few instances, sects have been able to endure over several generations while remaining fairly separate from society. Sociologist J. Milton Yinger (1970:226–273) uses the term *established sect* to describe a religious group that is the outgrowth of a sect, yet remains isolated from society. The Hutterites, Jehovah's Witnesses, Seventh-Day Adventists, and Amish are contemporary examples of established sects in the United States.

Cults As psychotherapist Irvin Doress and sociologist Jack Nusan Porter (1977:3–4) have suggested, the word *cult* has taken on a negative meaning in the United States and is used more to discredit religious minorities than to categorize them. They note that some groups, such as the Hare Krishnas, are labeled as "cults" because they seem to come from foreign (often nonwestern) lands and have customs perceived as "strange."

This reflects people's ethnocentric evaluations of that which differs from the commonplace.

It is difficult to distinguish sects from cults. A *cult* is a generally small, secretive religious group that represents either a new religion or a major innovation of an existing faith. Cults are similar to sects in that they tend to be small and are often viewed as less respectable than more established faiths.

However, unlike sects, cults normally do not result from schisms or breaks with established ecclesiae or denominations. Some cults, such as contemporary cults focused on UFO sightings or expectations of colonizing outer space, may be totally unrelated to the existing faiths in a culture. Even when a cult does accept certain fundamental tenets of a dominant faith—such as belief in the teachings of Jesus or Muhammad—it will offer new revelations or new insights to justify its claim to be a more advanced religion (Doress and Porter, 1977:3; 1981; Stark and Bainbridge, 1979; 1985:27).

As is true of sects, cults may undergo transformation over time into other types of religious organizations. An example is the Christian Science church, which began as a cult under the leadership of Mary Baker Eddy. Today, this church exhibits the characteristics of a denomination (Johnstone, 1988:88).

John C. Hillery

This photograph was not taken in the middle east. Actually, the Islamic center shown is found outside of Toledo, Ohio; note the Greyhound bus driving by. The presence of such a center in the midwest underscores the diversity of religious life in the United States.

TABLE 10-1 Characteristics of Ecclesiae, Denominations, Sects, and Cults

CHARACTERISTIC	ECCLESIA	DENOMINATION	SECT	CULT
Size	Very large	Large	Small	Small
Wealth	Extensive	Extensive	Limited	Variable
Religious services	Formal, little participation	Formal, little participation	Informal, emotional	Variable
Doctrines	Specific, but interpretation may be tolerated	Specific, but interpretation may be tolerated	Specific, purity of doctrine emphasized	Innovative, pathbreaking
Clergy	Well-trained, full-time	Well-trained, full-time	Trained to some degree	Unspecialized
Membership	By virtue of being a member of society	By acceptance of doctrine	By acceptance of doctrine	By an emotional commitment
Relationship to the state	Recognized, closely aligned	Tolerated	Not encouraged	Ignored

SOURCES: Adapted from G. Vernon, 1962; see also Chalfant et al., 1987:91–92.

Ecclesiae, denominations, and sects are best viewed as ideal types along a continuum; cults are outside the continuum because they generally define themselves as a new view of life rather than in terms of existing religious faiths.

Comparing Forms of Religious Organization
Clearly, it is no simple matter to determine whether a particular religious group falls into the sociological category of ecclesia, denomination, sect, or cult. Yet, as we have seen, these ideal types of religious organizations have somewhat different relationships to society. Ecclesiae are recognized as national churches; denominations, although not officially approved, are generally respected. By contrast, sects as well as cults are much more likely to be at odds with the larger culture.

Ecclesiae, denominations, and sects are best viewed as ideal types along a continuum rather than as mutually exclusive categories. Some of the primary characteristics of these ideal types are summarized in Table 10-1. Since the United States has no ecclesia, sociologists studying this nation's religions have naturally focused on the denomination and the sect. These religious forms have been pictured on either end of a continuum, with denominations accommodating to the secular world and sects making a protest against established religions. Cults have also been included in Table 10-1 but are outside the continuum because they generally define themselves as a new view of life rather than in terms of existing religious faiths (Chalfant et al., 1987:89–99).

SOCIOLOGICAL PERSPECTIVES ON EDUCATION

In the last 50 years, an increasing proportion of people in the United States have obtained high school diplomas, college degrees, and advanced professional degrees. As is shown in Figure 10-3 (page 272), the proportion of people 25 to 29 years of age with a high school diploma has increased from 38 percent in 1940 to more than 85 percent in 1991. Similarly, the proportion of 25- to 29-year-olds with a college degree has risen from less than 6 percent in 1940 to more than 23 percent in 1991 (Bureau of the Census, 1991a:138, 1992a:143). Currently, nearly 59 million people attend public or private schools—about 25 percent of the nation's population. As a result, education has become a major industry in the United States. More than 3 million people are employed as teachers, clerical staff, food service workers, groundskeepers, and full-time administrators.

FIGURE 10-3   Educational Attainment in the United States, Persons 25 to 29 Years Old, 1940–1991

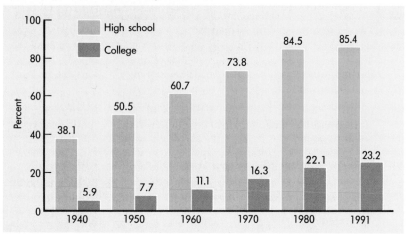

SOURCE: Bureau of the Census, 1991a:138, 1992a:143.

Since 1940, the proportion of people in the United States 25 to 29 years old with a high school diploma has more than doubled; the proportion with a college degree has nearly quadrupled.

Clearly, education has become a vast and complex social institution throughout the world. It prepares citizens for the various roles demanded by other social institutions, such as the family, government, and the economy. The functionalist, conflict, and interactionist perspectives each offer distinctive ways of examining education as a social institution.

Functionalist View

Like other social institutions, education has both manifest (open, stated) functions and latent (hidden) functions.

The most basic *manifest* function of education is the transmission of knowledge. Schools teach students how to read, speak foreign languages, and repair automobiles. Education has another important manifest function: bestowing status. Owing to widespread criticism of the differential way in which this function is performed, it will be considered later, in the section on the conflict view of education.

In addition to these manifest functions, schools perform a number of *latent* functions. Among these latent functions are transmitting culture, promoting social and political integration, maintaining social control, and serving as agents of change.

Transmitting Culture   As a social institution, education performs a rather conservative function—transmitting the dominant culture. Through schooling, each generation of young people is exposed to the existing beliefs, norms, and values of our culture. We learn respect for social control and reverence for established institutions, such as religion, the family, and the presidency. Of course, this is true in many other cultures as well. While schoolchildren in the United States are hearing about the greatness of George Washington and Abraham Lincoln, British children are hearing about the greatness of Queen Elizabeth I and Winston Churchill.

A dispute over Japanese textbooks provides an interesting case study of the transmission of culture through education. In 1982, Japanese newspapers reported that high school social studies textbooks dealing with the nation's wartime aggression and atrocities had been "watered down" by Japan's Ministry of Education. For example, where the expansion into Manchuria in the 1930s had previously been termed an "invasion," it was now to be called an "advance." Japanese atrocities in Korea in 1919 and later in Manchuria were rationalized as a "response to local resistance." Critics charged that these changes not only distorted history but might contribute to a revival of Japanese militarism. Despite vehement protests from

China and South Korea, the revised language was retained, but teachers were instructed to take these criticisms into account as they prepared their lessons (Seddon, 1987).

Debates over curricula have become common in the United States in the last decade. Such distinguished works of literature as Alice Walker's Pulitzer prize–winning novel *The Color Purple,* John Steinbeck's *Of Mice and Men,* and Arthur Miller's *Death of a Salesman* have been the target of censorship efforts in local school districts. An increasing proportion of challenges to school textbooks and library materials are being backed by groups with religious associations, such as the National Association of Christian Educators, and by national conservative groups such as Concerned Women of America and the Eagle Forum.

On the college level, there has been growing controversy over the general education or basic curriculum requirements of colleges and universities (refer back to the social policy section on multiculturalism in Chapter 2). Critics charge that standard academic curricula have failed to represent the important contributions of women and people of color to history, literature, and other fields of study. The underlying questions raised by this debate, still to be resolved, are: Which ideas and values are essential for instruction? Which culture should be transmitted by the schools and colleges of the United States?

Promoting Social and Political Integration

Education serves the latent function of promoting social and political integration by transforming diverse racial, ethnic, and religious groups into a society whose members share—to some extent at least—a common identity (Touraine, 1974:115). Schools in the United States have historically played an important role in socializing the children of immigrants into the norms, values, and beliefs of the dominant culture. From a functionalist perspective, the common identity and social integration fostered by education contribute to societal stability and consensus.

In the past, the integrative function of education was most obvious through its emphasis on promoting a common language. Immigrant children living in the United States were not only expected to learn, English; in some instances, they were forbidden to speak their native lan-

Courtesy Augustana College

Olaf the Viking serves as a reminder of the ethnic heritage of Augustana College, in Sioux Falls, South Dakota. This popular statue is often a site for student gatherings and celebrations.

guages on school grounds. More recently, bilingualism has been defended both for its educational value and as a means of encouraging cultural diversity. However, in the view of its critics, bilingualism undermines the social and political integration that education has traditionally promoted. The debate over bilingualism, like the discussion of Islamic day schools at the beginning of the chapter, underscores the fact that not everyone may want to be integrated into the dominant culture of the United States.

Maintaining Social Control

In performing the manifest function of transmitting knowledge, schools go far beyond teaching such skills as reading, writing, and mathematics. Schoolchildren are introduced to standards of proper conduct in public life which are quite different from the rules of behavior in their families. Like other social institutions such as the family and religion, education prepares young people to lead productive and orderly lives as adults by introducing them to the norms, values, and sanctions of the larger society.

Through the exercise of social control, students are taught various skills and values which will be essential in their future positions within the labor force. They learn, for example, punctuality, discipline, scheduling, and responsible work habits, as well as how to negotiate their way through the complexities of a bureaucratic organization. In effect, then, schools serve as a transitional agent of social control—between parents and employers—in the life cycle of most individuals. As a social institution, education reflects the interests of the family and in turn prepares young people for their participation in yet another social institution—the economy. Students are being trained for what is ahead, whether it be the assembly line or the office (Bowles and Gintis, 1976; M. Cole, 1988).

As will be discussed more fully later in the chapter, schools are highly bureaucratic organizations. Many teachers rely on the rules and regulations of schools to maintain order. Unfortunately, the need for control and discipline can take precedence over the learning process. Teachers may focus on obedience to the rules as an end in itself—a shift in priorities which reflects the type of goal displacement that was considered in Chapter 4. If this occurs, students and teachers alike become victims of what Philip Jackson (1968) has termed the *hidden curriculum*—the standards of behavior that are deemed proper by society. According to this subtle "curriculum," children must wait before speaking until the teacher calls on them and must regulate their activities according to the clock or bells. In addition, they are expected to concentrate on their own work rather than assist other students who learn more slowly.

In a classroom overly focused on obedience, value is placed on pleasing the teacher and remaining quiet—rather than on creative thought and academic learning (Leacock, 1969:59–61). If students become accustomed to habitual obedience to authority, the type of distressing behavior which was documented by Stanley Milgram in his classic obedience studies (see Chapter 5) may result.

The social-control function of education is not limited to patterns of rules and behavior. Schools direct and even restrict students' aspirations in a manner that reflects societal values and prejudices. School administrators may allocate substantial educational funds for athletic programs while giving much less support to music, art, and dance. Moreover, as we saw in Chapter 3, teachers and guidance counselors may encourage male students to pursue careers in the sciences but steer equally talented female students into careers as early childhood teachers. Such socialization into traditional gender roles can be viewed as a form of social control.

Education as an Agent of Change Thus far, this discussion has focused on conservative functions of education—on its role in transmitting the existing culture, promoting social and political integration, and maintaining social control. Yet education can stimulate or bring about desired social change. Sex education classes were introduced in public schools in response to the soaring pregnancy rate among teenagers. Affirmative action in education has been endorsed as a means of countering racial and sexual discrimination (see Chapter 7). Project Head Start—an early childhood program serving 400,000 children annually—has sought to compensate for the disadvantages in school readiness experienced by children from low-income families.

Education also promotes social change by serving as a meeting ground where each society's distinctive beliefs and traditions can be shared. In 1992, there were 420,000 foreign students in the United States, of whom about 72 percent were from developing nations (Watkins, 1992). Cross-cultural exchanges between these visitors and citizens of the United States ultimately broaden the perspective of both the hosts and their guests. The same is certainly true when students from the United States attend schools in Europe, Latin America, Africa, or the far east.

Numerous sociological studies have revealed that increased years of formal schooling are associated with openness to new ideas and more liberal social and political viewpoints. Sociologist Robin Williams (R. Williams et al., 1964:374–375) points out that better-educated people tend to have greater access to factual information, a

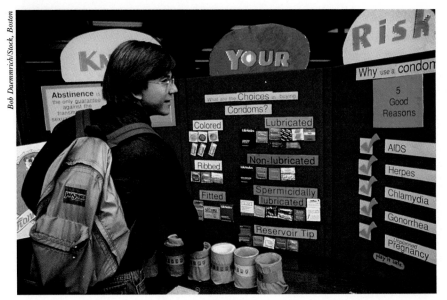

Education can stimulate or bring about desired social change. For example, sex education classes have been introduced in many schools to combat the soaring pregnancy rate among teenagers. In recent years, controversy has arisen over the distribution of condoms in schools, which defenders argue is necessary to prevent the spread of AIDS.

diversity of opinion, and subtle distinctions of analysis. Formal education stresses both the importance of qualifying statements and the need at least to question (rather than simply accept) established "truths" and practices. As we saw in Chapter 1, the scientific method relies on *testing* hypotheses and reflects the questioning spirit that characterizes modern education. For these reasons, education can make one less likely to champion outmoded beliefs and prejudices and more likely to promote and accept social change (Schaefer, 1976:127).

Conflict View

Sociologist Christopher Hurn (1985:48–76) has compared the functionalist and conflict views of schooling. According to Hurn, the functionalist perspective portrays the major features of contemporary education in fundamentally benign terms. For example, it argues that schools rationally sort and select students for future high-status positions, thereby meeting society's need for talented and expert personnel. By contrast, the conflict perspective views education as an instrument of elite domination. Schools convince subordinate groups of their inferiority, reinforce existing social class inequality, and discourage alternative and more democratic visions of society.

Conflict theorists take a critical view of the so-cial institution of education. They argue that the educational system socializes students into values dictated by the powerful, that schools stifle individualism and creativity in the name of maintaining order, and that the level of change promoted by education is relatively insignificant. From a conflict perspective, the inhibiting effects of education are particularly apparent in the creation of standards for entry into occupations, the differential way in which status is bestowed, and the treatment of women in education.

Credentialism Today, a college diploma has become virtually a minimum requirement for entry into the paid labor force of the United States, just as a high school diploma was 50 years ago. This change reflects the process of ***credentialism***—a term used to describe the increase in the lowest level of education needed to enter a field.

In recent decades, there has been a rise in the United States in the number of occupations viewed as professions. Credentialism is one symptom of this trend. Employers and occupational associations typically contend that such changes are a logical response to the increasing complexity of many jobs (R. Collins, 1979:5; Dore, 1976:5; Hurn, 1985:95). However, in many cases, employers raise degree requirements for a position simply because all applicants have achieved the existing minimum credential.

FIGURE 10-4   Education of Minority Group Students in the United States, 1991

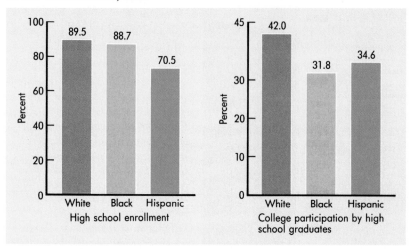

SOURCE: Bureau of the Census, 1992a:161, 163.

Although enrollment of racial and ethnic minorities in colleges in the United States increased throughout the 1970s and 1980s, these groups remain underrepresented at all levels of higher education.

Conflict theorists have observed that credentialism may reinforce social inequality. They note that applicants from poor and minority backgrounds are especially likely to suffer from the escalation of qualifications, since they lack the financial resources needed to obtain degree after degree. In addition, upgrading credentials serves the self-interest of the two groups most responsible for this trend. Educational institutions have a vested interest in prolonging the investment of time and money that people make by staying in school. Moreover, as Christopher Hurn (1985: 56–57) has suggested, current jobholders have a stake in raising occupational requirements. Credentialism can increase the status of an occupation and is crucial to demands for higher pay. Max Weber anticipated such possibilities as far back as 1916, concluding that the "universal clamor for the creation of educational certificates in all fields makes for the formation of a privileged stratum in businesses and in offices" (Gerth and Mills, 1958:240–241).

Bestowal of Status   Both functionalist and conflict theorists agree that education performs the important function of bestowing status. As noted earlier, an increasing proportion of people in the United States are obtaining high school diplomas, college degrees, and advanced professional de-

grees (refer back to Figure 10-3). From a functionalist perspective, this widening bestowal of status is beneficial not only to particular recipients but to the society as a whole. In our discussion of stratification in Chapter 6, we noted the view of Kingsley Davis and Wilbert Moore (1945) that society must distribute its members among a variety of social positions. Education can contribute to this process by sorting people into appropriate levels and courses of study that will prepare them for appropriate positions within the labor force.

Conflict sociologists are far more critical of the differential way education bestows status; they stress that schools sort pupils according to social class background. Although the educational system helps certain poor children to move into middle-class professional positions, it denies most disadvantaged children the same educational opportunities afforded children of the affluent (see Figure 10-4). In this way, schools tend to preserve social class inequalities in each new generation (Labaree, 1986; Mingle, 1987).

Money contributes to this disparity. In all but a few cases, public schools in the United States have been financed through local property taxes. Since the total value of property tends to be lower in areas with many low-income families, these school districts generally have less money available for education.

Class differences can also be reinforced within a single school. Working-class children are much more likely to be viewed as destined for subordinate positions and therefore placed in high school vocational or general tracks. The term *tracking* refers to the practice of placing students in specific curriculum groups on the basis of test scores and other criteria. Tracking begins very early in the classroom, often in reading groups during first grade. These tracks can reinforce the disadvantages that children from less affluent families may have if they have not been exposed to reading materials and writing instruments in their homes during early childhood years.

Tracking and differential access to higher education are evident not only in the United States but also in many nations around the world. For example, Japan's educational system mandates equality in school funding and insists that all schools use the same textbooks. Nevertheless, it is the more affluent Japanese families who can afford to send their children to *juku*, or cram schools. These afternoon schools assist high school students in preparing for examinations which determine admission into prestigious colleges (McGrath, 1983:66; Rohlen, 1983; M. White, 1987).

According to a study of teachers' attitudes toward students in the "outback" in rural Australia —an area where sheep vastly outnumber people— students are being prepared to stay in the "bush." Indeed, only a small minority seek out electives geared toward preparation for college. However, beginning in the 1980s, parents questioned this agriculture-oriented curriculum in view of rural Australia's declining employment base (Henry, 1989).

Conflict theorists hold that the educational inequalities resulting from funding disparities and tracking are designed to meet the needs of modern capitalist societies. Samuel Bowles and Herbert Gintis (1976:131–148) argue that capitalism requires a skilled, disciplined labor force and that the educational system of the United States is structured with this objective in mind. Citing numerous studies, they offer support for what they call the *correspondence principle*.

According to this approach, schools attended by different social classes promote the values expected of individuals in each class and perpetuate social class divisions from one generation to the next. Thus, working-class children, assumed to be destined for subordinate positions, are more likely to be placed in high school vocational and general tracks which emphasize close supervision and compliance with authority. By contrast, young people from more affluent families are largely directed to college preparatory tracks which stress leadership and decision-making skills—corresponding to their likely futures. While the correspondence principle continues to be persuasive, researchers have noted that the impact of race and gender on students' educational experiences may even overshadow that of class (M. Cole, 1988).

The relationship between education and status is nowhere more evident than in the college admissions process, as high school seniors compete for openings at prestigious colleges. Entry into an Ivy League school, for example, is a mark of high social status in itself, regardless of one's family background. In Box 10-2 (page 278), we examine the debate within a middle-class family over the status implications of attending such colleges.

Treatment of Women in Education The educational system of the United States, like many other social institutions, has long been characterized by discriminatory treatment of women. In 1833, Oberlin College became the first institution of higher learning to admit female students— some 200 years after the first men's college was established. But Oberlin believed that women should aspire to become wives and mothers, not lawyers and intellectuals. Female students washed men's clothing, cared for their rooms, and served them at meals. In the 1840s Lucy Stone, then an Oberlin undergraduate and later one of the nation's most outspoken feminist leaders, refused to write a commencement address because it would have had to be read to the audience by a male student (Fletcher, 1943; Flexner, 1972:29–30, 342).

In the twentieth century, sexism in education has been manifested in many ways—in textbooks with negative stereotypes of women, counselors' pressure on female students to prepare for "women's work," and unequal funding for women's and men's recreational programs. But perhaps nowhere has educational discrimination been more

BOX 10-2

A FAMILY PREPARES FOR COLLEGE

The status implications of the college selection and admissions process can spark intense debate within families. Psychologist Thomas Cottle (1991:83–84) observed Emma and Henry Leland (not their real names), a middle-class Boston couple, as they argued over their daughter Tara's college options. Tara had confided to friends that she was unsure she even wanted to go to college right after high school, but her father was anxious that she attend an Ivy League school. Emma, Harry's wife, was critical of his priorities:

"You want the status for yourself, Harry. Where Tara goes to school is something you think you can use somehow. *You* need it!"

"And you don't?"

"No, I don't. Tara's Tara. That's all there is to it. She'll be Tara at Harvard, Tara at a state university, Tara at no college at all."

Harry Leland is on fire. "That's a lie. You would die if she didn't go to college. You could never admit that to yourself. You were the one who got hot and bothered when her grades fell last year. *You,* not me!"

"I was concerned, but not for college." Emma Leland's voice remains surprisingly soft for a woman feeling such anger. "I

thought she was having a problem she wouldn't tell us about."

"And you never thought about what that might mean for college?"

"No."

"Never?"

"Never." . . .

"Damn it." Harry Leland has begun pulling off his tie. "Now you turn this into my liking Tara more if she goes to an Ivy League school. That maybe if she goes to some second-rate place I'll love her less. Or maybe I'll stop loving her altogether. Or maybe I don't love her at all. . . . Let's leave it at that, which will prove you were right. Tara goes to Dartmouth. I happily cough up the twenty-plus grand a year. Tara doesn't go to Dartmouth, I show my true colors and disown her. That's the proof you're looking for, isn't it?"

"She doesn't need proof." Emma's words are barely audible. Even Harry is straining to hear them. She has begun straightening the yellow throw pillows. "You just have to relax and let her lead her own life."

"Huh?"

"Let her lead her own life."

"You want me out of it, I'm out of it." His tie is off, Harry Leland is pacing in circles around the

small living room, tapping the television each time he passes it. "I'm an ogre, after all. I mean, how could I be so cruel as to want my daughter in a first-rate college. I mean, that has to qualify as abuse, doesn't it? It'd be better if I beat her, wouldn't it? Why don't we get a good psychiatrist to treat us? Father who wanted good school for daughter sentenced to life on death row,"

"Oh, stop it already! This whole thing is pitiful." Emma Leland barks out the words at the same time an upstairs door slams shut. For several moments no one speaks. The door slams a second time.

Tara has been listening to her parents. It is not the first time that a seemingly innocent discussion of college applications has erupted into this sort of argument. She cannot bear the scenes, nor the idea that this year seems to hold the confirmation of her parents' work for the last eighteen years. Everything they have tried to achieve seems to rest on the college admissions decision, and it does little good to mutter words like, why can't they just accept me for who I am, rather than where I get in. . . .

evident than in employment of teachers. The positions of university professor and college administrator, which hold relatively high status in the United States, have generally been reserved for men. Yet public school teachers, who have much lower status, are largely female. According to the American Association of University Women, as of 1991 about two-thirds of all public school teachers

in the United States were female. Yet women accounted for only 5 percent of the nation's school superintendents and held fewer than 350 of the 3000 college and university presidencies (J. Hicks, 1991:19).

Even when they hold the same degrees as men, women academics often receive lower salaries. According to data compiled by the National Re-

Shown is a law school class. In recent decades, there has been a significant increase in the proportion of women graduating from the law schools, medical schools, and dental schools of the United States.

search Council, in 1985 the median full-time salary for men with Ph.D. degrees in the humanities was $36,100, as compared with $30,900 for women with the same qualifications. In the sciences and engineering, the gap between men and women with Ph.D.s was still higher. The median salary for men was $46,100; for women, it was $35,600 (Rohter, 1987).

There has, however, been an increase in the proportion of women continuing their schooling. Whereas in the past, women were underrepresented in college enrollment, today 55 percent of undergraduate students in the United States are female. Access to graduate education for women has also increased dramatically; for example, the percentage of doctoral degrees awarded to women rose from 14 percent in 1950 to 37 percent in 1989. Professional schools, as well, have become much more open to women. The proportion of women graduates from medical schools has increased from 6 percent in 1960 to 33 percent in 1990. Twenty-six percent of all dental school graduates are now female, compared with less than 1 percent in 1960. Similarly, 40 percent of all law school graduates are women, compared with less than 3 percent in 1960. Pressure from the feminist movement (see Chapter 8) played a major role in opening the doors of these institutions (Bureau of the Census, 1992a:173–174).

Interactionist View

In George Bernard Shaw's play *Pygmalion*, later adapted into the hit Broadway musical *My Fair Lady*, flower girl Eliza Doolittle is transformed into a "lady" by Professor Henry Higgins. He changes her manner of speech and teaches her the etiquette of "high society."

Is it actually possible to change someone's behavior simply by treating the person differently? Because of their focus on micro-level classroom dynamics, interactionist researchers have been particularly interested in this question. The labeling approach (see Chapter 5) and the concept of the self-fulfilling prophecy (see Chapter 7) suggest that if we treat people in particular ways, they may fulfill our expectations. Children labeled as "troublemakers" come to view themselves as delinquents. A dominant group's stereotyping of racial minorities may limit their opportunities to break away from expected roles.

Can this labeling process operate in the classroom? Howard Becker (1952) studied public schools in low-income and more affluent areas of Chicago. He noticed that administrators expected less of students from poor neighborhoods, and he wondered if this view was being accepted by teachers. Subsequently, in *Pygmalion in the Classroom*, psychologist Robert Rosenthal and school principal Lenore Jacobson (1968) documented what they referred to as a *teacher-expectancy effect*—the impact that a teacher's expectations about a student's performance may have on the student's actual achievements.

Between 1965 and 1966, children in a San Francisco elementary school were administered a verbal and reasoning pretest. The researchers then randomly selected 20 percent of the sample and designated them as "spurters"—children of whom teachers could expect superior performance. On a later verbal and reasoning test, the spurters were found to score significantly higher than before. Moreover, teachers evaluated them as more interesting, more curious, and better-adjusted than their classmates. These results were striking, since the spurters—unbeknownst to the teachers—had been *arbitrarily* classified in the "superior" group. Apparently, teachers' perceptions that these students were exceptional led to noticeable improvements in performance.

Studies in the United States have revealed that teachers wait longer for an answer from a student believed to be a high achiever and are more likely to give such children a second chance. In one experiment, teachers' expectations were even shown to have an impact on students' athletic achievements. Teachers obtained better athletic performance—as measured in the number of sit-ups or push-ups performed—from those students of whom they expected higher numbers (R. Rosenthal and Babad, 1985).

The teacher-expectancy effect has been confirmed in a rather surprising setting: a training base for the Israeli army. Instructors for a combat command course were purposely given incorrect information about the "command potential" of 105 men about four days before the trainees arrived. Once the course began, the trainees who had been labeled "high in potential" did indeed learn more than others. These trainees also developed more favorable attitudes toward the combat command course (Eden and Shani, 1982).

Despite these findings, some researchers continue to question the validity of this "Pygmalion effect." Further research is needed to clarify the relationship between teachers' expectations and students' actual performance. Yet, drawing on the studies described above, interactionists emphasize that ability may not be so completely predictive of academic success as one might think.

SCHOOLS AS FORMAL ORGANIZATIONS

Nineteenth-century educators would be amazed at the scale of schools in the United States as we head toward the end of the twentieth century. For example, California's school system, the largest in the nation, currently enrolls as many children as there were in the entire country's secondary schools in 1930 (Bureau of the Census, 1975:368; 1992a:149). In many respects, today's schools, when viewed as an example of a formal organization, are similar to factories, hospitals, and business firms. The parallels between schools and these other organizations will become more apparent as we examine the bureaucratic nature of schools, teaching as an occupational role, and the student subculture.

Bureaucratization of Schools

The bureaucratization of schools in the United States has resulted not only from the growing number of students being served by individual schools and school systems but also from the greater degree of specialization required within a technologically complex society. It is simply not possible for a single teacher to transmit culture and skills to children of varying ages who will enter many diverse occupations (Goslin, 1965:132–142).

Chapter 4 examined Max Weber's insights on bureaucracy as an ideal type. Weber noted five basic characteristics of bureaucracy, all of which are evident in the vast majority of schools, whether at the elementary, secondary, or college level.

1 *Division of labor.* Specialized experts are employed to teach particular age levels of students and specific subjects. Public schools now employ teachers whose sole responsibility is to work with children who have learning disabilities or physical impairments. In a college sociology department, one instructor may specialize in sociology of religion, another in marriage and the family, and a third in industrial sociology.

2 *Hierarchy of authority.* Each employee of a school system is responsible to a higher authority. Teachers must report to principals and assistant principals and may also be supervised by department heads. Principals are answerable to a superintendent of schools, and the superintendent is hired and fired by a board of education. Even the students are hierarchically organized by grade and within clubs and organizations.

3 *Written rules and regulations.* Teachers and administrators must conform to numerous rules and regulations in the performance of their duties. This bureaucratic trait can become dysfunctional; the time invested in completing required forms could instead be spent in preparing lessons or conferring with students.

4 *Impersonality.* As was noted in Chapter 4, the university has been portrayed as a giant, faceless bureaucracy which cares little for the uniqueness of the individual. As class sizes have increased at schools and universities, it has become more difficult for teachers to give personal attention to each student. In fact, bureaucratic norms may actually encourage teachers to treat all students in the same way despite the fact that students have distinctive personalities and learning needs.

5 *Employment based on technical qualifications.* At least in theory, the hiring of teachers and college instructors is based on professional competence and expertise. Promotions are normally dictated by written personnel policies; people who excel may be granted lifelong job security through tenure. Teachers have achieved these protections partly because of the bargaining power of unions (Borman and Spring, 1984; W. Tyler, 1985).

Functionalists take a generally positive view of the bureaucratization of education. Teachers can master the skills needed to work with a specialized clientele, since they no longer are expected to cover a broad range of instruction. The chain of command within schools is clear; students are presumably treated in an unbiased fashion because of uniformly applied rules. Finally, security of office protects teachers from unjustified dismissal. In general, then, functionalists observe that bureaucratization of education increases the likelihood that students, teachers, and administrators will be dealt with fairly—that is, on the basis of rational and equitable criteria.

By contrast, conflict theorists argue that the trend toward more centralized education has harmful consequences for disadvantaged people.

The standardization of educational curricula, including textbooks, will generally reflect the values, interests, and lifestyles of the most powerful groups in our society and may ignore those of racial and ethnic minorities. In addition, the disadvantaged, more so than the affluent, will find it difficult to sort through complex educational bureaucracies and to organize effective lobbying groups. Therefore, in the view of conflict theorists, low-income and minority parents will have even less influence over citywide and statewide educational administrators than they have over local school officials (Bowles and Gintis, 1976; M. Katz, 1971).

Teachers: Employees and Instructors

Whether they serve as instructors of preschoolers or graduate students, teachers are employees of formal organizations with bureaucratic structures. There is an inherent conflict in serving as a professional within a bureaucracy. The organization follows the principles of hierarchy and expects adherence to its rules; professionalism demands the individual responsibility of the practitioner. This conflict is very real for teachers, who experience all the positive and negative consequences of working in bureaucracies (refer back to Table 4-2 on page 97).

On a day-to-day level, the occupational status of *teacher* brings with it many perplexing stresses. While teachers' academic assignments have become more specialized as a result of the increasing division of labor within education, the demands on their time remain diverse and contradictory. In analyzing the work of schoolteachers, sociologist C. Wayne Gordon (1955) noted the conflicts inherent in serving as an instructor, a disciplinarian, and an employee of a school district at the same time. For college instructors, different types of role strain arise. While formally employed as teachers, they are expected to work on committees and are encouraged to conduct scholarly research. In many colleges and universities, security of position (tenure) is based primarily on the publication of original scholarship. As a result, instructors must fulfill goals that compete for time.

College instructors rarely have to occupy themselves with the role of disciplinarian, but this task

On a day-to-day level, the occupational status of "teacher" has many rewards, but it also brings many demands and stresses.

has become a major focus of schoolteachers' work. Clearly, maintenance of order is essential in establishing an educational environment in which students can actually learn. Yet the nation's schools have been the scene of increasingly violent misbehavior in recent years. An estimated 135,000 pupils in the United States carry guns to school each day (J. Keen, 1991).

Given these difficulties, does teaching remain an attractive profession in the United States? In 1969, when teachers were already having difficulty finding jobs because of growing educational cutbacks, fully 75 percent of parents indicated that they would like their children to become public school teachers. By 1990, that figure had fallen to 51 percent. In the minds of parents, the status of teaching as a career for their children had declined. In 1991, 4.1 percent of first-year male college students and 12.7 percent of first-year female students indicated that they were interested in becoming teachers. While these figures reflect a modest upturn in the appeal of teaching in recent years, they are dramatically lower than the 12.7 percent of first-year male students and 37.5 percent of first-year female students who had such occupational aspirations in 1968 (Astin et al., 1987:46, 70; Astin et al., 1991:35; Elam, 1990:47).

Undoubtedly, students' feelings about the attractiveness of teaching have been influenced by the economics of the profession. In 1992, the average salary for all public elementary and secondary teachers was $34,213. This salary places teachers somewhere near the average of all wage earners in the United States. By contrast, university students in Japan line up for coveted teaching jobs. By law, Japanese teachers are paid 10 percent more than employees in the top-level civil service job, which places them among the top 10 percent of wage earners in the nation (Manning, 1992; Richburg, 1985).

As was noted in Chapter 6, the status of any job reflects several factors, including the level of education required, financial compensation, and the respect given the occupation within society. Teaching is feeling pressure in all three areas. The amount of formal schooling required for this profession remains high, but the public has begun to call for new competency examinations for teachers. Moreover, the statistics cited above demonstrate that teachers' salaries are significantly lower than those of many professionals and skilled workers. Finally, as we have seen, the prestige of the teaching profession has declined in the last decade. It is not surprising, then, to find that many teachers become disappointed and frustrated and leave the educational world for other careers. Many are simply "burned out" by the severe demands, limited rewards, and general sense of alienation that they experience on the job.

In 1987, a Rand Corporation report estimated attrition among teachers in the United States at 9 percent annually. The researchers noted that the "teacher burnout" rate had been as high as 17 percent per year in the 1960s. However, although the current rate is much lower, it has raised even greater concern among educators because the profession is no longer attracting a sufficient number of college graduates. Until 20 years ago, a steady supply of women and minority group members entered teaching. However, as career options have widened for these groups in recent decades (refer back to Chapters 7 and 8), many people have chosen to enter higher-paying occupations, rather than teaching (Grissmer and Kirby, 1987; Solórzano, 1986).

The Student Subculture

Earlier, various functions of education, such as transmitting culture, maintaining social control, and promoting social change, were described. An additional latent function which relates directly to student life can be identified: schools provide for students' social and recreational needs. Education helps toddlers and young children develop interpersonal skills that are essential during adolescence and adulthood. During high school and college years, students may meet future husbands and wives and may establish lifelong friendships (J. W. Coleman and Cressey, 1980:96).

When people observe high schools, community colleges, or universities from the outside, students appear to constitute a cohesive, uniform group. However, the student subculture is actually much more complex and diverse. High school cliques and social groups may be established on the basis of race, social class, physical attractiveness, placement in courses, athletic ability, and leadership roles in the school and community. Remarkably, in his study of Elmtown, allowing for the fact that an individual could belong to more than one social group, August Hollingshead (1975:154) found some 259 distinct cliques in a single high school. These cliques, whose average size was five, were centered on the school itself, on recreational activities, and on religious and community groups.

A similar diversity can be found at the college level. Burton Clark and Martin Trow (1966)—and, more recently, Helen Lefkowitz Horowitz (1987)—have identified distinctive subcultures among college students. Looking at their analyses together, we can present four ideal types of subcultures.

The *collegiate* subculture focuses on having fun and socializing. These students define what constitutes a "reasonable" amount of academic work (and what amount of work is "excessive" and leads to being labeled as a "grind"). Members of the collegiate subculture have little commitment to academic pursuits. By contrast, the *academic* subculture identifies with the intellectual concerns of the faculty and values knowledge for its own sake. The *vocational* subculture is primarily interested in career prospects and views college as a means of obtaining degrees which are essential for ad-

Bob Daemmrich/The Image Works

Shown is a high school class on newswriting in Austin, Texas. The student subculture of many schools in the United States includes young people with disabilities. According to federal legislature which took effect in 1980, children with disabilities must be educated in the atmosphere most similar to a regular classroom that is suitable for them. Mainstreaming is the practice of promoting maximum integration of disabled children with nondisabled children.

vancement. Finally, the *nonconformist* subculture is hostile to the college environment and seeks out ideas that may or may not relate to studies. Indeed, this subculture may be removed from the dominant college culture but may find outlets through campus publications or issue-oriented groups. Each college student is eventually exposed to these competing subcultures and must determine which (if any) seem most in line with his or her feelings and interests.

The typology used by these researchers reminds us that school is a complex social organization—almost like a community with different neighborhoods. However, it is important to note that these four subcultures are not the only ones evident on college campuses in the United States. For example, one might find subcultures of Vietnam veterans or former full-time homemakers at community colleges and four-year commuter institutions.

Sociologist Joe Feagin has studied a distinctive collegiate subculture: Black students at predominantly White universities. These students must function academically and socially within universities where there are few Black faculty members or Black administrators, where harassment of Blacks by campus police is common, and where the curricula place little emphasis on Black contributions. Indeed, Feagin (1989:11) suggests that "for minority students life at a predominantly white college or university means long-term encounters with *pervasive whiteness*." In Feagin's view, African American students at such institutions experience blatant and subtle racial discrimination which has a cumulative impact that can seriously damage students' confidence.

SOCIAL POLICY, RELIGION, AND EDUCATION
RELIGION IN THE SCHOOLS

- Is promoting religious observance a legitimate function of the social institution of education?
- How might organized school prayer be viewed from a conflict perspective?
- Why are advocates of a liberal education frightened by the effort to promote creationism in public schools?

Although most people in the United States support the general principle of separation of church and state as enunciated by Thomas Jefferson, legislative actions and judicial decisions concerning religion in the schools continue to provoke intense controversy. The Supreme Court has consistently interpreted the Constitution's First Amendment to mean that government should attempt to maximize religious freedom by maintaining a policy of neutrality. Thus government may not assist religion by financing a new church building, but it cannot obstruct religion by denying a church or synagogue adequate police and fire protection. In this section, we will focus on two issues involving religion in the schools that continue to provoke passionate debate: school prayer and creationism.

Should organized prayer be allowed in the public schools of the United States? In the key case of *Engel v. Vitale*, the Supreme Court ruled in 1962 that the use of nondenominational prayer in New York schools was "wholly inconsistent" with the First Amendment's prohibition against government establishment of religion. In finding that such organized school prayer violated the Constitution—even when no student was required to participate—the Court argued, in effect, that promoting religious observance was not a legitimate function of government or education.

Critics of this ruling insist that school prayer is a harmless ritual—although admittedly a religious ritual—that should be permitted to begin a school day. Prohibiting school prayer, in their view, forces too great a separation between what Émile Durkheim called the *sacred* and the *profane*. Moreover, supporters of school prayer insist that use of nondenominational prayer can in no way lead to the establishment of an ecclesia in the United States. Nevertheless, subsequent Supreme Court rulings overturned state laws requiring Bible reading in public schools, requiring recitation of the Lord's Prayer, and permitting a daily one-minute period of silent meditation or prayer.

In 1992, the Supreme Court ruled, by a narrow 5–4 vote, that a rabbi's invocation and dedication at a junior high school graduation in Providence, Rhode Island, violated the constitutional separation of church and state. The rabbi had given thanks to God for the "legacy of America, where diversity is celebrated and the rights of minorities are protected." The Bush administration had encouraged the Supreme Court to permit a greater role for religion in public schools, but the majority ruling emphasized that students were coerced into joining in these prayers. While this decision continues to allow *voluntary* school prayer by students, it forbids school officials to sponsor any prayer or religious observance at school events (Aikman, 1991:62; Elsasser, 1992).

Despite such judicial pronouncements, children in many public schools in the United States are led in regular prayer recitations or Bible reading. Many communities believe that schools should transmit the dominant culture of the United States by encouraging prayer. In a 1985 survey (the most recent available), 15 percent of school administrators (including 42 percent of school administrators in the south) reported that prayers are said in at least one of their schools. Moreover, according to a 1991 survey, 78 percent of adults in the United States favor allowing children to say prayers in public schools, while 89 percent of adults support silent meditation in schools (Aikman, 1991:64; J. Bacon, 1987).

Troubled by what they see as the growing secularization of our society, Christian fundamentalists have become the leading proponents of school prayer. (The term *fundamentalism* refers to adherence to earlier-accepted religious doctrines, often accompanied by a literal application of historical beliefs and scriptures to today's world.) Along with certain lay Catholic and Orthodox Jewish groups, they have advocated a constitutional amendment permitting organized prayer in public schools and other public institutions. Supporters of school prayer charge that, in outlawing any religious expression in public schools, the Supreme Court has violated the First Amendment clause protecting the "free exercise" of religion.

Opponents of organized school prayer include the mainline Christian denominations, represented by the National Council of Churches; most Jewish organizations; and secular groups, notably the American Civil Liberties Union (ACLU). They stress that no child is currently prevented from praying in school when eating lunch in the cafeteria, awaiting an examination, or preparing for a foul shot on the basketball court. What is prohibited—properly, in the view of these critics—is prayer *organized* by public officials. Opponents of such rituals insist that organizing prayer is not a legitimate function of the social institution of education.

Critics dismiss as unrealistic the argument that school prayer can remain truly voluntary. Drawing on the interactionist perspective and small-group re-

"TODAY'S AGENDA IS A TOUGH ONE, DEALING PRIMARILY WITH RELIGION IN THE PUBLIC SCHOOLS. BUT FIRST, LET US PRAY."

search, they suggest that children will face enormous social pressure to conform to the beliefs and practices of a religious majority. Opponents of school prayer add that a religious majority in a community might impose a prayer specific to its faith, at the expense of religious minorities. Viewed from a conflict perspective, organized school prayer could reinforce the religious beliefs, rituals, and interests of the powerful; violate the rights of the powerless; increase religious dissension; and threaten the cultural and religious pluralism of the United States.

A second area of continuing controversy regarding religion in the schools has been over whether the biblical account of creation should be presented in school curricula. As discussed earlier, *creationists* support a literal interpretation of the book of Genesis regarding the origin of the universe and argue that evolution should not be presented as established scientific fact. Their efforts recall the famous "monkey trial" of 1925, in which high school biology teacher John T. Scopes was convicted of violating a Tennessee law making it a crime to teach the scientific theory of evolution in public schools. However, contemporary creationists have gone beyond espousing fundamentalist religious doctrine; they attempt to reinforce their position regarding the origins of the universe with quasi-scientific data (Chalfant et al., 1987:236).

In 1968, the Supreme Court overturned an Arkansas law which barred any teaching of evolution in the state's public schools. This led creationists to a new strategy: they endorsed "balanced-treatment legislation" under which school systems would be forced to give the biblical account of creation equal weight in their curricula with scientific theories of evolution. However, in 1982, a federal district court judge ruled that an Arkansas balanced-treatment law violated the First Amendment guarantee of separation of church and state. Judge William Ray Overton declared that "creation science . . . has no scientific merit or educational value." Then, in 1987, the Supreme Court, by a 7–2 vote, held that states may not require the teaching of creationism alongside evolution in public schools if the primary purpose of such legislation is to promote a religious viewpoint (Stuart, 1982; S. Taylor, 1987).

The effort to promote creationist views is directly related to the rise of Christian fundamentalist belief and practice within the United States and the worldwide fundamentalist resurgence. Underlying this controversy is a more general question: "Whose ideas and values deserve a hearing in the nation's classrooms?" Critics of creationism see this campaign as one step toward sectarian religious control of public education. They worry that, at some point in the future, teachers may not be able to use books, or make statements, that conflict with fundamentalist interpretations of the Bible. For advocates of a liberal education, who are deeply committed to intellectual (and religious) diversity, this is a genuinely frightening prospect.

SUMMARY

Religion is found throughout the world because it offers answers to such ultimate questions as why we exist, why we succeed or fail, and why we die. *Education* is a process of learning in which some people consciously and formally teach while others adopt the social role of learner. This chapter examines the dimensions and functions of religion, types of religious organizations, sociological views of education, and schools as an example of formal organizations.

1 Émile Durkheim stressed the social aspect of religion and attempted to understand individual religious behavior within the context of the larger society.
2 From a Marxist point of view, religion lessens the possibility of collective political action that can end capitalist oppression and transform society.
3 Max Weber held that Calvinism (and, to a lesser extent, other branches of Protestantism) produced a type of person more likely to engage in capitalistic behavior.
4 Sociologists have identified four ideal types of religious organization: the *ecclesia,* the *denomination,* the *sect,* and the *cult.*
5 Transmission of knowledge and bestowal of status are manifest functions of education.
6 In the view of conflict theorists, schools "track" pupils according to their social class backgrounds, thereby preserving class-related inequalities.
7 Teacher expectations about a student's performance can sometimes have an impact on the student's actual achievements.

8 Today, most schools in the United States are organized in a bureaucratic fashion. Weber's five basic characteristics of bureaucracy are all evident in schools.
9 The issues of school prayer and creationism continue to provoke passionate debate regarding the proper role of religion in public schools.

CRITICAL THINKING QUESTIONS

1 Should atheists and agnostics be viewed as religious minorities in the United States? Do they have religious beliefs, rituals, or experiences? Are their rights protected—or even considered—in the many religious controversies evident across the country? How can the text material on the functions of religion be used to better understand the position of atheists and agnostics in the United States?
2 What are the functions and dysfunctions of tracking? Viewed from an interactionist perspective, how would tracking of high school students influence the interactions between students and teachers? In what ways might tracking have positive and negative impacts on the self-concepts of various students?
3 Are the student subcultures identified in the text evident on your campus? What other student subcultures are present? Which subcultures have the highest (and the lowest) social status? How might functionalists, conflict theorists, and interactionists view the existence of student subcultures on a college campus?

KEY TERMS

Correspondence principle A term used by Bowles and Gintis to refer to the tendency of schools to promote the values expected of individuals in each social class and to prepare students for the types of jobs typically held by members of their class. (page 277)

Creationists People who support a literal interpretation of the book of Genesis regarding the origin of the universe and argue that evolution should not be presented as established scientific fact. (267)

Credentialism An increase in the lowest level of education required to enter a field. (275)

Cult A generally small, secretive religious group that represents either a new religion or a major innovation of an existing faith. (270)

Cultural universals General practices found in every culture. (260)

Denomination A large, organized religion not officially linked with the state or government. (268)

Ecclesia A religious organization that claims to include most or all of the members of a society and is recognized as the national or official religion. (268)

Education A formal process of learning in which some people consciously teach while others adopt the social role of learner. (261)

Established sect J. Milton Yinger's term for a religious group that is the outgrowth of a sect, yet remains isolated from society. (270)

Fundamentalism Adherence to earlier-accepted religious doctrines, often accompanied by a literal application of historical beliefs and scriptures to today's world. (285)

Liberation theology Use of a church, primarily Roman Catholicism, in a political effort to eliminate poverty, discrimination, and other forms of injustice evident in secular society. (265)

Profane The ordinary and commonplace elements of life, as distinguished from the sacred. (262)

Protestant ethic Max Weber's term for the disciplined work ethic, this-worldly concerns, and rational orientation to life emphasized by John Calvin and his followers. (266)

Religion According to Émile Durkheim, a unified system of beliefs and practices relative to sacred things. (262)

Religious beliefs Statements to which members of a particular religion adhere. (267)

Religious experience The feeling or perception of being in direct contact with the ultimate reality, such as a divine being, or of being overcome with religious emotion. (267)

Religious rituals Practices required or expected of members of a faith. (267)

Sacred Elements beyond everyday life which inspire awe, respect, and even fear. (262)

Sect A relatively small religious group that has broken away from some other religious organization to renew what it views as the original vision of the faith. (268)

Secularization The process through which religion's influence on other social institutions diminishes. (260)

Teacher-expectancy effect The impact that a teacher's expectations about a student's performance may have on the student's actual achievements. (280)

Tracking The practice of placing students in specific curriculum groups on the basis of test scores and other criteria. (277)

ADDITIONAL READINGS

Carmody, Denise Lardner. *Women and World Religions* (2d ed.). Englewood Cliffs, N.J.: Prentice-Hall, 1989. A feminist examination of world religions and women's religious experiences.

Demerath, N. J., II, and Rhys H. Williams. *A Bridging of Faiths: Religions and Politics in a New England City.* Princeton, N.J.: Princeton University Press, 1992. An examination of the social transformation of Springfield, Massachusetts, from a city dominated by Protestants for three centuries to a largely Catholic community over the last 50 years.

Eve, Raymond A., and Francis B. Harrold. *The Creationist Movement in Modern America.* Boston: Twayne, 1991. The authors present a nonjudgmental analysis of the efforts of creationists to control school curricula.

Seider, John, and Katherine Meyer. *Conflict and Change in the Catholic Church.* New Brunswick, N.J.: Rutgers University Press, 1989. A study of the impact of wide-ranging changes in the Catholic church on both clergy and lay people.

Smith, Christian. *The Emergence of Liberation Theology: Radical Religion and Social Movement Theory.* Chicago: University of Chicago Press, 1991. A sociologist provides a brief history and an analysis of the liberation theology movement in Latin America.

White, Merry. *The Japanese Educational Challenge: A Commitment to Children.* New York: Free Press, 1987. A look at the strengths and weaknesses of the Japanese educational system, with an emphasis on the early years.

11

GOVERNMENT AND THE ECONOMY

LOOKING AHEAD

- How do capitalism, socialism, and communism differ as ideal types?
- How are systems of power and authority organized?
- Can people in the United States be considered apathetic in their political behavior?

- Is the United States run by a small ruling elite?
- How does a profession differ from an occupation?
- How common is sexual harassment in the United States?

By 1992, people across the United States were well-aware of the devastating crisis in the nation's savings and loan industry. The Resolution Trust Corporation, established by the federal government in 1989, had already overseen the closing of 721 savings and loan institutions and 585 banks that had gone bankrupt.

As the savings and loan crisis continued, there were varying, but ever-increasing, estimates as to the eventual cost of the government "bailout" of the industry. One of the lower estimates, $115 billion, was translated into comparative data by researchers. That figure would have funded the U.S. Food for Peace program at its 1989 level for 104 years. Similarly, $115 billion would have funded the Drug Enforcement Agency for 201 years; it would have supported the federal government's prenatal care programs for 549 years (M. Levinson and Thomas, 1992; Maraniss and Atkinson, 1989).

What led to this financial crisis? After achieving record profits in 1978, the savings and loan industry went into a tailspin in the early 1980s. Competition for consumers' savings had intensified after the creation of money market accounts and other high-interest investment opportunities by brokerage houses and mutual funds. At the same time, a 1982 federal law encouraged savings and loan companies to move away from the home mortgage business toward a new emphasis on riskier but potentially more profitable commercial and real estate loans. Finally, as part of a larger effort to streamline the federal bureaucracy and reduce government regulation of business, the

Reagan administration cut the number of federal examiners and auditors for the savings and loan industry by 75 percent over the period 1981–1985. By 1983, there were fewer than 800 examiners for the entire United States; because of low pay and high turnover, many of these examiners had been on the job less than two years (L. J. Davis, 1990:62; Maraniss and Atkinson, 1989; P. Taylor, 1990).

Consequently, the industry was simultaneously facing greater competition, was shifting toward riskier investments, and was increasingly without government supervision. In this environment, it became easy for unscrupulous owners and officers of savings and loan institutions to make fraudulent loans and exchanges of land—or to pay themselves astronomical salaries supplemented by lavish fringe benefits. Charles H. Keating, Jr., who ran the now infamous Lincoln Savings and Loan, determined that his own services to the institution were worth as much as $3.2 million per year. He hired almost his entire immediate family to work at Lincoln; regulators believe that the Keating family was paid a minimum of $34 million by Lincoln during the 1980s. According to a 1990 estimate, the failure of Lincoln Savings and Loan may cost taxpayers more than $2 billion (L. J. Davis, 1990:58–59).

The savings and loan crisis has clearly shaken the economic system of the United States. The term *economic system* refers to the social institution through which goods and services are produced, distributed, and consumed. As with social institutions such as the family, religion, and government, the economic system shapes other aspects of the social order and is, in turn, influenced by them. Throughout this textbook, we have been reminded of the economy's impact on social behavior—for example, individual and group behavior in factories and offices. We have studied the work of Karl Marx and Friedrich Engels (see Chapters 1 and 6), who emphasized that the economic system of a society can promote social inequality. And we learned (in Chapter 6) that foreign investment in developing countries can intensify inequality among residents.

Like the economic system, the political system of the United States has been shaken by the savings and loan crisis. The term *political system* refers to the social institution which relies on a recognized set of procedures for implementing and achieving the goals of a group. Each society must have a political system to maintain recognized procedures for allocating valued resources. Thus, like religion and the family, the economic and political systems are cultural universals; they are social institutions found in every society.

A society's economic system is deeply intertwined with its political system. In the example of the savings and loan crisis, the political system of the United States influenced the economy by encouraging the savings and loan industry to shift to riskier investments. At the same time, policymakers reduced government regulation of the industry by cutting the number of federal examiners and auditors. In the 1990s, the political system will have to face the consequences of the savings and loan crisis, for taxpayers will bear the burden of the bailout of the industry.

This chapter will present sociological analysis of the impact of government and the economy on people's lives. We will begin with macro-level analysis of the economic systems used by preindustrial and industrial societies to handle production and distribution. Next we will examine the sources of power in a political system and will describe three types of authority identified by Max Weber. In studying government and politics in the United States, we will give particular attention to political socialization, citizens' participation in political life, the changing role of women in politics, and the influence of interest groups on decision making. The question "Who really rules the United States?" will be posed, and the elite and

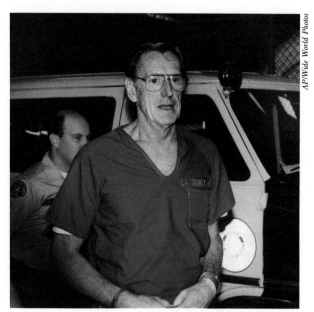

AP/Wide World Photos

In the aftermath of the savings and loan scandal, Charles H. Keating, Jr., who ran the now infamous Lincoln Savings and Loan, is shown in handcuffs in 1990 while facing a 42-count fraud indictment.

pluralist models of power will be contrasted. Then, using micro-level sociological analysis, we will consider work and the workplace. Finally, the social policy section will focus on sexual harassment, which has become an issue in both government and private-sector organizations.

ECONOMIC SYSTEMS

Preindustrial Societies

The earliest written documents known to exist, clay tablets from about 3000 B.C., were found in 1981 in Iran, Iraq, and Syria. It is fitting commentary on the importance of the economic sector that these tablets record units of land and agricultural products such as grain. Of course, economic life has grown exceedingly complex during the intervening 5000 years. One key factor in this change has been the development of increasingly sophisticated technology for tasks of production and distribution.

F. & H. Schreider/Photo Researchers

Preindustrial economic systems still exist in the 1990s. Shown here are Turkana fishermen in Kenya.

The term **technology** refers to the application of knowledge to the making of tools and the utilization of natural resources. The form that a particular economic system takes is not totally defined by the available technology. Nevertheless, the level of technology will limit, for example, the degree to which a society can depend on irrigation or complex machinery.

Sociologists Gerhard Lenski and Jean Lenski developed a scheme which categorizes societies on the basis of their economic systems. In their view, the first type to emerge is the **hunting-and-gathering society,** in which people simply rely on whatever foods and fiber are readily available. Technology in such societies is minimal. People are constantly on the move in search of food, and there is little division of labor into specialized tasks (Lenski et al., 1991).

Hunting-and-gathering societies are composed of small, widely dispersed groups. Each group consists almost entirely of people related to one another. As a result, kinship ties are the source of authority and influence, and the family takes on a particularly important role. Since resources are scarce, there is relatively little inequality in terms of material goods. Social differentiation within the hunting-and-gathering society is based on such ascribed characteristics as gender, age, and family background.

Horticultural societies, in which people plant seeds and crops rather than subsist merely on available foods, emerged perhaps 9000 years ago. In contrast to the hunters and gatherers, members of horticultural societies are much less nomadic. Consequently, they place greater emphasis on the production of tools and household objects. Yet technology within horticultural societies remains rather limited. Cultivation of crops is performed with the aid of digging sticks or hoes.

As farming in horticultural societies gradually becomes more efficient, a social surplus is created. The term **social surplus** refers to the production by a group of people of enough goods to cover their own needs, while at the same time sustaining other individuals who are not engaged in agricultural tasks. As a result of the emergence of a surplus, some individuals in horticultural societies begin to specialize in such tasks as governance, military defense, and leadership of religious observance. As was noted in Chapter 6, increasing division of labor can lead to a hierarchical social order and to differential rewards and power.

The last stage of preindustrial development in Lenski and Lenski's model is the **agrarian society.** As in horticultural societies, members of agrarian societies are primarily engaged in the production of food. However, because of the introduction of new technological innovations such as the plow, farmers dramatically increase their crop yield. It becomes possible to cultivate the same fields over generations, thereby allowing the emergence of still larger settlements.

The technology of the agrarian society continues to rely on the physical power of humans and animals. Nevertheless, there is more extensive division of labor than in horticultural societies. Individuals focus on specialized tasks, such as repair of fishing nets or work as a blacksmith. As human settlements become more established and stable, political institutions become more elaborate and concepts of property rights take on growing importance. The comparative permanence and greater surpluses of agrarian society make it more feasible to create artifacts such as statues, public monuments, and art objects and to pass them on from one generation to the next.

Industrial Societies

Although the industrial revolution did not topple monarchs, it produced changes as significant as those resulting from political revolutions. The **industrial revolution,** which took place largely in England during the period 1760–1830, was a scientific revolution focused on the application of nonanimal sources of power to labor tasks. It involved changes in the social organization of the workplace, as people left the homestead and began working in central locations such as factories.

As the industrial revolution proceeded, societies relied on new inventions that facilitated agricultural and industrial production and on new sources of energy such as steam. Many societies underwent an irrevocable shift from an agrarian-oriented economy to an industrial base. No longer did an individual or family typically make an entire product. Instead, the division of labor became increasingly complex, especially as manufacturing of goods became more common (Lenski et al., 1991).

The process of industrialization had distinctive social consequences. Families and communities could not continue to function as self-sufficient units. Individuals, villages, and regions began to exchange goods and services and become interde-

pendent. As people came to rely on the labor of members of other communities, the family lost its unique position as the source of power and authority. The need for specialized knowledge led to more formalized education, and education emerged as a social institution distinct from the family.

In general terms, an **industrial society** can be defined as a "society that relies chiefly on mechanization for the production of its economic goods and services" (Dushkin, 1991:283–284). There are two basic types of economic systems which distinguish contemporary industrial societies: capitalism and socialism. As described in the following sections, capitalism and socialism serve as ideal types of economic systems. No nation precisely fits either model. Instead, the economy of each industrial state represents a mixture of capitalism and socialism, although one type or the other will generally be more useful in describing a society's economic structure.

Capitalism   In the preindustrial societies described earlier, land functioned as the source of virtually all wealth. However, the industrial revolution required that certain individuals and institutions be willing to take substantial risks in order to finance new inventions, machinery, and business enterprises. Consequently, bankers, industrialists, and other holders of large sums of money replaced landowners as the most powerful economic force. These people invested their funds in the hope of realizing even greater profits and thereby became owners of property and business firms.

The transition to private ownership of business was accompanied by the emergence of the capitalist economic system. As we saw in Chapter 6, **capitalism** is an economic system in which the means of production are largely in private hands and the main incentive for economic activity is the accumulation of profits (Rosenberg, 1991). In practice, capitalist systems vary in the degree to which private ownership and economic activity are regulated by government.

During the period immediately following the industrial revolution, the prevailing form of capitalism was what is termed **laissez-faire** ("let them do"). Under the principle of laissez-faire, as expounded and endorsed by British economist

Adam Smith (1723–1790), people could compete freely with minimal government intervention in the economy. Business retained the right to regulate itself and essentially operated without fear of government regulation (Smelser, 1963:6–7).

Two centuries later, capitalism has taken on a somewhat different form. Private ownership and maximization of profits remain the most significant characteristics of capitalist economic systems. However, in contrast to the era of laissez-faire, contemporary capitalism features extensive government regulation of economic relations. Without restrictions, business firms can mislead consumers, endanger the safety of their workers, and even defraud the companies' investors—all in the pursuit of greater profits. As a result, the government of a capitalist nation often monitors prices, sets safety standards for industries, passes legislation to protect the rights of consumers, and regulates collective bargaining between labor unions and management. Yet, under capitalism as an ideal type, government rarely takes over ownership of an entire industry.

Contemporary capitalism also differs from laissez-faire in another important respect: the tolerance of monopolistic practices. A **monopoly** exists in a market when it is controlled by a single business firm. Domination of an industry allows the firm to effectively control a commodity so that it can dictate pricing, standards of quality, and availability. Buyers have little choice but to yield to the firm's decision; there is no other place to purchase the product or service. Clearly, monopolistic practices violate the ideal of free competition cherished by Adam Smith and other supporters of laissez-faire capitalism.

As is true in the United States, the government of a capitalist nation can outlaw monopolies through antitrust legislation. Such laws prevent any business from taking over so much of the competition in an industry that it gains control of the market. The federal government allows monopolies to exist only in certain exceptional cases, such as utilities and transportation. Even then, regulatory agencies are established to scrutinize these officially approved monopolies and protect the public. Yet, as conflict theorists point out, while *pure* monopolies are not a basic element of the economy of the United States, competition is much more restricted than one might expect in what is called a *free enterprise system*. In many industries, a few companies largely dominate the field and exclude new enterprises from entering the marketplace (see the discussion of multinational corporations in Chapter 6).

Socialism Socialist theory has its roots in the writings of Karl Marx and Friedrich Engels (see Chapter 1). These European radicals were disturbed by the exploitation of the working class as it emerged during the industrial revolution. In their view, capitalism forced large numbers of people to exchange their labor for wages. As was detailed in Chapter 6, the owners of an industry profit from the labor of their workers, primarily because they pay workers less than the value of the goods produced.

As an ideal type, a socialist economic system represents an attempt to eliminate such economic exploitation. Under *socialism,* the means of production and distribution in a society are collectively rather than privately owned. The basic objective of the economic system is to meet people's needs rather than to maximize profits. Socialists reject the laissez-faire philosophy that free competition benefits the general public. Instead, they believe that basic economic decisions should be made by the central government, which acts as the representative of the people. Therefore, government ownership of all major industries—including steel production, automobile manufacturing, and agriculture—is a major feature of socialism as an ideal type.

In practice, socialist economic systems vary in the extent to which private ownership is tolerated. For example, in Great Britain, a nation with certain aspects of both a socialist and a capitalist economy, passenger airline service is concentrated in the government-owned corporation British Airways. Yet private airline companies are allowed to compete with it.

Socialist societies also differ from capitalist nations in their commitment to social service programs. For example, the United States government provides health care and health insurance for the elderly and destitute through the Medicare and Medicaid programs. By contrast, socialist countries typically offer government-financed medical care for *all* citizens. In theory, the wealth of the people as a collectivity is used to provide health care, housing, education, and other key services for each individual and family.

In recent decades, the Soviet Union, the People's Republic of China, Vietnam, Cuba, and the nations of eastern Europe were popularly thought of as examples of communist economic systems. However, this is actually an incorrect usage of a term with sensitive political connotations. As an ideal type, **communism** refers to an economic system under which all property is communally owned and no social distinctions are made on the basis of people's ability to produce. In Marx's view, communist societies will naturally evolve out of the stage of socialism. The socialist state or government of each nation will eventually "wither away," as will all inequality and social class differentiation. Although the leaders of many twentieth-century revolutions—including the Russian Revolution of 1917 and the Chinese Revolution of 1949–1950—have proclaimed the goal of achieving a classless communist society, all nations known as *communist* in the twentieth century have remained far from this ideal.

In the late 1980s and the early 1990s, popular uprisings led to the overthrow of communist rule in the Soviet Union and many eastern European nations. Indeed, the Soviet Union officially dissolved in 1991; and by 1992, Yugoslavia was in the midst of a bloody civil war, and Czechoslovakia was moving toward dissolution. Nevertheless, as is discussed in Box 11-1 (on page 296), defenders of socialist ideals continue to argue that socialist planning and governmental intervention in economies are important in meeting people's basic needs and in effectively providing social services.

As we have seen, capitalism and socialism serve as ideal types of economic systems. In reality, the economy of each industrial society—including the United States, Great Britain, and Japan—includes certain elements of both capitalism and socialism. Whatever the differences, whether they more closely fit the ideal type of capitalism or socialism, all industrial societies rely chiefly on mechanization in the production of goods and services.

Postindustrial Societies

The significant changes in the occupational structure of industrial societies as their focus shifts from manufacturing to service industries have led social scientists to call technically advanced nations *postindustrial societies*. Sociologist Daniel Bell (1988:20) defines **postindustrial society** as a society whose economic system is based on the production of information rather than of goods. Large numbers of people become involved in occupations devoted to the teaching, generation, or dissemination of ideas—among them, engineers, educators, and scientists.

Sociologist Daniel Bell defines a postindustrial society *as one whose economic system is based on the production of information rather than goods.*

BOX 11-1

IN DEFENSE OF SOCIALIST PLANNING

As communism collapsed in the Soviet Union and eastern Europe, there was rejoicing not only within these countries but in the democracies of the west. Some observers viewed this collapse as a clear validation of unfettered "free market" policies that would prohibit governmental intervention in and regulation of national economies. However, economist Robert Pollin and political columnist Alexander Cockburn (1991) insist that socialist planning remains an essential tool for broadening democracy and making the world's economies better serve people's needs.

As part of their defense of socialist planning, Pollin and Cockburn identify and challenge what they see as three pervasive myths regarding socialist and free market economies:

MYTH 1: SOCIALIST
CENTRAL PLANNING
HAS BEEN A DISASTER
Pollin and Cockburn acknowledge that central planning under socialist governments had significant failures because the lack of democracy in these nations led to the creation of stifling, all-powerful bureaucracies. Nevertheless, socialist planning was responsible

for some substantial achievements. While western democracies suffered through an intense depression in the period 1929 to 1937, Soviet industrial growth averaged more than 12 percent. When the Communist party came to power in China in 1949, life expectancy was approximately 40 years; by 1988, it had reached 70 years. Over the period 1952 to 1978, industrial growth in China averaged 11.2 percent, thereby establishing the foundation for economic modernization in a previously agricultural nation. Finally, in terms of such health and social indicators as life expectancy, infant mortality, and rate of literacy, Cuba comes out far better than any other Latin American country.

MYTH 2: GOVERNMENT
INTERVENTION UNDER
CAPITALISM HAS ALSO
BEEN A FAILURE
In countering this myth, Pollin and Cockburn point to the example of Latin America. During the 1930s, most Latin American governments instituted interventionist policies intended primarily to encourage domestic manufacturing. These policies were fairly successful over a number of decades.

Mexico, Argentina, and Brazil all began producing consumer goods, developed machine-building capacity in the 1960s, and began to export on the world market in the 1970s. Per capita income in the region was generally high during the 1950s and 1960s. Although these interventionist policies eventually led to failure, it was primarily because the Latin American economies were never able to break their dependence on foreign capital from the United States and Europe.

MYTH 3: THE PARAGONS OF
FREE MARKET SUCCESS ARE
THE "MIRACLE" ECONOMIES
OF EAST ASIA
Pollin and Cockburn observe that, contrary to this myth, Japan and South Korea, the great "miracles" in the region, are not and never have been free market economies. In both nations, the state is dominant in planning and strategic financing; it provides business firms with export subsidies, protection, and cheap money. Moreover, the alleged "free market" was restricted, since both Japan and South Korea limited intervention by foreign corporations, especially during periods of rapid economic growth.

Taking a functionalist perspective, Bell views this transition from industrial society to postindustrial society as a positive development. He sees a general decline in organized working-class groups and a rise in interest groups concerned with such national issues as health, education, and the environment. Bell's outlook is functionalist because he portrays postindustrial society as basically consensual. Organizations and interest groups in such a society will engage in an open and competitive process of decision making. The level of conflict between diverse groups will diminish, and there will be much greater social stability.

Conflict theorists take issue with Bell's analysis of postindustrial society. For example, Michael Harrington (1980:125–126), who alerted the nation to the problems of the poor in his book *The Other America,* was critical of the significance Bell attached to the growing class of white-collar workers. Harrington conceded that scientists, engineers, and economists are involved in important political and economic decisions, but he disagreed with Bell's claim that they have a free hand in decision making, independent of the interests of the rich.

Harrington followed in the tradition of Marx by arguing that conflict between social classes will continue in postindustrial society. Other observers, reflecting a conflict perspective, have noted that the move to a postindustrial society in the United States has led to a loss of manufacturing jobs, a lessening of the role of unions in protecting and advocating the rights of workers, and an increase in the number of unemployed, underemployed, and homeless people.

In summary, postindustrial society may differ from industrial society in terms of the labor that people do, but perennial social problems will not disappear. As sociologist Paul Blumberg (1980: 217) has suggested, scarcity, poverty, inequality, and unemployment are still with us—despite the birth of a postindustrial world.

POLITICS AND GOVERNMENT

A cultural universal common to all economic systems is the exercise of power and authority. The struggle for power and authority inevitably involves *politics,* which political scientist Harold Lasswell (1936) defined as "who gets what, when, and how." In their study of politics and government, sociologists are concerned with social interactions among individuals and groups and their impact on the larger political and economic order.

Power

Power is at the heart of a political system. In Chapter 6, Max Weber's concept of power was examined, and *power* was defined as the ability to exercise one's will over others. To put it another way, if one party in a relationship can control the behavior of the other, that individual or group is exercising power. Power relations can involve large organizations, small groups, or even people in an intimate association.

There are three basic sources of power within any political system—force, influence, and authority. *Force* is the actual or threatened use of coercion to impose one's will on others. When leaders imprison or even execute political dissidents, they are applying force; so, too, are terrorists when they seize an embassy or assassinate a political leader. *Influence,* on the other hand, refers to the exercise of power through a process of persuasion. A citizen may change his or her position regarding a Supreme Court nominee because of a newspaper editorial, the expert testimony of a law school dean before the Senate Judiciary Committee, or a stirring speech at a rally by a political activist. In each case, sociologists would view such efforts to persuade people as examples of influence. The third source of power, *authority,* will be discussed in the next section of this chapter.

Types of Authority

The term *authority* refers to power that has been institutionalized and is recognized by the people over whom it is exercised. Sociologists commonly use the term in connection with those who hold legitimate power through elected or publicly acknowledged positions. It is important to stress that a person's authority is limited by the constraints of a particular social position. Thus, a referee has the authority to decide whether a penalty should be called during a football game but has no authority over the price of tickets to the game.

Max Weber (1947, original edition 1913) developed a classification system regarding authority that has become one of the most useful and frequently cited contributions of early sociology. He identified three ideal types of authority: traditional, legal-rational, and charismatic. Weber did not insist that only one type is accepted in a given society or organization. Rather, all can be present, but their relative importance will vary. Sociologists have found Weber's typology valuable in understanding different manifestations of legitimate power within a society.

A Yoruba king and elders in Nigeria. The king's young attendants carry his ceremonial swords, symbols of traditional authority.

Traditional Authority In a political system based on ***traditional authority,*** legitimate power is conferred by custom and accepted practice. The orders of one's superiors are felt to be legitimate because "this is how things have always been done." For example, a king or queen is accepted as ruler of a nation simply by virtue of inheriting the crown. The monarch may be loved or hated, competent or destructive; in terms of legitimacy, that does not matter. For the traditional leader, authority rests in custom, not in personal characteristics, technical competence, or even written law. Traditional authority is absolute in many instances because the ruler has the ability to determine laws and policies.

Legal-Rational Authority Power made legitimate by law is known as ***legal-rational authority.*** Leaders derive their legal-rational authority from the written rules and regulations of political systems. For example, the authority of the president of the United States and the Congress is legitimized by the Constitution. Generally, in societies that are based on legal-rational authority, leaders are conceived of as having specific areas of competence and authority. They are not viewed as having divine inspiration, as are the heads of certain societies with traditional forms of authority.

Charismatic Authority Weber also observed that power can be legitimized by the charisma of an individual. The term ***charismatic authority*** refers to power made legitimate by a leader's exceptional personal or emotional appeal to his or her followers. Charisma lets a person lead or inspire without relying on set rules or traditions. Interestingly, charismatic authority is derived more from the beliefs of followers than from the actual qualities of leaders. So long as people *perceive* a leader as having qualities setting him or her apart from ordinary citizens, that leader's authority will remain secure and often unquestioned.

Unlike traditional rulers, charismatic leaders often become well known by breaking with established institutions and advocating dramatic changes in the social structure and the economic system. Their strong hold over their followers makes it easier to build protest movements which challenge the dominant norms and values of a society. Thus, charismatic leaders such as Jesus, Joan of Arc, Mahatma Gandhi, Malcolm X, and Martin Luther King all used their power to press for changes in accepted social behavior. But so did Adolf Hitler, whose charismatic appeal turned people toward violent and destructive ends.

Weber used traditional, legal-rational, and charismatic authority as ideal types. In reality, particular leaders and political systems combine elements of two or more of these forms. Presidents Franklin D. Roosevelt, John F. Kennedy, and Ronald Reagan wielded power largely through legal-rational authority. At the same time, they were charismatic leaders who commanded the personal loyalty of large numbers of citizens.

POLITICAL BEHAVIOR IN THE UNITED STATES

As citizens of the United States, we take for granted many aspects of our political system. We are accustomed to living in a nation with a Bill of Rights, two major political parties, voting by secret ballot, an elected president, state and local governments distinct from the national government, and so forth.

Yet, of course, each society has its own ways of governing itself and making decisions. For example, just as we expect Democratic and Republican candidates to compete for public offices, residents of the People's Republic of China and Cuba are accustomed to the domination of the Communist party. In this section, we will examine a number of important aspects of political behavior within the United States.

Political Socialization

In Chapter 4, five functional prerequisites that a society must fulfill in order to survive were identified. Among these was the need to teach recruits to accept the values and customs of the group. In a political sense, this function is crucial; each succeeding generation must be encouraged to accept a society's basic political values and its particular methods of decision making.

Political socialization is the process by which individuals acquire political attitudes and develop patterns of political behavior. This involves not only learning the prevailing beliefs of a society but also coming to accept the surrounding political system despite its limitations and problems (Marger, 1981:321–323). In the United States, people are socialized to view representative democracy as the best form of government and to cherish such values as freedom, equality, patriotism, and the right of dissent.

Paul Conklin/Monkmeyer Press

In the United States, children are socialized to view representative democracy as the best form of government and to cherish such values as freedom, equality, and patriotism. One part of this socialization process is teaching children about symbols of the nation's political heritage.

The principal institutions of political socialization are those which also socialize us to other cultural norms—including the family, schools, and the media. Many observers see the family as playing a particularly significant role in the process. "The family incubates political man," observed political scientist Robert Lane (1959:204). In fact, parents pass on their political attitudes and evaluations to their sons and daughters through discussions at the dinner table and also through the example of their political involvement or apathy. Early socialization does not always *determine* a person's political orientation; there are changes over time and between generations. Yet research on political socialization continues to show that parents' views have an important impact on their children's outlook (Jennings and Niemi, 1981:384).

The schools can be influential in political socialization, since they provide young people with information and analysis of the political world. Unlike the family and peer groups, schools are easily susceptible to centralized and uniform control; consequently, totalitarian societies commonly use educational institutions for purposes of indoctrination. Yet, even in democracies, where local schools are not under the pervasive control of the national government, political education will generally reflect the norms and values of the prevailing political order.

In the view of conflict theorists, students in the United States learn much more than factual information about our political and economic way of life. They are socialized to view capitalism and representative democracy as the "normal" and most desirable ways of organizing a nation. At the same time, competing values and forms of government are often presented in a most negative fashion or are ignored. From a conflict perspective this type of political education serves the interests of the powerful and ignores the significance of the social divisions found within the United States (Marger, 1981:324–325).

Like the family and schools, the mass media can have obvious effects on people's thinking and political behavior—this is one reason why the media were included among the agents of socialization discussed in Chapter 3. Beginning with the Kennedy-Nixon presidential debates of 1960, television has given increasing exposure to political candidates. During the 1992 campaign, Democratic candidate Bill Clinton appeared on MTV and the *Arsenio Hall Show,* while independent challenger Ross Perot advocated use of electronic "town meetings." Today, many speeches given by our nation's leaders are designed not for immediate listeners but for the larger television audience.

Participation and Apathy

In theory, a representative democracy will function most effectively and fairly if there is an informed and active electorate communicating its views to government leaders. Unfortunately, this is hardly the case in the United States. Virtually all citizens are familiar with the basics of the political process, and most tend to identify to some extent with a political party (see Table 11-1), but only a small minority (often members of the higher social classes) actually participate in political organizations on a local or national level. Studies reveal that only 8 percent of people in the United States belong to a political club or organization. Not more than one in five has *ever* contacted an official of national, state, or local government about a political issue or problem (Orum, 1989:249).

TABLE 11-1 Political Party Preferences in the United States, 1991

PARTY IDENTIFICATION	PERCENTAGE OF POPULATION
Strong Democrat	15
Not very strong Democrat	21
Independent, close to Democrat	9
Independent	13
Independent, close to Republican	11
Not very strong Republican	19
Strong Republican	12

SOURCE: NORC, 1991:96.

According to the results of a national survey conducted in 1991, approximately 45 percent of the citizens of the United States identify to some extent with the Democratic party, while about 42 percent identify with the Republican party.

The failure of most citizens to become involved in political parties has serious implications for the functioning of our democracy. Within the political system of the United States, the political party serves as an intermediary between people and government. Through competition in regularly scheduled elections, the two-party system provides for challenges to public policies and for an orderly transfer of power. An individual dissatisfied with the state of the nation or a local community can become involved in the political party process many ways, such as by joining a political club supporting candidates for public office, or working to change the party's position on controversial issues. If, however, people do not take interest in the decisions of major political parties, public officials in a "representative" democracy will be chosen from two unrepresentative lists of candidates.

In the 1980s, it became clear that many people in the United States were turned off by political parties, politicians, and the specter of big government. The most dramatic indication of this growing alienation comes from voting statistics. Voters of all ages and races appear to be less enthusiastic than ever about elections, even presidential contests. For example, almost 80 percent of eligible voters in the United States went to the polls in the presidential election of 1896. Yet by the 1988 election, turnout had fallen to less than 58 percent of all eligible voters. By contrast, elections in the late 1980s brought out 84 percent or more of the voting-age population in Australia, France, Italy, the Netherlands, New Zealand, and Sweden (Cummings and Wise, 1989:349; Milbrath, 1981; Rodgers and Harrington, 1981:20–28).

Declining political participation allows institutions of government to operate with less of a sense of accountability to society. This issue is most serious for the least powerful individuals and groups within the United States. Voter turnout has been particularly low among younger adults and members of racial and ethnic minorities. In 1988, only 36 percent of eligible voters aged 18 to 20 went to the polls. According to a postelection survey, only 51.5 percent of Black voters and 28.8 percent of Hispanics reported that they had actually voted. Moreover, the poor—whose focus understandably is on survival—are traditionally underrepresented among voters as well. The low turnout

found among these groups is explained, at least in part, by their common feeling of powerlessness. Yet such voting statistics encourage political power brokers to continue to ignore the interests of the young, the less affluent, and the nation's minorities (Bureau of the Census, 1990a:439).

In 1992, the outpouring of support for Ross Perot's short-lived presidential candidacy underscored the fact that people were failing to vote or become involved in the political system because they were unhappy with both the Democratic and the Republican parties. According to a survey released in mid-1992 by pollster Gordon Black, based on questioning of a sample of 1600 likely voters, many people believe that the existing political parties are incapable of reform. Fifty-six percent of respondents stated that they were angry at *both* parties, while 69 percent agreed that current incumbents "will *never* reform" the political process (Ireland, 1992:8).

Cross-national comparisons, while confirming the relatively low level of voting in the United States, also suggest that we are *more* likely than citizens of other nations to be active at the community level, to contact local officials on behalf of ourselves or others, and to have worked for a political party. Perhaps this contrast reflects how unusual it is for people to be directly involved in national political decision making in the modern world. Nevertheless, it is possible that if tens of millions of people did not stay home on Election Day—and instead became more active in the nation's political life—the outcome of the political process might be somewhat different.

Women in Politics

In 1984, women in the United States achieved an unprecedented political breakthrough when Representative Geraldine Ferraro of New York became the Democratic nominee for vice president of the United States. Never before had a woman received the nomination of a major party for such high office.

Nevertheless, women continue to be dramatically underrepresented in the halls of government. The 103d Congress, which took office in January 1993, included 47 women (out of 435 members) in the House of Representatives and only 6 women (out of 100 members) in the Sen-

In 1992, in a dramatic breakthrough, California voters elected two women to the United States Senate: Diane Feinstein (left) and Barbara Boxer.

A new dimension of women and politics emerged beginning in the 1980s. Surveys detected a growing "gender gap" in the political preferences and activities of males and females. Women were more likely to register as Democrats than as Republicans and were also more critical of the policies of the Reagan and Bush administrations. According to political analysts, the Democratic party's continued support for the right to

FIGURE 11-1 Women in Government around the World

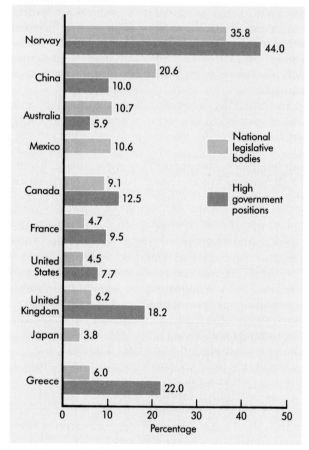

NOTE: Figure for "high government positions" in Mexico and Japan is zero.
SOURCES: Center for the American Woman and Politics, 1987; Inter-Parliamentary Union, 1990.

While women are more likely to hold top political offices in some countries than in others, nowhere do they reach parity with men. Shown above are figures for ten nations.

ate. While the number of women in state legislatures in 1993 was more than it was 20 years ago, only three states had women governors. As of 1992, women held no more than 18 percent of the available positions at any level of public office (Center for the American Woman and Politics, 1992a).

Sexism (see Chapter 8) has been the most serious barrier to women interested in holding office. Female candidates have had to overcome the prejudices of both men and women regarding women's fitness for leadership. Not until 1955 did a majority of people state that they would vote for a qualified woman for president. Moreover, women often encounter prejudice, discrimination, and abuse after they are elected.

Despite these problems, more women are being elected and more of them are identifying themselves as feminists. The traditional woman in politics was a widow who took office after her husband's death to continue his work and policies. However, women being elected in the 1990s are much more likely to view politics as their own career rather than as an afterthought. These trends are not restricted to the United States; Figure 11-1 shows the representation of women in the governments of 10 nations around the world.

choose a legal abortion is attracting women voters. At the same time, surveys show that women who hold public office are more feminist and more liberal than their male colleagues. While female officeholders are more likely to give priority to women's rights policies than are men, they are also more likely than men to show a distinctive concern for such areas as health care, children and the family, education, housing, and the elderly (Center for the American Woman and Politics, 1992b).

Politicians have begun to watch voting trends among women carefully, since women voters can prove decisive in close elections. In the 1990 elections for the House of Representatives, Election Day voter polls showed that women voted for Democratic candidates by a margin of 54 to 46 percent, while men split their votes evenly between Republican and Democratic candidates. Similarly, a gender gap was evident in the 1992 presidential race. Data from exit polls revealed that Bill Clinton won 45 percent of women's votes compared with 41 percent of men's votes. George Bush received 37 percent of women's votes and 38 percent of men's; independent candidate Ross Perot garnered 17 percent of women's votes and 21 percent of men's (S. Carroll, 1993; *New York Times*, 1990).

Interest Groups

This discussion of political behavior has focused primarily on individual participation (and nonparticipation) in decision-making processes of government and on involvement in the nation's political parties. However, there are other important ways that citizens can play a role in a nation's political arena. Because of common needs or common frustrations, people may band together in social movements such as the civil rights movement of the 1960s or the anti-nuclear power movement of the 1980s (A. Sherman and Kolker, 1987:17). We will consider social movements in more detail in Chapter 13. People can also influence the political process through membership in interest groups (some of which, in fact, may be part of larger social movements).

An *interest group* is a voluntary association of citizens who attempt to influence public policy. The National Organization for Women (NOW) is considered an interest group; so, too, are the Juvenile Diabetes Foundation and the National Rifle Association (NRA). Such groups are a vital part of the political process of the United States. Many interest groups (often known as *lobbies*) are national in scope and address a wide array of social, economic, and political issues.

One way in which interest groups influence the political process is through their political action committees. A *political action committee* (or *PAC*) is a political committee established by an interest group—a national bank, corporation, trade association, or cooperative or membership association—to accept voluntary contributions for candidates or political parties. The first political action committees were established in 1943 by organized labor. According to the Federal Election Commission, by 1976, there were 922 PACs; by 1990, there were more than 4000 (Minzesheimer, 1986).

These political action committees distribute substantial funds to candidates for public office. In the 1990 elections, for example, PACs gave congressional candidates nearly $159 million, of which $109 million was from PACs established by business groups and $37 million from labor PACs. The power of well-heeled PACs representing interest groups threatens the independence of lawmakers and, therefore, the integrity of the democratic process (*USA Today*, 1991a).

Interest groups are occasionally referred to as *pressure groups*—a term which implies that they attempt to force their will on a resistant public. In the view of functionalists, however, such groups play a constructive role in decision making by allowing orderly expression of public opinion and by increasing political participation. They also provide legislators with a useful flow of information.

Conflict theorists stress that although a very few organizations do work on behalf of the poor and disadvantaged, most interest groups in the United States represent affluent White professionals and business leaders. Studies show that Blacks running for public office receive substantially less money from PACs than do White candidates. From a conflict perspective, the overwhelming political clout of these powerful lobbies discourages participation by the individual citizen and raises serious questions about who actually rules a supposedly democratic nation (Wilhite and Theilmann, 1986).

By Mike Peters; reprinted by permission of UFS, Inc.

WHAT DO I DO? THIS CONGRESSMAN SAYS HE ALREADY SOLD HIS SOUL TO A POLITICAL ACTION COMMITTEE.

MODELS OF POWER STRUCTURE IN THE UNITED STATES

Who really holds power in the United States? Do "we the people" genuinely run the country through elected representatives? Or is it true that, behind the scenes, a small elite controls both the government and the economic system? It is difficult to determine the location of power in a society as complex as the United States. In exploring this critical question, social scientists have developed two basic views of our nation's power structure: the elite and the pluralist models.

Elite Model

Karl Marx essentially believed that nineteenth-century representative democracy was a sham. He argued that industrial societies were dominated by relatively small numbers of people who owned factories and controlled natural resources. In Marx's view, government officials and military leaders were essentially servants of the capitalist class and followed their wishes. Therefore, any key decisions made by politicians inevitably reflected the interests of the dominant bourgeoisie. Like others who hold an *elite model* of power relations, Marx thus believed that society is ruled by a small group of individuals who share a common set of political and economic interests.

The Power Elite In his pioneering work *The Power Elite*, sociologist C. Wright Mills described a small ruling elite of military, industrial, and governmental leaders who controlled the fate of the United States. Power rested in the hands of a few, both inside and outside government—the *power elite*. In Mills's words:

> The power elite is composed of men whose positions enable them to transcend the ordinary environments of ordinary men and women; they are in positions to make decisions having major consequences. . . . They are in command of the major hierarchies and organizations of modern society (1956:3–4).

In Mills's model, the power structure of the United States can be illustrated by the use of a pyramid (see Figure 11-2). At the top are the corporate rich, leaders of the executive branch of government, and heads of the military (whom Mills called the "warlords"). Below this triumvirate are local opinion leaders, members of the legislative branch of government, and leaders of special-interest groups. Mills contended that such individuals and groups would basically follow the wishes of the dominant power elite. At the bottom of society are the unorganized, exploited masses.

This power elite model is, in many respects, similar to the work of Karl Marx. The most striking difference is that Mills felt that the economically powerful coordinate their maneuvers with the military and political establishments in order to serve their mutual interests. Yet, reminiscent of Marx, Mills argued that the corporate rich were perhaps the most powerful element of the power elite (first among "equals"). And, of course, there is a further dramatic parallel between the work of these conflict theorists. The powerless masses at the bottom of Mills's power elite model certainly bring to mind Marx's portrait of the oppressed workers of the world, who have "nothing to lose but their chains."

A fundamental element in Mills's thesis is that the power elite not only has relatively few members but also operates as a self-conscious, cohesive unit. Although not necessarily diabolical or ruthless, the elite comprises similar types of people who regularly interact with one another and have essentially the same political and economic interests. Mills's power elite is not a conspiracy but rather a community of interest and sentiment among a small number of influential people (A. Hacker, 1964).

Admittedly, Mills failed to clarify when the elite acts against protests and when it tolerates them; he also failed to provide detailed case studies which would substantiate the interrelationship between members of the power elite. Nevertheless, his challenging theories forced scholars to look more critically at the "democratic" political system of the United States.

The Ruling Class Sociologist G. William Domhoff (1967, 1970, 1990) agreed with Mills that the United States is run by a powerful elite. But, rather than fully accepting Mills's power elite model, Domhoff (1983:1) argued that the nation is controlled by a social upper class "that is a ruling class by virtue of its dominant role in the economy and government." This socially cohesive ruling class owns 20 to 25 percent of all privately held wealth and 45 to 50 percent of all privately held common stock.

Unlike Mills, Domhoff (1983:17–55) was quite specific about who belongs to this social upper class. Membership comes through being part of a family recognized in *The Social Register*—the directory of the social elite in many cities in the United States. Attendance at prestigious private schools and membership in exclusive social clubs are further indications that a person comes from the social upper class. According to Domhoff, members of this class who hold leadership roles within the corporate community join with high-level employees of profit-making and nonprofit institutions controlled by the upper class to exercise power.

In Domhoff's view, the ruling class should not be seen in a conspiratorial way, as "sinister men lurking behind the throne." On the contrary they tend to hold public positions of authority. Almost all important appointive government posts— including those of diplomats and cabinet members—are filled by members of the social upper class. Domhoff contends that members of this class dominate powerful corporations, foundations, universities, and the executive branch of government. They control presidential nominations and the political party process through campaign contributions. In addition, the ruling class

FIGURE 11-2   C. Wright Mills's Model of the Power Structure of the United States

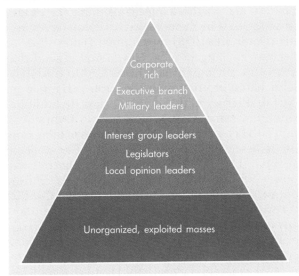

SOURCE: Adapted from Kornhauser, 1961:253.

In the view of sociologist C. Wright Mills, power in the United States rested in the hands of big business, the federal government, and the military. All other members of society played a secondary and largely irrelevant role in decision making.

exerts a significant (though not absolute) influence within Congress and units of state and local government (Domhoff, 1983:116–156; see also Steiber, 1979).

Perhaps the major difference between the elite models of Mills and Domhoff is that Mills insisted on the relative autonomy of the political elite and attached great significance to the independent power of the military. By contrast, Domhoff suggests that high-level government leaders and military leaders serve the interests of the social upper class. Both theorists, in line with a Marxian approach, assume that the rich are interested only in what benefits them financially. Furthermore, as advocates of elite models of power, Mills and Domhoff argue that the masses of people in the United States have no real influence on the decisions of the powerful (Eitzen, 1988:565–573).

Pluralist Model

Several social scientists have questioned the elite models of power relations proposed by Marx, Mills, Domhoff, and other conflict theorists. Quite simply, the critics insist that power in the United States is more widely shared than the elite model indicates. In their view, a pluralist model more accurately describes the nation's political system. According to the ***pluralist model,*** "many conflicting groups within the community have access to government officials and compete with one another in an effort to influence policy decisions" (Cummings and Wise, 1989:235).

Veto Groups David Riesman's *The Lonely Crowd* (Riesman et al., 1961) suggested that the political system of the United States could best be understood through examination of the power of veto groups. The term ***veto groups*** refers to interest groups that have the capacity to prevent the exercise of power by others. Functionally, they serve to increase political participation by preventing the concentration of political power. Examples cited by Riesman include farm groups, labor unions, professional associations, and racial and ethnic groups. Whereas Mills pointed to the dangers of rule by an undemocratic power elite, Riesman insisted that veto groups could effectively paralyze the nation's political processes by blocking *anyone* from exercising needed leadership functions. In Riesman's words, "The only leaders of national scope left in the United States are those who can placate the veto groups" (Riesman et al., 1961:247).

Dahl's Study of Pluralism Community studies of power have also supported the pluralist model. One of the most famous—an investigation of decision making in New Haven, Connecticut—was reported by Robert Dahl in his book, *Who Governs?* (1961). Dahl found that while the number of people involved in any important decision was rather small, community power was nonetheless diffuse. Few political actors exercised decision-making power on all issues. Therefore, one individual or group might be influential in a battle over urban renewal but at the same time might have little impact over educational policy. Several other studies of local politics, in such communities as Chicago and Oberlin, Ohio, further document that monolithic power structures do not operate on the level of local government.

Just as the elite model has been challenged on political and methodological grounds, the pluralist model has been subjected to serious questioning. Domhoff (1978) reexamined Dahl's study of decision making in New Haven and argued that Dahl and other pluralists had failed to trace how local elites prominent in decision making were part of a larger national ruling class. In addition, studies of community power, such as Dahl's work in New Haven, can examine decision making only on issues which become part of the political agenda. This focus fails to address the possible power of elites to keep certain matters entirely out of the realm of government debate. Conflict theorists contend that these elites will not allow any outcome of the political process which threatens their dominance. They may even be strong enough to block *discussion* of such measures by policymakers (P. Bachrach and Baratz, 1962:947–952; A. Sherman and Kolker, 1987:169–170).

We can end this discussion by reinforcing the one common point of the elite and pluralist perspectives—power in the political system of the United States is unequally distributed. All citizens may be equal in theory, yet those high in the nation's power structure are "more equal."

ASPECTS OF THE ECONOMY

Occupations and Professions

Whatever we call it—*job, work, occupation, gig, stint, position, duty,* or *vocation*—it is what we do for pay. The labor for which we are financially rewarded relates to our social behavior in a number of ways. As we saw in Chapter 3, preparation for work is a critical aspect of the socialization process. In addition, our social identities, or what Charles Horton Cooley termed the *looking-glass self,* are influenced by our work. A person who asks, "What do you do?" expects us to indicate our occupation. This underscores the importance of our work in defining who we are for others and, indeed, for ourselves. Of course, work has more than a symbolic significance; our positions in the stratification system are determined in good part by our occupations or those of the primary wage earners in our families.

In the United States and other contemporary societies, the majority of the paid labor force is involved in the service sector of the economy—providing health care, education, selling of goods, banking, and government. Along with the shift from manufacturing toward service industries, there has been a rise in the number of occupations that are viewed as professions. There is no single characteristic that defines a profession. In popular usage, the term *profession* is frequently used to convey a positive evaluation of work ("She's a real professional") or to denote full-time paid performance in a vocation (as in "professional golfer").

Sociologists use the term **profession** to describe an occupation requiring extensive knowledge which is governed by a code of ethics. Professionals tend to have a great degree of autonomy; they are not responsible to a supervisor for every action, nor do they have to respond to the customer's wishes. In general, professionals are their own authority in determining what is best for their clients.

It is widely agreed that medicine and law are professions, whereas driving a taxi is an occupation. However, when one considers such jobs as funeral director, firefighter, and pharmacist, it is not clear where "occupations" end and "professions" begin. Moreover, in recent decades, a growing number of occupational groups have claimed and even demanded professional status—often in an attempt to gain greater prestige and financial rewards. In certain instances, existing professions may object to the efforts of a related vocation to achieve designation as a profession. They may fear that a loss in business or clientele will result or that the status of their profession will

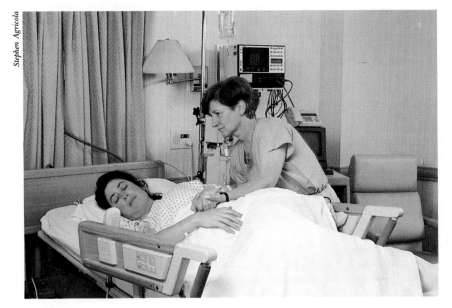

Stephen Agricola

The hostility of the medical profession toward midwives is an example of a conflict between an established profession and an occupation which has aspired to professional status. The photograph shows a midwife checking a pregnant woman in labor.

be downgraded if still more occupations are included. As we will see in Chapter 12, the hostility of the medical profession toward midwives is an example of such a conflict between an established profession and an occupation which has aspired to professional status.

In Chapter 4, it was noted that our society is increasingly dominated by large formal organizations with bureaucratic structures. Since autonomy is an important characteristic of professions, there is an inherent conflict in serving as a professional within a bureaucracy, such as being a staff physician in a hospital or a scientist in a corporation. The organization follows the principle of hierarchy and expects loyalty and obedience. Yet professionalism demands the individual responsibility of the practitioner. Bureaucracy fosters impersonality, yet professions emphasize close relations with one's professional colleagues. Consequently, working in a large organization represents a kind of trade-off for most professionals. While they resent limitations on their freedom and individual initiative, they appreciate the security that the organization provides (Pavalko, 1971:188–192; 1972:250–293).

Workers and the Workplace

For millions of men and women, work is a central activity of day-to-day life. Work may be satisfying or deadening; the workplace may be relatively democratic or totally authoritarian. Although the conditions and demands of people's work lives vary, there can be little doubt of the importance of work and workplace interactions in our society and others.

Work and Alienation: Marx's View All the pioneers of sociological thought were concerned that changes in the workplace resulting from the industrial revolution would have a negative impact on workers. Émile Durkheim (1933, original edition 1893) argued that as labor becomes more and more differentiated, individual workers will experience *anomie*, or a loss of direction. Workers cannot feel the same fulfillment from performing one specialized task in a factory as they did when they were totally responsible for creating a prod-

uct. As was noted in Chapter 4, Max Weber suggested that impersonality is a fundamental characteristic of bureaucratic organizations. One result is the cold and uncaring feeling often associated with contemporary bureaucracies. But the most penetrating analysis of the dehumanizing aspects of industrialization was offered by Karl Marx.

Marx believed that as the process of industrialization advanced within capitalist societies, people's lives became increasingly devoid of meaning. While Marx expressed concern about the damaging effects of many social institutions, he focused his attention on what he saw as a person's most important activity: labor. For Marx, the emphasis of the industrial revolution on specialization of factory tasks contributed to a growing sense of alienation among industrial workers (Erikson, 1986).

The term ***alienation*** refers to the situation of being estranged or disassociated from the surrounding society. The division of labor increased alienation because workers were channeled into monotonous, meaningless repetition of the same tasks. However, in Marx's view, an even deeper cause of alienation is the powerlessness of workers in a capitalist economic system. Workers have no control over their occupational duties, over the products of their labor, or over the distribution of profits. The very existence of private property within capitalism accelerates and intensifies the alienation of members of the working class, since they are constantly producing property which is owned by others (members of the capitalist class).

The solution to the problem of workers' alienation, according to Marx, is to give workers greater control over the workplace and over the products of their labor. Of course, Marx did not focus on limited reforms of factory life within the general framework of capitalist economic systems. Rather, he envisioned a revolutionary overthrow of capitalist oppression and a transition to collective ownership of the means of production (socialism) and eventually to the ideal of communism. Yet the actual trend in capitalist societies has been toward concentration of ownership by giant multinational corporations (refer back to Chapter 6).

BOX 11-2

FARM WORKERS AND THE ABOLITION OF THE SHORT-HANDLED HOE

Workers' dissatisfaction with a job often results from conditions unique to that industry. For farm workers in California, a hated implement, the short-handled hoe, was a central part of their dissatisfaction. Sociologist Douglas Murray (1982) studied the successful battle of farm workers to abolish use of this type of hoe.

Known to the overwhelmingly Mexican and Mexican American farm workers as *el cortito* (the "short one"), the short-handled hoe came to symbolize the oppressive working conditions of California farm labor. Growers claimed that the short-handled hoe enabled workers to achieve greater accuracy and efficiency than the long-handled hoe. However, farm workers believed that the true reason for growers' enthusiasm was that the short-handled hoe facilitated supervision of workers. One supervisor noted:

> With the long-handled hoe I can't tell whether they are working or just leaning on their hoes. With the short-handled hoe I know when they are not working by how often they stand up (Murray, 1982:28).

While the short-handled hoe may have been preferable for supervisors, workers quickly learned that use of this tool over a prolonged period could result in degeneration of the spine and permanent disabilities. Hector de la Rosa, a farm worker, said of *el cortito*:

> When I used the short-handled hoe my head would ache and my eyes hurt because of the pressure of bending down so long. My back would hurt whenever I stood up or bent over. I moved down the rows as fast as I could so I could get to the end and rest my back for a moment (Murray, 1982:29).

In hearings before California's Industrial Safety Board, physicians and medical specialists testified that use of the short-handled hoe had a damaging impact on a worker's spine. Nevertheless, growers continued to defend *el cortito*, in part because it increased turnover among farm workers.

The growers found it beneficial to rely on a steady (and steadily changing) supply of cheap labor coming from Mexico, along with Mexican Americans living in California.

Beginning in 1969, attorneys from California Rural Legal Assistance campaigned to prohibit the use of the short-handled hoe. They were supported by Cesar Chavez and the United Farm Workers union (UFW) and were opposed by growers and other agribusiness interests. After Jerry Brown, an ally of the UFW, became governor of California in 1975, the state's Division of Industrial Safety quickly issued a ruling banning use of the short-handled hoe.

The abolition of *el cortito* led to an important improvement in the working conditions of farm workers; some growers reported substantial decreases in workers' compensation claims for back injuries after the state ruling. Moreover, the farm workers' victory encouraged activism on other health-related issues, among them the hazards of workers' exposure to pesticides.

In the 1980s, the term *burnout* was increasingly being used to describe the occupational stress experienced by a wide variety of workers, including professionals, self-employed people, and even unpaid volunteers. Whereas Marx had focused on alienation among the proletarians, whom he viewed as powerless to effect change within capitalist institutions, the broader concept of work-related anxiety now covers alienation among more affluent workers who have a greater degree of control over their working conditions. From a conflict perspective, we have thereby masked the fact that alienation falls most heavily on the lower and working classes by making it appear to be endemic from the boardroom to the shop floor (Walker, 1986).

Workers' Satisfaction Workers' alienation (as measured by their dissatisfaction) is an admittedly elusive concept for researchers, since a worker can be more alienated at one job than at another without necessarily feeling unhappy. Most studies of alienation have focused on how structural changes in the economy serve to increase or decrease workers' satisfaction. In general, people with greater responsibility for a finished product (such as white-collar professionals and managers) experience less of a sense of alienation than those with little responsibility.

For both women and men working in blue-collar jobs, the repetitive nature of work can be particularly unsatisfying. Moreover, as is discussed in Box 11-2 (on page 309), the strain of day-to-day work in certain occupations not only alienates workers but can also lead to significant health hazards.

Robert Blauner's research (1964) revealed that printers—who often work in small shops and supervise apprentices—were more satisfied with their work than laborers on automobile assembly lines who performed repetitive tasks. However, William Form (1967) found that automobile workers in the United States, Italy, India, and Argentina were fairly satisfied with their work. In part, this may be because monotonous work does not *necessarily* lead to alienation. Sociologist Clark Molstad (1986) found that some workers prefer the safety and security of boring tasks. They want to avoid jobs with great responsibility and many "hassles."

How do we reconcile these positive reports with the concerns that were expressed by Durkheim, Weber, and Marx regarding alienation among workers?

A number of general factors can be identified which reduce the level of dissatisfaction of contemporary industrial workers. Higher wages give workers a sense of accomplishment apart from the task before them. A shortened workweek has increased the amount of time that people can devote to recreation and leisure, thereby reducing some of the discontent stemming from the workplace. For example, the average industrial worker spent 60 hours a week on the job in 1880, compared with the 40-hour workweek which began in the 1930s. Unions have given many workers an opportunity to exercise some influence in decision making. Finally, numerous studies from an interactionist perspective have shown that positive relationships with coworkers—often including the use of humor—can make a boring job tolerable or even enjoyable (Bureau of the Census, 1975; Seckman and Couch, 1989).

SOCIAL POLICY, GOVERNMENT, AND THE ECONOMY

SEXUAL HARASSMENT

- In legal terms, is sexual harassment considered a form of sex discrimination?

- Viewed from a conflict perspective, how do the data on sexual harassment reflect inequities based on gender and race?

- How have women's concerns about sexual harassment influenced the political system of the United States?

In 1991, the issue of sexual harassment received unprecedented attention in the United States, as Supreme Court nominee (now Associate Justice) Clarence Thomas was accused of repeatedly harassing a former aide, law professor Anita Hill, over a period of years. But Anita Hill is far from alone in making such a complaint about a coworker. Whether they hold managerial or clerical positions, whether they work in a voluntary association or a Fortune 500 corporation, women report being victimized by sexual harassment.

Dennis Brack/Black Star

Law professor Anita Hill is shown during her 1991 testimony before the Senate Judiciary Committee, in which she accused Supreme Court nominee (now Associate Justice) Clarence Thomas of repeatedly sexually harassing her over a period of years.

Under evolving legal standards, **sexual harassment** is recognized as any unwanted and unwelcome sexual advances that interfere with a person's ability to perform a job and enjoy the benefits of a job. The most blatant example is the boss who tells a subordinate: "Put out or get out!" However, the unwelcome advances which constitute sexual harassment may take the form of subtle pressures regarding sexual activity, inappropriate sexual language, inappropriate touching, attempted kissing or fondling, demands for sexual favors, or sexual assault.

Women of all ages and racial and ethnic groups—and men as well—have been the victims of sexual harassment. Attorney and political scientist Catharine MacKinnon (1979), the author of one of the first examinations of sexual harassment of working women, has observed that such harassment may occur as a single encounter or as a repeated pattern of behavior. Throughout the United States, sexual harassment occurs with alarming frequency. Studies suggest that anywhere from 42 to 90 percent of women—and at least 14 percent of men—will experience some form of harassment in their work outside the home. Obviously, experiencing sexual harassment can have a shattering impact on an employee's satisfaction on the job (Havemann, 1988; A. Hill, 1992).

In the 1986 case of *Meritor Savings Bank v. Vinson*, the Supreme Court unanimously held that sexual harassment by a supervisor violates federal law against sex discrimination in the workplace, as outlined in the 1964 Civil Rights Act. If sufficiently severe, sexual harassment constitutes a violation of the law even if the unwelcome sexual demands are not linked to concrete employment benefits such as a raise or a promotion. The justices ruled that the existence of a hostile or abusive work environment—in which a woman feels degraded as the result of unwelcome flirtation or obscene joking—may in itself constitute illegal sex discrimination. In 1991, a federal judge ruled that the public display of photographs of nude and partly nude women at a workplace constitutes sexual harassment (T. Lewin, 1991; Withers and Benaroya, 1989:6–7).

Sexual harassment has been commonly reported not only in the federal workplace and in private-sector organizations, but also in institutions of higher learning. According to a study conducted in the period 1982 to 1985, more than half of female students at the nation's colleges and universities experience some form of sexual harassment, ranging from verbal abuse to unwanted sexual contact or rape. More than 20 percent of female students are sexually propositioned or harassed by their instructors (Brodkey and Fine, 1988; Fitzgerald et al., 1988).

Whether it occurs in the federal bureaucracy, in the corporate world, or in universities, sexual harassment generally occurs in organizations in which the hierarchy of authority finds White males at the top. One survey in the private sector found that Black women were three times more likely than White women to experience sexual harassment. From a conflict perspective, it is not surprising that women, and especially women of color, are most likely to become victims of sexual harassment; these groups are typically an organization's most vulnerable employees in terms of job security (J. Jones, 1988).

While it is agreed that sexual harassment is widespread in the United States, it is nevertheless clear that most victims do not report these abuses to proper authorities. For example, in a survey of federal government employees conducted in 1988, only 5 percent of those who had been harassed stated that they had filed complaints. "It takes a lot of self-confidence to fight," suggests Catherine Broderick, a lawyer for the Securities and Exchange Commission (SEC) who won a sexual harassment complaint against the agency's Washington office. Broderick had refused her supervisor's advances and then had been repeatedly denied promotions. After a nine-year legal battle, Broderick was victorious in court and won a promotion and years of back pay. Still, her experience is a reminder that pursuing justice against those guilty of sexual harassment can be costly and draining (Havemann, 1988; Saltzman, 1988:56–57).

Even if the victim does have the will to fight, the process of making a sexual harassment complaint in the courts or in most bureaucracies is slow and burdensome. In early 1992, Evan Kemp, head of the federal Equal Employment Opportunity Commission (EEOC), admitted that a woman who has filed a complaint of sexual harassment may have to wait as long as *four years* to get a hearing before the EEOC. The agency has a huge caseload; it receives 60,000 complaints of discrimination each year and also oversees 50,000 others that are handled by state fair-employment agencies. Yet EEOC's funding is clearly inadequate to investigate all these cases (Hentoff, 1992:20–21).

Nevertheless, in the aftermath of Anita Hill's testimony before the Senate Judiciary Committee, women are speaking out as never before about sexual harassment. According to the EEOC, the number of complaints of sexual harassment filed in the first nine months of the 1992 fiscal year was higher than in all of fiscal 1991. Moreover, the political system is responding to allegations of sexual abuse in ways that were hardly common before the Senate hearings. In a recent example, the secretary of the Navy resigned in 1992—and Congress delayed hundreds of Navy and Marine Corps promotions—in reaction to a scandal that erupted after at least 26 naval women were harassed by 70 or more naval aviators at their annual Tailhook convention (Edmonds, 1992).

Some observers believe that public officials are taking the issue of sexual harassment more seriously because they believe their political futures are at stake. Indeed, the intense anger of many women about what they viewed as the (all-male) Senate Judiciary Committee's mistreatment of Anita Hill led to greatly increased support in 1992 for interest groups and political action committees backing female candidates for higher office. With the gender gap in evidence, four female candidates critical of the Judiciary Committee's actions defeated male opponents in 1992 Democratic senatorial primaries in California, Illinois, and Pennsylvania—and three were subsequently elected to office.

The battle against sexual harassment is being fought not only in the United States but around the world. In 1991, the European Economic Community established a code of conduct which holds employers ultimately responsible for combating such behavior. In 1992, France joined many European countries in banning sexual harassment. That same year, in an important victory for Japan's feminist movement, a district court ruled that a small publishing company and one of its male employees had violated the rights of a female employee because of crude remarks that led her to quit her job. The complainant had charged that her male supervisor had spread rumors about her, telling others that she was promiscuous. When she attempted to get him to stop making such comments, she was advised to quit her job. In the view of Yukido Tsunoda, a lawyer for the complainant: "Sexual harassment is a big problem in Japan, and we hope this will send a signal to men that they have to be more careful" (Riding, 1992; Weisman, 1992:A3).

SUMMARY

The **economic system** of a society has an important influence on social behavior and on other social institutions. Each society must have a **political system** in order to have recognized procedures for the allocation of valued resources. This chapter examines the economic systems found in preindustrial and **industrial societies;** it also examines the dimensions of the political system of the United States, and the social nature of the workplace.

1 Sociologists Gerhard Lenski and Jean Lenski have categorized preindustrial societies as **hunting-and-gathering societies, horticultural societies,** and **agrarian societies.**

2 Economic systems of **capitalism** vary in the degree to which private ownership and economic activity are regulated by government, but all emphasize the profit motive.

3 In a **postindustrial society,** large numbers of people become involved in teaching and disseminating ideas.

4 There are three basic sources of **power** within any political system: these sources are **force, influence,** and **authority.**

5 Max Weber provided one of the most useful and frequently cited contributions of early sociology by identifying three ideal types of authority: **traditional, legal-rational,** and **charismatic.**

6 The principal institutions of **political socialization** in the United States are the family, schools, and media.

7 Women are becoming more successful at winning election to public office.

8 Advocates of the **elite model** of the power structure of the United States see the nation as being ruled by a small group of individuals who share common political and economic interests, whereas advocates of a **pluralist model** believe that power is more widely shared among conflicting groups.

9 In comparison with other occupations, **professions** tend to have a great deal of autonomy.

10 Karl Marx believed that the powerlessness of workers under capitalism was a primary cause of **alienation.**

11 **Sexual harassment** has been commonly reported not only in the federal workplace and in private-sector organizations but also in institutions of higher education.

CRITICAL THINKING QUESTIONS

1 The United States has long been put forward as the model of a capitalist society. Drawing on material in earlier chapters of the textbook, discuss the values and beliefs that have led people in the United States to cherish a laissez-faire, capitalist economy. To what degree have these values and beliefs changed during the twentieth century? What aspects of socialism are now evident in the nation's economy? Have there been basic changes in our values and beliefs to support certain principles traditionally associated with socialist societies?

2 During the 1992 elections in the United States, many commentators referred to that year as the "Year of the Woman." How could you use experiments, observation research, surveys, and unobtrusive measures to study public attitudes toward electing women to high governmental office?

3 Who really holds power in the college or university that you attend? Describe the distribution of power at your school, drawing on the elite and pluralist models where they are relevant.

KEY TERMS

Agrarian society The most technologically advanced form of preindustrial society. Members are primarily engaged in the production of food but increase their crop yield through such innovations as the plow. (page 292)

Alienation The situation of being estranged or disassociated from the surrounding society. (308)

Authority Power that has been institutionalized and is recognized by the people over whom it is exercised. (297)

Capitalism An economic system in which the means of production are largely in private hands, and the main incentive for economic activity is the accumulation of profits. (293)

Charismatic authority Max Weber's term for power made legitimate by a leader's exceptional personal or emotional appeal to his or her followers. (298)

Communism As an ideal type, an economic system under which all property is communally owned and no social distinctions are made on the basis of people's ability to produce. (295)

Economic system The social institution through which goods and services are produced, distributed, and consumed. (290)

Elite model A view of society as ruled by a small group of individuals who share a common set of political and economic interests. (304)

Force The actual or threatened use of coercion to impose one's will on others. (297)

Horticultural societies Preindustrial societies in which people plant seeds and crops rather than subsist merely on available foods. (292)

Hunting-and-gathering society A preindustrial society in which people rely on whatever foods and fiber are readily available in order to live. (292)

Industrial revolution A scientific revolution, largely occurring in England between 1760 and 1830, which focused on the application of nonanimal sources of power to labor tasks. (293)

Industrial society A society which relies chiefly on mechanization for the production of its economic goods and services. (293)

Influence The exercise of power through a process of persuasion. (297)

Interest group A voluntary association of citizens who attempt to influence public policy. (303)

Laissez-faire A form of capitalism under which people compete freely, with minimal government intervention in the economy. (293)

Legal-rational authority Max Weber's term for power made legitimate by law. (298)

Monopoly Control of a market by a single business firm. (294)

Pluralist model A view of society in which many conflicting groups within a community have access to governmental officials and compete with one another in an attempt to influence policy decisions. (306)

Political action committee (PAC) A political committee established by an interest group—a national bank, corporation, trade association, or cooperative or membership association—to accept voluntary contributions for candidates or political parties. (303)

Political socialization The process by which individuals acquire political attitudes and develop patterns of political behavior. (299)

Political system The social institution which relies on a recognized set of procedures for implementing and achieving the goals of a group. (291)

Politics In Harold D. Lasswell's words, "who gets what, when, how." (297)

Postindustrial society As defined by Daniel Bell, a society whose economic system is based on the production of information rather than the production of goods. (295)

Power The ability to exercise one's will over others. (297)

Power elite A term used by C. Wright Mills for a small group of military, industrial, and government leaders who control the fate of the United States. (304)

Pressure groups A term sometimes used to refer to interest groups. (303)

Profession An occupation requiring extensive knowledge and governed by a code of ethics. (307)

Sexual harassment Any unwanted and unwelcome sexual advances that interfere with a person's ability to perform a job and enjoy the benefits of a job. (311)

Socialism An economic system under which the means of production and distribution are collectively owned. (294)

Social surplus The production by a group of people of enough goods to cover their own needs, while at the same time sustaining individuals who are not engaged in agricultural tasks. (292)

Technology The application of knowledge to the making of tools and the utilization of natural resources. (292)

Traditional authority Legitimate power conferred by custom and accepted practice. (298)

Veto groups David Riesman's term for interest groups that have the capacity to prevent the exercise of power by others. (306)

ADDITIONAL READINGS

Bensman, David, and Roberta Lynch. *Rusted Dreams: Hard Times in a Steel Community*. New York: McGraw-Hill, 1987. An analysis of a southeast Chicago neighborhood hit hard by plant closings that threw half the local labor force out of work.

DeVault, Marjorie L. *Feeding the Family: The Social Organization of Caring as Gendered Work*. Chicago: University of Chicago Press, 1991. On the basis of interviews in the United States, a sociologist explores the role of women in providing food for their families and how this single activity so defines their lives.

Enloe, Cynthia. *Bananas, Beaches, and Bases: Making Feminist Sense of International Politics*. Berkeley: University of California Press, 1990. Enloe studied the lives of women on military bases and diplomatic wives as part of her examination of the male-determined agenda of international politics.

Mills, C. Wright. *The Power Elite*. New York: Oxford University Press, 1956. Mills argues that the United States is ruled by an elite consisting of the "political directorate," "corporate rich," and "warlords."

Statham, Ann, Eleanor M. Miller, and Hans O. Mauksch (eds.). *The Worth of Women's Work*. Albany: State University of New York Press, 1988. An examination of women's work both inside and outside the home.

Terkel, Studs. *Working*. New York: Random House, 1974. The best-selling author presents the concerns and problems of men and women engaged in a variety of occupations.

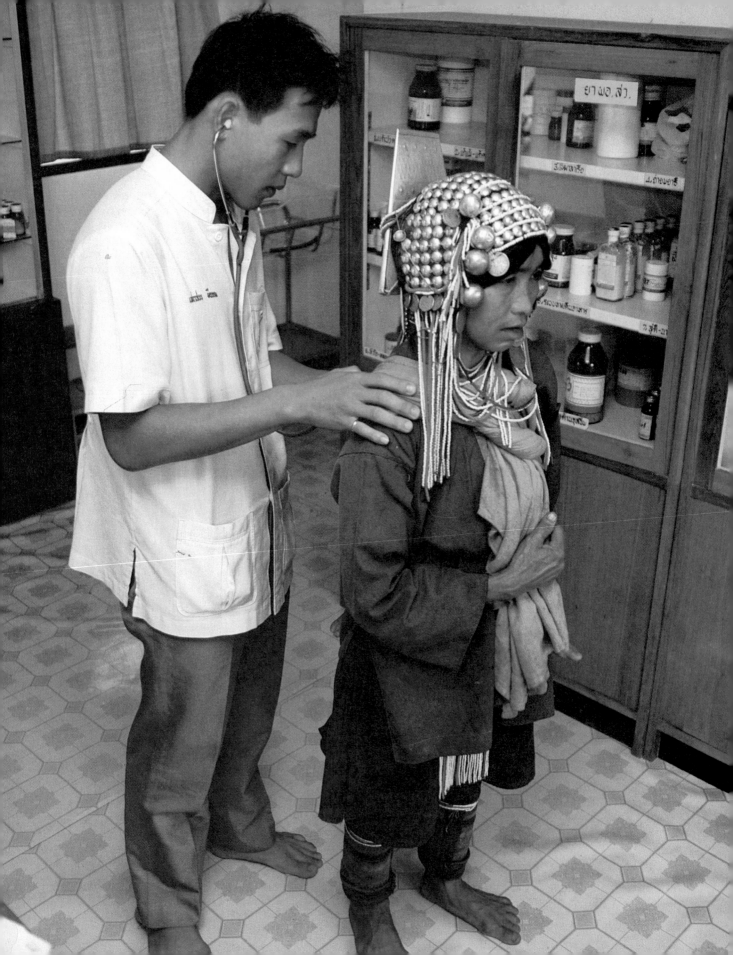

12

HEALTH AND POPULATION

LOOKING AHEAD

- In what ways are health and illness socially defined?
- How does medicine function as a mechanism of social control?
- Does gender, social class, race, or ethnicity influence a person's likelihood of experiencing illness, disease, and disability?
- What role has the federal government played in providing and financing health

care for United States citizens?
- Why did Karl Marx disagree with Thomas Robert Malthus's view that rising world population was the cause of social ills?
- How does the concept of demographic transition help us to understand world population history?
- Should the United States institute a program of national health insurance for all citizens?

Health care and population concerns are inevitably intertwined within a culture. In villages in Africa and other Third World regions where death is common among infants and children, villagers place a high cultural value on large families. By contrast, infant and child deaths are uncommon in the United States.

The population-related realities of these different types of societies lead to dramatically different demands on their health care systems. In industrialized nations, death is often a terminal event which follows a long series of debilitating chronic diseases. Consequently, the medical system is focused on providing extended care for a population which is increasingly aging and disabled. In developing countries, however, greater priority must be given to maternity and infant care—especially treatment of infectious and parasitic diseases. There is much less need for long-term hospitalization, in part because fewer people reach old age (W. Mosley and Cowley, 1991:3).

In this chapter, we will consider a sociological overview of health, illness, medicine as a social institution, and certain aspects of population as studied by sociologists. We will begin by examining how functionalists, conflict theorists, interactionists, and labeling theorists look at health-related issues. Then we will study the distribution of diseases in a society by gender, social class, and race and ethnicity. Sociologists are interested in the roles that people play within the health care system and the organizations that deal with issues of health and sickness. Therefore, we will analyze the interactions among doctors, nurses, and patients, and the role of government in providing health services to the needy.

In the second half of the chapter, we will examine the controversial analysis of population trends presented by Thomas Robert Malthus and the critical response of Karl Marx. The special terminology used in population research will be detailed, and a brief overview of world population history will be offered. Particular attention will be given to the current problem of overpopulation and to the prospects for and potential social consequences of stable population growth in the United States. Finally, the social policy section will consider whether the United States should follow the lead of other western democracies by establishing a national health care system or providing national health insurance.

SOCIOLOGICAL PERSPECTIVES ON HEALTH AND ILLNESS

From a sociological point of view, social factors contribute to the evaluation of a person as "healthy" or "sick." How, then, can we define health?

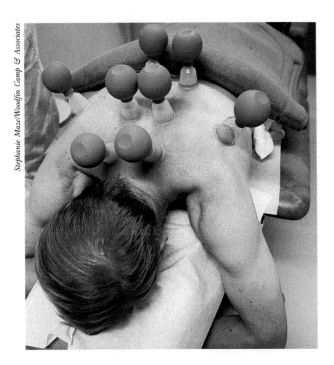

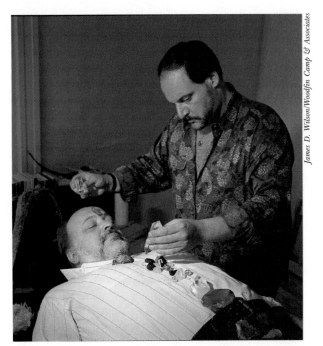

Health care takes many forms around the world. Cupping—a traditional practice used in ancient China, India, Egypt, Greece, and Rome—survives in modern Finland. Physiotherapists use suction cups to draw out blood in order to lower blood pressure, improve circulation, and relieve muscular pain. Also shown is a session of crystal healing in the United States.

We can imagine a continuum with health on one end and death on the other. In the preamble to its 1946 constitution, the World Health Organization defined *health* as a "state of complete physical, mental, and social well-being, and not merely the absence of disease and infirmity" (Leavell and Clark, 1965:14). With this definition in mind, the "healthy" end of our continuum represents an ideal toward which we are oriented rather than a precise condition that we expect to attain. Along the continuum, people define themselves as "healthy" or "sick" on the basis of criteria established by each individual, relatives, friends, co-workers, and medical practitioners. This relativistic approach to health allows us to view it in a social context and to consider how it varies in different situations or cultures (Twaddle, 1974; Wolinsky, 1980:64–98).

Who controls definitions of health and illness in our society, and for what ends? What are the consequences of viewing oneself (or being viewed) as ill or disabled? Drawing on four sociological perspectives—functionalism, conflict theory, interactionism, and labeling theory—we can gain greater insight into the social context shaping definitions of health and treatment of illness.

Functionalist Approach

Although illness is a phenomenon evident in all societies, functionalists contend that an overly broad definition of illness would impose serious difficulties on the workings of a society. Illness entails at least a temporary disruption in a person's social interactions both at work and at home. Consequently, from a functionalist perspective, "being sick" must be controlled so as to ensure that not too many people are released from their societal responsibilities at any one time.

"Sickness" requires that one take on a social role, even if temporarily. The term *sick role* refers to societal expectations about the attitudes and behavior of a person viewed as being ill (King, 1972). Sociologist Talcott Parsons (1951:428–

479; 1972; 1975), well known for his contributions to functionalist theory (see Chapter 1), has outlined the behavior required of people considered "sick." They are exempted from their normal, day-to-day responsibilities and generally are not blamed for their condition. Yet they are obligated to try to get well, and this may include seeking competent professional care. Attempting to get well is particularly important in the world's developing countries. In modern automated industrial societies, we can absorb a greater degree of illness or disability, but in horticultural or agrarian societies workers' availability is a much more critical concern (Mechanic, 1978:84–85; H. Schwartz, 1987:23–24).

According to Parsons' theory, physicians function as "gatekeepers" for the sick role, either verifying a patient's condition as "illness" or designating the patient as "recovered." The ill person becomes dependent on the doctor, because the latter can control valued rewards (not only treatment of illness, but also excused absences from work and school). Parsons suggests that the doctor-patient relationship is somewhat like that between parent and child. Like a parent, the physician grants the patient the privilege of returning to society as a full and functioning adult (Bloom and Wilson, 1979; Freidson, 1970:206; Parsons and Fox, 1952).

There have been a number of criticisms of the concept of the sick role. In the view of some observers, patients' judgments regarding their own state of health may be related to their gender, age, social class, and ethnic group. The sick role may be more applicable to people experiencing sudden, short-term illnesses than to those with recurring, long-term illnesses. Even simple factors such as whether a person is employed or not seem to affect willingness to assume the sick role. Nonetheless, sociologists continue to rely on Parsons' model for functionalist analysis of the relationship between illness and societal expectations for the sick.

Conflict Approach

Whereas functionalists seek to explain how health care systems meet the needs of society as well as those of individual patients and medical practitioners, conflict theorists take issue with this view.

They express concern that the profession of medicine has assumed a preeminence that extends well beyond whether to excuse a student from school or an employee from work. Sociologist Eliot Freidson (1970:5) has likened the position of medicine today "to that of state religions yesterday—it has an officially approved monopoly of the right to define health and illness and to treat illness." Conflict theorists use the term "medicalization of society" to refer to the growing role of medicine as a major institution of social control (Conrad and Schneider, 1980; McKinlay and McKinlay, 1977; Zola, 1972, 1983).

How is such social control manifested? First, medicine has greatly expanded its domain of expertise in recent decades. Society tolerates such expansion of the boundaries of medicine because we hope that these experts can bring new "miracle cures" to complex human problems as they have to the control of certain infectious diseases. Consequently, as the medicalization of society has proceeded in the twentieth century, physicians have become much more involved in examining a wide range of issues, among them sexuality (including homosexuality), old age, anxiety, obesity, child development, alcoholism, and drug addiction. The social significance of medicalization is that once a problem is viewed using a *medical model*—once medical experts become influential in proposing and assessing relevant public policies—it becomes more difficult for "common people" to join the discussion and to exert influence on decision making. It also becomes more difficult to view these issues as being shaped by social, cultural, or psychological factors, rather than by physical or medical factors (R. Caplan, 1989; Conrad and Kern, 1986:378; Conrad and Schneider, 1980; Starr, 1982).

Second, medicine serves as an agent of social control by retaining absolute jurisdiction over many health care procedures. It has even attempted to guard its jurisdiction by placing health care professionals such as chiropractors and nurse-midwives outside the realm of acceptable medicine. Despite the fact that midwives first brought professionalism to child delivery, they have been portrayed as having invaded the "legitimate" field of obstetrics. Nurse-midwives have sought licensing as a means of achieving professional respectability, but physicians continue to exert power to ensure that midwifery remains a subordinate occupation (M. Radosh, 1984; P. Radosh, 1986; Zia, 1990; Zola, 1972).

The medicalization of society is but one concern of conflict theorists as they assess the workings of health care institutions. As we have seen throughout this textbook, when analyzing any issue, conflict theorists seek to determine who benefits, who suffers, and who dominates at the expense of others. Viewed from a conflict perspective, there are certainly glaring inequalities in health care delivery. For example, there are 470 people per physician in the United States, while African nations have 26,000 to 80,000 people per physician. Within the United States, as well, there is an unequal distribution of medical services on the basis of both income and geographical location of facilities and personnel—an inequality that leaves poor and rural areas underserved (World Bank, 1992:272–273).

Conflict theorists emphasize that such inequities in health care resources have clear life-and-death consequences. For example, in the period 1990 to 1991, the *infant mortality rate* (the number of deaths of infants under 1 year of age per 1000 live births in a given year) ranged as high as 139 per 1000 live births in Ethiopia and 114 in Nigeria. By contrast, Sweden's infant mortality rate was only 5.8 infant deaths per 1000 live births and Japan's was only 4.6. From a conflict perspective, the dramatic differences in infant mortality rates around the world (see Figure 12-1) reflect, at least in part, unequal distribution of health care resources based on the wealth or poverty of various communities and nations.

In the period 1990 to 1991, the United States had a rate of 9.0 infant deaths per 1000 live births (although it is estimated that the rate in some poor, inner-city neighborhoods in this country exceeds 30 deaths per 1000 live births). Yet, despite the wealth of the United States, at least 26 nations have lower infant mortality rates, among them Great Britain, Canada, Taiwan, and Japan. Conflict theorists point out that, unlike the United States, many of these 26 countries offer some form of government-supported health care for all citizens, which typically leads to greater availability and greater use of prenatal care than is the case in this country (Haub and Yanagishita, 1992).

FIGURE 12-1   Infant Mortality Rates, 1990–1991

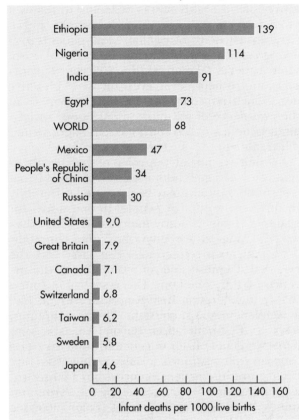

SOURCE: Haub and Yanagishita, 1992.

Infant mortality rates vary dramatically from nation to nation. The United States has a comparatively low rate, but several other nations (including Great Britain, Canada, Switzerland, Taiwan, Sweden, and Japan, as shown here) have still lower rates.

Interactionist Approach

In examining health, illness, and medicine as a social institution, interactionists generally focus on micro-level study of the roles played by health care professionals and patients. They emphasize that the patient should not always be viewed as passive, but instead as an actor who often shows a powerful intent to see the physician (Alonzo, 1989; Zola, 1983:59).

One way in which patients sometimes play an active role in health care is by failing to follow a physician's advice. For example, despite physicians' instructions, nearly half of all patients stop taking medications long before they should. Also, some patients take an incorrect dosage on purpose, and others never even fill their prescriptions. Such noncompliance results in part from the prevalence of self-medication: in our society, many people are accustomed to self-diagnosis and self-treatment.

In their studies of the roles played by physicians and patients, interactionists point out that the same symptoms may be presented differently by different groups of people. In one study, for example, patients were interviewed while they were waiting to see physicians; the symptoms these patients presented were compared with the eventual diagnosis and an evaluation of the urgency of the condition. The researchers found that first-generation Irish American patients had a tendency to understate their symptoms, whereas first-generation Italian American patients were more likely to generalize and overstate their symptoms. Such results remind us that health care interactions occur within a larger social context and are influenced by the norms and values of distinctive subcultures (Zola, 1966; see also Wolinsky, 1980:67–68).

Labeling Approach

In studying deviance, we used labeling theory to understand why certain people are *viewed* as deviants, "bad kids," or criminals whereas others whose behavior is similar are not (see Chapter 5). Labeling theorists also suggest that the designation "healthy" or "ill" generally involves social definition by significant others. Just as police, judges, and other regulators of social control have the power to define certain people as criminals, health care professionals (especially physicians) have the power to define certain people as "sick." Moreover, like labels that suggest nonconformity or criminality, labels associated with illness commonly reshape how we are treated by others and how we see ourselves. In our society serious consequences are attached to labels which suggest imperfect physical or mental health (Becker, 1963; C. Clark, 1983; H. Schwartz, 1987:82–84).

By the late 1980s, the power of a label— "person with AIDS"—had become quite evident. Once someone is told by a physician that he or she has tested positive for HIV, the virus associated with AIDS, immediate and difficult questions must then be faced. Should one tell one's family members, one's spouse or lover, one's friends, one's coworkers, one's employer? How will these people respond? As discussed in the social policy

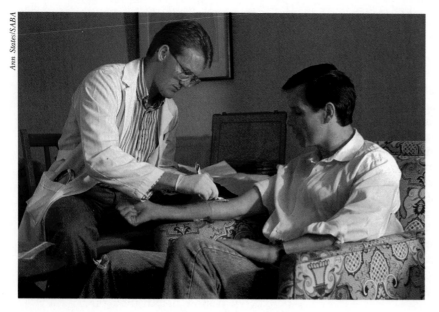

A physician is shown giving home care to a man with AIDS. A person who has AIDS must deal not only with the devastating medical consequences of the disease itself but also with the distressing social consequences of a feared label.

section of Chapter 4, people's intense fear of this deadly disease has led to prejudice and discrimination—even social ostracism—against those who have (or are suspected of having) AIDS. Consequently, a person who has AIDS must deal not only with the devastating medical consequences of the disease, but also with the distressing social consequences associated with this feared label.

Labeling theorists argue that even physical traits can, in a sense, be socially "created" through labels. Applying labeling theory to treatment of the blind, health statistician Marc Berk (1985) examined rates of reported blindness throughout New York State—where physicians and optometrists are required by law to report the names of blind patients. Berk found that in counties with a higher proportion of physicians and optometrists, a higher proportion of residents are classified as blind. He found no similar pattern involving the distribution of health care professionals and reported rates of infectious diseases. Berk's research suggests that deviance is indeed in the "eye of the beholder" (or, more accurately, in the "perceptions of the beholder," whether sighted or not). The prevalence of a condition such as blindness apparently depends in part on the number of official beholders available to apply this label (see also Scott, 1969).

An Overview

As has been noted throughout this book, the four sociological approaches described above should not be regarded as mutually exclusive. In the study of health-related issues, they share certain common themes. First, any person's health or illness is more than an organic condition, since it is subject to the interpretation of others. Owing to the impact of culture, family and friends, and the medical profession, health and illness are no longer purely biological occurrences but are sociological occurrences as well. Second, since members of a society (especially industrial societies) share the same health delivery system, health is a group and societal concern. Although health may be defined as the complete well-being of an individual, it is also the result of his or her social environment. As we will see in the next section, even such factors as gender, social class, race, and ethnicity can influence the likelihood of contracting a particular disease (Cockerham, 1989:171).

SOCIAL EPIDEMIOLOGY AND HEALTH

Social epidemiology is the study of the distribution of disease, impairment, and general health status across a population. In its earliest period, epidemiology concentrated on the scientific study of epidemics, focusing on how they started and spread. Contemporary social epidemiology is much broader in scope and is concerned not only with epidemics but also with nonepidemic diseases, injuries, drug addiction and alcoholism, suicide, and mental illness. Epidemiology draws on the work of a wide variety of scientists and researchers, among them physicians, sociologists, public health officials, biologists, veterinarians, demographers, anthropologists, psychologists, and (in studies of air pollution) meteorologists.

In social epidemiology, as well as in studies of population and crime victimization, two concepts are commonly employed: incidence and prevalence. *Incidence* refers to the number of new cases of a specific disorder occurring within a given population during a stated period of time, usually a year. For example, the incidence of AIDS in the United States in 1991 was 43,672 cases. By contrast, *prevalence* refers to the total number of cases of a specific disorder that exist at a given time. The prevalence of AIDS in 1991 was close to 200,000 cases (Bureau of the Census, 1992a:125).

When incidence figures are presented as rates, or as the number of reports per 100,000 people, they are called *morbidity rates.* Sociologists find morbidity rates useful because they reveal that a specific disease occurs more frequently among one segment of a population than another. The term *mortality rate* refers to the incidence of death in a given population. We will examine mortality rates in greater detail when we consider population issues later in the chapter.

Gender

A large body of research indicates that, in comparison with men, women experience a higher prevalence of many illnesses. There are variations—for example, men are more likely to have parasitic diseases whereas women are more likely to become diabetic—but, as a group, women appear to be in poorer health than men.

This seems noteworthy and surprising, especially in view of women's greater longevity rates and lower mortality rates at all ages. Sociologist Lois Verbrugge (1985:162–163) observes:

> In sum, women have more frequent illness and disability, but the problems are typically not serious (life threatening) ones. In contrast, men suffer more from life threatening diseases, and these cause more permanent disability and earlier death for them. One sex is "sicker" in the short run, and the other in the long run.

The apparent inconsistency between the "short-run" ill health of women and their greater longevity deserves an explanation, and researchers have advanced a theory. Women's lower rate of cigarette smoking (which reduces their risk of heart disease, lung cancer, and emphysema), lower consumption of alcohol (which reduces the risk of auto accidents and cirrhosis of the liver), and lower rates of employment in dangerous occupations explain about one-third of their greater longevity than men—despite women's otherwise poorer health record. Moreover, some clinical studies suggest that the genuine differences in morbidity between women and men may be less than is evident in the data on morbidity. Researchers argue that women are much more likely than men to seek treatment, to be diagnosed as having diseases, and thus to have their illnesses reflected in data examined by epidemiologists.

From a conflict perspective, women have been particularly vulnerable to the medicalization of society, with everything from birth to beauty treated in an increasingly medical context. Such medicalization may contribute to women's higher morbidity rates as compared with those of men (Conrad and Kern, 1986:25–26; Riessman, 1983; for a different view, see Gove and Hughes, 1979). Ironically, while women have been especially affected by medicalization, medical researchers have often excluded women from clinical studies. The controversy over this issue is discussed in Box 12-1.

Social Class

Social class is clearly associated with differences in morbidity and mortality rates. Although people from higher social classes have greater life expectancy than the less affluent, they are more likely to experience peptic ulcers. The lower classes, by contrast, are more likely to suffer from certain forms of cancer, as well as from problems related to alcoholism and drug abuse. Studies in the United States and in other countries have consistently shown that people in the lower classes have higher rates of mortality and disability. In general, there appears to be two to three times as much serious illness among low-income people as among the nation's population as a whole (Graham and Reeder, 1979:76; see also Lemkow, 1986).

Ted Cluterl/Photo Researchers

The occupations of people in the lower classes of the United States tend to be more dangerous than those of the more affluent.

BOX 12-1

SEXISM IN MEDICAL RESEARCH

One study, using 22,071 volunteer subjects, found that taking small doses of aspirin can reduce the risk of a heart attack. These results, reported in 1988, gave physicians in the United States a valuable piece of information. But there was a major problem: not one of the 22,071 subjects was a woman. Consequently, older women—the women most likely to experience heart problems—had no way of knowing if the results of the study would be applicable to them.

This male-only study is not unprecedented. A study designed to learn whether smoking increases the risk of getting cataracts involved 838 male subjects and no women. A research project exploring the links between heart disease and high cholesterol, lack of exercise, and smoking used 12,866 male subjects and, again, no women. Representative Patricia Schroeder, noting the absence of women in many medical studies, concludes: "At this point, doctors just aren't getting the kind of guidance they need when they try to prescribe to women" (Purvis, 1990:59–60).

Female physicians and researchers charge that sexism is at the heart of such research practices. "White men control these things," insists Dr. Kathy Anastos, a New York City internist. "When, for scientific reasons, they have to limit diversity, they choose to study themselves. Then when they get the results, they apply them to everyone. It's very unscientific" (Berney, 1990:27).

Even when women *are* the subjects of medical research, conclusions may be drawn and widely popularized despite fragmentary data. In 1990, the prestigious *New England Journal of Medicine* ran an editorial focusing on the relative inability of the female digestive system to metabolize alcohol as effectively as that of the male. This conclusion was based on a study of only 20 men and 23 women; moreover, 12 of the women were alcoholics, and all 23 had been hospitalized for surgery for gastric dysfunction. In criticizing this editorial, Jeanne Mager Stellman (1990:A23), a professor of clinical public health, and Joan E. Bertin, an executive of the Women's Rights Project of the American Civil Liberties Union, ask: "Where was the usual caution and prudence of the New England Journal in the overextrapolation of data from hospitalized patients to the healthy population, and why was this story front-page news?"

Critics of current medical research practices insist that there is a desperate need for studies with women subjects. Estelle Ramey, a recently retired physiology researcher, points out that researchers have far too little information on the impact of cholesterol and diet on women's health. Ramey adds that the lack of research on women and heart disease is especially shocking, since heart disease is the number one killer of women. There is also a shortage of data on women with AIDS— even though the proportion of AIDS patients who are female has increased. With such issues in mind, in 1992 the National Institutes of Health (NIH) established an Office of Research on Women. This office is charged with ensuring that adequate numbers of women serve both as researchers and as participants in taxpayer-supported studies (Berney, 1990:26–27; Cotton, 1990:1050, Painter, 1992).

Why is class linked to health? Crowded living conditions, substandard housing, poor diet, and stress all contribute to the ill health of many low-income people in the United States. In certain instances, poor education may lead to a lack of awareness of measures necessary to maintaining good health. Yet financial strains are certainly a major factor in the health problems of less affluent people. Given the high costs of high-quality medical care—which we will explore more fully later in the chapter—the poor have significantly less access to health care resources.

In addition to these factors, the occupations of people in the lower classes of the United States tend to be more dangerous than those of more affluent citizens. Miners, for example, must face the possibility of injury or death due to explosions and cave-ins; they are also likely to develop respiratory diseases such as black lung. To take another example, workers in textile mills may contract a variety of illnesses caused by exposure to toxic substances, including one disease commonly known as *brown lung disease* (R. Hall, 1982). In recent years, the public has learned of the perils of asbestos poisoning, which is a particular worry for construction workers.

In the view of Karl Marx and contemporary conflict theorists, capitalist societies such as the United States care more about maximizing profits than they do about providing for the health and safety of industrial workers. As a result, government agencies do not take forceful action to regulate conditions in the workplace, and workers suffer many preventable, job-related injuries and illnesses.

According to a 1988 analysis by health specialists in Great Britain, almost 40,000 adult deaths *each year* in that nation can be attributed to class differences. Members of the lower social classes experience higher mortality because of their greater vulnerability to such factors as dangerous jobs and inadequate housing. It is little wonder, then, that the World Health Organization has asked countries to reduce differences in health status due to economic advantages by at least 25 percent by the year 2000 (Scott-Samuel and Blackburn, 1988).

Race and Ethnicity

Health profiles of many racial and ethnic minorities reflect the social inequality evident in the United States. The poor economic and environmental conditions of groups such as Blacks, Hispanics, and Native Americans are manifested in high morbidity and mortality rates for these groups. It is true that some afflictions, such as sickle-cell anemia among Blacks, have a clear genetic basis. But in most instances, environmental factors contribute to the differential rates of disease and death.

Compared with Whites, Hispanics are more likely to live in poverty, to be unemployed, and to have little education. These factors contribute to Hispanics' increased risk of contracting a variety of diseases. For example, Hispanics are four times more likely than Whites to suffer from tuberculosis, are three times more likely to contract diabe-

tes, and are also more likely to have cancer of the stomach, pancreas, and cervix. Hispanic children suffer disproportionately from lead poisoning and measles. Although Hispanics constitute only about 8 percent of the population of the United States, they account for 14 percent of reported cases of AIDS, including nearly 21 percent of AIDS cases among women and 22 percent among children (Council on Scientific Affairs, 1991; Novello et al., 1991).

The morbidity rates and mortality rates for Blacks are also distressing. Compared with Whites, Blacks have higher death rates from diseases of the heart, pneumonia, diabetes, and cancer. The death rate from strokes is twice as high among African Americans as it is among Whites. Such epidemiological findings reflect in part the fact that a higher proportion of Blacks are found among the nation's lower classes. According to a study released in 1992 by the National Center for Health Statistics (1992a), Whites can expect to live 76.0 years. By contrast, life expectancy for Blacks is 69.2 years; indeed, for Black men life expectancy is only 64.8 years and has been *decreasing* since 1984.

What accounts for these racial differences? According to a national survey conducted in 1986, Blacks of all income levels are substantially worse off than Whites in terms of access to physicians. For example, African Americans had a lower rate of visits to physicians; this finding is especially disturbing, since rates of serious illness are higher among Blacks than Whites. The survey points to significantly less use of medical care by Blacks, and adds that Blacks are less likely than Whites to have medical insurance. Finally, in comparison with Whites, Blacks were found to be less satisfied with the health care they received from physicians and from hospital personnel (Blendon et al., 1989).

A study conducted in Massachusetts found that substantial racial inequalities exist in the provision of cardiac care. In comparison with Blacks, a significantly higher proportion of Whites admitted to Massachusetts hospitals with heart problems undergo cardiac bypass operations and cardiac catheterizations. Thus, racial differences are evident even among patients who are hospitalized with serious heart problems (Wenneker and Epstein, 1989).

FIGURE 12-2 **Total Health Care Expenditures in the United States, 1975–2000**

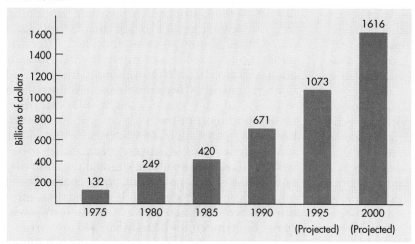

SOURCE: Hasson, 1992.

Expenditures for health care in the United States have continued to rise, reaching an all-time high of $809 billion in 1991. According to projections, expenditures for health care will reach $1.6 trillion by the year 2000.

Moreover, drawing on the conflict perspective, sociologist Howard Waitzkin (1986) suggests that racial tensions contribute to the medical problems of Blacks. In his view, the stress resulting from racial prejudice and discrimination helps to explain the higher rates of hypertension found among African Americans (and Hispanics) compared with Whites. Hypertension is twice as common in Blacks as in Whites; it is believed to be a critical factor in Blacks' high mortality rates from heart disease, kidney disease, and stroke. Although there is disagreement among medical experts, some argue that the stress resulting from racism and suppressed hostility exacerbates hypertension among Blacks (Goleman, 1990).

Just how significant is the impact of poorer health on the lives of the nation's less educated people, less affluent classes, and minorities? Drawing on a variety of research studies, population specialist Evelyn Kitagawa (1972) estimated the "excess mortality rate" to be 20 percent. In other words, 20 percent more people were dying than otherwise might have, because of differentially poor health linked to race and class. Using Kitagawa's model, we can calculate that if every person in the United States were White and had at least one year of college education, some 455,000 fewer people would die in 1995 (Bureau of the Census, 1991a:15).

HEALTH CARE IN THE UNITED STATES

As the entire nation is well-aware, the costs of health care have skyrocketed in recent years. For example, in 1990 total expenditures for health care in the United States reached $700 billion, a 65 percent increase over the 1985 figure (see Figure 12-2). Moreover, it is estimated that by the year 2000, total expenditures for health care will rise to $1.5 to $2 *trillion* (K. Anderson, 1991).

The rising costs of medical care are especially apparent in the event of catastrophic illnesses or confinement in a nursing home. Bills of tens of thousands of dollars are not unusual in the treatment of cancer, Alzheimer's disease, and other chronic diseases requiring custodial care. Moreover, according to a statement by a federal health official in mid-1992, the lifetime cost of treating an AIDS patient in the United States has reached $102,000, compared with $57,000 in 1988 (L. Altman, 1992b:B8).

The "graying of America" (see Chapter 8) is clearly a factor in rising health care costs. Older people typically have longer stays in the hospital than younger patients, and the elderly obviously account for an overwhelming percentage of nursing home expenditures. Insurance coverage and existing federal assistance programs, such as

Medicare, provide reimbursement for not quite half of all medical costs. For example, a 70-year-old who enters the hospital four times for heart problems and surgery can easily spend $6000 that will not be covered by Medicare. Proposals to fill this "medigap," as it has been called, reflect concern about unknown and potentially staggering costs (Mechanic, 1986; W. Stevens, 1987).

Clearly, the health care system of the United States has moved far beyond the days when general practitioners living in a neighborhood or community typically made house calls and charged modest fees. How did health care become big business involving nationwide hospital chains and marketing campaigns? How have these changes reshaped typical interactions between doctors, nurses, and patients? We will address these questions in the next section of the chapter.

A Historical View

According to sociologist Paul Starr (1982), writing in his critically acclaimed book, *The Social Transformation of American Medicine,* the authority of medical professionals rests on a system of standardized educational licensing. The establishment of such a system maintains authority from one generation to the next and transmits authority from the profession as a whole to its individual members. However, health care in the United States has not always followed this model.

The "popular health movement" of the 1830s and 1840s emphasized preventive care and what is termed "self-help." There was strong criticism of "doctoring" as a paid occupation. New medical philosophies or sects established their own medical schools and challenged the authority and methods of more traditional doctors. By the 1840s, most states had repealed medical licensing laws. However, through the leadership of the American Medical Association (AMA), founded in 1848, "regular" doctors attacked lay practitioners, sectarian doctors, and female physicians in general. (For a different view, see Navarro, 1984.)

The emergence of massive, organized philanthropy in the early twentieth century—administered by such organizations as the Rockefeller and Carnegie foundations—had a critical impact in reshaping and centralizing medicine in the United States. Beginning in 1903, extensive foundation support was allocated to create a respectable medical profession. A researcher employed by the Carnegie Corporation was sent to tour the nation in order to determine which medical schools should receive funding. After the publication of the Flexner report in 1910, numerous medical schools that he found unworthy of financial aid were forced to close. Among them were six of the nation's eight Black medical schools and most of the alternative schools which had been open to female students. In state after state, tough licensing laws were adopted to restrict medical practice to traditional doctors from approved institutions. As one result, babies could no longer be delivered by midwives in most states; the practice of obstetrics was restricted to physicians (Ehrenreich and English, 1973).

Once authority was institutionalized through standardized programs of education and licensing, it was conferred on all who successfully completed these programs. Recognition became relatively unambiguous. The authority of the physician no longer depended on lay attitudes or the person occupying the sick role; it was increasingly built into the structure of the medical profession and the health care system. As the institutionalization of health care proceeded, the medical profession gained control over both the market for its services and the various organizational hierarchies that govern medical practice, financing, and policymaking. By the 1920s, physicians controlled hospital technology, the division of labor of health personnel, and, indirectly, other professional practices such as nursing and pharmacy (R. Coser, 1984).

Physicians, Nurses, and Patients

The preeminence of physicians within the health care system of the United States has traditionally given them a position of dominance in their dealings with both patients and nurses. The functionalist and interactionist perspectives combine to offer a framework for understanding the professional socialization of physicians as it relates to patient care. Functionalists suggest that established physicians and medical school professors serve as mentors or role models who transmit knowledge, skills, and values to the passive learner—the medical student. Interactionists emphasize that students are molded by the medical school environment as they interact with their classmates. Both approaches argue that the typical training of physicians in the United States leads to rather dehumanizing physician-patient encounters. Despite many efforts to formally introduce a humanistic dimension of patient care into medical school curricula, patient overload and cost-containment efforts of hospitals tend to reduce positive relations. Moreover, widespread publicity concerning malpractice suits and high medical costs has further strained the physician-patient dyad (Becker et al., 1961; Merton et al., 1957; Mizrahi, 1986:14).

These problems in medicine have taken their toll on contemporary physicians. A survey conducted for the American Medical Association in 1989 revealed that 39 percent of doctors either definitely or probably would not go into medicine today if they were in college and knew what they now know about the field. This disenchantment is somewhat similar to the "burnout" experienced by teachers (refer back to Chapter 10), yet it is nevertheless surprising because physicians (unlike schoolteachers) enjoy substantial incomes and high prestige. Despite these benefits, the physicians surveyed report that they are disillusioned by the growing competition for patients, increased government regulation of medicine, and worrisome malpractice litigation (L. Altman and Rosenthal, 1990).

Interactionists have closely examined how compliance and negotiation occur between physician and patient. They concur with Talcott Parsons' view that the relationship is generally asymmetrical, with doctors holding a position of dominance and control of rewards. Just as physicians have maintained dominance in their interactions with patients, doctors have similarly controlled interactions with nurses. Despite their training and professional status, nurses commonly take orders from physicians. Traditionally, the relationship between doctors and nurses has paralleled the male dominance of the United States: most physicians have been male, whereas virtually all nurses have been female.

Like other women in subordinate roles, nurses have been expected to perform their duties without challenging the authority of men. Psychiatrist Leonard Stein (1967:699–700) refers to this pro-

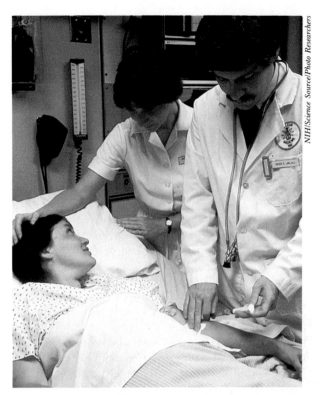

Like other women in subordinate roles, nurses have been expected to perform their duties without challenging the authority of men.

cess as the *doctor-nurse game.* According to the rules of this "game," the nurse must never disagree openly with the physician. When she has recommendations concerning a patient's care, she must communicate them indirectly in a deferential tone. For example, if asked by a hospital's medical resident, "What sleeping medication has been helpful to Mrs. Brown in the past?" (an indirect request for a recommendation), the nurse will respond with a disguised recommendation statement, such as "Pentobarbital mg 100 was quite effective night before last." Her careful response allows the physician to authoritatively restate the same prescription as if it were *his* idea.

By the 1980s nurses in the United States were increasingly speaking out, engaging in political action, walking picket lines, and joining lawsuits—all with the goals of better pay, more respect for their professional expertise, and transformation of the health care system. Margretta Styles, president of the American Nurses Association (ANA), notes: "Nursing is 97 percent female, and the problems we face are typical of those faced in women's professions, especially low pay and low status." Both inside the hospital and in the larger political system, nurses have organized to battle for autonomy, an improved image, and fair compensation for their skill and dedication (Holcomb, 1988:74).

Like nurses, female physicians find themselves in a subordinate position due to gender. According to a report issued in 1991 by the Feminist Majority Foundation and the American Medical Women's Association, women still receive disproportionately low pay and status within the medical profession. In 1988, for example, women doctors earned 63 cents for each dollar earned by a male doctor. This gap in earnings is not simply the result of differing levels of experience. The American Medical Association reports that in 1987, male doctors with one to four years' experience earned an average net income of $110,600, compared with $74,000 for women doctors with comparable experience. Male physicians with 10 to 20 years' experience earned an average net income of $158,800, compared with $99,400 for female physicians with similar experience.

The 1991 report notes that although 36 percent of all medical students in the United States are female, 79 percent of medical school faculty members, 98 percent of medical school chairpersons, and *all* medical school deans are male. The American Medical Association (AMA) has never had a woman as chief executive officer in its 144-year history (J. Gross, 1991b:10; Hilts, 1991:C7).

The Role of Government

Cindy Martin died in 1990 at age 26, after four months of surgery and intensive care at Presbyterian University Hospital in Pittsburgh. In the aftermath of her death, her husband's insurance company received a bill for $1.25 million. While accountants attempted to untangle the costs of seven surgical procedures performed on Cindy Martin—including heart, liver, and kidney transplants—this case underscored troubling issues regarding the high cost of health care. Who should pay for the expensive medical procedures

of the 1990s? What role, if any, should government play in providing medical care and health insurance for United States citizens? (Freudenheim, 1990).

The first significant involvement of the federal government in the financing of health care came with the 1946 Hill-Burton Act, which provided subsidies for building and improving hospitals, especially in rural areas. An even more important change came with the enactment of two wide-ranging government assistance programs: Medicare, which is essentially a compulsory health insurance plan for the elderly; and Medicaid, which is a noncontributory federal and state insurance plan for the poor. These programs greatly expanded federal involvement in health care financing for needy men, women, and children. In addition, over 1000 government-subsidized community health centers are located in low-income, medically underserved communities (Blendon, 1986).

Given rates of illness and disability among elderly people, Medicare has had a particularly noteworthy impact on the health care system of the United States. Initially, Medicare simply reimbursed health care providers such as physicians and hospitals for the costs of their services. However, as the overall costs of Medicare increased dramatically, the federal government introduced a price-control system in 1983. All illnesses were classified into 468 diagnostic-related groups (DRGs); a reimbursement rate was set for each condition and remained fixed regardless of the individual needs of any patient.

In effect, the federal government told hospitals and doctors that it would no longer be concerned with their costs in treating Medicare patients; it would reimburse them only to a designated level. If a patient is sicker than average (that is, the average set for a particular illness) and requires extra care, the hospital must absorb any expenses beyond its DRG allowance. However, if the patient is less ill than average for an illness, the hospital can essentially make a profit from the fixed level of reimbursement (Downs, 1987; Easterbrook, 1987:49).

The DRG system of reimbursement has contributed to the controversial practice of "dumping," under which patients whose treatment may be unprofitable are transferred by private hospitals to public facilities. Many private hospitals in the United States have begun to conduct routine "wallet biopsies" to investigate the financial status of potential patients; those judged as undesirable are then refused admission or are dumped. Since the introduction of DRGs, some urban public hospitals have reported 400 to 500 percent increases in the number of patients transferred from private hospitals (Feinglass, 1987).

Such dumping can have grave consequences for patients. In 1984, a Harvard Medical School team analyzed records of 458 patients transferred during a six-month period to a public hospital in Oakland, California. Researchers found that in 7.2 percent of cases, the patients were transferred before being stabilized medically; their care suffered as a result. Viewed from a conflict perspective, such practices are especially likely to hurt those people at the bottom of stratification hierarchies based on social class, race and ethnicity, gender, and age (P. Taylor, 1985:9).

During the twentieth century, one European nation after another has adopted government-sponsored national health insurance or created a national health service. By contrast, the United States government has been much less active in providing health care for its citizens. The social policy section at the end of the chapter will examine the issue of national health care insurance, which received renewed attention during the 1992 presidential campaign.

DEMOGRAPHY: THE STUDY OF POPULATION

As is true in the study of health and medicine, many natural and social scientists are involved in the study of population-related issues. The biologist explores the nature of reproduction and casts light on factors that affect *fertility* (the level of reproduction among women of childbearing age). The medical pathologist examines and analyzes trends in the causes of death. Geographers, historians, and psychologists also have distinctive contributions to make to our understanding of population (Wrong, 1977:6). Sociologists, more than these other researchers, focus on the *social* factors that influence population rates and trends.

In their study of population issues, sociologists are keenly aware that various elements of population—such as fertility, mortality (the amount of death), and migration—are profoundly affected by the norms, values, and social patterns of a society. Fertility is influenced by people's age of entry into sexual unions and by their use of contraception—both of which, in turn, reflect the social and religious values that guide a particular culture. Mortality is shaped by a nation's level of nutrition, acceptance of immunization, and provisions for sanitation, as well as its general commitment to health care and health education. Migration from one country to another can depend on marital and kinship ties, the relative degree of racial and religious tolerance in various societies, and people's evaluations of employment opportunities.

Demography is the scientific study of population. It draws on several components of population, including size, composition, and territorial distribution, to understand the social consequences of population. Demographers study geographical variations and historical trends in their effort to develop population forecasts. They also analyze the structure of a population in terms of such factors as the age, gender, race, and ethnicity of its members. A key figure in this type of analysis was Thomas Malthus.

Malthus's Thesis and Marx's Response

The Reverend Thomas Robert Malthus (1766–1834) was educated at Cambridge University and spent his life teaching history and political economy. He strongly criticized two major institutions of his time—the church and slavery—yet, his most significant legacy for contemporary scholars is his still-controversial *Essays on the Principle of Population,* published in 1798.

Essentially, Malthus held that the world's population was growing more rapidly than the available food supply. Malthus argued that food supply increases in an arithmetic progression (1, 2, 3, 4, and so on), whereas population expands by a geometric progression (1, 2, 4, 8, and so on). According to his analysis, the gap between food supply and population will continue to grow over time. Even though the food supply will increase, it will not increase nearly enough to meet the needs of an expanding world population.

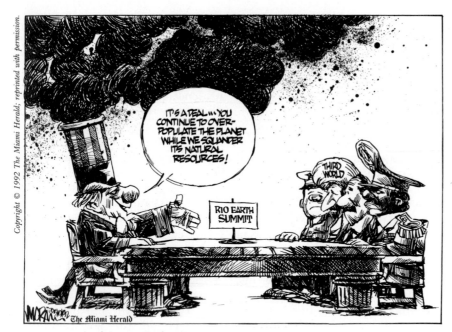

Copyright © 1992 The Miami Herald; reprinted with permission.

Neo-Malthusians condemn developed nations which consume a disproportionately large share of world resources. At the time of the United Nations' Earth Summit in Rio de Janeiro in 1992, the average resident of the United States used three times the energy of the average person in France and eight times that of the average person in China (Weisskopf, 1992).

Malthus saw population control as an answer to the gap between rising population and food supply, yet he explicitly denounced artificial means of birth control because they were not sanctioned by religion. For Malthus, the appropriate way to control population was to postpone marriage. He argued that couples must take responsibility for the number of children they choose to bear; without such restraint, the world would face widespread hunger, poverty, and misery (Malthus et al., 1960, original edition 1824; Petersen, 1979:192–194; Rashid, 1987).

Karl Marx strongly criticized Malthus's views on population. Marx saw the nature of economic relations in Europe's industrial societies as the central problem. He could not accept the Malthusian notion that rising world population, rather than capitalism, was the cause of social ills. In Marx's opinion, there was no special relationship between world population figures and the supply of resources (including food). If society were well-ordered, increases in population should lead to greater wealth, not to hunger and misery.

Of course, Marx did not believe that capitalism operated under these ideal conditions. He maintained that capitalism devoted its resources to the financing of buildings and tools rather than to

more equitable distribution of food, housing, and other necessities of life. Marx's work is important to the study of population because he linked overpopulation to the distribution of resources—a topic that will be taken up again later in this chapter. His concern with the writings of Malthus also testifies to the importance of population in political and economic affairs (Hawley, 1950; Meek, 1954; Petersen, 1975:165; 1979:74–77).

The insights of Malthus and Marx regarding population issues have come together in what is termed the *neo-Malthusian* view. This view is best exemplified by the work of Paul Ehrlich (1968; Ehrlich and Ehrlich, 1990). Neo-Malthusians agree with Malthus that world population growth is outstretching natural resources. However, in contrast to the British theorist, they insist that birth control measures are needed to regulate population increases. Neo-Malthusians have a Marxist flavor in their condemnation of developed nations which, despite their low birthrates, consume a disproportionately large share of world resources. While rather pessimistic about the future, these theorists stress that birth control and sensible use of resources are essential responses to rising world population (J. Tierney, 1990; Weeks, 1992).

Studying Population Today

The relative balance of births and deaths is no less important in the 1990s than it was during the lifetime of Malthus and Marx. The suffering that Malthus spoke of is certainly a reality for many people of the world who are hungry and poor. Malnutrition remains the largest contributing factor to illness and death among children in the developing countries. Almost 15 percent of these children will die before age 5—a rate nearly 14 times higher than in developed nations. Furthermore, warfare and large-scale migration have exacerbated the relationship between population and food supply. In order to combat world hunger, it may be necessary to reduce human births, dramatically increase the world's food supply, or perhaps do both at the same time. With this in mind, it seems essential to study population-related issues (World Bank, 1992:280–281).

In the United States and most other countries, the census is the primary mechanism for collecting population information. A *census* is an enumeration, or counting, of a population. The United States' Constitution requires that a census be held every 10 years in order to determine congressional representation. This periodic investigation is supplemented by *vital statistics;* these records of births, deaths, marriages, and divorces are gathered through a registration system maintained by government units. In addition, other governmental surveys provide up-to-date information on commercial developments, educational trends, industrial expansion, agricultural practices, and the status of such groups as children, the elderly, racial and ethnic minorities, and single parents.

In administering a nationwide census and conducting other types of research, demographers employ many of the skills and techniques described in Chapter 1, including questionnaires, interviews, and sampling. The precision of population projections is contingent on the accuracy of a series of estimates that demographers must make. First, they must determine past population trends and establish a base population as of the date for which the forecast began. Next, birth and death rates must be established, along with estimates of future fluctuations. In making projections for a nation's population trends, demographers must consider migration as well, since a significant number of individuals may enter and leave the country (D. Bogue, 1979:876–877).

Because of the difficulties of estimating future births, deaths, and migration, demographers usually specify a range of projections—from "high" through "medium" to "low." These statistical forecasts are useful to a wide range of concerned parties, including planners, public administrators, economists, and commercial interests.

Elements of Demography

Demographers employ the distinctive terminology of their science in analyzing and projecting population trends. Population facts are communicated with a language derived from the basic elements of human life—birth and death. The *birthrate* (or, more specifically, the *crude birthrate*) is the number of live births per 1000 population in a given year. In 1990, for example, there were 16 live births per 1000 people in the United States. The birthrate provides information on the actual reproductive patterns of a society.

One way demography can project future growth in a society is to make use of the *total fertility rate (TFR)*. The TFR is the average number of children born alive to any woman, assuming that she conforms to current fertility rates. The TFR reported for the United States in 1990 was 2.0 births, as compared with over 7.0 births per woman in such developing countries as Uganda, Iraq, and Bangladesh. Concerns in Japan about the nation's total fertility rate are explored in Box 12-2 on page 334.

Mortality, like fertility, is measured in several different ways. The *death rate* (also known as the *crude death rate*) is the number of deaths per 1000 population in a given year. In 1990, the United States had a death rate of 9.0 per 1000 population. As noted earlier, the *infant mortality rate* is the number of deaths of infants under 1 year of age per 1000 live births in a given year. This measure serves as an important indicator of a society's level of health care; it reflects prenatal nutrition, delivery procedures, and infant screening measures. The infant mortality rate is also a useful indicator of future population growth, since additional infants who survive to adulthood will contribute to further population increases.

BOX 12-2

JAPAN: THE 1.57 SHOCK

Beginning in 1990, Japanese newspapers, magazines, and television newscasts gave increasing attention to a phenomenon they called "1.57 shock." This phrase captured the widespread sense of disbelief over the fact that Japan's total fertility rate (TFR) had fallen to 1.57 births: Japanese women were averaging only slightly above 1½ children per lifetime. And the shocks kept coming. By 1991, Japan's TFR fell again, to 1.53 births. As of 1992, it was down to 1.5 births (Haub and Yanagishita, 1992; Yanagishita, 1992).

To put Japan's total fertility rate in perspective, the lowest TFR ever reached in the United States was 1.74 births in 1976. The lowest figure ever reported was 1.28 births in West Germany in 1985. Conversely, the Hutterites, a North American religious sect, averaged 12 children per woman in the 1930s by promoting early and universal marriage and by discouraging use of birth control measures (McFalls, 1991:4, 7).

According to official population estimates, Japan's annual growth rate fell to its lowest postwar level between 1989 and 1990—just 0.33 percent per year. Population projections released in 1992 suggest that its population will actually begin to decline after 2010. Japan is already experiencing some of the demographic consequences typically associated with low fertility, among them a shortage of younger workers and rises in the cost of health care for the elderly. Indeed, Tokyo Shoko Research reports that whereas only 1 percent of successful Japanese businesses had to close in 1988 due to a shortage of labor, this figure had increased to 6 percent by 1990.

Why has there been such a continuing decline in Japan's total fertility rate? While Japanese men continue to favor traditional gender roles both in the workplace and within marriage, an increasing proportion of Japanese women resent male dominance and view marriage as a "raw deal" that denies them opportunities available to men. In 1970, only 18 percent of women 25 to 29 years old were single, but by 1989, 38 percent of women in this age group were single (Yanagishita, 1992:3).

Even among couples that do marry, work and financial pressures have contributed to lower fertility. "People feel so much pressure on the job that they work until nine, ten o'clock at night," observes Kunio Kitamura, a Tokyo obstetrician. "Then they have another hour and a half home on the train, because most people can't afford a house anywhere near the office. You probably can't get a seat, and the train is full of drunks, singing and throwing up. After all that, who has the strength to get in bed and make a baby?" (J. Schwartz, 1991:20)

There is a wide disparity among nations in the rate of death of newborn children. In the period 1990 to 1991, the infant mortality rate for the United States was 9.0 deaths per 1000 live births, whereas for the world as a whole it was an estimated 68 per 1000 live births. As we noted earlier, at least 26 nations have lower rates of infant mortality than the United States, including Great Britain, Canada, Sweden, and Japan (Haub and Yanagishita, 1992; refer back to Figure 12-1 on page 321).

Another set of health-related measures are _morbidity rates,_ which measure the incidence of diseases in a given population. Sociologists are interested in morbidity rates because they reflect the standard of living and availability of medical technology in a society. The fact that morbidity rates are higher among lower-income segments of the population of the United States, as pointed out in Chapter 6, suggests that there is an uneven distribution of medical resources which favors those most able to pay for high-quality health care. In addition, as noted earlier in this chapter (see pages 325–326), less affluent people tend to be employed in jobs that leave them more susceptible to occupational hazards.

TABLE 12-1 For World Population, Estimated Time for Each Successive Increase of 1 Billion People

POPULATION LEVEL	TIME TAKEN TO REACH NEW POPULATION LEVEL	YEAR ATTAINED
First billion	2 to 5 million years	About A.D. 1800
Second billion	Approximately 130 years	1930
Third billion	30 years	1960
Fourth billion	15 years	1975
Fifth billion	12 years	1987
Sixth billion (projected)	11 years	1998

SOURCES: Gupte, 1982; Population Reference Bureau, reported in van der Tak et al., 1979:4.

A general measure of health used by demographers is *life expectancy*, the average number of years a person can be expected to live under current mortality conditions. Usually it is reported as life expectancy *at birth*. At present, Japan reports a life expectancy at birth of 76 years and Iceland reports 75 years, both slightly higher than the United States' figure of 72 years. By contrast, life expectancy at birth is less than 45 years in many developing nations, including The Gambia, Sierra Leone, and Afghanistan.

The *growth rate* of a society is the difference between births and deaths, plus the difference between *immigrants* (those who enter a country to establish permanent residence) and *emigrants* (those who leave a country permanently) per 1000 population. For the world as a whole, the growth rate is simply the difference between births and deaths per 1000 population, since worldwide immigration and emigration must of necessity be equal. In 1990, the United States had a growth rate of 1.0 percent, compared with an estimated 1.7 percent for the entire world (Haub and Yanagishita, 1992).

WORLD POPULATION PATTERNS

One important aspect of demographic work involves study of the history of population. However, this is made more difficult by the lack of reliable information for all but the modern era. For example, official national censuses were relatively rare before 1850. Researchers interested in early population therefore turn to archeological remains of settlements, burial sites, baptismal and tax records, and oral history sources.

During the twentieth century, the world population has expanded at a much faster rate than in earlier periods of history. Whereas it took roughly 130 years to reach the second billion in world population, it took only 30 years to reach the third billion and 12 years to reach the fifth billion.

We think of the world as having a large population—some 5.4 billion in 1992. Yet until modern times, there were relatively few humans living on this planet. One estimate placed the world population of a million years ago at only 125,000 people. As Table 12-1 indicates, the population has exploded in the last 200 years and continues to accelerate rapidly. Merely in the time it has taken you to read this far in this one paragraph, the world population has increased by 97 people!

Demographic Transition

The phenomenal growth of world population in recent times can be accounted for by changing patterns of births and deaths. Beginning in the late 1700s—and continuing until the middle 1900s—there was a gradual reduction in death rates in northern and western Europe. People were able to live longer because of advances in food production, sanitation, nutrition, and public health care. While death rates fell, birthrates remained high; as a result, there was unprecedented population growth during this period of European history. However, by the late 1800s, the birthrates of many European countries began to decline, and the rate of population growth also decreased (Matras, 1977:38–44; McKeown, 1976).

FIGURE 12-3 Demographic Transition

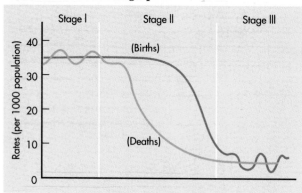

Demographers use the concept of demographic transition to describe changes in birthrates and death rates during stages of a nation's development. This graph shows the pattern that took place in presently developed nations. In the first stage, both birthrates and death rates were high, so that there was little population growth. In the second stage, the birthrate remained high while the death rate declined sharply, which led to rapid growth. By the last stage, which many developing nations have yet to enter, the birthrate also declined, and there was again little population growth.

The changes in birth- and death rates in nineteenth-century Europe serve as an example of demographic transition. Demographers use this term to describe an observed pattern in changing vital statistics. Specifically, **demographic transition** is the change from high birthrates and death rates to relatively low birthrates and death rates. This approach, which was first introduced in the 1920s, is now widely used in the study of population trends.

As illustrated in Figure 12-3 (above), demographic transition is typically viewed as a three-stage process:

1 High birth- and death rates with little population growth
2 Declining death rates, primarily the result of reductions in infant deaths, along with high to medium fertility—resulting in significant population growth
3 Low birth- and death rates with little population growth

Demographic transition should be regarded not as a "law of population growth," but rather as a generalization of the population history of industrialized nations. Through this concept, we can better understand the growth problems faced by the world in the 1990s. About two-thirds of the world's nations have yet to pass fully through the second stage of demographic transition, among them many of the developing countries. Even if such nations make dramatic advances in fertility control, their populations will nevertheless increase seriously because of the large base of people already at prime childbearing age.

The pattern of demographic transition varies from nation to nation. One particularly useful distinction is the contrast between the transition now occurring in developing nations—which include about two-thirds of the world's population—and that which occurred over almost a century in more industrialized countries. Demographic transition in developing nations has involved a rapid decline in death rates without adjustments in birthrates. Specifically, until the end of World War II, there was a very gradual decrease in the death rates of developing countries, due primarily to improved water supplies and other public sanitary measures. Yet the birthrates of these countries remained very high—about 30 per 1000 population in the 1940s (as compared with under 19 per 1000 in the United States during the same period).

In the post-World War II period, the death rates of developing nations began a sharp decline. This revolution in "death control" was triggered by antibiotics; immunization; insecticides (such as DDT, used to strike at malaria-bearing mosquitoes); and largely successful campaigns against such fatal diseases as smallpox. Substantial medical and public health technology was imported almost overnight from more developed nations. As a result, the drop in death rates that had taken a century in Europe was telescoped into two decades in many developing countries.

Birthrates scarcely had time to adjust. Cultural beliefs about the proper size of families could not possibly change as quickly as the falling death rates. For centuries, couples had given birth to as many as eight or more children with the realization that perhaps two or three would survive to adulthood. Consequently, whereas Europeans had had several generations to restrict their birthrates, peoples of developing nations needed to do the same in less than a lifetime. Many did not, as is evident from the astronomical "population explosion" that was already under way by the middle 1900s. Clearly, families were more willing to accept technological advances which prolonged life than to abandon fertility patterns which reflected centuries of tradition and religious training.

The Population Explosion

Apart from war, rapid population growth has been perhaps the dominant international social problem of the past 30 years. Often this issue is referred to in emotional terms as the "population explosion" or even the "population bomb." Such striking language is not surprising, given the staggering increases in world population during the last two centuries. As was detailed in Table 12-1, the population of our planet rose from 1 billion around the year 1800 to 5.4 billion by 1992. The United Nations projects that world population could rise to as high as 6.4 billion by 2000 (Haub and Yanagishita, 1992; Haupt, 1990).

By the middle 1970s, demographers had observed a slight decline in the growth rate of many developing nations. These countries were still experiencing population increases, yet their rates of increase had declined as death rates could not go much lower and birthrates began to fall. It appears that family planning efforts have been instrumental in this demographic change. Beginning in the early 1960s, governments in certain developing nations sponsored or supported campaigns to encourage family planning. For example, in good part as the result of government-sponsored birth control campaigns, Thailand's total fertility rate fell from 6.1 births per woman in 1970 to only 2.6 in 1990. Indonesia, Tunisia, Egypt, and Turkey have also made substantial progress in promoting contraceptive use and reducing fertility rates (Haub et al., 1990; Tsui and Bogue, 1978; Weeks, 1988; World Bank, 1990).

Shown is a family planning class in Pakistan. Family planning efforts in developing countries not only reduce unwanted population growth but can improve maternal health by helping women to time and space pregnancies.

Through the efforts of many governments (among them the United States and the People's Republic of China) and private agencies (among them Planned Parenthood), the fertility rates of many developing countries have declined. It would be incorrect, however, to suggest that the population bomb is being defused. Even if trends toward lower fertility rates continue, the momentum toward growing world population is well established.

The developing nations face the prospect of continued population growth, since a substantial portion of their population is approaching childbearing years. This is evident in Figure 12-4 (page 338), in which the population pyramids of the United States and Mexico are compared.

FIGURE 12-4   Population Structure of Mexico and the United States

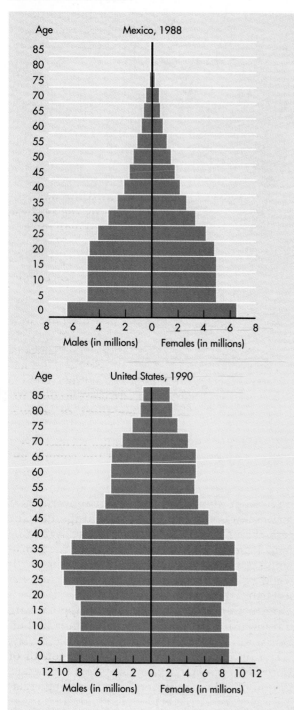

SOURCE: Weeks, 1992:230.

A ***population pyramid*** is a special type of bar chart that shows the distribution of population by gender and age; it is generally used to illustrate the population structure of a society. As Figure 12-4 illustrates, a substantial portion of the population of Mexico consists of children who are under the age of 15, with their childbearing years still to come.

By 1992, population specialists and policymakers, worried about the population explosion, were facing certain disturbing facts, among them the following:

- The world population rose by 93 million between mid-1988 and mid-1989, an all-time record increase.
- According to projections of the United Nations Food and Agriculture Organization, as many as 64 nations will experience critical food problems in the future. India now produces less food grain per person than it did in 1900 (Haub, 1988).
- Developing nations are not experiencing the declines in fertility that had been predicted earlier by researchers. Most seriously, a report published in late 1992 by the Population Crisis Committee suggests that neither China nor India is likely to stabilize growth until well into the next century, owing to serious shortcomings in these countries' family planning programs. China and India are the world's two most populous nations, and continued growth in these two countries is likely to result in substantial environmental damage, including soil and water depletion (Crossette, 1992).

This figure shows the population pyramids of Mexico and the United States. Developing countries like Mexico have high birthrates, but mortality takes its toll over the life cycle and there are relatively few people over the age of 65. By contrast, the United States continues to display the bulge of the "baby boom" of the 1950s and shows serious mortality only at older ages.

Population growth is not a problem in all industrialized nations. Indeed, a handful of countries are adopting policies which encourage growth—among them, Japan, which is considering offering benefits to families which have children and upgrading child care services (refer back to Box 12-2). Nevertheless, a global perspective underscores the dire consequences that could result from continued population growth (Reid, 1990).

A tragic new factor has emerged in the last decade which will restrict worldwide population growth: the spread of AIDS (refer back to the social policy section in Chapter 4). According to estimates, in certain African nations, as many as one-quarter to one-third of all adults in urban areas carry the HIV virus which destroys the body's immune system. It is projected that at least 10 million people in Asia will be infected with the HIV virus by the year 2000. Given the grim forecasts offered by researchers, the AIDS epidemic is likely to have increasing impact on world population patterns (Shenon, 1992).

Fertility Patterns in the United States

During the last four decades, the United States and other industrial nations have passed through two different patterns of population growth—the first marked by high fertility and rapid growth (stage II in the theory of demographic transition), the second marked by decline in fertility and little growth (stage III). Sociologists are keenly aware of the social impact of these fertility patterns.

The Baby Boom The most recent period of high fertility in the United States has often been referred to as the *baby boom*. After World War II—during which large numbers of military personnel were separated from their spouses—the annual number of births began to rise dramatically. Yet the baby boom was not a return to the large families common in the 1800s. In fact, there was only a slight increase in the proportion of couples having three or more children. The boom resulted from a striking decrease in the number of childless marriages and one-child families. Although a peak was reached in 1957, the nation maintained a relatively high birthrate of over 20 live births per 1000 population until 1964.

It would be a mistake to attribute the baby boom solely to the return home of large numbers of soldiers. High wages and general prosperity during the post-World War II period encouraged many married couples to have children and purchase homes. In addition, several sociologists—as well as feminist author Betty Friedan (1963)—have noted that there were pervasive pressures on women during the 1950s for marriage, homemaking, and motherhood (Bouvier, 1980).

Stable Population Growth Although the total fertility rate of the United States has remained low over the last two decades, the nation continues to grow in size because of two factors: the momentum built into our age structure by the postwar population boom, and the continued high rates of immigration. Because of the upsurge of births in the 1950s, there are now many more people in their childbearing years than in older age groups (where most deaths occur). This growth of population represents a "demographic echo" of the baby boom generation, many of whom are now parents. Consequently, the number of people born each year in the United States continues to exceed the number who die. In addition, the nation allows a large number of immigrants to enter each year; these immigrants currently account for between one-fourth and one-third of annual growth.

However, assuming relatively low fertility levels and moderate net migration in the coming decades, the United States may reach ***zero population growth (ZPG)***. ZPG is the state of a population where the number of births plus immigrants equals the number of deaths plus emigrants. For more than 99 percent of its history, humanity remained in the first stage of demographic transition and had little or no population growth (McFalls, 1991; McFalls et al., 1984; Population Reference Bureau, 1978).

The United States is not alone in approaching zero population growth. In 1991, more than 45 nations were at or approaching ZPG. Collectively, these countries account for about one-fourth of the world's people. In the recent past, although some nations have achieved ZPG, it has been relatively short-lived. However, given the current international concern over world population, more

The United States allows a large number of immigrants to enter the country each year; these immigrants currently account for between one-fourth and one-third of annual population growth.

nations may attempt to maintain ZPG in the late twentieth and early twenty-first centuries. Demographers estimate that it will probably take until the year 2200 for demographic transition to run its course worldwide, with the world's population reaching a peak of 11 to 13 billion (Day, 1978:2; Kent, 1991; McFalls, 1991:35).

What will a society with stable population growth be like? In demographic terms, it will be quite different from the United States of the 1990s. By the year 2040, there will be relatively equal numbers of people in each age group, and the median age of the population will be 37 (compared with 32.3 in 1988). As a result, the population pyramid will look more like a rectangle. Yet stable growth does not necessarily mean that people will be nonmobile. Internal migrations—whether "back to the city" or "back to the farm"—are still possible in a ZPG society (Bureau of the Census, 1990a:13; Day, 1978).

The impact of zero population growth goes far beyond demographic statistics. Day-to-day life will be somewhat different as countries cease to grow and the relative proportions of the population in various age groups remain constant. By itself, ZPG is no guarantee either of bounty or of economic ruin. There will be a much larger proportion of older people, especially aged 75 and over, a fact which will place a greater demand on the nation's social service programs and health care institutions. On a more positive note, the economy will be less volatile under ZPG, since the number of entrants to the labor market will be more stable (Spengler, 1978:187).

In industrial societies such as the United States, power and position in the work force have traditionally been determined in part by length of service. With ZPG, there will be less opportunity for promotion based on time of service, since a large part of the population will be older. For example, in 1988 the United States had 40 percent fewer people aged 50 to 55 than aged 20 to 25. By contrast, if the nation reaches ZPG, there will be only 5 to 10 percent fewer adults of age 50 than of age 20. Consequently, many more people with 20 to 30 years of work experience will be competing for the same desirable positions.

ZPG will also lead to changes in family life. Clearly, as fertility rates continue to decline, women will devote fewer years to childbearing and to the social roles of motherhood. The proportion of married women entering the paid labor force can be expected to rise (see Chapter 8). In addition, there may be further increases in the divorce rate in a ZPG society. As families have fewer children, unhappy couples may feel freer to seek separation and divorce (Day, 1978; McFalls, 1981; Weeks, 1992:251–258).

- Which people are especially likely to be without health insurance coverage?
- If the United States adopted nationalized health care, how would it change the position of physicians within the health care system?
- Viewed from a conflict perspective, why is it difficult to achieve basic change within the health care system of the United States?

Each year, people in the United States spend about $800 billion on health care, and that figure continues to rise dramatically (refer back to Figure 12-2). Health care has become a serious economic issue for many individuals and families, who fear (with reason) that illness can lead to economic catastrophe. Because of the skyrocketing costs of all medical services—but particularly hospitalization—the issue of health insurance is on the minds of many citizens and legislators in the United States.

At present, the United States remains the only western industrial democracy that does not treat health care as a basic right. Conflict theorists argue that this difference reflects an underlying and disturbing aspect of capitalism: illness may be exploited for profit. While other western democracies have adopted government-sponsored national health insurance or created a national health service, the American Medical Association (AMA) has played a major role in blocking such measures in the United States. The AMA has exacerbated fears about "socialized medicine" and has encouraged the public to believe that the "sacred doctor-patient relationship" would become less personal and intimate in any governmental health system. Yet even the editors of the *Journal of the American Medical Association,* writing of the institutional racism of the nation's health care system, have concluded that "it is not a coincidence that the United States of America and the Republic of South Africa . . ." are the only developed, institutionalized countries that do not ensure access to basic health care for all citizens (R. Harris, 1966; Lundberg, 1991:2566; Waitzkin and Waterman, 1974:14; Wohl, 1984).

Most people in the United States currently hold some form of private health insurance, such as Blue Cross (which covers many hospital costs) or Blue Shield (which covers doctors' fees during hospitaliza-

tion). Hundreds of firms supply such insurance to the public and reap substantial profits. In addition, millions of people are covered by Medicare and Medicaid, two programs passed by Congress in the 1960s to assist senior citizens and the poor in paying their health care bills. Moreover, as of 1990, 15 percent of people in the United States were enrolled in some type of *health maintenance organization (HMO).* In several respects, the HMO resembles a student health clinic at a residential college; it offers some of the same advantages (guaranteed health care, fixed costs, convenience) and disadvantages (impersonality, occasional long lines, lack of choice of physicians). Although HMOs are often less costly than private medical care, many individuals and families find it difficult to pay for either private health insurance or membership in an HMO (Freudenheim, 1991).

According to 1991 estimates, about 26 percent of the nation's people had no health insurance for at least one month during a 28-month period of study. The uninsured typically include self-employed people with limited incomes, illegal immigrants, and single and divorced mothers who are the sole providers for their families. Blacks and especially Hispanics are less likely than Whites to carry private health insurance. A study released by the National Council of La Raza and the Labor Council for Latin American Advancement reports that, in 1990, one-third of all Hispanics were uninsured, compared with 19.7 percent of African Americans and 12.9 percent of Whites. Currently, the proportion of the nation's population without health insurance is increasing, both because the costs of private coverage are rising sharply and because many private insurers now refuse to create policies for individuals and groups viewed as "high risks" because of their medical histories (Friedman, 1991; *New York Times,* 1992d:A23; Pear, 1991).

People without health insurance may be vulnerable to a lower quality of medical care than those who are covered. According to a study of nearly 600,000 patients hospitalized in 1987 in a national sample of hospitals, patients without health insurance are significantly more likely to die than are patients who have private health insurance. In 13 of 16 patient groups matched for age, gender, and race, the uninsured were found to be sicker when they arrived at the hospital and were 44 to 124 percent more likely to die at

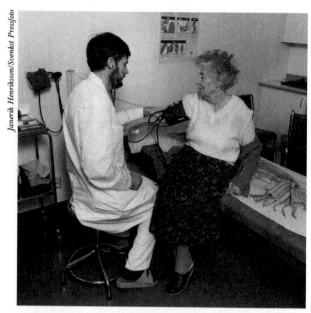

Under Sweden's national health system, medical care is delivered primarily by publicly funded hospitals and clinics, while a national health insurance system sets fees for health care services and reimburses providers of health care.

• *Tax credits and vouchers.* Each person would receive either a full tax credit to buy health coverage, a partial tax credit, or (in the case of the poor) a tax-supported voucher.

• *A managed market.* Employers and government would bargain with existing health care plans and with networks of physicians and hospitals to ensure affordable care for all and more effective control of health care costs.

• *Universal health care.* All residents would be entitled to health care funded primarily through tax revenues. People would choose their physicians, who would be paid by government (V. Cohn, 1992:7).

Opponents of broad national health insurance insist that any of these proposals would be extremely costly and lead to significant tax increases. Defenders of the proposals counter that people in the United States already spend more on health care than any other nation and that other countries have maintained broad governmental health coverage for decades. Great Britain's National Health Service is almost totally tax-supported, and health care services (including medical visits and hospitalization) are free to all citizens. Under Sweden's national health system, medical care is delivered primarily by publicly funded hospitals and clinics, while a national health insurance system sets fees for health care services and reimburses providers of health care. While Canadians rely on private physicians and hospitals for day-to-day treatment, health care is guaranteed as a right for all citizens. Income taxes are used to finance *public* medical insurance, medical fees are set by the government, and private health insurance is prohibited (Conrad and Kern, 1986; Marmor and Godfrey, 1992; Twaddle and Hessler, 1987:335–342; Vayda and Deber, 1984).

Critics point out that if the United States were to move in the direction of nationalized health care as in Great Britain or Sweden, there would be a marked transformation in the health care system as a social institution. With medicine under tight control by the federal government (which would own and operate all hospitals), the doctor-patient relationship would be altered, since an individual would not necessarily have a "family doctor." Physicians and dentists would no longer be self-employed professionals who would set their own fees. Instead, they would become salaried professionals working for the government. As one consequence, the dominant role of doctors in the health care system might be diminished somewhat. Under such a national health care service, physicians, nurses, technicians, and other health care staff would all work for a common "boss" in Washington.

the time of admission. Even after controlling for this difference, researchers found that uninsured patients in 11 of 16 cohorts were 1.2 to 3.2 times more likely to die than were patients with private insurance (Hadley et al., 1991:374–379).

With such disturbing inequities in mind, policymakers have expressed renewed interest in the possibility of national health insurance. *National health insurance* is a general term for legislative proposals that focus on ways to provide the entire population with health care services. First discussed by government officials in the 1930s, it has come to mean many different things, ranging from narrow health insurance coverage with minimal federal subsidies to broad coverage with large-scale federal funding. As of 1992, at least 20 health care bills were pending in Congress. Experts divide these proposals into four basic categories:

• *"Pay or play."* Employers either would provide basic health coverage for all workers or would be required to pay into a fund to assist government in extending coverage to those who are currently uninsured.

As conflict theorists suggest, the health care system, like other social institutions, resists basic change. In general, those who receive substantial wealth and power through the workings of an existing institution will have a strong incentive to keep things as they are. As explained earlier, private insurance companies are benefiting financially from the current system and have a clear interest in opposing certain forms of national health insurance. In addition, the American Medical Association, one of Washington's most powerful lobbying groups, has been successfully fighting national health insurance since the 1930s. Overall, there are more than 200 political action committees (PACs) which represent the medical, pharmaceutical, and insurance industries. These PACs contribute millions of dollars each year to members of Congress and use their influence to block any legislation that would threaten their interests (Dolbeare, 1982; Kemper and Novak, 1991).

SUMMARY

The meanings of *health,* sickness, and disease are shaped by social definitions of behavior. The size, composition, and distribution of the population of the United States can have an important influence on many of the policy issues that we have studied in this book. This chapter considers sociological perspectives on health and illness, the distribution of diseases in a society, the evolution of the health care system as a social institution, various elements of population, and the current problems of overpopulation.

1   According to Talcott Parsons, physicians function as "gatekeepers" for the *sick role,* either verifying a person's condition as "ill" or designating the person as "recovered."

2   Conflict theorists use the term *medicalization of society* to refer to medicine's growing role as a major institution of social control.

3   Labeling theorists suggest that the designation of a person as "healthy" or "ill" generally involves social definition by significant others.

4   Contemporary *social epidemiology* is concerned not only with epidemics but also with nonepidemic diseases, injuries, drug addiction and alcoholism, suicide, and mental illness.

5   Studies have consistently shown that people in the lower classes have higher rates of mortality and disability.

6   The preeminent role of physicians within the health care system of the United States has given them a position of dominance in their dealings with nurses and patients.

7   Thomas Robert Malthus suggested that the world's population was growing more rapidly than the available food supply and that this gap would increase over time. However, Karl Marx was critical of Malthus and saw capitalism rather than rising world population as the cause of social ills.

8   The primary mechanism for obtaining population information in the United States and most other countries is the *census*.

9   Roughly two-thirds of the world's nations have yet to pass fully through the second stage of *demographic transition,* and thus they continue to experience significant population growth.

10   By 2040, when most people born in the 1970s will be entering retirement age, the United States will be approaching *zero population growth (ZPG).*

11   At present, the United States remains the only western industrial democracy that does not treat health care as a basic right.

CRITICAL THINKING QUESTIONS

1   Sociologist Talcott Parsons has argued that the doctor-patient relationship is somewhat like that between parent and child. Does this view seem accurate? Should the doctor-patient relationship become more egalitarian? How might functionalist and conflict theorists differ in their views of the power of physicians within the health care system of the United States?

2   In the 1990s, what does it mean to carry a label associated with a disability, such as "blind," "deaf," or "wheelchair user"? Are there strong stigmas attached to labels which suggest physical or mental disabilities? Are students with disabilities generally accepted in your college and your community? Are there explicit challenges to negative labeling of such students?

3   Some European nations are now experiencing population declines. Their death rates are low and their birthrates are even lower than in stage III of the demographic transition model. Does this pattern suggest that there is now a fourth stage in the demographic transition? Even more important, what are the implications of negative population growth for an industrialized nation approaching the twenty-first century?

KEY TERMS

Birthrate The number of live births per 1000 population in a given year. Also known as the *crude birthrate*. (page 333)

Census An enumeration, or counting, of a population. (333)

Death rate The number of deaths per 1000 population in a given year. Also known as the *crude death rate*. (333)

Demographic transition A term used to describe the change from high birthrates and death rates to relatively low birthrates and death rates. (336)

Demography The scientific study of population. (331)

Fertility The amount of reproduction among women of childbearing age. (331)

Growth rate The difference between births and deaths, plus the difference between immigrants and emigrants, per 1000 population. (335)

Health As defined by the World Health Organization, a state of complete physical, mental, and social well-being, and not merely the absence of disease and infirmity. (319)

Health maintenance organization (HMO) An organization that provides comprehensive medical services to patients for a preestablished fee. (341)

Incidence The number of new cases of a specific disorder occurring within a given population during a stated period of time. (323)

Infant mortality rate The number of deaths of infants under 1 year of age per 1000 live births in a given year. (321)

Life expectancy The average number of years a person can be expected to live under current mortality conditions. (335)

Morbidity rates The incidence of diseases in a given population. (323)

Mortality rate The incidence of death in a given population. (323)

Population pyramid A special type of bar chart that shows the distribution of population by gender and age. (338)

Prevalence The total number of cases of a specific disorder that exist at a given time. (323)

Sick role Societal expectations about the attitudes and behavior of a person viewed as being ill. (319)

Social epidemiology The study of the distribution of disease, impairment, and general health status across a population. (323)

Total fertility rate (TFR) The average number of children born alive to a woman, assuming that she conforms to current fertility rates. (333)

Vital statistics Records of births, deaths, marriages, and divorces gathered through a registration system maintained by governmental units. (333)

Zero population growth (ZPG) The state of a population with a growth rate of zero, which is achieved when the number of births plus immigrants is equal to the number of deaths plus emigrants. (339)

ADDITIONAL READINGS

Ehrlich, Paul R., and Anne H. Ehrlich. *The Population Explosion*. New York: Simon and Schuster, 1990. Two biologists advance the neo-Malthusian thesis that unless interventionist policies are adopted to deal with the population bomb, the world will be subjected to natural forces (perhaps massive increases in death rates) that will bring world population back into balance.

Hine, Darlene Clark. *Black Women in White: Racial Conflict and Cooperation in the Nursing Profession, 1890–1950*. Bloomington: Indiana University Press, 1990. A historical look at racism that led to the exclusion and ultimately the second-class status of Black women within nursing.

Mizrahi, Terry. *Getting Rid of Patients*. New Brunswick, N.J.: Rutgers University Press, 1986. Based on a full year of observation research at a southern hospital and follow-up interviews six years later, Mizrahi's study explores the contradictions in the socialization of physicians.

Waitzkin, Howard. *The Second Sickness: Contradictions of Capitalist Health Care*. Chicago: University of Chicago Press, 1986. This indictment of medical care delivery in the United States offers interesting comparisons with health care in Cuba and the People's Republic of China.

Weeks, John R. *Population: An Introduction to Concepts and Issues* (5th ed.). Belmont, Calif.: Wadsworth, 1992. A sociological treatment of demography with consideration of such social issues as aging, urbanization, economic development, and food supply.

Zussman, Robert. *Intensive Care: Medical Ethics and the Medical Profession*. Chicago: University of Chicago Press, 1992. Intensive care units in hospitals—filled with critically ill patients and expensive technology—are testing grounds for fundamental ethical questions. Zussman examines the processes through which these questions are negotiated.

COLLECTIVE BEHAVIOR, SOCIAL CHANGE, AND URBANIZATION

LOOKING AHEAD

- How do contemporary sociological theorists view collective behavior?
- What functions do rumors perform for a society?
- What impact have social movements had on the course of history and the evolution of social structure?
- How have theorists analyzed the process

- of social change?
- How can urbanization be viewed as an example of social change?
- Why are efforts to promote social change likely to be met with resistance?
- How has the disability rights movement contributed to societal changes in treatment of people with disabilities?

The year 1989 brought tumultuous change in East Germany. That summer, both Hungary and Czechoslovakia began allowing visiting East Germans to continue on to the west. Tens of thousands began to use this escape route; by autumn, as many as 1 million East Germans had applied to emigrate. There were weekly demonstrations against Communist party rule; one demand of protestors was that all restrictions on travel be eliminated.

On October 18, East Germany's ruling Politburo responded to growing pressures for reform by removing Erich Honecker as head of state and replacing him with Egon Krenz. But protests against the Communist regime continued to intensify. Finally, on November 9, a government official announced a new travel decree, under which people who wanted to travel to the west could do so if they obtained visas from their local police stations. As word of the new policy spread that evening via radio and television, thousands of East Germans—most of whom had no visas— surged excitedly to the borders by car and by foot. With the approval of Krenz, the gates which had long separated the two Germanys, among them the hated Berlin Wall, were opened. Waves of East Germans were allowed to cross into the west, and West Germans were allowed to cross to the east (Moseley, 1990).

The norms, values, and social structure of Germany were forever altered that November as East and West Germans crossed the borders to see friends and relatives (and, in the case of many

East Germans, to begin new lives). Indeed, the entire world was deeply affected by photographs and television coverage of the celebrations at the Berlin Wall. Less than a year later, the world's superpowers consented to the reunification of Germany. The dramatic events of November 9 and 10—the rumors that the borders were open, the gathering of huge crowds, the capitulation of the Communist leadership to social forces they could no longer control—represent an example of both collective behavior and social change, the two focal points of this chapter.

Practically all group activity can be thought of as collective behavior, but sociologists have given distinct meaning to the term. Neil Smelser (1981:431), a sociologist who specializes in this field, has defined **collective behavior** as the "relatively spontaneous and unstructured behavior of a group of people who are reacting to a common influence in an ambiguous situation." The crowd behavior in the celebrations at the Berlin Wall is one example of collective behavior.

Social change has been defined by sociologist Wilbert Moore (1967:3) as significant alteration over time in behavior patterns and culture, including norms and values. But what constitutes a "significant" alteration? Certainly the dramatic rise in formal education documented in Chapter 10 is a change that has had profound social consequences. Other social changes that have had long-term and important consequences include the emergence of slavery as a system of stratification (see Chapter 6), the industrial revolution (Chap-

348

Jubilant Germans celebrate atop the Berlin Wall, near the Brandenburg Gate, on November 10, 1989. The celebration erupted after East German authorities opened border crossings to West Germany on November 9.

ters 6 and 11), the greatly increased participation of women in the paid labor force of the United States and Europe (Chapter 8), and the worldwide population explosion (Chapter 12).

This chapter begins with an examination of a number of theories used by sociologists to better understand collective behavior, including the emergent-norm, value-added, and assembling perspectives. Particular attention is given to certain types of collective behavior, among them crowd behavior, disaster behavior, fads and fashions, panics and crazes, rumors, public opinion, and social movements. Contemporary sociology acknowledges the crucial role that social movements can play in mobilizing discontented members of a society and initiating social change.

Efforts to explain long-term social changes have led to the development of theories of change, which will be studied in the second half of the chapter. We will examine some of the sources of change that sociologists see as contributing to significant alterations in behavior and culture, including physical environment, population, science and technology, strains of social inequality, and youth. The process of urbanization will be studied as an example of social change. Finally, in the social policy section, we will focus on changing societal treatment of people with disabilities and on the growing disability rights movement.

THEORIES OF COLLECTIVE BEHAVIOR

As Neil Smelser's definition suggests, collective behavior is usually unstructured and spontaneous. This fluidity makes it more difficult for sociologists to generalize about people's behavior in such situations. Nevertheless, sociologists have developed various theoretical perspectives which can help us to study—and deal with in a constructive manner—crowds, riots, fads, and other types of collective behavior.

Emergent-Norm Perspective

The early writings on collective behavior imply that crowds are basically ungovernable. However, this is not always the case. In many situations, crowds are effectively governed by norms and procedures and may even engage in such practices as queuing, or waiting in line. We routinely encounter queues when we await service, as in a fast-food restaurant or bank; or when we wish to enter or exit, as in a movie theater or football stadium. Normally, physical barriers, such as guardrails and checkout counters, help to regulate queuing. When massive crowds are involved, ushers or security personnel may also be present to assist in the orderly movement of the crowd.

On December 28, 1991, people began gathering outside a building at City College in New York City to see a heavily promoted charity basketball game involving rap stars and other celebrities. By late afternoon, more than 5000 people had gathered for the 6:00 P.M. game, even though the gym could accommodate only 2730 spectators. Although the crowd was divided into separate lines for ticket holders and those wishing to buy tickets at the door, restlessness and discontent swept through both lines and sporadic fights broke out. The arrival of celebrities only added to the commotion and the crowd's tension.

Doors to the gymnasium were finally opened one hour before game time, but only 50 people were admitted to the lobby at a time. Once their tickets had been taken, spectators proceeded down two flights of stairs, through a single unlocked entrance, and into the gym. Those further back in the crowd experienced the disconcerting feeling of moving forward, then stopping for a period of time, and then repeating this process again and again. Well past the publicized starting time, huge crowds were still outside, pressing to gain entrance to the building.

Finally, with the arena more than full, the doors to the gym were closed. As rumors spread outside the building that the game was beginning, more than 1000 frustrated fans, many with valid tickets, surged through glass doors into the building and headed for the stairs. Soon the stairwell became a horrifying mass of people surging against locked metal doors to the gym and crushed against concrete walls. The result was a tragedy: 9 young men and women eventually died and 29 were injured through the sheer pressure of bodies pressing against each other and against walls and doors (Mollen, 1992).

This was not the first time that violent crowding had led to tragedy. In 1979, 11 rock fans died of suffocation after a crowd outside Cincinnati's Riverfront Stadium pushed to gain entrance to a concert by The Who. In 1989, when thousands of soccer fans forced their way into a stadium to see the semifinals of the English Cup, more than 90 people were trampled to death or smothered. In 1991, three young people died of suffocation *inside* an arena in Salt Lake City as a crowd surged forward to get the best viewing point to hear the heavy metal group AC/DC (J. Gross, 1991a; D. L. Miller, 1988:46–47).

Sociologists Ralph Turner and Lewis Killian (1987) have offered a view of collective behavior which is helpful in assessing these events. Their emergent-norm perspective begins with the assumption that a large crowd, such as a group of rock or soccer fans, is governed by expectations of proper behavior just as much as four people playing doubles tennis. The *emergent-norm perspective* states that a collective definition of appropriate and inappropriate behavior emerges during episodes of collective behavior. Like other social norms, the emergent norm reflects shared convictions held by members of the group and is enforced through sanctions (see Chapter 2). These new norms of proper behavior may arise in what seem at first as ambiguous situations. There is latitude for a wide range of acts, yet within a general framework established by the emergent norms.

Using the emergent-norm perspective, we can see that fans outside the charity basketball game at City College found themselves in an ambiguous situation. Normal procedures of crowd control, such as orderly queues, were rapidly dissolving. A new norm was simultaneously emerging: it is acceptable to push forward, even if people in front protest. Some members of the crowd—especially those with valid tickets—may have felt that this push forward was justified as a way of ensuring that they would get to see the game. Others pushed forward simply to relieve the physical pressure of those pushing behind them. Even individuals who rejected the emergent norm may have felt afraid to oppose it, fearing ridicule or injury. Thus, conforming behavior, which we usually associate with highly structured situations (see Chapter 5), was evident in this rather chaotic crowd, as it had been earlier at the concerts by The Who and AC/DC and at the soccer game in England. It would be misleading to assume that these fans acted simply as a united, collective unit in creating a dangerous situation.

Value-Added Perspective

Neil Smelser (1962) continued the sociological effort to analyze collective behavior with his value-added theory. He uses the *value-added model* to explain how broad social conditions are transformed in a definite pattern into some form of collective behavior. This model outlines six important determinants of collective behavior.

The 1992 riots in south-central Los Angeles, during which 58 people were killed, were sparked by the acquittal of four White police officers charged after the videotaped beating of Rodney King, a Black construction worker.

Initially, in Smelser's view, certain elements must be present for an incident of collective behavior to take place. He uses the term *structural conduciveness* to indicate that the organization of society can facilitate the emergence of conflicting interests. Structural conduciveness makes collective behavior possible, though not inevitable.

The second determinant of collective behavior, *structural strain,* occurs when the conduciveness of the social structure to potential conflict gives way to a perception that conflicting interests do, in fact, exist. This type of strain was evident in East Germany in 1989: the intense desire of many East Germans to travel to or emigrate to the west placed great strain on the social control exercised by the ruling Communist party. Such structural strain contributes to what Smelser calls a *generalized belief*—a shared view of reality that redefines social action and serves to guide behavior. The overthrow of Communist rule in East Germany and other Soviet-bloc nations occurred in part as a result of a generalized belief that the Communist regimes were oppressive and that popular resistance *could* lead to social change.

Smelser suggests that a specific event or incident, known as a *precipitating factor,* triggers collective behavior. The event may grow out of the social structure, but whatever its origins, it contributes to the strains and beliefs shared by a group or community. For example, studies of race riots have found that interracial fights or arrests and searches of minority individuals by police officers often precede disturbances. The 1992 riots in south-central Los Angeles, during which 58 people were killed, were sparked by the acquittal of four White police officers charged after the videotaped beating of Rodney King, a Black construction worker.

According to Smelser, the presence of the four determinants identified above is necessary for collective behavior to occur. Nevertheless, the group must be *mobilized for action.* An extended thundershower or severe snowstorm may preclude such a mobilization. People are more likely to come together on weekends than on weekdays, in the evening rather than during the daytime.

The manner in which *social control is exercised*—both formally and informally—can be significant in determining whether the preceding factors will end in collective behavior. Stated simply, social control may prevent, delay, or interrupt a collective outburst. In some instances, forces of social control may be guilty of misjudgments that intensify the severity of an outbreak. In the view of many observers, the Los Angeles police did not respond fast enough as the initial rioting began in 1992, thereby creating a vacuum that allowed the level of violence to escalate.

The emergent-norm and value-added perspectives have both been questioned because of their imprecise definitions and the difficulty of testing them empirically. For example, the emergent-norm perspective of Turner and Killian has been criticized for being too vague in defining what constitutes a norm; the value-added model has been challenged because of its lack of specificity in defining generalized belief and structural strain. Of these two theories, the emergent-norm perspective appears to offer a more useful explanation of societywide episodes of collective behavior, such as crazes and fashions, than the value-added approach (M. Brown and Goldin, 1973; Quarantelli and Hundley, 1975; K. Tierney, 1980).

Nevertheless, Smelser's value-added model has been persuasive for many sociologists involved in the study of collective behavior. His perspective represents an advance over earlier theories that treated gatherings as dominated by irrational, extreme impulses. The value-added approach firmly relates episodes of collective behavior to the overall social structure of a society.

Assembling Perspective

As we have seen, one key determinant of collective behavior is mobilization for action. Some sociologists have given attention to the question of how people come together to undertake collective action. Clark McPhail, perhaps the most prolific researcher of collective behavior in the last 20 years, sees such behavior as involving people and organizations consciously responding to one another's actions. Drawing on the work of the interactionist approach to sociology, McPhail has observed that organized interactions occur during such diverse events as celebrations and revolutions. People may chant, sing, or gesture with respect to a common object. In the midst of waiting in line outside a rock concert, as we have already seen, they may accept an emergent norm and begin to push forward toward the doors.

Building on the interactionist approach, McPhail and Miller (1973) introduced the concept of the assembling process. Earlier theorists of collective behavior had been content to explain events such as riots without examining how gatherings of people actually came together. However, the *assembling perspective* sought for the first time to examine how and why people move from different points in space to a common location.

For example, sociologists David Snow, Louis Zurcher, and Robert Peters (1981) studied a series of football victory celebrations at the University of Texas that spilled over into the main streets of Austin. Some participants actively tried to recruit passersby for the celebrations by thrusting out open palms "to get five" or by yelling at drivers to honk their horns. In fact, encouraging still further assembling became a preoccupation of the celebrators. Whenever spectators were absent, those celebrating were relatively quiet.

A basic distinction has been made between two types of assemblies. *Periodic assemblies* include recurring, relatively routine gatherings of people such as work groups, college classes, and season ticket holders of an athletic series. These assemblies are characterized by advance scheduling and recurring attendance of the majority of participants. Thus, most members of an introductory sociology class may gather together for lectures every Monday, Wednesday, and Friday morning at a regular meeting time. By contrast, *nonperiodic assemblies* include demonstrations, parades, and gatherings at the scene of fires, accidents, and arrests. Such assemblies, for example, the 1989 celebrations at the Berlin Wall after the opening of Germany's borders, often result from word-of-mouth information and are generally less formal than periodic assemblies.

These three approaches to collective behavior give us deeper insight into relatively spontaneous and unstructured situations. While critics contend that certain key definitions are imprecise, thereby making it difficult to empirically test the validity of these theories, they nevertheless represent a significant advance over earlier views of collective behavior.

FORMS OF COLLECTIVE BEHAVIOR

Drawing on the emergent-norm, value-added, and assembling perspectives—and also on other aspects of sociological examination—sociologists have examined many forms of collective behavior. Among these forms are crowds, disaster behavior, fads and fashions, panics and crazes, rumors, public opinion, and social movements.

Crowds

Crowds are temporary groupings of people in close proximity who share a common focus or interest. Spectators at a baseball game, participants at a pep rally, and rioters are all examples of crowds. Sociologists have been interested in what characteristics are common to crowds. Of course, it can be difficult to generalize, since the nature of crowds varies dramatically. For example, in terms of the emotions shared by crowds, hostages on a hijacked airplane experience intense fear, whereas participants in a religious revival feel a deep sense of joy.

If we apply the emergent-norm perspective to crowds involved in urban rioting, we can suggest that a new social norm is accepted (at least temporarily) which condones looting. The norms of respect for private property—as well as obedience to the law—are replaced by a concept of all goods as community property. All desirable items, including those behind locked doors, can be used for the "general welfare." In effect, the emergent norm allows looters to take what they regard as properly theirs (Quarantelli and Dynes, 1970; see also C. McPhail, 1991).

Disaster Behavior

Newspapers, television reports, and even rumors bring us word of many disasters around the world. The term *disaster* refers to a sudden or disruptive event or set of events that overtaxes a community's resources so that outside aid is necessary (J. Thompson and Hawkes, 1962:268). Traditionally, disasters have been catastrophes related to nature, such as earthquakes, floods, and fires. Yet, in an industrial age, natural disasters have now been joined by such "technological disasters" as airplane crashes, industrial explosions, nuclear meltdowns, and massive chemical poisonings (M. Brown and Goldin, 1973:34; see also Kreps, 1984:311–313).

Sociologists have made enormous strides in disaster research despite the problems inherent in this type of investigation. The work of the Disaster Research Center at the University of Delaware has been especially important. The center has teams of trained researchers prepared to leave for the site of any disaster on four hours' notice.

Their field kits include material identifying them as staff members, recording equipment, and general interview guidelines for use in various types of disasters. En route to the scene, these researchers attempt to obtain news information in order to learn about the conditions they may encounter. On arrival, the team establishes a communication post to coordinate fieldwork and maintain contact with the center's headquarters.

The Disaster Research Center has conducted more than 520 field studies of natural and technological disasters in the United States and 24 in other nations. Its research has been used to develop effective planning and programming for dealing with disasters in such areas as delivery of emergency health care, establishment and operation of rumor-control centers, coordination of mental health services, and implementation of disaster-preparedness and emergency-response programs. The center has also provided extensive training and field research for over 100 graduate students. These students maintain a professional commitment to disaster research and often go on to work for such disaster service organizations as the Red Cross and civil defense agencies (D. L. Miller, 1988:55–56; Quarantelli and Wilson, 1980; see also Cisin and Clark, 1962).

Remarkably, in the wake of many natural and technological disasters, there is increased structure and organization rather than chaos. In the United States, disasters are often followed by the creation of an emergency "operations group" which coordinates public services and even certain services normally carried out by the private sector (such as food distribution). Decision making becomes more centralized than in normal times (Dynes, 1978).

Fads and Fashions

An almost endless list of objects and behavior patterns seems temporarily to catch the fancy of Americans. Examples include silly putty, Davy Crockett coonskin caps, hula hoops, *Star Wars* toys, the Rubik cube, break dancing, Cabbage Patch Kids, *The Simpsons* T shirts, and Nintendo games. Fads and fashions are sudden movements toward the acceptance of some lifestyle or particular taste in clothing, music, or recreation (Aguirre et al., 1988; R. Johnson, 1985).

Fads and fashions are sudden movements involving a particular lifestyle or taste in clothing, music, or recreation.

Fads are temporary patterns of behavior involving large numbers of people; they spring up independently of preceding trends and do not give rise to successors. By contrast, ***fashions*** are pleasurable mass involvements that feature a certain amount of acceptance by society and have a line of historical continuity (Lofland, 1981:442; 1985). Thus, punk haircuts would be considered a fashion, part of the constantly changing standards of hair length and style, whereas adult roller blading would be considered a fad of the early 1980s.

Fads and fashions allow people to identify with something different from the dominant institutions and symbols of a culture. Members of a subculture may break with tradition while remaining "in" with (accepted by) a significant reference group of peers. Fads are generally short-lived and tend to be viewed with amusement or lack of interest by most nonparticipants. Fashions, by contrast, often have wider implications because they can reflect (or falsely give the impression of) wealth and status.

Panics and Crazes

Panics and crazes both represent responses to some generalized belief. A ***craze*** is an exciting mass involvement which lasts for a relatively long period of time (Lofland, 1981:441; 1985).

For example, in late 1973, a press release from a Wisconsin congressman described how the federal bureaucracy had failed to contract for enough toilet paper for government buildings. Then, on December 19, as part of his nightly monologue on the *Tonight Show*, Johnny Carson suggested that it would not be strange if the entire nation experienced a shortage of toilet paper. Millions of viewers took his humorous comment seriously and immediately began stockpiling this item out of fear that it would soon be unavailable. Shortly thereafter, as a consequence of this craze, a shortage of toilet paper actually resulted. Its effects were felt into 1974 (Malcolm, 1974; *Money*, 1987).

By contrast, a ***panic*** is a fearful arousal or collective flight based on a generalized belief which may or may not be accurate. In a panic, people commonly perceive that there is insufficient time or inadequate means to avoid injury. Panics often occur on battlefields, in overcrowded burning buildings, or during stock market crashes. The key distinction between panics and crazes is that panics are flights *from* something whereas crazes are movements *to* something.

One of the most famous cases of panic in the United States was touched off by a media event: the 1938 Halloween eve radio dramatization of H. G. Wells's science fiction novel *The War of the Worlds*. This CBS broadcast realistically told of an invasion from Mars, with interplanetary visitors landing in New Jersey and taking over New York City 15 minutes later. The announcer indicated at the beginning of the broadcast that the account was fictional, but about 80 percent of the listeners tuned in late.

Clearly, a significant number of listeners became frightened by what they assumed to be a news report. However, some accounts have exaggerated people's reactions to *The War of the Worlds*. One report concluded that "people all over the United States were praying, crying, fleeing frantically to escape death from the Martians." In contrast, a CBS national survey of listeners found that only 20 percent were genuinely scared by the broadcast. Although perhaps a million people *reacted* to this program, many reacted by switching to other stations to see if the "news" was being carried elsewhere. This "invasion from outer space" set off a limited panic, rather than mass hysteria (R. W. Brown, 1954:871; Cantril, 1940:102–107; Houseman, 1972).

It is often believed that people engaged in panics or crazes are unaware of their actions, but this is certainly not the case. As the emergent-norm perspective suggests, people take cues from one another as to how to act during such forms of collective behavior. Even in the midst of an escape from a life-threatening situation, such as a fire in a crowded theater, people do not tend to run in a headlong stampede. Rather, they adjust their behavior on the basis of the perceived circumstances and the conduct of others who are assembling in a given location. To outside observers studying the events, people's decisions may seem foolish (pushing against a locked door) or suicidal (jumping from a balcony). Yet, for that individual at that moment, the action may genuinely seem appropriate—or the only desperate choice available (Quarantelli, 1957).

Rumors

"Paul McCartney is dead." According to a popular rumor in 1969, at the height of the Beatles' popularity, the singer died that year at the age of 27. (Or, according to another version of the rumor, he had died in 1966 in an automobile accident after leaving a recording studio tired, sad, and depressed.)

The evidence supporting this rumor seemed clear—at least to some. There was the funeral procession shown on the back of the Beatles' "Abbey Road" album, with McCartney (or perhaps a look-alike?) walking barefoot like a corpse. According to some listeners, if one pays careful attention at the end of the song "Strawberry Fields Forever," one can hear John Lennon say, "I buried Paul!" Moreover, if "Revolution No. 9" is played backwards, one can supposedly hear the terrifying sounds of a traffic accident. As radio stations carried these and other tidbits, Paul McCartney was interviewed by *Life* magazine, thereby establishing that he was indeed alive. But skeptics countered that when a McCartney look-alike contest had been held a few months earlier in Britain, a winner had never been announced. Perhaps *Life* had unwittingly interviewed an imposter standing in for the deceased McCartney? . . . (Kapferer, 1992:54; Neary, 1969; Rosnow, 1991:486).

Not all rumors that we hear are so astonishing, but none of us is immune from hearing or starting rumors. A **rumor** is a piece of information gathered informally which is used to interpret an ambiguous situation (R. Berk, 1974:78). Rumors serve a function by providing a group with a shared belief. As a group strives for consensus, members eliminate those rumors that are least useful or credible.

Although some rumors are begun with a specific intent to spread a falsehood, Jean-Noel Kapferer (1992:53), a professor of communication in France, suggests that rumors are typically "spontaneous social products, devoid of ulterior motives and underlying strategies." Kapferer argues that the existence and spreading of rumors reflect natural processes within social groups. In his view, it is misleading to project the responsibility for a rumor outside the group which hears the rumor, finds it meaningful, and mobilizes to pass it on. Kapferer (1992:54) concludes that "in the case of rumors, . . . the public is the main actor."

Rumors about celebrities—whether politicians, movie stars, or members of royal families—have long been a popular pastime around the world. Natural disasters, as well, tend to be a common subject for rumors. For example, after California was shaken (literally and figuratively) in mid-1992 by a series of powerful earthquakes and after-

BOX 13-1

PROCTER AND GAMBLE'S FIGHT AGAINST RUMORS OF SATANISM

Procter and Gamble is one of the leading consumer marketers in the United States. Its diverse products include Folger's coffee, Tide detergent, Ivory soap, Head and Shoulders shampoo, Crest toothpaste, Jif peanut butter, and Pampers disposable diapers. Yet, according to persistent rumors, the company that makes Ivory soap is engaged in Satanic activities!

At the center of this sweeping and completely unproven charge is Procter and Gamble's distinctive corporate trademark: the man in the moon and 13 stars. Adapted as the company's trademark in 1851, this presentation was developed by a nineteenth-century art director who drew 13 stars to represent the nation's original colonies. However, beginning in 1980, rumors reported that the trademark was a symbol of Satanism and that Procter and Gamble's

profits were channeled into satanic activities. One fallacious charge was that Procter and Gamble's chairman had appeared on television on *Donahue* and stated that he owed all his success to Satan.

As the rumor spread across the United States, Procter and Gamble took action. Press releases were issued denying that any Procter and Gamble executive had ever credited his own or the company's success to Satanism. Religious leaders—among them Billy Graham and Jerry Falwell—were enlisted to help combat the rumored link between the company and Satanism. At the height of its rumor-control efforts, Procter and Gamble employed 15 staff members to deal with as many as 15,000 monthly inquiries about possible ties to Satan.

By the early 1980s, this rumor seemed to be fading, but it resur-

faced in 1984. Procter and Gamble began a new initiative against these charges, including lawsuits against people who had allegedly spread "false and malicious" statements associating the company with Satanism. But, in the end, the fight against such rumors became so costly that Procter and Gamble regretfully decided upon a symbolic concession. In 1985, it announced that it would gradually remove the moon and stars trademark from some of Procter and Gamble's product packages. Subsequently, in 1991, Procter and Gamble adopted two new corporate logos. It announced that stationery, business cards, and other materials would feature either the symbol "P&G" or a scriptlike "Procter & Gamble."

SOURCES: P. Bacon, 1985; Koenig, 1985:39–54; Madigan, 1982; *New York Post*, 1991:16; Procter and Gamble, 1985, 1986.

---

shocks, rumors abounded that the long-dreaded "Big One" was imminent. According to one unfounded account, the California Institute of Technology in Pasadena—the site of the top seismology laboratory in the area—had ordered all its employees to leave town (*New York Times*, 1992f:A8; Rosnow, 1991).

Like celebrities, business firms find that rumors can be damaging. One type of rumor that is particularly worrisome for manufacturers involves ill-founded charges of contamination. In the late 1970s, it was rumored that General Foods' Pop Rocks and Cosmic Candy would explode in children's mouths with tragic results, yet no such ex-

plosions took place. Another popular theme of rumors in the marketplace focuses on the charge that a company is using its profits for evil purposes (Koenig, 1985). As is evident in Box 13-1, a corporation engaged in rumor control may find this process both time-consuming and expensive.

Publics and Public Opinion

The least organized and most individualized form of collective behavior is represented by publics. The term *public* refers to a dispersed group of people, not necessarily in contact with one another, who share interest in an issue.

As the term is used in the study of collective behavior, the public does not include everyone. Rather, it is a collective of people who focus on some issue, who engage in discussion, who agree or disagree, and who sometimes dissolve when the issue has been decided (Blumer, 1955:189–191, 1969:195–208; R. Turner and Killian, 1987:158–185).

The term *public opinion* refers to expressions of attitudes on matters of public policy which are communicated to decision makers. The last part of this definition is particularly important. From the point of view of theorists of collective behavior, there can be no public opinion unless there are both a public and a decision maker. We are not concerned here with the formation of an individual's attitudes on social and political issues; this question was explored in Chapter 11. Instead, in studying public opinion, we focus on the ways in which a public's attitudes are communicated to decision makers and on the ultimate outcome of the public's attempts to influence policymaking (R. Turner and Killian, 1987).

Polls and surveys play a major role in the assessment of public opinion. Using the same techniques that are essential in developing reliable questionnaire and interview schedules (see Chapter 1), survey specialists conduct studies of public opinion for business firms (market analyses), the government, the mass media (ratings of programs), and, of course, politicians. Survey data have become extremely influential not only in preselecting the products we buy but in determining which political candidates are likely to win election and even which possible Supreme Court nominees should be selected (Brower, 1988).

The earliest political polls lacked the scientific rigor that contemporary social scientists require. In a famous example of unscientific and misleading polling, the magazine *Literary Digest* sent over 18 million postcard ballots to Americans to assess voters' opinions on the 1936 presidential election. The 2 million replies indicated that Republican candidate Alf Landon would defeat Democratic incumbent Franklin D. Roosevelt. *Literary Digest* predicted a Landon victory, yet Roosevelt was reelected in a landslide.

Today, this method of polling would be considered completely unreliable. The magazine took its original sample from automobile registration lists and telephone books. Yet, in 1936, in the midst of the Depression, people with enough money to own a car or a private telephone were hardly a representative cross section of the nation's voters. Instead, those polled tended to be prosperous citizens who might be likely to support Republican candidates (Squire, 1988).

Current political polls use more precise and representative sampling techniques. As a result, their projections of presidential elections often fall within a few percentage points of the actual vote. The Gallup poll came within 3.7 percent of Ronald Reagan's vote in 1980, within 0.2 percent of Reagan's vote in 1984, and within 0.4 percent of George Bush's vote in 1988.

While political polling has improved dramatically since the *Literary Digest*'s 1936 fiasco, misleading surveys are still with us. Regrettably, telephone companies have marketed call-in "polls" using 1-900 area code numbers. Television viewers or newspaper readers are asked to call one number to register an opinion on an issue, or a second number to register an alternative opinion. There are many problems inherent in this type of "polling." The sample that emerges is hardly representative (refer back to Chapter 1) in that it includes only those people who happened to see the commercial or advertisement for the poll and who feel strongly enough about the issue to spend the typical charge of $1.

Social Movements

Social movements are the most all-encompassing type of collective behavior, because they may include aspects of other types such as crowds, rumors, publics, and public opinion. Although such factors as physical environment, population, technology, and social inequality serve as sources of change—as we will discuss more fully later in the chapter—it is the *collective* effort of individuals organized in social movements that ultimately leads to social change. Sociologists use the term *social movements* to refer to organized collective activities to bring about or resist fundamental change in existing society. Herbert Blumer (1955:119), a theorist of collective behavior, recognized the special importance of social movements when he defined them as "collective enterprises to establish a new order of life."

Moyer/Gamma Liaison

Social movements try to bring about fundamental changes in society. Shown are Chinese students demonstrating in Tianamen Square in 1989.

Social movements can be contrasted with the forms of collective behavior described earlier in the chapter. Like publics, social movements tend to focus on issues of public policy. Like crowds and fads, they involve social change—although social movements aim at more fundamental and long-lasting changes. Social movements persist over a longer time than other forms of collective behavior. In part, this is because social movements are more structured; their leadership is frequently well organized and ongoing. Ironically, as Robert Michels (1915) noted (see Chapter 4), political movements fighting for social change eventually take on bureaucratic forms of organization. Leaders dominate the decision-making process without directly consulting followers.

In many nations, including the United States, social movements have had a dramatic impact on history and the evolution of social structure. It would be naive to ignore the actions of abolitionists, suffragists, civil rights workers, and activists opposed to the war in Vietnam. Members of each social movement stepped outside traditional channels for bringing about social change and yet had a noticeable influence on public policy in the United States (J. Wilson, 1973:5).

Although change and conflict are implicit in the existence of social movements, their activities can also be analyzed from a functionalist perspective. Even when unsuccessful, social movements contribute to the formation of public opinion. Initially, the ideas of Margaret Sanger and other early advocates of birth control were viewed as "radical," yet contraceptives are now widely available in the United States. Moreover, social movements are viewed by functionalists as a training ground for leaders of the political establishment. Such heads of state as Cuba's Fidel Castro and Iran's Ayatollah Khomeini came to power after serving as leaders of revolutionary movements. More recently, Poland's Lech Walesa, Russia's Boris Yeltsin, and Czech playwright Vaclav Havel led protest movements against Communist rule and subsequently became leaders of their countries' governments (Heberle, 1968).

How and why do social movements emerge? Obviously, people are often discontented with the way things are. But what causes them to mobilize at a particular moment in a collective effort to work for change? Sociologists rely on two explanations: the relative-deprivation and resource-mobilization approaches.

Relative Deprivation Those members of a society who feel most frustrated and disgruntled by the social and economic conditions of their lives are not necessarily "worst off" in an objective sense. Social scientists have long recognized that what is most significant is how people *perceive* their situation. Karl Marx pointed out that although the misery of the workers was important in reflecting their oppressed state, so was their position relative to the capitalist ruling class (Marx and Engels, 1955:94, original edition 1847).

The term *relative deprivation* is defined as the conscious feeling of a negative discrepancy between legitimate expectations and present actualities (J. Wilson, 1973:69). It may be characterized by scarcity rather than lack of necessities (refer back to the distinction between absolute and relative poverty in Chapter 6). A relatively deprived person is dissatisfied because he or she feels downtrodden relative to some appropriate reference group. Thus, blue-collar workers who live in two-family houses with little lawn space—though hardly at the bottom of the economic ladder—may nevertheless feel deprived in comparison with corporate managers and professionals who live in lavish and exclusive suburbs.

In addition to the feeling of relative deprivation, two other elements must be present before discontent will be channeled into a social movement. People must feel that they have a right to their goals, that they deserve better than what they have. For example, the struggle against European colonialism in Africa (see Chapter 6) intensified when growing numbers of Africans decided that it was legitimate for them to have political and economic independence. At the same time, the disadvantaged group must perceive that it cannot attain its goals through conventional means. This belief may or may not be correct. Yet, whichever is the case, the group will not mobilize into a social movement unless there is a shared perception that its relative deprivation can be ended only through collective action (Morrison, 1971).

Critics of the relative-deprivation approach have noted that an increase in feelings of deprivation is not always necessary before people are moved to act. In addition, this approach fails to explain why certain feelings of deprivation are transformed into social movements, whereas in other situations there is no collective effort to reshape society. Consequently, in recent years sociologists have given increasing attention to the forces needed to bring about the emergence of social movements (Alain, 1985; Finkel and Rule, 1987; Orum, 1978).

Resource Mobilization Sociologist Anthony Oberschall (1973:199) has argued that to sustain social protest or resistance, there must be an "organizational base and continuity of leadership." The term *resource mobilization* is used to refer to the ways a social movement utilizes such resources as money, political influence, access to the media, and personnel. The success of a movement for change will depend in good part on how effectively it mobilizes its resources (see also Gamson, 1989; Staggenborg, 1989a, 1989b).

As people become part of a social movement, norms develop to guide their behavior. Members of the movement may be expected to attend regular meetings of organizations, pay dues, recruit new adherents, and boycott "enemy" products or speakers. The emergence of a new social movement can be evident from the rise of special language or new words for familiar terms. In recent years, social movements have been responsible for such new terms of self-reference as *Blacks* and *African Americans* (used to replace *Negroes*), *gays* (used to replace *homosexuals*), *people with AIDS* (used to replace *AIDS victims*), and *people with disabilities* (used to replace *the handicapped*).

Why do certain individuals join a social movement whereas others do not, when all share the same situation of relative deprivation and are subject to the same opportunities for resource mobilization? Karl Marx recognized the importance of recruitment when he called on workers to become aware of their oppressed status and develop a class consciousness (see Chapter 6). Like the contemporary resource-mobilization approach, Marx held that a social movement (specifically, the revolt of the proletariat) would require leaders to sharpen the awareness of the oppressed. They must help workers to overcome feelings of *false consciousness*, or attitudes that do not reflect workers' objective position, in order to organize a revolutionary movement. Similarly, one of the challenges faced by women's liberation activists of the late 1960s and early 1970s was to convince women that they were being deprived of their rights and of socially valued resources.

Unlike the relative-deprivation approach, the resource-mobilization perspective focuses on strategic difficulties facing social movements. Any movement for fundamental change will almost certainly arouse opposition; effective mobilization will depend in part on how the movement deals with resistance to its activities. Why people resist social change, and which tactics they employ in resisting, will be discussed later in the chapter. In the following section, we will examine a number of explanations for social change.

THEORIES OF SOCIAL CHANGE

It is clearly a challenge to explain social change in the diverse and complex world of the 1990s. Theorists from several disciplines have sought to analyze social change. In some instances, they have examined historical events to arrive at a better understanding of contemporary changes. We will review three theoretical approaches to change: evolutionary, functionalist, and conflict theory.

Evolutionary Theory

Nineteenth-century theories of social change reflect the influence of Charles Darwin's (1809–1882) pioneering work in biological evolution. According to his approach, there has been a continuing progression of successive life forms. For example, since human beings came at a later stage of evolution than reptiles, we represent a "higher" form of life. Social theorists sought an analogy to this biological model and originated *evolutionary theory,* which views society as moving in a definite direction. Early evolutionary theorists generally agreed that society was inevitably progressing to a higher state. As might be expected, they concluded in an ethnocentric fashion that their own behavior and culture were more advanced than those of earlier civilizations.

Auguste Comte (1798–1857), described in Chapter 1 as a founder of sociology, was an evolutionary theorist of change. He saw human societies as moving forward in their thinking from mythology to the scientific method. Similarly, Émile Durkheim (1933, original edition 1893) maintained that society progressed from simple to more complex forms of social organization.

The writings of Comte and Durkheim are examples of *unilinear evolutionary theory.* This approach contends that all societies pass through the same successive stages of evolution and inevitably reach the same end. English sociologist Herbert Spencer (1820–1903), also discussed in Chapter 1, used a similar approach: Spencer likened society to a living body with interrelated parts that were moving toward a common destiny. However, contemporary evolutionary theorists such as Gerhard Lenski, Jr., are more likely to picture social change as multilinear than to rely on the more limited unilinear perspective. *Multilinear evolutionary theory* holds that change can occur in several ways and that it does not inevitably lead in the same direction (Haines, 1988; J. Turner, 1985).

Multilinear theorists recognize that human culture has evolved along a number of lines. For example, the theory of demographic transition graphically demonstrates that population change in developing nations has not necessarily followed the model evident in industrialized nations (see Chapter 12). Medical and public health technology was introduced gradually in the developed nations, which gave them time to adjust to falling death rates and resulting rises in population. However, such technology was imported much more rapidly by developing nations, leading to dramatic population growth and severe pressure on social services and natural resources, including food production (R. Appelbaum, 1970:15–64).

Functionalist Theory

As has been stressed throughout this textbook, functionalist sociologists are concerned with the role of cultural elements in preserving the social order as a whole. They focus on what maintains a system, not on what changes it. This might seem to suggest that functionalists can offer little of value to the study of social change. Yet, as the work of sociologist Talcott Parsons demonstrates, functionalists have made a distinctive contribution to this area of sociological investigation.

Parsons (1902–1979), a leading proponent of functionalist theory (refer back to Chapter 1), viewed society as naturally being in a state of equilibrium. By "equilibrium," he meant that society tends toward a state of stability or balance. Parsons would view even prolonged labor strikes or civilian riots as temporary disruptions in the status quo rather than as significant alterations in social structure. Therefore, according to his *equilibrium model,* as changes occur in one part of society, there must be adjustments in other parts. If this does not take place, the society's equilibrium will be threatened and strains will occur.

Reflecting an evolutionary approach, Parsons (1966:21–24) maintained that four processes of social change are inevitable. The first, *differentiation,* refers to the increasing complexity of social organization. A change from "medicine man" to physician, nurse, and pharmacist is an illustration of differentiation in the field of health. This process is accompanied by *adaptive upgrading,* whereby social institutions become more specialized in their purposes. The division of labor among physicians into obstetricians, internists, surgeons, and so forth is an example of adaptive upgrading.

The third process identified by Parsons is the *inclusion* of groups into society which were previously excluded by virtue of such factors as gender, race, and social class background. Medical schools have practiced inclusion by admitting increasing numbers of women and Blacks. Finally, Parsons contends that societies experience *value generation,* the development of new values that tolerate and legitimate a greater range of activities. The acceptance of preventive medicine is an example of value generation; our society has broadened its view of health care. All four processes identified by Parsons stress consensus—societal agreement on the nature of social organization and values (B. Johnson, 1975; R. Wallace and Wolf, 1980:50–51).

Parsons's approach explicitly incorporates the evolutionary notion of continuing progress. However, the dominant theme in his model is balance and stability. Society may change, but it remains stable through new forms of integration. In place of the kinship ties that provided social cohesion in the past, there will be laws, judicial processes, and new values and belief systems.

As noted by critics, the functionalist approach virtually disregards the use of coercion by the powerful to maintain the illusion of a stable, well-integrated society. Functionalists assume that social institutions will not persist unless they continue to contribute to the overall society. This leads functionalists to conclude that altering institutions will threaten societal equilibrium (Gouldner, 1960).

Conflict Theory

The functionalist perspective minimizes change. It emphasizes the persistence of social life and views change as necessary in order to maintain the equilibrium (or balance) of a society. By contrast, conflict theorists contend that social institutions and practices continue because powerful groups have the ability to maintain the status quo. Change has crucial significance, since it is needed to correct social injustices and inequalities.

An example of the process of inclusion, *as described by Talcott Parsons, is the admission of women, African Americans, and Jews into exclusive clubs (including golf clubs) that were previously restricted.*

Karl Marx accepted the evolutionary argument that societies develop along a particular path. However, unlike Comte and Spencer, he did not view each successive stage as an inevitable improvement over the previous one. History, according to Marx, proceeds through a series of stages, each of which has an exploited class of people. Ancient society exploited slaves; the estate system of feudalism exploited serfs; modern capitalist society exploits the working class. Ultimately, through a socialist revolution led by the proletariat, human society will move toward the final stage of development: a classless communist society, or "community of free individuals" as Marx described it in *Das Kapital* (original edition 1867; Bottomore and Rubel, 1956:250).

361

COLLECTIVE BEHAVIOR, SOCIAL CHANGE, AND URBANIZATION

As was noted earlier in this book, Karl Marx had an important influence on the development of sociology. His thinking offered insights into such institutions as the economy, the family, religion, and government. The Marxist view of social change is appealing because it does not restrict people to a passive role in responding to inevitable cycles or changes in material culture. Rather, Marxist theory offers a tool for those who wish to seize control of the historical process and gain their freedom from injustice. In contrast to functionalists' emphasis on stability, Marx argues that conflict is a normal and desirable aspect of social change. Indeed, change must be encouraged as a means of eliminating social inequality (Lauer, 1982).

One conflict sociologist, Ralf Dahrendorf (1959), has noted that the contrast between the functionalist perspective's emphasis on stability and the conflict perspective's focus on change reflects the contradictory nature of society. Human societies are stable and long-lasting, yet they also experience serious conflict. Indeed, Parsons spoke of new functions that result from social change, and Marx recognized the need for change so that societies could function more equitably. According to Dahrendorf's view, the functionalist approach and the conflict approach are ultimately compatible despite their many areas of disagreement.

SOURCES OF SOCIAL CHANGE

The theoretical approaches to social change presented above underscore the multidimensional nature of change as a social phenomenon. This section will examine sources of change identified by sociologists as being particularly significant in reshaping behavior and social structure. Earlier, in Chapter 2, we saw that the general processes of innovation and diffusion contribute to the expansion of human culture. In addition to these processes of change, sociologists have determined that physical environment, population, science and technology, inequality, and youth are key sources of change. We will examine each of these factors in turn.

Physical Environment

The dust storms and erosion which became critical in the 1930s helped people in the United States to realize that soil was not an inexhaustible resource. These "dust bowl" days also precipitated a migration out of farm areas in Nebraska and Oklahoma. Many rural residents moved to the cities in search of better living conditions. The difficulties of life in the "dust bowl" did not dictate *where* migrants went; nevertheless, the environmental calamities of the region certainly limited the kinds of living patterns that were possible in the area.

Recent assessments of the availability of natural resources have reaffirmed the effects of physical environment in directing change in behavior. Debates over depletion of fossil fuels such as coal and oil, global warming from the greenhouse effect, the loss of rain forests, and the extinction of animals and plants have all precipitated protests and social movements demanding change.

Population

Changes in the size, density, and composition of a population have an important impact on social change. This is evident when one studies the problems of our nation's central cities. As affluent residents and business firms leave the cities, it becomes much more difficult to support public transportation and social services. Even if the size of a population remains stable, shifts in its composition lead to different demands on government. School buildings may stand empty, while health care facilities become overburdened.

Population changes affect many of the social policy issues that have been considered in this book. High rates of immigration from Latin American and Asian nations have contributed to the expansion of multicultural educational programs (see Chapter 2). An increase in the birthrate of the United States will add to the need for child care facilities (see Chapter 3).

Science and Technology

History chronicles the instances in which changes have been set in motion by advances in science and technology.

The term **science** refers to the body of knowledge obtained by methods based on systematic observation. **Technology,** as was noted in Chapter 11, refers to the application of such knowledge to the making of tools and the utilization of natural resources.

Technological developments are closely associated with historical changes. For example, the use of three-masted, seagoing galleons and cannons facilitated European conquest of the world during the sixteenth through nineteenth centuries. Advances in agricultural technology, ranging from the iron-tipped plow to the three-crop rotation system, made possible the creation of a social surplus—thereby leading to the emergence of the preindustrial cities (L. White, 1962:78). More recently, computers have become an important factor in social change in the United States. As one example, work at home with computers linked to an office, known as *telecommuting*, offers an attractive new option for some people with disabilities or limited mobility.

Social Inequality

As we saw in Chapter 6, people receive unequal amounts of wealth, income, status, and power. This inequality leads those who perceive themselves as deprived to seek a redistribution of valued social rewards. Earlier in the book, we considered movements for social change initiated by racial minorities (Chapter 7), women (Chapter 8), and the elderly (Chapter 8); in the social policy section of this chapter, we will examine the disability rights movement. These movements share a common opposition to social inequality and a desire to transform long-standing patterns of prejudice and discrimination.

Without question, the persistence of social inequality in a society can stimulate efforts toward social change. Sociologist Theda Skocpol (1979) has stressed the role of revolution in rapid yet basic transformation of a society's class structure. Obviously, such revolutions are carried out from below; the powerful have a stake in maintaining the existing stratification systems. Yet, as Karl Marx was well-aware, people may remain oppressed for a long time without calling for change, much less for rebellion and revolution.

Like other sources of social change, the strains of inequality do not necessarily lead to actual changes. The discontented must be *mobilized* if change is to occur (W. Moore, 1974:87–90).

Youth

Young people have traditionally been viewed as the vanguard of social change. Throughout the history of the United States, youth has played a prominent role in many diverse movements fighting for change. According to historian David Donald (1956:26–27), the median age of abolitionist leaders opposing slavery was 29. Similarly, many young Blacks and Whites joined the civil rights movement of the 1960s. Dr. Martin Luther King, Jr., was only 24 when he began working as an organizer on behalf of civil rights.

It is not simply youth in itself that leads one to become committed to change. The young are less directly involved in established social institutions than their elders and have fewer social and economic ties to the existing social structure. Consequently, they can be mobilized to join movements for change more easily than those who have a greater stake in the status quo.

URBANIZATION AS SOCIAL CHANGE: A CASE STUDY

The worldwide growth in the number and size of dense urban settlements has been influenced by many of the sources of social change discussed above—including changes in physical environment, population, technology, inequality, and age distribution. The emergence of urban areas began centuries ago as people gradually changed from living together in nomadic bands to participating in larger permanent settlements.

Early Communities

For most of human history, people used **subsistence technology**—the tools, processes, and knowledge that a society requires to meet its basic needs for survival. Thus, the need for an adequate food supply was satisfied through hunting, foraging for fruits or vegetables, fishing, and herding.

In comparison with later industrial societies, early civilizations were much more dependent on the physical environment and much less able to alter that environment to their advantage. As we saw in Chapter 11, the emergence of horticultural societies, in which people actually cultivated food rather than merely gathered fruits and vegetables, led to many dramatic changes in human social organization.

Significantly, people no longer had to move from place to place in search of food. In fact, group cultivation required that people remain in specific locations and thereby encouraged the development of more stable and enduring communities. Ultimately, as agricultural techniques became more and more sophisticated, a cooperative division of labor involving both family members and others developed. It gradually became possible for people to produce more food than they actually needed for themselves. Consequently, food could be given, perhaps as part of an exchange, to others who might be involved in nonagricultural labor. This transition from subsistence to surplus represented a critical step in the emergence of cities.

The term *social surplus* refers to the production by a group of people of enough goods to cover their own needs, while at the same time sustaining people who are not engaged in agricultural tasks. Initially, the social surplus of early communities was limited to agricultural products, but it gradually evolved to include all types of goods and services. Residents of a city came to rely on community members who provided crafts products and means of transportation, gathered information, and so forth (Lenski et al., 1991; F. Wilson, 1984:297–298).

Preindustrial Cities

It is estimated that, beginning about 10,000 B.C., permanent settlements free from dependence on crop cultivation emerged. Yet, by today's standards of population, these early communities would barely qualify as cities. The *preindustrial city,* as it is termed, had only a few thousand people living within its borders. These residents relied on perhaps 100,000 farmers and their own part-time farming to provide them with the needed agricultural surplus. The Mesopotamian city of Ur, for instance, had a population of about 10,000 and was limited to roughly 220 acres of land, including the canals, the temple, and the harbor.

Why were these early cities so small and relatively few in number? Urbanization was restricted by a number of key factors:

1 *Reliance on animal power (both humans and beasts of burden) as a source of energy for economic production.* This limited the ability of humans to make use of and alter the physical environment.

2 *Modest levels of surplus produced by the agricultural sector.* Sociologist Kingsley Davis (1949) has estimated that between 50 and 90 farmers were required to support 1 city resident.

3 *Problems in transportation and storage of food and other goods.* Even an excellent crop could easily be lost as a result of such difficulties.

4 *Hardships of migration to the city.* For many peasants, migration was both physically and economically impossible. A few weeks of travel was out of the question without more sophisticated techniques of food storage.

5 *Dangers of city life.* Concentrating a society's population in a small area left a society open to attack from outsiders, as well as more susceptible to extreme damages from plagues and fires.

A sophisticated social organization is an essential precondition for urban existence. Specialized social roles emerge more fully in industrial societies than in earlier communities. These roles bring people together in new ways through the exchange of goods and services. A well-developed social organization ensures that these relationships are clearly defined and generally acceptable to all parties. This function becomes even more crucial as cities become larger and more industrialized.

Industrial Cities

Advances in agricultural technology led to dramatic changes in community life, but so did the process of industrialization. As was noted in Chapter 11, the *industrial revolution,* which began in the middle of the eighteenth century, focused on the application of nonanimal sources of power to labor tasks.

Like other types of social change, urbanization has not always been met with enthusiasm. This bumper sticker, evident in San Diego in the 1990s, reflects hostility to urban development and population increases.

Industrialization had a wide range of effects on people's lifestyles as well as on the structure of communities. Emerging urban settlements became centers not only of industry but also of banking, finance, and industrial management.

The factory system which developed during the industrial revolution led to a much more refined division of labor than was evident in early preindustrial cities. Many new occupations were created, and one by-product was a more complex set of relationships among workers. Thus, the ***industrial city*** was not only more populous than its preindustrial predecessors; it was also based on very different principles of social organization.

In comparison with industrial cities, preindustrial cities had relatively closed class systems and limited social mobility as well as a much more rigid division of labor by gender. Status in these early cities was based on ascribed characteristics such as family background. Education was limited to members of the elite. However, in industrial cities, formal education gradually became available to many children from poor and working-class families. There was a much greater opportunity for a talented or skilled individual to better his or her social position. In these and other respects, the industrial city is genuinely a "different world" from the preindustrial urban community.

The 1990 census was the first to demonstrate that more than half the population of the United States lives in 39 metropolitan areas—each with 1 million or more residents. In only three states (Mississippi, Vermont, and West Virginia) do more than half the residents live in rural areas. Clearly, urbanization has become a central aspect of life in the United States. In Box 13-2 (pages 366–367), we examine a number of theories devised by social scientists to explain the process of urban growth.

It is important to emphasize that urbanization is evident not only in the United States, but throughout the world. In 1920, only 14 percent of the world's people lived in urban areas, but by 1990 that proportion had risen to 41 percent, and by the year 2025 it is expected to reach as high as 62 percent. During the nineteenth and early twentieth centuries, urbanization occurred primarily in European and North American cities; however, since World War II, there has been an urban "explosion" in the world's developing countries. The dramatic growth in urban populations has been fueled by natural increase (excess of births over deaths) and by migration. In Mexico, for example, migration accounts for one-fourth of the expansion of urban areas (Fox, 1987:32–33; Haub et al., 1990; Newland, 1980).

BOX 13-2

THEORIES OF URBAN GROWTH

Human ecology is concerned with the interrelationships between people in their spatial setting and physical environment. Human ecologists have long been interested in how the physical environment shapes people's lives (rivers can serve as a barrier to residential expansion) and also how people influence the surrounding environment (the advent of air conditioning has played a critical role in the growth of major metropolitan areas in the southwest). *Urban ecology* focuses on such interrelationships as they emerge in urban areas.

Early urban ecologists such as Robert Park (1916, 1936) and Ernest Burgess (1925) concentrated on city life but drew on the approaches used by ecologists in studying plant and animal communities. With few exceptions, urban ecologists trace their work back to the *concentric-zone theory* devised in the 1920s by Burgess. Using the city of Chicago as an example, Burgess offered a framework for describing land use in industrial cities. At the center, or nucleus, of such a city is the central business district. Large department stores, hotels, theaters, and financial institutions occupy this highly valued land. Surrounding this urban center are succeeding zones that contain other types of land use and that illustrate the growth of the urban area over time.

Encircling the central business district is the "zone of transition," which has a temporary character, since its residents are in the immediate path of business and industrial expansion. Homes in this area are generally unpopular; most people do not wish to live next to a factory. The zone of transition is populated by those at the bottom of the nation's social hierarchies, including recent immigrants and the poor. When people living in this zone achieve upward mobility, they frequently move to the outer zones of residential housing.

It must be stressed that the creation of zones is a *social* process, not the result of nature alone. Families and business firms compete for the most valuable land; those possessing the most wealth and power are generally the winners. The concentric-zone theory proposed by Burgess also represented a dynamic model of urban growth. As urban growth proceeded, each zone would move even further from the central business district.

By the middle of the twentieth century, urban populations had spilled beyond the traditional city limits. No longer could urban ecologists focus exclusively on *growth* in the central city, for large numbers of urban residents were abandoning the cities to live in suburban areas. As a response to the emergence of more than one focal point in some metropolitan areas, C. D. Harris and Edward L. Ullman (1945) presented the *multiple-nuclei theory.* In their view, all urban growth does not radiate outward from a central business district. Instead, a metropolitan area may have many centers of development, each of which reflects a particular urban need or activity. Thus, a city may have a financial district, a manufacturing zone, a waterfront area, an entertainment center, and so forth. Certain types of business firms and certain types of housing will naturally cluster around each distinctive nucleus.

The rise of suburban shopping malls is a vivid example of the phenomenon of multiple nuclei within metropolitan areas. Initially, all major retailing in cities was located in the central business district. Each residential neighborhood had its own grocers, bakers, and butchers, but people traveled to the center of the city to make major purchases at department stores. However, as major metropolitan areas expanded and the suburbs became more populous, an increasing number of people began to shop nearer their homes. Today, the suburban mall is a significant retailing and social center for communities across the United States.

In a refinement of multiple-nuclei theory, contemporary urban ecologists have begun to study what journalist Joel Garreau (1991) has called "edge cities." These communities, which have grown up on the outskirts of major metropolitan areas, are economic and social centers with identities of their own. (The edge cities surrounding Phoenix, Arizona, are shown in the figure on the opposite page.) By any standard of measurement—height of buildings, amount of office space, presence of medical facilities, presence of leisure-time facilities, or, of course, population—edge cities qualify as urban areas rather than as large suburbs (B. O'Hare, 1992).

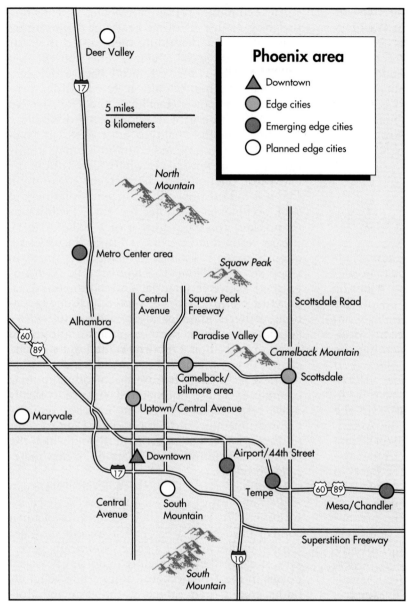

Phoenix area

▲ Downtown

● Edge cities

● Emerging edge cities

○ Planned edge cities

Deer Valley

5 miles
8 kilometers

North
Mountain

Metro Center area

Squaw Peak

Central
Avenue

Squaw Peak
Freeway

Scottsdale Road

Alhambra

Paradise Valley

Camelback Mountain

Camelback/
Biltmore area

Scottsdale

Maryvale

Uptown/Central Avenue

Downtown

Airport/44th Street

Central
Avenue

South
Mountain

Tempe

Mesa/Chandler

Superstition Freeway

South
Mountain

SOURCE: Garreau, 1991:181.

This figure shows the downtown area of Phoenix, Arizona, along with edge cities, emerging edge cities, and planned edge cities. Edge cities *are economic and social centers with identities of their own which have grown up on the outskirts of major metropolitan areas.*

As part of the worldwide urban expansion, some metropolitan areas have spread so far that they have connected with other urban centers. Such a densely populated area, containing two or more cities and their suburbs, has become known as a **megalopolis.** An example is the 500-mile corridor stretching from Boston south to Washington, D.C., and including New York City, Philadelphia, and Baltimore, which accounts for one-sixth of the total population of the United States. Even when it is divided into autonomous political jurisdictions, the megalopolis can be viewed as a single economic identity. The megalopolis is not unique to the United States; such areas are now seen in Great Britain, Germany, Italy, Egypt, India, Japan, and China.

RESISTANCE TO SOCIAL CHANGE

As has been stressed throughout this chapter, efforts to promote social change are likely to be met with resistance. In the midst of rapid scientific and technological innovations, many people are emotionally frightened by the demands of an ever-changing society. However, certain individuals and groups have a stake in maintaining the existing state of affairs.

Social economist Thorstein Veblen (1857–1929) coined the term **vested interests** to refer to those people or groups who will suffer in the event of social change. For example, the American Medical Association (AMA) has taken strong stands against national health insurance and the professionalization of midwifery (refer back to Chapter 12). National health insurance could lead to limits on the income of physicians, and a rise in the status of midwives could threaten the preeminent position of doctors as the nation's deliverers of babies. In general, those with a disproportionate share of society's wealth, status, and power, such as members of the American Medical Association, have a vested interest in preserving the status quo (Starr, 1982; Veblen, 1919).

Economic factors play an important role in resistance to social change. For example, it can be expensive for manufacturers to meet the highest possible standards for the safety of products and of industrial workers. Conflict theorists argue that, in a capitalist economic system, many firms are not willing to pay the price of meeting strict safety standards. They may resist social change by cutting corners within their plants or by pressuring the government to ease regulations.

An economic refrain involving "protecting property values" is often heard in communities that claim to be defending their vested interests as they resist social change. The abbreviation "NIMBY" stands for "not in my backyard," a cry often heard when people protest landfills, prisons, nuclear power facilities, and even group homes for those with developmental disabilities. The need for the facility is not necessarily challenged, but the targeted community may simply insist that it be located elsewhere. The "not in my backyard" phenomenon has become so common that it is almost impossible for policy planners to find acceptable locations for such facilities as dump sites for hazardous wastes (Piller, 1991).

Like economic factors, cultural factors frequently shape resistance to change. As noted in Chapter 2, William F. Ogburn (1922) distinguished between material and nonmaterial aspects of culture. *Material culture* includes inventions, artifacts, and technology; *nonmaterial culture* encompasses ideas, norms, communication, and social organization. Ogburn pointed out that one cannot devise methods for controlling and utilizing new technology before the introduction of a technique. Thus, nonmaterial culture typically must respond to changes in material culture. Ogburn introduced the term **culture lag** to refer to the period of maladjustment during which the nonmaterial culture is still adapting to new material conditions.

In certain cases, changes in material culture can add strain to the relationships between social institutions. For example, new techniques of birth control have been developed in recent decades. Large families are no longer economically necessary, nor are they commonly endorsed by social norms in the United States. But certain religious faiths, among them Roman Catholicism and Mormonism, continue to extol large families and to view methods of limiting family size such as contraception and abortion as undesirable. This represents a lag between aspects of material culture (technology) and nonmaterial culture (religious beliefs). Conflicts may emerge between religion

The abbreviation "NIMBY" stands for "not in my backyard," a cry often heard when people protest landfills, prisons, nuclear power facilities, and even group homes for those with developmental disabilities.

and other social institutions, such as government and the educational system, over the dissemination of birth control and family planning information (Lauer, 1982:152).

Today, social movements often seem to question the traditional basis for a culture. The feminist and gay liberation movements have challenged cultural beliefs long accepted as "natural"—that the male is the dominant member of the species, that heterosexuality is the only healthy form of sexual orientation, and so forth. Not surprisingly, resistance to such movements is often very strong. The resource-mobilization approach has focused not only on how social movements mobilize but also on how resistance to change is expressed (R. Roberts and Kloss, 1974:153–157; Zald and McCarthy, 1979). Forms of resistance to social movements include:

- *Ridicule.* The women's movement was tagged with the derisive label "women's lib" by its detractors. At the same time, feminists were stereotyped as "bra burners."
- *Cooptation.* One way to pacify members of a social movement is to appear to incorporate, or coopt, its goals or leaders into the political structure. In 1991, while facing strong criticism from Black civil rights groups, President George Bush nominated Judge Clarence Thomas to fill a vacancy on the Supreme Court.

- *Formal social control.* During the 1950s, southern communities passed legislation banning civil rights marches. More recently, certain colleges have denied official recognition of lesbian and gay male student organizations.
- *Violence.* If all other measures used to stop a social movement are unsuccessful, its opponents may resort to violence. When National Guard troops shot and killed four Kent State college students during a 1970 demonstration opposing the United States' invasion of Cambodia, a generation of young protestors learned that participation in a social movement can be extremely risky.

Social movements face a difficult challenge in their struggle for social change. Almost inevitably, powerful individuals and groups in society have a vested interest in opposing change. While members of a social movement attempt to mobilize their resources, the powerful do the same—and the powerful often have more money, more political influence, and greater access to the media. Nevertheless, human history is a history of change; resistance by those in power has often been overcome. In the social policy section which follows, we will see that disability rights activists have overcome resistance, to force important changes in society's treatment of people with disabilities.

COLLECTIVE BEHAVIOR, SOCIAL CHANGE, AND URBANIZATION

- How does the medical model of disability compare with the civil rights model?
- In what ways do people with disabilities experience prejudice, discrimination, and other forms of social inequality?
- What difficulties does the disability rights movement face in mobilizing as a political bloc?

Throughout history, people with disabilities have often been subjected to cruel and inhuman treatment. For example, in the early twentieth century the disabled were frequently viewed as subhuman creatures who were a menace to society. As one result, many state legislatures passed compulsory sterilization laws aimed at handicapped people. Drawing on similar prejudices against the disabled, Adolf Hitler's Nazi regime persecuted and put to death perhaps as many as 1 million people with disabilities. In a chilling reminder of this legacy, neo-Nazi groups in Germany launched more than 40 attacks on physically and mentally disabled people during the first two months of 1993 (Hahn, 1987:200; M. Rebell, 1986; Waldrop, 1993).

Today, such blatantly hostile treatment of disabled people has generally been replaced by a *medical model* which focuses on the functional impairments of the person. Those with disabilities are therefore viewed as chronic patients. In an adaptation of Talcott Parsons's sick role (refer back to Chapter 12), we can say that society assigns the disabled a "handicapped role." They are viewed as helpless, childlike people who are expected to assume a cheerful and continuing dependence on family members, friends, and health care professionals.

Increasingly, however, people concerned with the rights of the disabled have criticized this medical model. In the view of these activists, it is the unnecessary and discriminatory barriers present in the environment—both physical and attitudinal—that stand in the way of people with disabilities, more than their biological limitations do. Applying a *civil rights model*, activists emphasize that those with disabilities face widespread prejudice, discrimination, and segregation. For example, most voting places are architecturally inaccessible to wheelchair users and fail to offer ballots that can be used by people unable to read print. Many states continue to deny blind and deaf citizens the right to serve on juries. City and state government hearings, school board meetings, and other important public events are typically held in inaccessible locations and without sign language interpreters. Viewed from a conflict perspective, such public policies reflect unequal treatment that helps to keep people with disabilities in a subservient position (A. Asch, 1986:219; Hahn, 1987:194).

Labeling theorists, drawing on the earlier work of Erving Goffman (1963), have suggested that society attaches a stigma to many forms of disability and that this stigma leads to prejudicial treatment. Indeed, people with disabilities frequently observe that the nondisabled see them only as blind, deaf, wheelchair users, and so forth, rather than as complex human beings with individual strengths and weaknesses whose blindness or deafness is merely one aspect of their lives. In this regard, a review of studies of women with disabilities disclosed that most academic research on the disabled does not differentiate by gender—thereby perpetuating the view that when a disability is present, no other personal characteristic can matter. Consequently, as noted in Chapter 4, disability serves as a master status (Fine and Asch, 1981, 1988a, 1988b; Gove, 1980:237; R. Smith, 1980).

The mass media have contributed to stereotyping of people with disabilities by treating them with a mixture of pity and fear. Nationwide charity telethons promote negative images of the disabled by showing them as childlike, incompetent, and nonproductive. By contrast, in literature and film, "evil" characters with disabilities (from Captain Hook to Dr. Strangelove) reinforce the view that disability is a punishment for evil and that the handicapped, out of a desire for revenge, would destroy the nondisabled if they could. Even ostensibly more favorable treatments of disabled characters tend to focus on unusually courageous and inspirational individuals who achieve striking personal successes against great odds—rather than on the impact of prejudice and discrimination on "ordinary" disabled people (Biklen, 1986; Krossel, 1988; Longmore, 1985; Zola, 1987).

By 1970, a strong social movement for disability rights—drawing on the experiences of the Black civil rights movement, the women's liberation movement, and various self-help movements—had emerged

Disability rights activists are shown heading toward a protest at a federal government building in Atlanta. Without question, people with disabilities occupy a subordinate position in the United States.

across the United States. This movement now includes organizations of people with a single disability (such as the National Federation of the Blind), organizations of people with different disabilities (such as New York City's Disabled in Action), a legal advocacy organization (the Disability Rights Education and Defense Fund), and an activist publication (the *Disability Rag*). Ironically, the war in Vietnam served as a major factor in advancing the disability rights movement. Because of war-related injuries, a large number of disabled Vietnam veterans joined forces with other people with disabilities in demanding full civil rights.

Women and men involved in the disability rights movement are working to challenge negative views of disabled people; to gain a greater voice for the disabled in all agency and public policy decisions that affect them; and to reshape laws, institutions, and environments so that people with disabilities can be fully integrated into mainstream society. Disability rights activists argue that there is an important distinction between organizations *for* disabled people and organizations *of* disabled people. The former include service providers, charitable associations, and parental groups. Some activists maintain that since these organizations are not controlled by people with disabilities, they do not give priority to the goals of independence and self-help emphasized by the disability rights movement (Scotch, 1984:33–37; 1989).

Without question, people with disabilities occupy a subordinate position in the United States. According to Mitchell LaPlante, director of the Disability Statistics Program at the University of California at San Francisco, 23 percent of disabled adults in the United States are poor—almost three times the rate for the rest of the population. Many of these low-income people with disabilities survive largely on Social Security payments, Medicaid, and food stamps. Even among the disabled, racial differences are evident. A 1992 study by the federal government's General Accounting Office found that African Americans have more difficulty than others in obtaining benefits from the two largest federal programs for people with severe disabilities: Disability Insurance and Supplementary Security Income (Kilborn, 1992:24; Labaton, 1992).

Architectural barriers and transportation difficulties often add to the problems of disabled people who seek or obtain employment. Simply getting around city streets can be quite difficult; many streets are not properly equipped with curb cuts for wheelchair users. A genuinely barrier-free building needs more than a ramp; it should also include automatic doors, raised letters and braille on signs, and toilets that are accessible to the disabled. But even if a disabled person finds a job, and even if the job is in a barrier-free building, he or she still faces the problem of getting to work in a society where most rail stations and buses remain inaccessible to wheelchair users and others with disabilities.

With such issues in mind, the disability rights movement won an important victory in 1990 when President Bush signed the Americans with Disabilities Act (ADA). This civil rights law was passed only after a long legislative struggle, behind-the-scenes lobbying to weaken the bill by business groups, and demonstrations at the Capitol Rotunda by disability rights activists. The ADA will affect some 43 million people with a disability (defined as a condition that "substantially limits" a "major life activity" such as walking or sight).

This law, which is the most sweeping antidiscrimination law to be approved since the 1964 Civil Rights Act, began to go into effect in 1992. It prohibits bias in employment, transportation, public accommodations, and telecommunications against people with disabilities. Businesses with more than 25 employees will be forbidden to refuse to hire a disabled applicant; these companies will be expected to make a "reasonable accommodation" to permit such a worker to do the job. Commercial establishments such as office buildings, hotels, theaters, supermarkets, and dry cleaners have been barred from denying service to people with disabilities (Kilborn, 1992).

With passage of the ADA, the disability rights movement has begun to emphasize the issue of attendant services. Lack of affordable and reliable home care leaves thousands of severely disabled people powerless to benefit from the ADA—and forces others unnecessarily into nursing homes. Yet state support for home care services varies dramatically: whereas California provides personal assistants for more than 93,000 disabled people, Virginia does so for only 36 people. Disability rights activists view attendant services as a civil rights issue. In their view, advances in employment or accessible transportation are meaningless if a disabled person cannot get needed assistance to get up, get ready for work, and get out of the house (*Disability Rag*, 1990; Holmes, 1990c; see also Longmore, 1988).

In order to win future victories, the disability rights movement will need to become stronger as a political bloc. Yet the social movement for disability rights must overcome certain difficulties related to mobilization. Those with disabilities are geographically, socially, and economically dispersed; there is danger of fragmentation because of the diversity evident in the different types and levels of disability. Moreover, many of these individuals—especially those who are successfully employed—may not identify themselves consciously with the movement. Still, activists remain encouraged after passage of the ADA. Mary Johnson (1989:446), editor of the *Disability Rag*, has written: "Discrimination against people with disabilities has now been officially acknowledged. We've got a foot—or a wheel or a cane—in the door" (Bradley, 1990; Scotch, 1988).

SUMMARY

Collective behavior is the relatively spontaneous and unstructured behavior of a group that is reacting to an ambiguous situation. *Social change* is significant alteration over time in behavior patterns and culture, including norms and values. This chapter examines sociological theories that are used to understand collective behavior, forms of collective behavior, theories of social change, sources of social change, and resistance to social change.

1 Turner and Killian's *emergent-norm perspective* suggests that new norms of proper behavior may arise in ambiguous situations.

2 Smelser's *value-added model* of collective behavior outlines six important determinants of such behavior: structural conduciveness, structural strain, generalized belief, precipitating factor, mobilization of participants for action, and operation of social control.

3 The *assembling perspective* introduced by McPhail and Miller sought for the first time to examine how and why people move from different points in space to a common location.

4 Unlike certain situations involving collective behavior, *crowds* require people to be in relatively close contact and interaction.

5 The key distinction between a *panic* and a *craze* is that a panic is a flight *from* something whereas a craze is a movement *to* something.

6 A *rumor* serves a social function by providing a group with a shared belief.

7 *Social movements* are more structured than other forms of collective behavior and persist over longer periods of time.

8 Talcott Parsons, a leading advocate of functionalist theory, viewed society as naturally being in a state of equilibrium or balance.

9 Conflict theorists see change as having crucial significance, since it is needed to correct social injustices and inequalities.

10 Urbanization is evident not only in the United States, but throughout the world.

11 In general, those with a disproportionate share of society's wealth, status, and power have a *vested interest* in preserving the status quo.

12 By the 1970s, a strong movement for disability rights had emerged across the United States.

CRITICAL THINKING QUESTIONS

1 Are the emergent-norm, value-added, and assembling perspectives aligned with or reminiscent of functionalism, conflict theory, or interactionism? What aspects of each of these theories of collective behavior (if any) seem linked to the broader theoretical perspectives of sociology?

2 Without using any of the examples presented in the textbook, list at least two examples of each of the following types of collective behavior: crowds, disasters, fads, fashions, panics, crazes, rumors, publics, and social movements. Explain why each example belongs in its assigned category. Distinguish between each type of collective behavior based on the type and degree of social structure and interaction that are present.

3 Select one social movement that is currently working for change in the United States. Analyze that movement, drawing on the concepts of relative deprivation, resource mobilization, and false consciousness. Discuss whether the equilibrium model and the conflict theory of social change are useful in analyzing the social movement you have chosen.

KEY TERMS

Assembling perspective A theory of collective behavior introduced by McPhail and Miller which seeks to examine how and why people move from different points in space to a common location. (page 352)

Collective behavior In the view of sociologist Neil Smelser, the relatively spontaneous and unstructured behavior of a group of people who are reacting to a common influence in an ambiguous situation. (348)

Concentric-zone theory A theory of urban growth devised by Ernest Burgess which sees growth in terms of a series of rings radiating from the central business district. (366)

Craze An exciting mass involvement which lasts for a relatively long period of time. (354)

Crowds Temporary gatherings of people in close proximity who share a common focus or interest. (353)

Culture lag Ogburn's term for a period of maladjustment during which the nonmaterial culture is still adapting to new material conditions. (368)

Disaster A sudden or disruptive event or set of events that overtaxes a community's resources so that outside aid is necessary. (353)

Emergent-norm perspective A theory of collective behavior proposed by Turner and Killian which holds that a collective definition of appropriate and inappropriate behavior emerges during episodes of collective behavior. (350)

Equilibrium model Talcott Parsons's functionalist view of society as tending toward a state of stability or balance. (360)

Evolutionary theory A theory of social change which holds that society is moving in a definite direction. (360)

Fads Temporary movements toward the acceptance of some particular taste or lifestyle that involve large numbers of people and are independent of preceding trends. (354)

False consciousness A term used by Karl Marx to describe an attitude held by members of a class that does not accurately reflect its objective position. (359)

Fashions Pleasurable mass involvements in some particular taste or lifestyle that have a line of historical continuity. (354)

Human ecology An area of study concerned with the interrelationships between people in their spatial setting and physical environment. (366)

Industrial city A city characterized by relatively large size, open competition, an open class system, and elaborate specialization in the manufacturing of goods. (365)

Industrial revolution A scientific revolution, largely occurring in England between 1760 and 1830, which focused on the application of nonanimal sources of power to labor tasks. (364)

Megalopolis A densely populated area containing two or more cities and their surrounding suburbs. (368)

Multilinear evolutionary theory A theory of social change which holds that change can occur in several ways and does not inevitably lead in the same direction. (360)

Multiple-nuclei theory A theory of urban growth developed by Harris and Ullman, which views growth as emerging from many centers of development, each of which may reflect a particular urban need or activity. (366)

Nonperiodic assemblies Nonrecurring gatherings of people which often result from word-of-mouth information. (352)

Panic A fearful arousal or collective flight based on a generalized belief which may or may not be accurate. (354)

Periodic assemblies Recurring, relatively routine gatherings of people, such as college classes. (352)

Preindustrial city A city with only a few thousand people living within its borders and characterized by a relatively closed class system and limited mobility. (364)

Public A dispersed group of people, not necessarily in contact with one another, who share an interest in an issue. (356)

Public opinion Expressions of attitudes on matters of public policy which are communicated to decision makers. (357)

Relative deprivation The conscious feeling of a negative discrepancy between legitimate expectations and present actualities. (359)

Resource mobilization The ways in which a social movement utilizes such resources as money, political influence, access to the media, and personnel. (359)

Rumor A piece of information gathered informally which is used to interpret an ambiguous situation. (355)

Science The body of knowledge obtained by methods based on systematic observation. (363)

Social change Significant alteration over time in behavior patterns and culture, including norms and values. (348)

Social movements Organized collective activities to bring about or resist fundamental change in existing society. (357)

Social surplus The production by a group of people of enough goods to cover their own needs, while at the same time sustaining people who are not engaged in agricultural tasks. (364)

Subsistence technology The tools, processes, and knowledge that a society requires to meet its basic needs for survival. (363)

Technology Application of knowledge to the making of tools and the utilization of natural resources. (363)

Unilinear evolutionary theory A theory of social change which holds that all societies pass through the same successive stages of evolution and inevitably reach the same end. (360)

Urban ecology An area of study which focuses on the interrelationships between people and their environment as they emerge in urban areas. (366)

Value-added model A theory of collective behavior proposed by Neil Smelser to explain how broad social conditions are transformed in a definite pattern into some form of collective behavior. (350)

Vested interests Veblen's term for those people or groups who will suffer in the event of social change and who have a stake in maintaining the status quo. (368)

ADDITIONAL READINGS

Brunvand, Jan Harold. *Curses! Broiled Again!* New York: Norton, 1989. The author, an English professor, has collected another series of rumors which have become such an accepted part of our culture that they can perhaps be considered legends or folklore.

Davis, Fred. *Fashions, Culture, and Identity*. Chicago: University of Chicago Press, 1992. A sociologist considers how fashion reflects our sense of identity and is influenced by consumer selection.

Fine, Michelle, and Adrienne Asch (eds.). *Women with Disabilities: Essays in Psychology, Culture, and Politics*. Philadelphia: Temple University Press, 1988. An anthology exploring scholarly and activist concerns on issues ranging from prejudice to employment policy, from friendship to social justice.

Jasper, James M., and Dorothy Nelkin. *The Animal Rights Crusade: The Growth of a Moral Protest*. New York: Free Press, 1992. Two sociologists provide a history and an analysis of a social movement whose members range from associations of kindly pet lovers concerned with "animal welfare" to passionate groups of activists fighting for "animal rights."

Johnson, Mary, and the editors of the *Disability Rag* (eds.). *People with Disabilities Explain It All for You*. Louisville, Ky.: Avocado Press, 1992. Written after the passage of the Americans with Disabilities Act, this manual explains how people with disabilities face discrimination in public accommodations and how businesses can comply with the requirements of this new civil rights law.

Miller, David L. *Introduction to Collective Behavior*. Prospect Heights, Ill.: Waveland, 1988. The author, associated with the assembling perspective, covers all the major theoretical approaches of the field. He examines rumors, riots, social movements, immigration, and other forms of collective behavior.

Walton, John. *Western Times and Water Wars: State, Culture, and Rebellion in California*. Berkeley: University of California Press, 1992. A sociological analysis of environmental protests and social movements that developed in the Owens Valley of California.

GLOSSARY

Note: Numbers following the definitions indicate pages where the terms were identified.
Consult the index for further page references.

Absolute poverty A standard of poverty based on a minimum level of subsistence below which families should not be expected to exist. (150)

Achieved status A social position attained by a person largely through his or her own effort. (84, 155)

Activity theory An interactionist theory of aging which argues that elderly people who remain active will be best-adjusted. (219)

Adoption In a legal sense, a process that allows for the transfer of the legal rights, responsibilities, and privileges of parenthood from legal parents to new legal parents. (241)

Affirmative action Positive efforts to recruit minority group members or women for jobs, promotions, and educational opportunities. (194)

Age grades Cultural categories that identify the stages of biological maturation. (218)

Ageism A term coined by Robert N. Butler to refer to prejudice and discrimination against the elderly. (222)

Agrarian society The most technologically advanced form of preindustrial society. Members are primarily engaged in the production of food but increase their crop yield through such innovations as the plow. (292)

Alienation The situation of being estranged or disassociated from the surrounding society. (308)

Amalgamation The process by which a majority group and a minority group combine through intermarriage to form a new group. (182)

Anomie Durkheim's term for the loss of direction felt in a society when social control of individual behavior has become ineffective. (117)

Anomie theory of deviance A theory developed by Robert Merton which explains deviance as an adaptation either of socially prescribed goals or of the norms governing their attainment. (117)

Anticipatory socialization Processes of socialization in which a person "rehearses" for future positions, occupations, and social relationships. (68)

Anti-Semitism Anti-Jewish prejudice. (192)

Apartheid The policy of the South African government designed to maintain the separation of Blacks, Coloureds, and Asians from the dominant Whites. (182)

Argot Specialized language used by members of a group or subculture. (44)

Ascribed status A social position "assigned" to a person by society without regard for the person's unique talents or characteristics. (83, 140)

Assembling perspective A theory of collective behavior introduced by McPhail and Miller which seeks to examine how and why people move from different points in space to a common location. (352)

Assimilation The process by which a person forsakes his or her own cultural tradition to become part of a different culture. (182)

Authority Power that has been institutionalized and is recognized by the people over whom it is exercised. (297)

Bilateral descent A kinship system in which both sides of a person's family are regarded as equally important. (236)

Birthrate The number of live births per 1000 population in a given year. Also known as the *crude birthrate*. (333)

Black power A political philosophy promoted by many younger Blacks in the 1960s which supported the creation of Black-controlled political and economic institutions. (186)

Bourgeoisie Karl Marx's term for the capitalist class, comprising the owners of the means of production. (141)

Bureaucracy A component of formal organization in which rules and hierarchical ranking are used to achieve efficiency. (96)

Bureaucratization The process by which a group, organization, or social movement becomes increasingly bureaucratic. (100)

Capitalism An economic system in which the means of production are largely in private hands, and the main incentive for economic activity is the accumulation of profits. (141, 293)

Castes Hereditary systems of rank, usually religiously dictated, that tend to be relatively fixed and immobile. (137)

Census An enumeration, or counting, of a population. (333)

Charismatic authority Max Weber's term for power made legitimate by a leader's exceptional personal or emotional appeal to his or her followers. (298)

Class A term used by Max Weber to refer to people who have a similar level of wealth and income. (142)

Class consciousness In Karl Marx's view, a subjective awareness held by members of a class regarding their common vested interests and need for collective political action to bring about social change. (141)

Classical theory An approach to the study of formal organizations which views workers as being motivated almost entirely by economic rewards. (101)

Class system A social ranking based primarily on economic position in which achieved characteristics can influence mobility. (139)

Closed system A social system in which there is little possibility or no possibility of individual mobility. (155)

Code of ethics The standards of acceptable behavior developed by and for members of a profession. (21)

Cognitive theory of development Jean Piaget's theory explaining how children's thought progresses through four stages. (66)

Cohabitation The practice of living together as a male-female couple without marrying. (249)

Collective behavior In the view of sociologist Neil Smelser, the relatively spontaneous and unstructured behavior of a group of people who are reacting to a common influence in an ambiguous situation. (348)

Colonialism The maintenance of political, social, economic, and cultural dominance over a people by a foreign power for an extended period of time. (157)

Commune A small, self-supporting community joined voluntarily by people dedicated to cooperative living. (252)

Communism As an ideal type, an economic system under which all property is communally owned and no social distinctions are made on the basis of people's ability to produce. (295)

Concentric-zone theory A theory of urban growth devised by Ernest Burgess which sees growth in terms of a series of rings radiating from the central business district. (366)

Conflict perspective A sociological approach which assumes that social behavior is best understood in terms of conflict or tension between competing groups. (11)

Conformity Going along with one's peers, individuals of a person's own status, who have no special right to direct that person's behavior. (111)

Contact hypothesis An interactionist perspective which states that interracial contact of people with equal status in noncompetitive circumstances will reduce prejudice. (179)

Content analysis The systematic coding and objective recording of data, guided by some rationale. (16)

Control group Subjects in an experiment who are not introduced to the independent variable by the researcher. (19)

Correspondence principle A term used by Bowles and Gintis to refer to the tendency of schools to promote the values expected of individuals in each social class and to prepare students for the types of jobs typically held by members of their class. (277)

Counterculture A subculture that rejects societal norms and values and seeks an alternative lifestyle. (45)

Craze An exciting mass involvement which lasts for a relatively long period of time. (354)

Creationists People who support a literal interpretation of the book of Genesis regarding the origin of the universe and argue that evolution should not be presented as established scientific fact. (267)

Credentialism An increase in the lowest level of education required to enter a field. (275)

Crime A violation of criminal law for which formal penalties are applied by some governmental authority. (122)

Crowds Temporary gatherings of people in close proximity who share a common focus or interest. (353)

Cult A generally small, secretive religious group that represents either a new religion or a major innovation of an existing faith. (270)

Cultural relativism The viewing of people's behavior from the perspective of their own culture. (47)

Cultural transmission A school of criminology which argues that criminal behavior is learned through social interactions. (119)

Cultural universals General practices found in every culture. (34, 260)

Culture The totality of learned, socially transmitted behavior. (32)

Culture lag Ogburn's term for a period of maladjustment during which the nonmaterial culture is still adapting to new material conditions. (368)

Culture shock The feeling of surprise and disorientation that is experienced when people witness cultural practices different from their own. (46)

Death rate The number of deaths per 1000 population in a given year. Also known as the *crude death rate*. (333)

Degradation ceremony An aspect of the socialization process within total institutions, in which people are subjected to humiliating rituals. (68)

Demographic transition A term used to describe the change from high birthrates and death rates to relatively low birthrates and death rates. (336)

Demography The scientific study of population. (331)

Denomination A large, organized religion not officially linked with the state or government. (268)

Dependent variable The variable in a causal relationship which is subject to the influence of another variable. (16)

Deviance Behavior that violates the standards of conduct or expectations of a group or society. (115)

Differential association A theory of deviance proposed by Edwin Sutherland which holds that violation of rules results from exposure to attitudes favorable to criminal acts. (119)

Diffusion The process by which a cultural item is spread from group to group or society to society. (36)

Disaster A sudden or disruptive event or set of events that overtaxes a community's resources so that outside aid is necessary. (353)

Discovery The process of making known or sharing the existence of an aspect of reality. (36)

Discrimination The process of denying opportunities and equal rights to individuals and groups because of prejudice or for other arbitrary reasons. (180)

Disengagement theory A functionalist theory of aging introduced by Cumming and Henry which contends that society and the aging individual mutually sever many of their relationships. (218)

Dominant ideology A set of cultural beliefs and practices that help to maintain powerful social, economic, and political interests. (49)

Dramaturgical approach A view of social interaction, popularized by Erving Goffman, under which people are examined as if they were theatrical performers. (13, 64)

Dysfunction An element or a process of society that may disrupt a social system or lead to a decrease in stability. (11, 97)

Ecclesia A religious organization that claims to include most or all of the members of a society and is recognized as the national or official religion. (268)

Economic system The social institution through which goods and services are produced, distributed, and consumed. (290)

Education A formal process of learning in which some people consciously teach while others adopt the social role of learner. (261)

Egalitarian family An authority pattern in which the adult members of the family are regarded as equals. (237)

Elite model A view of society as

ruled by a small group of individuals who share a common set of political and economic interests. (304)

Emergent-norm perspective A theory of collective behavior proposed by Turner and Killian which holds that a collective definition of appropriate and inappropriate behavior emerges during episodes of collective behavior. (350)

Endogamy The restriction of mate selection to people within the same group. (239)

Equilibrium model Talcott Parsons's functionalist view of society as tending toward a state of stability or balance. (360)

Established sect J. Milton Yinger's term for a religious group that is the outgrowth of a sect, yet remains isolated from society. (270)

Estate system A system of stratification under which peasants were required to work land leased to them by nobles in exchange for military protection and other services. Also known as *feudalism*. (139)

Esteem The reputation that a particular individual has within an occupation. (145)

Ethnic group A group which is set apart from others because of its national origin or distinctive cultural patterns. (173)

Ethnocentrism The tendency to assume that one's own culture and way of life are superior to all others. (46, 179)

Evolutionary theory A theory of social change which holds that society is moving in a definite direction. (360)

Exogamy The requirement that people select mates outside certain groups. (240)

Experiment An artificially created situation which allows the researcher to manipulate variables. (19)

Experimental group Subjects in an experiment who are exposed to an independent variable introduced by a researcher. (19)

Exploitation theory A Marxist theory which views racial subordination in the United States as a manifestation of the class system inherent in capitalism. (178)

Expressiveness A term used by Parsons and Bales to refer to concern for maintenance of harmony and the internal emotional affairs of the family. (206)

Extended family A family in which relatives in addition to parents and children—such as grandparents, aunts, or uncles—live in the same home. (234)

Face-work A term used by Erving Goffman to refer to people's efforts to maintain the proper image and avoid embarrassment in public. (65)

Fads Temporary movements toward the acceptance of some particular taste or lifestyle that involve large numbers of people and are independent of preceding trends. (354)

False consciousness A term used by Karl Marx to describe an attitude held by members of a class that does not accurately reflect its objective position. (141, 359)

Familism Pride in the extended family expressed through the maintenance of close ties and strong obligations to kinfolk. (244)

Family A set of people related by blood, marriage (or some other agreed-upon relationship), or adoption who share the responsibility for reproducing and caring for members of society. (232)

Fashions Pleasurable mass involvements in some particular taste or lifestyle that have a line of historical continuity. (354)

Fertility The amount of reproduction among women of childbearing age. (331)

Folkways Norms governing everyday social behavior whose violation raises comparatively little concern. (41)

Force The actual or threatened use of coercion to impose one's will on others. (297)

Formal norms Norms which have generally been written down and which involve strict rules for punishment of violators. (39)

Formal organization A special-purpose group designed and structured in the interests of maximum efficiency. (96)

Formal social control Social control carried out by authorized agents, such as police officers, judges, school administrators, and employers. (114)

Functionalist perspective A sociological approach which emphasizes the way that parts of a society are structured to maintain its stability. (10)

Fundamentalism Adherence to earlier-accepted religious doctrines, often accompanied by a literal application of historical beliefs and scriptures to today's world. (285)

Gemeinschaft A term used by Ferdinand Tönnies to describe close-knit communities, often found in rural areas, in which strong personal bonds unite members. (95)

Gender identity The self-concept of a person as being male or female. (203)

Gender roles Expectations regarding the proper behavior, attitudes, and activities of males and females. (70, 203)

Generalized others A term used by George Herbert Mead to refer to the child's awareness of the attitudes, viewpoints, and expectations of society as a whole. (64)

Genocide The deliberate, systematic killing of an entire people or nation. (181)

Gerontology The scientific study of the sociological and psychological aspects of aging and the problems of the aged. (218)

Gesellschaft A term used by Ferdinand Tönnies to describe communities, often urban, that are large and impersonal, with little commitment to the group or consensus on values. (96)

Goal displacement Overzealous conformity to official regulations within a bureaucracy. (99)

Group Any number of people with similar norms, values, and expectations who regularly and consciously interact. (87)

Growth rate The difference between births and deaths, plus the difference between immigrants and emigrants, per 1000 population. (335)

Hawthorne effect The unintended influence that observers or experiments can have on their subjects. (19)

Health As defined by the World Health Organization, a state of complete physical, mental, and social well-being, and not merely the absence of disease and infirmity. (319)

Health maintenance organization (HMO) An organization that provides comprehensive medical services to patients for a preestablished fee. (341)

Hominids Primates that had characteristics of human beings. (34)

Homophobia Fear of and prejudice against homosexuality. (105)

Horizontal mobility The movement of an individual from one social position to another of the same rank. (155)

Horticultural societies Preindustrial societies in which people plant seeds and crops rather than subsist merely on available foods. (292)

Human ecology An area of study concerned with the interrelationships between people in their spatial setting and physical environment. (366)

Human relations approach An approach to the study of formal organizations which emphasizes the role of people, communication, and participation within a bureaucracy and tends to focus on the informal structure of the organization. (101)

Hunting-and-gathering society A preindustrial society in which people rely on whatever foods and fiber are readily available in order to live. (292)

Hypothesis A speculative statement about the relationship between two or more variables. (16)

Ideal type A construct or model that serves as a measuring rod against which actual cases can be evaluated. (7)

Impression management A term used by Erving Goffman to refer to the altering of the presentation of the self in order to create distinctive appearances and satisfy particular audiences. (64)

Incest taboo The prohibition of sexual relationships between certain culturally specified relatives. (240)

Incidence The number of new cases of a specific disorder occurring within a given population during a stated period of time. (323)

Income Salaries and wages. (136)

Independent variable The variable in a causal relationship which, when altered, causes or influences a change in a second variable. (16)

Index crimes The eight types of crime reported annually by the FBI in the *Uniform Crime Reports*. These eight are murder, rape, robbery, assault, burglary, theft, motor vehicle theft, and arson. (122)

Industrial city A city characterized by relatively large size, open competition, an open class system, and elaborate specialization in the manufacturing of goods. (365)

Industrial revolution A scientific revolution, largely occurring in England between 1760 and 1830, which focused on the application of nonanimal sources of power to labor tasks. (293, 364)

Industrial society A society which relies chiefly on mechanization for the production of its economic goods and services. (293)

Infant mortality rate The number of deaths of infants under 1 year of age per 1000 live births in a given year. (321)

Influence The exercise of power through a process of persuasion. (297)

Informal norms Norms which are generally understood but which are not precisely recorded. (39)

Informal social control Social control carried out by people casually through such means as laughter, smiles, and ridicule. (114)

In-group Any group or category to which people feel they belong. (89)

Innovation The process of introducing new elements into a culture through either discovery or invention. (36)

Institutional discrimination The denial of opportunities and equal rights to individuals or groups which results from the normal operations of a society. (180, 209)

Instrumentality A term used by Parsons and Bales to refer to emphasis on tasks, focus on more distinct goals, and a concern for the external relationship between one's family and other social institutions. (206)

Interactionist perspective A sociological approach which generalizes about fundamental or everyday forms of social interaction. (13)

Interest group A voluntary association of citizens who attempt to influence public policy. (303)

Intergenerational mobility Changes in the social position of children relative to their parents. (155)

Interview A face-to-face or telephone questioning of a respondent in order to obtain desired information. (18)

Intragenerational mobility Changes in a person's social position within his or her adult life. (155)

Invention The combination of existing cultural items into a form that did not previously exist. (36)

Iron law of oligarchy A principle of organizational life developed by Robert Michels under which even democratic organizations will become bureaucracies ruled by a few individuals. (101)

Issei The early Japanese immigrants to the United States. (189)

Kibbutz A collective society in Israel in which individuals and groups join together in an economic and social community. (252)

Kinship The state of being related to others. (235)

Labeling theory An approach to deviance popularized by Howard S. Becker which attempts to explain why certain people are *viewed* as deviants while others engaging in the same behavior are not. (120)

Laissez-faire A form of capitalism under which people compete freely, with minimal government intervention in the economy. (293)

Language An abstract system of word meanings and symbols for all aspects of culture. It also includes gestures and other nonverbal communication. (38)

Latent functions Unconscious or unintended functions; hidden purposes. (10)

Law In a political sense, the body of rules made by government for society, interpreted by the courts, and backed by the power of the state. (39, 114)

Legal-rational authority Max Weber's term for power made legitimate by law. (298)

Liberation theology Use of a church, primarily Roman Catholicism, in a political effort to eliminate poverty, discrimination, and other forms of injustice evident in a secular society. (265)

Life chances Max Weber's term for people's opportunities to provide themselves with material goods, positive living conditions, and favorable life experiences. (151)

Life expectancy The average number of years a person can be expected to live under current mortality conditions. (335)

Looking-glass self A phrase used by Charles Horton Cooley to emphasize that the self is the product of our social interactions with others. (63)

Machismo A sense of virility, personal worth, and pride in one's maleness. (244)

Manifest functions Open, stated, and conscious functions. (10)

Marital power A term used by Blood and Wolfe to describe the manner in which decision making is distributed within families. (237)

Master status A status that dominates others and thereby determines a person's general position within society. (84)

Material culture The physical or technological aspects of our daily lives. (36)

Matriarchy A society in which women dominate in family decision making. (236)

Matrilineal descent A kinship system which favors the relatives of the mother. (236)

Matrilocal A pattern of residence in which a married couple lives with the wife's parents. (236)

Mechanical solidarity A term used by Émile Durkheim to describe a society in which people generally all perform the same tasks and in which relationships are close and intimate. (94)

Megalopolis A densely populated area containing two or more cities and their surrounding suburbs. (368)

Minority group A subordinate group whose members have significantly less control or power over their own lives than the members of a dominant or majority group have over theirs. (173)

Modernization The far-reaching process by which a society moves from traditional or less developed institutions to those characteristic of more developed societies. (159)

Monogamy A form of marriage in which one woman and one man are married only to each other. (234)

Monopoly Control of a market by a single business firm. (294)

Morbidity rates The incidence of diseases in a given population. (323)

Mores Norms deemed highly necessary to the welfare of a society. (41)

Mortality rate The incidence of death in a given population. (323)

Multiculturalism The effort to revise school and college curricula to give greater emphasis to the contributions and experiences of African Americans, other racial and ethnic minorities, women, and nonwestern peoples. (50)

Multilinear evolutionary theory A theory of social change which holds that change can occur in several ways and does not inevitably lead in the same direction. (360)

Multinational corporations Commercial organizations which, while headquartered in one country, own or control other corporations and subsidiaries throughout the world. (161)

Multiple-nuclei theory A theory of

urban growth developed by Harris and Ullman, which views growth as emerging from many centers of development, each of which may reflect a particular urban need or activity. (366)

Neocolonialism Continuing dependence of former colonies on foreign countries. (157)

Neolocal A pattern of residence in which a married couple establishes a separate residence. (236)

Nisei Japanese born in the United States who were descendants of the Issei. (191)

Nonmaterial culture Cultural adjustments to material conditions, such as customs, beliefs, patterns of communication, and ways of using material objects. (36)

Nonperiodic assemblies Nonrecurring gatherings of people which often result from word-of-mouth information. (352)

Nonverbal communication The sending of messages through the use of posture, facial expressions, and gestures. (13)

Norms Established standards of behavior maintained by a society. (39)

Nuclear family A married couple and their unmarried children living together. (233)

Obedience Compliance with higher authorities in a hierarchical structure. (111)

Objective method A technique for measuring social class that assigns individuals to classes on the basis of criteria such as occupation, education, income, and place of residence. (145)

Observation A research technique in which an investigator collects information through direct involvement with and observation of a group, tribe, or community. (18)

Open system A social system in which the position of each individual is influenced by his or her achieved status. (155)

Organic solidarity A term used by Émile Durkheim to describe a society in which members are mutually dependent and in which a complex division of labor exists. (95)

Organized crime The work of a group that regulates relations between various criminal enterprises involved in smuggling and sale of drugs, prostitution, gambling, and other activities. (123)

Out-group A group or category to which people feel they do not belong. (89)

Panic A fearful arousal or collective flight based on a generalized belief which may or may not be accurate. (354)

Patriarchy A society in which men are expected to dominate family decision making. (236)

Patrilineal descent A kinship system which favors the relatives of the father. (236)

Patrilocal A pattern of residence in which a married couple lives with the husband's parents. (236)

Periodic assemblies Recurring, relatively routine gatherings of people, such as college classes. (352)

Personality In everyday speech, a person's typical patterns of attitudes, needs, characteristics, and behavior. (58)

Peter principle A principle of organizational life, originated by Laurence J. Peter, according to which each individual within a hierarchy tends to rise to his or her level of incompetence. (100)

Pluralism Mutual respect between the various groups in a society for one another's cultures, which allows minorities to express their own cultures without experiencing prejudice. (183)

Pluralist model A view of society in which many conflicting groups within a community have access to governmental officials and compete with one another in an attempt to influence policy decisions. (306)

Political action committee (PAC) A political committee established by an interest group—a national bank, corporation, trade association, or cooperative or membership association—to accept voluntary contributions for candidates or political parties. (303)

Political socialization The process by which individuals acquire political attitudes and develop patterns of political behavior. (299)

Political system The social institution which relies on a recognized set of procedures for implementing and achieving the goals of a group. (291)

Politics In Harold D. Lasswell's words, "who gets what, when, how." (297)

Polyandry A form of polygamy in which a woman can have several husbands at the same time. (235)

Polygamy A form of marriage in which an individual can have several husbands or wives simultaneously. (234)

Polygyny A form of polygamy in which a husband can have several wives at the same time. (234)

Population pyramid A special type of bar chart that shows the distribution of the population by gender and age. (338)

Postindustrial society As defined by Daniel Bell, a society whose economic system is based on the production of information rather than the production of goods. (295)

Power The ability to exercise one's will over others. (142, 297)

Power elite A term used by C. Wright Mills for a small group of military, industrial, and government leaders who control the fate of the United States. (304)

Preindustrial city A city with only a few thousand people living within its borders and characterized by a relatively closed class system and limited mobility. (364)

Prejudice A negative attitude toward an entire category of people, such as a racial or ethnic minority. (179)

Pressure groups A term sometimes used to refer to interest groups. (303)

Prestige The respect and admiration with which an occupation is regarded by society. (145)

Prevalence The total number of cases of a specific disorder that exist at a given time. (323)

Primary group A small group characterized by intimate, face-to-face association and cooperation. (87)

Profane The ordinary and commonplace elements of life, as distinguished from the sacred. (262)

Profession An occupation requiring extensive knowledge and governed by a code of ethics. (307)

Professional criminal A person who pursues crime as a day-to-day occupation, developing skilled techniques and enjoying a certain degree of status among other criminals. (122)

Proletariat Karl Marx's term for the working class in a capitalist society. (141)

Protestant ethic Max Weber's term for the disciplined work ethic, this-worldly concerns, and rational orientation to life emphasized by John Calvin and his followers. (266)

Public A dispersed group of people, not necessarily in contact with one another, who share an interest in an issue. (356)

Public opinion Expressions of attitudes on matters of public policy which are communicated to decision makers. (357)

Questionnaire A printed research instrument employed to obtain desired information from a respondent. (18)

Racial group A group which is set apart from others because of obvious physical differences. (173)

Racism The belief that one race is

supreme and all others are innately inferior. (179)

Random sample A sample for which every member of the entire population has the same chance of being selected. (17)

Reference group A term used when speaking of any group that individuals use as a standard in evaluating themselves and their own behavior. (90)

Relative deprivation The conscious feeling of a negative discrepancy between legitimate expectations and present actualities. (359)

Relative poverty A floating standard of deprivation by which people at the bottom of a society, whatever their lifestyles, are judged to be disadvantaged in comparison with the nation as a whole. (150)

Religion According to Émile Durkheim, a unified system of beliefs and practices relative to sacred things. (262)

Religious beliefs Statements to which members of a particular religion adhere. (267)

Religious experience The feeling or perception of being in direct contact with the ultimate reality, such as a divine being, or of being overcome with religious emotion. (267)

Religious rituals Practices required or expected of members of a faith. (267)

Representative sample A selection from a larger population that is statistically found to be typical of that population. (17)

Research design A detailed plan or method for obtaining data scientifically. (17)

Resocialization The process of discarding former behavior patterns and accepting new ones as part of a transition in one's life. (68)

Resource mobilization The ways in which a social movement utilizes such resources as money, political

influence, access to the media, and personnel. (359)

Reverse socialization The process whereby people normally being socialized are at the same time socializing their socializers. (71)

Rites of passage Rituals marking the symbolic transition from one social position to another. (67)

Role conflict Difficulties that occur when incompatible expectations arise from two or more social positions held by the same person. (85)

Role exit The process of disengagement from a role that is central to one's self-identity, and reestablishment of an identity in a new role. (86)

Role taking The process of mentally assuming the perspective of another, thereby enabling one to respond from that imagined viewpoint. (63)

Rumor A piece of information gathered informally which is used to interpret an ambiguous situation. (355)

Sacred Elements beyond everyday life which inspire awe, respect, and even fear. (262)

Sanctions Penalties and rewards for conduct concerning a social norm. (42, 111)

Sapir-Whorf hypothesis A hypothesis concerning the role of language in shaping cultures. It holds that language is culturally determined and serves to influence our mode of thought. (38)

Science The body of knowledge obtained by methods based on systematic observation. (363)

Scientific management approach Another name for the *classical theory* of formal organizations. (101)

Scientific method A systematic, organized series of steps that ensures maximum objectivity and consistency in researching a problem. (15)

Secondary group A formal, impersonal group in which there is little social intimacy or mutual understanding. (89)

Sect A relatively small religious group that has broken away from some other religious organization to renew what it views as the original vision of the faith. (268)

Secularization The process through which religion's influence on other social institutions diminishes. (260)

Segregation The act of physically separating two groups; often imposed on a minority group by a dominant group. (182)

Self According to George Herbert Mead, the sum total of people's conscious perception of their identity as distinct from others. (63)

Self-fulfilling prophecy The tendency of people to respond to and act on the basis of stereotypes, a predisposition which can lead to validation of false definitions. (175)

Serial monogamy A form of marriage in which a person can have several spouses in his or her lifetime but can have only one spouse at one time. (234)

Sexism The ideology that one sex is superior to the other. (209)

Sexual harassment Any unwanted and unwelcome sexual advances that interfere with a person's ability to perform a job and enjoy the benefits of a job. (311)

Sick role Societal expectations about the attitudes and behavior of a person viewed as being ill. (319)

Significant others A term used by George Herbert Mead to refer to those individuals who are most important in the development of the self, such as parents, friends, and teachers. (64)

Single-parent families Families in which there is only one parent present to care for children. (251)

Slavery A system of enforced servitude in which people are legally owned by others and in which enslaved status is transferred from parents to children. (137)

Social change Significant alteration over time in behavior patterns and culture, including norms and values. (348)

Social control The techniques and strategies for regulating human behavior in any society. (111)

Social epidemiology The study of the distribution of disease, impairment, and general health status across a population. (323)

Social inequality A condition in which members of a society have different amounts of wealth, prestige, or power. (136)

Social institutions Organized patterns of beliefs and behavior centered on basic social needs. (91)

Social interaction The ways in which people respond to one another. (82)

Socialism An economic system under which the means of production and distribution are collectively owned. (294)

Socialization The process whereby people learn the attitudes, values, and actions appropriate to individuals as members of a particular culture. (58)

Social mobility Movement of individuals and groups from one position of a society's stratification system to another. (155)

Social movements Organized collective activities to bring about or resist fundamental change in existing society. (357)

Social network A series of social relationships that link a person directly to others and therefore indirectly to still more people. (90)

Social role A set of expectations of people who occupy a given social position or status. (85)

Social structure The way in which a society is organized into predictable relationships. (83)

Social surplus The production by a group of people of enough goods to cover their own needs, while at the same time sustaining people who are not engaged in agricultural tasks. (292, 364)

Societal-reaction approach Another name for *labeling theory.* (120)

Society A fairly large number of people who live in the same territory, are relatively independent of people outside it, and participate in a common culture. (33)

Sociobiology The systematic study of the biological bases of social behavior. (62)

Sociological imagination An awareness of the relationship between an individual and the wider society. (3)

Sociology The systematic study of social behavior and human groups. (2)

Status A term used by sociologists to refer to any of the full range of socially defined positions within a large group or society. (83)

Status group A term used by Max Weber to refer to people who have the same prestige or lifestyle, independent of their class positions. (142)

Stereotypes Unreliable generalizations about all members of a group that do not recognize individual differences within the group. (175)

Stratification A structured ranking of entire groups of people that perpetuates unequal economic rewards and power in a society. (136)

Subculture A segment of society which shares a distinctive pattern of mores, folkways, and values which differ from the pattern of the larger society. (44)

Subsistence technology The tools, processes, and knowledge that a society requires to meet its basic needs for survival. (363)

Survey A study, generally in the form of interviews or questionnaires, which provides sociologists and other researchers with information concerning how people think and act. (17)

Symbols The gestures, objects, and language which form the basis of human communication. (63)

Teacher-expectancy effect The impact that a teacher's expectations about a student's performance may have on the student's actual achievements. (280)

Technology The application of knowledge to the making of tools and the utilization of natural resources. (292, 363)

Total fertility rate (TFR) The average number of children born alive to a woman, assuming that she conforms to current fertility rates. (333)

Total institutions A term coined by Erving Goffman to refer to institutions which regulate all aspects of a person's life under a single authority, such as prisons, the military, mental hospitals, and convents. (68)

Tracking The practice of placing students in specific curriculum groups on the basis of test scores and other criteria. (277)

Traditional authority Legitimate power conferred by custom and accepted practice. (298)

Trained incapacity The tendency of workers in a bureaucracy to become so specialized that they develop blind spots and cannot notice obvious problems. (97)

Underclass Long-term poor people who lack training and skills. (149)

Unilinear evolutionary theory A theory of social change which holds that all societies pass through the same successive stages of evolution and inevitably reach the same end. (360)

Unobtrusive measures Research techniques in which the method of study has no influence on the subjects under investigation. (20)

Urban ecology An area of study which focuses on the interrelationships between people and their environment as they emerge in urban areas. (366)

Value-added model A theory of collective behavior proposed by Neil Smelser to explain how broad social conditions are transformed in a definite pattern into some form of collective behavior. (350)

Value neutrality Max Weber's term for objectivity of sociologists in the interpretation of data. (24)

Values Collective conceptions of what is considered good, desirable, and proper—or bad, undesirable, and improper—in a culture. (43)

Variable A measurable trait or characteristic that is subject to change under different conditions. (16)

Verstehen The German word for "understanding" or "insight"; used by Max Weber to stress the need for sociologists to take into account people's emotions, thoughts, beliefs, and attitudes. (6)

Vertical mobility The movement of a person from one social position to another of a different rank. (155)

Vested interests Veblen's term for those people or groups who will suffer in the event of social change and who have a stake in maintaining the status quo. (368)

Veto groups David Riesman's term for interest groups that have the capacity to prevent the exercise of power by others. (306)

Victimization surveys Questionnaires or interviews used to determine whether people have been victims of crime. (127)

Victimless crimes A term used by sociologists to describe the willing exchange among adults of widely desired, but illegal, goods and services. (126)

Vital statistics Records of births, deaths, marriages, and divorces gathered through a registration system maintained by governmental units. (333)

Wealth An inclusive term encompassing all of a person's material assets, including land and other types of property. (136)

White-collar crimes Crimes committed by affluent individuals or corporations in the course of their daily business activities. (123)

World systems theory Immanuel Wallerstein's view of the global economic system as divided between certain industrialized nations who control wealth and developing countries who are controlled and exploited. (159)

Xenocentrism The belief that the products, styles, or ideas of one's society are inferior to those that originate elsewhere. (48)

Zero population growth (ZPG) The state of a population with a growth rate of zero, which is achieved when the number of births plus immigrants is equal to the number of deaths plus emigrants. (339)

REFERENCES

Abercrombie, Nicholas, Stephen Hill, and Bryan S. Turner. 1980. *The Dominant Ideology Thesis.* London: Allen and Unwin.

——, ——, and —— (eds.). 1990. *Dominant Ideologies.* Cambridge, Mass.: Unwin Hyman.

Aberle, David F., A. K. Cohen, A. K. Davis, M. J. Leng, Jr., and F. N. Sutton. 1950. "The Functional Prerequisites of a Society," *Ethics,* **60**(January):100–111.

Abrahamse, Allan F., Peter A. Morrison, and Linda J. Waite. 1988. *Beyond Stereotypes: Who Becomes a Single Teenage Mother?* Santa Monica, Calif.: Rand Corp.

Abrahamson, Mark. 1978. *Functionalism.* Englewood Cliffs, N.J.: Prentice-Hall.

Adam, Barry D. 1992. "Sociology and People Living with AIDS," in Joan Huber and Beth E. Schneider (eds.), *The Social Context of AIDS.* Newbury Park, Calif.: Sage, pp. 3–18.

Aguirre, B. E., E. L. Quarantelli, and Jorge L. Mendoza. 1988. "The Collective Behavior of Fads: The Characteristics, Effects, and Career of Streaking," *American Sociological Review,* **53**(August):569–584.

Aikman, David. 1991. "America's Holy War," *Time,* **138**(December 9):60–66, 68.

Alain, Michel. 1985. "An Empirical Validation of Relative Deprivation," *Human Relations,* **38**(8):739–749.

Alam, Sultana. 1985. "Women and Poverty in Bangladesh," *Women's Studies International Forum,* **8**(4):361–371.

Alba, Richard D. 1990. *Ethnic Identity: The Transformation of White America.* New Haven, Conn.: Yale University Press.

—— and Gwen Moore. 1982. "Ethnicity in the American Elite," *American Sociological Review,* **47**(June):373–383.

Albas, Daniel, and Cheryl Albas. 1988. "Aces and Bombers: The Post-exam Impression Management Strategies of Students," *Symbolic Interaction,* **11**(Fall):289–302.

Alexander, Vicki, Linda Kahn, Sushaun Robb, and Melanie Tervalon. 1987. "Teenage Mothers: Setting the Record Straight," *AAWO Discussion Paper,* **8**(June):1–8.

Allen, Bem P. 1978. *Social Behavior: Fact and Falsehood.* Chicago: Nelson Hall.

Allport, Gordon W. 1979. *The Nature of Prejudice* (25th anniversary ed.). Reading, Mass.: Addison-Wesley.

Alonzo, Angelo A. 1989. "Health and Illness and the Definition of the Situation: An Interactionist Perspective." Paper presented at the annual meeting of the Society for the Study of Social Problems, Berkeley, Calif.

Altman, Dennis. 1986. *AIDS in the Mind of America: The Social, Political, and Psychological Impact of a New Epidemic.* Garden City, N.Y.: Anchor/Doubleday.

Altman, Lawrence K. 1992a. "Women Worldwide Nearing Higher Rate for AIDS than Men," *New York Times* (July 21), p. C3.

—— 1992b. "Cost of Treating AIDS Patients Is Soaring," *New York Times* (July 23), p. B8.

—— and Elisabeth Rosenthal. 1990. "Changes in Medicine Bring Pain to

Healing Profession," *New York Times* (February 18), pp. 1, 20.

American Association of University Women. 1992. *How Schools Shortchange Girls*. Washington, D.C.: American Association of University Women.

American Medical Association. 1992. "Physicians and Domestic Violence: Ethical Considerations," *Journal of the American Medical Association*, **267**(June 17):3190–3193.

American Sociological Association. 1989. *Code of Ethics*. Washington, D.C.: American Sociological Association.

——. 1991. *Careers in Sociology*. Washington, D.C.: American Sociological Association.

Anderson, Cheryl, and Linda Rouse. 1988. "Intervention in Cases of Woman Battering: An Application of Symbolic Interactionism and Critical Theory," *Clinical Sociological Review*, **6**:134–137.

Anderson, Kevin. 1991. "Health Care Costs More, Serves Fewer," *USA Today* (March 11), pp. B1, B2.

Anderson, Roy M., and Robert M. May. 1992. "Understanding the AIDS Pandemic," *Scientific American*, **266**(May): 58–61, 64–66.

Andersson-Brolin, Lillemor. 1988. "Ethnic Residential Segregation: The Case of Sweden," *Scandinavian Journal of Development Alternatives*, **7**(March):33–45.

Anti-Defamation League of B'nai B'rith. 1992. *Audit of Anti-Semitic Incidents*. New York: Anti-Defamation League.

Appelbaum, Richard P. 1970. *Theories of Social Change*. Chicago: Markham.

Archer, Margaret. 1988. *Culture and Agency: The Place of Culture in Social Theory*. Cambridge, Eng.: Cambridge University Press.

Aronson, Elliot. 1972. *The Social Animal*. San Francisco: Freeman.

Asante, Molefi Kete. 1992. "Afrocentric Systematics," *Black Issues in Higher Education*, **9**(August 13):16–17, 21–22.

Asch, Adrienne. 1986. "Will Populism Empower Disabled People?" in Harry G. Boyte and Frank Riessman (eds.), *The New Populism: The Politics of Empowerment*. Philadelphia: Temple University Press, pp. 213–228.

Astin, Alexander W., Eric L. Day, William S. Korn, and Ellyne R. Riggs. 1991. *The American Freshman: National Norms for Fall 1991*. Los Angeles: Higher Education Research Institute, University of California at Los Angeles.

——, Kenneth C. Green, and William S. Korn. 1987. *The American Freshman: Twenty Year Trends*. Los Angeles: Cooperative Institutional Research Program, University of California at Los Angeles.

Atchley, Robert C. 1985. *The Social Forces in Later Life: An Introduction to Social Gerontology* (4th ed.). Belmont, Calif.: Wadsworth.

Aytac, Isik A. 1987. "Wife's Decision-Making at Work and Contribution to Family Income as Determinate of How Domestic Chores Are Shared." Paper presented at the annual meeting of the Eastern Sociological Society, Boston.

Azumi, Koya, and Jerald Hage. 1972. *Organizational Systems*. Lexington, Mass.: Heath.

Babbie, Earl R. 1980. *Sociology: An Introduction* (2d ed.). Belmont, Calif.: Wadsworth.

Bachrach, Christine A. 1986. "Adoption Plans, Adopted Children, and Adoptive Mothers," *Journal of Marriage and the Family*, **48**(May):243–253.

Bachrach, Peter, and Morton S. Baratz. 1962. "Two Faces of Power," *American Political Science Review*, **56**(December):947–952.

Bacon, John. 1987. "Court Ruling Hasn't Quieted School Prayer," *USA Today* (April 3), p. 34.

Bacon, Phil. 1985. "Facts behind the Trademark," *Moonkeans* (June), pp. 3–5.

Balswick, Jack, and Charles Peek. 1971. "The Inexpressive Male: A Tragedy of American Society," *Family Coordinator*, **20**(October)363–368.

Barlett, Donald L., and James B. Steele. 1981. *Empire: The Life, Legend, and Madness of Howard Hughes*. New York: Norton.

Barnet, Richard J. 1990. "But What about Africa?" *Harper's*, **280**(May):43–51.

—— and Ronald E. Müller. 1974. *Global Reach: The Power of the Multinational Corporation*. New York: Simon and Schuster.

Baron, James N., and William T. Bielby. 1986. "The Proliferation of Job Titles in Organizations," *Administrative Science Quarterly*, **31**(December):561–586.

Bartlett, Kay. 1988. "Sociologist Researches 'Role Exiting' Process," *Galesburg Register-Mail* (August 11), sec. C, p. 1.

Baruch, Grace, Rosalind Barnett, and Caryl Rivers. 1980. "A New Start for Women at Midlife," *New York Times Magazine* (December 7), pp. 196–201.

——, ——, and ——. 1983. *Lifeprints: New Patterns of Love and Work for Today's Women*. New York: McGraw-Hill.

Basso, Keith H. 1972. "Ice and Travel among the Fort Norman Slave: Folk Taxonomies and Cultural Rules," *Language in Society*, **1**(March):31–49.

Baumann, Marty. 1992. "Abortion Poll," *USA Today* (June 10), p. 4A.

Becker, Howard S. 1952. "Social Class Variations in the Teacher-Pupil Relationship," *Journal of Educational Sociology*, **25**(April):451–465.

——. 1963. *The Outsiders: Studies in the Sociology of Deviance*. New York: Free Press.

—— (ed.). 1964. *The Other Side: Perspectives on Deviance*. New York: Free Press.

——. 1973. *The Outsiders: Studies in the Sociology of Deviance* (rev. ed.). New York: Free Press.

——, Blanche Greer, Everett C. Hughes, and Anselm Strauss. 1961. *Boys in White: Student Culture in Medical School*. Chicago: University of Chicago Press.

Beeghley, Leonard. 1978. *Social Stratification in America: A Critical Analysis of Theory and Research*. Santa Monica, Calif.: Goodyear.

Belknap, Penny, and Wilbert Leonard II. 1991. "A Conceptual Replication and Extension of Erving Goffman's Study of Gender Advertisements," *Sex Roles*, **25**(3,4):103–118.

Bell, Daniel. 1953. "Crime as an American Way of Life," *Antioch Review*, **13**(Summer):131–154.

——. 1988. *The End of Ideology* (with a new afterword). Cambridge, Mass.: Harvard University Press.

Bell, Wendell. 1981a. "Modernization," in *Encyclopedia of Sociology*. Guilford, Conn.: DPG Publishing, pp. 186–187.

——. 1981b. "Neocolonialism," in *Encyclopedia of Sociology*. Guilford, Conn.: DPG Publishing, p. 193.

Bellah, Robert, Richard Madsen, Anne Swidler, William M. Sullivan, and Steven M. Tipton. 1985. *Habits of the Heart: Individualism and Commitment in American Life*. Berkeley: University of California Press.

Bem, Sandra Lipsitz. 1978. "Beyond Androgyny," in Julia A. Sherman and Florence L. Dennsk (eds.), *The Psychology of Women: Future Directions of Research*. New York: Psychological Dimensions, pp. 3–23.

Bendix, B. Reinhard. 1968. "Max Weber," in David L. Sills (ed.), *International Encyclopedia of the Social Sciences*. New York: Macmillan, pp. 493–502.

Benner, Richard S., and Susan Tyler Hitchcock. 1986. *Life after Liberal Arts.* Charlottesville: Office of Career Planning and Placement, University of Virginia.

Bensman, David, and Roberta Lynch. 1987. *Rusted Dreams: Hard Times in a Steel Community.* New York: McGraw-Hill.

Berg, Philip L. 1975. "Racism and the Puritan Mind," *Phylon,* **36**(Spring): 1–7.

Berger, Bennett M. 1981. *The Survival of a Counterculture.* Berkeley: University of California Press.

Berger, Peter, and Thomas Luckmann. 1966. *The Social Construction of Reality.* New York: Doubleday.

Berk, Marc. 1985. "Medical Manpower and the Labeling of Blindness," *Deviant Behavior,* **6**(3):253–265.

Berk, Richard A. 1974. *Collective Behavior.* Dubuque, Iowa: Brown.

Berkeley Wellness Letter. 1990. "The Nest Refilled," **6**(February):1–2.

Berlin, Brent, and Paul Kay. 1991. *Basic Color Terms: Their Universality and Evolution.* Berkeley: University of California Press.

Berman, Paul (ed.). 1992. *Debating P.C.: The Controversy over Political Correctness on College Campuses.* New York: Dell.

Bernard, Jessie. 1972. "The Paradox of the Happy Marriage," in Vivian Gornick and Barbara K. Moran (eds.), *Women in Sexist Society: Studies in Power and Powerlessness.* New York: Basic Books, pp. 145–162.

Berney, Barbara. 1990. "In Research, Women Don't Matter," *The Progressive,* **54**(October):24–27.

Bettelheim, Bruno, and Morris Janowitz. 1964. *Social Change and Prejudice.* New York: Free Press.

Biggart, Nicole Woolsey. 1989. *Charismatic Capitalism: Direct Selling Organizations in America.* Chicago: University of Chicago Press.

Biklen, Douglas. 1986. "Framed: Journalism's Treatment of Disability," *Social Policy,* **16**(Winter):45–51.

Black, C. E. 1966. *The Dynamics of Modernization: A Study in Comparative History.* New York: Harper and Row.

Blakey, G. Robert, Ronald Goldstock, and Charles H. Rogarin. 1978. *Rackets Bureaus: Investigation and Prosecution of Organized Crime.* Report of National Institute of Law Enforcement and Criminal Justice. Washington, D.C.: U.S. Government Printing Office.

Blanc, Ann Klimas. 1984. "Nonmarital Cohabitation and Fertility in the United States and Western Europe," *Population Research and Policy Review,* **3**:181–193.

Blanchard, Fletcher A., Teri Lilly, and Leigh Ann Vaughan. 1991. "Reducing the Expression of Racial Prejudice," *Psychological Science,* **2**(March): 101–105.

Blau, Peter M., and Otis Dudley Duncan. 1967. *The American Occupational Structure.* New York: Wiley.

——— and Marshall W. Meyer. 1987. *Bureaucracy in Modern Society* (3d ed.). New York: Random House.

Blauner, Robert. 1964. *Alienation and Freedom.* Chicago: University of Chicago Press.

———. 1972. *Racial Oppression in America.* New York: Harper and Row.

Blendon, Robert J. 1986. "The Problems of Cost, Access, and Distribution of Medical Care," *Daedalus,* **115** (Spring):119–135.

——— et al. [4 authors]. 1989. "Access to Medical Care for Black and White Americans," *Journal of the American Medical Association,* **261**(January 13): 278–281.

Blood, Robert O., Jr., and Donald M. Wolfe. 1960. *Husbands and Wives: The Dynamics of Married Living.* New York: Free Press.

Bloom, Samuel W., and Robert N. Wilson. 1979. "Patient-Practitioner Relationship," in Howard E. Freeman, Sol Levine, and Leo G. Reider (eds.), *Handbook of Medical Sociology* (3d ed.). Englewood Cliffs, N.J.: Prentice-Hall, pp. 275–296.

Bluestone, Barry, and Bennett Harrison. 1982. *The Deindustrialization of America.* New York: Basic Books.

Blumberg, Paul. 1980. *Inequality in an Age of Decline.* New York: Oxford University Press.

Blumer, Herbert. 1955. "Collective Behavior," in Alfred McClung Lee (ed.), *Principles of Sociology* (2d ed.). New York: Barnes and Noble, pp. 165–198.

———. 1969. *Symbolic Interactionism: Perspective and Method.* Englewood Cliffs, N.J.: Prentice-Hall.

Blumstein, Philip, and Pepper Schwartz. 1983: *American Couples: Money, Work, Sex.* New York: Morrow.

Bogue, Donald. 1979. *Principles of Demography.* New York: Wiley.

Bohannan, Paul. 1970. "The Six Stations of Divorce," in Paul Bohannan (ed.), *Divorce and After.* New York: Doubleday, pp. 33–62.

Borgatta, Edgar F., and Marie L. Borgatta (eds.). 1992. *Encyclopedia of Sociology.* New York: Macmillan.

Borman, Kathryn M., and Joel H.

Spring. 1984. *Schools in Central Cities: Structure and Process.* New York: Longman.

Bornschier, Volker, Christopher Chase-Dunn, and Richard Rubinson. 1978. "Cross-National Evidence of the Effects of Foreign Investment and Aid on Economic Growth and Inequality: A Survey of Findings and a Reanalysis," *American Journal of Sociology,* **84**(November):651–683.

Boserup, Ester. 1977. "Preface," in Wellesley Editorial Committee (ed.), *Women and National Development: The Complexities of Change.* Chicago: University of Chicago Press, pp. xi–xiv.

Bottomore, Tom (ed.). 1983. *A Dictionary of Marxist Thought.* Cambridge, Mass.: Harvard University Press.

——— and Maximilien Rubel (eds.). 1956. *Karl Marx: Selected Writings in Sociology and Social Philosophy.* New York: McGraw-Hill.

Bouchard, Thomas J., Jr. 1991. "A Twice-Told Tale: Twins Reared Apart," in W. Grove and D. Ciccehetti (eds.), *Thinking Clearly about Psychology: Essays in Honor of Paul Everett Meehl,* vol. 2: *Personality and Psychopathology.* Minneapolis: University of Minnesota, pp. 188–215.

Bouvier, Leon F. 1980. "America's Baby Boom Generation: The Fateful Bulge," *Population Bulletin,* **35**(April).

——— and Cary B. Davis. 1982. *The Future Racial Composition of the United States.* Washington, D.C.: Demographic Information Services Center of the Population Reference Bureau.

——— and Carol J. De Vita. 1991. "The Baby Boom: Entering Midlife," *Population Bulletin,* **46**(November):1–34.

Bowles, Samuel, and Herbert Gintis. 1976. *Schooling in Capitalist America: Educational Reforms and the Contradictions of Economic Life.* New York: Basic Books.

Bradley, Phil. 1990. "The Growing Clout of Voters with Disabilities," *Illinois Issues,* **16**(April):34.

Bradshaw, York W. 1988. "Reassessing Economic Dependency and Uneven Development: The Kenyan Experience," *American Sociological Review,* **53**(October):693–708.

Braun, Denny. 1991. *The Rich Get Richer.* Chicago: Nelson-Hall.

Brazil. 1981. *Ix Recenseamento Geral do Brasil—1980, 1, Pt. 1.* Rio de Janeiro: Secretaria de Planejamento da Presidência da República, Fundação Instituto Brasilerio de Geografia e Estatistica.

Brewer, Rose M. 1989. "Black Women and Feminist Sociology: The Emerging Perspective," *American Sociologist,* **20**(Spring):57–70.

Brinton, Mary C. 1992. *Women and the Economic Miracle: Gender and Work in Postwar Japan.* Berkeley: University of California Press.

Brodkey, Linda, and Michelle Fine. 1988. "Presence of Mind in the Absence of Body," *Journal of Education,* **170**(Fall):84–99.

Bronfenbrenner, Urie. 1970. *Two Worlds of Childhood: U.S. and U.S.S.R.* New York: Russell Sage.

Brower, Brock. 1988. "The Pernicious Power of the Polls," *Money,* **17**(March):144–163.

Brown, Michael, and Amy Goldin. 1973. *Collective Behavior: A Review and Reinterpretation of the Literature.* Pacific Palisades, Calif.: Goodyear.

Brown, Robert McAfee. 1980. *Gustavo Gutierrez.* Atlanta: John Knox.

Brown, Roger W. 1954. "Mass Phenomena," in Gardner Lindzey (ed.), *Handbook of Social Psychology,* vol. 2. Reading Mass.: Addison-Wesley, pp. 833–873.

———. 1965. *Social Psychology.* New York: Free Press.

Brozan, Nadine. 1985. "Rate of Pregnancies for U.S. Teenagers Found High in Study," *New York Times* (March 13), pp. A1, C7.

Brunvand, Jan Harold. 1989. *Curses! Broiled Again!* New York: Norton.

Bulle, Wolfgang F. 1987. *Crossing Cultures? Southeast Asian Mainland.* Atlanta: Centers for Disease Control.

Bumpass, Larry L., James A. Sweet, and Teresa Castro Martin. 1990. "Changing Patterns of Remarriage," *Journal of Marriage and the Family,* **52**(August):747–756.

Burciaga, Cecilia Preciado de, Viola Gonzales, and Ruth A. Hepburn. 1977. "The Chicana as Feminist," in Alice G. Sargent (ed.), *Beyond Sex Roles.* St. Paul, Minn.: West, pp. 266–273.

Bureau of the Census. 1975. *Historical Statistics of the United States, Colonial Times to 1970.* Washington, D.C.: U.S. Government Printing Office.

———. 1986. "Household Wealth and Asset Ownership: 1984," *Current Population Reports,* ser. P-70, no. 7. Washington, D.C.: U.S. Government Printing Office.

———. 1990a. *Statistical Abstract of the United States: 1990.* Washington, D.C.: U.S. Government Printing Office.

———. 1990b. *Money Income and Poverty in the United States, 1989,* ser. P-60, no. 168. Washington, D.C.: U.S. Government Printing Office.

———. 1990c. *Transitions in Income and Poverty Status: 1985–86,* ser. P-70, no. 18. Washington, D.C.: U.S. Government Printing Office.

———. 1990d. "Household and Family Characteristics: March 1990 and 1989," *Current Population Reports.* Washington, D.C.: U.S. Government Printing Office.

———. 1991a. *Statistical Abstract of the United States, 1991.* Washington, D.C.: U.S. Government Printing Office.

———. 1991b. *Money Income of Households, Families, and Persons in the United States: 1990,* ser. P-60, no. 174. Washington, D.C.: U.S. Government Printing Office.

———. 1991c. *Poverty in the United States: 1990,* ser. P-60, no. 175. Washington, D.C.: U.S. Government Printing Office.

———. 1991d. "1990 Census Counts on Specific Racial Groups." News release, June 12, Washington, D.C.: United States Department of Commerce.

———. 1991e. *The Hispanic Population in the United States: March 1990,* ser. P-20, no. 449. Washington, D.C.: U.S. Government Printing Office.

———. 1991f. "Fertility of American Women: June 1990," *Current Population Reports,* ser. P-20, no. 454. Washington, D.C.: U.S. Government Printing Office.

———. 1991g. "Marital Status and Living Arrangements: March 1990," *Current Population Reports.* ser. P-2, no. 450. Washington, D.C.: U.S. Government Printing Office.

———. 1992a. *Statistical Abstract of the United States: 1992.* Washington, D.C.: U.S. Government Printing Office.

———. 1992b. "School Enrollment— Social and Economic Characteristics of Students: October 1990," ser. P-20, no. 460. Washington, D.C.: U.S. Government Printing Office.

Burgess, Ernest W. 1925. "The Growth of the City," in Robert E. Park, Ernest W. Burgess, and Roderick D. McKenzie (eds.), *The City.* Chicago: University of Chicago Press, pp. 47–62.

Burgess, John. 1989. "Exporting Our Office Work," *Washington Post National Weekly Edition,* **6**(May 1):22.

Butler, Robert N. 1975. *Why Survive? Being Old in America.* New York: Harper and Row.

———. 1980. "Ageism: A Forward," *Journal of Social Issues,* **36**(Spring):8–11.

———. 1989. "Dispelling Ageism: The Cross-Cutting Intervention," *Annals,* **503**(May):138–147.

Cahill, Spencer E. 1986. "Language

Practices and Self Definition: The Case of Gender Identity Acquisition," *Sociological Quarterly,* **27**(September): 295–312.

Cancian, Francesca. 1986. "The Feminization of Love," *Signs,* **11**(Summer): 692–708.

Cantril, Hadley. 1940. *The Invasion from Mars: A Study in the Psychology of Panic.* Princeton, N.J.: Princeton University Press.

Caplan, Arthur L. (ed.). 1978. *The Sociobiology Debate; Readings on Ethical and Scientific Issues.* New York: Harper and Row.

Caplan, Ronald L. 1989. "The Commodification of American Health Care," *Social Science and Medicine,* **28**(11):1139–1148.

Cargan, Leonard, and Matthew Melko. 1991. "Being Single on Noah's Ark," in Leonard Cargan and Jeanne H. Ballantine (eds.), *Sociological Footprints* (5th ed.). Belmont, Calif.: Wadsworth, pp. 161–165.

Carmichael, Stokely, and Charles V. Hamilton. 1967. *Black Power: The Politics of Liberation in America.* New York: Random House.

Carmody, Denise Lardner. 1989. *Women and World Religions* (2d ed.). Englewood Cliffs, N.J.: Prentice-Hall.

Carroll, John B. 1953. *The Study of Language.* Cambridge, Mass.: Harvard University Press.

———. 1956. *Language, Thought, and Reality: Selected Writings of Benjamin Lee Whorf.* Cambridge, Mass.: M.I.T. Press.

Carroll, Susan. 1993. "The Gender Gap in the Presidential Race," *CAWP News and Notes,* **9**(Winter):5–6.

Carter, Keith. 1989. "Networking Is the Key to Jobs," *USA Today* (August 7), p. B1.

Cauchon, Dennis. 1991. "Study Shows Bias in Sentencing Laws," *USA Today* (August 23), p. 8A.

CBS News. 1979. Transcript of *Sixty Minutes* segment, "I Was Only Following Orders," March 31, pp. 2–8.

Center for the American Woman and Politics. 1987. *Women in Government around the World.* New Brunswick, N.J.: Center for the American Woman and Politics.

———. 1992a. *Women in Elective Office 1992.* New Brunswick, N.J.: Center for the American Woman and Politics.

———. 1992b. *The Impact of Women in Public Office: Findings at a Glance.* New Brunswick, N.J.: Center for the American Woman and Politics.

Centers for Disease Control. 1992a. "Sexual Behavior among High School

Students: United States, 1990," *Morbidity and Mortality Weekly Report*, **40**(January 3):885–889.

———. 1992b. "The Second 100,000 Cases of Acquired Immunodeficiency Syndrome," *Morbidity and Mortality Weekly Report*, **40**(January 3):885–889.

———. 1992c. "Projections of the Number of Persons Diagnosed with AIDS and the Number of Immunosuppressed HIV-Infected Persons—United States, 1992–1994," *Morbidity and Mortality Weekly Report*, **41**(December 25):1–28.

Chafetz, Janet Saltzman. 1988. *Feminist Sociology: An Overview of Contemporary Theories*. Itasca, Ill.: Peacock.

Chalfant, H. Paul, Robert E. Beckley, and C. Eddie Palmer. 1987. *Religion in Contemporary Society* (2d ed.). Palo Alto, Calif.: Mayfield.

——— et al. [5 others]. 1990. "The Clergy as a Resource for Those Encountering Psychological Distress," *Review of Religious Research*, **31** (March):305–315.

Chambliss, William. 1972. "Introduction," in Harry King, *Box Man*. New York: Harper and Row, pp. ix–xi.

———. 1973. "The Saints and the Roughnecks," *Society*, **11**(November–December):24–31.

——— and Robert B. Seidman. 1971. *Law, Order, and Power*. Reading, Mass.: Addison-Wesley.

Changing Times. 1981. "When Family Anger Turns to Violence," **35** (March):66–70.

Chapman, Fern Schumer. 1987. "Executive Guilt: Who's Taking Care of the Children," *Fortune*, **115**(February 16): 30–37.

Cherlin, Andrew S. (ed.). 1988. *The Changing American Family and Public Policy*. Washington, D.C.: Urban Institute Press.

Chinoy, Ely. 1954. *Sociological Perspectives: Basic Concepts and Their Applications*. New York: Random House.

Chudacoff, Howard P. 1989. *How Old Are You?* Princeton, N.J.: Princeton University Press.

Cicone, Michael V., and Diane N. Ruble. 1978. "Beliefs about Males," *Journal of Social Issues*, **34**(Winter):5–16.

Cisin, Ira H., and Walter B. Clark. 1962. "The Methodological Challenge of Disaster Research," in George W. Baker and Dwight W. Chapman (eds.), *Man and Society in Disaster*. New York: Basic Books, pp. 23–40.

Clark, Burton R., and Martin Trow. 1966. "The Organizational Context," in Theodore M. Newcomb and Everett K. Wilson (eds.), *The Study of College Peer Groups*. Chicago: Aldine, pp. 17–70.

Clark, Candace. 1983. "Sickness and Social Control," in Howard Robboy and Candace Clark (eds.), *Social Interaction: Readings in Sociology* (2d ed.). New York: St. Martin's, pp. 346–365.

Clines, Francis X. 1989. "There's a Crime Wave, or a Perception Wave, in the Soviet Union," *New York Times* (August 17), p. E2.

Cloward, Richard A. 1959. "Illegitimate Means, Anomie, and Deviant Behavior," *American Sociological Review*, **24**(April):164–176.

Cockerham, William C. 1989. *Medical Sociology* (4th ed.). Englewood Cliffs, N.J.: Prentice-Hall.

Cohn, Bob. 1991. "The Q-Word Charade," *Newsweek*, **117**(June 3):16–18.

Cohn, Victor. 1992. "How Can We Fix a Broken System? *Washington Post National Weekly Edition*, **9**(February):6–7.

Colasanto, Diane. 1989. "Public Wants Civil Rights Widened for Some Groups, Not for Others," *Gallup Poll Monthly*, **291**(December):13–22.

Cole, Elizabeth S. 1985. "Adoption: History, Policy, and Program," in Joan Laird and Ann Hartman (eds.), *A Handbook of Child Welfare*. New York: Free Press, pp. 638–666.

Cole, Mike. 1988. *Bowles and Gintis Revisited: Correspondence and Contradiction in Educational Theory*. Philadelphia: Falmer.

Coleman, James William, and Donald R. Cressey. 1980. *Social Problems*. New York: Harper and Row.

Collins, Glenn. 1987. "As Nation Grays, a Mighty Advocate Flexes Its Muscles," *New York Times* (April 2), pp. C1, C8.

Collins, Randall. 1975. *Conflict Sociology: Toward an Explanatory Sociology*. New York: Academic.

———. 1979. *The Credential Society: An Historical Sociology of Education and Stratification*. New York: Academic.

———. 1980. "Weber's Last Theory of Capitalism: A Systematization," *American Sociological Review*, **45**(December):925–942.

——— and Michael Makowsky. 1978. *The Discovery of Society*. New York: Random House.

Commission on Civil Rights. 1976. *A Guide to Federal Laws and Regulations Prohibiting Sex Discrimination*. Washington, D.C.: U.S. Government Printing Office.

———. 1981. *Affirmative Action in the 1980s: Dismantling the Process of Discrimination*. Washington, D.C.: U.S. Government Printing Office.

———. 1992. *Civil Rights Issues Facing Asian Americans in the 1990s*. Washington, D.C.: U.S. Government Printing Office.

Conklin, John E. 1981. *Criminology*. New York: Macmillan.

Conly, Catherine H., and J. Thomas McEwen. 1990. "Computer Crime," *NIJ Reports* (January–February), pp. 2–7.

Conniff, Ruth. 1992. "Cutting the Lifeline: The Real Welfare Fraud," *The Progressive*, **56**(February):25–31.

Conover, Pamela J., and Virginia Gray. 1983. *Feminism and the New Right Conflict over the American Family*. New York: Praeger.

Conrad, Peter, and Rochelle Kern (eds.). 1986. *The Sociology of Health and Illness: Critical Perspectives* (2d ed.). New York: St. Martin's.

——— and Joseph W. Schneider. 1980. *Deviance and Medicalization: From Badness to Sickness*. St. Louis: Mosby.

Cooley, Charles H. 1902. *Human Nature and the Social Order*. New York: Scribner.

Cooper, B. Lee. 1992. "Popular Songs, Military Conflict, and Public Perceptions of the United States at War," *Social Education*, **56**(March):160–168.

Coser, Lewis A. 1956. *The Functions of Social Conflict*. New York: Free Press.

———. 1977. *Masters of Sociological Thought: Ideas in Historical and Social Context* (2d ed.). New York: Harcourt Brace Jovanovich.

Coser, Rose Laub. 1984. "American Medicine's Ambiguous Progress," *Contemporary Sociology*, **13**(January):9–13.

COSSA (Consortium of Social Science Associations). 1991. "Social Science Triumphs in Congress after Setback on American Teenage Study," *Washington Update*, **15**(August):1–4.

Cottle, Thomas J. 1991. "A Family Prepares for College," *Journal of Higher Education*, **62**(January–February):79–86.

Cotton, Paul. 1990. "Is There Still Too Much Extrapolation from Data on Middle-Aged White Men?" *Journal of the American Medical Association*, **263**(February 23):1049–1050.

Council on Scientific Affairs. 1991. "Hispanic Health in the United States," *Journal of the American Medical Association*, **265**(January 9):248–252.

Courtney, Alice E., and Thomas W. Whipple. 1983. *Sex Stereotyping in Advertising*. Lexington, Mass.: Lexington.

Cowan, Neil M., and Ruth Schwartz Cowan. 1989. *Our Parents' Lives: The*

Americanization of Eastern European Jews. New York: Basic Books.

Cowgill, Donald O. 1986. *Aging around the World*. Belmont, Calif.: Wadsworth.

Cox, Oliver C. 1948. *Caste, Class and Race: A Study in Social Dynamics*. Detroit: Wayne State University Press.

———. 1976. *Race Relations: Elements and Social Dynamics*. Detroit: Wayne State University Press.

Craig, Steve (ed.). 1992. *Men, Masculinity, and the Media*. Newbury Park, Calif.: Sage.

Cressey, Donald R. 1960. "Epidemiology and Individual Contact: A Case from Criminology," *Pacific Sociological Review*, **3**(Fall):47–58.

Crossette, Barbara. 1992. "Population Policy in Asia Is Faulted," *New York Times* (September 16), p. A9.

Crow, Ben, and Alan Thomas. 1983. *Third World Atlas*. Milton Keynes, Eng.: Open University Press.

Cuff, E. C., and G. C. F. Payne. 1979. *Perspectives on Sociology*. Boston: G. Allen.

Cullen, Francis T., Jr., and John B. Cullen. 1978. *Toward a Paradigm of Labeling Theory*, ser. 58. Lincoln: University of Nebraska Studies.

Cumming, Elaine, and William E. Henry. 1961. *Growing Old: The Process of Disengagement*. New York: Basic Books.

Cummings, Milton C., Jr., and David Wise. 1989. *Democracy under Pressure: An Introduction to the American Political System* (6th ed.). San Diego: Harcourt Brace Jovanovich.

Currie, Elliot. 1985. *Confronting Crime: An American Challenge*. New York: Pantheon.

Dahl, Robert A. 1961. *Who Governs?* New Haven, Conn.: Yale University Press.

Dahrendorf, Ralf. 1958. "Toward a Theory of Social Conflict," *Journal of Conflict Resolution*, **2**(June):170–183.

———. 1959. *Class and Class Conflict in Industrial Sociology*. Stanford, Calif.: Stanford University Press.

———. 1990. *Reflections on the Revolution in Europe*. New York: Random House.

Darnton, Nina. 1992. "A Split Verdict on America's Marital Future," *Newsweek*, **119**(January 13):52.

Davies, Christie. 1989. "Goffman's Concept of the Total Institution: Criticisms and Revisions," *Human Studies*, **12**(June):77–95.

Davis, Fred. 1992. *Fashions, Culture and Identity*. Chicago: University of Chicago Press.

Davis, James. 1982. "Up and Down

Opportunity's Ladder," *Public Opinion*, **5**(June–July):11–15, 48–51.

Davis, Kingsley. 1937. "The Sociology of Prostitution," *American Sociological Review*, **2**(October):744–755.

———. 1940. "Extreme Social Isolation of a Child," *American Journal of Sociology*, **45**(January):554–565.

———. 1947. "Final Note on a Case of Extreme Isolation," *American Journal of Sociology*, **52**(March):432–437.

———. 1949. *Human Society*. New York: Macmillan.

——— and Wilbert E. Moore. 1945. "Some Principles of Stratification," *American Sociological Review*, **10**(April): 242–249.

Davis, L. J. 1990. "Chronicle of a Debacle Foretold: How Deregulation Begat the S&L Scandal," *Harper's*, **281**(September):50–66.

Davis, Mike. 1992. "In L.A., Burning All Illusions," *The Nation*, **254**(June 1): 743–746.

Davis, Nancy J., and Robert V. Robinson. 1988. "Class Identification of Men and Women in the 1970s and 1980s," *American Sociological Review*, **53**(February):103–112.

Davis, Nanette J. 1975. *Sociological Constructions of Deviance: Perspectives and Issues in the Field*. Dubuque, Iowa: Brown.

Day, Lincoln H. 1978. "What Will a ZPG Society Be Like?" *Population Bulletin*, **33**(June).

de Beauvoir, Simone. 1953. *The Second Sex*. New York: Knopf.

Deegan, Mary Jo. 1988. "Transcending a Patriarchal Past: Teaching the History of Women in Sociology," *Teaching Sociology*, **16**(April):141–150.

Degler, Carl N. 1971. *Neither Black nor White: Slavery and Race Relations in Brazil and the United States*. New York: Macmillan.

Demerath, N. J., II, and Rhys H. Williams. 1992. *A Bridging of Faiths: Religion and Politics in a New England City*. Princeton, N.J.: Princeton University Press.

Denisoff, R. Serge, and Ralph Wahrman. 1983. *An Introduction to Sociology* (3d ed.). New York: Macmillan.

Dentan, Robert. 1968. *The Semai: A Nonviolent People of Malaya*. New York: Holt.

DeParle, Jason. 1992a. "Why Marginal Changes Don't Rescue the Welfare System," *New York Times* (March 1), p. E3.

———. 1992b. "'88 Welfare Act Is Falling Short, Researchers Say," *New York Times* (March 30), pp. A1, A11.

———. 1992c. "Welfare Plan Linked to

Jobs Is Paying Off, a Study Shows," *New York Times* (April 23), pp. A1, D25.

Department of Justice. 1987. *White Collar Crime*. Washington, D.C.: U.S. Government Printing Office.

———. 1989. *BJS Data Report, 1988*. Washington, D.C.: U.S. Government Printing Office.

———. 1990. *Criminal Victimization in the United States, 1988*. Washington, D.C.: U.S. Government Printing Office.

———. 1991. *Criminal Victimization in the United States, 1989*. Washington, D.C.: U.S. Government Printing Office.

———. 1992. *Crime in the United States, 1991*. Washington, D.C.: U.S. Government Printing Office.

Department of Labor. 1980. *Perspectives on Working Women: A Datebook*. Washington, D.C.: U.S. Government Printing Office.

Desforges, Donna M., et al. [8 authors]. 1991. "Effects of Structured Cooperative Contact on Changing Negative Attitudes toward Stigmatized Social Groups," *Journal of Personality and Social Psychology*, **60**(4):531–544.

Desroches, Frederick J. 1990. "Tearoom Trade: A Research Update," *Qualitative Sociology*, **13**(1):39–61.

DeStefano, Linda, and Diane Colasanto. 1990. "Unlike 1975, Today Most Americans Think Men Have It Better," *Gallup Poll Monthly*, **293**(February):25–36.

DeVault, Marjorie L. 1991. *Feeding the Family: The Social Organization of Caring as Gendered Work*. Chicago: University of Chicago Press.

Devine, Don. 1972. *Political Culture of the United States: The Influence of Member Values on Regime Maintenance*. Boston: Little, Brown.

DiMaggio, Paul. 1990. "Review of *Charismatic Capitalism: Direct Selling Organizations in America*," *Contemporary Sociology*, **19**(March):218–220.

Disability Rag. 1990. "The Fight Is On!" (September–October):4–7.

Dittersdorf, Harriet. 1990. "Domestic Partnership: What Used to Define a Traditional Family," *NOW-NYC News*, **14**(July–August):6.

Dolbeare, Kenneth M. 1982. *American Public Policy: A Citizen's Guide*. New York: McGraw-Hill.

Domhoff, G. William. 1967. *Who Rules America?* Englewood Cliffs, N.J.: Prentice-Hall.

———. 1970. *The Higher Circles: The Governing Class in America*. New York: Random House.

———. 1978. *Who Really Rules? New Haven and Community Power Reexam-*

ined. New Brunswick, N.J.: Transaction.

———. 1983. *Who Rules America Now? A View for the '80s.* Englewood Cliffs, N.J.: Prentice-Hall.

———. 1990. *The Power Elite and the State: How Policy Is Made in America.* New York: Aldine De Gruyter.

Donald, David. 1956. *Lincoln Reconsidered: Essays on the Civil War Era.* New York: Knopf.

Dore, Ronald P. 1976. *The Diploma Disease: Education, Qualification and Development.* Berkeley: University of California Press.

Doress, Irwin, and Jack Nusan Porter. 1977. *Kids in Cults: Why They Join, Why They Stay, Why They Leave.* Brookline, Mass.: Reconciliation Associates.

Dornbusch, Sanford M. 1989. "The Sociology of Adolescence," in W. Richard Scott and Judith Blake (eds.), *Annual Review of Sociology, 1989.* Palo Alto, Calif.: Annual Reviews, pp. 233–259.

Dowd, James J. 1980. *Stratification among the Aged.* Monterey, Calif.: Brooks/Cole.

Downs, Peter. 1987. "Your Money or Your Life," *The Progressive,* **51**(January):24–28.

Driscoll, Anne. 1988. "For Salem, a Reminder of a Dark Past," *New York Times* (October 30), p. 51.

Drosnin, Michael. 1985. *Citizen Hughes.* New York: Holt.

Duberman, Lucille. 1976. *Social Inequality: Class and Caste in America.* Philadelphia: Lippincott.

Du Bois, W. E. B. 1909. *The Negro American Family.* Atlanta University (reprinted 1970, Cambridge, Mass.: M.I.T. Press).

Dumas, Kitty. 1992. "Vote Likely Buries Anti-crime Bill," *Congressional Quarterly Weekly Report,* **50**(March 21):732.

Duncan, Greg J., and Ken R. Smith. 1989. "The Rising Affluence of the Elderly: How Far, How Fair, and How Frail," in W. Richard Scott and Judith Blake (eds.), *Annual Review of Sociology, 1989.* Palo Alto, Calif.: Annual Reviews, pp. 261–289.

Durkheim, Émile. 1933. *Division of Labor in Society.* Translated by George Simpson. New York: Free Press (originally published in 1893).

———. 1947. *The Elementary Forms of the Religious Life.* Glencoe, Ill.: Free Press (originally published in 1912).

———. 1951. *Suicide.* Translated by John A. Spaulding and George Simpson. New York: Free Press (originally published in 1897).

———. 1964. *The Rules of Sociological*

Method. Translated by Sarah A. Solovay and John H. Mueller. New York: Free Press (originally published in 1895).

Durning, Alan B. 1990. "Life on the Brink," *World Watch,* **3**(March–April):22–30.

Dushkin Publishing Group. 1991. *Encyclopedic Dictionary of Sociology* (4th ed.). Guilford, Conn.: Dushkin.

Duster, Troy. 1991. "Understanding Self-Segregation on the Campus," *Chronicle of Higher Education,* **38**(September 25):B1, B2.

Dworkin, Rosalind J. 1982. "A Woman's Report: Numbers Are Not Enough," in Anthony Dworkin and Rosalind Dworkin (eds.), *The Minority Report.* New York: Holt, pp. 375–400.

Dynes, Russell R. 1978. "Interorganizational Relations in Communities under Stress," in E. L. Quarantelli (ed.), *Disasters: Theory and Research.* Beverly Hills, Calif.: Sage, pp. 50–64.

Dzidzienyo, Anani. 1987. "Brazil," in Jay A. Sigler (ed.), *International Handbook on Race and Race Relations.* New York: Greenwood, pp. 23–42.

Easterbrook, Gregg. 1987. "The Revolution in Medicine," *Newsweek,* **109**(January 26):40–44, 49–54, 56–59, 61–64, 67–68, 70–74.

Ebaugh, Helen Rose Fuchs. 1988. *Becoming an Ex: The Process of Role Exit.* Chicago: University of Chicago Press.

Eckholm, Erik. 1992. "The Riots Bring a Rush to Arm and New Debate," *New York Times* (May 17), p. E18.

Economist. 1990a. "By Any Other Name," **314**(January 6):42.

———. 1990b. "Thick Skins," **314**(February 24):26.

———. 1991. "The Reincarnation of Caste," **319**(June 8):21–23.

Eden, Dov, and Abraham B. Shani. 1982. "Pygmalion Goes to Boot Camp: Expectancy, Leadership, and Trainee Performance," *Journal of Applied Psychology,* **67**(April):194–199.

Eder, Donna. 1985. "The Cycle of Popularity: Interpersonal Relations among Female Adolescents," *Sociology of Education,* **58**(July):154–165.

Edin, Kathryn. 1991. "Surviving the Welfare System: How AFDC Recipients Make Ends Meet in Chicago," *Social Problems,* **38**(November):462–474.

Edmonds, Patricia. 1992. "Year Later, Harassment's 'Real to More People,'" *USA Today* (October 2), p. 6A.

Education Week. 1991. "The Cost of Raising a Child" (May 8), p. 7.

Edwards, Harry. 1984. "The Black 'Dumb Jock,'" *College Board Review,* **131**(Spring):8–13.

Egeland, Janice A., et al. 1987. "Bipolar Affective Disorders Linked to DNA Markers on Chromosome 11," *Nature,* **325**(February 26):783–787.

Ehrenreich, Barbara, and Deidre English. 1973. *Witches, Midwives, and Nurses: A History of Women Healers.* Old Westbury, N.Y.: Feminist Press.

——— and Annette Fuentes. 1981. "Life on the Global Assembly," *Ms.,* **9**(January):53–59, 71.

Ehrlich, Paul R. 1968. *The Population Bomb.* New York: Ballantine.

——— and Anne H. Ehrlich. 1990. *The Population Explosion.* New York: Simon and Schuster.

Eitzen, D. Stanley. 1978. *In Conflict and Order: Understanding Society.* Boston: Allyn and Bacon.

———, with Maxine Baca Zinn. 1988. *In Conflict and Order: Understanding Society.* (4th ed.). Boston: Allyn and Bacon.

Ekman, Paul, Wallace V. Friesen, and John Bear. 1984. "The International Language of Gestures," *Psychology Today,* **18**(May):64–69.

Elam, Stanley M. 1990. "The 22nd Annual Gallup Poll of the Public Schools," *Phi Delta Kappan,* **72**(September):41–55.

Elias, Marilyn. 1991. "More Kids in Declining Day Care," *USA Today* (November 7), p. D1.

Elkin, Frederick, and Gerald Handel. 1989. *The Child and Society: The Process of Socialization* (5th ed.). New York: Random House.

Ellison, Ralph. 1952. *Invisible Man.* New York: Random House.

Elsasser, Glen. 1992. "School Prayer Ban Upheld," *Chicago Tribune* (June 25), pp. 1, 10.

Emerson, Rupert. 1968. "Colonialism: Political Aspects," in David L. Sills (ed.), *International Encyclopedia of the Social Sciences,* vol. 3. New York: Macmillan, pp. 1–5.

Engels, Friedrich. 1884. "The Origin of the Family, Private Property and the State." Excerpted in Lewis Feuer (ed.), *Marx and Engels: Basic Writings on Politics and Philosophy.* Garden City, N.Y.: Anchor, 1959, pp. 392–394.

Enloe, Cynthia. 1990. *Bananas, Beaches, and Bases: Making Feminist Sense of International Politics.* Berkeley: University of California Press.

Erickson, J. David, and Tor Bjerkedal. 1982. "Fetal and Infant Mortality in Norway and the United States," *Journal of the American Medical Association,* **247**(February 19):987–991.

Erikson, Kai. 1966. *Wayward Puritans: A*

Study in the Sociology of Deviance. New York: Wiley.

———. 1986. "On Work and Alienation," *American Sociological Review,* **51**(February):1–8.

Espinosa, Dula. 1987. "The Impact of Affirmative Action Policy on Ethnic and Gender Employment Inequality." Paper presented at the annual meeting of the American Sociological Association, Chicago.

Etzioni, Amitai. 1964. *Modern Organization.* Englewood Cliffs, N.J.: Prentice-Hall.

———. 1985. "Shady Corporate Practices," *New York Times* (November 15), p. A35.

———. 1990. "Going Soft on Corporate Crime," *Washington Post* (April 1), p. C3.

Evans, Sara. 1980. *Personal Politics: The Roots of Women's Liberation in the Civil Rights Movement and the New Left.* New York: Vintage.

Eve, Raymond A., and Francis B. Harrold. 1991. *The Creationist Movement in Modern America.* Boston: Twayne.

Fager, Marty, Mike Bradley, Lonnie Danchik, and Tom Wodetski. 1971. *Unbecoming Men.* Washington, N.J.: Times Change.

Faludi, Susan. 1991. *Backlash: The Undeclared War against Women.* New York: Crown.

Family Economics Research Group. 1992. "Expenditures on a Child by Husband-Wife Families," *Family Economics Review,* **5**(1):33–36.

Fannin, Leon F. 1989. "Thuggee and Professional Criminality," *Michigan Sociological Review,* **3**(Fall):34–44.

Feagin, Joe R. 1989. *Minority Group Issues in Higher Education: Learning from Qualitative Research.* Norman: Center for Research on Minority Education, University of Oklahoma.

Featherman, David L., and Robert M. Hauser. 1978. *Opportunity and Change.* New York: Aeodus.

Featherstone, Mike. 1990. *Global Culture: Nationalism, Globalization, and Modernity.* London: Sage.

Feinglass, Joe. 1987. "Next, the McDRG," *The Progressive,* **51**(January):28.

Fenigstein, Alan. 1984. "Self-Consciousness and the Over-perception of self as a Target," *Journal of Personality and Social Psychology,* **47**(4):860–870.

Ferguson, Kathy E. 1983. "Bureaucracy and Public Life: The Feminization of the Polity," *Administration and Society,* **15**(November):295–322.

———. 1984. *The Feminist Case against*

Bureaucracy. Philadelphia: Temple University Press.

Fergusson, D. M., L. J. Horwood, and F. T. Shannon. 1984. "A Proportional Hazards Model of Family Breakdown," *Journal of Marriage and the Family,* **46**(August):539–549.

Ferrell, Tom. 1979. "More Choose to Live outside Marriage," *New York Times* (July 1), p. E7.

Feuer, Lewis S. (ed.). 1959. *Karl Marx and Friederich Engels: Basic Writings on Politics and Philosophy.* Garden City, N.Y.: Doubleday.

Fine, Michelle, and Adrienne Asch. 1981. "Disabled Women: Sexism without Pedestal," *Journal of Sociology and Social Welfare,* **8**(July):233–248.

——— and ——— (eds.). 1988a. *Women with Disabilities: Essays in Psychology, Culture, and Politics.* Philadelphia University Press.

——— and ———. 1988b. "Disability beyond Stigma: Social Interaction, Discrimination, and Activism," *Journal of Social Issues,* **44**(1):3–21.

Fineberg, Harvey. 1988. "The Social Dimensions of AIDS," *Scientific American,* **259**(October):128–134.

Fingerhut, Lois A., and Joel C. Kleinman. 1990. "International and Interstate Comparisons of Homicide among Young Males," *Journal of the American Medical Association,* **263**(June 27):3292–3295.

Finkel, Steven E., and James B. Rule. 1987. "Relative Deprivation and Related Psychological Theories of Civil Violence: A Critical Review," *Research in Social Movements,* **9**:47–69.

Firestone, Shulamith. 1970. *The Dialectic of Sex: The Case for Feminist Revolution.* New York: Bantam.

Fischer, Claude S. 1988. "Gender and the Residential Telephone, 1890–1940: Technologies of Sociability," *Sociological Forum,* **3**(Spring):211–233.

Fisher, Arthur. 1992. "Sociobiology: Science or Ideology?" *Society,* **29**(July–August):67–79.

Fitzgerald, Louise F., Lauren M. Weitzman, Yael Gold, and Mimi Ormerod. 1988. "Academic Harassment: Sex and Denial in Scholarly Garb," *Psychology of Women Quarterly,* **12**(September):329–340.

Flacks, Richard. 1971. *Youth and Social Change.* Chicago: Markham.

Fletcher, Robert S. 1943. *History of Oberlin College to the Civil War.* Oberlin, Ohio: Oberlin College Press.

Flexner, Eleanor. 1972. *Century of Struggle: The Women's Rights Movement in the United States.* New York: Atheneum.

Foner, Nancy. 1984. *Ages in Conflict.* New York: Columbia University Press.

Fong-Torres, Ben. 1986. "The China Syndrome," *Moviegoer,* **5**(July):6–7.

Footlick, Jerrold K. 1990. "What Happened to the Family?" special issue of *Newsweek,* **114**(Winter–Spring):14–18, 20.

Forer, Lois G. 1984. *Money and Justice: Who Owns the Courts.* New York: Norton.

Form, William H. 1967. "Occupational and Social Integration of Automobile Workers in Four Countries," in William A. Faunce and W. Form (eds.), *Comparative Perspectives on Industrial Society.* Boston: Little, Brown, pp. 222–244.

Fox, Robert. 1987. *Population Images* (2d ed.). New York: United Nations Fund for Population Activities.

France, David. 1988. "ACT-UP Fires Up," *Village Voice,* **33**(May 3):36.

Franklin, John Hope, and Alfred A. Moss, Jr. 1988. *From Slavery to Freedom* (6th ed.). New York: Knopf.

Freeman, Jo. 1973. "The Origins of the Women's Liberation Movement," *American Journal of Sociology,* **78**(January):792–811.

———. 1975. *The Politics of Women's Liberation.* New York: McKay.

Freeman, Linton C. 1958. "Marriage without Love: Mate Selection in Nonwestern Societies," in Robert F. Winch (ed.), *Mate Selection.* New York: Harper and Row, pp. 20–30.

Freidson, Eliot. 1970. *Profession of Medicine.* New York: Dodd, Mead.

Freudenheim, Milt. 1990. "Employers Balk at High Cost of High-Tech Medical Care," *New York Times* (April 29), pp. 1, 16.

———. 1991. "In a Stronghold for H.M.O.'s, One Possible Future Emerges," *New York Times* (August 30), pp. 1, 28.

Friedan, Betty. 1963. *The Feminine Mystique.* New York: Norton.

Friedman, Emily. 1991. "The Uninsured from Dilemma to Crisis," *Journal of the American Medical Association,* **265**(May 15):2491–2495.

Galinsky, Ellen. 1986. *Investing in Quality Child Care.* Basking Ridge, N.J.: AT&T.

Gallup (Opinion Index). 1975. "Vietnamese Refugees," **119**(May):6.

———. 1978. "Religion in America, 1977–78," **145**(January).

Gamson, Josh. 1989. "Silence, Death, and the Invisible Enemy: AIDS Activism and Social Movement 'Newness,'" *Social Problems,* **36**(October):351–367.

Gans, Herbert J. 1991. *People, Plans, and Policies: Essays on Poverty, Racism, and Other National Urban Problems.* New York: Columbia University Press and Russell Sage Foundation.

Ganzeboom, Harry B. G., Ruud Luijkx, and Donald J. Treiman. 1989. "Intergenerational Class Mobility in Comparative Perspective," in Arne L. Kalleberg (ed.), *Research in Social Stratification and Mobility.* Greenwich, Conn.: JAI Press, pp. 3–84.

———, Donald J. Treiman, and Wout C. Ultee. 1991. "Comparative Intergenerational Stratification Research," in W. Richard Scott (ed.), *Annual Review of Sociology, 1991.* Palo Alto, Calif.: Annual Reviews, pp. 277–302.

Garber, H., and F. R. Herber. 1977. "The Milwaukee Project: Indications of the Effectiveness of Early Intervention in Preventing Mental Retardation," in Peter Mittler (ed.), *Research to Practice in Mental Retardation,* vol. 1. Baltimore: University Park Press, pp. 119–127.

Gardner, Carol Brooks. 1989. "Analyzing Gender in Public Places: Rethinking Goffman's Vision of Everyday Life," *American Sociologist,* **20**(Spring): 42–56.

Garfinkel, Harold. 1956. "Conditions of Successful Degradation Ceremonies," *American Journal of Sociology,* **61** (March):420–424.

Gargan, Edward A. 1992. "Bound to Looms by Poverty and Fear, Boys in India Make a Few Men Rich," *New York Times* (July 9), p. A8.

Garreau, Joel. 1991. *Edge City: Life on the New Frontier.* New York: Doubleday.

Gates, Henry Louis, Jr. 1991. "Delusions of Grandeur," *Sports Illustrated,* **75**(August 19):78.

———. 1992. "Whose Canon Is It, Anyway?" in Paul Berman (ed.), *Debating P.C.: The Controversy over Political Correctness on College Campuses.* New York: Dell, pp. 190–200.

Gecas, Viktor. 1981. "Concepts of Socialization," in Morris Rosenberg and Ralph H. Turner (eds.), *Social Psychology: Sociological Perspectives.* New York: Basic Books, pp. 165–199.

———. 1982. "The Self-Concept," in Ralph H. Turner and James F. Short, Jr. (eds.), *Annual Review of Sociology, 1982.* Palo Alto, Calif.: Annual Reviews, pp. 1–33.

Gelles, Richard J., and Claire Pedrick Cornell. 1990. *Intimate Violence in Families* (2d ed.). Newbury Park, Calif.: Sage.

———, Murray A. Straus, and John W. Harrop. 1988. "Has Family Violence Decreased? A Response to J. Timothy Stocks," *Journal of Marriage and the Family,* **50**(February):286–291.

Gelman, David. 1985. "Who's Taking Care of Our Parents?" *Newsweek,* **105**(May 6):60–64, 68.

George, Susan. 1988. *A Fate Worse Than Debt.* New York: Grove.

Georges, Christopher. 1992. "Old Money," *Washington Monthly,* **24**(June): 16–21.

Gerstel, Naomi. 1987. "Divorce and Stigma," *Social Problems,* **34**(April): 172–186.

Gerth, H. H., and C. Wright Mills. 1958. *From Max Weber: Essays in Sociology.* New York: Galaxy.

Gesensway, Deborah, and Mindy Roseman. 1987. *Beyond Words: Images from American Concentration Camps.* Ithaca, N.Y.: Cornell University Press.

Gest, Ted. 1985. "Are White-Collar Crooks Getting Off Too Easy?" *U.S. News and World Report,* **99**(July 1):43.

Giago, Tim, and Sharon Illoway. 1982. "Dying Too Young," *Civil Rights Quarterly Perspective,* **14**(Fall):29, 31, 33.

Giddens, Anthony. 1991. *Introduction to Sociology.* New York: Norton.

Giddings, Paula. 1984. *When and Where I Enter.* New York: Morrow.

Gilligan, Carol. 1982. *In a Different Voice.* Cambridge, Mass.: Harvard University Press.

Gilly, M. C. 1988. "Sex Roles in Advertising: A Comparison of Television Advertisements in Australia, Mexico, and the United States," *Journal of Marketing,* **52**(April):75–85.

Gilmore, David. 1990. "Men and Women in Southern Spain: 'Domestic Power' Revisited," *American Anthropologist,* **92**(December):953–970.

Gimenez, Martha E. 1987. "Black Family: Vanishing or Unattainable," *Humanity and Society,* **11**(November):420–439.

Gittelsohn, John. 1987. "An Asian Norma Rae," *U.S. News and World Report,* **103**(September 14):52.

Godwin, Deborah D., and John Scanzoni. 1989. "Couple Consensus during Marital Joint Decision-Making: A Context, Process, Outcome Model," *Journal of Marriage and the Family,* **31**(November):943–956.

Goffman, Erving. 1959. *The Presentation of Self in Everyday Life.* New York: Doubleday.

———. 1961. *Asylums: Essays on the Social Situation of Mental Patients and Other Inmates.* Garden City, N.Y.: Doubleday.

———. 1963. *Stigma: Notes on Manage-ment of Spoiled Identity.* Englewood Cliffs, N.J.: Prentice-Hall.

———. 1977. "The Arrangement between the Sexes," *Theory and Society,* 4:301–331.

———. 1979. *Gender Advertisements.* New York: Harper and Row.

Goldman, Ari L. 1992. "Reading, Writing, Arithmetic, and Arabic," *New York Times* (October 3), pp. 25–26.

Goleman, Daniel. 1990. "Anger over Racism Is Seen as a Cause of Blacks' High Blood Pressure," *New York Times* (April 24), p. C3.

———. 1991. "New Ways to Battle Bias: Fight Acts, Not Feelings," *New York Times* (July 16), pp. C1, C8.

Goodale, Jane C. 1971. *Tiwi Wives: A Study of Women of Melville Island, North Australia.* Seattle: University of Washington Press.

Goode, William J. 1959. "The Theoretical Importance of Love," *American Sociological Review,* **24**(February):38–47.

———. 1976. "Family Disorganization," in Robert Merton and Robert Nisbet (eds.), *Contemporary Social Problems* (4th ed.). New York: Harcourt Brace Jovanovich, pp. 511–554.

Goodman, Ellen. 1977. "Great (Male) Expectations," *Washington Post* (September 3), p. A11.

Goodman, Norman, and Gary T. Marx. 1978. *Society Today* (3d ed.). New York: CRM/Random House.

Gordon, C. Wayne. 1955. "The Role of the Teacher in the School Structure of the High School," *Journal of Educational Sociology,* **29**(September):21–29.

Gordus, Jeanne Prial, and Karen Yamakawa. 1988. "Incomparable Losses: Economic and Labor Market Outcomes for Unemployed Female versus Male Autoworkers," in Patricia Voydanoff and Linda C. Majka (eds.), *Families and Economic Distress.* Newbury Park, Calif.: Sage, pp. 38–54.

Goslin, David A. 1965. *The Schools in Contemporary Society.* Glenview, Ill.: Scott, Foresman.

Gough, E. Kathleen. 1974. "Nayar: Central Kerala," in David Schneider and E. Kathleen Gough (eds.), *Matrilineal Kinship.* Berkeley: University of California Press, pp. 298–384.

Gouldner, Alvin. 1950. *Studies in Leadership.* New York: Harper and Row.

———. 1960. "The Norm of Reciprocity," *American Sociological Review,* **25**(April):161–177.

———. 1962. "Anti-Minotaur: The Myth of a Value-Free Sociology," *Social Problems,* **9**(Winter):199–213.

———. 1970. *The Coming Crisis of Western Sociology.* New York: Basic Books.

Gove, Walter R. (ed.). 1980. *The Labelling of Deviance* (2d ed.). Beverly Hills, Calif.: Sage.

———. 1987. "Sociobiology Misses the Mark: An Essay on Why Biology but Not Sociobiology Is Very Relevant to Sociology," *American Sociologist,* **18**(Fall):258–277.

——— and Michael Hughes. 1979. "Possible Causes of the Apparent Sex Differences in Physical Health: An Empirical Investigation," *American Sociological Review,* **44**(February):126–146.

Graham, Saxon, and Leo G. Reeder. 1979. "Social Epidemiology of Chronic Diseases," in Howard E. Freeman, Sol Levine, and Leo G. Reeder (eds.), *Handbook in Medical Sociology* (3d ed.). Englewood Cliffs, N.J.: Prentice-Hall.

Gramsci, Antonio. 1929. In Quintin Hoare and Geoffrey Nowell Smith (eds.), *Selections from the Prison Notebooks.* London: Lawrence and Wishort.

Gray, Jane. 1991. "Tea Room Revisited: A Study of Male Homosexuals in a Public Setting." Paper presented at the annual meeting of the American Criminal Justice Society, Nashville.

Greeley, Andrew M. 1989. "Protestant and Catholic: Is the Analogical Imagination Extinct?" *American Sociological Review,* **54**(August):485–502.

Greene, Elizabeth. 1987. "Jail!" *Chronicle of Higher Education,* **34**(November 4):A42–A44.

Greenfield, Sheldon, Dolores M. Blanco, Robert M. Elashoff, and Patricia A. Ganz. 1987. "Patterns of Care Related to Age of Breast Cancer Patients," *Journal of the American Medical Association,* **257**(May 22–29):2766–2770.

Greenhouse, Linda. 1991. "5 Justices Uphold U.S. Rule Curbing Abortion Advice," *New York Times* (May 24), pp. A1, A18.

Grissmer, David, and Sheila Kirby. 1987. *Teacher Attrition: The Uphill Climb to Staff the Nation's Schools.* Santa Monica, Calif.: Rand Corp.

Gross, Edward, and Gregory P. Stone. 1964. "Embarrassment and the Analysis of Role Requirements," *American Journal of Sociology,* **70**(July):1–15.

Gross, Jane. 1987. "An Ever-Widening Epidemic Tears at the City's Life and Spirit," *New York Times* (March 16), p. 17.

———. 1991a. "Surge of Rock Fans, Then Death, Grief, and Anger," *New York Times* (January 25), pp. A1, A16.

———. 1991b. "Female Surgeon's Quitting Touches Nerve at Medical Schools," *New York Times* (July 14), p. 10.

Grusky, David B., and Robert M. Hauser. 1984. "Comparative Social Mobility Revisited: Models of Convergence and Divergence in 16 Countries," *American Sociological Review,* **49**(February):19–38.

Gupte, Pranay B. 1982. "U.N. Lowers Estimate of Population in 2000," *New York Times* (June 13), p. 4.

Gutiérrez, Gustavo. 1990. "Theology and the Social Sciences," in Paul E. Sigmund, *Liberation Theology at the Crossroads: Democracy or Revolution?* New York: Oxford University Press, pp. 214–225.

Hacker, Andrew. 1964. "Power to Do What?" in Irving Louis Horowitz (ed.), *The New Sociology.* New York: Oxford University Press, pp. 134–146.

———. 1992. *Two Nations: Black and White, Separate, Hostile, Unequal.* New York: Scribner.

Hacker, Helen Mayer. 1973. "Sex Roles in Black Society: Caste versus Caste." Paper presented at the annual meeting of the American Sociological Association, New York City, August 30.

Hadley, Jack, Earl P. Steinberg, and Judith Feder. 1991. "Comparison of Uninsured and Privately Insured Hospital Patients: Condition on Admission, Resource Use, and Outcome," *Journal of the American Medical Association,* **265**(January 16):374–379.

Hagan, John, and Patricia Parker. 1985. "White-Collar Crime and Punishment: The Class Structure and Legal Sanctioning of Securities Violations," *American Sociological Review,* **50**(June):302–316.

Hahn, Harlan. 1987. "Civil Rights for Disabled Americans: The Foundation of a Political Agenda," in Alan Gartner and Tom Joe (eds.), *Images of the Disabled, Disabling Images.* New York: Praeger, pp. 181–203.

Haines, Valerie A. 1988. "Is Spencer's Theory an Evolutionary Theory?" *American Journal of Sociology,* **93**(March):1200–1223.

Hall, Richard H. 1963. "The Concept of Bureaucracy: An Empirical Assessment," *American Journal of Sociology,* **69**(July):32–40.

Hall, Robert H. 1982. "The Truth about Brown Lung," *Business and Society Review,* **40**(Winter 1981–1982):15–20.

Haller, Max, Wolfgang König, Peter Krause, and Karin Kurz. 1990. "Pat-

terns of Career Mobility and Structural Positions in Advanced Capitalist Societies: A Comparison of Men in Austria, France, and the United States," *American Sociological Review,* **50**(October):579–603.

Halliday, M. A. K. 1978. *Language as Social Semiotic.* Baltimore: University Park Press.

Haney, Craig, Curtis Banks, and Philip Zimbardo. 1973. "Interpersonal Dynamics in a Simulated Prison," *International Journal of Criminology and Penology,* **1**(February):69–97.

Hanson, Sandra L. and Ooms, Theodora. 1991. "The Economic Costs and Rewards of Two-Earner, Two-Parent Families," *Journal of Marriage and the Family,* **53**(August):622–634.

Harap, Louis. 1982. "Marxism and Religion: Social Functions of Religious Belief," *Jewish Currents,* **36**(January):12–17, 32–35.

Harlow, Harry F. 1971. *Learning to Love.* New York: Ballantine.

Harrington, Michael. 1980. "The New Class and the Left," in B. Bruce-Briggs (ed.), *The New Class.* New Brunswick, N.J.: Transaction, pp. 123–138.

Harris, Chauncy D., and Edward Ullman. 1945. "The Nature of Cities," *Annals of the American Academy of Political and Social Sciences,* **242**(November):7–17.

Harris, Diana K., and William E. Cole. 1980. *The Sociology of Aging.* Boston: Houghton Mifflin.

Harris, Lou. 1987. *Inside America.* New York: Vintage.

Harris, Marlys. 1988. "Where Have All the Babies Gone?" *Money,* **17**(December):164–176.

Harris, Marvin. 1958. *Minorities in the New World: Six Case Studies.* New York: Columbia University Press.

———. 1980. *Culture, People, Nature* (3d ed.). New York: Harper and Row.

Harris, Richard. 1966. *The Sacred Trust.* New York: New American Library.

Harrison, Bennett, and Barry Bluestone. 1988. *The Great U-Turn.* New York: Basic Books.

Hartjen, Clayton A. 1978. *Crime and Criminalization* (2d ed.). New York: Praeger.

Hasson, Judi. 1992. "No Simple Cure for Sick System," *USA Today* (October 15), p. 5A.

Haub, Carl. 1988. "The World Population Crisis Was Forgotten, but Not Gone," *Washington Post National Weekly Edition,* **5**(September 5):23.

———, Mary Mederios Kent, and

Machiko Yanagishita. 1990. *World Population Data Sheet, 1990*. Washington, D.C.: Population Reference Bureau.

——— and Machiko Yanagishita. 1992. *World Population Data Sheet, 1992*. Washington, D.C.: Population Reference Bureau.

Haupt, Arthur. 1979. "World's Refugees Finding No Refuge," *Intercom*, **7**(June–July):1, 15.

———. 1990. "UN Projections Rise Slightly Higher than 1989," *Population Today*, **18**(November):4.

Hauser, Robert M., and David B. Grusky. 1988. "Cross-National Variation in Occupational Distributions, Relative Mobility Chances, and Intergenerational Shifts in Occupational Distributions," *American Sociological Review*, **53**(October):723–741.

Havemann, Judith. 1988. "Sexual Harassment: The Personnel Problem That Won't Go Away," *Washington Post National Weekly Edition*, **5**(July 11–17):30–31.

Haviland, William A. 1985. *Cultural Anthropology* (5th ed.). New York: Holt.

Hawley, Amos H. 1950. *Human Ecology: A Theory of Community Structure*. New York: Ronald.

Heberle, Rudolf. 1968. "Social Movements: Types and Functions," in David Sills (ed.), *International Encyclopedia of the Social Sciences*, vol. 14. New York: Macmillan, pp. 438–444.

Heisel, Marsel A. 1985. *Aging in the Context of Population Policies in Developing Countries*. New York: United Nations.

Heller, Scott. 1987. "Research on Coerced Behavior Leads Berkeley Sociologist to Key Role as Expert Witness in Controversial Lawsuits," *Chronicle of Higher Education*, **33**(March 8):1, 13.

Hellmich, Nanci. 1990. "Day-Care Workers' Low Pay 'Horrifying,'" *USA Today* (February 28), p. A1.

Hendricks, Jon. 1982. "The Elderly in Society: Beyond Modernization," *Social Science History*, **6**(Summer):321–345.

Hendry, Joy. 1981. *Marriage in Changing Japan*. New York: St. Martin's.

Henkoff, Ronald. 1989. "Is Creed Dead?" *Fortune*, **120** (August 14):40–43, 46, 49.

Henley, Nancy, Mykol Hamilton, and Barrie Thorne. 1985. "Womanspeak and Manspeak: Sex Differences and Sexism in Communication, Verbal and Nonverbal," in Alice G. Sargent (ed.), *Beyond Sex Roles* (2d ed.). St. Paul, Minn.: West, pp. 168–185.

Henry, Mary E. 1989. "The Function of Schooling: Perspectives from Rural Australia," *Discourse*, **9**(April):1–21.

Henshaw, Stanley K., and Jennifer Van Vort. 1989. "Teenage Abortion, Birth and Pregnancy Statistics: An Update," *Family Planning Perspective*, **21**(March–April):85–88.

Henslin, James M. (ed.). 1972. *Down to Earth Sociology*. New York: Free Press.

Hentoff, Nat. 1992. "The Silence of Anita Hill," *Village Voice*, **37**(January 21):20–21.

Herek, Gregory M., and Eric K. Glunt. 1988. "An Epidemic of Stigma," *American Psychologist*, **43**(November): 886–891.

Herskovits, Melville J. 1930. *The Anthropometry of the American Negro*. New York: Columbia University Press.

———. 1941. *The Myth of the Negro Past*. New York: Harper.

———. 1943. "The Negro in Bahia, Brazil: A Problem in Method," *American Sociological Review*, **8**(August):394–402.

Hess, Beth B., and Elizabeth W. Markson. 1980. *Aging and Old Age: An Introduction to Social Gerontology*. New York: Macmillan.

Hetherington, E. Mavis. 1979. "Divorce: A Child's Perspective," *American Psychologist*, **34**(October):851–858.

Hiatt, Fred. 1988. "Japanese Kids Are Licking Their Chopsticks," *Washington Post National Weekly Edition*, **5**(March 14–20):19.

Hicks, Jonathan P. 1991. "Women in Waiting," *New York Times* (November 3), sec. 4A, p. 19.

Hill, Anita. 1992. "The Nature of the Beast," *Ms.*, **2**(January–February): 32–33.

Hill, Robert B. 1972. *The Strengths of Black Families*. New York: Emerson.

———. 1987. "The Future of Black Families," *Colloqui* (Spring), pp. 22–28.

Hillebrand, Barbara. 1992. "Midlife Crisis," *Chicago Tribune* (May 10), sec. 6, pp. 1, 11.

Hilts, Philip J. 1990. "New Study Challenges Estimates of Adopting a Child," *New York Times* (December 10), p. B10.

———. 1991. "Women Still Behind in Medicine," *New York Times* (September 10), p. C7.

———. 1992. "More Teen-Agers Being Slain by Guns," *New York Times* (June 10), p. A19.

Hine, Darlene Clark. 1990. *Black Women in White: Racial Conflict and Cooperation in the Nursing Profession, 1890–1950*. Bloomington: Indiana University Press.

Hiro, Dilip. 1973. *Black British, White British* (rev. ed.). New York: Monthly Review Press.

Hively, Robert (ed.). 1990. *The Lurking Evil: Racial and Ethnic Conflict on the College Campus*. Washington, D.C.: American Association of State Colleges and Universities.

Hochschild, Arlie Russell. 1990. "The Second Shift: Employed Women and Putting In Another Day of Work at Home," *Utne Reader*, **38**(March–April):66–73.

———, with Anne Machung. 1989. *The Second Shift: Working Parents and the Revolution at Home*. New York: Viking Penguin.

Hodge, Robert W., and Peter H. Rossi. 1964. "Occupational Prestige in the United States, 1925–1963," *American Journal of Sociology*, **70**(November): 286–302.

Hoebel, E. Adamson. 1949. *Man in the Primitive World: An Introduction to Anthropology*. New York: McGraw-Hill.

Hoffman, Lois Wladis. 1977. "Changes in Family Roles, Socialization, and Sex Differences," *American Psychologist*, **32**(August):644–657.

———. 1985. "The Changing Genetics/Socialization Balance," *Journal of Social Issues*, **41**(Spring):127–148.

——— and F. Ivan Nye. 1975. *Working Mothers*. San Francisco: Jossey-Bass.

Holcomb, Betty. 1988. "Nurses Fight Back," *Ms.*, **16**(July):72–78.

Hollingshead, August B. 1975. *Elmtown's Youth and Elmtown Revisited*. New York: Wiley.

Holmes, Steven A. 1990a. "House, 265–145, Votes to Widen Day Care Programs in the Nation," *New York Times* (March 30), pp. A1, A14.

———. 1990b. "Day Care Bill Marks a Turn toward Help for the Poor," *New York Times* (April 8), p. E4.

———. 1990c. "Disabled People Say Home Care Is Needed to Use New Rights," *New York Times* (October 14), p. 22.

Homans, George C. 1979. "Nature versus Nurture: A False Dichotomy," *Contemporary Sociology*, **8**(May):345–348.

Horn, Jack C., and Jeff Meer. 1987. "The Vintage Years," *Psychology Today*, **21**(May):76–77, 80–84, 88–90.

Hornblower, Margot. 1988. "Gray Power!" *Time*, **131**(January 4):36–37.

Horowitz, Helen Lefkowitz. 1987. *Campus Life*. Chicago: University of Chicago Press.

Horowitz, Irving Louis, and Lee Rainwater. 1970. "Journalistic Moralizers," *Transaction,* **7**(May):5–8.

Hosokawa, William K. 1969. *Nisei: The Quiet Americans.* New York: Morrow.

Houseman, John. 1972. *Run Through.* New York: Simon and Schuster.

Hout, Michael. 1988. "More Universalism, Less Structural Mobility: The American Occupational Structure in the 1980s," *American Journal of Sociology,* **93**(May):1358–1400.

Howard, Michael C. 1989. *Contemporary Cultural Anthropology* (3d ed.). Glenview, Ill.: Scott, Foresman.

Howe, Marvine. 1991. "Sex Discrimination Persists, U.N. Says," *New York Times* (June 16), p. 7.

Howlett, Debbie, and Judy Keen. 1991. "Role in Military Splits Minorities," *USA Today* (February 18), p. 2A.

Huang, Gary. 1988. "Daily Addressing Ritual: A Cross-Cultural Study." Paper presented at the annual meeting of the American Sociological Association, Atlanta.

Huber, Bettina J. 1985. *Employment Patterns in Sociology: Recent Trends and Future Prospects.* Washington, D.C.: American Sociological Association.

———. 1987. "Graduate Education and the Academic Job Market," *American Sociologist,* **18**(Spring):46–52.

Huber, Joan, and Beth E. Schneider (eds.). 1992. *The Social Context of AIDS.* Newbury Park, Calif.: Sage.

Huesmann, L. Rowell, and Neil M. Malamuth (eds.). 1986. "Media Violence and Antisocial Behavior," special issue of the *Journal of Social Issues,* **42**(3).

Hughes, Everett. 1945. "Dilemmas and Contradictions of Status," *American Journal of Sociology,* **50**(March):353–359.

Humphreys, Laud. 1970a. "Tearoom Trade," *Transaction,* **7**(January):10–25.

———. 1970b. *Tearoom Trade: Impersonal Sex in Public Places.* Chicago: Aldine.

———. 1975. *Tearoom Trade: Impersonal Sex in Public Places* (enlarged ed.). Chicago: Aldine.

Hunter, Herbert M., and Sameer Y. Abraham. 1987. *Race, Class, and the World Systems: The Sociology of Oliver C. Cox.* New York: Monthly Review.

Hurh, Won Moo, and Kwang Chung Kim. 1989. "The 'Success' Image of Asian Americans: Its Validity, and Its Practical and Theoretical Implications," *Ethnic and Racial Studies,* **12**(October):512–538.

Hurn, Christopher J. 1985. *The Limits and Possibilities of Schooling* (2d ed.). Boston: Allyn and Bacon.

Inter-Parliamentary Union. 1990. *Sharp Drop in the Number of Women Holding Seats in Europe's Parliaments.* Geneva: Inter-Parliamentary Union.

Ireland, Doug. 1992. "The Party's Over," *Village Voice,* **37**(June 16):8.

Isaacson, Walter. 1989. "Should Gays Have Marriage Rights?" *Time,* **134**(November 20):101–102.

Jackson, Elton F., Charles R. Tittle, and Mary Jean Burke. 1986. "Offense-Specific Models of the Differential Association Process," *Social Problems,* **33**(April):335–356.

Jackson, Philip W. 1968. *Life in Classrooms.* New York: Holt.

Jacobs, Jerry A. 1990. *Revolving Doors: Sex Segregation in Women's Careers.* Palo Alto, Calif.: Stanford University Press.

Jacobs, Paul, and Saul Landau (eds.). 1966. *The New Radicals.* New York: Vintage.

Jaffe, Peter G., David A. Wolfe, and Susan Kaye Wilson. 1990. *Children of Battered Women.* Newbury Park, Calif.: Sage.

Jaimes, M. Annette (ed.). 1992. *The State of Native America.* Boston: South End.

Jasper, James M., and Dorothy Nelkin. 1992. *The Animal Rights Crusade: The Growth of a Moral Protest.* New York: Free Press.

Jennings, M. Kent, and Richard G. Niemi. 1981. *Generations and Politics.* Princeton, N.J.: Princeton University Press.

Johnson, Benton. 1975. *Functionalism in Modern Sociology: Understanding Talcott Parsons.* Morristown, N.J.: General Learning.

Johnson, Charles S. 1939. "Race Relations and Social Change," in Edgar T. Thompson (ed.), *Race Relations and the Race Problem.* Durham, N.C.: Duke University Press, pp. 217–303.

Johnson, Dirk. 1987. "Fear of AIDS Stirs New Attacks on Homosexuals," *New York Times* (April 24), p. 12.

———. 1991. "Census Finds Many Claiming New Identity: Indian," *New York Times* (March 5), pp. A1, A16.

Johnson, Mary. 1989. "Enabling Act," *The Nation,* **249**(October 23):446.

——— and the editors of the *Disability Rag* (eds.). 1992. *People with Disabilities Explain It All for You.* Louisville, Ky.: Avocado.

Johnson, Richard A. 1985. *American Fads.* New York: Beech Tree.

Johnstone, Ronald L. 1988. *Religion in Society* (3d ed.). Englewood Cliffs, N.J.: Prentice-Hall.

Joint Center for Political Studies. 1992. *National Roster of Black Elected Officials, 1992.* Washington, D.C.: Joint Center for Political Studies.

Jones, Elise F., et al. [8 authors]. 1985. "Teenage Pregnancy in Developed Countries: Determinants and Policy Implications," *Family Planning Perspectives,* **17**(March–April):53–63.

———. 1986. *Teenage Pregnancy in Industrialized Countries.* New Haven, Conn., and London: Yale University Press.

Jones, James T., IV. 1988. "Harassment Is Too Often Part of the Job." *USA Today* (August 8), p. 5D.

Kagay, Michael M. 1991. "Poll Finds AIDS Causes Single People to Alter Behavior," *New York Times* (June 18), p. C3.

Kalette, Denise, et al. 1987. "The Family Changes Shape," *USA Today* (April 13), p. 4D.

Kalleberg, Arne L. 1988. "Comparative Perspectives on Work Structures and Inequality," in W. Richard Scott and Judith Blake (eds.), *Review of Sociology, 1988.* Palo Alto, Calif.: Annual Reviews, pp. 203–225.

Kalter, Neil. 1989. "Effects of Divorce on Boys versus Girls," *Medical Aspects of Human Sexuality,* **23**(November):26, 31–34.

Kanter, Rosabeth Moss. 1977. *Men and Women of the Corporation.* New York: Basic Books.

Kantrowitz, Barbara. 1988. "And Thousands More," *Newsweek,* **112**(December 12):58–59.

Kapferer, Jean-Noël. 1992. "How Rumors Are Born," *Society,* **29**(July–August):53–60.

Kaplan, David A. 1991. "The Bank Robbery Boom," *Newsweek,* **119**(December 9):62–63.

Karlins, Marvin, Thomas Coffman, and Gary Walters. 1969. "On the Fading of Social Stereotypes: Studies in Three Generations of College Students," *Journal of Personality and Social Psychology,* **13**(September):1–16.

Katovich, Michael A. 1987. Correspondence, June 1.

Katz, Michael. 1971. *Class, Bureaucracy, and the Schools: The Illusion of Educational Change in America.* New York: Praeger.

Katznelson, Ira, and Mark Kesselman. 1979. *The Politics of Power: A Critical Introduction to American Government* (2d ed.). New York: Harcourt Brace Jovanovich.

Kaufman, Gladis. 1985. "Power Relations in Middle-Class American Families," *Wisconsin Sociology*, **22**(Winter):13–23.

Kay, Paul, and Willett Kempton. 1984. "What Is the Sapir-Whorf Hypothesis?" *American Anthropologist*, **86**(March):65–79.

Keen, Judy. 1991. "Student Searches Yield Fear," *USA Today* (November 12), pp. A1, A2.

Kemper, Vicki, and Viveca Novak. 1991. "Health Care Reform: Don't Hold Your Breath," *Washington Post National Weekly Edition*, **8**(October 28):28.

Kent, Mary M. 1991. Correspondence.

Kephart, William M., and William M. Zellner. 1991. *Extraordinary Groups: An Examination of Unconventional Lifestyles* (4th ed.). New York: St. Martin's.

Kerbo, Harold R. 1991. *Social Stratification and Inequality*. New York: McGraw-Hill.

Kessler, Ronald C., J. Blake Turner, and James S. House. 1989. "Unemployment, Reemployment, and Emotional Functioning in a Community Sample," *American Sociological Review*, **54**(August):648–657.

Kilborn, Peter T. 1992. "Big Change Likely as Law Bans Bias toward Disabled," *New York Times* (July 19), pp. 1, 24.

Kimball, Roger. 1992. "The Periphery v. the Center: The MLA in Chicago," in Paul Berman (ed.), *Debating P.C.: The Controversy over Political Correctness on College Campuses*. New York: Dell, pp. 61–84.

Kimmel, Michael S. (ed.). 1987. *Changing Men*. Newbury Park, Calif.: Sage.

King, Stanley H. 1972. "Social-Psychological Factors in Illness," in Howard E. Freeman, Sol Levine, and Leo G. Reeder (eds.), *Handbook of Medical Sociology* (2d ed.). Englewood Cliffs, N.J.: Prentice-Hall, pp. 129–147.

Kinsella, Kevin. 1988. *Aging in the Third World*. International Population Reports, ser. P-95, no. 79. Washington, D.C.: U.S. Government Printing Office.

Kitagawa, Evelyn. 1972. "Socioeconomic Differences in the United States and Some Implications for Population Policy," in Charles F. Westoff and Robert Parke, Jr. (eds.), *Demographic and Social Aspects of Population Growth*. Washington, D.C.: U.S. Government Printing Office, pp. 87–110.

Klausner, Samuel Z. 1988. "Anti-Semitism in the Executive Suite: Yesterday, Today, and Tomorrow," *Moment*, **13**(September):32–39, 55.

Klein, Abbie Gordon. 1992. *The Debate over Child Care 1969–1990: A Sociohistorical Analysis*. Albany: State University of New York Press.

Knight, Franklin W. 1974. *The African Dimension in Latin American Societies*. New York: Macmillan.

Koenig, Frederick W. 1985. *Rumor in the Marketplace*. Dover, Mass.: Auburn House.

Kohlberg, Lawrence. 1963. "Development of Children's Orientation toward a Moral Order (Part 1): Sequence in the Development of Moral Thought," *Vita Humana*, **6**:11–36.

———. 1981. *The Philosophy of Moral Development: Moral Stages and the Idea of Justice*, vol. 1: *Essays on Moral Development*. San Francisco: Harper and Row.

Kohn, Alfie. 1988. "Girltalk, Guytalk," *Psychology Today*, **22**(February):65–66.

Kohn, Melvin L. 1970. "The Effects of Social Class on Parental Values and Practices," in David Reiss and H. A. Hoffman (eds.), *The American Family: Dying or Developing*. New York: Plenum, pp. 45–68.

Komarovsky, Mirra. 1991. "Some Reflections on the Feminist Scholarship in Sociology," in W. Richard Scott and Judith Blake (eds.), *Annual Review of Sociology, 1991*. Palo Alto, Calif.: Annual Reviews, pp. 1–25.

Kornblum, William. 1991. "Who Is the Underclass?" *Dissent*, **38**(Spring):202–211.

Kornhauser, William. 1961. "'Power Elite' or 'Veto Groups'?" in Seymour Martin Lipset and Leo Lowenthal (eds.), *Culture and Social Character*. New York: Free Press, pp. 252–267.

Kotulak, Ronald. 1986. "Youngsters Lose Way in Maze of Family Interstability," *Chicago Tribune* (December 14), sec. 6, pp. 1, 4–5.

Kralewski, John E., Laura Pitt, and Deborah Shatin. 1985. "Structural Characteristics of Medical Group Practices," *Administrative Science Quarterly*, **30**(March):34–45.

Kraybill, Donald B. 1989. *The Riddle of Amish Culture*. Baltimore: Johns Hopkins University Press.

Kreps, G. A. 1984. "Sociological Inquiry and Disaster Research," in Ralph Turner (ed.), *Annual Review of Sociology, 1984*. Palo Alto, Calif.: Annual Reviews, pp. 309–330.

Kroeber, Alfred L. 1923. *Anthropology: Culture Patterns and Processes*. New York: Harcourt Brace and World.

Krossel, Martin. 1988. "'Handicapped Heroes' and the Knee-Jerk Press," *Columbia Journalism Review*, **27**(May–June):46–47.

Kwong, Peter. 1992. "The First Multicultural Riots," *Village Voice*, **37**(June 9):29–32.

——— and JoAnn Lum. 1988. "Chinese-American Politics: A Silent Minority Tests Its Clout," *The Nation*, **246**(January 16):49–50, 52.

Labaree, David F. 1986. "Curriculum, Credentials, and the Middle Class: A Case Study of a Nineteenth Century High School," *Sociology of Education*, **59**(January):42–57.

Labaton, Stephen. 1992. "Benefits Are Refused More Often to Disabled Blacks, Study Finds," *New York Times* (May 11), p. A1.

Ladner, Joyce. 1986. "Black Women Face the 21st Century: Major Issues and Problems," *Black Scholar*, **17**(September–October):12–19.

La Gory, Mark, Russell Ward, and Thomas Juravich. 1980. "The Age Segregation Process: Explanation for American Cities," *Urban Affairs Quarterly*, **16**(September):79–80.

———, ———, and ———. 1981. "Patterns of Age Segregation," *Sociological Focus*, **14**(January):1–13.

———, ———, and Susan Sherman. 1985. "The Ecology of Aging: Neighborhood Satisfaction in an Older Population," *Sociological Quarterly*, **26**(3): 405–418.

Lamm, Bob. 1977. "Men's Movement Hype," in Jon Snodgrass (ed.), *For Men against Sexism: A Book of Readings*. Albion, Calif.: Times Change, pp. 153–157.

Lamont, Michéle, and Marcel Fournier. 1993. *Cultivating Differences: Symbolic Boundaries and the Making of Inequality*. Chicago: University of Chicago Press.

Landtman, Gunnar. 1968. *The Origin of Inequality of the Social Class*. New York: Greenwood (original edition 1938, Chicago: University of Chicago Press).

Lane, Robert E. 1959. *Political Life*. New York: Free Press.

Lantz, Herman, Martin Schultz, and May O'Hare. 1977. "The Changing American Family from the Preindustrial to the Industrial Period: A Final Report," *American Sociological Review*, **42**(June):406–421.

Lasswell, Harold D. 1936. *Politics: Who Gets What, When, How*. New York: McGraw-Hill.

Lauer, Robert H. 1982. *Perspectives on Social Change* (3d ed.). Boston: Allyn and Bacon.

Lawson, Carol. 1989. "How France Is Providing Child Care to a Nation," *New York Times* (November 9), pp. C1, C14.

———. 1991. "Getting Congress to Support Adoption," *New York Times* (March 28), pp. C1, C5.

Leacock, Eleanor Burke. 1969. *Teaching and Learning in City Schools.* New York: Basic Books.

Leavell, Hugh R., and E. Gurney Clark. 1965. *Preventive Medicine for the Doctor in His Community: An Epidemiologic Approach* (3d ed.). New York: McGraw-Hill.

Leland, John. 1992. "Rap and Race," *Newsweek,* **119**(June 29):46–52.

Lemann, Nicholas. 1991. "The Other Underclass," *Atlantic Monthly,* **268**(December):96–102, 104, 107–108, 110.

Lemkow, Louis. 1986. "Socio-Economic Status Differences in Health," *Social Science and Medicine,* **22**(11):1257–1262.

Lenski, Gerhard. 1966. *Power and Privilege: A Theory of Social Stratification.* New York: McGraw-Hill.

———, Jean Lenski, and Patrick Nolan. 1991. *Human Societies: An Introduction to Macrosociology.* New York: McGraw-Hill.

Leo, John. 1987. "Exploring the Traits of Twins," *Time,* **129**(January 12):63.

Leslie, Gerald R., and Sheila K. Korman. 1989. *The Family in Social Context* (7th ed.). New York: Oxford University Press.

Letkemann, Peter. 1973. *Crime as Work.* Englewood Cliffs, N.J.: Prentice-Hall.

Levin, Jack, and William C. Levin. 1980. *Ageism.* Belmont, Calif.: Wadsworth.

Levin, William C. 1988. "Age Stereotyping: College Student Evaluations," *Research on Aging,* **10**(March):134–148.

Levinson, Arlene. 1984. "Laws for Live-In Lovers," *Ms.,* **12**(June):101.

Levinson, Marc, and Rich Thomas. 1992. "Salvation Too Soon?" *Newsweek,* **120**(October 19):48–49.

Levy, Judith A. 1988. "Intersections of Gender and Aging," *Sociological Quarterly,* **29**(4):479–486.

Lewin, Tamar. 1990a. "Strategies to Let Elderly Keep Some Control," *New York Times* (March 28), pp. A1, A22.

———. 1990b. "Too Much Retirement Time? A Move Is Afoot to Change It," *New York Times* (April 22), pp. 1, 26.

———. 1990c. "Abortions Harder to Get in Rural Areas of Nation," *New York Times* (June 28), p. A18.

———. 1991a. "Nude Pictures Are Ruled Sexual Harassment," *New York Times* (January 23), p. A14.

———. 1991b. "Older Women Face Bias in Workplace," *New York Times* (May 11), p. 8.

———. 1992. "Hurdles Increase for Many Women Seeking Abortions," *New York Times* (March 15), pp. 1, 18.

Lewis, Robert. 1973. "A Longitudinal Test of a Developmental Framework for Premarital Dyadic Formation," *Journal of Marriage and the Family,* **35**(February):16–25.

Lewis, Suzan, Dafna N. Izraeli, and Helen Hootsmans. 1991. *Dual-Earner Families: International Perspectives.* Newbury Park, Calif.: Sage.

Lin, Na, and Wen Xie. 1988. "Occupational Prestige in Urban China," *American Journal of Sociology,* **93**(January):793–832.

Lindsey, Robert. 1987. "Adoption Market: Big Demand, Tight Supply," *New York Times* (April 5), pp. 1, 30.

Linton, Ralph. 1936. *The Study of Man: An Introduction.* New York: Appleton-Century.

Lipset, Seymour Martin. 1990. *Continental Divide: The Values and Institutions of the United States and Canada.* New York: Routledge.

Lofland, John. 1977. *Doomsday Cult* (enlarged ed.). New York: Irvington.

———. 1981. "Collective Behavior: The Elementary Forms," in Morris Rosenberg and Ralph Turner (eds.), *Social Psychology: Sociological Perspectives.* New York: Basic Books, pp. 441–446.

———. 1985. *Protest: Studies of Collective Behavior and Social Movements.* Rutgers, N.J.: Transaction.

London, Kathryn A. 1991. *Cohabitation, Marriage, Marital Dissolution, and Remarriage: United States, 1988.* Washington, D.C.: National Center for Health Statistics.

Longmore, Paul K. 1985. "Screening Stereotypes: Images of Disabled People," *Social Policy,* **16**(Summer):31–37.

———. 1988. "Crippling the Disabled," *New York Times* (November 26), p. 23.

Los Angeles Times. 1992. *Understanding the Riots.* Los Angeles: *Los Angeles Times.*

Lott, Bernice. 1987. *Women's Lives: Themes and Variations in Gender Learning.* Monterey, Calif.: Brooks/Cole.

Lukacs, Georg. 1923. *History and Class Consciousness.* London: Merlin.

Luker, Kristin. 1984. *Abortion and the Politics of Motherhood.* Berkeley: University of California Press.

Lum, Joanne, and Peter Kwong. 1989. "Surviving in America: The Trials of a Chinese Immigrant Woman," *Village Voice,* **34**(October 31):39–41.

Lundberg, George D. 1991. "National Health Care Reform: An Aura of Inevitability Is upon Us," *Journal of the American Medical Association,* **265**(May 15):2565–2566.

Luster, Tom, Kelly Rhoades, and Bruce Haas. 1989. "The Relation between Parental Values and Parenting Behavior: A Test of the Kohn Hypothesis," *Journal of Marriage and the Family,* **51**(February):139–147.

Luxenburg, Joan, and Lloyd Klein. 1984. "CB Radio Prostitution: Technology and the Displacement of Deviance," *Journal of Offender Counseling, Service, and Rehabilitation,* **9**(Fall–Winter):71–87.

Mack, Raymond W., and Calvin P. Bradford. 1979. *Transforming America: Patterns of Social Change* (2d ed.). New York: Random House.

Mackenzie, Hilary. 1991. "David vs. Goliath," *Maclean* (May 6), pp. 24–25.

Mackey, Wade C. 1987. "A Cross-Cultural Perspective on Perceptions of Paternalist Deficiencies in the United States: The Myth of the Derelict Daddy," *Sex Roles,* **12**(March):509–534.

MacKinnon, Catharine A. 1979. *Sexual Harassment of Working Women: A Case of Sex Discrimination.* New Haven, Conn.: Yale University Press.

Madigan, Charles. 1982. "A Story of Satan That Is Rated P&G," *Chicago Tribune* (July 18), p. 1.

Maguire, Brendan. 1988. "The Applied Dimension of Radical Criminology: A Survey of Prominent Radical Criminologists," *Sociological Spectrum,* **8**(2):133–151.

Maher, Timothy. 1991. "Race, Class and Trash: Whose Backyard Do We Dump In?" Paper presented at the annual meeting of the North Central Sociological Association, Dearborn, Mich.

Majors, Richard, and Janet Mancini Bellson. 1992. *Cool Pose: The Dilemmas of Black Manhood in America.* New York: Lexington.

Makepeace, James M. 1986. "Gender Differences in Courtship Violence Victimization," *Family Relations,* **35**(July):383–388.

Malcolm, Andrew H. 1974. "The 'Shortage' of Bathroom Tissue: A Classic Study in Rumor," *New York Times* (February 3), p. 29.

Malcolm X, with Alex Haley. 1964. *The Autobiography of Malcolm X.* New York: Grove.

Malinowski, Michael J. 1990. "Federal

Enclaves and Local Law: Carving Out a Domestic Violence Exception to Exclusive Legislative Jurisdiction," *Yale Law Journal,* **100**:189–208.

Malthus, Thomas, Julian Huxley, and Frederick Osborn. 1960. *Three Essays on Population.* New York: New American Library (originally published in 1824).

Mangalmurti, Sandeep, and Robert Allan Cooke. 1991. *State Lotteries: Seducing the Less Fortunate.* Chicago: Heartland Institute.

Mann, James. 1983. "One-Parent Family: The Troubles—And the Joys," *U.S. News and World Report,* **95**(November 28):57–58, 62.

Manning, Anita. 1992. "Economy Weakens Teacher Pay Gains," *USA Today* (August 28), p. D1.

Manson, Donald A. 1986. *Tracking Offenders: White-Collar Crime.* Bureau of Justice Statistics Special Report. Washington, D.C.: U.S. Government Printing Office.

Maraniss, David, and Rick Atkinson. 1989. "The Texas S&L Meltdown," *Washington Post National Weekly Edition,* **6**(June 26):6–8.

Marger, Martin. 1981. *Elites and Masses: An Introduction to Political Sociology.* New York: Van Nostrand.

Margolick, David. 1992. "Legal System Is Assailed on AIDS Crisis," *New York Times* (January 19), p. 16.

Marmor, Theodore R., and John Godfrey. 1992. "Canada's Medical System Is a Model. That's a Fact," *New York Times* (July 23), p. A23.

Marsden, Peter V. 1990. "Network Data and Measurement," in W. Richard Scott (ed.), *Annual Review of Sociology, 1990.* Palo Alto, Calif.: Annual Reviews, pp. 435–463.

Martin, Douglas. 1987. "Indians Seek a New Life in New York," *New York Times* (March 22), p. 17.

Martin, Linda G. 1989. "The Graying of Japan," *Population Bulletin,* **44**(July): 1–43.

Martin, Teresa Castro, and Larry L. Bumpass. 1989. "Recent Trends in Marital Disruption," *Demography,* **26**(February):37–51.

Martineau, Harriet. 1962. *Society in America.* Edited, abridged, with an introductory essay by Seymour Martin Lipset. Garden City, N.Y.: Doubleday (originally published in 1837).

Martyna, Wendy. 1983. "Beyond the He/Man Approach: The Case for Nonsexist Language," in Barrie Thorne, Cheris Kramorae, and Nancy Henley (eds.), *Language, Gender and Society.* Rowley, Mass.: Newly House, pp. 25–37.

Marx, Karl, and Friedrich Engels. 1955. *Selected Work in Two Volumes.* Moscow: Foreign Languages Publishing House (original edition 1847).

Masland, Tim. 1992. "Slavery," *Newsweek,* **199**(May 4):30–32, 37–39.

Mason, Marie K. 1942. "Learning to Speak after Six and One-Half Years of Silence," *Journal of Speech Disorders,* **7**(December):295–304.

Massey, Douglas S., and Nancy A. Denton. 1989a. "Residential Segregation of Mexicans, Puerto Ricans, and Cubans in Selected U.S. Metropolitan Areas," *Sociology and Social Research,* **73**(January):73–83.

——— and ———. 1989b. "Hypersegregation in U.S. Metropolitan Areas: Black and Hispanic Segregation along Five Dimensions," *Demography,* **26**(August):373–391.

Matras, Judah. 1977. *Introduction to Population: A Sociological Approach.* Englewood Cliffs, N.J.: Prentice-Hall.

Mayer, Egon. 1983. *Children of Intermarriage.* New York: American Jewish Committee.

———. 1985. *Love and Tradition: Marriage between Jews and Christians.* New York: Plenum.

Mayer, Karl Ulrich, and Urs Schoepflin. 1989. "The State and the Life Course," in W. Richard Scott and Judith Blake (eds.), *Annual Review of Sociology, 1989.* Palo Alto, Calif.: Annual Reviews, pp. 187–209.

McCaghy, Charles H. 1980. *Crime in American Society.* New York: Macmillan.

McCord, Colin, and Harold P. Freeman. 1990. "Excess Mortality in Harlem," *New England Journal of Medicine,* **322**(January 18):173–177.

McCormick, Kenelm F. 1992. "Attitudes of Primary Case Physicians toward Corporal Punishment," *Journal of the American Medical Association,* **267**(June 17):3161–3165.

McEnroe, Jennifer. 1991. 'Split-Shift Parenting," *American Demographics,* **13**(February):50–52.

McFalls, Joseph A., Jr. 1981. "Where Have All the Children Gone?" *USA Today* (March):30–33.

———. 1991. "Population: A Lively Introduction," *Population Bulletin,* **46**(October).

———, Brian Jones, and Bernard J. Gallegher, III. 1984. "U.S. Population Growth: Prospects and Policy," *USA Today* (January), pp. 30–34.

McGrath, Ellie. 1983. "Schooling for the Common Good," *Time,* **122**(August 1):66–67.

McGuire, Meredith B. 1981. *Religion: The Social Context.* Belmont, Calif.: Wadsworth.

McGuire, Randall M., and Robert Paynter (eds.). 1991. *The Archaeology of Inequality.* Oxford, Eng.: Basil Blackwell.

McKeown, Thomas. 1976. *The Role of Medicine: Dream, Mirage, or Nemesis?* London: Nuffield Provincial Hospitals Trust.

McKinlay, John B., and Sonja M. McKinlay. 1977. "The Questionable Contribution of Medical Measures to the Decline of Mortality in the United States in the Twentieth Century," *Milbank Memorial Fund Quarterly,* **55**(Summer):405–428.

McLean, Elys A. 1992. "Gun Control Lobby Outgunned," *USA Today* (July 31):A1.

McNamara, Patrick H. (ed.). 1984. *Religion: North American Style* (2d ed.). Belmont, Calif.: Wadsworth.

McPhail, Clark. 1991. *The Myth of the Madding Crowd.* New York: De Gruyther.

——— and David Miller. 1973. "The Assembling Process: A Theoretical and Empirical Examination," *American Sociological Review,* **38**(December):721–735.

McPhail, Thomas L. 1981. *Electronic Colonialism: The Future of International Broadcasting and Communication.* Beverly Hills, Calif.: Sage.

McRoberts, Flynn, and Susan Kuczka. 1992. "Morton Grove Gun Ban Failed to Catch U.S. Fancy," *Chicago Tribune* (April 29), pp. 1, 8.

McWilliams, Carey. 1951. *Brothers under the Skin* (rev. ed.). Boston: Little, Brown.

Mead, George H. 1930. "Cooley's Contribution to American Social Thought," *American Journal of Sociology,* **35**(March):693–706.

———. 1934. In Charles W. Morris (ed.), *Mind, Self and Society.* Chicago: University of Chicago Press.

———. 1964a. In Anselm Strauss (ed.), *On Social Psychology.* Chicago: University of Chicago Press.

———. 1964b. "The Genesis of the Self and Social Control," in Andrew J. Reck (ed.), *Selected Writings: George Herbert Mead.* Indianapolis: Bobbs-Merrill, pp. 267–293.

Mead, Margaret. 1963. *Sex and Temperament in Three Primitive Societies.* New York: Morrow (originally published 1935).

———. 1966. "Marriage in Two Steps," *Redbook,* **127**(July):48–49, 84–85.

———. 1970. *Culture and Commitment: A Study of the Generation Gap.* New York: Doubleday.

———. 1973. "Does the World Belong to Men—Or to Women?" *Redbook,* **141**(October):46–52.

Mechanic, David. 1978. *Medical Sociology* (2d ed.). New York: Free Press.

———. 1986. *From Advocacy to Allocation: American Health Care.* New York: Free Press.

Meek, Ronald L. (ed.). 1954. *Marx and Engels on Malthus: Selections from the Writings of Marx and Engels Dealing with the Theories of Thomas Robert Malthus.* New York: International Publishers.

Melson, Robert. 1986. "Provocation or Nationalism: A Critical Inquiry into the Armenian Genocide of 1915," in Richard G. Hovannisian (ed.), *The Armenian Genocide in Perspective.* New Brunswick, N.J.: Transaction, pp. 61–84.

Memmi, Albert. 1967. *The Colonizer and the Colonized.* Boston: Beacon.

Merton, Robert K. 1968. *Social Theory and Social Structure.* New York: Free Press.

——— and Alice S. Kitt. 1950. "Contributions to the Theory of Reference Group Behavior," in Robert K. Merton and Paul L. Lazarsfeld (eds.), *Continuities in Social Research: Studies in the Scope and Method of the American Soldier.* New York: Free Press, pp. 40–105.

———, G. C. Reader, and P. L. Kendall. 1957. *The Student Physician.* Cambridge, Mass.: Harvard University Press.

Meyrowitz, Joshua. 1985. *No Sense of Place.* New York: Oxford University Press.

Michalowski, Raymond J., and Ronald C. Kramer. 1987. "The Space between Laws: The Problem of Corporate Crime in a Transnational Context," *Social Problems,* **34**(February):34–53.

Michel, Andrée. 1989. "Marina, Sarah, Michel and Jean," *Unesco Courier* (July), pp. 34–37.

Michels, Robert. 1915. *Political Parties.* Glencoe, Ill.: Free Press (reprinted 1949).

Mifflin, Lawrie. 1984. "56 Seasons of Loving a Game," *New York Times* (November 22), pp. B11, B12.

Milbrath, Lester. 1981. "Political Participation," in S. L. Long (ed.), *Handbook of Political Behavior,* vol. 4. New York: Plenum, pp. 197–240.

Milgram, Stanley. 1963. "Behavioral Study of Obedience," *Journal of Abnormal and Social Psychology,* **67**(October):371–378.

———. 1975. *Obedience to Authority: An Experimental View.* New York: Harper and Row.

Miller, Annetta. 1992. "The World 'S' Ours," *Newsweek,* **114**(March 23):46–47.

Miller, David L. 1988. *Introduction to Collective Behavior.* Prospect Heights, Ill.: Waveland.

Miller, Delbert C. 1991. *Handbook of Research Design and Social Measurement* (5th ed.). Newbury Park, Calif.: Sage.

Mills, C. Wright. 1956. *The Power Elite.* New York: Oxford University Press.

———. 1959. *The Sociological Imagination.* London: Oxford University Press.

Mindel, Charles H., Robert W. Habenstein, and Roosevelt Wright, Jr. (eds.). 1988. *Ethnic Families in America: Patterns and Variations* (3d ed.). New York: Elsevier.

Mingle, James R. 1987. *Focus on Minorities.* Denver: Education Commission of the States and the State Higher Education Executive Officers.

Mintz, Steven, and Susan Kellogg. 1988. *Domestic Revolutions: A Social History of American Family Life.* New York: Free Press.

Minzesheimer, Bob. 1986. "Senate Votes on PAC Limits," *USA Today* (August 12), p. 7A.

Mishel, Lawrence, and David M. Frankel. 1991. "Hard Times for Working America," *Dissent,* **38**(Spring):282–285.

Miyazawa, Setsuo. 1992. *Policing in Japan: A Study on Making Crime.* Albany: State University of New York Press.

Mizrahi, Terry. 1986. *Getting Rid of Patients.* New Brunswick, N.J.: Rutgers University Press.

Mokhiber, Russell, Julie Gozan, and Holley Knaus. 1992. "The Corporate Rap Sheet: The 10 Worst Corporations of 1992," *Multinational Monitor,* **13**(December):7–16.

Mollen, Milton. 1992. *A Failure of Responsibility: Report to Mayor David N. Dinkins on the December 28, 1991, Tragedy at City College of New York.* New York: Office of the Deputy Mayor for Public Safety.

Molstad, Clark. 1986. "Choosing and Coping with Boring Work," *Urban Life,* **15**(July):215–236.

Money. 1987. "A Short History of Shortages," special issue, **16**(Fall):42.

Moore, Joan, and Harry Pachon. 1985. *Hispanics in the United States.* Englewood Cliffs, N.J.: Prentice-Hall.

Moore, Wilbert E. 1967. *Order and Change: Essays in Comparative Sociology.* New York: Wiley.

———. 1968. "Occupational Socialization," in David A. Goslin (ed.), *Handbook of Socialization Theory and Research.* Chicago: Rand McNally, pp. 861–883.

———. 1974. *Social Change* (2d ed.). Englewood Cliffs, N.J.: Prentice-Hall.

Moran, Theodore. 1978. "Multinational Corporations and Dependency: A Dialogue for Dependentistas and Non-Dependentistas," *International Organization,* **32**(Winter):79–100.

Morin, Richard. 1989. "Bringing Up Baby the Company Way," *Washington Post National Weekly Edition,* **6**(September 11–17):37.

———. 1990. "Women Asking Women about Men Asking Women about Men," *Washington Post National Weekly Edition,* **7**(January 21):37.

Morris, Michael. 1989. "From the Culture of Poverty to the Underclass: An Analysis of a Shift in Public Language," *American Sociologist,* **20**(Summer):123–133.

Morrison, Denton E. 1971. "Some Notes toward Theory on Relative Deprivation, Social Movements, and Social Change," *American Behavioral Scientist,* **14**(May–June):675–690.

Mortenson, Thomas G. 1992. "College Participation Rates by Family Income," *Postsecondary Education Opportunity* (April):1–4.

Mortimer, Jeylan E., and Roberta G. Simmons. 1978. "Adult Socialization," in Ralph H. Turner, James Coleman, and Renee C. Fox (eds.), *Annual Review of Sociology, 1978.* Palo Alto, Calif.: Annual Reviews, pp. 421–454.

Moseley, Ray. 1990. "The Night the Wall Fell," *Chicago Tribune* (October 28), pp. 1–10.

Moskos, Charles. 1991. "How Do They Do It?" *New Republic,* **205**(August 5):20.

Mosley, Leonard. 1971. *Backs to the Wall: London under Fire.* London: Weidenfeld and Nicolson.

Mosley, W. Henry, and Peter Cowley. 1991. "The Challenge of World Health," *Population Bulletin,* **46**(December).

Murdock, George P. 1945. "The Common Denominator of Cultures," in Ralph Linton (ed.), *The Science of Man in the World Crisis.* New York: Columbia University Press, pp. 123–142.

———. 1949. *Social Structure.* New York: Macmillan.

———. 1957. "World Ethnographic Sample," *American Anthropologist,* **59**(August):664–687.

Murray, Douglas L. 1982. "The Abolition of El Cortito, the Short-Handled Hoe: A Case Study in Social Conflict and State Policy in California Agriculture," *Social Problems,* **30**(October):26–39.

Muskrat, Joe. 1972. "Assimilate or Starve!" *Civil Rights Digest,* **8**(October):27–34.

Mydans, Seth. 1989. "TV Unites, and Divides, Hispanic Groups," *New York Times* (August 2), p. E4.

Nader, Laura. 1986. "The Subordination of Women in Comparative Perspective," *Urban Anthropology,* **15**(Fall–Winter):377–397.

Nader, Ralph. 1985. "America's Crime without Criminals," *New York Times* (May 19), p. F3.

Nakao, Keiko, and Judith Treas. 1990a. "Occupational Prestige in the United States Revisited: Twenty-Five Years of Stability and Change." Paper presented at the annual meeting of the American Sociological Association, Washington, D.C.

——— and ———. 1990b. *Computing 1989 Occupational Prestige Scores.* Chicago: NORC.

Nasar, Sylvia. 1992. "Even among the Well-Off, the Richest Get Richer," *New York Times* (March 5), pp. A1, D24.

Nash, Manning. 1962. "Race and the Ideology of Race," *Current Anthropology,* **3**(June):285–288.

National Advisory Commission on Criminal Justice. 1976. *Organized Crime.* Washington, D.C.: U.S. Government Printing Office.

National Association of Scholars. 1992. Paid advertisement in *New York Times* (April 5), p. E17.

National Center for Health Statistics. 1974. *Summary Report: Final Divorce Statistics, 1974.* Washington, D.C.: U.S. Government Printing Office.

———. 1990. *Annual Survey of Births, Marriages, Divorces, and Deaths: United States, 1989.* Washington, D.C.: U.S. Government Printing Office.

———. 1992a. "Advance Report of Final Mortality Statistics, 1989," *Monthly Vital Statistics Report,* **40**(January 7).

———. 1992b. "Births, Marriages, Divorces, and Deaths for April, 1992," *Monthly Vital Statistics Report,* **41**(September 17):1–24.

National Center on Women and Family Law. 1991. *Marital Rape Exemption Chart: State-by-State Analysis.* New York: National Center on Women and Family Law.

Navarro, Vicente. 1984. "Medical History as Justification Rather than Explanation: A Critique of Starr's *The Social Transformation of American Medicine,*" *International Journal of Health Services,* **14**(4):511–528.

Neary, John. 1969. "The Magical McCartney Mystery," *Life,* **67**(November 7):103–106.

Neuborne, Ellen. 1991. "Gift Wrap Says: Lousy Christmas," *USA Today* (November 19), p. B1.

Newland, Kathleen. 1980. *City Limits: Emerging Constraints on Urban Growth.* Washington, D.C.: Worldwatch Institute.

Newman, William M. 1973. *American Pluralism: A Study of Minority Groups and Social Theory.* New York: Harper and Row.

New York Post. 1991. "Did the Devil Make Them Do It? Procter and Gamble Redesigns Its Trademark" (July 11), p. 16.

New York Times. 1990. "Portrait of the Electorate: U.S. House Vote" (November 8), p. B7.

———. 1991. "U.S. Reports AIDS Deaths Exceed 100,000" (January 25), p. A18.

———. 1992a. "100,000 Kenyans Stage Protest Rally" (January 19), p. 3.

———. 1992b. "California Rancher to Pay $1.5 Million in Enslavement Case" (March 25), p. A17.

———. 1992c. "Young Indians Prone to Suicide, Study Finds" (March 25), p. D24.

———. 1992d. "Hispanic Residents Often Lack Health Coverage" (May 5), p. A23.

———. 1992e. "Doctors Are Advised to Screen Women for Abuse" (June 17), p. A26.

———. 1992f. "Californians Confront Wave of Quake Rumors" (July 20), p. A8.

Neysmith, Sheila, and Joey Edwardh. 1984. "Economic Dependency in the 1980s: Its Impact on Third World Elderly," *Ageing and Society,* **4**(1):21–44.

Noble, Barbara Presley. 1992. "Legal Victories for Gay Workers," *New York Times* (June 21), p. F23.

Noble, Kenneth B. 1984. "Plight of Black Family Is Studied Anew," *New York Times* (January 29), p. E20.

NORC (National Opinion Research Center). 1991. *General Social Surveys 1972–1991: Cumulative Codebook.* Chicago: National Opinion Research Center.

Novello, Antonia C., Paul H. Wise, and Dushanka V. Kleinman. 1991. "Hispanic Health: Time for Date, Time for Action," *Journal of the American Medical Association,* **265**(January 9): 253–255.

Oberschall, Anthony. 1973. *Social Conflict and Social Movements.* Englewood Cliffs, N.J.: Prentice-Hall.

Office of the Federal Register. 1991. *United States Government Manual, 1991–1992.* Washington, D.C.: U.S. Government Printing Office.

Ogburn, William F. 1922. *Social Change with Respect to Culture and Original Nature.* New York: Huebsch (reprinted 1966, New York: Dell).

——— and Clark Tibbits. 1934. "The Family and Its Functions," in Research Committee on Social Trends (ed.), *Recent Social Trends in the United States.* New York: McGraw-Hill, pp. 661–708.

O'Hare, Barbara. 1992. "Review of 'Edge City,'" *Population,* **20**(June):11.

O'Hare, William P., and Brenda Curry-White. 1992. "Is There a Rural Underclass?" *Population Today,* **20**(March): 6–8.

Ohnuma, Keiko. 1991. "Study Finds Asians Unhappy at CSU," *Asian Week,* **12**(August 8):5.

Oliver, Melvin L. 1988. "The Urban Black Community as Network: Toward a Social Network Perspective," *Sociological Quarterly,* **29**(4):623–645.

Olson, Laura Katz. 1982. *The Political Economy of Aging: The State, Private Power, and Social Welfare.* New York: Columbia University Press.

Olson, Philip. 1987. "A Model of Eldercare in the People's Republic of China," *International Journal of Aging and Human Development,* **24**(4): 279–300.

———. 1988. "Modernization in the People's Republic of China: The Politicization of the Elderly," *Sociological Quarterly,* **29**(2):241–262.

Orfield, Gary. 1987. *School Segregation in the 1980s.* Chicago: National School Desegregation Report.

Ornstein, Norman J., and Mark Schmitt. 1990. "The New World of Interest Politics," *American Enterprise,* **1**(January–February):46–51.

Orum, Anthony M. 1978. *Introduction to Political Sociology: The Social Anatomy of the Body Politic.* Englewood Cliffs, N.J.: Prentice-Hall.

———. 1989. *Introduction to Political Sociology: The Social Anatomy of the Body Politic* (3d ed.). Englewood Cliffs, N.J.: Prentice Hall.

Osborne, Lynn T., Anne H. Rhu, and

Ronald W. Smith. 1985. "Labelers in Education: Their Perceptions about Learning Disabilities," *Free Inquiry in Creative Sociology*, **13**:117–122.

Oved, Yaacov. 1992. *Two Hundred Years of American Communes*. Rutgers, N.J.: Transaction.

Oxnam, Robert B. 1986. "Why Asians Succeed Here," *New York Times Magazine* (November 30), pp. 72, 74–75, 88–89, 92.

Page, Charles H. 1946. "Bureaucracy's Other Face," *Social Forces*, **25**(October):89–94.

Painter, Kim. 1992. "A Better Prognosis for Women's Medical Research," *USA Today* (September 24), p. 6D.

Paneth, Nigel. 1982. "Editorial: Infant Mortality Reexamined," *Journal of the American Medical Association*, **247**(February 19):1027–1028.

Park, Robert E. 1916. "The City: Suggestions for the Investigation of Human Behavior in the Urban Environment," *American Journal of Sociology*, **20**(March):577–612.

———. 1936. "Succession, an Ecological Concept," *American Sociological Review*, **1**(April):171–179.

Parsons, Talcott. 1951. *The Social System*. New York: Free Press.

———. 1966. *Societies: Evolutionary and Comparative Perspectives*. Englewood Cliffs, N.J.: Prentice-Hall.

———. 1972. "Definitions of Health and Illness in the Light of American Values and Social Structure," in E. Gartley Jaco (ed.), *Patients, Physicians and Illness*. New York: Free Press, pp. 166–187.

———. 1975. "The Sick Role and the Role of the Physician Reconsidered," *Milbank Medical Fund Quarterly, Health and Society*, **53**(Summer):257–278.

——— and Robert Bales. 1955. *Family, Socialization, and Interaction Process*. Glencoe, Ill.: Free Press.

——— and Renee Fox. 1952. "Therapy and the Modern Family," *Journal of Social Issues*, **8**(Fall):31–44.

Paternoster, Raymond. 1991. *Capital Punishment in America*. New York: Lexington.

Pavalko, Ronald M. 1971. *Sociology of Occupations and Professions*. Itasca, Ill.: Peacock.

——— (ed.). 1972. *Sociological Perspectives on Occupations*. Itasca, Ill.: Peacock.

Pear, Robert. 1983. "$1.5 Billion Urged for U.S. Japanese Held in War," *New York Times* (June 17), pp. A1, D16.

———. 1991. "34.7 Million Lack Health Insurance, Studies Say Number Is Highest since '65," *New York Times* (December 19), p. B17.

———. 1992. "Ranks of U.S. Poor Reach 35.7 Million, the Most since 1964, *New York Times* (September 4), pp. A1, A14.

Peirce, Kate. 1989. "Sex-Role Stereotyping of Children on Television: A Content Analysis of the Roles and Attributes of Child Characters," *Sociological Spectrum*, **9**(3):321–328.

Perlez, Jane. 1991. "In Kenya, the Lawyers Lead the Call for Freedom," *New York Times* (March 10), p. E2.

Perrow, Charles. 1986. *Complex Organizations* (3d ed.). New York: Random House.

Petchesky, Rosalind. 1990. "Giving Women a Real Choice," *The Nation*, **250**(May 28):732–735.

Peter, Laurence J., and Raymond Hull. 1969. *The Peter Principle*. New York: Morrow.

Peters, John F. 1985. "Adolescents as Socialization Agents to Parents," *Adolescence*, **2**(Winter):921–933.

Petersen, William. 1975. *Population* (3d ed.). New York: Macmillan.

———. 1979. *Malthus*. Cambridge, Mass.: Harvard University Press.

Peterson, Felix. 1987. "Vietnam 'Battle Deaths': Is There a Race or Class Issue?" *Focus*, **15**(July):3–4.

Piaget, Jean. 1954. *The Construction of Reality in the Child*. Translated by Margaret Cook. New York: Basic Books.

Pieterse, Jan Nederveen. 1992. *White on Black: Images of Africa and Blacks in Western Populous Culture*. New Haven, Conn.: Yale University Press.

Piller, Charles. 1991. *The Fail-Safe Society: Community Defiance and the End of American Technological Optimism*. New York: Basic Books.

Pleck, Joseph H. 1981. *The Myth of Masculinity*. Cambridge, Mass.: M.I.T. Press.

———. 1985. *Working Wives, Working Husbands*. Beverly Hills, Calif.: Sage.

Plomin, Robert. 1989. "Determinants of Behavior," *American Psychologist*, **44**(February):105–111.

———. 1990. "The Role of Inheritance in Behavior," *Science*, **248**(April 13): 183–187.

Pogrebin, Letty Cottin. 1981. *Growing Up Free: Raising Your Child in the 80's*. New York: McGraw-Hill.

Police Foundation. 1992. *States with Handgun Purchase Laws*. Washington, D.C.: Police Foundation.

Polk, Barbara Bovee. 1974. "Male Power and the Women's Movement," *Journal of Applied Behavioral Sciences*, **10**(July):415–431.

Pollin, Robert, and Alexander Cockburn. 1991. "The World, the Free Market and the Left," *The Nation*, **252**(February 25):224–232, 234–236.

Population Crisis Committee. 1988. *Country Rankings of the Status of Women: Poor, Powerless and Pregnant*. Washington, D.C.: Population Crisis Committee.

Population Reference Bureau. 1978. "World Population: Growth on the Decline," *Interchange* **7**(May):1–3.

Powers, Mary G., and Joan J. Holmberg. 1978. "Occupational Status Scores: Changes Introduced by the Inclusion of Women," *Demography*, **15**(May): 183–204.

President's Commission on Law Enforcement and Administration of Justice. 1967. *Task Force Report: Organized Crime*. Washington, D.C.: U.S. Government Printing Office.

Princeton Religion Research Center. 1990a. *Religion in America, 1990 Report*. Princeton, N.J.: Princeton Religion Research Center.

———. 1990b. "Ranks of the 'Born-Again' Faithful Continue to Grow," *Emerging Trends*, **12**(September):1.

Procter and Gamble. 1985. "News from Procter & Gamble." News release, May 16.

———. 1986. *Procter and Gamble's Symbol of Quality*. Cincinnati: Procter and Gamble.

Prud'homme, Alex. 1991a. "A Blow to the N.R.A." *Time*, **137**(May 20):26.

———. 1991b. "Chicago's Uphill Battle," *Time*, **137**(June 17):30.

Psychology Today. 1992. "Why Do They Stay?" **25**(May–June):22.

Purvis, Andrew. 1990. "Research for Men Only," *Time*, **135**(March 5):59–60.

Quadagno, Jill. (ed.). 1980. *Aging, the Individual and Society: Readings in Social Gerontology*. New York: St. Martin's.

Quarantelli, E. L. 1957. "The Behavior of Panic Participants," *Sociology and Social Research*, **41**(January):187–194.

——— and Russell R. Dynes. 1970. "Property Norms and Looting: Their Patterns in Community Crises," *Phylon*, **31**(Summer):168–182.

——— and James R. Hundley, Jr. 1975. "A Test of Some Propositions about Crowd Formation and Behavior," in Robert R. Evans (ed.), *Readings in Collective Behavior*. Chicago: Rand McNally, pp. 538–554.

——— and Elizabeth A. Wilson. 1980.

"History and Current Activities of the Disaster Research Center." Miscellaneous report no. 26 of Disaster Research Center, Columbus, Ohio.

Quinn, Bernard, Herman Anderson, Martin Bradley, Paul Goetting, and Peggy Shriver. 1982. *Churches and Church Membership in the United States, 1980.* Atlanta: Glenmary Research Center.

Quinn, Kathleen, Polly Roskin, and Joyce M. Pruitt. 1984. *Cultural Violence: There Are Many Causes.* Springfield, Ill.: Illinois Coalition Against Sexual Assault and the Illinois Coalition Against Domestic Violence.

Quinney, Richard. 1970. *The Social Reality of Crime.* Boston: Little, Brown.

———. 1974. *Criminal Justice in America.* Boston: Little, Brown.

———. 1979. *Criminology* (2d ed.). Boston: Little, Brown.

———. 1980. *Class, State and Crime* (2d ed.). New York: Longman.

Radosh, Mary Flannery. 1984. "The Collapse of Midwifery: A Sociological Study of the Decline of a Profession." Unpublished Ph.D. dissertation, Southern Illinois University, Carbondale.

Radosh, Polly F. 1986. "Midwives in the United States: Past and Present," *Population Research and Policy Review,* 5:129–145.

Randall, Teri. 1990a. "Domestic Violence Intervention Calls for More Than Treating Injuries," *Journal of the American Medical Association,* 264(August 22):939–940.

———. 1990b. "Domestic Violence Begets Other Problems of Which Physicians Must Be Aware to Be Effective," *Journal of the American Medical Association,* 264(August 22):940, 943–944.

Rashid, Salim. 1987. "Malthus's *Essay on Population:* The Facts of 'Super-Growth' and the Rhetoric of Scientific Persuasion," *Journal of the History of the Behavioral Sciences,* 23(January):22–36.

Rathje, William L. 1974. "The Garbage Project," *Archaeology,* 27(October): 236–241.

Ravitch, Diane. 1992. "Multiculturalism: E Pluribus Plures," in Paul Berman (ed.), *Debating P.C.: The Controversy over Political Correctness on College Campuses.* New York: Dell, pp. 271–298.

Rawlings, Steve W. 1989. "Single Parents and Their Children," in *Studies in Marriage and the Family. Current Population Reports,* ser. P-23, no. 162, pp. 13–25.

Reardon, Patrick. 1989. "Study Ties Poor Child Care to Low Wages," *Chicago Tribune* (October 18), p. 5.

Rebell, Michael A. 1986. "Structural Discrimination and the Rights of the Disabled," *Georgetown Law Journal,* 74(June):1435–1489.

Rebell, Susan. 1987. "National Survey: Americans Call for Child Care," *Ms.,* 15(March):44.

Rebelsky, Freda, and Cheryl Hanks. 1973. "Fathers' Verbal Interaction with Infants in the First Three Months of Life," in Freda Rebelsky and Lyn Dorman (eds.), *Child Development and Behavior* (2d ed.). New York: Knopf, pp. 145–148.

Reid, T. R. 1990. "Japan Is Making Everything but Babies," *Washington Post National Weekly Edition,* 8(November 5):18.

Reiman, Jeffrey H. 1984. *The Rich Get Richer and the Poor Get Prison* (2d ed.). New York: Wiley.

Reisman, Barbara, Amy J. Moore, and Karen Fitzgerald. 1988. *Child Care, the Bottom Line: An Economic and Child Care Policy Paper.* New York: Child Care Action Campaign.

Reskin, Barbara, and Francine Blau. 1990. *Job Queues, Gender Queues: Explaining Women's Inroads into Male Occupations.* Philadelphia: Temple University Press.

Rheingold, Harriet L. 1969. "The Social and Socializing Infant," in David A. Goslin (ed.), *Handbook of Socialization Theory and Research.* Chicago: Rand McNally, pp. 779–790.

Richburg, Keith B. 1985. "Learning What Japan Has to Teach," *Washington Post National Weekly Edition,* 3(November 4):9.

Riddle, Lyn. 1988. "Shaker Village Buoyed by New Blood," *New York Times* (August 28), p. 43.

Riding, Alan. 1992. "Harassment or Flirting? Europe Tries to Decide," *New York Times* (November 3), p. A8.

Riesman, David, with Nathan Glazer and Reuel Denny. 1961. *The Lonely Crowd.* New Haven, Conn.: Yale University Press.

Riessman, Catherine Kohler. 1983. "Women and Medicalization: A New Perspective," *Social Policy,* 14(Summer): 3–18.

Riley, Matilda White. 1987. "On the Significance of Age in Sociology," *American Sociological Review,* 52(February): 1–14.

Ritzer, George. 1977. *Working: Conflict and Change* (2d ed.). Englewood Cliffs, N.J.: Prentice-Hall.

Roberts, D. F. 1975. "The Dynamics of Racial Intermixture in the American Negro—Some Anthropological Considerations," *American Journal of Human Genetics,* 7(December):361–367.

Roberts, Keith A. 1984. *Religion in Sociological Perspective.* Homewood, Ill.: Dorsey.

Roberts, Robert E. Lee. 1987. "Those Who Do Not Watch Television," *Sociology and Social Research,* 71(January): 105–107.

Roberts, Ron E. 1991. "Social Control," in Dushkin Publishing Group, *Encyclopedic Dictionary of Sociology* (4th ed.). Guilford, Conn.: Dushkin, p. 274.

——— and Robert March Kloss. 1974. *Social Movements: Between the Balcony and the Barricade.* St. Louis: Mosby.

Robertson, Roland. 1988. "The Sociological Significance of Culture: Some General Considerations," *Theory, Culture, and Society,* 5(February):3–23.

Robinson, John P. 1988. "Who's Doing the Housework?" *American Demographics,* 10(December):24–28, 63.

Robinson, Tracey. 1989. "African Heritage Pulses in Brazil's Salvador de Bahia," *Chicago Sun-Times* (April 23), p. D3.

Rodgers, Harrell R., Jr., and Michael Harrington. 1981. *Unfinished Democracy: The American Political System.* Glenview, Ill.: Scott, Foresman.

Roethlisberger, Fritz J., and W. J. Dickson. 1939. *Management and the Worker.* Cambridge, Mass.: Harvard University Press.

Rohlen, Thomas P. 1983. *Japan's High Schools.* Berkeley: University of California Press.

Rohter, Larry. 1987. "Women Gain Degrees, but Not Tenure," *New York Times* (January 4), p. E9.

Rosaldo, Renato. 1985. "Chicano Studies, 1970–1984," in Bernard J. Seigal (ed.), *Annual Review of Anthropology, 1985.* Palo Alto, Calif.: Annual Reviews, pp. 405–427.

Rosario, Ruben, and Tony Marcano. 1989. "A Killer Is Freed," *New York Daily News* (April 1), p. 2.

Rose, Arnold. 1951. *The Roots of Prejudice.* Paris: UNESCO.

Rose, Peter I. (ed.). 1979. *Socialization and the Life Cycle.* New York: St. Martin's.

———, Myron Glazer, and Penina Migdal Glazer. 1979. "In Controlled Environments: Four Cases of Intense Resocialization," in Peter I. Rose (ed.), *Socialization and the Life Cycle.* New York: St. Martin's, pp. 320–338.

Rosenberg, Douglas H. 1991. "Capitalism," in Dushkin Publishing Group, *Encyclopedic Dictionary of Sociology* (4th ed.). Guilford, Conn.: Dushkin, pp. 33–34.

Rosenthal, Robert, and Elisha Y. Babad. 1985. "Pygmalion in the Gymnasium," *Educational Leadership*, **45**(September): 36–39.

—— and Lenore Jacobson. 1968. *Pygmalion in the Classroom*, New York: Holt.

Rosnow, Ralph L. 1991. "Inside Rumor: A Personal Journey," *American Psychologist*, **46**(May):484–496.

Rossi, Alice S. 1968. "Transition to Parenthood," *Journal of Marriage and the Family*, **30**(February):26–39.

——. 1984. "Gender and Parenthood," *American Sociological Review*, **49**(February):1–19.

Rossi, Peter H. 1987. "No Good Applied Social Research Goes Unpunished," *Society*, **25**(November–December): 73–79.

Rossides, Daniel W. 1990. *Social Stratification: The American Class System in Comparative Perspective*. Englewood Cliffs, N.J.: Prentice-Hall.

Roszak, Theodore. 1969. *The Making of a Counterculture*. Garden City, N.Y.: Doubleday.

Rothenberg, Paula S. 1988. *Racism and Sexism: An Integrated Study*. New York: St. Martin's.

——. 1992. "Critics of Attempts to Democratize the Curriculum Are Waging a Campaign to Misrepresent the Work of Responsible Professors," in Paul Berman (ed.), *Debating P.C.: The Controversy over Political Correctness on College Campuses*. New York: Dell, pp. 262–268.

Rothschild-Whitt, Joyce. 1979. "The Collectivist Organization: An Alternative to Rational-Bureaucratic Models," *American Sociological Review*, **44**(August):509–527.

Rousseau, Ann Marie. 1981. *Shopping Bag Ladies*. New York: Pilgrim.

Rovner, Julie. 1990. "Congress Wraps Up Decision on Child-Care Legislation," *Congressional Quarterly Weekly Report*, **48**(October 27):3605–3606.

Rudolph, Ellen. 1991. "Women's Talk," *New York Times Magazine* (September 1), p. 8.

Ruggles, Patricia. 1991. "Short- and Long-Term Poverty in the United States: Measuring the American 'Underclass,'" in Lars Osberg (ed.), *Economic Inequity and Poverty: International Perspectives*. Armonk, N.Y.: Sharpe, pp. 157–193.

Rugh, Andrea B. 1984. *Family in Contemporary Egypt*. Syracuse, N.Y.: Syracuse University Press.

Ryan, William. 1976. *Blaming the Victim* (rev. ed.). New York: Random House.

Saarinen, Thomas F. 1988. "Centering of Mental Maps of the World," *National Geographic Research*, **4**(Winter): 112–127.

Sack, Kevin. 1992. "New, and Volatile, Politics of Welfare," *New York Times* (March 15), p. 24.

Sadker, Myra, and David Sadker. 1985. "Sexism in the Schoolroom of the '80s," *Psychology Today*, **19**(March):54–57.

Sagarin, Edward, and Jose Sanchez. 1988. "Ideology and Deviance: The Case of the Debate over the Biological Factor," *Deviant Behavior*, **9**(1):87–99.

Salem, Richard, and Stanislaus Grabarek. 1986. "Sociology B.A.s in a Corporate Setting: How Can They Get There and of What Value Are They," *Teaching Sociology*, **14**(October):273–275.

Salholz, Eloise. 1990. "Teenagers and Abortion," *Newsweek*, **115**(January 8): 32–33, 36.

Saltzman, Amy. 1988. "Hands Off at the Office," *U.S. News and World Report*, **105**(August 1):56–58.

Salvatore, Diane. 1986. "Babies for Sale," *Ladies Home Journal*, **103**(July): 54, 56, 60, 64, 136.

Sampson, Anthony. 1973. *The Sovereign State of I.T.T.* New York: Stein and Day.

Sampson, Robert J. 1986. "Effects of Socioeconomic Context on Official Reaction to Juvenile Delinquency," *American Sociological Review*, **51**(December):876–885.

Samuelson, Paul A., and William D. Nordhaus. 1992. *Economics* (14th ed.). New York: McGraw-Hill.

Sanders, Clinton. 1989. *Customizing the Body: The Art and Culture of Tatooing*. Philadelphia: Temple University Press.

Sapir, Edward. 1929. "The Status of Linguistics as a Science," *Language*, **5**(4):207–214.

Schaefer, Richard T. 1976. *The Extent and Content of Race Prejudice in Great Britain*. San Francisco: R and E Research Association.

——. 1992. "People of Color: The 'Kaleidoscope' May Be a Better Way to Describe America than 'the Melting Pot,'" *Peoria Journal Star* (January 19), p. A7.

——. 1993. *Racial and Ethnic Groups* (5th ed.). New York: Harper Collins.

—— and Robert P. Lamm (eds.).

1987. *Introducing Sociology*. New York: McGraw-Hill.

—— and Sandra L. Schaefer. 1975. "Reluctant Welcome: U.S. Responses to the South Vietnamese Refugees," *New Community*, **4**(Autumn):366–370.

Scheff, Thomas J. 1992. *Microsociology: Discourse, Emotion, and Structure*. Chicago: University of Chicago Press.

Schlenker, Barry R. (ed.). 1985. *The Self and Social Life*. New York: McGraw-Hill.

Schmid, Carol. 1980. "Sexual Antagonism: Roots of the Sex-Ordered Division of Labor," *Humanity and Society*, **4**(November):243–261.

Schramm, Wilbur, Lyle M. Nelson, and Mere T. Betham. 1981. *Bold Experiment: The Story of Educational Television in American Samoa*. Stanford, Calif.: Stanford University Press.

Schultz, Terri. 1977. "Though Legal, Abortions Are Not Always Available," *New York Times* (January 1), p. E8.

Schur, Edwin M. 1965. *Crimes without Victims: Deviant Behavior and Public Policy*. Englewood Cliffs, N.J.: Prentice-Hall.

——. 1968. *Law and Society: A Sociological View*. New York: Random House.

——. 1983. *Labeling Women Deviant: Gender, Stigma, and Social Control*. Philadelphia: Temple University Press.

——. 1985. "'Crimes without Victims': A 20 Year Reassessment." Paper presented at the annual meeting of the Society for the Study of Social Problems.

Schwartz, Howard D. (ed.). 1987. *Dominant Issues in Medical Sociology* (2d ed.). New York: Random House.

Schwartz, Joe. 1991. "Why Japan's Birthrate Is So Low," *American Demographics*, **13**(April):20.

Scotch, Richard K. 1984. *From Good Will to Civil Rights: Transforming Federal Disability Policy*. Philadelphia: Temple University Press.

——. 1988. "Disability as the Basis for a Social Movement: Advocacy and the Politics of Definition," *Journal of Social Issues*, **44**(1):159–172.

——. 1989. "Politics and Policy in the History of the Disability Rights Movement," *Milbank Quarterly*, **67**(Suppl. 2):380–400.

Scott, Robert A. 1969. *The Making of Blind Men: A Study of Adult Socialization*. New York: Russell Sage.

Scott-Samuel, Alex, and Paul Blackburn. 1988. "Crossing the Health Divide—Mortality Attributable to Social Inequality in Great Britain," *Health Promotion*, **2**(3):243–245.

Searle, John. 1992. "The Storm over the University," in Paul Berman (ed.), *Debating P.C.: The Controversy over Political Correctness on College Campuses*. New York: Dell, pp. 85–123.

Seckman, Mark A., and Carl J. Couch. 1989. "Jocularity, Sarcasm, and Relationships: An Empirical Study," *Journal of Contemporary Ethnography*, **18**(October):327–344.

Seddon, Terri. 1987. "Politics and Curriculum: A Case Study of the Japanese History Textbook Dispute, 1982," *British Journal of Sociology of Education*, **8**(2):213–226.

Seider, John, and Katherine Meyer. 1989. *Conflict and Change in the Catholic Church*. New Brunswick, N.J.: Rutgers University Press.

Senter, Richard, Terry Miller, Larry T. Reynolds, and Tim Shaffer. 1983. "Bureaucratization and Goal Succession in Alternative Organizations," *Sociological Focus*, **16**(October):239–253.

Shaw, Susan. 1988. "Gender Differences in the Definition and Perception of Household Labor," *Family Relations*, **37**(July):333–337.

Shell, Louise I. 1988. "Babies in Day Care," *Atlantic*, **262**(August):73–74.

Shenon, Philip. 1992. "After Years of Denial, Asia Faces Scourge of AIDS," *New York Times* (November 8), pp. 1, 12.

Sherman, Arnold K., and Aliza Kolker. 1987. *The Social Bases of Politics*. Belmont, Calif.: Wadsworth.

Sherman, Lawrence W. 1992. *Policing Domestic Violence*. New York: Free Press.

Shilts, Randy. 1987. *And the Band Played On: Politics, People, and the AIDS Epidemic*. New York: St. Martin's.

———. 1989. "The Era of Bad Feelings," *Mother Jones*, **14**(November):32–36, 58–60.

Shupe, Anson D., and David G. Bromley. 1980. "Walking a Tightrope," *Qualitative Sociology*, **2**:8–21.

——— and ———. 1985. "Social Response to Cults," in Phillip E. Hammond (ed.), *The Sacred in a Secular Age*. Berkeley: University of California Press, pp. 58–72.

Sigmund, Paul E. 1990. *Liberation Theology at the Crossroads: Democracy or Revolution?* New York: Oxford University Press.

Silva, Nelson De Valle. 1985. "Updating the Cost of Not Being White in Brazil," in Pierre-Michel Fontaine (ed.), *Race, Class, and Power in Brazil*. Los Angeles: Center for Afro-American Studies, University of California at Los Angeles, pp. 42–55.

Simon, John L. 1992. *Population and Development in Poor Countries*. Princeton, N.J.: Princeton University Press.

Simons, Marlise. 1988. "Brazil's Blacks Feel Prejudice 100 Years after Slavery's End," *New York Times* (May 14), pp. 1, 6.

———. 1989. "Abortion Fight Has New Front in Western Europe," *New York Times* (June 28), pp. A1, A9.

Skafte, Peter. 1979. "Smoking Out Secrets of the Mysterious 'Snakers' in India," *Smithsonian*, **10**(October):120–127.

Skocpol, Theda. 1979. *States and Social Revolutions*. Cambridge, Eng.: Cambridge University Press.

Skogan, Wesley G. 1981. *Issues in the Measurement of Victimization*. U.S. Department of Justice. Washington, D.C.: U.S. Government Printing Office.

Sloan, John Henry, et al. [9 authors]. 1988. "Handgun Regulations, Crime, Assaults, and Homicide: A Tale of Two Cities," *New England Journal of Medicine*, **319**(November 10):1256–1262.

Smelser, Neil. 1962. *Theory of Collective Behavior*. New York: Free Press.

———. 1963. *The Sociology of Economic Life*. Englewood Cliffs, N.J.: Prentice-Hall.

———. 1981. *Sociology*. Englewood Cliffs, N.J.: Prentice-Hall.

Smith, Christian. 1991. *The Emergence of Liberation Theology: Radical Religion and Social Movement Theory*. Chicago: University of Chicago Press.

Smith, James P. 1986. *The Distribution of Wealth*. Ann Arbor, Mich.: Survey Research Center.

Smith, Richard T. 1980. "Societal Reaction and Physical Disability: Contrasting Perspectives," in Walter R. Gove (ed.), *The Labelling of Deviance*. Beverly Hills, Calif.: Sage, pp. 227–236.

Smoler, Fredric. 1992. "What Should We Teach Our Children about American History?" *American Heritage*, **43**(February–March):45–50.

Smothers, Ronald. 1992. "Many State Lotteries Feel the Pinch of Recession, and Perhaps Monotony," *New York Times* (February 2), p. 16.

Snow, David A., Louis A. Zurcher, Jr., and Robert Peters. 1981. "Victory Celebrations as Theater: A Dramaturgical Approach to Crowd Behavior," *Symbolic Interaction*, **4**:21–42.

Solórzano, Lucia. 1986. "Teaching in Trouble," *U.S. News and World Report*, **100**(May 26):52–57.

Son, In Soo, Suzanne W. Model, and Gene A. Fisher. 1989. "Polarization and Progress in the Black Community: Earnings and Status Gains for Young Black Males in the Era of Affirmative Action," *Sociological Forum*, **4**(September):309–327.

Sorokin, Pitirim A. 1959. *Social and Cultural Mobility*. New York: Free Press (original edition 1927, New York: Harper).

Sorrentino, Constance. 1990. "The Changing Family in International Perspective," *Monthly Labor Review*, **113**(March):41–56.

Spanier, Graham B. 1983. "Married and Unmarried Cohabitation in the United States, 1980," *Journal of Marriage and the Family*, **45**(May):277–288.

Spencer, Gregory. 1989. *Projections of the Population of the United States, by Age, Sex, and Race: 1988 to 2080*. Current Population Reports, ser. P-25, no. 1018. Washington, D.C.: U.S. Government Printing Office.

Spengler, Joseph J. 1978. *Facing Zero Population Growth: Reactions and Interpretations, Past and Present*. Durham, N.C.: Duke University Press.

Spradley, James P., and David W. McCurdy. 1980. *Anthropology: The Cultural Perspective* (2d ed.). New York: Wiley.

Squire, Peverill. 1988. "Why the 1936 *Literary Digest* Poll Failed," *Public Opinion Quarterly*, **52**(Spring):125–133.

Staggenborg, Suzanne. 1988. "Consequences of Professionalization and Formalization," *American Sociological Review*, **53**(August):585–606.

———. 1989a. "Stability and Innovation in the Women's Movement: A Comparison of Two Movement Organizations," *Social Problems*, **36**(February):75–92.

———. 1989b. "Organization and Environmental Influences on the Development of the Pro-Choice Movement," *Social Forces*, **68**(September):204–240.

Stanley, J. P. 1977. "Paradigmatic Women: The Prostitute," in B. Shores and C. P. Hines (eds.), *Papers in Language Variation*. University, Alabama: University of Alabama Press, pp. 303–321.

Stark, Rodney, and William Sims Bainbridge. 1979. "Of Churches, Sects, and Cults: Preliminary Concepts for a Theory of Religious Movements,"

Journal for the Scientific Study of Religion, **18**(June):117–131.

———— and ————. 1985. *The Future of Religion.* Berkeley: University of California Press.

Starr, Paul. 1982. *The Social Transformation of American Medicine.* New York: Basic Books.

Statham, Ann, Eleanor M. Miller, and Hans O. Mauksch (eds.). 1988. *The Worth of Women's Work.* Albany: State University of New York Press.

Steiber, Steven R. 1979. "The World System and World Trade: An Empirical Exploration of Conceptual Conflicts," *Sociological Quarterly,* **20**(Winter):23–36.

Stein, Leonard. 1967. "The Doctor-Nurse Game," *Archives of General Psychiatry,* **16**:699–703.

Stein, Peter J. 1975. "Singlehood: An Alternative to Marriage," *Family Coordinator,* **24**(October):489–503.

———— (ed.). 1981. *Single Life: Unmarried Adults in Social Context.* New York: St. Martin's.

Stellman, Jeanne Mager, and Joan E. Bertin. 1990. "Science's Anti-Female Bias," *New York Times* (June 4), p. A23.

Stenning, Derrick J. 1958. "Household Viability among the Pastoral Fulani," in John R. Goody (ed.), *The Developmental Cycle in Domestic Groups.* Cambridge, Eng.: Cambridge University Press, pp. 92–119.

Stets, Jan E., and Maureen A. Pirog-Good. 1987. "Violence in Dating Relationships," *Social Psychology Quarterly,* **50**(September):237–246.

Stevens, Evelyn P. 1973. "Machismo and Marianismo," *Society,* **10**(September–October):57–63.

Stevens, William K. 1987. "Reagan Insurance Plan Appears Helpful to Few," *New York Times* (March 8), p. 24.

Stimpson, Catharine R. 1992. "On Differences: Modern Language Association Presidential Address 1990," in Paul Berman (ed.), *Debating P.C.: The Controversy over Political Correctness on College Campuses.* New York: Dell, pp. 40–60.

Stocks, J. Timothy. 1988. "Has Family Violence Decreased? A Reassessment of the Straus and Gelles Data," *Journal of Marriage and the Family,* **50**(February):281–285.

Stone, Andrea. 1991. "Welfare Slash Worst in 10 Years," *USA Today* (December 19), p. A1.

Stone, Gregory P. 1977. "Personal Acts," *Symbolic Interaction,* **1**(Fall):1–21.

Strasser, Steven, et al. 1981. "A Survival Summit," *Newsweek,* **98**(October 26): 36–44.

Straus, Murray A., and Richard J. Gelles (eds.). 1990. *Physical Violence in American Families.* New Brunswick, N.J.: Transaction.

Straus, Roger (ed.). 1985. *Using Sociology.* Bayside, N.Y.: General Hall.

Strauss, Anselm. 1985. "Work and the Division of Labor," *Sociological Quarterly,* **26**(Spring):1–19.

Stuart, Reginald. 1982. "Judge Overturns Arkansas Law on Creationism," *New York Tiems* (January 6), pp. A1, B7, B8.

Sumner, William G. 1906. *Folkways.* New York: Ginn.

Sutherland, Edwin H. 1937. *The Professional Thief.* Chicago: University of Chicago Press.

————. 1940. "White-Collar Criminality," *American Sociological Review,* **5**(February):1–11.

————. 1949. *White Collar Crime.* New York: Dryden.

————. 1983. *White Collar Crime: The Uncut Version.* New Haven, Conn.: Yale University Press.

———— and Donald R. Cressey. 1978. *Principles of Criminology* (10th ed.). Philadelphia: Lippincott.

Sweet, James A., and Larry L. Bumpass. 1987. *American Families and Households.* New York: Russell Sage.

Swinton, David. 1987. "Economic Status of Blacks, 1986," in Janet Dewart (ed.), *The State of Black America.* New York: National Urban League, pp. 49–73.

Szulc, Tad. 1988. "How Can We Help Ourselves Age with Dignity?" *Parade* (May 29), pp. 4–7.

Szymanski, Albert. 1983. *Class Structure: A Critical Perspective.* New York: Praeger.

Tachibana, Judy. 1990. "Model Minority Myth Presents Unrepresentative Portrait of Asian Americans, Many Educators Say," *Black Issues in Higher Education,* **6**(March 1): 1, 11.

Takaki, Ronald. 1989. *Strangers from a Different Shore: A History of Asian Americans.* Boston: Little, Brown.

————. 1990. "The Harmful Myth of Asian Superiority," *New York Times* (June 16), p. 21.

Tannen, Deborah. 1990. *You Just Don't Understand: Women and Men in Conversation.* New York: Ballantine.

Taylor, Paul. 1985. "Uninsured? Find Another Hospital," *Washington Post National Weekly Edition,* **2**(July 22): 8–9.

————. 1990. "The Democrats Discover the Savings and Loan Scandal," *Washington Post National Weekly Edition,* **7**(June 4):13.

————. 1991. "Baby Steps toward Being Family-Friendly," *Washington Post National Weekly Edition,* **9**(November 25):21.

Taylor, Stuart, Jr. 1987. "High Court Voids Curb on Teaching Evolution Theory," *New York Times* (June 20), pp. 1, 7.

Telsch, Kathleen. 1991. "New Study of Older Workers Finds They Can Become Good Investments," *New York Times* (May 21), p. A16.

Terkel, Studs. 1974. *Working.* New York: Random House.

Thomas, William I. 1923. *The Unadjusted Girl.* Boston: Little, Brown.

Thompson, James D., and Robert W. Hawkes. 1962. "Disaster, Community Organization, and Administrative Process," in G. W. Baker and D. W. Chapman (eds.), *Man and Society in Disaster.* New York: Basic Books, pp. 268–300.

Thompson, Linda, and Alexis J. Walker. 1989. "Gender in Families: Women and Men in Marriage, Work, and Parenthood," *Journal of Marriage and the Family,* **51**(November):845–871.

Thompson, William E. 1983. "Hanging Tongues: A Sociological Encounter with the Assembly Line," *Qualitative Sociology,* **6**(Fall):215–237.

Thomson, Elizabeth, and Ugo Colella. 1992. "Cohabitation and Marital Stability: Quality or Commitment?" *Journal of Marriage and the Family,* **54**(May):259–267.

Thorne, Barrie. 1987. "Re-Visioning Women and Social Change: Where Are the Children?" *Gender and Society,* **1**(March):85–109.

Thornton, Arland. 1985. "Changing Attitudes toward Separation and Divorce: Causes and Consequences," *American Journal of Sociology,* **90**(January):856–872.

Tiano, Susan. 1987. "Gender, Work, and World Capitalism: Third World Women's Role in Development," in Beth B. Hess and Myra Marx Ferree (eds.), *Analyzing Gender: A Handbook of Social Science Research.* Newbury Park, Calif.: Sage, pp. 216–243.

Tierney, John. 1990. "Betting the Planet," *New York Times Magazine* (December 2), pp. 52–53, 71, 74, 76, 78, 80–81.

Tierney, Kathleen. 1980. "Emergent Norm Theory as 'Theory': An Analysis and Critique of Turner's Formulation," in Meredith David Pugh (ed.), *Collective Behavior: A Source Book.* St. Paul, Minn.: West, pp. 42–53.

Time. 1982. "Out Front on Arms Control," **119**(February 1):19.

Tinker, Irene (ed.). 1990. *Persistent Inequalities: Women and World Development.* New York: Oxford University Press.

Tipps, Havens C., and Henry A. Gordon. 1983. "Inequality at Work: Race, Sex, and Underemployment." Paper presented at the annual meeting of the American Sociological Association, Detroit.

Tonkinson, Robert. 1978. *The Mardudjara Aborigines.* New York: Holt.

Tönnies, Ferdinand. 1988. *Community and Society.* Rutgers, N.J.: Transaction (originally published in 1887).

Touraine, Alain. 1974. *The Academic System in American Society.* New York: McGraw-Hill.

Treiman, Donald J. 1977. *Occupational Prestige in Comparative Perspective.* New York: Academic.

Tsui, Amy Ong, and Donald J. Bogue. 1978. "Declining World Fertility: Trends, Causes, Implications," *Population Bulletin,* **33**(October).

Tumin, Melvin M. 1953. "Some Principles of Stratification: A Critical Analysis," *American Sociological Review,* **18**(August):387–394.

———. 1985. *Social Stratification* (2d ed.). Englewood Cliffs, N.J.: Prentice-Hall.

Turner, J. H. 1985. *Herbert Spencer: A Renewed Application.* Beverly Hills, Calif.: Sage.

Turner, Margery, Michael Fix, and Raymond J. Struyck. 1991. *Opportunities Denied, Opportunities Diminished: Discrimination in Hiring.* Washington, D.C.: Urban Institute.

Turner, Ralph. 1962. "Role Taking: Process vs. Conformity," in Arnold Rose (ed.), *Human Behavior and Social Processes.* Boston: Houghton Mifflin, pp. 20–40.

——— and Lewis M. Killian. 1987. *Collective Behavior* (3d ed.). Englewood Cliffs, N.J.: Prentice-Hall.

Twaddle, Andrew. 1974. "The Concept of Health Status," *Social Science and Medicine,* **8**(January):29–38.

——— and Richard M. Hessler. 1987. *A Sociology of Health* (2d ed.). New York: Macmillan.

Tyler, Charles. 1991. "The World's Manacled Millions," *Geographical Magazine,* **63**(1):30–35.

Tyler, William B. 1985. "The Organizational Structure of the School," in Ralph H. Turner (ed.), *Annual Review of Sociology, 1985.* Palo Alto, Calif.: Annual Reviews, pp. 49–73.

Udy, Stanley H., Jr. 1959. "Bureaucracy and Rationality in Weber's Organizational Theory: An Empirical Study," *American Sociological Review,* **24**(December):791–795.

USA Today. 1991a. "Business PACs Kept Dems in the Money" (May 3), p. 11A.

———. 1991b. "Study: Women Hold 2.6% of Top Jobs" (August 27), p. 1A.

van den Berghe, Pierre. 1978. *Race and Racism: A Comparative Perspective* (2d ed.). New York: Wiley.

van der Tak, Jean, Carl Haub, and Elaine Murphy. 1979. "Our Population Predicament: A New Look," *Population Bulletin,* **34**(December).

Vanneman, Reeve, and Lynn Weber Cannon. 1987. *The American Perception of Class.* Philadelphia: Temple University Press.

Vayda, Eugene, and Ralsa B. Deber. 1984. "The Canadian Health Care System: An Overview," *Social Science and Medicine,* **18**:191–197.

Veblen, Thorstein. 1919. *The Vested Interests and the State of the Industrial Arts.* New York: Huebsch.

Verbrugge, Lois M. 1985. "Gender and Health: An Update on Hypotheses and Evidence," *Journal of Health and Social Behavior,* **26**(September):156–182.

Vernon, Glenn. 1962. *Sociology and Religion.* New York: McGraw-Hill.

Vernon, Raymond. 1977. *Storm over the Multinationals: The Real Issues.* Cambridge, Mass.: Harvard University Press.

Von Hoffman, Nicholas. 1970. "Sociological Snoopers," *Transaction* **7**(May): 4, 6.

Waitzkin, Howard. 1986. *The Second Sickness: Contradictions of Capitalist Health Care.* Chicago: University of Chicago Press.

——— and Barbara Waterman. 1974. *The Exploitation of Illness in Capitalist Society.* Indianapolis: Bobbs-Merrill.

Waldrop, Theresa. 1993. "'Slapping Spastis': German Neo-Nazis Turn on the Handicapped," *Newsweek* (March 1), p. 26.

Walker, Gillian A. 1986. "Burnout: From Metaphor to Ideology," *Canadian Journal of Sociology,* **11**(Spring): 35–55.

Wallace, Ruth A., and Alison Wolf. 1980. *Contemporary Sociological Theory.* Englewood Cliffs, N.J.: Prentice-Hall.

Wallace, Stephen. 1984. "Macro and Micro Issues in Intergenerational Relationships within the Latino Family and Community." Paper presented at the annual meeting of the Society for the Study of Social Problems, San Antonio, Tex.

Wallerstein, Immanuel. 1974. *The Modern World System.* New York: Academic Press.

———. 1979. *Capitalist World Economy.* Cambridge, Eng.: Cambridge University Press.

———. 1991. *Geopolitics and Geoculture: Essays on the Changing World System.* Cambridge, Eng.: Cambridge University Press.

Wallerstein, Judith, and Sandra Blakeslee. 1989. *Second Chances: Men, Women, and Children a Decade after Divorce.* New York: Ticknor and Fields.

Wallis, Claudia. 1981. "Southward Ho for Jobs," *Time,* **117**(May 11):23.

———. 1987. "Is Mental Illness Inherited?" *Time,* **129**(March 9):67.

Walton, John. 1992. *Western Times and Water Wars: State, Culture, and Rebellion in California.* Berkeley: University of California Press.

Waring, Marilyn. 1988. *If Women Counted: A New Feminist Economics.* San Francisco: Harper and Row.

Washington Post. 1984. "The Congressional Checkoff," *Washington Post National Weekly Edition,* **1**(October 15):14–15.

Watkins, Beverly T. 1992. "Foreign Enrollment at U.S. Colleges and Universities Totaled 419,585 in 1991–92, an All-Time High," *Chronicle of Higher Education,* **49**(November 25):A28–A29.

Watson, Kenneth M. 1986. "Birth Families: Living with the Adoption Decision," *Public Welfare,* **44**(Spring):5–10.

Watson, Russell. 1984. "A Hidden Epidemic," *Newsweek,* **103**(May 14):30–36.

Watson, Tracey. 1987. "Women Athletes and Athletic Women: The Dilemmas and Contradictions of Managing Incongruent Identities," *Sociological Inquiry,* **57**(Fall):431–446.

Watts, W. David, and Ann Marie Ellis. 1989. "Assessing Sociology Educational Outcomes: Occupational Status and Mobility of Graduates," *Teaching Sociology,* **17**(July):297–306.

Webb, Eugene J., Donald T. Campbell, Richard D. Schwartz, Lee Sechrest, and Janet Belew Grove. 1981. *Nonreactive Measures in the Social Sciences* (2d ed.). Boston: Houghton Mifflin.

Weber, Max. 1922. *Wirtschaft und Gesellschaft.* Tübingen, Ger.: Mohr.

———. 1947. *The Theory of Social and Economic Organization.* Translated by A. Henderson and T. Parsons. New York: Free Press (originally published during the period 1913–1922).

———. 1949. *Methodology of the Social Sciences.* Translated by Edward A.

Shils and Henry A. Finch. Glencoe, Ill.: Free Press (originally published in 1904).

————. 1958a. *The Protestant Ethic and the Spirit of Capitalism.* Translated by Talcott Parsons. New York: Scribner (originally published in 1904).

————. 1958b. *The Religion of India: The Sociology of Hinduism and Buddhism.* New York: Free Press (originally published in 1916).

Webster, Peggy Lovell, and Jeffrey W. Dwyer. 1988. "The Cost of Being Nonwhite in Brazil," *Social Science Research,* **72**(January):136–142.

Weeks, John R. 1988. "The Demography of Islamic Nations," *Population Bulletin,* **43**(December).

————. 1992. *Population: An Introduction to Concepts and Issues* (5th ed.). Belmont, Calif.: Wadsworth.

Weigard, Bruce. 1992. *Off the Books: A Theory and Critique of the Underground Economy.* Dix Hills, N.Y.: General Hall.

Weinstein, Deeva. 1992. *Heavy Metal: A Cultural Sociology.* New York: Lexington.

Weisburd, David, Stanton Wheeler, Elin Waring, and Nancy Bode. 1991. *Crimes of the Middle Classes: White-Collar Offenders in the Federal Courts.* New Haven, Conn.: Yale University Press.

Weisman, Steven R. 1992. "Landmark Harassment Case in Japan," *New York Times* (April 17), p. A3.

Weisskopf, Michael. 1992. "Doing Things the Old-Fashioned Way," *Washington Post National Weekly Edition,* **9**(June 8):8–9.

Weitz, Shirley. 1977. *Sex Roles: Biological, Psychological, and Social Foundations.* New York: Oxford University Press.

Wenneker, Mark B., and Arnold M. Epstein. 1989. "Racial Inequalities in the Use of Procedures for Patients with Ischemic Heart Disease in Massachusetts," *Journal of the American Medical Association,* **261**(January 13):253–257.

West, Candace. 1984. "When the Doctor Is a 'Lady': Power, Status, and Gender in Physician-Patient Encounters," *Symbolic Interaction,* **7**(Spring):87–106.

———— and Don H. Zimmerman. 1983. "Small Insults: A Study of Interruptions in Cross Sex Conversations between Unacquainted Persons," in Barrie Thorne, Cheris Kramarae, and Nancy Henley (eds.), *Language, Gender, and Society.* Rowley, Mass.: Newbury House, pp. 86–111.

———— and ————. 1987. "Doing Gender," *Gender and Society,* **1**(June):125–151.

White, Lynn, Jr. 1962. *Medieval Technology and Social Change.* New York: Oxford University Press.

White, Merry. 1987. *The Japanese Educational Challenge: A Commitment to Children.* New York: Free Press.

Whyte, William Foote. 1981. *Street Corner Society: Social Structure of an Italian Slum* (3d ed.). Chicago: University of Chicago Press.

Wickman, Peter M. 1991. "Deviance," in Dushkin Publishing Group, *Encyclopedic Dictionary of Sociology* (4th ed.). Guilford, Conn.: Dushkin, pp. 85–87.

Wiener, Jon. 1990. "Frosh Activists," *The Nation,* **250**(April 16):513.

Wilhite, Allen, and John Theilmann. 1986. "Women, Blacks, and PAC Discrimination," *Social Science Quarterly,* **67**(July):283–298.

Wilkerson, Isabel. 1991. "Black-White Marriages Rise, but Social Acceptance Lags," *New York Times* (December 2), pp. A1, B6.

Wilkinson, Doris K. 1980. "A Synopsis: Projections for the Profession in the 1980's," *ASA Footnotes,* **8**(April 1):6–7.

Will, George F. 1992. "Radical English," in Paul Berman (ed.), *Debating P.C.: The Controversy over Political Correctness on College Campuses.* New York: Dell, pp. 258–261.

Will, J. A., P. A. Self, and N. Datan. 1976. "Maternal Behavior and Perceived Sex of Infant," *American Journal of Orthopsychiatry,* **46**:135–139.

Williams, Lena. 1986. "Older Women Are Found Struggling," *New York Times* (May 8), p. A21.

Williams, Robin M., Jr. 1970. *American Society* (3d ed.). New York: Knopf.

————, in collaboration with John P. Dean and Edward A. Suchman. 1964. *Strangers Next Door: Ethnic Relations in American Communities.* Englewood Cliffs, N.J.: Prentice-Hall.

Williams, Simon Johnson. 1986. "Appraising Goffman," *British Journal of Sociology,* **37**(September):348–369.

Willis, Ellen. 1980. (Untitled column), *Village Voice,* **25**(March 3):8.

Willis, John. 1975. "Variations in State Casualty Rates in World War II and the Vietnam War," *Social Problems,* **22**(April):558–568.

Wilson, Craig. 1991. "Still Havens for Security, Spirituality," *USA Today* (October 15), pp. D1, D2.

Wilson, Edward O. 1975. *Sociobiology: The New Synthesis.* Cambridge, Mass.: Harvard University Press.

————. 1977. "Biology and the Social Sciences," *Daedalus,* **106**(Spring):127–140.

————. 1978. *On Human Nature.* Cambridge, Mass.: Harvard University Press.

Wilson, Franklin D. 1984. "Urban Ecology: Urbanization and Systems of Cities," in Ralph Turner (ed.), *Annual Review of Sociology, 1984.* Palo Alto, Calif.: Annual Reviews, pp. 283–307.

Wilson, John. 1973. *Introduction to Social Movements.* New York: Basic Books.

————. 1978. *Religion in American Society: The Effective Presence.* Englewood Cliffs, N.J.: Prentice-Hall.

Wilson, Warner, Larry Dennis, and Allen P. Wadsworth, Jr. 1976. "Authoritarianism Left and Right," *Bulletin of the Psychonomic Society,* **7**(March):271–274.

Wilson, William Julius. 1980. *The Declining Significance of Race: Blacks and Changing American Institutions* (2d ed.). Chicago: University of Chicago Press.

————. 1987a. *The Truly Disadvantaged: The Inner City, the Underclass and Public Policy.* Chicago: University of Chicago Press.

————. 1987b. "The Ghetto Underclass and the Social Transformation of the Inner City." Paper presented at the annual meeting of the American Association for the Advancement of Science, Chicago.

————. 1988. "The Ghetto Underclass and the Social Transformation of the Inner City," *The Black Scholar,* **19**(May–June):10–17.

———— (ed.). 1989. *The Ghetto Underclass: Social Science Perspectives.* Newbury Park, Calif.: Sage.

————. 1991. "Poverty, Joblessness, and Family Structure in the Inner City: A Comparative Perspective." Paper presented at the Chicago Urban Poverty and Family Life Conference, Chicago.

Winter, J. Alan. 1977. *Continuities in the Sociology of Religion.* New York: Harper and Row.

Withers, Claudia, and Anne Benaroya. 1989. *Sexual Harassment Update 1989: Selected Issues.* Washington, D.C.: Women's Legal Defense Fund.

Wohl, Stanley. 1984. *Medical Industrial Complex.* New York: Harmony.

Wolinsky, Fredric P. 1980. *The Sociology of Health.* Boston: Little, Brown.

Wong, Raymond Sin-Kwok. 1990. "Understanding Cross-National Variation in Occupational Mobility," *American Sociological Review,* **55**(August):560–573.

Wood, Charles, and José de Carvalho.

1988. *The Demography of Inequality in Brazil.* Cambridge, Eng.: Cambridge University Press.

World Bank. 1990. *World Development Report 1990: Poverty.* New York: Oxford University Press.

————. 1992. *World Development Report 1992.* New York: Oxford University Press.

World Development Forum. 1990. "The Danger of Television," **8**(July 15):4.

Wright, Erik Olin, David Hachen, Cynthia Costello, and Joy Sprague. 1982. "The American Class Structure," *American Sociological Review,* **47**(December):709–726.

Wright, Susan. 1993. "Blaming the Victim, Blaming Society, or Blaming the Discipline: Fixing Responsibility for Homelessness," *Sociological Quarterly,* **33**(1): forthcoming.

Wrong, Dennis H. 1977. *Population and Society* (4th ed.). New York: Random House.

Wuthnow, Robert, and Marsha Witten. 1988. "New Directions in the Study of Culture," in W. Richard Scott and Judith Blake (eds.), *Annual Review of Sociology, 1988.* Palo Alto, Calif.: Annual Reviews, pp. 49–67.

Yanagishita, Machiko. 1992. "Japan's Declining Fertility: '1.53 Shock,'" *Population Today,* **20**(April):3–4.

Yates, Ronald E. 1985. "Japanese Merrily Leave the Christ out of 'Kurisumasu,'" *Chicago Tribune* (December 22), p. 13.

Yinger, J. Milton. 1960. "Counterculture and Subculture," *American Sociological Review,* **25**(October):625–635.

————. 1970. *The Scientific Study of Religion.* New York: Macmillan.

————. 1974. "Religion, Sociology of," in *Encyclopedia Britannica,* vol. 15. Chicago: Encyclopedia Britannica, pp. 604–613.

Zablocki, Benjamin. 1980. *Alienation and Charisma: A Study of Contemporary American Communes.* New York: Free Press.

Zald, Mayer N., and John D. McCarthy (eds.). 1979. *The Dynamics of Social Movements.* Cambridge, Mass.: Winthrop.

Zaslow, Martha J. 1988. "Sex Differences in Children's Response to Parental Divorce: 1. Research Methodology and Postdivorce Family Forms," *American Journal of Orthopsychiatry,* **58**(July):355–378.

————. 1989. "Sex Differences in Children's Response to Parental Divorce: 2. Samples, Variables, Ages, and Sources," *American Jouranl of Orthopsychiatry,* **59**(January):118–141.

Zeitlin, Maurice, Kenneth G. Lutterman, and James W. Russell. 1973. "Death in Vietnam: Class, Poverty and the Risks of War," *Politics and Society,* **3**(Spring):313–328.

Zellner, William M. 1978. "Vehicular Suicide: In Search of Incidence." Unpublished M.A. thesis, Western Illinois University, Macomb.

Zelnick, Melvin, and J. Kim Young. 1982. "Sex Education and Its Association with Teenage Sexual Activity, Pregnancy, and Contraceptive Use," *Family Planning Perspectives,* **14**:117–126.

Zia, Helen. 1990. "Midwives: Talking about a Revolution," *Ms.,* **1**(November–December):91.

Zimbardo, Philip C. 1972. "Pathology of Imprisonment," *Society,* **9**(April):4, 6, 8.

————. 1974. "On the Ethics of Intervention in Human Psychological Research: With Special Reference to the Stanford Prison Experiment," *Cognition,* **2**(2):243–256.

Zola, Irving K. 1966. "Culture and Symptoms: An Analysis of Patients Presenting Complaints," *American Sociological Review,* **31**(October):615–630.

————. 1972. "Medicine as an Institution of Social Control," *Sociological Review,* **20**(November):487–504.

————. 1983. *Socio-Medical Inquiries.* Philadelphia: Temple University Press.

————. 1987. "The Portrayal of Disability in the Crime Mystery Genre," *Social Policy,* **17**(Spring):34–39.

Zussman, Robert. 1992. *Intensive Care: Medical Ethics and the Medical Profession.* Chicago: University of Chicago Press.

ACKNOWLEDGMENTS

CHAPTER 1

Chapter-opening photograph: State fair in Dallas—Bob Daemmrich/Stock, Boston.

Figure 1-3: David Watts and Ann Marie Ellis. 1989. "Where Sociology Graduates Find Employment" in "Assessing Sociology Educational Outcomes: Occupational Status and Mobility of Graduates," *Teaching Sociology*, **17** (July):301. Reprinted by permission of the publisher and authors.

Box 1-2: John Lofland. 1977. *Doomsday Cult.* Copyright Irvington Publishers, 195 McGregor St., Manchester, NH 03102. Reprinted by permission.

Excerpts on page 24: Peter Rossi, 1987. "No Good Applied Social Research Goes Unpunished," *Society*, **25**(November–December):73, 79. Reprinted by permission of Transactional Periodicals Consortium.

CHAPTER 2

Chapter-opening photograph: Vietnamese woman—Anna Clopet/Rea/SABA.

Figure 2-2: Thomas F. Saarinen. 1988. "Centering the Mental Maps of the World," *National Geographic Research*, **4**(Winter):124. Reprinted by permission of Thomas F. Saarinen.

CHAPTER 3

Chapter-opening photograph: Burmese boy's head is shaved before he enters a monastery—Bruno Barbey/Magnum.

Box 3-1: Daniel Albas and Cheryl Albas. 1988. "Aces and Bombers: The Post-Exam Impression Management Strategies of Students," *Symbolic Interaction*, **11**(Fall):289–302. Reprinted by permission of JAI Press, Inc.

CHAPTER 4

Chapter-opening photograph: Kurosawa on set of *Dreams*—Sygma.

Box 4-2: William E. Thompson. 1983. "Hanging Tongues: A Sociological Encounter with the Assembly Line," *Qualitative Sociology*, **6**(Fall):215–237. Reprinted by permission of Human Sciences Press, Inc.

Excerpt on pages 104–105: Adapted from Barry Adam. 1992. "Sociology and People Living with AIDS." In Joan Huber and Beth E. Schneider (eds.), *The Social Context of AIDS*, pp. 5–15. Reprinted by permission of Sage Publications, Inc.

CHAPTER 5

Chapter-opening photograph: Boy "train-surfing" in Rio de Janeiro—Miguel Fairbanks.

Table 5-1: Adapted from Robert Merton. 1968. "Modes of Individual Adaptation" *Social Theory and Social Structure,* pp. 400, 488. Copyright © 1967, 1968 by Robert K. Merton. Adapted by permission of The Free Press, a division of Macmillan, Inc.

Box 5-1: Russell Mokhiber et al. 1992. "The 10 Worst Corporations of 1992," *Multinational Monitor* (December):7–16. Reprinted with permission of Multinational Monitor, P.O. Box 19405, Washington, D.C. 20036. Individual subscription $25/year.

CHAPTER 6

Chapter-opening photograph: Caracas, Venezuela—Peter Menzel/Stock, Boston.

Figure 6-4: Ben Crow and Alan Thomas. 1983. "Worldwide Gross National Product Per Capita," *World Population Data Sheet, 1990.* Reprinted by permission of Open University Press and Population Reference Bureau, Inc.

Figure 6-5: World Bank, 1992. "Distribution of Income in Seven Nations," *World Development Report 1992,* pp. 276–277. Reprinted by permission of Oxford University Press, New York.

Table 6-2: Keiko Nakao and Judith Treas. 1990. "Occupational Prestige in the United States Revisited: Twenty-Five Years of Stability and Change," paper presented at the annual meeting of the American Sociological Association, Washington, D.C. Reprinted by permission of the authors.

Box 6-2: William Ryan. 1971. *Blaming the Victim.* Copyright © 1971, 1976 by William Ryan. Reprinted by permission of Pantheon Books, a division of Random House, Inc.

Excerpt on page 167: Kathryn Edin. 1992. "Surviving the Welfare System: How AFDC Recipients Make Ends Meet in Chicago," *Social Problems,* 38(November):462–473. © 1992 by the Society for the Study of Social Problems. Reprinted by permission of University of California Press and the author.

CHAPTER 7

Chapter-opening photograph: Native American woman—J.B. Diederich/Woodfin Camp & Associates.

Figure 7-1: Richard T. Schaefer. 1993. "The Self-Fulfilling Prophecy," from *Racial and Ethnic Groups,* 5th edition. Reprinted by permission of HarperCollins Publishers.

Table 7-3: Richard D. Alba and Gwen Moore. 1982. "Ethnicity in the American Elite," *American Sociological Review,* 47(June):373–383. Reprinted by permission of the publisher and authors.

CHAPTER 8

Chapter-opening photograph: Dr. Desforges of Tufts Medical School—Paula Lerner/Woodfin Camp & Associates.

Figure 8-2: Linda DeStefano and Diane Colasanto. 1990. "Unlike 1975, Today Most Americans Think Men Have It Better," *The Gallup Poll Monthly,* 293(February):31. Reprinted by permission of The Gallup Poll Monthly.

Box 8-1: Marvine Howe. 1991. "Sex Discrimination Persists, U.N. Says," *New York Times* (16 June):7, Copyright © 1991 by The New York Times Company. Reprinted by permission.

CHAPTER 9

Chapter-opening photograph: Hmong family in Fresno, California—Mickey Pfleger/Photo 20-20.

Table 9-1: Adapted from William J. Goode. 1976. "Family Disorganization" in Robert Merton and Robert Nisbet (eds.), *Contemporary Social Problems,* 4th ed., pp. 537–538. Copyright © 1976 by Harcourt Brace Jovanovich, Inc. Reprinted by permission of the publisher.

Table 9-3: Adapted from Peter J. Stein. 1975. "Singlehood: An Alternative to Marriage," *Family Relations,* 24(October). Reprinted by permission of the National Council on Family Relations and the author.

Excerpt on pages 246–247: Paul Bohannan (ed). "The Six Stations of Divorce," *Divorce and After,* pp. 33–62. Copyright © 1970 by Paul Bohannan. Used by permission of Doubleday, a division of Bantam Doubleday Dell Publishing Group, Inc.

Excerpt on page 254: *Psychology Today,* 1992. "Why Do They Stay?" *Psychology Today,* 25(May/June):22. Copyright © 1992 Sussex Publishers, Inc. Reprinted by permission of Psychology Today Magazine.

CHAPTER 10

Chapter-opening photograph: Nun tutoring a student—Paul Conklin/Monkmeyer Press.

Table 10-1: Glenn Vernon. 1962. *Sociology of Religion.* New York: McGraw-Hill Book Company.

Box 10-2: Thomas Cottle. 1991. "A Family Prepares for College," *Journal of Higher Education,* 62(January–February):83–84. Reprinted by permission of Ohio State University Press.

Excerpt on pages 280–281: Ralph H. Turner (ed.). 1985. "Organizational Structure of the School," *Annual Review of Sociology:*49–73.

Excerpt on pages 280–281: Adapted in part from Kathryn M. Borman and Joel H. Spring. 1984. *Schools in Central Cities: Structure and Process.* Adapted by permission of the authors. And adapted in part from William B. Tyler. 1985. "The Organizational Structure of the School" in Ralph H. Turner (ed.), *Annual Review of Sociology,* 11:49–73. © 1985 by Annual Reviews Inc. Adapted by permission of the publisher.

CHAPTER 11

Chapter-opening photograph: Bill Clinton in a Washington, D.C., neighborhood just after his election—Brad Markel/Gamma Liaison.

Box 11-2: Douglas Murray. 1982. "The Abolition of El Cortito, the Short-Handled Hoe: A Case Study in Social Conflict and State Policy in California Agriculture," *Social Problems,* **30**(October):26–39. © 1982 by the Society for the Study of Social Problems. Reprinted by permission of the publisher and author.

CHAPTER 12

Chapter-opening photograph: Health clinic in Thailand—David R. Austen/Stock, Boston.

Figure 12-4: Adapted from John R. Weeks. 1992. "Population Structure of Mexico and the United States," *Population: An Introduction to Concepts and Issues,* 5th edition, p. 230. Used by permission of Wadsworth, Inc.

Box 12-2: Joe Schwartz. 1991. "Why Japan's Birthrate Is So Low," *American Demographics,* **13**(April):20. © 1991 American Demographics. Reprinted with permission.

Excerpt on page 342: Victor Cohn. 1992. "How Can We Fix a Broken System?" *The Washington Post* (March 2):7. © 1992 The Washington Post. Reprinted with permission.

CHAPTER 13

Chapter-opening photograph: Demonstrators protesting the parental-consent rule—Ron Haviv/SABA.

Figure in Box 13-2: Joel Garreau. 1991. "The Phoenix Area," *Edge City: Life on the New Frontier,* p. 181. Copyright 1991 by Joel Garreau. Used by permission of Doubleday, a division of Bantam Doubleday Dell Publishing Group, Inc.

INDEXES

NAME INDEX

SUBJECT INDEX